The Lime Street Guide to Lloyd's

Edited by
Barbara Schurer

Foreword by
Michael Meacock

Lime Street Publications

The Lime Street Guide to Lloyd's is published by
Lime Street Publications
10 Gledhow Gardens
London SW5 0AY

www.limestreetpublications.co.uk

978-0-9563314-0-3

This edition published 2009

A CIP catalogue record for this book is available from the British Library.

Printed and bound in Great Britain by Service Point UK.

This book has been produced using paper that contains wood from well-managed forests and recycled fibres made from post-consumer waste.

The Lime Street Guide to Lloyd's
– an homage to its people

It was the entrepreneurial spirit of Lloyd's that captured my imagination back in 1988, as I left a career in Merchant Banking and took up Membership of Lloyd's. It has fascinated me ever since.

No one can disagree that it remains one of the most remarkable and enduring market places in the world and, in my opinion, that is because of the calibre of the people who work in the Lloyd's Market and apply amazing skill and diligence to arrange risk transfer in the modern global environment. Their forebears like John Julius Angerstein and Cuthbert Heath would look on amazed at today's complex risk transfer mechanisms and indeed the nature of risks considered as insurable at Lloyd's today. The enduring entrepreneurial spirit of Lloyd's people is still most invigorating.

It is my own experiences as a Name at Lloyd's, good and bad, that has led me to compile **The Lime Street Guide to Lloyd's** as my personal homage to Lloyd's and these remarkable people.

There are plenty of individual points of reference about Lloyd's, its underwriting businesses and all their financial data, available to observers. However, nowhere is there a reference book which records the position in this community of all the key people who make Lloyd's what it is. Of course, they are the ones behind the continued success of Lloyd's. This Guide introduces these key players of the Lloyd's market collectively for the first time.

The Guide has two main sections; the 'People at Lloyd's' and those Companies arranging the underwriting in the 'Lloyd's Market'. There are other aspects of Lloyd's as well; in particular the social and charitable sides with a whole section on the various Societies at work within the market. These Clubs and Societies all add to the community and cohesiveness of the market and, in turn, add to the lives of the participants.

The 'People at Lloyd's' section contains those detailed personal profiles returned to us. Where we do not have detailed profiles, all the Members, Directors and Senior Management in the Council, Managing, Run-off and Members' Agencies and the Corporation Staff are included as "Mini-Profiles" with data drawn from publicly available sources.

The 'Lloyd's Market' section covers the Governance of Lloyd's, the companies trading in the market place and the details of all Managing, Run-off and Members' Agents and their various syndicates.

The details recorded here are believed to be accurate as at the beginning of 2009, updated at the time of going to press where we have been given further information. Of course, change is the one constant at Lloyd's and there will be some imperfections for which I apologise, as a result of people moving around.

Hopefully **The Lime Street Guide to Lloyd's** will be a unique and valuable reference point for all those with an interest in Lloyd's and its people.

Barbara Schurer

Editor – The Lime Street Guide to Lloyd's
Associate Member, Lloyd's Market Association
Lloyd's Member since 1988

Foreword

My grandfather formed Syndicate 727 to underwrite the 1910 account for just six unlimited liability Lloyd's Names. Next year will be our family centenary of that small beginning as my father was also the underwriter and I have spent all my working life at Lloyd's, taking over as the underwriter of our syndicate in 1966. It could be said Lloyd's is in our genes.

There has been plenty of turbulence throughout that period including two world wars as well as incredible growth in the world economy. Lloyd's has grown significantly to meet all the challenges. Lloyd's has been close by when calamity has struck; helping its clients at their time of greatest need. It is a fascinating business in which to spend one's working life, assessing a wide variety of risks in the company of people whom I am always pleased to see.

Some of the brightest people in the City of London have sat at the boxes in Lloyd's underwriting rooms over these years and they have found innovative ways to insure some very unusual and interesting risks. There is much that might be considered dull about some forms of insurance but at Lloyd's it really is very different.

The underwriters of today, who are at the heart of the market, all need the very best sources of accurate information to assist them in running their syndicates and in knowing their marketplace.

It is to all those people in this great underwriting market that Barbara Schurer has dedicated this book, and in so doing, she brings us that most valuable tool of all – well researched, relevant facts that will be useful in our everyday life within Lloyd's.

I am happy to commend this book to you.

[signature]

Underwriting Director and Active Underwriter Syndicate 727

SA Meacock & Company Limited

Acknowledgements

I wish to dedicate this first edition of **The Lime Street Guide to Lloyd's** to all those practising their skill, diligence and professionalism in the name of their companies, and in the name of Lloyd's.

There are innumerable friends and Market colleagues I wish to thank for helping me to bring the first **Lime Street Guide to Lloyd's** to publication.

I am particularly grateful to Brian Caudle who launched the Personal Profiles section with me over a very long lunch at the Lloyds (no apostrophe!) Club. Over such memorable lunches are new ideas developed every day throughout EC3 – long may that continue. I am also grateful to Michael Meacock, 'Father of the House' as the longest serving Active Underwriter, whose Foreword highlights the personal nature of the Lloyd's Market. To all those others who so kindly responded to subsequent requests for a Personal Profile, I give my special thanks. Hopefully there will be even more next year.

There are so very many secretaries, personal assistants, Company Secretaries and others working within the Market, who have been so very patient and helpful but, sadly, are far too many to mention individually here. I am extremely grateful to you all nevertheless. Others who put in such a lot of work as the Guide evolved were my many researchers, which included my godson Philip Schauss. They were very often university friends of my daughter, Philomena, whose support and patience has been just wonderful.

I would particularly like to thank Keith Hodgson, alias Ant Creative, who designed and produced the layouts, and made the many changes and refinements, with patience and good humour. Also my thanks to Paul Whitby of Kurtzdesign who provided us with our quill logo and to Ben James who took my portrait.

The historic profile of John Julius Angerstein has been very kindly supplied by Dr Anthony Twist, the author of 'A Life of John Julius Angerstein, 1735 - 1823'. He supplied the Sir Brook Watson profile as well. Also, my thanks go to Jane Gilbert of Brokers E.S.J.G. Ltd, for supplying the profile on her great great uncle, Cuthbert Heath. Thank you all.

There are a small number of people who have been very close to this project for a long time and whose enthusiasm kept me moving forward. They are too modest to wish to have any mention here, but know who they are. I will be eternally grateful to them.

And lastly, to my Mother, I also dedicate this book with my very grateful thanks for all her parental guidance, which has seen me through to the conclusion.

Picture Credits

The portraits of Sir Brook Watson, John Julius Angerstein and Cuthbert Heath are courtesy of Lloyd's.

Individual photos have been provided by those featured or their companies. Other photos are published here again by courtesy of Lloyd's.

All reasonable effort has been made to contact the owners of copyright in all the images featured in this book. Owners of copyright not credited are invited to inform the publishers, who will be pleased to rectify any such oversights in the next editions of the Guide.

Editorial

The Lloyd's market has changed considerably over the last twenty years, having gone through extreme adversity in the early 1990s. There is now a need for a guide that identifies and lists all the people involved in the continuing evolution of this marketplace. **The Lime Street Guide to Lloyd's** provides a single reference point where all the information about who is who and where they work can be found.

Lime Street Publications has been established solely to publish all this information. The mission has been to provide the Market, and all those who do business in it, with the most up-to-date listings of the key people and their companies as is possible, in a place where the one constant is change.

There are very many differing facets to the way businesses are run at Lloyd's and this Guide brings out some of those interesting differences. There appear to be no absolute rules about the composition of the Boards of Directors other than the fact they must be up to the job. Boards can vary from six to twenty directors depending on the nature and size of these companies, which may be very sensible but initially at least is very confusing to a poor editor. Some roles and titles are more fully embracing of certain functions in one company when compared to another. Add into the melting pot the requirements of the Financial Services Authority and the task gets no easier for creating a standard listing.

If our valiant effort in defining 'Senior Management', using the Companies House and FSA records, has mistakenly raised or lowered someone's responsibilities within their world, please do accept our apologies and please tell us, so the mistake is not repeated. Also, where we do not have data such as qualifications we would be pleased to be sent such information for the next edition of the Guide. Our starting date for 'Current and Previous Major Positions' is 2001, unless advised otherwise.

The Guide is designed to allow the reader a chance to compare who fulfils comparable roles through the many listings of all Chairmen, CEOs, CFOs etc. In addition, there are more detailed profiles of every one of the individuals in those listings. In some cases, the individual has supplied us with information and in all cases we have checked publicly available sources to enable us to provide the information herein. Not everyone is on the listings as some roles do not reach these levels of senior management just yet.

As is well understood within the Market, Lloyd's is very much more than the people working in the market place today, impressive though they most certainly are. Lloyd's has a strong social side, as well as a strong social conscience all of which we have sought to bring out with a section providing details and contact points of all the diverse Clubs, Societies and Charities. These are brought together here in one place for the first time.

Finally, the history of Lloyd's and our formidable forbears, who helped to create the reputation of 'Lloyd's of London' over the last three centuries, cannot be left out of any Guide to Lloyd's. We have attempted to provide an appropriate reflection of this noble record together with some detailed facts on the heritage of this remarkable place.

A Short Explanation of the Lloyd's Market

Structure

Lloyd's is not an insurance company. It is a Society of Members. It is still and always has been an insurance market place with very many 'Members of Lloyd's'. As the oldest continuously active insurance market place in the world, Lloyd's has retained some unusual structures and practices that differ from all other insurance providers today.

The Society of Lloyd's does not underwrite insurance business, leaving that role to its members, who group themselves together into syndicates in order to achieve the scale needed in today's large scale world. Instead, the Society of Lloyd's operates as a market place supervisor and manager; setting rules under which the members operate and providing a range of centralised administrative services to those members. Additionally, The Society of Lloyd's holds the essential international licences on behalf of its Members, which allows them to underwrite business in virtually every country throughout the world.

Structurally, Lloyd's is governed by the Council of Lloyd's, an eighteen member body that is roughly equivalent to the board of directors of a company. The Council administers the Corporation of Lloyd's, which runs the various services and administrative operations of the market place. The Council delegates many of its day to day oversight roles, in respect of the insurance business being undertaken by the Members, to its Franchise Board.

While Lloyd's supervises the operation of the market place and the members within it, the whole market and those working there are regulated according to rules laid down by the UK Financial Services Authority.

The Businesses at Lloyd's

There are various different groups of people active within the Businesses at Lloyd's.

Firstly there are the **Members** who provide the capital to back the risks underwritten.

The capital of these Members is contracted by **Managing Agents** each year to provide backing to **Syndicates**. In these Syndicates each member takes on risks – 'each underwriting member for his own part and not one for another' (Lloyd's Act 1982). Each Syndicate has its own **Underwriter** who is an employee of the Managing Agent as well as, very often, class or specialist underwriters.

To administer the affairs of Members who are not aligned to a Managing Agent there are **Members' Agents**. Such agents deliver capital and often provide their members' capital backing to new ventures.

The insurance risks are brought to the Lloyd's market place by the **Brokers**, who act on behalf of their clients (the insured) seeking, across the range of Lloyd's syndicates, the best available insurance cover.

The Members

Throughout Lloyd's history wealthy individuals, often known as 'Names', backed the policies underwritten at Lloyd's with all of their personal wealth. They had unlimited liability.

In 1994, alongside these traditional members, Lloyd's allowed Corporate Members with limited liability into the market place, while at the same time building up the Lloyd's Central Fund to cover any shortfalls that might ever occur. This change to the membership came about following some very severe losses in the early 1990s which devastated the finances of many Names.

The introduction of corporate capital has resulted in the market growing quite significantly and, by 2009, traditional non-aligned Names provide about 14% of this larger market's capital with many Names now underwriting their Lloyd's business within their own Namecos or Limited Liability Partnerships (privately owned companies that back Lloyd's syndicates).

No new Names with unlimited liability are now admitted: only seven hundred and seventy three such Members remain active.

The Managing Agents

Managing Agents create and manage the Syndicates at Lloyd's. They canvass members for commitments of capacity each year, create the syndicate, hire underwriters, and oversee all of the syndicate's activities. Many Managing Agents run more than one syndicate.

The Syndicates

Members do not write insurance policies directly, but through syndicates. In the 2009 account there are over eighty syndicates competing against each other for business.

Some syndicates specialise in niche insurance areas (such as aviation, marine hull, motor etc.) while others are composite syndicates with different underwriting divisions focusing on their specialty areas, as part of a larger unit. Syndicates employ Underwriters who decide which policies and at what prices the syndicate should write business.

A syndicate at Lloyd's is not in any way a partnership. Members just take their proportion of the risks and rewards for their own account alone and are not responsible if another Member cannot meet its obligations. Any such failure is dealt with by payments from the Lloyd's Central Fund.

Members of a syndicate can underwrite very different levels of business based on their capital provided and appetite for risk.

The Underwriters

The Underwriters are the key people in each Managing Agent, as they are the employees given the responsibility of taking on the risks for their Syndicates.

Whether it is spaceships, drilling rigs in 6,000 metres (18,000 feet) of water, copper mines in Chile liable to floods or helicopters flying into Afghanistan, it is to these Underwriters that the Brokers go to secure insurance cover for their clients.

As Lloyd's is often the world's last resort for high risks, complex risks, new risks, big risks and dangerous risks it is to these Underwriters that the Brokers go when all other avenues are closed.

In the Lloyd's Underwriter there is a vast depth of risk wisdom. Collectively across all the Syndicates, this is the Lloyd's insurance market. It fits no tick boxes and never will.

The Members' Agents

Members' Agents are companies specifically established to provide services and perform duties for Members. They look after those members who are not aligned to any particular Managing Agent.

These services and duties include researching all Lloyd's Syndicates and Managing Agents. They then advise their Members on which Syndicates they should participate and at what level.

Additionally, Members' Agents work with Managing Agents to assess capital provision from Members for new ventures at Lloyd's.

The risks attaching to membership are such that external Members of Lloyd's must have this experienced interface with their underwriting business.

The Brokers

Brokers act as the intermediary between their clients seeking insurance cover and the underwriters willing to carry, on behalf of the Members, the risks being laid off.

Lloyd's has over the years had a large number of authorised Brokers where their affairs were monitored by the Society of Lloyd's and their personnel were regulated as well. Until 1984, some Lloyd's Brokers also controlled Managing Agents but the Lloyd's Act 1982 forced them to withdraw from such ownership. That position has recently changed but, as yet, no new Broker-controlled Managing Agent has appeared.

London is an international insurance centre with enormous expertise available. There are many very specialised Brokers arranging a vast array of risk transfer, a lot of which finds its way to Lloyd's.

Some Brokers are large enough to have different divisions dealing with the different classes of insurance and reinsurance. Lloyd's, as a market place, is well known to underwrite very large and complex risks which, by their very nature, have to be divided into smaller, more manageable sizes.

The Brokers, with their knowledge of the market, arrange the placements over several syndicates. This in turn creates the reinsurance market where underwriters lay off their own exposure to accumulations of catastrophe risk, which these Brokers also arrange.

Contents

Contents

Lloyd's Origins

A Brief History

1688	Coffee arrived in London in 1650 and became the fashionable drink of the day and lots of coffee houses opened up. The river by the Tower was the port of London and the first known mention of Edward Lloyd's coffee house in Tower Street is in the 'London Gazette' of 18-21 February 1688. Edward Lloyd made his coffee house a meeting place for merchants and insurers. He built on this by arranging a network of correspondents in ports throughout Britain and on the Continent who could provide him with news of shipping movements. Edward Lloyd only provided the services for shipowners who went round to lay off their risks. Those who accepted these risks were known as underwriters as one signed underneath the other.

The Lombard Street plaque

1691   Edward Lloyd moved his business to Lombard Street.

1696   Edward Lloyd started a regular bulletin 'Lloyd's News'.

1713   Edward Lloyd died. The coffee house management had been taken over by Newton and then Sheppard while the City was gripped by the South Sea Bubble speculation.

1720   The South Sea Bubble burst. King George I asked for a £300,000 favour of Parliament to approve an Insurance Act to restrict insurance to two chartered companies, the Royal Exchange Assurance Corporation and the London Assurance Corporation. However, individuals were exempt from the duopoly granted to the two companies. Also the two companies seemed to lack the experience of insurance that the individuals operating at Lloyds had, so the duopoly tended to concentrate on fire and life policies and Lloyd's underwriters on shipping and commerce.

1734   Jemson, who had taken over management of the Coffee House in 1727, revived the idea of a newspaper and in April 1734 Richard Baker, the new proprietor, produced Lloyd's List for the first time. However, his coffee house began to fall into disrepute and became the haunt of gamblers and speculators, as well as underwriters.

1769   On 21 March Thomas Fielding opened up a rival coffee house called 'The New Lloyd's'. The more serious Members of Lloyd's then left Richard Baker's coffee house to frequent this new establishment.

1771   At a significant meeting on 13th December in Pope's Head Alley seventy-nine Lloyd's underwriters drew up an agreement to subscribe £100 each and form a committee by ballot. The committee was charged with either building or finding new premises. One of the original subscribers was John Julius Angerstein. (A full profile of him can be found in the Lloyd's Personal Profile section.) However, they were unable to make any progress until John Julius Angerstein arranged on his own account two large rooms in the Royal Exchange which had been occupied by the British Herring Fishery.

The second Royal Exchange

1774   Lloyd's ceased to be a coffee house and became the property of the subscribers. The Society of Lloyd's moved into the first floor of the second Royal Exchange building. The first Master of the new premises was Thomas Taylor, who was appointed in 1774 to see to the smooth running of the rooms and the publications of Lloyd's List, as well as communication with correspondents. The first Committee of Lloyd's was elected and comprised nine subscribers.

1779   The General Meeting approved the adoption of a standard Lloyd's policy.

1780   A subscriber, John Weskitt, complained: "Litigation has become so rife that there is a necessity for the daily attendance of no less than four or five attorneys at Lloyd's."

1796   The Committee resolved that two ordinary general meetings should be held each year and an annual report and accounts should be presented. During the American War of Independence and the Napoleonic Wars, Lloyd's had a turbulent time with many fortunes being made and lost.

1798   After the Battle of the Nile, the Lloyd's Committee raised the sum of £38,000 to help the wounded and bereaved, and also donated a silver dinner service to Admiral Lord Nelson. He understood that Britain's prosperity depended on the protection of its sea-borne trade. Likewise Lloyd's and the rest of the English commercial world were deeply conscious of the debt they owed to the Royal Navy and to Nelson in particular.

Nelson leaves England for the last time on 14 September 1805

1803   The Lloyd's Patriotic Fund was established to raise funds for victims of the Napoleonic Wars. The meeting was chaired by Brook Watson. (Please see the profile of Brook Watson in the Personal Profiles section and details of the Patriotic Fund in the Charities section.)

1804   John Bennett Jnr became the first Secretary to Lloyd's.

1810   A Bill was brought before Parliament to break the 1720 duopoly enjoyed by the two companies but was defeated by one vote.

1811   A general meeting of subscribers adopted a trust deed giving Lloyd's a constitution. This regulated more strictly admission to Lloyd's.

1824   Nathan Rothschild together with Alexander Baring, Samuel Gurney and Sir Moses Montefiore successfully petitioned Parliament again for the removal of restrictions on marine underwriting. They had formed the 'Alliance British & Foreign Fire & Life Assurance Company' and wanted it to be able to participate in the lucrative marine premiums. Parliament allowed the existence of insurance companies other than Royal Exchange and London Assurance.

1829   The Lloyd's Benevolent Fund was set up to assist those in need in the Lloyd's community. (Please see details of the Benevolent Fund in the Charities section.)

1838	The premises at the Royal Exchange were destroyed by a fire which had started in the Captain's Room kitchen. For the next seven years, Lloyds became tenants of the South Sea Company. Many early Lloyd's records were destroyed by the fire.
1844	Lloyd's Market returned to the rebuilt third Royal Exchange building.
1857	First deposit for security made with Committee by an underwriting member.
1871	Lloyd's was incorporated by a private Act of Parliament. This Act was supplemented by Acts in 1888 (including one on Lloyd's Signal Stations), 1911, 1925, 1951 and 1982.
1873	The Lloyd's seal with the motto 'Fidentia' was affixed to every Lloyd's policy.
1880	Cuthbert Heath became an underwriting member and started writing risks other than marine risks. (His profile can be found in the Personal Profiles section.) A side effect of this departure was the formation of syndicates with underwriting agents introducing 'Names' to active underwriters.
1887	Cuthbert Heath wrote the first Lloyd's reinsurance policy on American risks for a British company doing business in the US.
1903	The Lloyd's Committee accepted the first non-marine deposit establishing the non-marine alongside marine business.
1904	The first Lloyd's motor insurance policy was issued.
1906	San Francisco earthquake claims were met by Lloyd's underwriters, so establishing Lloyd's reputation in the US.
1906-7	Cuthbert Heath devised excess loss reinsurance following the San Francisco claims.
1908	Annual audit and the premiums trust fund was introduced and made compulsory by law under the Assurance Companies Acts 1909-1946.
1911	The first aviation insurance policy was issued at Lloyd's.
1923	The underwriters led by Cuthbert Heath had pressed for an annual audit to determine solvency of each syndicate. The Harrison syndicate defaulted and at the subsequent General Meeting underwriters voted to protect the policyholder and each contributed to pay the debt.
1925	The Lloyd's Central Fund was created.
1928	The requirement for more space grew constantly and in 1928 Lloyd's transferred to Sir Edwin Cooper's elegant building on the corner of Leadenhall Street and Lime Street, which was opened by HM King George V and HM Queen Mary.
1939	The Lloyd's American Trust Fund was established for US Dollar premiums.

The third Royal Exchange

The Lloyd's Seal

The Leadenhall Street building

1953   The Lloyd's Charities Trust was established to donate to a number of charities. (Please see details of the Charities Trust in the Charities section.)

1958   Lloyd's transferred to the new Lime Street building which had been officially opened by HM Queen Elizabeth The Queen Mother on 14th November 1957.

1965   Hurricane Betsy was the first hurricane to cause over a billion US Dollars in damage (1965 Dollars not adjusted for inflation) in the United States and earned the nickname 'Billion-Dollar Betsy'. It led to unprecedented losses at Lloyd's and a decline in membership. A committee was established under the Chairmanship of Lord Cromer to report on changes necessary to improve the Society and to increase membership.

The Lime Street building

1968   The Lloyd's Committee admitted non-UK or Commonwealth Members.

1978   A general meeting of Members agreed the establishment of a working party to examine self-regulation at Lloyd's, to be chaired by Sir Henry Fisher.

1979   HM Queen Elizabeth The Queen Mother opened Lloyd's administration headquarters building in Chatham, Kent.

1980   A draft Lloyd's Act of Parliament based on the Fisher proposals was approved at an Extraordinary General Meeting of the Members.

1982   The Lloyd's Act 1982 received Royal Assent. This led to Lloyd's brokers having to divest their businesses of their Lloyd's underwriting interests. The first Council of Lloyd's was established.

1983   At the first meeting of the Council of Lloyd's, the first Chief Executive was appointed. (Please see listings of all Lloyd's Chairmen, Deputy Chairmen and Chief Executive Officers in the Lloyd's History section.)

1986   Space demands and better communications forced Lloyd's to move again. The iconic building at Number One Lime Street, designed by Richard Rogers, was opened by HM Queen Elizabeth in November.

1988   The Lloyd's Tercentenary Foundation was set up to commemorate Lloyd's 300th anniversary. (Please see details of the Tercentenary Foundation in the Charities section.)

1989   Lloyd's Community Programme was set up to provide volunteering opportunities for individuals and companies at Lloyd's to support the local community. (Please see details of the Community Programme in the Lloyd's Charities section.)

1991   The Lloyd's Council commissioned a Task Force under the chairmanship of David Rowland to look beyond the immediate future and identify the framework within which the Society should be trading.

The current Lime Street building

1993	David Rowland was appointed as the first full-time remunerated Chairman of Lloyd's.
1994	Corporate Members were accepted for the first time and commenced underwriting with £1.6 billion capacity.
1997	Conclusion of 'Reconstruction and Renewal'. The Lloyd's settlement proposals were accepted by 95 per cent of Members and Equitas became the reinsurer of all Lloyd's members' liabilities emanating from policies underwritten before 1993.
1998	The Government announced the independent regulation of Lloyd's by the Financial Services Authority effective from 30 November 2001.
2002	Lloyd's Members approved the proposals of the Chairman's Strategy Group. These outlined major changes to transform Lloyd's into a modern dynamic marketplace attractive to capital providers and policyholders.
2003	The Franchise Board was set up and the first ever Franchise Performance Director, Rolf Tolle, was appointed. (His profile can be found in the Franchise section.)
2005	In the aftermath of Hurricane Katrina, the largest insured loss in history, which swamped New Orleans, Lloyd's emerged with only a small market loss and reinforced its commitment to help a devastated region to rebuild.
2007	Equitas secured reinsurance from a division of Berkshire Hathaway Inc as the first part of a deal to remove all reinsured liabilities from Lloyd's Members.
2008	Lloyd's maintained its financial strength and rating despite the turmoil in the financial markets.
2009	A transaction between Equitas and Berkshire Hathaway Inc was approved by the UK Courts and completed. It ended the residual liabilities of Lloyd's Members under UK Law to business underwritten prior to 1993.

Publication of the first edition of *The Lime Street Guide to Lloyd's*.

Key People in History –
Chairmen
Deputy Chairmen
Chief Executive Officers
Honorary Members
Gold & Silver Medal Holders

Chairmen

1771-1777	Martin Kuyck Van Mierop	
1778-1781	Alderman George Hayley	
1782-1794	During this period the following people acted at various times as Chairmen of General Meetings; Brook Watson, Joshua Readshaw, John Julius Angerstein, John Ewer and Godfrey Thornton	
1795	John Julius Angerstein	Chairman of Lloyd's Patriotic Fund 1810-1813
1796-1806	Sir Brook Watson	Bart Lord Mayor of London 1796 Chairman of Provisional Committee Lloyd's Patriotic Fund 1803
1807	William Bell	
1808-1809	George Curling	
1809-1811	William Bell	
1811-1824	Joseph Marryat MP	
1824-1825	Benjamin Shaw	
1825-1833	Alderman William Thompson MP	Lord Mayor of London 1828
1834-1850	George Richard Robinson MP	
1851-1868	Thomas Baring MP	
1869-1886	Right Hon George Joachim Goschen MP	Created Viscount Goschen 1900
1887-1892	Right Hon Edward Charles Baring	Lord Revelstoke
1893-1901	Charles Hermann Goschen	
1902	Sir John Henry Luscombe	
1903	Joseph Edward Street	
1904	Herbert de Rougemont	Chairman of Lloyd's Patriotic Fund 1901 to 1915
1905	Edward Beauchamp	MP 1906 to 1910 and 1910 to 1922 Created a Baronet 1911
1906	Sir Frederic Bolton	Knighted 1908
1907	William Hegley Byas	
1908-1909	Sir John Henry Luscombe	
1910-1911	Sir Raymond Beck	Knighted 1911
1912	Sir John Henry Luscombe	
1913	Sir Edward Beauchamp Bart MP	
1914	Sir John Henry Luscombe	
1915-1917	Sir Raymond Beck	
1918-1919	Charles Irving de Rougemont	Chairman of Lloyd's Patriotic Fund 1927 to 1939
1920-1921	Sidney Alexander Boulton	
1922-1923	Arthur Lloyd Sturge	
1924	Ernest Edward Adams	
1925	Percy Graham MacKinnon	
1926	Eustace Ralph Pulbrook	
1927-1928	Sir Percy Graham MacKinnon	Knighted June 1928

Chairmen (continued)

1929	Arthur Reginald Mountain	
1930	Percy Hargreaves	
1931	Charles Neville Douglas Dixey	
1932-1933	Sir Percy Graham MacKinnon	Chairman of Lloyd's Patriotic Fund 1939 to 1955
1934	Charles Neville Douglas Dixey	
1935	Sir Stanley James Aubrey	
1936	Charles Neville Douglas Dixey	
1937	Robert Walker Roylance	
1938-1939	Sir Stanley James Aubrey	Knighted July 1939
1940-1946	Sir Eustace Ralph Pulbrook	Knighted July 1943
1947	Sir Philip D'Ambrumenil	
1948	Sir Eustace Ralph Pulbrook	
1949-1952	Matthew Watt Drysdale	
1953-1954	Walter Barrie	
1955-1956	Sir Matthew Watt Drysdale	Knighted February 1953
1957-1958	Sir Walter Barrie	Knighted February 1958
1959-1960	Sir Anthony Charles Grover	Knighted June 1973
1961	George Ewart Thomson	
1962	Patrick Ward Milligan	
1963	John Nalton Sharpe Ridgers	
1964-1966	Raymond Wilson Sturge	
1967-1968	Ralph Hiscox OBE	
1969-1972	Sir Henry Stenhouse Mance	Knighted January 1971
1973-1974	Paul Arthur Groser Dixey	
1975-1977	Sir Havelock Henry Trevor Hudson	Knighted January 1977
1978-1979	Ian Herbert Fyfe Findlay	
1980-1983	Sir Peter James Frederick Green	Knighted June 1982
1984-1987	Peter North Miller	
1988-1990	Walter Nicholas Murray Lawrence	
1991-1992	David Ean Coleridge	
1993-1997	Sir John David Rowland	Knighted January 1997
1998-2000	Max Taylor	
2001-2002	Saxon Riley	

Deputy Chairmen

1881-1882	Michael Wills	1933	Charles Neville Douglas Dixey
1883	Leonard Charles Wakefield	1934	Stanley James Aubrey
1884	Solomon Israel Da Costa	1935	Arthur James Whittall
1885	William Young	1936	Robert Walker Roylance
1886	Marmaduke Hart Brooking	1937	Harold Guylee Chester
1887-1888	Henry Nixon	1938-1939	Thomas Augustus Miall
1889	Marmaduke Hart Brooking	1940-1942	Harold Guylee Chester
1890	Augustus Octavius Robinson	1943-1944	Sir Stanley James Aubrey
1891	Marmaduke Hart Brooking	1945-1946	Sir Philip D'Ambrumenil
1892	Gerard Frederick Miller	1947	Matthew Watt Drysdale
1893	Leonard Charles Wakefield	1948-1950	Sir Stanley James Aubrey
1894	Joseph Edward Street	1951-1952	Walter Barrie
1895	Herbert de Rougemont	1953	George MacGowan Harper
1896	George Dalton Hardy	1954-1955	Kenneth Gordon McNeil
1897	William Hegley Byas	1956	George Ewart Thomson
1898	Solomon Israel Da Costa	1957	Anthony Eugene Myddelton Gale (to 16th January)
1899	Gerard Frederick Miller		Patrick Ward Milligan (from 23rd January)
1900	Edward Beauchamp		
1901	Henry Sampson Atkins	1958	Anthony Charles Grover
1912-1913	Sir Raymond Beck	1959	Ralph Hiscox OBE
1915-1916	Sir Edward Beauchamp Bart MP	1960	Patrick Ward Milligan
1917	Charles Irving de Rougemont	1961	Raymond Alfred James Porter
1918-1919	Cecil Charles Blogg	1962	John Nalton Sharpe Ridgers
1920	Ernest Edward St Quintin	1963	Raymond Wilson Sturge
1921	Arthur Lloyd Sturge	1964	Peter Ralph MacKinnon DSC
1922	Henry John Fairrie Dumas	1965	Kenneth Gordon McNeil CBE JP
1923	Ernest Edward Adams	1966	Charles Trevor Letts
1924	Percy Graham MacKinnon	1967	Paul Arthur Groser Dixey Henry Stenhouse Mance
1925	Eustace Ralph Pulbrook	1968	Henry Stenhouse Mance Havelock Henry Trevor Hudson
1926	Percy Janson (to 19th May) Chairman of Lloyd's Patriotic Fund 1916-1927 Arthur Reginald Mountain (from 19th May)	1969	Paul Arthur Groser Dixey Arthur Collwyn Sturge MC
1927	Ernest Edward Adams	1970	Arthur Collwyn Sturge MC Charles Nugent Close-Smith
1928	Charles Irving de Rougemont	1971	Havelock Henry Trevor Hudson Leslie Robert Dew
1929	Percy Hargreaves		
1930	Charles Neville Douglas Dixey	1972	Paul Arthur Groser Dixey Jack Norman Creswell
1931-1932	Austin Wilfrid Street		

Deputy Chairmen (continued)

1973	Havelock Henry Trevor Hudson Thomas Bennett Langton MC		1989	David Ean Coleridge Colin Keith Murray
1974	Jack Norman Creswell Thomas Bennett Langton MC		1990	Colin Keith Murray Alan Francis Jackson
1975	Leslie Robert Dew Alec Wilfred Higgins MBE MC DL JP		1991	Alan Francis Jackson John Scott Greig
1976	Alec Wilfred Higgins MBE MC DL JP Peter Lawrence Foden-Pattinson		1992	John Scott Greig Richard Dennis Hazell
1977	Leslie Robert Dew (to 2nd March) Ian Herbert Fyfe Findlay Adam Bruce Gray (from 3rd March)		1993-1993	Stephen Roy Merrett Resigned - September 1993
1978	Adam Bruce Gray Charles Oliver Gibb		1993-1995	Robert Ralph Scrymgeour Hiscox
1979	Charles Oliver Gibb Peter James Frederick Green1980 Charles Oliver Gibb Alec Wilfred Higgins MBE MC DL JP		1993-1993	Brian Pattison Garraway* Deceased - September 1993
			1993-1994	Richard John Ratcliffe Keeling
			1993-1997	Sir Alan Hardcastle FCA*
1981	Alec Wilfred Higgins MBE MC DL JP Brian John Brennan MC		1995-1996	John Lawrence Stace
1982	Brian John Brennan MC Walter Nicholas Murray Lawrence		1996-1997	John Robert Charman
1983	Brian John Brennan MC Frank Barber		1997-1999	Ian Charles Agnew
1984	Frank Barber Walter Nicholas Murray Lawrence		1997-2002	John Robert Chester Young CBE*
			1998-1998	Elvin Ensor Patrick
1985	Walter Nicholas Murray Lawrence David Ean Coleridge		1999-2000	Saxon Riley
1986	Walter Nicholas Murray Lawrence Michael Henry Cockell		2000-2000	Paul Nicholas Archard
			2001-2005	David John Coldman
1987	Walter Nicholas Murray Lawrence Alan Parry		2001-2006	Bronislaw Edmund Masojada
1988	David Ean Coleridge Alan Parry		2002-2008	William John Langford Knight*

Also Deputy Chairman of the Council

Chief Executive Officers

ALSO LLOYD'S DEPUTY CHAIRMAN

1993-1995	Peter James Middleton		1999-2005	Nicholas Edward Tucker Prettejohn
1995-1999	Ronald Arnon Sandler			

Honorary Members

1824	James William Freshfield MP	Solicitor to Lloyd's
1824	James William Freshfield, Jnr.	
1845	Sir William Tite CB MP FRS	Architect of the Royal Exchange 1841-1844
1871	Edwin Freshfield LL D FSA	Solicitor to the Corporation of Lloyd's
1871	Charles Walton	Solicitor to the Corporation of Lloyd's
1884	Henry Caspar Heintz	
1889	Viscount Goschen	Chairman of Lloyd's from 1869 to 1886
1891	Sir William Walton KBE	late of Waltons & Co Solicitors to the Corporation of Lloyd's
1906	Colonel Sir Henry Montague Hozier KCB	Secretary of Lloyd's from 1874 to 1906
1919	Marchese Guglielmo Marconi GCVO LL D DSc	
1919	Admiral of the Fleet The Earl Beatty GGB OM GCVO	
1920	Field-Marshal The Earl Haig KT GCB OM GCVO KCLE	
1920	Admiral of the Fleet Sir Frederick Charles Doyeton-Sturdee Bt GCB KCMG GVO	
1921	Samuel Garrett	late of Parker Garrett & Co Solicitors
1922	Rear-Admiral Sir Edward Fitzmaurice Inglefield KBE	Secretary of Lloyd's from 1906 to 1921
1922	Hugh de Heriz Whatton	late of Waltons & Co Solicitors to the Corporation of Lloyd's
1923	Sidney Alexander Boulton	Chairman of Lloyd's from 1920 and 1921
1924	William Clifton	late of WA Crump & Son Solicitors
1924	Sir Joseph Lowrey KBE	Secretary, The Salvage Association, London
1928	Sir Edwin Cooper ARA (RA 1937)	Architect of the Lloyd's Building 1924-1928
1932	Sir John Henry Luscombe JP	Chairman of Lloyd's 1902, 1908, 1909, 1912, 1914
1944	The Right Honourable Winston Spencer Churchill CH MP	
1946	Oscar Dibble Duncan	The first General Counsel appointed by Lloyd's for USA
1948	Field-Marshal The Right Hon. J. C. Smuts OM CH KC DTD	
1952	William Blanc Mendes	Senior Partner, Mendes & Mount, General Counsel for Lloyd's in the USA
1957	Terence Ernest Heysham FRIBA	Architect of Lloyd's New Building 1951-1958
1965	David Matthew	of Waltons Bright & Co. Solicitors to the Corporation of Lloyd's
1966	The Right Honourable Sir Robert Menzie KT CH QC FRS	
1974	Her Majesty Queen Elizabeth The Queen Mother	
1983	The Honourable Sir Henry Fisher	
1988	Edward Ian Walker-Arnott	Nominated Member of the Council of Lloyd's 1983-1988
1989	Her Royal Highness The Princess Royal GCVO	
2004	Brian Walter Pomeroy	Nominated Member of the Council of Lloyd's July 1987 to December 1992 January 1996 to December 2004

Gold Medal Holders

Awarded for services to Lloyd's

1919	Sir Raymond Beck JP	Chairman of Lloyd's 1910, 1911, 1915, 1916, 1917
1920	Sir John Henry Luscome JP	Chairman of Lloyd's 1902, 1908, 1909, 1912, 1914
1923	Arthur Lloyd Sturge	Chairman of Lloyd's 1922, 1923
1928	Sir Percy Graham MacKinnon	Chairman of Lloyd's 1925, 1927, 1928, 1932, 1933
1932	Sir Eustace Ralph Pulbrook	Knighted July 1943 Chairman of Lloyd's 1926, 1940 to 1946, 1948
1939	Sir Stanley James Aubrey	Chairman of Lloyd's 1935, 1938, 1939
1943	Sir Philip D'Ambrumenil Chairman of Lloyd's 1947	Knighted January 1945
1945	Sir Walter Ernest Hargreaves KBE	
1952	Sir Matthew Watt Drysdale	Knighted February 1953 Chairman of Lloyd's 1949, 1950, 1951, 1952, 1955, 1956
1957	Sir Walter Barrie	Knighted February 1958 Chairman of Lloyd's 1953, 1954, 1957, 1958
1965	David Eric Wilson Gibb	
1972	Sir Henry Stenhouse Mance	Chairman of Lloyd's 1969, 1970, 1971, 1972
1977	Sir Havelock Henry Trevor Hudson	Chairman of Lloyd's 1975, 1976, 1977
1983	Sir Peter James Frederick Green	Chairman of Lloyd's 1980, 1981, 1982, 1983
1988	Sir Peter North Miller	Knighted June 1988 Chairman of Lloyd's 1984, 1985, 1986, 1987
1996	Sir John David Rowland	Knighted January 1997 Chairman of Lloyd's 1993, 1994, 1995, 1996, 1997

Silver Medal Holders

Awarded for services to Lloyd's

1976	Ernest Blain Parke MBE	
1978	Raymond Alfred James Porter	
1986	Charles Brandon Gough MA FCA	
1991	Gerald Ralph Auchinleck Darling RD DL QC MA	
1996	Ronald Arnon Sandler	Chief Executive Officer 1995
1996	Robin Anthony Charles Hewes	Director of Finance 1994-2000
1996	Richard Ratcliffe Keeling	Chairman Reserve Group
1996	Barry John O'Brien	Partner, Freshfield
2005	Saxon Riley	Chairman 2001-2002
2005	Nicholas Edward Tucker Prettejohn	Chief Executive Officer 1999-2005

People at Lloyd's

Profiles – Council

Lord Levene of Portsoken, KBE
Chairman of Lloyd's
(Working member)

Dr Richard Ward
Chief Executive Officer
(Nominated member)

Ewen Gilmour
Deputy Chairman of Lloyd's
(Working member)

Dr Andreas Prindl, CBE
Deputy Chairman of Lloyd's
(Nominated member)

Graham White
Deputy Chairman of Lloyd's
(Working member)

Rupert Atkin
(Working member)

Michael Deeny
(External member)

Celia Denton
(Nominated member)

Sir Robert Finch
(Nominated member)

Christopher Harman
(Working member)

Dr Reg Hinkley
(Nominated member)

Martin Hudson
Representative of
Aprilgrange Limited
(External member)

Paul Jardine
Representative of
Catlin Syndicate Limited
(External member)

The Honorable Philip Lader
(Nominated member)

Alan Lovell
(External member)

Nick Marsh
(Working member)

Eileen McCusker
Representative of Dornoch Limited
(External member)

Barbara Merry
Representative of Hardy
Underwriting Limited
(External member)

Council Secretariat

Secretary	Gavin Steele
Address	One Lime Street
	London EC3M 7HA
Telephone	+44 (0)20 7327 6032
Fax	+44 (0)20 7327 6156
Email	gavin.steele@lloyds.com
Website	www.lloyds.com

Lord Levene of Portsoken, KBE

Chairman (Working Member)

Appointed/Elected	2002
Telephone	+44 (0)20 7327 6556
Fax	+44 (0)20 7327 5926
Email	peter.levene@lloyds.com
Secretary/PA	Barbara Addison
Telephone	+44 (0)20 7327 6556

Full Name	Lord Peter Keith Levene, KBE
Year of Birth	1941
Qualifications	BA Econ, QMW, CCMI, FCIPS, Hon.FCII, Hon.DSc

PROFESSIONAL INFORMATION

CURRENT MAJOR POSITIONS/APPOINTMENTS

Liveryman	The Worshipful Company of	
	Information Technologists	1993 -
Director	Haymarket Group Ltd	1997-
Peer	Portsoken Ward	1998 -
Chairman	International Financial Services London	2000 -
Chairman	General Dynamics UK Ltd	2001 -
Board Member	Total SA	2005 -
Director	China Construction Bank	2006 -
Board Member	The House of Lords Select Committee	
	on Economic Affairs	2008 -
Alderman	Aldgate Ward	2005 -

PREVIOUS MAJOR POSITIONS/APPOINTMENTS

Managing Director	United Scientific Holding	1968 - 1985
Member	SE Asia Trade Advisory Group	1979 - 1983
Chairman	United Scientific Holding	1982 - 1985
Council	Defence Manufacturers' Association	1982 - 1985
Vice-Chairman	Defence Manufacturers' Association	1983 - 1984
Chairman	Defence Manufacturers' Association	1984 - 1985
Personal Advisor	Secretary of State for Defence	1984 - 1984
Member Board of Management	London Homes for the Elderly	1984 - 1993
Chief of Defence Procurement	Ministry of Defence	1985 - 1991

UK National Armaments Director	Ministry of Defence	1988 - 1991
Chairman	European National Armaments	1989 - 1990
Chairman	London Homes for the Elderly	1990 - 1993
Personal Advisor	Secretary of State for the Environment	1991 - 1992
Chairman	Docklands Light Railway	1991 - 1994
Deputy Chairman	Wasserstein Perella & Co Ltd	1991 - 1994
Personal Advisor	Chancellor of the Exchequer on Competition & Purchasing	1992 - 1992
Advisory Panel Member	Citizen's Charter	1992 - 1993
Personal Advisor	President of Board of Trade	1992 - 1995
Personal Advisor	Prime Minister on Efficiency and Effectiveness	1992 - 1997
Chairman and Chief Executive	Canary Wharf Ltd	1993 - 1996
Senior Advisor	Morgan Stanley & Co Ltd	1996 - 1998
Lord Mayor of London		1998 - 1999
Chairman	Bankers Trust International plc	1998 - 1999
International Advisory Board	Singapore Government International Laboratories	1998 - 1999
Chairman's Council	Alcatel	2000 - 2003
Vice-Chairman	Deutsche Bank, Investment Banking Europe	2001 - 2002
Director	Sainsbury plc	2001 - 2004
Chairman	World Trade Centre Disaster Fund (UK)	2001 - 2006

Main Interests and Recreation	Skiing, watching Association football, travel
Clubs/Memberships	Guildhall, City Livery, Royal Automobile Club

Dr Richard Ward

Chief Executive Officer (Nominated Member)

Appointed/Elected	2006
Telephone	+44 (0)20 7226 6930
Fax	+44 (0)20 7327 5926
Email	richard.ward@lloyds.com
Secretary/PA	Lesley Penney
Telephone	+44 (0)20 7226 6920

Full Name	Richard Churchill Ward
Year of Birth	1957
Qualifications	PHD

PROFESSIONAL INFORMATION

CURRENT MAJOR POSITIONS/APPOINTMENTS
See above

PREVIOUS MAJOR POSITIONS/APPOINTMENTS

Senior Physicist	Science and Engineering Research Council	1982 - 1988
Senior Manager	BP Research	1988 - 1991
Head of Business Development	BP Oil Trading International	1991 - 1994
Head of Marketing	Tradition Financial Services	1994 - 1995
Director, Product Development	ICE Futures	1995 - 1996
Vice-President	ICE Futures	1996 - 1999

Dr Richard Ward (continued)

| Chief Executive Officer | ICE Futures | 1999 - 2005 |
| Vice-Chairman | ICE Futures | 2005 - 2006 |

| Main Interests and Recreation | Capsizing small dinghies, hockey, skiing, tennis |

Ewen H Gilmour

Deputy Chairman of Lloyd's (Working Member)

Appointed/Elected	2006
Telephone	+44 (0)20 7105 8080
Fax	+44 (0)20 7105 8300
Email	c/o Secretariat
Secretary/PA	Diane Mackey
Telephone	+44 (0)20 7105 8054

| PERSONAL PROFILE | A profile can be found in the People at Lloyd's, Managing Agents section. |

Dr Andreas R Prindl, CBE

Deputy Chairman of Lloyd's (Nominated Member)

Appointed/Elected	2003
Telephone	+44 (0)20 7638 9382
Fax	+44 (0)20 7327 6156
Email	c/o Secretariat

Full Name	Andreas Robert Prindl, CBE
Year of Birth	1939
Qualifications	BA Princeton University, MA, PHD University of Kentucky , Hon DSc

PROFESSIONAL INFORMATION

CURRENT MAJOR POSITIONS/APPOINTMENTS

| Liveryman | The Worshipful Company of Musicians | 1999 - |
| Visiting Professor | People's University of China | 2000 - |

PREVIOUS MAJOR POSITIONS/APPOINTMENTS

General Manager	Morgan Guaranty Trust Company, New York and Frankfurt	1964 - 1970
Vice-President	IMM, London	1970 - 1976
General Manager	IMM, Tokyo	1976 - 1980
Chief Executive Officer	Saudi International Bank, London	1980 - 1982
Vice-President	Morgan Guaranty Trust Company	1982 - 1984
Managing Director	Nomura Bank International	1984 - 1986
President	Chartered Institute of Bankers	1994 - 1995
Chairman	Banking Industry Training and Development Council	1994 - 1996
President	Association of Corporate Treasurers	1996 - 1996
Chairman	Nomura Bank International	1990 - 1997
Provost	Gresham College	1996 - 1999

Master	The Worshipful Company of Musicians	2006 - 2007
Governor	Yehudi Menuhin School	Unknown
Trustee	Good Vibrations (Charity)	2008-
Main Interests and Recreation	Classical music, Asian art and history	
Clubs/Memberships	Reform Club	

Graham J White

Deputy Chairman of Lloyd's (Working Member)

Appointed/Elected	2006
Telephone	+44 (0)20 7825 7182
Fax	+44 (0)20 7825 7299
Email	c/o Secretariat
Secretary/PA	Ann Kisberg
Telephone	+44 (0)20 7825 7136

PERSONAL PROFILE   A profile can be found in the People at Lloyd's, Personal section.

Rupert Atkin

Working Member

Appointed/Elected	2007
Contact	c/o Secretariat

PERSONAL PROFILE   A profile can be found in the People at Lloyd's, Personal section.

Michael EM Deeny

External Member

Appointed/Elected	2009
Contact	c/o Secretariat

PERSONAL PROFILE   A profile can be found in the People at Lloyd's, Personal section.

Celia Denton

Nominated Member

Appointed/Elected	2005
Contact	c/o Secretariat

Full Name	Celia Denton
Year of Birth	1952
Qualifications	ACA

PROFESSIONAL INFORMATION

CURRENT MAJOR POSITIONS/APPOINTMENTS

No other information available

Celia Denton (continued)

PREVIOUS MAJOR POSITIONS/APPOINTMENTS

Non-Executive Director	Esano London Friendly Society	2001 - 2004
Senior Audit Partner	Deloitte & Touche	Unknown
Head of General Insurance Practice	Deloitte & Touche	Unknown

Sir Robert Finch
Nominated Member

Appointed/Elected	2008
Contact	c/o Secretariat

Full Name	Sir Robert Gerard Finch
Year of Birth	1944
Qualifications	Information not available

PROFESSIONAL INFORMATION

CURRENT MAJOR POSITIONS/APPOINTMENTS

Chairman	Royal Brompton and Harefield Hospital	2009 -
Director	FF&P Russia Real Estate Ltd	Unknown -

PREVIOUS MAJOR POSITIONS/APPOINTMENTS

Partner	Linklaters	1974 - 2005
Head of Real Estate	Linklaters	1997 - 2005
Director	International Financial Services London	2001 - 2003
Lord Mayor of London		2003 - 2004
Church Commissioner		2003 - 2008
Chairman	Liberty International Plc	2005 - 2008

Main Interests and Recreation	Sailing, ski-ing, climbing
Clubs/Memberships	Ski Club of GB, Alpine Ski, City Livery, East India, Itchenor Sailing (W Sussex)

Christopher G Harman
Working Member

Appointed/Elected	2007
Contact	c/o Secretariat

Full Name	Christopher Gill Harman
Year of Birth	1950
Qualifications	Information not available

PROFESSIONAL INFORMATION

CURRENT MAJOR POSITIONS/APPOINTMENTS

Executive Director	Harman Kemp North America Limited	2005 -

PREVIOUS MAJOR POSITIONS/APPOINTMENTS

Non-Executive Director	The Griffin Insurance Association Limited	2002 - 2008
Executive Director	BDB Limited	2005 - 2006
Executive Director	Harman Wicks & Swayne International Limited	2005 - 2008
Chief Executive	Harman Wicks & Swayne Ltd	2005 - 2008

Dr Raymond (Reg) K Hinkley

Nominated Member

Appointed/Elected	2007
Contact	c/o Secretariat

Full Name	Raymond Keith Hinkley
Year of Birth	Information not available
Qualifications	Information not available

PROFESSIONAL INFORMATION

CURRENT MAJOR POSITIONS/APPOINTMENTS

See above

PREVIOUS MAJOR POSITIONS/APPOINTMENTS

Non-Executive Director	BP Oil UK Limited	2002 - 2004
Non-Executive Director	BP Japan Trading Limited	2002 - 2005
Non-Executive Director	BP Oil International Limited	2002 - 2005
Non-Executive Director	Britannic Energy Trading Limited	2002 - 2005
Non-Executive Director	Britannic Trading Ltd	2002 - 2005
Chief Executive Officer	BP's UK Pension Fund	Unknown - 2007

Martin P Hudson

Representative of Aprilgrange Limited (External Member)

Appointed/Elected	2009
Contact	c/o Secretariat

PERSONAL PROFILE	A profile can be found in the People at Lloyd's, Managing Agents section.

Paul A Jardine

Representative of Catlin Syndicates Limited (External Member)

Appointed/Elected	2008
Contact	c/o Secretariat

PERSONAL PROFILE	A profile can be found in the People at Lloyd's, Managing Agents section.

The Honorable Philip Lader

Nominated Member

Appointed/Elected	2004
Contact	c/o Secretariat

Full Name	Philip Lader
Year of Birth	Information not available
Qualifications	Information not available

PROFESSIONAL INFORMATION

CURRENT MAJOR POSITIONS/APPOINTMENTS

Chairman	WPP Group plc	2001 -
Senior Advisor	Morgan Stanley & Co Ltd	2001 -
Board Member	Marathon Oil	2001 -
Board Member	RAND	2001 -
Board Member	Rusal	2001 -
Board Member	AES	2002 -
Board Member	Songbird Estates	2006 -
Board Member	The Atlantic Council	Unknown
Board Member	The Smithsonian Museum of American History	2006 -

PREVIOUS MAJOR POSITIONS/APPOINTMENTS

Member	President Clinton's Cabinet
US Ambassador	Court of St James

Alan C Lovell

External Member

Appointed/Elected	2007
Contact	c/o Secretariat

PERSONAL PROFILE	A profile can be found in the People at Lloyd's, Members' Agents section.

Nick Marsh

Working Member

Appointed/Elected	2008
Contact	c/o Secretariat

PERSONAL PROFILE	A profile can be found in the People at Lloyd's, Managing Agents section.

Eileen E McCusker

External Member

Appointed/Elected	2009
Contact	c/o Secretariat

PERSONAL PROFILE   A profile can be found in the People at Lloyd's, Managing Agents section.

Barbara J Merry

External Member

Appointed/Elected	2007
Contact	c/o Secretariat

PERSONAL PROFILE   A profile can be found in the People at Lloyd's, Personal section.

Profiles – Franchise Board

**Lord Levene of
Portsoken, KBE**
Chairman

Luke Savage
Executive Director

Rolf Tolle
Executive Director
Franchise Performance

Dr Richard Ward
Executive Director

Nicholas H Furlonge
Non-Executive Director

David Shipley
Non-Executive Director

Andrew J Kendrick
Non-Executive Director

Dipesh J Shah, OBE
Non-Executive Director

Claire Ighodaro, CBE
Non-Executive Director

James Stretton
Non-Executive Director

Franchise Board Secretariat

Secretary	Gavin Steele
Address	One Lime Street
	London EC3M 7HA
Telephone	+44 (0)20 7327 6032
Fax	+44 (0)20 7327 6156
Email	gavin.steele@lloyds.com
Website	www.lloyds.com

Lord Levene of Portsoken, KBE
Chairman

Appointed/Elected	2003
Telephone	+44 (0)20 7327 6556
Fax	+44 (0)20 7327 6156
Email	peter.levene@lloyds.com
PERSONAL PROFILE	A profile can be found in the People at Lloyd's, Council section.

Dr Richard Ward
Executive Director

Appointed/Elected	2007
Telephone	+44 (0)20 7226 6930
Fax	+44 (0)20 7327 6156
Email	richard.ward@lloyds.com
PERSONAL PROFILE	A profile can be found in the People at Lloyd's, Council section.

Nicholas H Furlonge
Non-Executive Director

Appointed/Elected	2008
Contact	c/o Secretariat
PERSONAL PROFILE	A profile can be found in the People at Lloyd's, Personal section.

Claire Ighodaro, CBE

Non-Executive Director

Appointed/Elected	2008
Contact	c/o Secretariat

Full Name	Claire Aimie Ighodaro
Year of Birth	Information not available
Qualifications	Information not available

PROFESSIONAL INFORMATION

CURRENT MAJOR POSITIONS/APPOINTMENTS

Board Member	British Council	2007 -
Board Member	The Banking Code Standards Board	Unknown
Board Member	UK Trade & Investment	Unknown
Committee Member	The Learning and Skills Council	Unknown
Committee Member	The Open University	Unknown
Board Member	The Department for Business, Enterprise and Regulatory Reforms	Unknown

PREVIOUS MAJOR POSITIONS/APPOINTMENTS

President	Chartered Institute of Management Accountants	2003 - 2004

Andrew J Kendrick

Non-Executive Director

Appointed/Elected	2007
Contact	c/o Secretariat

Full Name	Andrew James Kendrick
Year of Birth	1957
Qualifications	Information not available

PERSONAL PROFILE   A profile can be found in the People at Lloyd's, Managing Agents section.

Luke Savage

Executive Director

Appointed/Elected	2004
Tel/Fax	c/o Secretariat
Email	luke.savage@lloyds.com

PERSONAL PROFILE   A profile can be found in the People at Lloyd's, Corporation section.

Dipesh J Shah, OBE

Non-Executive Director

Appointed/Elected	2008
Contact	c/o Secretariat

Full Name	Dipesh Jayantilal Shah
Year of Birth	Information not available
Qualifications	Information not available

PROFESSIONAL INFORMATION

CURRENT MAJOR POSITIONS/APPOINTMENTS

Non-Executive Director	Thames Water and Kemble Water	2007 -
Non-Executive Director	Babcock International Group Plc	1999 -
Non-Executive Director	JKX Oil and Gas Plc	Unknown

PREVIOUS MAJOR POSITIONS/APPOINTMENTS

Chairman	Viridian Group plc	Unknown
Chairman	Hg Capital Renewable Power Partners LLP	Unknown
Chief Executive	UK Atomic Energy Authority	1994 - 2002

David Shipley

Non-Executive Director

Appointed/Elected	2009
Contact	c/o Secretariat

PERSONAL PROFILE	A profile can be found in the People at Lloyd's, Personal section.

James Stretton

Non-Executive Director

Appointed/Elected	2003
Contact	c/o Secretariat

Full Name	James Stretton
Year of Birth	Information not available
Qualifications	Information not available

PROFESSIONAL INFORMATION

CURRENT MAJOR POSITIONS/APPOINTMENTS

Chairman	The Wise Group	Unknown

PREVIOUS MAJOR POSITIONS/APPOINTMENTS

Executive Director	Standard Life Pension Funds Limited	2001 - 2001
Executive Director	Standard Life Bank Plc	2001 - 2001
Executive Director	The Standard Life Assurance Company 2006	2001 - 2001

Non-Executive Director	Standard Life Investment Funds Limited	2001 - 2001
Non-Executive Director	Standard Life Investments Limited	2001 - 2001
Non-Executive Director	Standard Life Savings Limited	2001 - 2001
Member	Court of the Bank of England	1998 - 2003

Rolf AW Tolle*

Executive Director – Franchise Performance

Appointed/Elected	2003
Tel/Fax	c/o Secretariat
Email	rolf.tolle@lloyds.com

Full Name	Rolf Albert Wilhelm Tolle
Year of Birth	1947
Qualifications	Information not available

PROFESSIONAL INFORMATION

CURRENT MAJOR POSITIONS/APPOINTMENTS

Non-Executive Director	Xchanging Claims Services Board	Unknown

PREVIOUS MAJOR POSITIONS/APPOINTMENTS

Senior Position	Storebrand	Unknown
Senior Position	Unipolaris	Unknown
Managing Director	Polaris	Unknown
Chief Executive	Europa Re	1991 - 2001
Executive Director	Faraday Underwriting Limited	2001 - 2003
Executive Director	Faraday Reinsurance Co Limited	2002 - 2003

*To be replaced by Tom Bolt on 01.01.2010

Profiles – Corporation

**Lord Levene of
Portsoken, KBE**
Chairman

Dr Richard Ward
Chief Executive Officer

Ewen H Gilmour
Deputy Chairman
of Lloyd's

Dr Andreas R Prindl, CBE
Deputy Chairmen
of Lloyd's

Graham J White
Deputy Chairmen
of Lloyd's

Luke Savage
Director of Finance,
Risk Management,
and Operations

Rolf Tolle
Franchise Performance
Director

Sean G McGovern
Director &
General Counsel

Jose Ribeiro
Director of International
Markets and Business
Development

Susan (Sue) C Langley
Director of
Market Operations and
North America

Address	One Lime Street London EC3M 7HA
Website	www.lloyds.com

Lord Levene of Portsoken, KBE

Chairman

Appointed	2002
Telephone	+44 (0)20 7327 6556
Fax	+44 (0)20 7327 5926
Email	peter.levene@lloyds.com
Secretary/PA	Barbara Addison
Telephone	+44 (0)20 7327 6556

PERSONAL PROFILE	A profile can be found in the People at Lloyd's, Council section.

Dr Richard Ward

Chief Executive Officer

Appointed	2006
Telephone	+44 (0)20 7327 6930
Fax	+44 (0)20 7327 5926
Email	richard.ward@lloyds.com
Secretary/PA	Lesley Penney
Telephone	+44 (0)20 7327 6920

PERSONAL PROFILE	A profile can be found in the People at Lloyd's, Council section.

Ewen H Gilmour

Deputy Chairman of Lloyd's

Appointed	2006
Telephone	+44 (0)20 7105 8080
Fax	+44 (0)20 7105 8300
Email	ewen.gilmour@chaucerplc.com
Secretary/PA	Diane Mackey
Telephone	+44 (0)20 7105 8054

PERSONAL PROFILE	A profile can be found in the People at Lloyd's, Managing Agents section.

Dr Andreas R Prindl, CBE

Deputy Chairmen of Lloyd's

Appointed	2003
Telephone	+44 (0)20 7638 9382
Fax	+44 (0)20 7825 7299
Email	andreas.prindl@lloyds.com
PERSONAL PROFILE	A profile can be found in the People at Lloyd's, Council section.

Graham J White

Deputy Chairmen of Lloyd's

Appointed	2006
Telephone	+44 (0)20 7825 7182
Fax	+44 (0)20 7825 7299
Email	graham.white@lloyds.com
Website	www.lloyds.com
Secretary/PA	Ann Kisberg
Telephone	+44 (0)20 7825 7136
PERSONAL PROFILE	A profile can be found in the People at Lloyd's, Personal section.

Luke Savage

Director of Finance, Risk Management, and Operations

Appointed	2004
Telephone	+44 (0)20 7327 6711
Fax	+44 (0)20 7327 6604
Email	luke.savage@lloyds.com
Secretary/PA	Stephen Bancroft
Telephone	+44 (0)20 7327 6752
Full Name	Luke Savage
Year of Birth	Information not available
Qualifications	ACA accounting
	Degree in Electrical and Electronic Engineering, Imperial College London, University of London

PROFESSIONAL INFORMATION

CURRENT MAJOR POSITIONS/APPOINTMENTS

Executive Director	Lioncover Insurance Company Limited	2006 -
Executive Director	Centrewrite Limited	2008 -

PREVIOUS MAJOR POSITIONS/APPOINTMENTS

Financial Controller	Morgan Stanley	1991 - 2000
Global Head of Equity Control	Deutsche Bank	2000 - 2004
Clubs	Lloyd's Yacht Club, Honorary Treasurer	

Rolf AW Tolle*

Franchise Performance Director

Appointed	2003
Telephone	+44 (0)20 7327 6743
Fax	+44 (0)20 7327 6604
Email	rolf.tolle@lloyds.com
Secretary/PA	Sarah Brown
Telephone	+44 (0)20 7327 6742

PERSONAL PROFILE   A profile can be found in the People at Lloyd's, Franchise Board section.

*To be replaced by Tom Bolt on 01.01.2010

Sean G McGovern

Director & General Counsel

Appointed	2002
Telephone	+44 (0)20 7327 6142
Fax	+44 (0)20 7327 5414
Email	sean.mcgovern@lloyds.com
Website	www.lloyds.com
Secretary/PA	Liz Humberstone
Telephone	+44 (0)20 7327 5598
Full Name	Sean Gerard McGovern
Year of Birth	1970
Qualifications	Degree in Law, Manchester University

PROFESSIONAL INFORMATION

CURRENT MAJOR POSITIONS/APPOINTMENTS

Non Executive Director	Equitas Limited	2007 -
Non Executive Director	Equitas Reinsurance Limited	2007 -
Director	Lloyd's Reinsurance Company China Limited	2007 -
Non Executive Director	Xchanging Insurance Services Limited	2008 -
Non Executive Director	Equitas Insurance Limited	2009 -

PREVIOUS MAJOR POSITIONS/APPOINTMENTS

Solicitor	Clifford Chance	1992 - 1996
Solicitor	Lloyd's Legal Department	1996 - 2000
Head of Legal Department	Society of Lloyd's	2000 - 2008

Jose Ribeiro

Director of International Markets and Business Development

Appointed	2007
Telephone	+44 (0)20 7327 6179
Fax	+44 (0)20 7327 6604
Email	jose.ribeiro@lloyds.com
Secretary/PA	Sophie Thorne
Telephone	+44 (0)20 7327 6136
Full Name	Jose Ribeiro
Year of Birth	1961
Qualifications	Information not available

PROFESSIONAL INFORMATION

CURRENT MAJOR POSITIONS/APPOINTMENTS

Executive Director	Society of Lloyd's	2007 -

PREVIOUS MAJOR POSITIONS/APPOINTMENTS

Chief Executive Officer	AIG Life Companies	1994 - 1998
President	AIG Life Companies	1995 - 1999
Chief Executive Officer	Delphos Group	1997 - 2001
President	Delphos Group	1998 - 2002
Managing Director	Willis Group Limited	2002 - 2007

Susan (Sue) C Langley

Director of Market Operations and North America

Appointed	2007
Telephone	+44 (0)20 7327 6200
Fax	+44 (0)20 7327 6604
Email	sue.langley@lloyds.com
Secretary/PA	Laura Cole
Telephone	+44 (0)20 7327 6213
Full Name	Susan Carol Langley
Year of Birth	1963
Qualifications	Information not available

PROFESSIONAL INFORMATION

CURRENT MAJOR POSITIONS/APPOINTMENTS

Executive Director	Society of Lloyd's	2007 -

PREVIOUS MAJOR POSITIONS/APPOINTMENTS

Management Consultant	Thomson Tour Operations	1990 - 1996
Management Consultant	Price Waterhouse	1996 - 1998
Chief Information Officer	Hiscox	1998 - 2001
Group Operations Director	Hiscox	2001 - 2004
Chief Operating Officer	Hiscox	2004 - 2007

Profiles – Personal

John Julius Angerstein

Insurance Broker and Underwriter

Full Name	John Julius Angerstein

Lived

Julius Angerstein was born in 1735 in St Petersburg, Russia and was baptised there in the Lutheran Church. His father was possibly Johan Angerstein, a surgeon from Coburg, Germany but more probably Andrew Thomson, a British merchant. His mother was very likely Mrs Eva Angerstein (wife of Johan) who came from Archangel, but there are suggestions that he might have been the illegitimate son of a Russian princess. He died in 1823 and is buried in a vault under St Alfege's Church, Greenwich.

Nationality

John Julius Angerstein was naturalised in 1770 by Act of Parliament, as was required at that time.

PROFESSIONAL INFORMATION

Elected to Lloyd's

1771

Career

John Julius Angerstein started business in 1756 as junior partner to Alexander Dick at Cowper's Court, Cornhill and is likely to have specialised in Baltic risks for Thomson & Peters. From about 1768 until 1777 John Julius Angerstein was a sole principal with his office at 71 Old Broad Street.

In 1771 John Julius Angerstein was one of the original 79 subscribers to New Lloyd's but not on the original Committee. He negotiated the lease of premises for Lloyd's in the Royal Exchange two years later and took Thomas Lewis into partnership in 1777 with their address being Throgmorton Street until 1786 when they moved to rooms in the Royal Exchange and Angerstein joined the Committee.

The position of Chairman was ill-defined at this time and meetings, which took place irregularly, tended to be chaired by one or other senior Committee member. On this basis Angerstein can fairly be described as Chairman of Lloyd's for 1795/96. He left the Committee in September 1796 but continued as a Subscriber for a further 15 years.

Thomas Lewis retired circa 1792 and Peter Warren was Angerstein's partner from 1785 to 1799. Vincent Francis Rivaz then joined him and after Angerstein's retirement continued the business in partnership with Charles Richard Harford. Two family members were also briefly in partnership with Angerstein.

Principal Underwriting Area/
Main area of Expertise

Marine Insurance. He was one of the principal witnesses before the Parliamentary Committee on Marine Insurance in 1810. He was also both a shipbroker and a shipowner around the time of the American War, and was involved with the Lloyd's Register of Shipping for many years.

John Julius Angerstein (continued)

Most Interesting Policies/Claims	In 1799 Angerstein placed the insurance on Lutine (for a full story on Lutine and the Lutine bell please see Lloyd's Yacht Club in Lloyd's Clubs and Societies section) and was one of the underwriters. In 1807 he placed the insurance on a cargo of bullion and specie carried by the frigate Diana from Vera Cruz. The sum involved was a record £656,800 – about £45 million at today's prices. The voyage was completed safely. Between 1788 and 1810 he placed insurances amounting to almost £8.5 million for a 'very respectable and honourable house' (probably Sir Robert Wigram) and recovered almost £500,000 in losses, averages and returns.
Longest Customer Relationship(s)	Andrew Thomson
Major Achievements whilst at Lloyd's	Lloyd's did not emerge from the Coffee House stage until the last quarter of the eighteenth century. Under the guidance of Angerstein, it took up its position in the old Royal Exchange and, after the fire, in the present Royal Exchange (opened by Her Majesty Queen Victoria in 1844). John Julius Angerstein largely moulded both broking and underwriting so that he is traditionally known as the 'Father of Lloyd's'.
	John Julius Angerstein was one of a small group of men who acted as loan contractors during the Napoleonic period, underwriting and placing large sums of Government stock in the London market. Angerstein often worked with Sir Francis Baring and subsequently the latter's son Alexander.

PERSONAL INFORMATION

Home	In 1774 he built Woodlands, Blackheath. He also leased 100 Pall Mall which subsequently became the home of the first National Gallery and contained many pictures from his own collection.
Charitable/Voluntary Activities	John Julius Angerstein supported innumerable good causes. In 1802 he took the lead in arranging for Lloyd's to put up £2,000 – about £135,000 at today's prices – for encouraging the development of lifeboats.
	He was closely concerned with almost all the funds raised at Lloyd's for the benefit of seamen and their families following the various battles during the Napoleonic Wars and especially with the Lloyd's Patriotic Fund, of which he was a prime mover from 1803 onwards. In 1801 Nelson wrote to Angerstein calling him "one of the very best men of the age we live in" and in 1802 'The Times' described "The Gentleman of Lloyd's Coffee-House" as the father of every seaman's orphan.

(continued)

John Julius Angerstein (continued)

Main Interests and Recreation

John Julius Angerstein was an enthusiastic rider. He also enjoyed gardening and had a very fine greenhouse at Woodlands. He had a wide range of family and business friends and his circle also extended to Royalty. He knew Princess Caroline of Wales well and entertained the Prince Regent at Woodlands. John Julius Angerstein was also close to many people in the art world especially Sir Thomas Lawrence and built up a remarkable collection of pictures.
The most important pictures were kept in what was effectively a private art gallery at 100 Pall Mall. He had a son also called John and a daughter, Juliana.

John was the main heir and he was not as interested in art as his father had been. Together with his trustees, he decided upon the death of his father, that the pictures should be sold. An elaborate catalogue of 42 paintings was produced and the Government stepped in and bought 38 of them for £57,000 – one family portrait shouldn't have been included and three they didn't buy.

These paintings formed the nucleus of the National Gallery, which initially opened at 100 Pall Mall when the Government had taken over Angerstein's lease. His personal property was sworn to be under £500,000 but this figure excluded his real property, which comprised estates in Lincolnshire, Norfolk, Suffolk, along with in and around Blackheath. His total worth was certainly more than that of the cargo on the Diana, which he had once insured.

Lord Ashton of Hyde

Chairman and Chief Executive Officer
Faraday Underwriting Limited

Address (Office)	5th Floor
	Corn Exchange
	55 Mark Lane
	London EC3R 7NE
Telephone	+44 (0)20 7680 4239
Fax	+44 (0)20 7680 4369
Email	henry.ashton@faraday.com
Secretary/PA	Louise Dunning
Telephone	+44 (0)20 7680 4300
Email	louise.dunning@faraday.com
Website	www.faraday.com
Full Name	Thomas Henry Ashton (Lord Ashton of Hyde)
Born	1958
Nationality	British
Secondary Education	Eton College, Berkshire
Further Education	Trinity College, Oxford

PROFESSIONAL INFORMATION

Career	CT Bowring Reinsurance: 1982 - 1990
	Guy Carpenter & Co, New York: 1990 - 1993
	DP Mann Ltd/Faraday Underwriting Ltd: 1994 - 1996
	Faraday Underwriting Ltd, Director: 1996 - 2005
	Faraday Underwriting Ltd, Chief Executive Officer: 2005 -
	Faraday Underwriting Ltd, Executive Chairman: 2005 -
	Faraday Reinsurance Co Ltd, Executive Chairman: 2005 -

PERSONAL INFORMATION

Home	Gloucestershire
Armed Forces	Short service volunteer commission with The Royal Hussars (PWO)

Rupert Atkin

Chief Executive Officer
Talbot Underwriting Ltd

Address (Office)	Gracechurch House
	55 Gracechurch Street
	London EC3V 0JP
Telephone	+44 (0)20 7550 3535
Fax	+44 (0)20 7550 3555
Email	rupert.atkin@talbotuw.com
Secretary/PA	Sarah Rollings
Telephone	+44 (0)20 7550 3546
Email	sarah.rollings@talbotuw.com
Website	www.talbotuw.com

Full Name	Charles Neville Rupert Atkin
Born	1958
Nationality	British
Secondary Education	Marlborough College, Wiltshire
Further Education	University of Oxford, Modern History MA (Hons)

PROFESSIONAL INFORMATION

Elected to Lloyd's	1985
Career	Alexander Howden Group: 1980 - 1983
	Posgate & Denby, Underwriting Assistant: 1983 - 1984
	Catlin Underwriting Agency Ltd, Syndicate 1003,
	Deputy Underwriter: 1984 - 1990
	Talbot Underwriting Ltd, Syndicate 1183,
	Active Underwriter: 1995 - 2007
	Syndicate 376, Active Underwriter: 2000 - 2001
	Talbot Underwriting Ltd, Director of Underwriting: 2002 - 2007
	Talbot Underwriting Ltd, Chief Executive Officer: 2007 -
Main Area(s) of Expertise	Marine, War and Terrorism
First Policy Written	1982
Most interesting Policies/Claims	War risk for vessel used in Iraqi troop landings
	Sri Lankan Government war cover following Tamil Tiger attack on
	Sri Lankan Airport in 2001
Current Major Appointments/	Talbot Underwriting Holdings Ltd, Director
Committees	Talbot 2002 Underwriting Capital Ltd, Director
	Talbot Underwriting Capital Ltd (dormant), Director
	Talbot Underwriting Ltd, Director
	Underwriting Risk Services Ltd, Director
	Talbot Underwriting Services Ltd, Director
	Talbot Risk Services Pte Ltd, Director
	1384 Capital Ltd, Director
	Yachtsure Ltd (dormant), Director
	Shrewsbury Holdings Ltd, Director
	Shrewsbury Underwriting Capital (Bermuda) Ltd, Director
	Shrewsbury Underwriting Capital Ltd, Director
	Lloyd's Underwriters' Association: 1996 -

Rupert Atkin (continued)

	Lloyd's Market Association Marine Committee: 1996 -
	Lloyd's Professional Standards Committee: 2005 -
	Nominations Committee of International Union of Marine Insurers: 2006 -
	Council of Lloyd's, Working Member: 2007 -
Previous Major Appointments/ Committees	Joint War Risk Committee, Chairman: 1996 - 2006
	Lloyd's Insurance Services Board: 1997 - 1998
	Lloyd's War and Financial Risks Committee: 1998 - 1999
	Lloyd's Market Association Committee: 1999 - 2000
	Lloyd's Underwriters' Association, Chairman: 1999 - 2000
	Lloyd's Regulatory Board: 2001 - 2002
	London Market Faculty: 2005 - 2006
Major Achievements while at Lloyd's	Implementation of Market Risk Code Triangles
	Introduction of Underwriter Cancellation Clauses in Marine Market
	Raising money for Salvage Association Pensioners from Market
Mentor(s)	Ian Posgate, Stephen Catlin, Jeremy Venton

PERSONAL INFORMATION

Home	East Sussex
Main Interests and Recreation	Skiing, windsurfing, shooting, golf
Favourite Book(s)	'Tess of the d'Urbervilles' by Thomas Hardy
Favourite Gadget(s)	Road Angel
Favourite Music	'The Pearl Fishers' by Bizet, 'The Harder They Come' by Jimmy Cliff
Livery Companies	The Worshipful Company of Gunmakers
Clubs/Memberships	Royal Ashdown Forest Golf Club, City of London Club

Richard Bardwell

Underwriting Director and Active Underwriter Syndicate 1221
Navigators Underwriting Agency Ltd

Address (Office)	7th Floor
	2 Minster Court
	Mincing Lane
	London EC3R 7BB
Telephone	+44 (0)20 7220 6920
Email	rbardwell@navg.com
Website	www.navg.com
Full Name	Richard Paxton Bardwell
Born	1958
Nationality	British
Secondary Education	Seaford College, West Sussex

PROFESSIONAL INFORMATION

Career	PW Hardy, Syndicate 30/382: 1976
	CJ Mander, Syndicate 552/1221: 1980
	Navigators Underwriting Agency Ltd, Syndicate 1221,
	Active Underwriter: 2005 -
	Navigators Underwriting Agency Ltd, Underwriting Director: 2005 -
Main Area(s) of Expertise	Marine and Energy
Underwriting Speciality	Marine and Offshore Energy liabilities
Mentor(s)	Colin Mander

PERSONAL INFORMATION

Home	Hampshire
Clubs/Memberships	Lloyd's Yacht Club

Ed Barker

Senior Underwriter
Syndicate 382, Hardy (Underwriting Agencies) Ltd

Address (Office)	4th Floor
	40 Lime Street
	London EC3M 7AW
Telephone	+44 (0)20 7105 3325
Fax	+44 (0)20 7283 4677
Email	edward.barker@hardygroup.co.uk
Website	www.hardygroup.co.uk

Full Name	John Edward Gerald Barker
Born	1958
Nationality	British
Secondary Education	Radley College, Oxfordshire: 1972 - 1976
Further Education	University of Reading, Agriculture BSc (Hons): 1977 - 1980
Professional Qualifications	FCII: 1988

PROFESSIONAL INFORMATION

Elected to Lloyd's	1985
Career	RK Carvill, Broker Support: 1982
	Birrell-Smith Underwriting Agency, Underwriter: 1985
	Hardy (Underwriting Agencies) Ltd, Syndicate 382: 1992 -
	Hardy (Underwriting Agencies) Ltd, Executive Director: 2004 - 2008
	Hardy (Underwriting Agencies) Ltd, Syndicate 382,
	Deputy Underwriter: 2004 - 2008
	Hardy (Underwriting Agencies) Ltd, Syndicate 382,
	Senior Underwriter: 2009 -
Main Area(s) of Expertise	Cargo and Specie
First Policy Written	Marine Hull: 1986
Previous Major Appointments/ Committees	Lloyd's Market Association Binding Authorities Committee
Lloyd's Connections (inc family)	Father, a Member's Agent; Sister, an ex-Underwriter
Mentor(s)	Colin Mabey, Peter Hardy

PERSONAL INFORMATION

Home	Hampshire
Main Interests and Recreation	Polo, shooting

Andrew Bathurst

Executive Director
SSL Insurance Services Ltd

Address (Office)	6th Floor
	140 Leadenhall Street
	London EC3V 4QT
Telephone	+44 (0)20 7220 1110
Fax	+44 (0)20 7220 1120
Email	bathurst@sslins.com
Secretary/PA	Liz O'Connor
Telephone	+44 (0)20 7220 1132
Email	oconnor@sslins.com
Website	www.sslins.com
Full Name	Andrew Eric Bathurst
Born	1954
Nationality	British

PROFESSIONAL INFORMATION

Career	IR Posgate: 1973 - 1982
	AJ Archer: 1982 - 1992
	Bankassure, Managing Director: 1992 - 1998
	Benfield Ellinger, Director: 1998 - 2007
	Argenta Syndicate Management Ltd, Chief Executive Officer: 2007 - 2008
	Hampden Agencies Ltd, Consultant: 2008
	SSL Insurance Brokers Limited, Executive Director: 2008 -
Current Major Appointments/ Committees	The Insurance Institute of London, Marine Committee, Chairman
Major Achievements while at Lloyd's	Founder of Lloyd's Fly Fishing Society
Mentor(s)	AJ (Fred) Archer

PERSONAL INFORMATION

Home	Kent
Main Interests and Recreation	Tennis, fishing, six children
Favourite Music	Leonard Cohen
Livery Companies	The Worshipful Company of Shipwrights
Clubs/Memberships	Lloyd's Fly Fishing Society

Paul Battagliola

Chief Operating Officer
Argo Managing Agency Ltd

Address (Office)	47 Mark Lane
	London EC3R 7QQ
Telephone	+44 (0)20 7712 7662
Fax	+44 (0)20 7712 7601
Mobile	+44 (0)7802 278 559
Email	paul.battagliola@argo-int.com
Secretary/PA	Sandra Swan
Website	www.argo-int.com

Full Name	Paul David Battagliola
Born	1954
Nationality	British
Secondary Education	Buckhurst Hill County High School, Essex: 1965 - 1972
Further Education	PCL, Business Studies BA (Hons)
Professional Qualifications	CIMA: 1984
	MBA: 1994

PROFESSIONAL INFORMATION

Career	Gibbs Hartley Cooper: 1979 - 1984
	Aon Ltd: 1984 - 2004
	Consultant: 2005
	Argo Managing Agency Ltd, Chief Operating Officer: 2006 -

PERSONAL INFORMATION

Home	Essex
Clubs/Memberships	Royal Corinthian Yacht Club

Simon Beale

Underwriting Director, Amlin London and
Active Underwriter Syndicate 2001
Amlin Underwriting Ltd

Address (Office)	St Helen's
	1 Undershaft
	London EC3A 8ND
Telephone	+44 (0)20 7746 1000
Fax	+44 (0)20 7746 1890
Email	simon.beale@amlin.co.uk
Secretary/PA	Margaret Lilley
Telephone	+44 (0)20 7746 1000
Email	margaret.lilley@amlin.co.uk
Website	www.amlin.com

Full Name	Simon Charles Waldegrave Beale
Born	1961
Nationality	British
Secondary Education	Radley College, Oxfordshire
Further Education	University of St Andrews, BSc
Professional Qualifications	ACII
Nickname	Bealey

PROFESSIONAL INFORMATION

Elected to Lloyd's	1987
Career	RJ Bromley Syndicate 475: 1984 - 1991
	Lloyd Roberts & Gilkes Syndicate 1088: 1992 - 1994
	Amlin Underwriting Ltd, Syndicates 40 and 2001: 1994
	Amlin Underwriting Ltd, Syndicate 2001, Divisional Underwriter: 2001 - 2008
	Amlin Underwriting Ltd, Underwriting Director, Amlin London: 2008 -
	Amlin Underwriting Ltd, Syndicate 2001, Active Underwriter: 2008 -
Main Area(s) of Expertise	Marine
Underwriting Speciality	Marine Hull
Most interesting Policies/Claims	Most interesting claims are still ongoing
Longest Customer Relationship(s)	Valles Steamship
Current Major Appointments/ Committees	Lloyd's Market Association Marine Committee
	International Union of Marine Insurance Executive Committee
	Lloyd's Joint Hull Committee
	Lloyd's Register General Committee
Previous Major Appointments/ Committees	Lloyd's Joint Hull Committee, Chairman
	International Union of Marine Insurance Ocean Hull Committee, Chairman
Lloyd's Connections (inc family)	To come
Mentor(s)	My Father

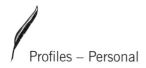

Simon Beale (continued)

PERSONAL INFORMATION

Home	London
Charitable/Voluntary Activities	Maritime London Cadet Scheme
	Royal National Lifeboat Institution
	City of London 2008 Appeal
Main Interests and Recreation	Family
Favourite Book(s)	'Jude the Obscure' by Thomas Hardy
Favourite Car(s)	Land Rover
Favourite Gadget(s)	Sky Plus
Favourite Music	Cello Concerto by Elgar
Livery Companies	The Worshipful Company of Tallow Chandlers
	The Worshipful Company of Shipwrights
Clubs/Memberships	City of London Club, Telford Park Lawn Tennis Club

Andrew Beazley

Executive Director
Beazley Furlonge Limited

Address (Office)	Plantation Place South
	60 Great Tower Street
	London EC3R 5AD
Telephone	+44 (0)20 7667 0623
Email	andrew.beazley@beazley.com
Secretary/PA	Gemma Adams
Telephone	+44 (0)20 7674 7501
Email	gemma.adams@beazley.com
Website	www.beazley.com
Full Name	Andrew Frederick Beazley
Born	1953
Nationality	British

PROFESSIONAL INFORMATION

Elected to Lloyd's	1979
Career	Price Forbes, Insurance Broker
	RA Edwards Syndicate 219, Casualty Underwriter
	Beazley, Furlonge & Hiscox Ltd, Co-founder: 1985
	AF Beazley & Ors Syndicate 623, Active Underwriter: 1986 - 2008
	Beazley Group plc, Chief Executive: 2000 - 2008
	AF Beazley & Ors Syndicate 2623, Active Underwriter: 2002 - 2008
	Beazley Furlonge Ltd, Executive Director: 1985 -
	Beazley Group plc, Deputy Chairman: 2008 -
Main Area(s) of Expertise	Non-Marine Liabilities
Underwriting Speciality	Professional Indemnity
First Policy Written	Cannot recall, but it would have been in 1975 – a long time ago – and probably ran clean!
Most interesting Policies/Claims	An Irish architect who wanted to buy a policy because he had a claim
Previous Major Appointments/ Committees	Rowland Task Force
	Lloyd's Market Board
	Lloyd's Chairman's Strategy Group
Major Achievements while at Lloyd's	Made good money for capital providers and gathered some of the most talented colleagues to work with in a fun environment
Mentor(s)	Charles Skey

PERSONAL INFORMATION

Home	London
Charitable/Voluntary Activities	Brambletye School Trust
Main Interests and Recreation	Tennis, travel, flyfishing, gardening
Favourite Book(s)	Too many to mention
Favourite Car(s)	Morris Minor, one of my first cars and an ex police vehicle!
Favourite Gadget(s)	Anything with many moving parts
Favourite Music	Puccini, Saint-Saëns, Grieg
Important and Interesting Aspects of Lloyd's	Lloyd's is a strong constant brand that allows creativeness and regeneration behind the scenes – a truly unique combination

Gilles Bonvarlet

Former Chief Operating Officer
Talbot Underwriting Ltd

Contact Details	tba

Full Name	Gilles Alex Maxime Bonvarlet
Born	1964
Nationality	French
Secondary Education	Saint Erembert, France
Further Education	Institut Supérieur d'Electronique de Paris (ISEP)
	ESSEC Business School, Paris, MBA

PROFESSIONAL INFORMATION

Career	XL London Market Ltd, Managing Director: 2000 - 2004
	XL London Market Group, Chief Financial Officer: 2001 - 2004
	Talbot Underwriting Ltd, Chief Operating Officer: 2004 - 2009
Current Major Appointments/ Committees	Lloyd's Market Association Risk Management Committee: 2006 -
Previous Major Appointments/ Committees	Lloyd's Market Board: 2001 - 2002

PERSONAL INFORMATION

Home	London

James Brandon

Finance Director
ICP General Partner Limited

Address (Office)	Unit C25
	Jack's Place
	6 Corbet Place
	London E1 6NN
Telephone	+44 (0)20 7392 8480
Fax	+44 (0)20 7392 8481
Mobile	+44 (0)7963 218 009
Email	james.brandon@inscap.co.uk
Website	www.inscap.co.uk

Full Name	James Roderick Vivian Brandon
Born	1956
Nationality	British
Secondary Education	Winchester College, Hampshire: 1970 - 1974
Further Education	University of Exeter, LLB: 1975 - 1978
Professional Qualifications	ACA: 1987

PROFESSIONAL INFORMATION

Career	Littlejohn Frazer: 1982 - 1987
	Corporation of Lloyd's, General Review: 1988 - 1990
	RF Bailey Underwriting Agencies Ltd, Finance Director,
	Company Secretary and Compliance Officer: 1991 - 1999
	Heritage Underwriting Agency PLC, Finance Director: 1999 - 2000
	Consultant: 2001 - 2006
	ICP General Partner Ltd, Finance Director: 2007 -
	ICP Holdings Ltd, Finance Director: 2007 -
Major Achievements while at Lloyd's	Helped set up Heritage Managing Agency
Mentor(s)	Barbara Schurer

PERSONAL INFORMATION

Home	London
Main Interests and Recreation	Public debates, cycling, walking, swimming
Favourite Book(s)	'The Ten Second Miracle' by Gay Hendricks
Clubs/Memberships	Cogers

Stuart Bridges

Group Chief Financial Officer
Hiscox Limited

Address (Office)	1 Great St Helen's
	London EC3A 6HX
Telephone	+44 (0)20 7488 6003
Fax	+44 (0)20 7488 6598
Mobile	+44 (0)7818 070 077
Email	stuart.bridges@hiscox.com
Secretary/PA	Anna Skelton
Telephone	+44 (0)20 7448 6013
Email	anna.skelton@hiscox.com
Website	www.hiscox.com
Full Name	Stuart John Bridges
Born	1960
Nationality	British
Secondary Education	Dalriada School, Ballymoney: 1972 - 1979
Further Education	Gonville & Caius College, Cambridge,
	Engineering MA (Hons): 1980 - 1983
Professional Qualifications	ACA: 1986

PROFESSIONAL INFORMATION

Career	Arthur Anderson & Co: 1983 - 1989
	Richard Ellis: 1989 - 1991
	Henderson Investors plc: 1991 - 1994
	Jacobs Holdings plc, Executive Director: 1995 - 1997
	Lowri Beck, Executive Director: 1997 - 1998
	Hiscox Ltd, Group Chief Financial Officer: 1999 -
	Hiscox Syndicates Ltd, Executive Director: 1999 -
	Hiscox Underwriting Ltd, Executive Chairman: 2003 -
Current Major Appointments/	Lloyd's Market Association Finance Committee, Deputy Chairman
Committees	Association of British Insurers, Financial Regulation and Taxation Committee
	Institute of Chartered Accountants in England and Wales,
	Business Advisory Board, Chairman

PERSONAL INFORMATION

Home	Berkshire
Main Interests and Recreation	Golf, sailing
Clubs/Memberships	Lloyd's Yacht Club, Marylebone Cricket Club (MCC)

Reg Brown

Former Active Underwriter Syndicate 702 (retired)
Octavian Syndicate Management Ltd

Telephone	+44 (0)20 8300 4991
Fax	+44 (0)20 8300 4991
Email	rebel.702@virgin.net

Full Name	Reginald Brown
Born	1942
Nationality	British
Secondary Education	Barnsbury Boys School, London: 1953 - 1959
Further Education	University College London, External Student: 1970 - 1975
Professional Qualifications	FCII LLB(London): 1975

PROFESSIONAL INFORMATION

Elected to Lloyd's	1981
Career	Reliance Fire & Accident Insurance Corporation Ltd: 1959 - 1966
	FAI Insurance Group, London Manager: 1966 - 1976
	Frank Barber & Ors, Class Underwriter: 1976 - 1977
	Dugdale/Octavian Syndicate 702, Deputy Underwriter: 1977 - 1984
	Dugdale/Octavian Syndicate 702, Active Underwriter: 1984 - 2000
Main Area(s) of Expertise	Professional Indemnity, D&O, Legal Expenses
Underwriting Speciality	Non-US Legal Liability
First Policy Written	Cannot remember
Most interesting Policies/Claims	The World's first Vasectomy Insurance policy; in at the beginning of UK D&O and Legal Expenses Markets
Previous Major Appointments/ Committees	Lloyd's Underwriters' Non-Marine Assocation, Chairman: 1993 - 1994
	Insurance Institute of London, President: 1994 - 1995
	Chartered Insurance Institute, President: 2000
	British Insurance Law Association, President: 2003
Major Achievements while at Lloyd's	Surviving the Crisis!

PERSONAL INFORMATION

Home	London
Armed Forces	Too Young!
Awards/Honours	London Phoenix Orchestra, President
Charitable/Voluntary Activities	Mentoring in Tower Hamlets as part of Lloyd's Community Programme
Main Interests and Recreation	Deltiology, expert witness work, mentoring, football, travelling
Favourite Book(s)	'Fever Pitch' by Nick Hornby
Favourite Car(s)	None
Favourite Music	Anything played by London Phoenix Orchestra
Livery Companies	The Worshipful Company of Insurers
Clubs/Memberships	Langbourn Ward Club

Steven Burns

Chief Executive Officer
QBE Underwriting Limited

Address (Office)	Plantation Place
	30 Fenchurch Street
	London EC3M 3BD
Telephone	+44 (0)20 7105 4058
Fax	+44 (0)20 7105 5020
Mobile	+44 (0)7887 767 707
Email	steven.burns@uk.qbe.com
Secretary/PA	Sally Amos
Telephone	+44 (0)20 7105 4515
Email	sally.amos@uk.qbe.com
Website	www.qbeeurope.com

Full Name	Steven Paul Burns
Born	1958
Nationality	British
Further Education	University of Cambridge, MA: 1977 - 1980
Professional Qualifications	ACCA: 1980
	FCA: 1998

PROFESSIONAL INFORMATION

Started at Lloyd's	1987
Elected to Lloyd's	1991
Career	Harbour Insurance (London market captive of a major US multinational), Financial Controller: 1980
	Janson Green Ltd, Financial Controller and Company Secretary: 1987
	Janson Green Ltd, Finance Director: 1990
	LIMIT Underwriting Ltd, Finance Director: 1996
	LIMIT Group (following takeover by QBE), Chief Executive Officer: 2000
	QBE Underwriting Ltd (formerly LIMIT Underwriting Ltd),
	Chief Executive Officer: 1999 -
	QBE European Operations (formerly LIMIT Group),
	Chief Executive Officer: 2000 -
Previous Major Appointments/ Committees	Council of Lloyd's, External Member: 2001 - 2004
	Lloyd's Franchise Board, one of three Market practitioners appointed as Non-Executive Directors: 2005 - 2007

PERSONAL INFORMATION

Home	London

Brian Carpenter

Underwriting Director, UK Commercial and
Joint Active Underwriter Syndicate 2001
Amlin Underwriting Ltd

Address (Office)	Amlin House
	Parkway
	Chelmsford
	Essex CM2 0UR
Telephone	+44 (0)1245 214 875
Fax	+44 (0)1245 396 489
Email	brian.carpenter@amlin.co.uk
Secretary/PA	Carmen Wigg
Telephone	+44 (0)1245 214 875
Email	cwigg@amlin-insurance.co.uk
Website	www.amlin.com
Full Name	Brian Douglas Carpenter
Born	1957
Nationality	British
Secondary Education	Loughton School, Essex
	Buckhurst Hill County High, Essex

PROFESSIONAL INFORMATION

Started at Lloyd's	1975
Elected to Lloyd's	1986
Category of Lloyd's Membership	Name
Career	MW Drysdale, Claims Negotiator: 1975 - 1976
	FE Wright, Lloyd's Broker: 1976 - 1978
	Sedgwick (UK) Ltd, Lloyd's Broker: 1978 - 1985
	Marsh (UK), Associate Director: 1985 - 1989
	Summit at Lloyd's Motor Syndicate 887, Underwriter: 1989
	MW Drysdale, Underwriter: 1999
	Amlin Underwriting Ltd, Divisional Underwriter, UK Commercial: 2000 -
	Amlin Underwriting Ltd, Underwriting Director, UK Commercial: 2000 -
	Amlin Underwriting Ltd, Syndicate 2001, Joint Active Underwriter: 2000 -
	Amlin plc, Executive Director: 2002 -
	Amlin Insurance Services, Divisional Underwriter: 2003 -
Main Area(s) of Expertise	UK Commercial Insurance
Underwriting Speciality	Motor Fleet
First Policy Written	Drive & Survive, Motor Fleet: 1989
Most interesting Policies/Claims	Angelina Jolie's motorcycle; London Duck Tours
Longest Customer Relationship(s)	Mars

Brian Carpenter (continued)

Current Major Appointments/ Committees	Lloyd's Market Association Motor Committee: 1987 -
Previous Major Appointments/ Committees	Lloyd's Business Development Unit Board, Member: 1997 - 2000
	Lloyd's Market Board, Member: 2000 - 2002
	Lloyd's Training and Advisory Group, Chairman: 2001 - 2002
	London Market Underwriting Agency Finance Committee, Chairman: 2000 - 2006
Major Achievements while at Lloyd's	Improved performance of Summit and MW Drysdale from bottom to top quartile
	Longest serving motor underwriter (20 years)
	Co-founder of Amlin

PERSONAL INFORMATION

Home	Essex
Awards/Honours	100 metres swimming badge
Charitable/Voluntary Activities	Supporter of Little Havens Children's Hospice
Main Interests and Recreation	Coaching, watching rugby and football
Favourite Book(s)	'Lord of the Rings' by JRR Tolkien
Favourite Film	Zulu
Favourite Car(s)	Mini Cooper
Favourite Music	Guns and Roses
Clubs/Memberships	West Ham United

Michael Carpenter

Chairman
Talbot Underwriting Ltd

Address (Office)	Gracechurch House
	55 Gracechurch Street
	London EC3V 0JP
Telephone	+44 (0)20 7550 3500
Fax	+44 (0)20 7550 3555
Email	michael.carpenter@talbotuw.com
Secretary/PA	Lisa Love
Telephone	+44 (0)20 7550 3659
Email	lisa.love@talbotuw.com
Website	www.talbotuw.com
Full Name	Michael Edward Arscott Carpenter
Born	1949
Nationality	British
Secondary Education	Westminster School, London: 1963 - 1967
Further Education	Magdalene College, Cambridge, MA (Cantab): 1969 - 1971
Professional Qualifications	FCA

PROFESSIONAL INFORMATION

Elected to Lloyd's	1983
Category of Lloyd's Membership	Non-Underwriting Working Member
Career	Binder Hamlyn: 1971 - 1977
	WJ Towell, Kuwait: 1978 - 1979
	Samuel Montagu & Co Ltd: 1979 - 1993
	LIMIT plc: 1993 - 2000
	EO PLC: 2000 - 2001
	Talbot Underwriting Ltd, Non-Executive Chairman: 2001 -
Previous Major Appointments/	Lloyd's Corporate Capital Association
Committees	Lloyd's Underwriting Agents' Association
	Lloyd's Community Programme
	Lloyd's Corporation Budget Review Group

Brian Caudle

Former Executive Director and Active Underwriter Syndicate 780
Advent Underwriting Limited

Address (Office)	10th Floor
	1 Minster Court
	Mincing Lane
	London EC3R 7AA
Telephone	+44 (0)20 7743 8202
Fax	+44 (0)20 7743 8244
Email	brian.caudle@adventgroup.co.uk
Secretary/PA	Joanne Tang
Telephone	+44 (0)20 7743 8201
Email	joanne.tang@adventgroup.co.uk
Website	www.adventgroup.co.uk
Full Name	Brian Frank Caudle
Born	1935
Nationality	British
Secondary Education	Leyton County Grammar High School, Essex
Nickname	Lord Leyton

PROFESSIONAL INFORMATION

Started at Lloyd's	1958
Elected to Lloyd's	1971
Career	Leslie & Godwin Insurance Brokers: 1952 - 1953
	Leslie & Godwin Insurance Brokers: 1956 - 1958
	GW Price & Ors Syndicate 164: 1958 - 1964
	Leslie & Godwin Insurance Brokers: 1964 - 1968
	Bellew Parry and Raven Reinsurance Brokers: 1968 - 1974
	BF Caudle Agency, Founder: 1975
	Syndicate 760, Founder and Active Underwriter: 1979
	BF Caudle Syndicate 780, Founder and Active Underwriter: 1974 - 1999
	Advent Capital (Holdings) PLC, Executive Chairman : 1995 -
Main Area(s) of Expertise	Reinsurance
First Policy Written	Vermont Mutual
Most interesting Policies/Claims	Elizabeth Taylor, jewellery iro 'Cleopatra'; Billy Graham, abandonment policy
Longest Customer Relationship(s)	Vermont Mutual
Previous Major Appointments/ Committees	Advent Underwriting Ltd, Director of Underwriting
Major Achievements while at Lloyd's	Over 50 years experience in the Lloyd's market
	Voted 'Underwriter of the Year 2001' by the Association of Lloyd's Members
Lloyd's Connections (inc family)	Olive Pattenden (aunt) started with Keith Shipton as secretary in 1938
Mentor(s)	GW Price (Underwriter)

(continued)

Brian Caudle (continued)

PERSONAL INFORMATION

Home	Essex
Armed Forces	Royal Army Pay Corps
Charitable/Voluntary Activities	Kim Caudle Charity
Main Interests and Recreation	Restoring old buildings, old timers, carriage clocks, pocket watches, cornet playing, golf
Favourite Book(s)	Historical and autobiographies
Favourite Car(s)	1928 Austin 7
Favourite Gadget(s)	Lloyd's/Reinsurance
Favourite Music	Brass band
Clubs/Memberships	City of London Club, Lloyds Club, Chelmsford Golf Club, Lloyd's Golf Club, President of Lloyd's Football Club
Important and Interesting Aspects of Lloyd's	That it maintains its huge history and successfully evolves during the years ahead

David Constable

Executive Director and Active Underwriter Syndicate 386
QBE European Operations

Address (Office)	Plantation Place
	30 Fenchurch Street
	London EC3M 3BD
Telephone	+44 (0)20 7105 4000
Fax	+44 (0)20 7105 4009
Email	david.constable@uk.qbe.com
Secretary/PA	Anita Edwards
Telephone	+44 (0)20 7105 4848
Email	anita.edwards@uk.qbe.com
Website	www.qbeeurope.com

Full Name	David Andrew Constable
Born	1957
Nationality	British
Secondary Education	Eltham College, London: 1971 - 1974
	Bury Grammar School, Lancashire: 1974 - 1976
Professional Qualifications	FCII
	Institute of Directors, Diploma in Company Direction

PROFESSIONAL INFORMATION

Career	Sun Alliance: 1976 - 1991
	Janson Green and Limit Underwriting Limited, Syndicate 386: 1991 - 1999
	QBE European Operations, Casualty Syndicate 386: 1991
	QBE European Operations, Casualty Syndicate 386,
	Joint Managing Director: 2008
	QBE European Operations, Casualty Syndicate 386,
	Active Underwriter: 2000 -
Main Area(s) of Expertise	Underwriting Casualty
Underwriting Speciality	Direct Insurance, International Casualty
First Policy Written	Household Insurance: 1976
Major Achievements while at Lloyd's	Over 30 years in Insurance with 17 years in Lloyd's, voted '2006 Underwriting Team of the Year' by Insurance Times
Mentor(s)	Bob Wallace (Underwriter)

PERSONAL INFORMATION

Home	London
Charitable/Voluntary Activities	Church youth work
Main Interests and Recreation	Sport, rugby, golf
Favourite Book(s)	History books
Favourite Car(s)	Saab
Favourite Music	Classical tunes

Edward Creasy

Chairman
R J Kiln & Co Limited

Address (Office)	106 Fenchurch Street
	London EC3M 5NR
Telephone	+44 (0)20 7360 1600
Fax	+44 (0)20 7295 0098
Mobile	+44 (0)7879 625 456
Email	edward.creasy@kilngroup.com
Secretary/PA	Jill Bamber
Telephone	+44 (0)20 7360 1602
Email	jill.bamber@kilngroup.com
Website	www.kilnplc.com

Full Name	Edward George Creasy
Born	1955
Nationality	British
Secondary Education	Eton College, Berkshire
Further Education	Trinity College, Cambridge, MA (Cantab)
Professional Qualifications	City University Business School, MBA
	FCII

PROFESSIONAL INFORMATION

Elected to Lloyd's	1984
Career	Investment Insurance International, Broker: 1978 - 1982
	AA Cassidy & Ors, Underwriter: 1982 - 1992
	Cassidy Davis Ltd, Managing Director: 1992 - 2000
	Kiln Ltd, Group Chief Executive Officer: 2001 - 2008
	R J Kiln & Co Ltd, Executive Chairman: 2000 -
	Kiln Ltd, Group Chairman: 2009 -
Previous Major Appointments/	Lloyd's Market Association, Founding Director: 2001 - 2009
Committees	Lloyd's Franchise Board, Market Representative Director: 2003 - 2008
	Lloyd's Underwriting Agents' Association, Deputy Chairman
	Franchise Liaison Group, Chairman
	Lloyd's Prudential Supervision Committee

PERSONAL INFORMATION

Home	Suffolk
Main Interests and Recreation	The countryside and everything connected to it
Favourite Book(s)	History biographies
Favourite Car(s)	Anything that gets me from A to B safely
Favourite Gadget(s)	A good pair of binoculars
Favourite Music	Nothing too serious
Clubs/Memberships	Boodle's

Simon Curtis

Former Group Finance Director
Atrium Underwriters Ltd

Address (Office)	c/o Atrium Underwriting plc
	Room 790
	Lloyd's
	One Lime Street
	London EC3M 7DQ
Website	www.atrium-uw.com

Full Name	Simon Peter Curtis
Born	1970
Nationality	British
Secondary Education	Great Cornard Upper School, Suffolk (10 O-Levels and 4 A-Levels): 1983 - 1988
Further Education	Durham University, Mathematics BSc II(i): 1988 - 1991
Professional Qualifications	ACA: 1995
Nickname	Dracula (!)

PROFESSIONAL INFORMATION

Career	Atrium Underwriters Ltd, Group Finance Director: 2000 - 2007
Previous Major Appointments/ Committees	Lloyd's Market Association Finance Committee
Major Achievements while at Lloyd's	Moving from three years accounting to annual accounting and then IFRS

PERSONAL INFORMATION

Home	Surrey
Main Interests and Recreation	Poker, horse racing, music
Favourite Book(s)	'Big Deal' by Anthony Holden
Favourite Car(s)	Aston Martin DBS
Favourite Gadget(s)	iPod
Favourite Music	Bruce Springsteen, U2

David Dale

Active Underwriter Syndicate 2525
Max at Lloyd's Ltd

Address (Office)	4th Floor
	70 Gracechurch Street
	London EC3V 0XL
Telephone	+44 (0)20 3102 3180
Fax	+44 (0)20 3102 3200
Mobile	+44 (0)7901 646 547
Email	ddale@syndicate2525.co.uk
Website	www.syndicate2525.co.uk

Full Name	David Lionel Dale
Born	1958
Nationality	British
Secondary Education	Haileybury College, Hertfordshire
Professional Qualifications	9/10 ACII (still going!)
Nickname	Pratty

PROFESSIONAL INFORMATION

Elected to Lloyd's	1987
Category of Lloyd's Membership	Member of Lloyd's-Unlimited: 1988 - 1995
	Limited: 2004 - 2005
Career	EO Walklin & Ors Syndicate: 1978
	MW Payne/RJ Wallace Syndicate 386: 1979 - 2002
	Max at Lloyd's Ltd, Syndicate 2525, Active Underwriter: 2003 -
Main Area(s) of Expertise	UK/ROI, Employers' Liability, Third Party Liability
Underwriting Speciality	Offshore Employers' Liability
First Policy Written	Italian Army PA cover during Lebanon Crisis: 1980s
Most interesting Policies/Claims	HMS Edinburgh gold bullion diving recovery: 1980s
Longest Customer Relationship(s)	Waveney Insurance Brokers, Norfolk; Houlder Insurance Services, Windsor; Central Insurance Brokers
Major Achievements while at Lloyd's	30 years profitable underwriting – out of a possible 31!
Lloyd's Connections (inc family)	Norman Clarke, Sedgwick/Marsh
Mentor(s)	Michael Payne, Bob Wallace

PERSONAL INFORMATION

Home	Kent
Main Interests and Recreation	Golf, walking, gardening, astronomy
Favourite Book(s)	'A Prayer for Owen Meany' by John Irving
Favourite Car(s)	Jaguar Sovereign Series III V12
Favourite Music	Classical
Clubs/Memberships	Cooden Beach Golf Club, Wine Society
Important and Interesting Aspects of Lloyd's	A society that engenders long, strong and close relationships on a personal/professional basis

Christine Dandridge
Non-Executive Director
Managing Agency Partners Limited

Address (Office)	c/o Managing Agency Partners Ltd
	1st Floor 110 Fenchurch Street
	London EC3M 5JT
Telephone	+44 (0)20 7709 3860
Fax	+44 (0)20 7709 3861
Secretary/PA	Kathryn Brown (for liaison only)
Email	kathryn.brown@atrium-uw.com
Website	www.mapunderwriting.co.uk

Full Name	Christine Elaine Dandridge
Born	1956
Nationality	British
Secondary Education	Kingsbridge School, Devon
Further Education	University College London, BSc (Hons): 1975 - 1978
Professional Qualifications	ACII: 1983
Nickname	Maestro

PROFESSIONAL INFORMATION

Elected to Lloyd's	1983
Career	Stewart Wrightson: 1978
	Holmes Hulbert Bloodstock: 1980
	Posgate & Denby: 1982
	Atrium Cockell Underwriting Ltd, Syndicate 609: 1986 - 1997
	Atrium Underwriters Ltd, Syndicate 609, Active Underwriter: 1997 - 2007
	RFIB Group Ltd, Non-Executive Director: 2008 -
	Managing Agency Partners Ltd, Non-Executive Director: 2008 -
Main Area(s) of Expertise	War Risks
Underwriting Speciality	Generalist
First Policy Written	Cannot remember
Current Major Appointments/ Committees	Lloyd's Underwriters' Association, Underwriting and Claims Committee
Previous Major Appointments/ Committees	Lloyd's Underwriters' Association, Member and past Chair
	Lloyd's Market Board
	Lloyd's Market Association
	Council of Lloyd's
	Lloyd's Charities Trust, Trustee
Major Achievements while at Lloyd's	Decent results, being a 'good citizen'!
Lloyd's Connections (inc family)	None
Mentor(s)	Myself

(continued)

Christine Dandridge (continued)

PERSONAL INFORMATION

Home	Hampshire
Charitable/Voluntary Activities	Lloyd's Charities Trust
Main Interests and Recreation	Country life, skiing
Favourite Car(s)	Porsche 911
Favourite Gadget(s)	My Aga
Favourite Music	Simon and Garfunkel
Clubs/Memberships	Royal Society of Arts

Andrew Davies

Finance Director
Markel Syndicate Management Limited

Address (Office)	The Markel Building
	49 Leadenhall Street
	London EC3A 2EA
Telephone	+44 (0)20 7953 6400
Fax	+44 (0)20 7953 6927
Mobile	+44 (0)7778 069 855
Email	andy.davies@markelintl.com
Secretary/PA	Samantha Chrismas
Telephone	+44 (0)20 7953 6417
Email	samantha.chrismas@markelintl.com
Website	www.markelintl.com
Full Name	Andrew John Davies
Born	1966
Nationality	British
Secondary Education	Wrekin College, Shropshire: 1979 - 1984
Further Education	Loughborough University, Economics BSc: 1984 - 1987
Professional Qualifications	ACA

PROFESSIONAL INFORMATION

Career	PricewaterhouseCoopers: 1987 - 1994
	Markel International Ltd, Group Finance Director: 1994 -
	Markel Syndicate Management Ltd, Finance Director: 2002 -
Current Major Appointments/	Lloyd's Market Association Finance Committee
Committees	Lloyd's Market Association Exchanging Review Board
Mentor(s)	Tony Markel

PERSONAL INFORMATION

Home	Hampshire
Main Interests and Recreation	Travel, wine, golf, rugby, tennis
Favourite Book(s)	'World Atlas of Wine' by Hugh Johnson and Jancis Robinson
Favourite Car(s)	Mercedes 500 SL AMG
Favourite Gadget(s)	Sky remote
Favourite Music	Rolling Stones
Clubs/Memberships	Lloyd's Golf Club, Stoneham Golf Club, Barnes Rugby Club, Looe Golf Club

Bill Davis

Non-Executive Director
Novae Syndicates Limited

Address (Office)	71 Fenchurch Street
	London EC3M 4HH
Telephone	+44 (0)20 7903 3745
Fax	+44 (0)20 7903 7333
Email	bdavis@novae.com
Website	www.novae.com

Full Name	William John Davis
Born	1939
Nationality	British
Secondary Education	Sherborne School, Dorset: 1953 - 1957
Further Education	City of London College
Professional Qualifications	FCII: 1963
Nickname	Bill

PROFESSIONAL INFORMATION

Started at Lloyd's	1957
Elected to Lloyd's	1962
Category of Lloyd's Membership	Sole Trader, Nameco
Career	Leslie Langton & Sons: 1957 - 1958
	NR Frizzell & Ors: 1958 - 1964
	Stewart Smith (Australia): 1964 - 1966
	Edward Lumley (Australia): 1966 - 1969
	Frizzell and JK Buckenham: 1969 - 1975
	RG Vernon & Ors: 1975 - 1977
	Cassidy Davis Ltd: 1977 - 1990
	SVB & Novae Syndicates Ltd, presently Non-Executive Director: 1986 -
Main Area(s) of Expertise	Kidnap and Ransom
First Policy Written	First Kidnap and Ransom: 1975
Most interesting Policies/Claims	Many but highly secret

PERSONAL INFORMATION

Home	London
Main Interests and Recreation	Previously rugby and cricket, now golf and shooting
Clubs/Memberships	City of London Club

Michael Deeny

Chairman
Association of Lloyd's Members

Address (Office)	100 Fenchurch Street London EC3M 5LG
Telephone	+44 (0)20 7488 0033
Fax	+44 (0)20 7488 7555
Website	www.alm.ltd.uk

Full Name	Michael Eunan McLarnon Deeny
Born	1944
Nationality	British and Irish
Secondary Education	Clongowes Wood College, County Kildare, Ireland: 1956 - 1962
Further Education	Magdalen College, Oxford, Modern History MA
Professional Qualifications	FCA

PROFESSIONAL INFORMATION

Elected to Lloyd's	1985
Career and Current Major Appointments	**Promoter and manager for concerts by U2, Bruce Springsteen, Pavarotti, The Eagles and many others: 1971 -** **Equitas Trust, Deputy Chairman of Trustees: 1996 -** **Equitas Ltd, Non-Executive Director: 1996 -** **Association of Lloyd's Members, Executive Chairman: 1998 -** **Council of Lloyd's, External Member: 2009 -**
Previous Major Appointments/ Committees	Gooda Walker Action Group, Chairman: 1993 - 2007 Litigating Names Committee, Chairman: 1994 - 1997 Council of Lloyd's, External Member: 1995 - 1997
Major Achievements while at Lloyd's	Managed Gooda Walker Action Group, resulting in largest damages awarded in English legal history. As Chairman of LNC and GWAG, negotiated Lloyd's settlement offer on behalf of Names.

PERSONAL INFORMATION

Home	Wiltshire
Main Interests and Recreation	Taking risks and living to tell the tale
Favourite Book(s)	'Vanity Fair' by William M Thackeray
Favourite Car(s)	1968 Mercedes 280 SL
Favourite Gadget(s)	The telephone
Favourite Music	1940s French
Clubs/Memberships	Les Bains Douches, Paris

Nick Denniston

Chief Financial Officer
Argo Managing Agency Ltd

Address (Office)	47 Mark Lane
	London EC3R 7QQ
Telephone	+44 (0)20 7712 7658
Fax	+44 (0)20 7712 7601
Mobile	+44 (0)7748 933 276
Email	nick.denniston@argo-int.com
Website	www.argo-int.com

Full Name	Nicholas Geoffrey Alastair Denniston
Born	1955
Nationality	British
Secondary Education	Westminster School, London: 1968 - 1973
Further Education	University of Oxford: 1974 - 1978
Professional Qualifications	ACA

PROFESSIONAL INFORMATION

Career	Heritage Managing Agency Ltd, Interim Chief Executive Officer: 2008 - 2009
	Argo Managing Agency Ltd, Chief Financial Officer: 2003 -

PERSONAL INFORMATION

Home	London

Emilio Di Silvio

Managing Director & Underwriter Syndicate 5555
QBE Underwriting Limited

Address (Office)	Plantation Place
	30 Fenchurch Street
	London EC3M 3BD
Telephone	+44 (0)20 7105 5714
Fax	+44 (0)20 7105 5732
Mobile	+44 (0)7785 257 836
Email	emilio.disilvio@uk.qbe.com
Secretary/PA	Kay Cross
Telephone	+44 (0)20 7105 5172
Email	kay.cross@uk.qbe.com
Website	www.qbeeurope.com
Full Name	Emilio Antonio Di Silvio
Born	1953
Nationality	Italian
Secondary Education	Kennington Boys, Lambeth, London
Professional Qualifications	ACII

PROFESSIONAL INFORMATION

Elected to Lloyd's	1987
Career	EO Walklin & Ors Aviation Syndicate 312: 1975 - 1980
	LG Cox and Co Ltd Aviation Syndicate 734: 1980 - 1986
	LG Cox and Co Ltd Aviation Syndicate 734,
	Deputy Underwriter: 1984 - 1986
	Sturge Aviation Syndicate Managment Ltd, Syndicate 960/998: 1986 - 1991
	LG Cox and Co Ltd Aviation Syndicate 734, Active Underwriter: 1991 - 2002
	Allianz Insurance Plc: 2002 - 2006
	QBE Underwriting Ltd, Underwriting Director: 2006 -
	QBE Aviation Syndicate 5555, Managing Director and Underwriter: 2006 -
Main Area(s) of Expertise	Aviation
First Policy Written	1976
Most interesting Policies/Claims	All of them
Longest Customer Relationship(s)	20+ years
Current Major Appointments/ Committees	QBE Insurance (Europe) Ltd, Director: 2008 -
	Lloyd's Market Association Aviation Group: 2008 -
Previous Major Appointments/ Committees	Lloyd's Aviation Underwriters' Association, Chairman: 2001
Major Achievements while at Lloyd's	Active Underwriter of 734 E Di Silvio & Ors: 1991 - 2002,
	now Active Underwriter of Syndicate 5555
Mentor(s)	EO (Ted) Walklin, Michael Charlesworth, Brian Beagley

(continued)

Emilio Di Silvio (continued)

PERSONAL INFORMATION

Home	London
Main Interests and Recreation	Season ticket holder Tottenham Hotspur, my family
Favourite Book(s)	'La Divinia Comedia' by Dante Alleghieri
Favourite Car(s)	Fiat 500 (original version)
Favourite Gadget(s)	Many
Favourite Music	General
Clubs/Memberships	Three Rooms Club, Lloyd's Shotgun Club, Chartered Insurance Institute
Important and Interesting Aspects of Lloyd's	The market is unique and respected. An environment that in the past has enabled entrepreneurial ability to flourish irrespective of class and background and which hopefully will be allowed to continue.

Dane Douetil, CBE

Chief Executive Officer
Brit Syndicates Limited

Address (Office)	2nd Floor
	55 Bishopsgate
	London EC2N 3AS
Telephone	+44 (0)20 7984 8800
Fax	+44 (0)20 7984 8801
Email	dane.douetil@britinsurance.com
Secretary/PA	Annie Jenkins/Lisa Zeffie
Telephone	+44 (0)20 7984 8595
Email	annie.jenkins@britinsurance.com
Website	www.britinsurance.com

Full Name	Dane Jonathan Douetil, CBE
Born	1960
Nationality	British
Secondary Education	Marlborough College, Wiltshire
Further Education	University of Birmingham, Commerce BA (Hons): 1982

PROFESSIONAL INFORMATION

Career	Willis Faber & Dumas Ltd, Director of Political and Financial Risks: 1982 - 1988
	Special Risk Services Ltd, Founding Shareholder/Director: 1989 - 1994
	Benfield Group, Consultant: 1994 - 1997
	Benfield Group, Full-time Consultant: 1997 - 1998
	Brit Insurance Holdings PLC, Director: 1999 - 2005
	Brit Insurance Ltd, Chief Executive Officer: 1998 -
	Brit Syndicates Ltd, Chief Executive Officer: 2002 -
	Brit Insurance Holdings PLC, Chief Executive Officer: 2005 -
Current Major Appointments/ Committees	Association of British Insurers, Member of the Board: 2009 -
Previous Major Appointments/ Committees	Lloyd's Market Association, Chairman
	Market Reform Group (MRG), Chairman
	Contract Certainty Steering Group, Chairman
Major Achievements while at Lloyd's	Awarded CBE in 2007

PERSONAL INFORMATION

Home	West Sussex
Awards/Honours	CBE
Main Interests and Recreation	Fishing, shooting
Favourite Book(s)	Science fiction
Favourite Car(s)	Mercedes SL
Favourite Gadget(s)	Scag Sabre Tooth Tiger
Favourite Music	From The Doors to Mozart
Clubs/Memberships	Boodle's

Mark Everest

Chief Legal Counsel
Spectrum Syndicate Management Ltd

Address (Office)	2nd Floor
	6 Bevis Marks
	London EC3A 7HL
Telephone	+44 (0)20 7283 2646
Fax	+44 (0)20 7621 0975
Mobile	+44 (0)7734 101 372
Email	mark.everest@spectrumins.com
Secretary/PA	Dawn Beamish
Email	dawn.beamish@spectrumins.com
Website	www.spectrumins.com

Full Name	Christopher Mark Everest
Born	1963
Nationality	British and Australian
Secondary Education	King's College, Taunton, Somerset
Further Education	Trinity College, Cambridge, Law BA and MA
Professional Qualifications	Barrister, England and Wales: 1992
	Solicitor, Australia: 1993
	Solicitor, Australia and High Court: 1994
	Solicitor, England and Wales: 1998

PROFESSIONAL INFORMATION

Career	Oswald Hickson Collier & Co, London: 1990 - 1991
	Brisbane Bar: 1993 - 1994
	Clayton Utz: 1994 - 1995
	Lovell White Durrant: 1995 - 1999
	Eversheds: 1999 - 2001
	Barlow Lyde & Gilbert: 2001 - 2006
	Spectrum Syndicate Management Ltd, Chief Legal Counsel: 2006 -
Most interesting Policies/Claims	Bonner v. Cox (AON 77 Cover), acted for a party in the litigation in London
Longest Customer Relationship(s)	Confidential…

PERSONAL INFORMATION

Home	London
Awards/Honours	Major sports scholarship on entry to King's College, Taunton
Main Interests and Recreation	Boxing, driving, rugby
Favourite Book(s)	'Pickwick Papers' by Charles Dickens
Favourite Car(s)	TVR Tuscan S Convertible (my own!)
Favourite Music	Italian opera

Richard Finn

Independent Review Director
Advent Underwriting Limited

Address (Office)	10th Floor
	1 Minster Court
	Mincing Lane
	London EC3R 7AA
Telephone	+44 (0)1622 890 327
Fax	+44 (0)1622 891 288
Mobile	+44 (0)7801 570 453
Email	finnr@hotmail.co.uk
Website	www.adventgroup.co.uk
Full Name	Richard George Maxwell Finn
Born	1945
Nationality	British
Nickname	Finny

PROFESSIONAL INFORMATION

Started at Lloyd's	1965
Elected to Lloyd's	1977
Career	RA Norman Syndicate 917: 1965 - 1968
	ER Wood & Co, UK Property Broker: 1969
	RA Edwards Syndicate 219,
	Assistant to Casualty Underwriter: 1969 - 1973
	RA Edwards Syndicate 219,
	Assistant/Deputy Treaty/Treaty Underwriter: 1973 - 1990
	RA Edwards Syndicate 219, Active Underwriter: 1990 - 1998
	Wren Non-Marine Syndicate 250 (subsequently merged to create Brit Composite
	Syndicate 2987 for 2002), Active Underwriter: 1999 - 2001
	Brit Insurance Ltd, Reinsurance Underwriting Director: 2002 - 2005
	Brit Insurance Ltd, Reinsurance Division, Consultant: 2005 - 2007
	Advent Underwriting Ltd, Independent Review Director: 2007 -
Main Area(s) of Expertise	Non-Marine, All Lines Insurance and Reinsurance
Underwriting Speciality	All Lines Reinsurance (ex Marine)
First Policy Written	1975
Longest Customer Relationship(s)	Farm Mutual Reinsurance Bureau (Canada): 1970 - 2007
	Zenith Insurance Company (California WCA): 1970 - 2006
	Many R/I Relationships with customers: 1970 - 2007
Previous Major Appointments/	Lloyd's Underwriters' Non-Marine Association: 1993 - 1995
Committees	1986 Building Redevelopment Committee
	Asbestos Working Party: 1991 - 1995
	Syndicate Underwriting Management Ltd, Director
Lloyd's Connections (inc family)	Brother in law (deceased) Duncan AN Allen; Partner Fothergill and Hartung,
	merged Greigs 1973
Mentor(s)	Charles Skey

(continued)

Richard Finn (continued)

PERSONAL INFORMATION

Home	Kent
Main Interests and Recreation	Squash, cricket, golf, tennis, gardening, travel
Favourite Book(s)	John Grisham for travel
Favourite Music	50s-60's/80's Pop, light classical
Clubs/Memberships	Band of Brothers Cricket Club, Marylebone Cricket Club (MCC), FF, Boodle's, City of London Club, St Enodoc Golf Club, Royal St Georges Golf Club, Rye Golf Club
Important and Interesting Aspects of Lloyd's	Camaraderie, networking worldwide, friends, travel, variety, market change 1965 - 2009

David Foreman

Group Director of Underwriting
Ark Syndicate Management Limited

Address (Office)	8th Floor
	St Helen's
	1 Undershaft
	London EC3A 8EE
Telephone	+44 (0)20 3023 4002
Fax	+44 (0)20 3023 4000
Mobile	+44 (0)7768 973 107
Email	david.foreman@arkunderwriting.com
Secretary/PA	Lianne Walker
Telephone	+44 (0)20 3023 4014
Email	lianne.walker@arkunderwriting.com
Website	www.arkunderwriting.com
Full Name	David Peter Foreman
Born	1952
Nationality	British
Secondary Education	Hazelwick Comprehensive School, West Sussex: 1969
Further Education	Crawley College of Education: 1969 - 1972
Nickname	Unprintable

PROFESSIONAL INFORMATION

Elected to Lloyd's	1979
Career	SA Meacock & Ors: 1973 - 1976
	Harvey Bowring & Ors: 1976 - 1992
	IC Agnew Syndicate 672: 1993 - 1996
	IC Agnew Syndicate 672, Deputy Underwriter: 1996 - 1999
	Wellington Underwriting Agencies Ltd, Syndicate 2020,
	Active Underwriter: 1999 - 2006
	Ark Syndicate Management Ltd, Chief Underwriting Officer: 2007 - 2008
	Ark Syndicate Management Ltd, Group Director of Underwriting: 2009 -
Main Area(s) of Expertise	All, but Non-Marine mainly
Underwriting Speciality	Property Direct and Reinsurance
First Policy Written	Circa 1975 – probably a US Autotrucking PD
Most interesting Policies/Claims	All of them, but the WTC claim takes some beating
Longest Customer Relationship(s)	Brown Forman (Jack Daniels): 15 years. Many, many more
Current Major Appointments/ Committees	Ark Group Holding Board. No committees – hooray!
Previous Major Appointments/ Committees	Lloyd's Underwriters' Non-Marine Association, Chairman
	Lloyd's Market Board
	Lloyd's Market Association Underwriting Committee
Major Achievements while at Lloyd's	Starting Ark from scratch
Lloyd's Connections (inc family)	None
Mentor(s)	Michael Meacock, Richard Keeling, Ian Agnew, Louise Foreman

(continued)

David Foreman   (continued)

PERSONAL INFORMATION

Home	Surrey
Awards/Honours	Black Belt, 2nd Dan Shiotokan Karate
Charitable/Voluntary Activities	Organise Leadenhall Ball (10) for children's charities
Main Interests and Recreation	Tennis, golf, Manchester United, gardening. But mostly family
Favourite Book(s)	'The Boy in the Striped Pyjamas' by John Boyne
Favourite Car(s)	Mercedes E320 Diesel
Favourite Gadget(s)	Lawn mowers – I have six
Favourite Music	80s Soul, The Eagles
Clubs/Memberships	Reigate Tennis Club
Important and Interesting Aspects of Lloyd's	Lloyd's spirit of community and friendship

Matthew Fosh

Chief Executive
Novae Group plc

Address (Office)	71 Fenchurch Street
	London EC3M 4HH
Telephone	+44 (0)20 7903 7326
Fax	+44 (0)20 7903 7333
Email	mfosh@novae.com
Secretary/PA	Susan Wasmuth
Telephone	+44 (0)20 7903 7326
Email	swasmuth@novae.com
Website	www.novae.com

Full Name	Matthew Kailey Fosh
Born	1957
Nationality	British
Secondary Education	Harrow School, Middlesex: 1971 - 1975
Further Education	Magdalene College, Cambridge: 1976 - 1979
Professional Qualifications	MSI
Nickname	Foshy

PROFESSIONAL INFORMATION

Career	Strauss Turnbull Stockbrokers: 1981 - 1986
	Gartmore Investment Management: 1987
	Sheppards: 1987 - 1988
	Seagray Fosh Futures (sold to ICAP plc in Mar 2000): 1988 - 2002
	Novae Group plc, Chief Executive: 2002 -
Previous Major Appointments/ Committees	Seagray Fosh, Chief Executive Officer
Major Achievements while at Lloyd's	Completing successful turnaround of Novae Group
Mentor(s)	Rupert Villers

PERSONAL INFORMATION

Home	London
Awards/Honours	Double Blue (Rugby and Cricket) Cambridge
	England Cricketer of the Year 1977
Charitable/Voluntary Activities	Harrow School, Board of Governors
Main Interests and Recreation	Sport, acting, writing music
Favourite Book(s)	Historical novels
Favourite Car(s)	Triumph Stag
Favourite Gadget(s)	Cappuccino machine
Favourite Music	Mozart, Status Quo
Livery Companies	The Worshipful Company of Stationers and Newspaper Makers
Clubs/Memberships	The Hawks' Club Cambridge, Essex County Cricket Club,
	Cambridge University Rugby Union Football Club (RUFC)
Important and Interesting Aspects of Lloyd's	Lloyd's ability to adapt

Nick Furlonge

Director of Risk Management
Beazley Furlonge Limited

Address (Office)	Plantation Place South
	60 Great Tower Street
	London EC3R 5AD
Telephone	+44 (0)20 7674 7002
Fax	+44 (0)20 7674 7100
Email	nicholas.furlonge@beazley.com
Secretary/PA	Rachel Harrington
Telephone	+44 (0)20 7674 7267
Email	rachel.harrington@beazley.com
Website	www.beazley.com

Full Name	Nicholas Hill Furlonge
Born	1950
Nationality	British
Secondary Education	Redrice School, Hampshire
Further Education	The London Academy of Music and Dramatic Art (LAMDA)

PROFESSIONAL INFORMATION

Started at Lloyd's	1971
Elected to Lloyd's	1985
Career	Willis Faber & Dumas Ltd, Broker: 1971
	CE Heath & Co Ltd, Broker: 1974
	RA Edwards Syndicate 219: 1977
	Beazley Furlonge & Hiscox Ltd, Co-founder: 1985
	AF Beazley & Ors Syndicate 2623, Deputy Underwriter: 2002 - 2008
	Beazley Furlonge Ltd, Executive Director: 1985 -
	AF Beazley & Ors Syndicate 623, Deputy Underwriter: 1986 -
	Beazley Furlonge Ltd, Director of Risk Management: 1998 -
Main Area(s) of Expertise	Treaty Reinsurance (Non Marine)
First Policy Written	Excess Australian Liability Policy: 1977
Current Major Appointments/	Lloyd's Market Association Board: 2005 -
Committees	Lloyd's Community Programme, Chairman: 2007 -
	Lloyd's Franchise Board, Non-Executive Independent Director: 2008 -
Previous Major Appointments/	Business Development Unit Board: 1977
Committees	Standards & Protocol Committee (LMP): 2000
	Lloyd's Com/Kinnect: 2001
	Franchise Performance Management Group: 2002
Major Achievements while at Lloyd's	Co-founded and helped build Beazley
Mentor(s)	Charles Skey

Nick Furlonge (continued)

PERSONAL INFORMATION

Home	Kent
Main Interests and Recreation	Music (guitar), windsurfing, skiing, art, sport, music
Favourite Car(s)	My first car – a very old MG
Favourite Music	Rodrigo, Rachmaninov, Brahms, Clapton
Important and Interesting Aspects of Lloyd's	In 1986 we were able to sit down at a box in Lloyd's with a stamp capacity of £10 million and trade with all the world's major brokers. Our security was accepted without question. Extraordinary! This land of opportunity must be guarded and preserved.

Jeffery Gilbert

Gentleman, Scrutineer
Atrium Syndicate 609

Prefers to be incognito

Address (Office)	Room 790
	Lloyd's
	One Lime Street
	London EC3M 7DQ
Telephone	+44 (0)20 7327 8347
Mobile	'Mobile what? Of course I'm mobile'
Secretary/PA	'Don't be daft. No one would take it on'
Website	www.atrium-uw.com

Full Name	Jeffery Gilbert
Born	1943
Nationality	English (Not Foreign)
Secondary Education	Don't think any, have I?'
Further Education	Lloyd's. Membership 1969 - 1997 and 2001 - 2008.
	Will probably rejoin 2010
Professional Qualifications	Restricted 'D' (Can't fly jumbos)
Nickname	Madman

PROFESSIONAL INFORMATION

Elected to Lloyd's	1969
Career	1961 until asked to leave
	Agnew: 1982 - 2000
	Atrium: 2000 -
Main Area(s) of Expertise	(Marine) Anything that can bump into something else
Underwriting Speciality	Underwater Motorcycling Accident?
First Policy Written	1973 D.N.K
Most interesting Policies/Claims	How long have you got? Isaac Ibrahim de Hullu (PA Claim): 1976
Longest Customer Relationship(s)	I don't think anyone likes me that much
Previous Major Appointments/ Committees	Lloyd's Joint Hull Committee: 1994 - 1998
Major Achievements while at Lloyd's	Still employed 48 years later
Lloyd's Connections (inc family)	About 260 Gilbert/Man/Years of which 46 Underwriting, 214 Broking.
	Uncle, Father, Cousins, Son and so on.
	Married Cuthbert Heath's Great-Great Niece: 2001
Mentor(s)	Don't understand the question. You are asking a Lloyd's Name
	for goodness' sake.

Jeffery Gilbert (continued)

PERSONAL INFORMATION

Home	England
Armed Forces	Yes. Wholly in favour.
Awards/Honours	55 court appearances to date. PSSSST! Won them all but one.
Charitable/Voluntary Activities	Mowing the lawn
Main Interests and Recreation	Smashing up cars, dreaming, writing to the Mayor of London about urban foxes, making fireworks
Favourite Book(s)	My underwriter motorcycle PA book
Favourite Car(s)	The silver one. No, the red and white one. No, the Maclaren, Oh I don't know.
Favourite Gadget(s)	Wife no.2
Favourite Music	Louis James Alfred Lefébure-Wély
Livery Companies	No. Don't drink.
Favourite Car(s)	Jaguar
Favourite Gadget(s)	Blackberry
Favourite Music	Various

David Gittings
Chief Executive
Lloyd's Market Association

Address (Office)	Suite 358
	One Lime Street
	London EC3M 7DQ
Telephone	+44 (0)20 7327 4151
Fax	+44 (0)20 7327 4443
Mobile	+44 (0)7714 995 749
Email	david.gittings@lmalloyds.com
Secretary/PA	Louise Maisey
Telephone	+44 (0)20 7327 4938
Email	louise.maisey@lmalloyds.com
Website	www.lmalloyds.com

Full Name	David Howard Gittings
Born	1954
Nationality	British
Secondary Education	Colfe's School, Greenwich, London
Further Education	University of London (External Student), LLB (Hons): 1973-1976
Professional Qualifications	Barrister: 1977

PROFESSIONAL INFORMATION

Career	Lloyd's, Director of Regulation: 1995-2002
	Wellington Underwriting PLC, Group Head of Risk: 2002-2006
	Lloyd's Market Association, Chief Executive: 2006-
Current Major Appointments/ Committees	Financial Services Skills Council, Director: 2003-
	Chartered Insurance Institute, London Market Faculty Board, Chairman: 2006-
	Lloyd's Charities Trust, Trustee: 2007-
	JMD Specialist Insurance Services, Non-Executive Director: 2009-
Previous Major Appointments/ Committees	Lloyd's Regulatory Board: 1995-2002
	General Insurance Standards Council: 1999-2002
	Lloyd's Market Board: 2000-2002
Major Achievements while at Lloyd's	Transfer of Broker Regulation to GISC: 1999, Transfer of Managing Agent Regulation to FSA: 2001
Mentor(s)	John RC Young, CBE (former Chief Executive of The Securities and Investments Board)

PERSONAL INFORMATION

Home	Kent
Awards/Honours	Insurance Institute of London, Vice President
Main Interests and Recreation	Music, ballet, literature
Favourite Book(s)	Anything by John le Carré

Peter Grove

Chief Underwriting Officer
QBE Underwriting Limited

Address (Office)	Plantation Place
	30 Fenchurch Street
	London EC3M 3BD
Telephone	+44 (0)20 7105 4000
Fax	+44 (0)20 7105 5020
Email	peter.grove@uk.qbe.com
Secretary/PA	Andra Giles
Telephone	+44 (0)20 7105 4516
Email	andra.giles@uk.qbe.com
Website	www.qbeeurope.com

Full Name	Peter Ernest Grove
Born	1949
Nationality	British
Secondary Education	Heathcote Secondary Modern, Essex

PROFESSIONAL INFORMATION

Elected to Lloyd's	1984
Career	Willis Faber & Dumas Ltd: 1966
	Syndicates 561, 566 and 197/726, Deputy Underwriter: 1982
	Bankside Syndicates Ltd, Syndicate 561, Active Underwriter: 1988
	LIMIT Underwriting Ltd, Underwriting Director: 1999
	QBE Underwriting Ltd, Active Underwriter, Syndicate 2999: 2003 - 2009
	QBE Underwriting Ltd, Underwriting Director: 2003 -
	QBE European Operations, Chief Underwriting Officer: 2004 -
Main Area(s) of Expertise	Reinsurance
Underwriting Speciality	Retrocession business
First Policy Written	1977
Longest Customer Relationship(s)	BF Caudle & Ors: 1977
Major Achievements while at Lloyd's	Survival
Mentor(s)	BP Johnson, Elvin Patrick

PERSONAL INFORMATION

Home	Essex
Charitable/Voluntary Activities	Helen Rollason Heal Cancer Charity
Main Interests and Recreation	Sleeping
Favourite Book(s)	'Modern Chess Openings' by Walter Korn and Nick Defirmian
Favourite Car(s)	Bentley Continental
Favourite Gadget(s)	Blackberry
Favourite Music	Bob Dylan
Important and Interesting Aspects of Lloyd's	The most important thing to me about Lloyd's is that it is the ultimate trading market place

Nigel Hanbury

Chairman
Hampden Agencies Ltd

Address (Office)	85 Gracechurch Street
	London EC3V 0AA
Telephone	+44 (0)20 7863 6500
Fax	+44 (0)20 7863 6587
Email	nigel.hanbury@hampden.co.uk
Secretary/PA	Liz Coe
Telephone	+44 (0)20 7863 6521
Email	liz.coe@hampden.co.uk
Website	www.hampden.co.uk

Full Name	Nigel John Hanbury
Born	1957
Nationality	British
Secondary Education	Stanbridge Earls School, Hampshire: 1970 - 1975
Further Education	Royal Military Academy, Sandhurst: 1975 - 1976

PROFESSIONAL INFORMATION

Elected to Lloyd's	1978
Career	JH Minet, Broker: 1981 - 1983
	CT Bowring, Broker: 1983 - 1985
	RW Sturge Members Agency, Director: 1985 - 1991
	Stewart Members Agency, Director: 1991 - 1994
	Venton Underwriting Agency Ltd: 1994
	Hampden Agencies Ltd, Director and Chief Executive Officer: 1995 - 2008
	Hampden Agencies Ltd, Executive Chairman: 2008 -
Longest Customer Relationship(s)	30 years
Current Major Appointments/ Committees	Association of Lloyd's Members, Director
Previous Major Appointments/ Committees	Council of Lloyd's, Working Member: 1999 - 2001, 2005 - 2008
Major Achievements while at Lloyd's	Since the troubles culminating in R&R, private capital's ability to participate at Lloyd's has been under severe threat. Along with others I have done my bit to ensure that any such threats have not been successful.
Lloyd's Connections (inc family)	Father a Member since 1950
Mentor(s)	David Coleridge

Nigel Hanbury   (continued)

PERSONAL INFORMATION

Home	Hampshire
Armed Forces	Welsh Guards: 1976 - 1980
Charitable/Voluntary Activities	Oliver Whitby Educational Foundation, Vice Chairman and Governor
	Red Squirrel Survival Trust, Trustee
Main Interests and Recreation	Hiking, skiing, shooting, farming, forestry, conservation
Favourite Book(s)	'Stalingrad' by Anthony Beevor, 'Moscow 1812: Napoleon's Fatal March' by Adam Zamoyski, 'Lord of the Rings' by JRR Tolkien
Favourite Gadget(s)	No gadgets, gizmos or toys, but my dogs (currently four terriers) give me enormous pleasure
Favourite Music	70s Rock music
Clubs/Memberships	City of London Club
Important and Interesting Aspects of Lloyd's	Lloyd's is an institution that has for over 300 years provided a vital service to millions of clients as well as an enjoyable and profitable career for countless others. Investors in whatever form, have also made substantial profits over time. My hope is that this will continue for another 300 years.

Cuthbert Heath, OBE

Underwriter and Insurance Broker

Address (Office)	Heaven by way of Coldharbour Churchyard
	Dorking
	Surrey

Full Name	Cuthbert Eden Heath
Lived	1859-1939
Nationality	British
Secondary Education	Brighton College 1869-1872/3
Further Education	Niort, France and the University of Bonn, Germany where he studied Chemistry in a very mild way
Professional Qualifications	What?!! Gentlemen didn't have these things!
Nickname	Bertie

PROFESSIONAL INFORMATION

Elected to Lloyd's	1880 with the support of his father
Career	Started at Henry Head in about 1878 and then founded CE Heath & Co, which was incorporated in 1910
Main Areas of Expertise	Non-Marine at a time when Lloyd's was the world's foremost marine market
Underwriting Speciality	Why not?
First Policy	A lot of the risks he broked, and subsequently wrote, were the first of their type.
Interesting Policies	Following the 1906 San Francisco earthquake, Cuthbert Heath sent a telegram to his Agent saying, "Pay all our policy holders in full, irrespective of the terms of their policies."
	An entertainer asked Cuthbert Heath to insure his monkey as being essential to his act. Cuthbert Heath did so. Some years later, the monkey died and the entertainer returned to claim his money. The claim was settled in full and the entertainer left the monkey at Heath's, who had it stuffed.
Longest Customer Relationship	His assureds
Major Appointments/Committees	At Lloyd's all his life
	Elected to Lloyd's Committee in a contested election: 1912
	Lloyd's Patriotic Fund, Trustee: 1915
	Labour Department, Member of the Committee: 1919
Major Achievements whilst at Lloyd's	Took Lloyd's to the man on the street, woke it up and he is credited with the founding of the Non-Marine Market at Lloyd's which is now greater in size than the Marine market.
Lloyd's Connections (inc family)	His father and two of his brothers
Mentor	Secret (probably his father and mother – but more his father)

PERSONAL INFORMATION

Armed Forces	There's a painting of him in an unidentified uniform, probably the Home Guard. He didn't get into the Navy because of his deafness.
Charitable/Voluntary Posts	Apparently he was amazingly generous to people who asked him for money – they came from all quarters.

Robert Hiscox

Chairman
Hiscox Syndicates Limited

Address (Office)	1 Great St Helen's
	London EC3A 6HX
Telephone	+44 (0)20 7448 6011
Fax	+44 (0)20 7448 6900
Email	robert.hiscox@hiscox.com
Secretary/PA	Jade Hallam
Telephone	+44 (0)20 7448 6011
Email	jade.hallam@hiscox.com
Website	www.hiscox.com

Full Name	Robert Ralph Scrymgeour Hiscox
Born	1943
Nationality	British
Secondary Education	Rugby School, Warwickshire: 1956 - 1961
Further Education	Corpus Christi College, Cambridge, MA: 1961 - 1964
Professional Qualifications	ACII

PROFESSIONAL INFORMATION

Elected to Lloyd's	1967
Career	Durtnell & Fowler Ltd, Lloyd's Broker: 1964 - 1965
	Hiscox Ltd: 1965 -
	Hiscox Ltd, Executive Chairman: 1996 -
	Hiscox Syndicates Ltd, Executive Chairman: 1991 -
Main Area(s) of Expertise	Non-Marine
Underwriting Speciality	PA, Fine Art and general Non-Marine business: 1967 - 1988
Current Major Appointments/ Committees	Grainger plc, Director: 2002 -
Previous Major Appointments/ Committees	Lloyd's Underwriters Agents' Association, Chairman: 1991
	Lloyd's, Deputy Chairman: 1993 - 1995
	Lloyd's Corporate Capital Association, Chairman: 1998 - 1999
	Lloyd's Market Association, Chairman: 1999 - 2000
Major Achievements while at Lloyd's	For others to judge
Lloyd's Connections (inc family)	Ralph Hiscox, CBE (father) was an Underwriter and Chairman of Lloyd's: 1967 - 1968

(continued)

Robert Hiscox   (CONTINUED)

PERSONAL INFORMATION

Home	Wiltshire
Charitable/Voluntary Activities	Friends of the Tate Gallery, Treasurer: 1990 - 1993
	St Francis School Pewsey, Governor: 1994 - 1997
	Museums and Galleries Commission Treasurer: 1996 - 2000
	Wiltshire Bobby Van Trust, Trustee: 1998 - 2002
	Campaign for Museums, Trustee and Treasurer: 1998 - 2004
	24 Hour Museum, Trustee: 2000 - 2001
	Wiltshire Bobby Van Trust, Chairman: 2002 -
	Public Catalogue Foundation: 2004 -
	Bermuda Society: 2007 -
Main Interests and Recreation	Art, country life, family
Favourite Gadget(s)	Blackberry
Clubs/Memberships	Boodle's, Queen's
Important and Interesting Aspects of Lloyd's	That it remains a vibrant force in international insurance and reinsurance.

Paul Hunt

Underwriting Director and Active Underwriter Syndicate 2121
Argenta Syndicate Management Limited

Address (Office)	Fountain House
	130 Fenchurch Street
	London EC3M 5DJ
Telephone	+44 (0)20 7825 7110
Fax	+44 (0)20 7825 7155
Mobile	+44 (0)7770 886 586
Email	paul.hunt@argentaplc.com
Secretary/PA	Debbie Bryan
Telephone	+44 (0)20 7825 7206
Email	debbie.bryan@argentaplc.com
Website	www.argentaplc.com
Full Name	Paul Hunt
Born	1950
Nationality	British
Secondary Education	East Ham Grammar School, London
Nickname	Bunker

PROFESSIONAL INFORMATION

Elected to Lloyd's	1980
Career	Hartley, Cooper & Co Ltd, Junior Claims Broker: 1967
	GL Towers & Ors, Syndicate 406: 1973 (and connected with underwriting ever since)
	Hiscox Syndicates Ltd, Syndicate 52, Active Underwriter: 1990
	RM Pateman Underwriting Agencies Ltd, Director
	Hiscox Syndicates Ltd, Director
	Hunt Underwriting Ltd, Founder: 2001
	Argenta Syndicate Management Ltd, Underwriting Director and Active Underwriter, Syndicate 2121: 2006 -
Main Area(s) of Expertise	Marine and Energy
Underwriting Speciality	Marine Liability
First Policy Written	1980
Most interesting Policies/Claims	Panama Canal Commission, Package Insurance
Longest Customer Relationship(s)	McDermott International
Previous Major Appointments/ Committees	Lloyd's Underwriters' Association, Committee Member
	The Salvage Association, Committee Member
Major Achievements while at Lloyd's	Forty years in the Lloyd's Market!
Mentor(s)	My wife Sandra

PERSONAL INFORMATION

Home	Essex
Main Interests and Recreation	Skiing, fishing, walking
Favourite Book(s)	Stephen King novels
Favourite Car(s)	Any Mercedes!
Favourite Gadget(s)	My car
Favourite Music	Motown
Important and Interesting Aspects of Lloyd's	Its history

James Illingworth

Chief Risk Officer
Amlin Underwriting Ltd

Address (Office)	St Helen's
	1 Undershaft
	London EC3A 8ND
Telephone	+44 (0)20 7746 1000
Fax	+44 (0)20 7746 1311
Mobile	+44 (0)7921 038 059
Email	james.illingworth@amlin.co.uk
Secretary/PA	Carol Simmons
Telephone	+44 (0)20 7746 1765
Email	carol.simmons@amlin.co.uk
Website	www.amlin.com

Full Name	James Le Tall Illingworth
Born	1961
Nationality	British
Secondary Education	Millfield School, Somerset
Further Education	Royal Holloway College, University of London, History BA (Hons)

PROFESSIONAL INFORMATION

Category of Lloyd's Membership	Non-Underwriting Working Member: 2000 -
Career	Greig Fester Ltd: 1983 - 1991
	Stace Barr Ltd, Director: 1991 - 1996
	Stace Barr Insurance Capital, Managing Director: 1995 - 1997
	Angerstein Underwriting Trust PLC, Director: 1998
	Amlin Underwriting Ltd, Chairman: 1999 - 2000
	Amlin Underwriting Ltd, Executive Director: 1999 -
	Amlin Plus Ltd, Non-Executive Director: 2005 -
	Amlin Marine Services Ltd, Non-Executive Director: 2005 -
	Amlin plc, Chief Risk Officer: 2006 -
	Amlin Underwriting Ltd, Chief Risk Officer: 2006 -
Current Major Appointments/ Committees	Lloyd's Market Association Risk Management Committee, Chairman: 2008 -
	Leadenhall Capital Partners, Director
Previous Major Appointments/ Committees	Lloyd's Underwriting Agents' Association: 2000
Major Achievements while at Lloyd's	Formed Stace Barr Insurance Capital, which became the largest Lloyd's corporate spread capital adviser
Mentor(s)	John Ballard (Broker), Mike Andrews (Banker and Non-Executive Director)

PERSONAL INFORMATION

Home	London
Main Interests and Recreation	Family, sport, opera, countryside, history, travel
Favourite Book(s)	'Birdsong' by Sebastian Faulks and all books by Ian McEwan
Favourite Music	Operas by Verdi and Puccini, Mozart, most Rock music
Clubs/Memberships	Marylebone Cricket Club (MCC), Lloyd's Golf Club,
	Chartered Insurance Institute (CII), Hurlingham Club

Robin Jackson

Chairman
Marketform Managing Agency Limited

Address (Office)	8 Lloyd's Avenue
	London EC3N 3EL
Telephone	+44 (0)20 7488 7700
Fax	+44 (0)20 7488 7800
Email	ragj@btinternet.com
Website	www.marketform.com
Full Name	Robin Anthony Gildart Jackson
Born	1935
Nationality	British
Secondary Education	Millfield School, Somerset
Nickname	Giraffe

PROFESSIONAL INFORMATION

Elected to Lloyd's	1977
Career	CT Bowring Group, Lloyd's Broker, Life Pensions and Personal Accident departments: 1956 - 1960
	General Reinsurance Corporation (New York), Casualty Facultative Department, Underwriter: 1960 - 1971
	General Reinsurance Corporation (New York), Vice-President: 1970 - 1971
	Unionamerica Insurance Company (London), Founder and Managing Director: 1971 - 1976
	Merrett Group at Lloyd's: 1976 - 1992
	Merrett Group, Syndicate 799, Active Underwriter: 1976 - 1988
	Centrewrite Ltd, Chairman and Chief Executive: 1992 - 1994
	RF Bailey Underwriting Agencies Ltd, Non-Executive Director: 1992 - 2003
	Newline Syndicate Management Ltd, Non-Executive Director: 1996 - 2001
	Marketform Managing Agency Ltd, Non-Executive Director: 1998
	Tawa PLC, Non-Executive Director: 2001
	Reinsurance Disputes in UK, US and Australia, Appointed Arbitrator: 1999 -
	Marketform Managing Agency Ltd, Non-Executive Chairman: 2002 -
	Tawa PLC, Non-Executive Chairman: 2007 -
Main Area(s) of Expertise	Non-Marine
Underwriting Speciality	Reinsurance
First Policy Written	In Lloyd's: September 1976; in USA: January 1961
Most interesting Policies/Claims	Golden Parachutes: circa 1982
Previous Major Appointments/ Committees	Lloyd's Underwriters' Non-Marine Association Committee, Member: 1980 - 1988
	Lloyd's Underwriters' Non-Marine Association Committee, Chairman: 1986

(continued)

Robin Jackson (continued)

London Market Asbestos Working Party, Chairman: 1984 - 1996
London Market Claims Services Ltd, Chairman: 1988 - 1998
Equitas Project Core Reserve Group at Lloyd's, Chairman of one of the
    underwriting teams: 1993 - 1996
Lloyd's Special Claims Unit, Chairman: 1994 - 1996

Major Achievements while at Lloyd's Attempts to sort out the Asbestos problem – a lot of work – no thanks!
    (Another Lloyd's tradition)

PERSONAL INFORMATION

Home	Herefordshire
Armed Forces	National Service, Intelligence Corps Egypt/Libya: 1953 - 1955
Awards/Honours	General Service Medal (Suez Canal Zone)
Main Interests and Recreation	Travel and (watching these days) cricket, golf, rugby; helping get rid of Labour Government and UK membership of EU
Favourite Book(s)	History and biographies
Favourite Gadget(s)	Do not like gadgets!
Favourite Music	Almost anything other than modern and loud rubbish
Clubs/Memberships	A number of golf and cricket clubs

Nick Jones

Former Executive Director and Active Underwriter Syndicate 1200
Heritage Managing Agency Limited

Contact Details	tba

Full Name	Nicholas Gavin Jones
Born	1971
Nationality	British
Secondary Education	St Dunstan's College, London: 1979 - 1989
Further Education	University of Manchester (UMIST), Mathematics and Statistics BSc (Hons): 1989 - 1992
Professional Qualifications	ACII, Chartered Insurer: 2004

PROFESSIONAL INFORMATION

Started at Lloyd's	1993
Career	DP Mann Ltd, Syndicate 435, Underwriting Assistant: 1993
	DP Mann Ltd, Syndicate 435, Property Underwriter: 1994 - 2003
	Heritage Managing Agency Ltd, Syndicate 1200, Deputy Underwriter: 2003 - 2006
	Heritage Managing Agency Ltd, Executive Director: 2006 - 2008
	Heritage Managing Agency Ltd, Syndicate 1200, Active Underwriter: 2006 - 2008
Main Area(s) of Expertise	Direct and Facultative Property
Underwriting Speciality	Mortgage Impairment
First Policy Written	US Fire theft collision on trucking fleets: 1994
Most interesting Policies/Claims	Lloyd's Leader on $500 million xs $1.0 billion on Silverstein World Trade Center Twin Towers Placement at time of loss
Longest Customer Relationship(s)	Insurmark, Ohio; Proctor Financial, Detroit
Major Achievements while at Lloyd's	Over 15 years underwriting experience. Represented Lloyd's Market in New York Federal Court in World Trade Center/Silverstein trial.
Mentor(s)	Les Rock (Underwriter)

PERSONAL INFORMATION

Home	Kent
Main Interests and Recreation	Family (two sons)
Clubs/Memberships	Chartered Insurance Institute

James Mackay

New Business Director
Argenta Private Capital Limited

Address (Office)	Fountain House
	130 Fenchurch Street
	London EC3M 5DJ
Telephone	+44 (0)20 7825 7288
Fax	+44 (0)20 7825 7212
Email	james.mackay@argentaplc.com
Secretary/PA	Sarah Capon
Telephone	+44 (0)20 7825 7160
Email	sarah.capon@argentaplc.com
Website	www.argentaplc.com

Full Name	James Anthony Mackay
Born	1969
Nationality	British
Secondary Education	King's School, Rochester, Kent: 1978 - 1988
Further Education	Queen Mary College, University of London, BSc (Hons)
Professional Qualifications	IMC

PROFESSIONAL INFORMATION

Category of Lloyd's Membership	Shareholder in a NameCo from 2006 Account onwards
Career	Bankside Underwriting Agency: 1993 - 1995
	Argenta Private Capital Ltd, New Business Director: 1995 -
Mentor(s)	Chris Murphy

PERSONAL INFORMATION

Home	Kent
Main Interests and Recreation	Golf, photography, wine
Favourite Book(s)	'Lord of the Rings' by JRR Tolkien
Favourite Car(s)	M5 BMW
Favourite Gadget(s)	Nikon Digital SLR
Favourite Music	Rock, Pop
Clubs/Memberships	Lloyd's Golf Club
Important and Interesting Aspects of Lloyd's	I have always been fascinated by the unique way in which private investors are able to underwrite risk through syndicates at Lloyd's. Despite ups and downs in performance, it is the most interesting investment I have ever known.

Lord Marland of Odstock

Chairman
Jubilee Managing Agency Limited

Address (Office)	c/o ICP Holdings Ltd
	Unit C25
	Jack's Place
	6 Corbet Place
	London E1 6NN
Telephone	+44 (0)20 7392 8480
Fax	+44 (0)20 7392 8481
Email	marland@parliament.uk
Secretary/PA	Laura Westgate
Email	laura@odstock.net
Full Name	Jonathan Peter Marland (Lord Marland of Odstock)
Born	1956
Nationality	British

PROFESSIONAL INFORMATION

Elected to Lloyd's	1981
Career	Willis Faber Ltd: 1975 - 1982
	Lloyd Thompson Ltd, Reinsurance Division, Board Director and Shareholder: 1982
	Lloyd Thompson Ltd, Member of Executive Committee to organise flotation: 1987
	Lloyd Thompson Group PLC, Director: 1987
	Lloyd Thompson, Reinsurance Division, Chairman: 1997
	Jardine Lloyd Thompson Group PLC, Executive Director : 1997 - 1999
	Jardine Lloyd Thompson Reinsurance Ltd, Chief Executive: 1997 - 1999
	Jubilee Managing Agency Ltd and Subsidiaries, Non-Executive Director: 2004 - 2009
	Jardine Lloyd Thompson Group PLC, Consultant: 1999 -
	ICP Holdings Ltd & ICP Capital Ltd, Non-Executive Director: 2007 -
	ICP General Partner Ltd, Non-Executive Director: 2007 -
	Jubilee Managing Agency Ltd, Non-Executive Chairman: 2009 -
Current Major Appointments/ Committees	Herriot Ltd – family investment and consultancy business, Chairman
	Janspeed Ltd
	Jubilee Motor Policies, Director
	Clareville Capital LLP (hedge fund)
	Hunter Boot Ltd, Director
	Insurance Capital Partners LLP, Director
	WH Ireland, Stockbroker, Director
Mentor(s)	John Lloyd, Ian Agnew – they taught me nearly everything they know

(continued)

Lord Marland of Odstock   (continued)

PERSONAL INFORMATION

Home	London
Awards/Honours	Fellow of the Royal Society of Arts
Charitable/Voluntary Activities	Atlantic Partnership, Treasurer/Trustee
	St Bartholomew's Church, Dinard, France, Board Member
	C&UCO Properties, Director
	Guggenheim UK Charitable Trust, Trustee
	Peggy Guggenheim Museum, Venice, Trustee
	Harnham Watermeadows Trust, Chairman
	International Churchill Society, Trustee
	Invercauld Estate, Trustee
	JP Marland Charitable Trust, Trustee
	Royal Academy of Arts, Development Committee
	Salisbury FC, President
	The Sports Nexus, Founder and Chairman
	The Conservative Party, former Treasurer and involvement in Boris Johnson's Mayoral Campaign
	Wiltshire Churches, Patron
Clubs/Memberships	Brooks's, Marylebone Cricket Club (MCC)

Bronek Masojada

Chief Executive Officer
Hiscox Syndicates Limited

Address (Office)	1 Great St Helen's
	London EC3A 6HX
Telephone	+44 (0)20 7448 6012
Fax	+44 (0)20 7448 6598
Email	bronek.masojada@hiscox.com
Secretary/PA	Jane Curle
Telephone	+44 (0)20 7448 6012
Email	jane.curle@hiscox.com
Website	www.hiscox.com

Full Name	Bronislaw Edmund Masojada
Born	1961
Nationality	South African
Secondary Education	Durban High School, South Africa: 1975 - 1978
Further Education	University of Natal, Durban,
	Civil Engineering BSc (Cum Laude): 1979 - 1983
	Trinity College, Oxford, Management Studies MPhil: 1985 - 1987

PROFESSIONAL INFORMATION

Category of Lloyd's Membership	Non-Underwriting Working Member
Career	South African Defence Force, National Service: 1983 - 1984
	Pim Goldby Management Consultants: 1988
	McKinsey: 1989 - 1993
	Hiscox Syndicates Ltd, Chief Executive Officer: 1993 -
	Hiscox Group, Chief Executive Officer: 2000 -
Current Major Appointments/	Lloyd's Croquet Society, President: 2004 -
Committees	Lloyd's Tercentenary Foundation, Chairman: 2008 -
Previous Major Appointments/	Lloyd's, Deputy Chairman: 2001 - 2007
Committees	Insurance Institute of London, President: 2004 - 2005
	Lloyd's Tercentenary Foundation, Trustee: 2006

PERSONAL INFORMATION

Home	Surrey
Awards/Honours	Rhodes Scholar
Main Interests and Recreation	Kite surfing
Livery Companies	The Worshipful Company of Insurers
Clubs/Memberships	Stormriders Kitesurfing Club

Michael Meacock

Underwriting Director and Active Underwriter Syndicate 727
SA Meacock & Company Limited

Address (Office)	4th Floor
	15 St Helen's Place
	London EC3A 6DE
Telephone	+44 (0)20 7374 6727
Fax	+44 (0)20 7374 4727
Email	michael.meacock@sameacock.com
Secretary/PA	Linda Mailoudi
Email	linda.mailoudi@sameacock.com
Full Name	Michael John Meacock
Born	1937
Nationality	British
Secondary Education	Haileybury College, Hertfordshire: 1951 - 1955
Nickname	Nigel (as in Nigel Lawson)

PROFESSIONAL INFORMATION

Elected to Lloyd's	1958
Category of Lloyd's Membership	Name
Career	**Syndicate 727, Active Underwriter: 1966 -**
	SA Meacock & Company Ltd, Underwriting Director: 1996 -
Main Area(s) of Expertise	Non-Marine
Underwriting Speciality	Jack of all trades
First Policy Written	Twins Insurance
Longest Customer Relationship(s)	Jersey Mutual
Major Achievements while at Lloyd's	An attractive return on Names' capital over six underwriting cycles
Lloyd's Connections (inc family)	SA Meacock (grandfather) at Lloyd's: 1873 - 1950; John Meacock (father) at Lloyd's: 1929 - 1970

PERSONAL INFORMATION

Home	Hertfordshire
Awards/Honours	Voted 'Lloyd's Personality of Year 2001' by the Association of Lloyd's Members
Charitable/Voluntary Activities	Much Hadham Cricket Club, President
Main Interests and Recreation	My family, most sports, Lloyd's – the risk, the people
Favourite Book(s)	'Churchill' by Roy Jenkins
Favourite Car(s)	London taxi (I hate all cars!)
Favourite Gadget(s)	My Wisden cricket bat autographed by Denis Compton
Favourite Music	New World Symphony by Dvořák, any Mozart
Clubs/Memberships	City of London Club, Lloyds Club, Marylebone Cricket Club (MCC), Forty Club
Important and Interesting Aspects of Lloyd's	I regard myself as very fortunate to have had the opportunity to be at the coalface of a very special and unique institution for over 50 years

Brian Merfield

Former Non-Executive Director
Equity Syndicate Management Ltd

Address (Office)	c/o Equity Syndicate Management Ltd
	Library House
	New Road
	Brentwood
	Essex CM14 4GD
Telephone	+44 (0)1732 700 664
Fax	+44 (0)1732 700 664
Mobile	+44 (0)7774 859 664
Email	bcmerfield@aol.com
Website	www.equitygroup.co.uk

Full Name	Brian Cuthbert Merfield
Born	1945
Nationality	British
Secondary Education	Archbishop Tennison's Grammar School, London: 1956 - 1961
Professional Qualifications	ACIB

PROFESSIONAL INFORMATION

Career	Samuel Montagu & Co Ltd, Director Specialised Financing
	HSBC Investment Bank plc
	Equity Syndicate Management Ltd, Non-Executive Director: 1999 - 2008

PERSONAL INFORMATION

Home	Kent
Charitable/Voluntary Activities	Sevenoaks Table Tennis League, President
Main Interests and Recreation	Cycling, tennis, swimming
Favourite Book(s)	'Lord of the Rings' by JRR Tolkien
Favourite Car(s)	Jaguar XJ Series
Favourite Gadget(s)	Laptop
Favourite Music	1960's

Barbara Merry

Chief Executive Officer
Hardy (Underwriting Agencies) Ltd

Address (Office)	4th Floor
	40 Lime Street
	London EC3M 7AW
Telephone	+44 (0)20 7105 3302
Fax	+44 (0)20 7283 4677
Email	barbara.merry@hardygroup.co.uk
Secretary/PA	Tieri Tizard-Varcoe
Telephone	+44 (0)20 7105 3303
Email	tieri@hardygroup.co.uk
Website	www.hardygroup.co.uk

Full Name	Barbara Jane Merry
Born	1957
Nationality	British
Secondary Education	Great Yarmouth High School for Girls, Norfolk: 1968 - 1975
Further Education	London School of Economics: 1975 - 1979
Professional Qualifications	ACA: 1982

PROFESSIONAL INFORMATION

Career	Corporation of Lloyd's, various roles including General Manager, Regulatory Policy: 1985 - 1999
	Omega Group, Managing Director: 1999 - 2001
	Hardy Underwriting Bermuda Ltd, Chief Executive Officer: 2002 -
	Hardy (Underwriting Agencies) Ltd, Chief Executive Officer: 2002 -
Main Area(s) of Expertise	Management
Current Major Appointments/ Committees	Lloyd's Market Association Professional Standards Committee (PSC), Chair: 2008 -
	Council of Lloyd's, External Member: 2007 -
Previous Major Appointments/ Committees	Lloyd's Market Association, Elected Board Member: 2003 - 2008
Mentor(s)	Graeme King, Nigel Pantling

PERSONAL INFORMATION

Home	Kent
Main Interests and Recreation	Reading, cooking, walking, travelling, terrible and infrequent golf, watching rugby, any games which my young son likes
Favourite Book(s)	Changes all the time – recent favourites are: 'The Vanishing Act of Esme Lennox' by Maggie O'Farrell, 'A Thousand Splendid Suns' by Khaled Hosseini and 'The Boy in the Striped Pyjamas' by John Boyne
Favourite Car(s)	My old Jaguar
Favourite Gadget(s)	My PDA thing: see! I don't even know its proper name!
Favourite Music	At the moment, Take That
Livery Companies	The Worshipful Company of Insurers

Peter Morgan, MBE

Director
Association of Lloyd's Members

Address (Office)	c/o Association of Lloyd's Members
	100 Fenchurch Street
	London EC3M 5LG
Telephone	+44 (0)20 7488 0033
Fax	+44 (0)1428 643 684
Mobile	+44 (0)7973 162 810
Email	petermorgan@cleeves2.demon.co.uk
Website	www.alm.ltd.uk

Full Name	Peter William Lloyd Morgan, MBE
Born	1936
Nationality	British
Secondary Education	Llandovery College, South Wales (A-Levels: History, Latin, English)
Further Education	Trinity Hall, Cambridge, History Tripos MA

PROFESSIONAL INFORMATION

Elected to Lloyd's	1986
Career and Current Major Appointments	IBM UK and IBM Europe: 1959 - 1989
	IBM UK, London, Sales Director: 1971 - 1974
	IBM Europe, Paris, Marketing Director: 1975 - 1980
	IBM UK, London, Executive Director: 1980 - 1987
	IBM UK Holdings PLC, Director: 1987 - 1989
	The Institute of Directors, Director General: 1989 - 1994
	SWALEC, Director: 1989 - 1996
	NPI, Director and Chairman: 1990 - 1999
	SWALEC, Chairman: 1996
	Pace Micro Technology PLC, Chairman: 1996 - 2000
	Baltimore Technologies PLC, Director and Chairman: 1999 - 2003
	Association of Lloyd's Members, Director: 1997 -
	Oxford Instruments plc, Director: 1999 -
	Hyder Consulting plc, Director: 2002 -
	Strategic Thought plc, Chairman: 2004 -
	European Economic and Social Committee, Brussels, UK Delegate: 2006 -
Previous Major Appointments/ Committees	Lloyd's Audit Committee
	Lloyd's Market Board
	Lloyd's Chairman's Strategy Group, Member
	European Economic and Social Committee, Brussels, UK Delegate: 1994 - 2002
	Council of Lloyd's, External Member: 2000 - 2009
	Lloyd's Nominations and Compensation Committee: 2000 - 2009

(continued)

Peter Morgan, MBE (continued)

PERSONAL INFORMATION

Home	Surrey
Armed Forces	Royal Signals, 2nd Lieutenant (National Service): 1954 - 1956
Awards/Honours	MBE in 2003
Charitable/Voluntary Activities	Church Housing Trust, Patron
	Past Master of the Worshipful Company of Information Technologists
Main Interests and Recreation	Wine, history, lurchers, rugby, gardening, skiing, travelling
Favourite Book(s)	'Alarming Drum – Britain's European Dilemma', which I wrote
Favourite Car(s)	Maserati Quattroporte
Favourite Gadget(s)	Sky+ for recording Rugby
Favourite Music	Mozart, Stan Getz, Welsh Hymns
Clubs/Memberships	Oxford and Cambridge Club
Important and Interesting Aspects of Lloyd's	Managing the cycle

Scott Moser

Non-Executive Director
Atrium Underwriters Ltd

Address (Office)	c/o Resolute Management Services Ltd
	Exchequer Court
	33 St Mary Axe
	London EC3A 8LL
Telephone	+44 (0)20 7342 2118
Fax	+44 (0)20 7342 2001
Email	scott.moser@resmsl.co.uk
Secretary/PA	Kathy Allington
Email	kathy.allington@resmsl.co.uk

Full Name	Scott Peter Moser
Born	1951
Nationality	American
Further Education	Columbia University School of Law
	Clark University, Phi Beta Kappa, Government
	(Magna Cum Laude with High Honours)

PROFESSIONAL INFORMATION

Career	Simpson Thacher & Bartlett, Associate: 1975 - 1976
	Day Berry and Howard, Associate: 1976 - 1982
	Day Berry and Howard, Partner: 1983 - 1994
	Aetna Casualty & Surety Co, Vice President: 1994 - 1996
	Envision Claims Management Corporation, President: 1996 - 1997
	Equitas Ltd, Claims Director: 1997 - 2003
	Equitas Ltd, Chief Executive Officer: 2003 - 2007
	Resolute Management Services Ltd, Chief Executive Officer: 2007 -
	Atrium Underwriters Ltd, Non Executive Director: 2008 -

PERSONAL INFORMATION

Home	Surrey
Awards/Honours	Kent Scholar: 1973 - 1974
	Archie O Dawson Prize for Excellence in Advocacy: 1974
	Stone Scholar: 1974 - 1975
	Property Teaching Fellow: 1975

Allan Nichols

Chairman
Novae Syndicates Limited

Address (Office)	71 Fenchurch Street
	London EC3M 4HH
Telephone	+44 (0)20 7903 7300
Fax	+44 (0)20 7903 7333
Email	anichols@novae.com
Secretary/PA	Kathy Whitehead
Telephone	+44 (0)20 7903 7327
Email	kwhitehead@novae.com
Website	www.novae.com

Full Name	Allan Malcolm Nichols
Born	1954
Nationality	British
Secondary Education	High Pavement Grammar School, Nottingham
Further Education	University College, Oxford: 1972 - 1976

PROFESSIONAL INFORMATION

Career	Grieveson, Grant & Co, Research Department: 1976 - 1978
	Grieveson, Grant & Co, Insurance Analyst: 1978 - 1985
	James Capel & Co, Insurance Analyst: 1985 - 1993
	LIMIT plc, Research Director: 1993 - 1999
	Novae Group plc, Underwriting Review Director: 2000 -
	Novae Syndicates Ltd, Executive Chairman: 2003 -

PERSONAL INFORMATION

Home	London
Charitable/Voluntary Activities	Parochial Church Council, Treasurer
Main Interests and Recreation	Walking, travelling around Britain
Favourite Book(s)	History books, selected fiction
Clubs/Memberships	Oxford and Cambridge Club

Peter Nutting JP DL

Former Chairman
Hampden Agencies Ltd

Address (Office)	c/o Hampden Agencies Ltd
	85 Gracechurch Street
	London EC3V 0AA
Telephone	+44 (0)1420 562 703
Mobile	+44 (0)7957 855 008
Email	pnut@uwclub.net

Full Name	Peter Robert Nutting
Born	1935
Nationality	British
Secondary Education	Cheam School, Berkshire: 1944 - 1948
	Eton College, Berkshire: 1948 - 1953

PROFESSIONAL INFORMATION

Elected to Lloyd's	1972
Career	Outhwaite, Chairman: 1982
	Names Association: 1987 - 2003
	Association of Lloyd's Members, Director: 1990 - 2005
	Council of Lloyd's: 1990 - 1994, 1996 - 1998
	Aberdeen Lloyd's Insurance Trust Plc (Chaucer plc): 1995 - 2000
	Hampden Agencies Ltd, Chairman: 1996 - 2007
Previous Major Appointments/ Committees	Lloyd's Solvency and Reporting Committee, Chairman: 1991 - 1992
	Lloyd's Regulatory Board, Deputy Chairman: 1991 - 1994
	Lloyd's Regulatory Board, Member: 1995 - 1999
	Prudential Supervision Committee: 1998 - 2001
Major Achievements while at Lloyd's	Against fierce opposition from Lloyd's and the City generally, I led the first successful litigation against an Underwriter. Other successful Action Groups followed us. I was Acting Chairman of the Regulatory Board at the time of introduction of corporate capital. I chaired the first meeting at Lloyd's to discuss risk-based capital.
Mentor(s)	Never really had one!

(continued)

Peter Nutting JP DL (continued)

PERSONAL INFORMATION

Home	Hampshire, formerly Surrey
Armed Forces	Irish Guards, Lieutenant: 1953 - 1956
Awards/Honours	High Sheriff of Surrey: 1999 - 2000
	Deputy Lieutenant (DL) of Surrey
Charitable/Voluntary Activities	Cranleigh Village Hospital Trust, Chairman
	NSPCC, Chairman of Full Stop in Surrey
Other Activities	Justice of the Peace: 1978 - 2005
Main Interests and Recreation	Golf, sailing, shooting, fishing
Favourite Book(s)	'Bonfire of the Vanities' by Tom Wolfe
Favourite Car(s)	Mercedes 500
Favourite Gadget(s)	My vegetable garden
Favourite Music	Mahler, Puccini
Clubs/Memberships	Royal Yacht Squadron, Boodle's, Swinley Forest Golf Club,
	Walton Heath Golf Club, Pratt's
Important and Interesting Aspects of Lloyd's	I was not a Lloyd's man, having worked as a stockbroker, merchant banker and in industry. I became active at Lloyd's late in my business career when it all went wrong and profits became huge losses. I did something about it, learned a lot about it and persevered. I hope I contributed a bit towards making Lloyd's the very professional and successful operation it is today.

Tim Oliver

Chairman
Hampden Capital Plc

Address (Office)	85 Gracechurch Street
	London EC3V 0AA
Telephone	+44 (0)1494 489 000
Fax	+44 (0)1494 488 686
Mobile	+44 (0)7775 501 248
Email	tim.oliver@hampden.co.uk
Secretary/PA	Sue Passaro
Telephone	+44 (0)1494 489 042
Email	sue.passaro@hampden.co.uk
Website	www.hpcgroup.co.uk

Full Name	Timothy Patrick Camroux Oliver
Born	1944
Nationality	British and Canadian
Secondary Education	Christ's Hospital, West Sussex: 1952 - 1962

PROFESSIONAL INFORMATION

Elected to Lloyd's	1977
Career	**Hampden Group, Founder and Principal Shareholder: 1983 -**
	Hampden Capital Plc, Executive Chairman: 2001 -
First Policy Written	Shell Oil, Rotterdam: 1963 (exploded shortly thereafter!)
Longest Customer Relationship(s)	Fenton: 1974
	Overseas Union: 1982
	Sampo (now IF): 1983
Major Achievements while at Lloyd's	Keeping my head below the parapet!
Mentor(s)	Len Toomey

PERSONAL INFORMATION

Home	Buckinghamshire
Awards/Honours	Oxford Business Alumni
Charitable/Voluntary Activities	Bishopsgate Foundation Campaign, Chairman
Main Interests and Recreation	Shooting, fishing, skiing, restoration of old buildings
Favourite Book(s)	'City of Djinns: A Year in Delhi' by William Dalrymple, history books
Favourite Car(s)	Bentley Flying Spur, Ferrari Dino
Favourite Gadget(s)	Palm
Favourite Music	Classical
Livery Companies	The Worshipful Company of Ironmongers, Master: 2003
Clubs/Memberships	Brooks's, City of London Club, City Livery Yacht Club,
	Institute of Directors
Important and Interesting Aspects of Lloyd's	Preservation of Private Capital at Lloyd's

Jonathan Parry

Managing Director and Underwriter Syndicate 566
QBE Underwriting Limited

Address (Office)	Plantation Place
	30 Fenchurch Street
	London EC3M 3BD
Telephone	+44 (0)20 7105 4077
Fax	+44 (0)20 7105 4037
Email	jonathan.parry@uk.qbe.com
Secretary/PA	Lisa Margrie
Telephone	+44 (0)20 7105 4652
Fax	+44 (0)20 7105 4037
Email	lisa.margrie@uk.qbe.com
Website	www.qbeeurope.com

Full Name	Jonathan Wyn Parry
Born	1963
Nationality	British
Secondary Education	Merchant Taylors' School, Middlesex: 1975 - 1980
Nickname	JP

PROFESSIONAL INFORMATION

Elected to Lloyd's	1984
Career	Wigham Poland, Reinsurance Broker: 1981 - 1985
	Steel Burrill Jones, Reinsurance Broker: 1985 - 1989
	Alexander Howden, Reinsurance Broker: 1989 - 2000
	QBE Reinsurance Syndicate 566: 2000 -
	QBE Underwriting Ltd, Underwriting Director: 2005 -
	QBE Reinsurance Syndicate 566, Managing Director and Underwriter: 2005 -
	QBE Re Europe, Managing Director: 2007 -
	QBE Insurance (Europe) Ltd, Director: 2008 -
Main Area(s) of Expertise	Non-Marine Reinsurance
Underwriting Speciality	Retro
First Policy Written	US Risk XL (totalled by WTC): November 2000
Most interesting Policies/Claims	2006 hurricane risks due to dire predictions following 'Katrina', 'Rita' and 'Wilma' in 2005
Longest Customer Relationship(s)	Advent Group – broked account from 1989 - 2000 and have reinsured Syndicate 780 ever since
Major Achievements while at Lloyd's	28 years not out!
Lloyd's Connections (inc family)	Father worked at Lloyd's for 40 years
Mentor(s)	Peter Grove

Jonathan Parry (continued)

PERSONAL INFORMATION

Home	Essex
Main Interests and Recreation	Family, racehorse ownership
Favourite Book(s)	'Catch 22' by Joseph Heller
Favourite Car(s)	Mercedes
Favourite Gadget(s)	Nintendo Wii
Favourite Music	The Clash
Clubs/Memberships	Lloyd's Ski Club, Lloyd's Croquet Society
Important and Interesting Aspects of Lloyd's	Many great friendships over 28 years

Nicholas Pawson

Chairman
Starr Managing Agents Ltd

Address (Office)	3rd Floor
	140 Leadenhall Street
	London EC3V 4QT
Telephone	+44 (0)20 7337 3550
Fax	+44 (0)20 7337 3551
Email	nicholas.pawson@fmi.co.uk
Website	www.cvstarrco.com

Full Name	Nicholas Charles Thoresby Pawson
Born	1952
Nationality	British
Secondary Education	Rugby School, Warwickshire
Further Education	Trinity Hall, Cambridge, MA
Professional Qualifications	FCA: 1977
	FIA: 1978

PROFESSIONAL INFORMATION

Elected to Lloyd's	1983
Career	Marlborough Underwriting Agency Ltd, Non-Executive Director: 1998 - 2000
	Marlborough Underwriting Agency Ltd, Non-Executive Chairman: 2000 - 2009
	Centrewrite Ltd, Executive Chairman: 1994 -
	Starr Managing Agents Ltd, Non-Executive Chairman: 2007 -
	Marlborough Underwriting Agency Ltd, Deputy Chairman: 2009 -
Current Major Appointments/ Committees	Lloyd's Pension Fund, Trustee: 1994-
Previous Major Appointments/ Committees	Council of Lloyd's: 1990 - 1992
	Lloyd's Market Board: 1993 - 1996
	Lloyd's Central Services Unit/Members' Services Unit, Chairman: 1993 - 2001
	Finance and General Purposes Committee
	Underwriting Agents Registration Committee
	Hardship Committee
Major Achievements while at Lloyd's	Part of Reconstruction and Renewal (R&R)
Lloyd's Connections (inc family)	Father was a Name

Nicholas Pawson (continued)

PERSONAL INFORMATION

Home	Yorkshire
Armed Forces	Ex Cambridge University Officer Training Corps (OTC)
Charitable/Voluntary Activities	UK Forum for Genetics and Insurance, Treasurer
	Community Projects at Molema, Botswana
	Hurlingham Club, main committee (and two others)
Main Interests and Recreation	Shooting, fishing, tennis, conservation, bridge
Favourite Book(s)	'Narcissus and Goldmund' by Hermann Hesse
Favourite Car(s)	Alvis TE 21
Favourite Gadget(s)	Citrix
Favourite Music	'Enigma Variations' by Elgar
Clubs/Memberships	Hawks Club, Hurlingham Club, Royal Geographical Society

Charles Pender
Group Company Secretary
Amlin plc

Address (Office)	St Helen's
	1 Undershaft
	London EC3A 8ND
Telephone	+44 (0)20 7746 1000
Fax	+44 (0)20 7746 1696
Email	charles.pender@amlin.co.uk
Website	www.amlin.co.uk

Full Name	Charles Christopher Tresilian Pender
Born	1956
Nationality	British
Secondary Education	Eton College, Berkshire: 1969 - 1974
Further Education	Magdalene College, Cambridge, History and Law BA and MA (Hons): 1975 - 1978
Professional Qualifications	London Stock Exchange, Member: 1986 FCIS: 2003, FSI

PROFESSIONAL INFORMATION

Career	NatWest Markets (and other firms), Investment Banker, Corporate Stockbroker: 1981 - 1997
	Angerstein Underwriting Trust PLC: 1997
	Amlin plc, Group Company Secretary: 2000 -
Longest Customer Relationship(s)	Amlin plc – involved in its flotation, as Angerstein, when at NatWest Markets: 1993
Current Major Appointments/ Committees	LSF Pensions Management Ltd (the trustee of Lloyd's Superannuation Fund), Director: 2004 -
	LSF Pensions Management Ltd, Deputy Chairman: 2005 -
	Institute of Chartered Secretaries and Administrators (invited representatives of FTSE100 and FTSE250 Company Secretaries), Company Secretaries' Forum, Member: 2007 -
Previous Major Appointments/ Committees	Stace Barr Angerstein PLC, Director: 2004 - 2006
Major Achievements while at Lloyd's	To have been part of Lloyd's when it started joining the modern world
	To have played a very small part in creating the success of Amlin to date
Lloyd's Connections (inc family)	BWT Pender (father, d. 1989) was an external Name. My connection started with advice to potential corporate capital.

Charles Pender (continued)

PERSONAL INFORMATION

Home	London
Charitable/Voluntary Activities	Former Borough Councillor (Kensington and Chelsea): 1982 - 1986 I retain an interest in politics, but now mostly 'armchair'
	Local Residents' Association in London, Chairman
Main Interests and Recreation	Theatre, golf, all aspects of London
Favourite Book(s)	19th Century novels, history books
Favourite Car(s)	Travelling in the back of a black cab
Favourite Music	Mozart
Clubs/Memberships	Coningsby Club
Important and Interesting Aspects of Lloyd's	Human-scale business in a world-scale industry

Brian Pomeroy, CBE

Non-Executive Director
QBE Underwriting Limited

Address (Office)	Plantation Place
	30 Fenchurch Street
	London EC3M 3BD
Telephone	+44 (0)20 7435 2584
Mobile	+44 (0)7785 304 368
Email	pomeroybw@aol.com
Website:	www.qbeeurope.com
Full Name	Brian Walter Pomeroy, CBE
Born	1944
Nationality	British
Secondary Education	King's School, Canterbury, Kent
Further Education	Magdalene College, Cambridge
Professional Qualifications	FCA

PROFESSIONAL INFORMATION

Career	Deloitte Consulting, Partner: 1975 - 1995
	Deloitte Consulting, Senior Partner: 1995 - 1999
	QBE Insurance (Europe) Ltd, Deputy Chairman: 2006 -
	QBE Underwriting Limited, Non-Executive Director (Independent): 2006 -
Current Major Appointments/ Committees	Money Advice Trust, Trustee: 1999 -
	Social Market Foundation, Director: 2000 -
	Lloyd's Charities Trust, Trustee: 2004 -
	Financial Inclusion Task Force, HM Treasury, Chairman: 2005 -
	Photographers' Gallery, Chairman: 2006 -
	Payments Council, Chairman: 2007 -
	Gambling Commission, Chairman: 2007 -
Previous Major Appointments/ Committees	Council of Lloyd's, Nominated Member: 1987 - 1992 and 1996 - 2004
	Centrepoint, Chairman: 1993 - 2001
	National Lottery Commission, Chairman: 1999 - 2000 and 2002 - 2003
	Homeless Link, Chairman: 2001 - 2005
	Lloyd's Regulatory Board, Deputy Chairman: 2001 - 2002
	Lloyd's Audit Committee, Member: 2001 - 2002
Lloyd's Connections (inc family)	Formerly a Nominated Member of the Council of Lloyd's, made an Honorary Member of Lloyd's in 2005

PERSONAL INFORMATION

Home	London
Awards/Honours	CBE in 1996
Main Interests and Recreation	Photography, music, theatre
Livery Companies	The Worshipful Company of Management Consultants
Clubs/Memberships	Commonwealth Club

Mark Rayner

Chief Underwriting Officer and Active Underwriter Syndicate 435
Faraday Underwriting Limited

Address (Office)	5th Floor
	Corn Exchange
	55 Mark Lane
	London EC3R 7NE
Telephone	+44 (0)20 7680 4236
Email	mark.rayner@faraday.com
Secretary/PA	Joanna Gridley
Telephone	+44 (0)20 7680 4292
Email	joanna.gridley@faraday.com
Website	www.faraday.com

Full Name	Mark Jonathan Rayner
Born	1968
Nationality	British
Secondary Education	Westcliff High School for Boys, Essex: 1979 - 1986
Further Education	University College London
Professional Qualifications	ACII Chartered Insurer: 1990
Nickname	Pavarotti

PROFESSIONAL INFORMATION

Career	TG Holloway & Ors Syndicate 604/605, Underwriting Assistant: 1986 - 1990
	DP Mann Ltd, Syndicate 435, Underwriting Assistant: 1990 - 1992
	NA Barton Syndicate 1192, Property Underwriter: 1992 - 1993
	Faraday Underwriting Ltd, Chief Underwriting Officer and
	Active Underwriter Syndicate 435: 1993 -
Main Area(s) of Expertise	Property, Casualty and Aviation
Underwriting Speciality	Catastrophe XL
First Policy Written	Far Horizon Properties: 17th July 1991
Most interesting Policies/Claims	Once got Warren Buffett out of lunch for a live catastrophe opportunity during Hurricane Rita
Longest Customer Relationship(s)	Liberty Mutual, Hartford; Wawanesa: since syndicate was formed in 1983
Current Major Appointments/ Committees	Faraday Underwriting Ltd, Executive Director: 2003 -
	Faraday Reinsurance Co Ltd, Executive Director: 2003 -
Previous Major Appointments/ Committees	Lloyd's North American Property Reinsurance Group, Member
Major Achievements while at Lloyd's	Lloyd's youngest Active Underwriter when appointed aged 35 in 1993
Lloyd's Connections (inc family)	My Godfather, Robin Maynard, introduced me to Lloyd's. He ran Sedgwick Far East at the time and was Lloyd's Representative in Japan until 2008.
Mentor(s)	David Mann

PERSONAL INFORMATION

Home	Essex

Martin Reith

Non-Executive Director
Ascot Underwriting Ltd

Address (Office)	Plantation Place
	30 Fenchurch Street
	London EC3M 3BD
Telephone	+44 (0)20 7743 9602
Fax	+44 (0)20 7743 9601
Email	martin.reith@ascotuw.com
Secretary/PA	Sarah Neale
Telephone	+44 (0)20 7743 9624
Email	sarah.neale@ascotuw.com
Website	www.ascotuw.com
Full Name	Martin Robert Davidson Reith
Born	1965
Nationality	British

PROFESSIONAL INFORMATION

Elected to Lloyd's	1988
Career	Alston Brockbank Ltd: 1984
	Mid Ocean Ltd: 1995
	XL Capital London Market: 1998
	Ascot Underwriting Ltd, Founder and Chief Executive: 2001 - 2008
	Ascot Underwriting Ltd, Syndicate 1414 Reith, Active Underwriter: 2001 - 2008
	Ascot Underwriting Ltd, Non-Executive Director: 2008 -
Main Area(s) of Expertise	All short tail classes, principally reinsurance, property, terrorism,
	energy and cargo
Previous Major Appointments/	Joint War Committee
Committees	War, Civil War and Financial Guarantees Committee
	Lloyd's Underwriters' Association
	Prudential Supervision Committee
	Lloyd's Joint Hull Committee
	Cargo War Risks Rating Committee
	Lloyd's Market Association Underwriting and Claims Committee
	Lloyd's Capital Committee
	Political Risk and Financial Contingencies Committee

PERSONAL INFORMATION

Home	Hertfordshire
Charitable/Voluntary Activities	Noah's Ark Children's Hospice

Sir Adam Ridley

Chairman of Trustees
Equitas Trust

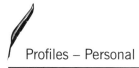

Address (Office)	c/o Equitas Trust
	33 St Mary Axe
	London EC3A 8LL
Telephone	+44 (0)20 7863 6581
Email	adam.ridley@equitastrust.com
Secretary/PA	Janice Clarke
Telephone	+44 (0)20 7863 6582
Full Name	Sir Adam Nicholas Ridley
Born	1942
Nationality	British
Further Education	University of Oxford, Politics, Philosophy, Economics: 1961 - 1965
	University of California, Berkeley, Mathematical Economics and
	Statistics: 1968 - 1969

PROFESSIONAL INFORMATION

Elected to Lloyd's	1976
Category of Lloyd's Membership	LLP
Career	Department of Economic Affairs, Treasury and Central Policy Review Staff,
	The Economist: 1965 - 1974
	Conservative Party, Economic Adviser to Leader, Geoffrey Howe and
	the Shadow Cabinet: 1974 - 1979
	Conservative Research Department, Director: 1979
	HM Treasury, Special Adviser to Sir Geoffrey Howe and
	Nigel Lawson: 1979 - 1985
	Hambros Bank PLC, Executive Director: 1985 - 1997
	Association of Lloyd's Members, Deputy Chairman: 1994 -
	Equitas Trust, Executive Chairman of Trustees: 1996 -
	Morgan Stanley Bank International, Non-Executive Director: 2006 -
	Hampden Agencies Ltd, Non-Executive Director: 2007 -
Previous Major Appointments/	Lloyd's Morse Committee, alternate for Neil Shaw,
Committees	Acting Chairman: 1993 - 1994
	Lloyd's Names Committee, Chairman: 1995 - 1996
	Lloyd's Hardcastle Committee, Member: 1997 - 1998
	Council of Lloyd's, External Member: 1997 - 1999
	Lloyd's Regulatory Board: 1997 - 1999
	Lloyd's Prudential Supervision Committee: 1997 - 1999
	Lloyd's Nomination and Remuneration Committee: 1997 - 1999
	London Investment Banking Association, Director-General: 2000 - 2005
Major Achievements while at Lloyd's	Reconstruction and Renewal (R&R), supporting Equitas in successful negotiation
	of reinsurance by National Indemnity/Berkshire Hathaway

(continued)

Sir Adam Ridley (continued)

PERSONAL INFORMATION

Awards/Honours	Knighthood in 1985
Charitable/Voluntary Activities	Windsor Group of fund-raising charities: 1990 - 1992
	National Lottery Charities Board, Founder Member and
	Deputy Chairman: 1994 - 2000
	St Christopher's Hospice, Trustee: 1985 -
Main Interests and Recreation	Playing the violin
Favourite Music	Berlioz, Dvorák, Smetana, Schubert
Important and Interesting Aspects of Lloyd's	Ensuring the full-hearted honouring and delivery of R&R whereby Names committed to support the settlement in exchange for guaranteed continuing rights to participate on civilised terms

John Robinson
Underwriting Director & Active Underwriter Syndicate 958
Omega Underwriting Agents Limited

Address (Office)	4th Floor
	New London House
	6 London Street
	London EC3R 7LP
Telephone	+44 (0)20 7767 3000
Fax	+44 (0)20 7488 9639
Email	john.robinson@omegauw.com
Secretary/PA	Lucy Tulacz
Telephone	+44 (0)20 7767 3022
Email	lucy.tulacz@omegauw.com
Website	www.omegauw.com
Full Name	John David Robinson
Born	1953
Nationality	British
Secondary Education	Giggleswick School, Settle, North Yorkshire
Nickname	Not knowingly but must have one being in Lloyd's since 1972

PROFESSIONAL INFORMATION

Elected to Lloyd's	1980
Category of Lloyd's Membership	Non-Underwriting Working Member
Career	CE Heath, Underwriting Assistant: 1972
	GS Christensen & Others Non-Marine Syndicate 958, Co-Founder & Deputy Underwriter: 1979
	GS Christensen & Others Non-Marine Syndicate 958, Active Underwriter: 1995-
	Omega Underwriting Agents Ltd, Executive Director: 1998 -
	Omega Group: Founder Shareholder: 2005 -
	Omega Insurance Holdings Ltd, Bermuda, Executive Director: 2006 -
Main Area(s) of Expertise	Short-tail Property Insurance and Reinsurance
Underwriting Speciality	Generalist
First Policy Written	Hatton Garden Jewellers Block
Most Interesting Policies/Claims	All are interesting!
Longest Customer Relationship(s)	Antilles Insurance Company, April 1980
Current Major Appointments/ Committees	Not a committee person

PERSONAL INFORMATION

Home	London
Charitable/Voluntary Activities	Privately contributing to a number of Charities
Main Interests and Recreation	Motor racing (used to be a racing driver), any competitive sport
Favourite Book(s)	'Churchill' by Roy Jenkins
Favourite Car(s)	Any car which is technically interesting
Favourite Gadget(s)	Gadgets drive me potty!
Favourite Music	Rock & Roll, Heavy Metal
Important and Interesting Aspects of Lloyd's	On the business side the subscription market, on the human side the camaraderie

Paul Sandilands
Non-Executive Director
Argenta Private Capital Limited

Address (Office)	Fountain House
	130 Fenchurch Street
	London EC3M 5DJ
Telephone	+44 (0)1280 850 666
Fax	+44 (0)1280 850 470
Mobile	+44 (0)7775 741 833
Email	paul@pulse-on-line.com
Secretary/PA	Debbie Lane
Telephone	+44 (0)1280 850 666
Email	admin@pulse-on-line.com
Website	www.argentaplc.com

Full Name	Paul Francis Sandilands
Born	1946
Nationality	British
Secondary Education	Eton College, Berkshire
Further Education	University of Cambridge, Law MA
Professional Qualifications	Barrister-At-Law

PROFESSIONAL INFORMATION

Elected to Lloyd's	1983
Career	**Talisman Corporate Underwriting Ltd,**
	Non-Executive Director: 1997 -
	Argenta Private Capital Ltd, Non-Executive Director: 2000 -
	Pulse Insurance Ltd (Cover Holder for Kiln Life Syndicate 308),
	Managing Director: 2005 -
Main Area(s) of Expertise	Term Life Cover for individuals and groups who find it difficult to obtain life cover due to a pre-existing medical condition, lifestyle or due to the location or nature of their work.

PERSONAL INFORMATION

Home	Northamptonshire

Roger Sedgwick Rough

Executive Director
Hampden Capital Plc

Address (Office)	85 Gracechurch Street
	London EC3V 0AA
Telephone	+44 (0)20 7863 6547
Fax	+44 (0)20 7863 6744
Mobile	+44 (0)7732 192 244
Email	roger.sr@hampden.co.uk
Secretary/PA	Abigail McMorrow
Telephone	+44 (0)20 7863 6575
Email	abigail.mcmorrow@hampden.co.uk
Website	www.hampden.co.uk

Full Name	William Roger Peter Sedgwick Rough
Born	1951
Nationality	British
Secondary Education	Cheam School, Berkshire: 1960 - 1964
	Wellington College, Berkshire: 1964 - 1968
Professional Qualifications	None except speaking French, German and Spanish
Nickname	Scruff

PROFESSIONAL INFORMATION

Elected to Lloyd's	1972
Category of Lloyd's Membership	LLP
Career	CT Bowring & Co Ltd: 1971
	CT Bowring & Co Ltd, Broker/Director of Aviation and Non-Marine Department, looking after Spanish speaking areas as Treaty Reinsurance: 1971 - 1985
	Bowring Members Agency, Director: 1985
	Wellington Members Agency Ltd: 1994 - 1999
	CBS Private Capital Ltd: 1999 - 2005
	Hampden Agencies Ltd, Names Executive and Consultant: 2005 -
	Hampden Capital Plc, Executive Director: 2005 -
Longest Customer Relationship(s)	I still look after clients who were with me in 1985
Major Achievements while at Lloyd's	Lloyd's Golf Club, Captain: 2004, President: 2008
Lloyd's Connections (inc family)	Grandfather's uncle, HB Sedgwick, founded Sedgwick Collins
	Grandfather and Father worked for Sedgwicks
Mentor(s)	Charles Cullum

Roger Sedgwick Rough

PERSONAL INFORMATION

Home	Hertfordshire
Main Interests and Recreation	Skiing, golf, tennis, travel
Favourite Book(s)	'Touching the Void' by Joe Simpson (and many others!)
Favourite Car(s)	1973 Carrera RS Porsche (mine), 1937 Austin Seven (originally Grandmother's!)
Favourite Music	Classical, Latin American and some Pop!
Clubs/Memberships	White's, Pratt's, City Golf Club, Marylebone Cricket Club (MCC), Pilgrims, Royal St George's Golf Club, Royal Worlington Golf Club
Important and Interesting Aspects of Lloyd's	That it should remain a market place where 'people skills' remain an important factor.

Bruce Shepherd

Executive Director and Deputy Underwriter Syndicate 807
R J Kiln & Co Limited

Address (Office)	106 Fenchurch Street
	London EC3M 5NR
Telephone	+44 (0)20 7886 9000
Email	bruce.shepherd@kilngroup.com
Website	www.kilnplc.com
Full Name	Bruce Donald Shepherd
Born	1949
Nationality	British

PROFESSIONAL INFORMATION

Elected to Lloyd's	1982
Category of Lloyd's Membership	LLP/Nameco
Career	**Kiln Mathers Syndicate 807, Deputy Underwriter: 1982 -**
	R J Kiln & Co Limited, Executive Director: 1993 -
Main Area(s) of Expertise	North American business
Underwriting Speciality	Most classes of Non-Marine business
Longest Customer Relationship(s)	NAS Insurance Services California since 1977
Mentor(s)	Robin Wilshaw

PERSONAL INFORMATION

Home	Surrey

David Shipley

Chairman
Managing Agency Partners Limited

Address (Office)	1st Floor
	110 Fenchurch Street
	London EC3M 5JT
Telephone	+44 (0)20 7709 3860
Fax	+44 (0)20 7709 3861
Email	dshipley@mapunderwriting.co.uk
Secretary/PA	Brenda Wallington
Telephone	+44 (0)20 7709 3872
Email	bwallington@mapunderwriting.co.uk
Website	www.mapunderwriting.co.uk

Full Name	David Endon Stuart Shipley
Born	1955
Nationality	British
Secondary Education	Dr Challoner's Grammar School, Buckinghamshire
	(A-Levels: Maths, Further Maths, English): 1965 - 1972
Further Education	Keble College, Oxford, Mathematics BA (Hons): 1973 - 1976
Professional Qualifications	None at all
Nickname	Not at my age

PROFESSIONAL INFORMATION

Elected to Lloyd's	1983
	Name: 1984 - 1998
	SLP: 1999 - 2000
	Corporate (LLP 2007): 2001 -
Career	Harvey Bowring & Ors Syndicate 362: 1976 - 1993
	Harvey Bowring & Ors Syndicate 362, Deputy Underwriter: 1993 - 1995
	Harvey Bowring & Ors Syndicate 362, Active Underwriter: 1996 - 1999
	Managing Agency Partners Ltd, Syndicate 2791,
	Active Underwriter: 2000 - 2007
	Managing Agency Partners Ltd, Non-Executive Chairman: 2007 -
Main Area(s) of Expertise	North America
Underwriting Speciality	Medical Malpractice/Professional Liability
First Policy Written	MacArthur Life Insurance Co, Personal Accident Cat Excess: 1978
Most interesting Policies/Claims	Policy: Deportivo la Coruña qualifying for group stage of Champions League
	Claims: Dr Miofsky, the rogue anaethesiologist (don't ask); Shake 'n' bake,
	the flaky funeral directors
Longest Customer Relationship(s)	Various 'Doctor Mutuals' since 1980 – State Volunteer Mutual, Medical Mutual
	of Maryland, Texas Medical Liability Trust
Current Major Appointments/ Committees	Lloyd's Franchise Board, Non-Executive Director: 2009 -
Previous Major Appointments/ Committees	Equitas Reserve Group: 1993 - 1996
	Regulatory Review Working Party
	North American User Board
	Lloyd's Market Association Underwriting and Claims Committee
	Council of Lloyd's, External Member: 2003 - 2009

David Shipley (continued)

Major Achievements while at Lloyd's	Equitas Reserve Group Member (1993 - 1996) bringing to a successful conclusion
	Co-founded Managing Agency Partners Ltd: 2000
Lloyd's Connections (inc family)	Father is Financial Adviser to some Names
Mentor(s)	Murray Lawrence, Richard Keeling, Ian Sinclair, Professor Adrian Smith

PERSONAL INFORMATION

Home	Hertfordshire
Main Interests and Recreation	Reading, running, cycling, epidemiology, watching sport (especially Tottenham Hotspur)
Favourite Book(s)	'Terra Nostra' by Carlos Fuentes, 'The Good Soldier Svejk and His Fortunes in the World War' by Jaroslav Hasek, 'A Place of Greater Safety' by Hilary Mantel
Favourite Car(s)	BMW 650i Convertible
Favourite Gadget(s)	(sadly) i-Pod
Favourite Music	African dance music, electronic rock/dance, Van Morrison, late 60s/early 70s rock
Clubs/Memberships	Three Rooms Club, Tottenham Hotspur Supporters Club
Important and Interesting Aspects of Lloyd's	We did not get where we are today by not being childish. Please keep the fun in Lloyd's.

Karen Sinden

Managing Director
Marketform Managing Agency Limited

Address (Office)	8 Lloyd's Avenue
	London EC3N 3EL
Telephone	+44 (0)20 7488 7700
Fax	+44 (0)20 7488 7800
Email	underwriters@marketform.com
Secretary/PA	Catherine Smith
Telephone	+44 (0)20 7488 7616
Email	catherine.smith@marketform.com
Website	www.marketform.com

Full Name	Karen Sinden
Born	1962
Nationality	British
Secondary Education	Fort Pitt Grammar School, Kent

PROFESSIONAL INFORMATION

Elected to Lloyd's	1987
Career	Lloyd's Market: 1980
	RW Sturge: 1991 - 1995
	Lloyd's Auctions, Manager: 1995 - 1996
	Numis Securities Limited: 1996 - 1997
	Leadenhall Insurance Consultants: 1997 - 2003
	Marketform Managing Agency Ltd: 2004
	Marketform Managing Agency Ltd, Managing Director: 2005 -

PERSONAL INFORMATION

Home	Kent
Main Interests and Recreation	Golf, Italian wine and cooking
Favourite Book(s)	With pictures!
Favourite Car(s)	1962 Austin Healey Sprite
Favourite Gadget(s)	My pasta machine
Clubs/Memberships	Rochester and Cobham Park Golf Club

Keith Thompson

Managing Director
Advent Underwriting Limited

Address (Office)	10th Floor
	1 Minster Court
	Mincing Lane
	London EC3R 7AA
Telephone	+44 (0)20 7743 8203
Fax	+44 (0)20 7743 8244
Email	keith.thompson@adventgroup.co.uk
Secretary/PA	Joanne Tang
Telephone	+44 (0)20 7743 8201
Email	joanne.tang@adventgroup.co.uk
Website	www.adventgroup.co.uk
Full Name	Keith Donald Thompson
Born	1957
Nationality	British
Secondary Education	Gillingham Grammar School, Kent

PROFESSIONAL INFORMATION

Elected to Lloyd's	1986
Category of Lloyd's Membership	Non-Underwriting Working Member
Career	Corporation of Lloyd's: 1976
	Scott Underwriting Agencies Ltd: 1983
	Scott Underwriting Agencies Ltd, Director: 1987
	Vantage Underwriting Ltd, Managing Director: 1993
	Advent Capital (Holdings) PLC, Founder Director: 1994
	Advent Capital (Holdings) PLC, Chief Operating Officer: 1995 -
	Advent Underwriting Ltd, Managing Director: 1995 -
Main Area(s) of Expertise	Managing our day-to-day Lloyd's operations
Major Achievements while at Lloyd's	Forming Advent Capital and becoming one of the first dedicated capital providers in 1995 and 10 years later taking the company onto the London Stock Exchange (AIM)
Mentor(s)	Brian Caudle

PERSONAL INFORMATION

Home	Kent
Main Interests and Recreation	Golf, following Gillingham Football Club, holidaying in Portugal
Favourite Book(s)	'Gulliver's Travels' by Jonathan Swift
Favourite Car(s)	Mercedes
Favourite Gadget(s)	Mobile phone
Favourite Music	Motown
Clubs/Memberships	Sittingbourne Golf Club
Important and Interesting Aspects of Lloyd's	Lloyd's history and uniqueness.

Sir Brook Watson, Bt

Member of the First Committee of Lloyd's &
Founder Member of the Lloyd's Patriotic Fund

Full Name	Sir Brook Watson

Lived

Brook Watson was born in Plymouth in 1735/6 as the only son of John Watson of Hull and his second wife Sarah nee Schofield. At the age of six he was orphaned and sent to a distant relative in Boston, Massachusetts. When he was 14, he lost a leg to a shark in Havana Harbour, an incident later commemorated in John Singleton Copley's well-known painting 'Watson and the Shark'. He subsequently made his way to Nova Scotia.

In 1760 Brook Watson married Helen, daughter of Colin Campbell, an Edinburgh goldsmith but there were no surviving children. He died in 1807 at East Sheen and was buried at Mortlake, where there is a memorial tablet. The baronetcy passed successively to the two sons of Watson's niece Ann Webber and her husband William Kay of Montreal and became extinct on the death in action in France of Sir William Kay, 6th Bart, in 1918.

Nationality

English

PROFESSIONAL INFORMATION

Elected to Lloyd's

Brook Watson was one of the original 79 subscribers to 'New Lloyd's' in 1771 and one of the nine men on the original Committee.

Career

In 1759, after some nine years in Nova Scotia, Brook Watson moved to London and joined Joseph Mauger in business, later forming several partnerships relating to commercial interests in Nova Scotia and Quebec. He made a good impression on Lieutenant Governor Guy Carleton when he visited Quebec in 1766-67.

He handled business in fish, fur, timber, whales and ironworks and in 1773 he acted as guarantor, together with Robert Rashleigh, of the tea shipped to Boston for what became known as the Boston Tea Party.

In 1775 he visited New York and talked in conciliatory terms to several future rebels while privately condemning the British Government for lack of firmness. He then continued to Quebec and renewed his connection with Guy Carleton.

In 1781 Brook Watson took the chair at a General Meeting of Lloyd's. At this time there was no Chairman of Lloyd's as such and a senior member of the committee presided at General Meetings which were held irregularly.

Following his appointment as Commander in Chief in North America, Guy Carleton arrived in New York in May 1782 accompanied by Brook Watson as Commissary-General. Brook Watson was responsible for supplies of food, etc. for the British forces and he also oversaw the evacuation of 35,000 Loyalists to Nova Scotia. In December 1783 he left New York with Guy Carleton and William Smith, the last Loyalist Chief Justice of New York. As soon as he reached London he prepared to stand for Parliament and was elected MP for the City of London

Sir Brook Watson, Bt (continued)

later in 1784. He also became a Director of the Bank of England and was Alderman for Cordwainer Ward from 1784 until his death and a Sheriff for the year 1785-86. His office was in Garlick Hill.

In 1786 and again in 1791, he took the chair at a General Meeting of Lloyd's. In 1786 he and Guy Carleton received Parliamentary pensions in their wives' names on the same day. Guy Carleton was made Lord Dorchester and went to Canada as Governor-General, taking William Smith with him as Chief Justice. Brook Watson was Agent for New Brunswick in London from 1786-1795.

From 1793 to 1796, Brook Watson was Commissary-General to the army in Flanders. He was responsible directly to William Pitt as First Lord of the Treasury and corresponded with him.

In 1798 Brook Watson was appointed to the newly-created position of Commissary-General of Great Britain and in 1803 he was made a baronet. His friends ranged from literary ones to members of the Royal Family. In 1805 the Prince of Wales disapproved strongly when Watson called him 'My Prince' on a convivial occasion, but the Duke of York dined with him at East Sheen in 1806.

Major Achievements whilst at Lloyd's	On 20th July 1803 Brook Watson was Chairman of the meeting to inaugurate the Lloyd's Patriotic Fund. Once the Fund was established the chairmanship was taken by Sir Francis Baring.

PERSONAL INFORMATION

Home	East Sheen and a leasehold town house in Adelphi Terrace.
Honours	Granted Baronetcy in 1803
Charitable/Voluntary Activities	He was a Freemason and a Governor of Christ's Hospital to which he bequeathed the painting 'Watson and the Shark', and was involved with a number of good causes. Brook Watson acted for many individuals claiming compensation and organized charitable subscription for the indigent. He was described as having a high character of integrity and Lord Liverpool called him 'one of the most honourable men ever known'.
Main Interests and Recreation	Brook Watson had varied interests, he enjoyed cricket matches and was Master of the Musicians' Company. He became Colonel of the London and Westminster Light Horse Volunteers. In 1803 he was given the responsibility for moving all the 'treasure' of the Bank of England to Worcester Cathedral in 30 wagons, escorted from county to county by the Volunteers due to fear of a French invasion.

Mark Wheeler

Underwriting Director and Active Underwriter Syndicate 4000
Pembroke Managing Agency Limited

Address (Office)	2nd Floor
	3 Minster Court
	Mincing Lane
	London EC3R 7DD
Telephone	+44 (0)20 7337 4400
Fax	+44 (0)20 7337 4401
Mobile	+44 (0)7834 600 065
Email	mark.wheeler@pembrokeunderwriting.com
Secretary/PA	Jane Meijer
Telephone	+44 (0)20 7337 4510
Email	jane.meijer@pembrokeunderwriting.com
Website	www.pembrokeunderwriting.com

Full Name	Mark Handley Wheeler
Born	1965
Nationality	British
Secondary Education	King's School, Bruton, Somerset: 1978 - 1983
Professional Qualifications	ACII

PROFESSIONAL INFORMATION

Category of Lloyd's Membership	Non-Underwriting Working Member
Career	RW Sturge: 1987
	SVB Syndicate 1007: 1990
	SVB Syndicate 1007, Active Underwriter: 2000 - 2003
	Pembroke Managing Agency Ltd, Syndicate 4000, Active Underwriter: 2004 -
	Pembroke Managing Agency Ltd, Underwriting Director: 2007 -
Main Area(s) of Expertise	Specialist Lines Insurance
Underwriting Speciality	Financial Institutions
First Policy Written	Bank of New York: 1990
Longest Customer Relationship(s)	HSBC
Mentor(s)	Rupert Villers

PERSONAL INFORMATION

Home	London
Main Interests and Recreation	Sailing, skiing
Favourite Book(s)	'Like The Roman' by Simon Heffer
Favourite Car(s)	Blue ones
Favourite Gadget(s)	Corkscrew
Favourite Music	Schubert
Clubs/Memberships	City of London Club, Brooks's

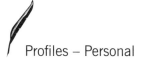

Graham White

Managing Director
Argenta Private Capital Limited

Address (Office)	Fountain House
	130 Fenchurch Street
	London EC3M 5DJ
Telephone	+44 (0)20 7825 7182
Fax	+44 (0)20 7825 7299
Email	graham.white@argentaplc.com
Secretary/PA	Ann Kisberg
Telephone	+44 (0)20 7825 7136
Email	ann.kisberg@argentaplc.com
Website	www.argentaplc.com
Full Name	Graham John White
Born	1946
Nationality	British
Secondary Education	University College School, London: 1959 - 1964
Further Education	Caius College, Cambridge, Law (Hons): 1965 - 1968
	Cranfield School of Management, Cranfield University,
	Business Administration MBA: 1972 - 1973
Nickname	Blofeldt

PROFESSIONAL INFORMATION

Elected to Lloyd's	1971
Career	Willis Faber Group: 1968
	Willis Faber Group, Director Principal Subsidiary: 1976
	Willis Faber Group, Company Secretary: 1980 - 1983
	Richard Beckett Underwriting Agencies Ltd,
	Managing Director: 1983 - 1986
	Merrett Holdings plc, New York representative: 1986
	Merrett Holdings plc, Group Company Secretary: 1986 - 1988
	Jardine Insurance Group, Director of Reinsurance
	Broking subsidiary: 1988 - 1996
	CBS Insurance Holdings plc (and predecessor companies), Director and
	Chairman of Members Agency: 1996 - 2006
	Argenta Private Capital Ltd, Executive Director: 2006 - 2008
	Sportscover Underwriting Ltd, Non-Executive Director: 2008 - 2009
	Argenta Syndicate Management Ltd, alternating between Executive and
	(presently) Non-Executive Deputy Chairman: 2007 -
	Argenta Private Capital Ltd, Managing Director: 2008 -
	Argenta Holdings plc, Executive Director: 2008 -
Current Major Appointments/	Lloyd's Charities Trust, Trustee: 2004 -
Committees	Lloyd's Charities Trust, Chairman: 2008 -
	Council of Lloyd's, Working Member: 2006 -
	Lloyd's, Deputy Chairman: 2007 -
	Lloyd's Members' Agency Services Limited, Non-Executive Director, 2006 -

(continued)

Graham White (continued)

Previous Major Appointments/	Lloyd's Market Association, Director: 2002 - 2006
Committees	Lloyd's Chairman's Strategy Group, Member: 2003
Major Achievements while at Lloyd's	Becoming Deputy Chairman of Lloyd's
Lloyd's Connections (inc family)	Father was a Lloyd's Broker: 1926 - 1971
Mentor(s)	My father and David Palmer

PERSONAL INFORMATION

Home	Cambridgeshire
Charitable/Voluntary Activities	Lloyd's Charities Trust, Trustee
	Music Platform, Director
	City of London Festival, Director
Main Interests and Recreation	Golf, theatre, opera, watching Tottenham Hotspur FC, skiing
Favourite Book(s)	'The Masters' by Charles Percy Snow
Favourite Car(s)	Smart
Favourite Gadget(s)	Blackberry
Favourite Music	Opera
Livery Companies	The Worshipful Company of Upholders
Clubs/Memberships	City of London Club, Travellers Club, Kandahar Ski Club
Important and Interesting Aspects of Lloyd's	Lloyd's is a fantastic career opportunity for anyone.

Kevin Wilkins

Executive Director and Active Underwriter Syndicate 570
Atrium Underwriters Ltd

Address (Office)	Room 790
	Lloyd's
	One Lime Street
	London EC3M 7DQ
Telephone	+44 (0)20 7327 8137
Fax	+44 (0)20 7327 4878
Email	kevin.wilkins@atrium-uw.com
Website	www.atrium-uw.com
Full Name	Kevin William Wilkins
Born	1961
Nationality	British

PROFESSIONAL INFORMATION

Elected to Lloyd's	1986
Career	Methuen Underwriting Ltd, Syndicate 47: 1979
	MH Cockell Syndicate 570: 1986
	MH Cockell & Partners, Partner: 1987
	MH Cockell Syndicate 570, Deputy Underwriter: 1989
	Atrium Underwriters Ltd, Co-founding Director: 1997 -
	Atrium Underwriters Ltd, Syndicate 570,
	Active Underwriter : 2005 -
Main Area(s) of Expertise	Non-Marine
Underwriting Speciality	Concentrate on Property Treaty but still keep a hand in all areas

PERSONAL INFORMATION

Home	Surrey

David Young

Non-Executive Director
Marlborough Underwriting Agency Limited

Address (Office)	Birchin Court
	20 Birchin Lane
	London EC3V 9DU
Telephone	+44 (0)20 7456 1800
Fax	+44 (0)20 7456 1810
Email	overhall@waitrose.com
Website	www.marlborough.co.uk

Full Name	David Tyrrell Young
Born	1938
Nationality	British
Secondary Education	Charterhouse, Surrey: 1951 - 1955
Professional Qualifications	FCA

PROFESSIONAL INFORMATION

Started at Lloyd's	1993
Category of Lloyd's Membership	Non-Underwriting Working Member (Agency Director)
Career	Gérard van de Linde & Son, Trainee Accountant: 1955 - 1961
	James, Edwards & Co, Audit Manager: 1961 - 1965
	Spicer and Pegler, Partner, Managing Partner and
	Senior Partner: 1965 - 1990
	Touche Ross, Deputy Chairman: 1990 - 1993
	Marlborough Underwriting Agency Ltd, Non-Executive Director: 2001 -
Current Major Appointments/	Berkshire Hathaway International Insurance Ltd, Non-Executive Director: 2001 -
Committees	Nomura Bank International Plc, Non-Executive Chairman: 2001 -
Previous Major Appointments/	Lombard Insurance Group plc, Chairman
Committees	Archer Dedicated plc, Chairman
	GW Run-Off Ltd, Chairman: 1993 - 1998
	Capita Syndicate Management Ltd, Non-Executive Chairman: 2001 - 2008

PERSONAL INFORMATION

Home	Essex
Armed Forces	First Regiment Honourable Artillery Company (RHA),
	Captain: 1955 - 1967
Awards/Honours	Fellow of the Royal Society of Arts
	Honorary Fellow of City and Guilds of London Institute
Charitable/Voluntary Activities	City and Guilds of London Institute, Chairman: 1999 - 2006
	Gresham's School, Holt, Chairman: 1999 - 2005
Main Interests and Recreation	Golf
Livery Companies	The Worshipful Company of Fishmongers, Prime Warden
	The Worshipful Company of Chartered Accountants in
	England and Wales, Master
Clubs/Memberships	City of London Club, Honourable Artillery Company, Royal St George's Golf Club,
	Royal Worlington Golf Club

Profiles – Managing Agents

Richard D Abbott

Position	Non-Executive Director
Company	Hardy (Underwriting Agencies) Ltd
Address (Office)	4th Floor
	40 Lime Street
	London EC3M 7AW
Telephone	+44 (0)20 7626 0382
Fax	+44 (0)20 7283 4677
Email	info@hardygroup.co.uk
Website	www.hardygroup.co.uk
Full Name	Richard David Abbott
Year of Birth	1954
Professional Qualifications	ACII

PROFESSIONAL INFORMATION

CURRENT MAJOR POSITIONS/APPOINTMENTS

Non-Executive Director	Hardy (Underwriting Agencies) Ltd	2008 -

PREVIOUS MAJOR POSITIONS/APPOINTMENTS

Non-Executive Director	St Helen's Capital Plc	2004 - 2007
Director	Knight Frank Corporate Finance Limited	2005 - 2007

Jeremy R Adams

Position	Chief Executive Officer
Company	Novae Syndicates Limited
Address (Office)	71 Fenchurch Street
	London EC3M 4HH
Telephone	+44 (0)20 7903 7300
Fax	+44 (0)20 7903 7333
Email	jadams@novae.com
Website	www.novae.com
Full Name	Jeremy Richard Adams
Year of Birth	1956
Professional Qualifications	MA Oxon, ACII

PROFESSIONAL INFORMATION

CURRENT MAJOR POSITIONS/APPOINTMENTS

Executive Director	Novae Syndicates Limited	2001 -
Chief Executive	Novae Syndicates Limited	2002 -
Executive Director	Novae Insurance Company Ltd	2007 -

PREVIOUS MAJOR POSITIONS/APPOINTMENTS

Information not available

Andrew J Adie

Position	Managing Director
Company	Omega Underwriting Agents Ltd
Address (Office)	4th Floor
	New London House
	6 London Street
	London EC3R 7LP
Telephone	+44 (0)20 7767 3000
Fax	+44 (0)20 7488 9639
Email	andrew.adie@omegauw.com
Website	www.omegauw.com

Full Name	Andrew James Adie
Year of Birth	1961
Professional Qualifications	Information not available

PROFESSIONAL INFORMATION

CURRENT MAJOR POSITIONS/APPOINTMENTS

Executive Director	Omega Underwriting Agents Ltd	2006 -

PREVIOUS MAJOR POSITIONS/APPOINTMENTS

Executive Director	AEGIS Managing Agency Ltd	2001 - 2006

Jonathan GW Agnew

Position	Chairman
Company	Beazley Furlonge Ltd
Address (Office)	Plantation Place South
	60 Great Tower Street
	London EC3R 5AD
Telephone	+44 (0)20 7667 0623
Fax	+44 (0)20 7674 7100
Email	jonathan.agnew@beazley.com
Website	www.beazley.com

Full Name	Jonathan Geoffrey William Agnew
Year of Birth	1941
Professional Qualifications	Information not available

PROFESSIONAL INFORMATION

CURRENT MAJOR POSITIONS/APPOINTMENTS

Non-Executive Director	Beazley Furlonge Ltd	2002 -
Chairman	Nationwide Building Society	2007 -
Executive Director	Jarvis plc	Unknown -

PREVIOUS MAJOR POSITIONS/APPOINTMENTS

Non-Executive Director	Nationwide Building Society	2001 - 2007
Executive Director	Soditic Limited	2001 - 2004
Chief Executive Officer	Kleinwort Benson Group	1987 - 1993
Managing Director	Morgan Stanley	1973 - 1982

| Chairman | LIMIT plc | Unknown |
| Chairman | Gerrard Group plc | Unknown |

Theodore TM Agnew

Position	Deputy Chairman
Company	Jubilee Managing Agency Limited
Address (Office)	4th Floor
	50 Fenchurch Street
	London EC3M 3JY
Telephone	+44 (0)20 7220 8728
Fax	+44 (0)20 7220 8732
Email	theodore.agnew@jubilee-insurance.com
Website	www.jubilee-insurance.com

Full Name	Theodore Thomas More Agnew
Year of Birth	1961
Professional Qualifications	Information not available

PROFESSIONAL INFORMATION

CURRENT MAJOR POSITIONS/APPOINTMENTS

| Deputy Chairman | Jubilee Managing Agency Limited | 2009 - |

PREVIOUS MAJOR POSITIONS/APPOINTMENTS

| Chief Executive Officer | Town and Country Assistance | 1989 - 2002 |
| Chief Executive | Jubilee Managing Agency Limited | 2004 - 2009 |

Graham K Allen

Position	Finance Director
Company	Argenta Syndicate Management Limited
Address (Office)	Fountain House
	130 Fenchurch Street
	London EC3M 5DJ
Telephone	+44 (0)20 7825 7243
Fax	+44 (0)20 7825 7155
Email	graham.allen@argentaplc.com
Website	www.argentaplc.com

Full Name	Graham Kevin Allen
Year of Birth	1965
Professional Qualifications	ACA

PROFESSIONAL INFORMATION

CURRENT MAJOR POSITIONS/APPOINTMENTS

| Executive Director | Argenta Syndicate Management Limited | 2002 - |

PREVIOUS MAJOR POSITIONS/APPOINTMENTS

| | Information not available |

Les F Allen

Position	Underwriting Director & Active Underwriter Syndicate 1861
Company	Marlborough Underwriting Agency Ltd
Address (Office)	Birchin Court
	20 Birchin Lane
	London EC3V 9DU
Telephone	+44 (0)20 7456 1800
Fax	+44 (0)20 7456 1810
Email	leslie.allen@marlborough.co.uk
Website	www.marlborough.co.uk

Full Name	Leslie Francis Allen
Year of Birth	1953
Professional Qualifications	Information not available

PROFESSIONAL INFORMATION

CURRENT MAJOR POSITIONS/APPOINTMENTS

Executive Director	Marlborough Underwriting Agency Ltd	2001 -

PREVIOUS MAJOR POSITIONS/APPOINTMENTS

Information not available

J Michael G Andrews

Position	Non-Executive Director
Company	Cathedral Underwriting Limited
Address (Office)	5th Floor
	Fitzwilliam House
	10 St Mary Axe
	London EC3A 8EN
Telephone	+44 (0)20 7170 9000
Fax	+44 (0)20 7170 9001
Email	info@cathedralcapital.com
Website	www.cathedralcapital.com

Full Name	John Michael Geoffrey Andrews
Year of Birth	1926
Professional Qualifications	Information not available

PROFESSIONAL INFORMATION

CURRENT MAJOR POSITIONS/APPOINTMENTS

Non-Executive Director	Cathedral Underwriting Limited	2000 -

PREVIOUS MAJOR POSITIONS/APPOINTMENTS

Non-Executive Director	UBS Wealth Management (UK) Ltd	2001 - 2004
Non-Executive Director	QBE Underwriting Limited	2001 - 2006
Non-Executive Director	Atrium Underwriters Limited	2001 - 2007
Non-Executive Director	Beaufort Underwriting Agency Limited	2001 - 2008
Head of Corporate Finance	Samuel Montagu & Company Limited	Unknown

Andrew J Annandale

Position	Managing Director
Company	Argenta Syndicate Management Limited
Address (Office)	Fountain House
	130 Fenchurch Street
	London EC3M 5DJ
Telephone	+44 (0)20 7825 7239
Fax	+44 (0)20 7825 7155
Email	andrew.annandale@argentaplc.com
Website	www.argentaplc.com

Full Name	Andrew John Annandale
Year of Birth	1963
Professional Qualifications	Information not available

PROFESSIONAL INFORMATION

CURRENT MAJOR POSITIONS/APPOINTMENTS

Non-Executive Director	Argenta Private Capital Limited	2008 -
Chief Executive	Argenta Syndicate Management Limited	2008 -

PREVIOUS MAJOR POSITIONS/APPOINTMENTS

Executive Director	Richmond Underwriting Limited	2001 - 2006
Chief Executive	Argenta Private Capital Limited	2001 - 2008
Executive Director	Argenta Private Capital Limited	2001 - 2008
Non-Executive Director	The Stop Loss Mutual Insurance Association Ltd	2002 - 2004

Simon R Arnold

Position	Chairman
Company	Markel Syndicate Management Limited
Address (Office)	The Markel Building
	49 Leadenhall Street
	London EC3A 2EA
Telephone	+44 (0)20 7953 6000
Fax	+44 (0)20 7953 6001
Email	simon.arnold@markelintl.com
Website	www.markelintl.com

Full Name	Simon Rory Arnold
Year of Birth	1933
Professional Qualifications	Information not available

PROFESSIONAL INFORMATION

CURRENT MAJOR POSITIONS/APPOINTMENTS

Non-Executive Director	Markel Syndicate Management Limited	1996 -
Non-Executive Director	Markel International Insurance Company Limited	2003 -

PREVIOUS MAJOR POSITIONS/APPOINTMENTS

	Information not available

Thomas E Artmann

Position	Non-Executive Director
Company	Munich Re Underwriting Limited
Address (Office)	St Helen's
	1 Undershaft
	London EC3A 8EE
Telephone	+44 (0)20 7886 3900
Fax	+44 (0)20 7886 3901
Email	central@mrunderwriting.com
Website	www.watkins-syndicate.co.uk

Full Name	Thomas Eduard Artmann
Year of Birth	1962
Professional Qualifications	Information not available

PROFESSIONAL INFORMATION

CURRENT MAJOR POSITIONS/APPOINTMENTS

Non-Executive Director	Munich Re Underwriting Limited	2003 -

PREVIOUS MAJOR POSITIONS/APPOINTMENTS

Information not available

Lord Ashton of Hyde

Position	Chairman & Chief Executive Officer
Company	Faraday Underwriting Limited
Address (Office)	5th Floor
	Corn Exchange
	55 Mark Lane
	London EC3R 7NE
Telephone	+44 (0)20 7680 4239
Fax	+44 (0)20 7680 4369
Email	henry.ashton@faraday.com
Website	www.faraday.com

PERSONAL PROFILE	A profile can be found in the People at Lloyd's, Personal section.

CN Rupert Atkin

Position	Chief Executive Officer
Company	Talbot Underwriting Ltd
Address (Office)	Gracechurch House
	55 Gracechurch Street
	London EC3V 0JP
Telephone	+44 (0)20 7550 3500
Fax	+44 (0)20 7550 3555
Email	rupert.atkin@talbotuw.com
Website	www.talbotuw.com

PERSONAL PROFILE	A profile can be found in the People at Lloyd's, Personal section.

Andrew M Baddeley

Position	Chief Financial Officer
Company	Atrium Underwriters Limited
Address (Office)	Room 790
	Lloyd's
	One Lime Street
	London EC3M 7DQ
Telephone	+44 (0)20 7327 4877
Fax	+44 (0)20 7327 4878
Email	info@atrium-uw.com
Website	www.atrium-uw.com
Full Name	Andrew Martin Baddeley
Year of Birth	1964
Professional Qualifications	Information not available

PROFESSIONAL INFORMATION

CURRENT MAJOR POSITIONS/APPOINTMENTS

Executive Director	Atrium Underwriters Limited	2007 -
Executive Director	Atrium Insurance Agency Limited	2008 -

PREVIOUS MAJOR POSITIONS/APPOINTMENTS

Executive Director	Faraday Reinsurance Co Limited	2006 - 2007
Executive Director	Faraday Underwriting Limited	2006 - 2007
Executive Director	General Reinsurance UK Limited	2006 - 2007
Executive Director	General Star International Indemnity Ltd	2006 - 2007

Kim Barber

Position	Executive Director & Head of Motor Division
Company	Chaucer Syndicates Limited
Address (Office)	Plantation Place
	30 Fenchurch Street
	London EC3M 3AD
Telephone	+44 (0)1227 284 700
Fax	+44 (0)20 7397 9710
Email	kim.barber@chaucerplc.com
Website	www.chaucerplc.com
Full Name	Kim Barber
Year of Birth	1953
Professional Qualifications	Information not available

PROFESSIONAL INFORMATION

CURRENT MAJOR POSITIONS/APPOINTMENTS

Executive Director	Chaucer Syndicates Limited	2005 -
Chief Executive	Chaucer Insurance Services Ltd	2007 -

PREVIOUS MAJOR POSITIONS/APPOINTMENTS

Information not available

Richard P Bardwell

Position	Underwriting Director & Active Underwriter Syndicate 1221
Company	Navigators Underwriting Agency Ltd
Address (Office)	7th Floor
	2 Minster Court
	Mincing Lane
	London EC3R 7BB
Telephone	+44 (0)20 7220 6900
Fax	+44 (0)20 7220 6901
Email	rbardwell@navg.com
Website	www.navg.com
PERSONAL PROFILE	A profile can be found in the People at Lloyd's, Personal section.

Andrew A Barnard

Position	Chairman
Company	Newline Underwriting Management Ltd
Address (Office)	Suite 5/4
	London Underwriting Centre
	3 Minster Court
	Mincing Lane
	London EC3R 7DD
Telephone	+44 (0)20 7090 1700
Fax	+44 (0)20 7090 1701
Email	abarnard@odysseyre.com
Website	www.newlineuml.com
Full Name	Andrew Acheson Barnard
Year of Birth	1955
Professional Qualifications	BA

PROFESSIONAL INFORMATION

CURRENT MAJOR POSITIONS/APPOINTMENTS

Non-Executive Director	Newline Underwriting Management Ltd	1999 -
Executive Director	Newline Insurance Company Limited	2006 -

PREVIOUS MAJOR POSITIONS/APPOINTMENTS
Information not available

Gillian E Barnes

Position	Claims Director
Company	Pembroke Managing Agency Ltd
Address (Office)	2nd Floor
	3 Minster Court
	Mincing Lane
	London EC3R 7DD
Telephone	+44 (0)20 7337 4400
Fax	+44 (0)20 7337 4401

| Email | gillian.barnes@pembrokeunderwriting.com |
| Website | www.pembrokeunderwriting.com |

Full Name	Gillian Elizabeth Barnes
Year of Birth	1962
Professional Qualifications	BA (Hons), FCII

PROFESSIONAL INFORMATION

CURRENT MAJOR POSITIONS/APPOINTMENTS

| Executive Director | Pembroke Managing Agency Ltd | 2008 - |

PREVIOUS MAJOR POSITIONS/APPOINTMENTS

Information not available

Luke N Barnett

Position	Chief Operating Officer & Compliance Officer
Company	Whittington Capital Management Limited
Address (Office)	33 Creechurch Lane
	London EC3A 5EB
Telephone	+44 (0)20 7743 0900
Fax	+44 (0)20 7743 0901
Email	luke.barnett@whittingtoninsurance.com
Website	www.whittingtoninsurance.com

Full Name	Luke Nicholas Barnett
Year of Birth	1966
Professional Qualifications	Information not available

PROFESSIONAL INFORMATION

CURRENT MAJOR POSITIONS/APPOINTMENTS

| Executive Director | Whittington Capital Management Limited | 2008 - |

PREVIOUS MAJOR POSITIONS/APPOINTMENTS

Information not available

Simon C Barrett

Position	Chief Financial Officer
Company	XL London Market Limited
Address (Office)	XL House
	70 Gracechurch Street
	London EC3V 0XL
Telephone	+44 (0)20 7933 7000
Fax	+44 (0)20 7469 1071
Email	simon.barrett@xlgroup.com
Website	www.xlinsurance.co.uk

Full Name	Simon Christopher Barrett
Year of Birth	1963
Professional Qualifications	Information not available

PROFESSIONAL INFORMATION

CURRENT MAJOR POSITIONS/APPOINTMENTS

Executive Director	XL London Market Limited	2003 -
Executive Director	XL Insurance Company Limited	2005 -

PREVIOUS MAJOR POSITIONS/APPOINTMENTS

Executive Director	Brockbank Personal Lines Limited	2004 - 2007

Adam J Barron

Position	Non-Executive Director
Company	Canopius Managing Agents Limited
Address (Office)	Gallery 9
	One Lime Street
	London EC3M 7HA
Telephone	+44 (0)20 7337 3700
Fax	+44 (0)20 7337 3999
Email	adam.barron@canopius.com
Website	www.canopius.com

Full Name	Adam James Barron
Year of Birth	1968
Professional Qualifications	Information not available

PROFESSIONAL INFORMATION

CURRENT MAJOR POSITIONS/APPOINTMENTS

Non-Executive Director	Canopius Managing Agents Limited	2004 -

PREVIOUS MAJOR POSITIONS/APPOINTMENTS
Information not available

Bruce P Bartell

Position	Executive Director & Active Underwriter Syndicate 1084
Company	Chaucer Syndicates Limited
Address (Office)	Plantation Place
	30 Fenchurch Street
	London EC3M 3AD
Telephone	+44 (0)20 7397 9700
Fax	+44 (0)20 7397 9710
Email	bruce.bartell@chaucerplc.com
Website	www.chaucerplc.com

Full Name	Bruce Philip Bartell
Year of Birth	1957
Professional Qualifications	Information not available

PROFESSIONAL INFORMATION

CURRENT MAJOR POSITIONS/APPOINTMENTS

Executive Director	Chaucer Syndicates Limited	1992 -

PREVIOUS MAJOR POSITIONS/APPOINTMENTS
Information not available

R John O Barton

Position	Chairman
Company	Brit Syndicates Limited
Address (Office)	2nd Floor
	55 Bishopsgate
	London EC2N 3AS
Telephone	+44 (0)20 7984 8500
Fax	+44 (0)20 7984 8501
Email	john.barton@britinsurance.com
Website	www.britinsurance.com
Full Name	Robert John Orr Barton
Year of Birth	1944
Professional Qualifications	Information not available

PROFESSIONAL INFORMATION

CURRENT MAJOR POSITIONS/APPOINTMENTS

Non-Executive Director	Brit Syndicates Limited	2008 -
Non-Executive Director	BRIT Insurance Limited	2008 -
Chairman	Next PLC	Unknown -
Non-Executive Director	WH Smith PLC	Unknown -

PREVIOUS MAJOR POSITIONS/APPOINTMENTS

Non-Executive Director	Catlin (Wellington) Underwriting Agencies Limited	2001 - 2003
Chief Executive	JIB Group plc	Unknown
Chairman	Jardine Lloyd Thompson Group plc	Unknown
Chairman	Wellington Underwriting PLC	Unknown

H Clay Bassett Jr

Position	Non-Executive Director
Company	Navigators Underwriting Agency Ltd
Address (Office)	7th Floor
	2 Minster Court
	Mincing Lane
	London EC3R 7BB
Telephone	+44 (0)20 7220 6900
Fax	+44 (0)20 7220 6901
Email	cbassett@navg.com
Website	www.navg.com
Full Name	Henry Clay Bassett Jr
Year of Birth	1965
Professional Qualifications	Information not available

PROFESSIONAL INFORMATION

CURRENT MAJOR POSITIONS/APPOINTMENTS

Non-Executive Director	Navigators Underwriting Agency Ltd	2008 -

PREVIOUS MAJOR POSITIONS/APPOINTMENTS

Information not available

Ashis M Bathia

Position	Underwriting Director
Company	QBE Underwriting Limited
Address (Office)	Plantation Place
	30 Fenchurch Street
	London EC3M 3BD
Telephone	+44 (0)20 7105 4000
Fax	+44 (0)20 7105 4019
Email	enquiries@uk.qbe.com
Website	www.qbeeurope.com
Full Name	Ashis Mathuradas Bathia
Year of Birth	1960
Professional Qualifications	Information not available

PROFESSIONAL INFORMATION

CURRENT MAJOR POSITIONS/APPOINTMENTS

Executive Director	QBE Insurance (Europe) Limited	2005 -
Executive Director	QBE Underwriting Limited	2008 -

PREVIOUS MAJOR POSITIONS/APPOINTMENTS

Executive Director	QBE Insurance Company (UK) Limited	2005 - 2006

Shingo Batori

Position	Executive Director
Company	R J Kiln & Co Limited
Address (Office)	106 Fenchurch Street
	London EC3M 5NR
Telephone	+44 (0)20 7886 9000
Fax	+44 (0)20 7488 1848
Email	shingo.batori@kilngroup.com
Website	www.kilnplc.com
Full Name	Shingo Batori
Year of Birth	1967
Professional Qualifications	Information not available

PROFESSIONAL INFORMATION

CURRENT MAJOR POSITIONS/APPOINTMENTS

Executive Director	R J Kiln & Co Limited	2008 -

PREVIOUS MAJOR POSITIONS/APPOINTMENTS
Information not available

Paul D Battagliola

Position	Chief Operating Officer
Company	Argo Managing Agency Ltd
Address (Office)	47 Mark Lane
	London EC3R 7QQ
Telephone	+44 (0)20 7712 7600
Fax	+44 (0)20 7712 7601
Email	paul.battagliola@argo-int.com
Website	www.argo-int.com

PERSONAL PROFILE   A profile can be found in the People at Lloyd's, Personal section.

Alexander R Baugh

Position	Non-Executive Director
Company	Ascot Underwriting Limited
Address (Office)	Plantation Place
	30 Fenchurch Street
	London EC3M 3BD
Telephone	+44 (0)20 7743 9600
Fax	+44 (0)20 7743 9601
Email	enquiries@ascotuw.com
Website	www.ascotuw.com

Full Name	Alexander Ross Baugh
Year of Birth	Information not available
Professional Qualifications	Information not available

PROFESSIONAL INFORMATION

CURRENT MAJOR POSITIONS/APPOINTMENTS

Executive Director	AIG UK Limited	2008 -
Executive Director	AIG UK Services Limited	2008 -
Non-Executive Director	Ascot Underwriting Limited	2008 -
Chief Executive	AIG UK Limited	2008 -

PREVIOUS MAJOR POSITIONS/APPOINTMENTS
Information not available

Paul Baynham

Position	Underwriting Director, Liability & CAR
Company	HCC Underwriting Agency Ltd
Address (Office)	Walsingham House
	35 Seething Lane
	London EC3N 4AH
Telephone	+44 (0)20 7680 3009

Fax	+44 (0)20 7977 7350
Email	pbaynham@hccual.com
Website	www.hccual.com

Full Name	Paul Baynham
Year of Birth	1967
Professional Qualifications	Information not available

PROFESSIONAL INFORMATION

CURRENT MAJOR POSITIONS/APPOINTMENTS

Executive Director	HCC Insurance Services Ltd	2005 -
Executive Director	HCC Underwriting Agency Ltd	2007 -

PREVIOUS MAJOR POSITIONS/APPOINTMENTS

Information not available

Simon CW Beale

Position	Underwriting Director, Amlin London & Joint Active Underwriter Syndicate 2001
Company	Amlin Underwriting Limited
Address (Office)	St Helen's
	1 Undershaft
	London EC3A 8ND
Telephone	+44 (0)20 7746 1000
Fax	+44 (0)20 7746 1696
Email	simon.beale@amlin.co.uk
Website	www.amlin.com

PERSONAL PROFILE	A profile can be found in the People at Lloyd's, Personal section.

Ian E Beaton

Position	Chief Executive Officer
Company	ARK Syndicate Management Limited
Address (Office)	8th Floor
	St Helen's
	1 Undershaft
	London EC3A 8EE
Telephone	+44 (0)20 3023 4001
Fax	+44 (0)20 3023 4000
Email	ian.beaton@arkunderwriting.com
Website	www.arkunderwriting.com

Full Name	Ian Eric Beaton
Year of Birth	1970
Professional Qualifications	Information not available

PROFESSIONAL INFORMATION

CURRENT MAJOR POSITIONS/APPOINTMENTS

Executive Director	ARK Syndicate Management Limited	2007 -
Chief Executive	ARK Syndicate Management Limited	2007 -

PREVIOUS MAJOR POSITIONS/APPOINTMENTS
Information not available

Andrew F Beazley

Position	Group Deputy Chairman
Company	Beazley Furlonge Ltd
Address (Office)	Plantation Place South
	60 Great Tower Street
	London EC3R 5AD
Telephone	+44 (0)20 7667 0623
Fax	+44 (0)20 7674 7100
Email	andrew.beazley@beazley.com
Website	www.beazley.com

PERSONAL PROFILE   A profile can be found in the People at Lloyd's, Personal section.

Baron Clemens ATW von Bechtolsheim

Position	Non-Executive Director
Company	Max at Lloyd's Ltd
Address (Office)	4th Floor
	70 Gracechurch Street
	London EC3V 0XL
Telephone	+44 (0)20 3102 3100
Fax	+44 (0)20 3102 3200
Email	clemens.vonbechtolsheim@maxatlloyds.com
Website	www.maxatlloyds.com

Full Name	Baron Clemens Anton Theodor Wolf von Bechtolsheim
Year of Birth	1945
Professional Qualifications	Information not available

PROFESSIONAL INFORMATION

CURRENT MAJOR POSITIONS/APPOINTMENTS

Non-Executive Director	Allianz Insurance Plc	2006 -
Non-Executive Director	Max at Lloyd's Ltd	2007 -
Non-Executive Director	Tokio Marine Global Ltd	2007 -

PREVIOUS MAJOR POSITIONS/APPOINTMENTS

Chief Executive	Muenchener Rueckversicherungs-Gesellschaft AG, Muenchen	2001 - 2005
Non-Executive Director	Great Lakes Reinsurance (UK) Plc	2001 - 2003
Executive Director	Munich Re General Services Ltd	2004 - 2005

W Marston (Marty) Becker

Position	Chairman
Company	Max at Lloyd's Ltd
Address (Office)	4th Floor
	70 Gracechurch Street
	London EC3V 0XL
Telephone	+44 (0)20 3102 3100
Fax	+44 (0)20 3102 3200
Email	william.becker@maxatlloyds.com
Website	www.maxatlloyds.com
Full Name	William Marston Becker
Year of Birth	Information not available
Professional Qualifications	Information not available

PROFESSIONAL INFORMATION

CURRENT MAJOR POSITIONS/APPOINTMENTS

Executive Director	Max at Lloyd's Ltd	2008 -

PREVIOUS MAJOR POSITIONS/APPOINTMENTS

Information not available

Ian D Beckerson

Position	Compliance & Risk Management Director
Company	QBE Underwriting Limited
Address (Office)	Plantation Place
	30 Fenchurch Street
	London EC3M 3BD
Telephone	+44 (0)20 7105 4000
Fax	+44 (0)20 7105 4019
Email	enquiries@uk.qbe.com
Website	www.qbeeurope.com
Full Name	Ian David Beckerson
Year of Birth	1967
Professional Qualifications	Information not available

PROFESSIONAL INFORMATION

CURRENT MAJOR POSITIONS/APPOINTMENTS

Executive Director	QBE Underwriting Limited	2000 -
Executive Director	Greenhill Sturge Underwriting Ltd	2005 -
Executive Director	Greenhill International Ins Holdings Ltd	2005 -
Executive Director	Greenhill Underwriting Espana Ltd	2005 -
Executive Director	QBE (Stafford) Limited	2005 -
Executive Director	QBE Insurance (Europe) Limited	2005 -
Executive Director	QBE Reinsurance (UK) Ltd	2005 -
Executive Director	The Minibus and Coach Club Ltd	2005 -

PREVIOUS MAJOR POSITIONS/APPOINTMENTS

Executive Director	QBE Insurance Company (UK) Limited	2005 - 2006

David C Bendle

Position	Operations Director
Company	Chaucer Syndicates Limited
Address (Office)	Plantation Place
	30 Fenchurch Street
	London EC3M 3AD
Telephone	+44 (0)20 7397 9700
Fax	+44 (0)20 7397 9710
Email	david.bendle@chaucerplc.com
Website	www.chaucerplc.com
Full Name	David Clifford Bendle
Year of Birth	1964
Professional Qualifications	Information not available

PROFESSIONAL INFORMATION

CURRENT MAJOR POSITIONS/APPOINTMENTS

Executive Director	Chaucer Syndicates Limited	2005 -

PREVIOUS MAJOR POSITIONS/APPOINTMENTS

Information not available

Roger A Bickmore

Position	Executive Director
Company	R J Kiln & Co Limited
Address (Office)	106 Fenchurch Street
	London EC3M 5NR
Telephone	+44 (0)20 7886 9000
Fax	+44 (0)20 7488 1848
Email	roger.bickmore@kilngroup.com
Website	www.kilnplc.com
Full Name	Roger Antony Bickmore
Year of Birth	1961
Professional Qualifications	Information not available

PROFESSIONAL INFORMATION

CURRENT MAJOR POSITIONS/APPOINTMENTS

Executive Director	R J Kiln & Co Limited	2006 -

PREVIOUS MAJOR POSITIONS/APPOINTMENTS

Executive Director	SLE Worldwide Ltd	2005 - 2006

John D Birney

Position	Independent Review Director
Company	Canopius Managing Agents Limited
Address (Office)	Gallery 9
	One Lime Street
	London EC3M 7HA
Telephone	+44 (0)20 7337 3700
Fax	+44 (0)20 7337 3999
Email	john.birney@canopius.com
Website	www.canopius.com
Full Name	John David Birney
Year of Birth	1944
Professional Qualifications	Information not available

PROFESSIONAL INFORMATION

CURRENT MAJOR POSITIONS/APPOINTMENTS

Non-Executive Director	Canopius Managing Agents Limited	2004 -

PREVIOUS MAJOR POSITIONS/APPOINTMENTS

Information not available

John H Bishop

Position	Chairman
Company	HCC Underwriting Agency Ltd
Address (Office)	Walsingham House
	35 Seething Lane
	London EC3N 4AH
Telephone	+44 (0)20 7680 3000
Fax	+44 (0)20 7977 7350
Email	info@hccual.com
Website	www.hccual.com
Full Name	John Henry Bishop
Year of Birth	1945
Professional Qualifications	Information not available

PROFESSIONAL INFORMATION

CURRENT MAJOR POSITIONS/APPOINTMENTS

Non-Executive Director	Berkshire Hathaway International Insurance Ltd	2001 -
Non-Executive Director	HCC Underwriting Agency Ltd	2003 -
Non-Executive Director	Lancashire Insurance Company (UK) Ltd	2008 -

PREVIOUS MAJOR POSITIONS/APPOINTMENTS

Information not available

Ashley R Bissett

Position	Executive Director
Company	Chaucer Syndicates Limited

Address (Office)	Plantation Place
	30 Fenchurch Street
	London EC3M 3AD
Telephone	+44 (0)20 7397 9700
Fax	+44 (0)20 7397 9710
Email	ashley.bissett@chaucerplc.com
Website	www.chaucerplc.com

Full Name	Ashley Raymond Bissett
Year of Birth	1964
Professional Qualifications	Information not available

PROFESSIONAL INFORMATION

CURRENT MAJOR POSITIONS/APPOINTMENTS

Executive Director	Chaucer Syndicates Limited	2005 -
Executive Director	Chaucer Insurance Services Ltd	2007 -

PREVIOUS MAJOR POSITIONS/APPOINTMENTS
Information not available

Henry JM Blakeney

Position	Chairman
Company	Navigators Underwriting Agency Ltd
Address (Office)	7th Floor
	2 Minster Court
	Mincing Lane
	London EC3R 7BB
Telephone	+44 (0)20 7220 6900
Fax	+44 (0)20 7220 6901
Email	hblakeney@navg.com
Website	www.navg.com

Full Name	Henry John Mervyn Blakeney
Year of Birth	1938
Professional Qualifications	Information not available

PROFESSIONAL INFORMATION

CURRENT MAJOR POSITIONS/APPOINTMENTS

Non-Executive Director	Navigators Underwriting Agency Ltd	1993 -

PREVIOUS MAJOR POSITIONS/APPOINTMENTS

Non-Executive Director	Creechurch Underwriting Limited	2001 - 2006
Non-Executive Director	BA (GI) Limited	2001 - 2003
Executive Director	Alba Life Limited	2003 - 2003

Steven G Blakey

Position	Chief Executive Officer
Company	Starr Managing Agents Limited

Address (Office)	3rd Floor
	140 Leadenhall Street
	London EC3V 4QT
Telephone	+44 (0)20 7337 3550
Fax	+44 (0)20 7337 3551
Email	steven.blakey@cvstarrco.com
Website	www.cvstarrco.com
Full Name	Steven George Blakey
Year of Birth	1957
Professional Qualifications	Information not available

PROFESSIONAL INFORMATION

CURRENT MAJOR POSITIONS/APPOINTMENTS

Chief Executive	Starr Underwriting Agents Limited	2007 -
Chief Executive	Starr Managing Agents Limited	2007 -

PREVIOUS MAJOR POSITIONS/APPOINTMENTS

Information not available

George P Blunden

Position	Non-Executive Director
Company	Beazley Furlonge Ltd
Address (Office)	Plantation Place South
	60 Great Tower Street
	London EC3R 5AD
Telephone	+44 (0)20 7667 0623
Fax	+44 (0)20 7674 7100
Email	george.blunden@beazley.com
Website	www.beazley.com
Full Name	George Patrick Blunden
Year of Birth	1952
Professional Qualifications	Information not available

PROFESSIONAL INFORMATION

CURRENT MAJOR POSITIONS/APPOINTMENTS

Non-Executive Director	Beazley Furlonge Ltd	1993 -

PREVIOUS MAJOR POSITIONS/APPOINTMENTS

Executive Director	ACM Investments Limited	2001 - 2004
Executive Director	AllianceBernstein Fixed Income Limited	2001 - 2004

Thomas (Tom) A Bolt*

Position	Managing Director
Company	Marlborough Underwriting Agency Ltd
Address (Office)	Birchin Court
	20 Birchin Lane
	London EC3V 9DU

Telephone	+44 (0)20 7456 1800
Fax	+44 (0)20 7456 1810
Email	thomas.bolt@marlborough.co.uk
Website	www.marlborough.co.uk

Full Name	Thomas Allen Bolt
Year of Birth	1956
Professional Qualifications	Information not available

PROFESSIONAL INFORMATION

CURRENT MAJOR POSITIONS/APPOINTMENTS

Chief Executive	Marlborough Underwriting Agency Ltd	2001 -
Chief Executive	NRG Victory Reinsurance Limited	2008 -
Non-Executive Director	Berkshire Hathaway International Insurance Ltd	2009 -
Non-Executive Director	Kyoei Fire & Marine Insurance Co (UK) Limited	2009 -
Non-Executive Director	Tenecom Limited	2009 -
Non-Executive Director	Transfercom Limited	2009 -
Non-Executive Director	Resolute Management Limited	2009 -

PREVIOUS MAJOR POSITIONS/APPOINTMENTS

Executive Director	Berkshire Hathaway International Insurance Ltd	2001 - 2008
Executive Director	Tenecom Limited	2001 - 2008
Chief Executive	Berkshire Hathaway International Insurance Ltd	2001 - 2008
Chief Executive	Tenecom Limited	2001 - 2008
Chief Executive	Transfercom Limited	2006 - 2008
Executive Director	Resolute Management Limited	2007 - 2008

* Lloyd's Underwriting Performance Director Designate from 01.01.2010

Nicholas (Nick) K Bonnar

Position	Chief Underwriting Officer & Active Underwriter
	Syndicates 4020 & 6105
Company	ARK Syndicate Management Limited
Address (Office)	8th Floor
	St Helen's
	1 Undershaft
	London EC3A 8EE
Telephone	+44 (0)20 3023 4003
Fax	+44 (0)20 3023 4000
Email	nick.bonnar@arkunderwriting.com
Website	www.arkunderwriting.com

Full Name	Nicholas Kershaw Bonnar
Year of Birth	1964
Professional Qualifications	Information not available

PROFESSIONAL INFORMATION

CURRENT MAJOR POSITIONS/APPOINTMENTS

Executive Director	ARK Syndicate Management Limited	2007 -

PREVIOUS MAJOR POSITIONS/APPOINTMENTS

Executive Director	XL London Market Limited	2001 - 2002
Executive Director	Aspen Insurance UK Limited	2006 - 2006

John M Boylan

Position	Executive Director
Company	Max at Lloyd's Ltd
Address (Office)	4th Floor
	70 Gracechurch Street
	London EC3V 0XL
Telephone	+44 (0)20 3102 3100
Fax	+44 (0)20 3102 3200
Email	john.boylan@maxatlloyds.com
Website	www.maxatlloyds.com

Full Name	John Macartan Boylan
Year of Birth	Information not available
Professional Qualifications	Information not available

PROFESSIONAL INFORMATION

CURRENT MAJOR POSITIONS/APPOINTMENTS

Executive Director	Max at Lloyd's Ltd	2008 -
Executive Director	Max UK Underwriting Services Ltd	2008 -

PREVIOUS MAJOR POSITIONS/APPOINTMENTS

Information not available

Jonathan A Boyns

Position	Group Claims Director
Company	Novae Syndicates Limited
Address (Office)	71 Fenchurch Street
	London EC3M 4HH
Telephone	+44 (0)20 7903 7300
Fax	+44 (0)20 7903 7333
Email	jboyns@novae.com
Website	www.novae.com

Full Name	Jonathan Andrew Boyns
Year of Birth	1952
Professional Qualifications	Information not available

PROFESSIONAL INFORMATION

CURRENT MAJOR POSITIONS/APPOINTMENTS

Executive Director	Novae Syndicates Limited	2004 -
Non-Executive Director	Novae Insurance Company Ltd	2008 -

PREVIOUS MAJOR POSITIONS/APPOINTMENTS

Executive Director	Denham Syndicate Management Ltd	2001 - 2002
Executive Director	BRIT Insurance (UK) Ltd	2002 - 2003

Jeremy W Brazil

Position	Director of London Underwriting & Active Underwriter Syndicate 3000
Company	Markel Syndicate Management Limited
Address (Office)	The Markel Building
	49 Leadenhall Street
	London EC3A 2EA
Telephone	+44 (0)20 7953 6000
Fax	+44 (0)20 7953 6001
Email	jeremy.brazil@markelintl.com
Website	www.markelintl.com
Full Name	Jeremy William Brazil
Year of Birth	1962
Professional Qualifications	BSc (Hons), ACII

PROFESSIONAL INFORMATION

CURRENT MAJOR POSITIONS/APPOINTMENTS

Executive Director	Markel Syndicate Management Limited	2001 -
Executive Director	Markel International Insurance Company Limited	2005 -
Executive Director	Markel (London) Limited	2005 -
Chief Executive	Markel Syndicate Management Limited	2008 -
Chief Executive	Markel International Insurance Company Limited	2008 -

PREVIOUS MAJOR POSITIONS/APPOINTMENTS

Information not available

Iain J Bremner

Position	Managing Director
Company	Max at Lloyd's Ltd
Address (Office)	4th Floor
	70 Gracechurch Street
	London EC3V 0XL
Telephone	+44 (0)20 3102 3100
Fax	+44 (0)20 3102 3200
Email	iain.bremner@maxatlloyds.com
Website	www.maxatlloyds.com
Full Name	Iain James Bremner
Year of Birth	1964
Professional Qualifications	FCA

PROFESSIONAL INFORMATION

CURRENT MAJOR POSITIONS/APPOINTMENTS

Executive Director	Max at Lloyd's Ltd	2001 -
Chief Executive	Max at Lloyd's Ltd	2002 -
Chief Executive	Max UK Underwriting Services Ltd	2006 -

PREVIOUS MAJOR POSITIONS/APPOINTMENTS

Chief Executive	Imagine Underwriting Limited	2006 - 2007

| Chief Executive | Danish Re Syndicates Ltd | 2006 - 2006 |
| Executive Director | Abacus Syndicates Ltd | Unknown |

Jerome Breslin

Position	Non-Executive Director
Company	Spectrum Syndicate Management Limited
Address (Office)	2nd Floor
	6 Bevis Marks
	London EC3A 7HL
Telephone	+44 (0)20 7283 2646
Fax	+44 (0)20 3003 6999
Email	newbusiness@spectrumins.com
Website	www.spectrumins.com

Full Name	Jerome Breslin
Year of Birth	1966
Professional Qualifications	Information not available

PROFESSIONAL INFORMATION

CURRENT MAJOR POSITIONS/APPOINTMENTS

| Executive Director | Spectrum Syndicate Management Limited | 2008 - |

PREVIOUS MAJOR POSITIONS/APPOINTMENTS

Information not available

Richard M Brewster

Position	Non-Executive Director
Company	Argenta Syndicate Management Limited
Address (Office)	Fountain House
	130 Fenchurch Street
	London EC3M 5DJ
Telephone	+44 (0)20 7825 7200
Fax	+44 (0)20 7825 7155
Email	richard.brewster@argentaplc.com
Website	www.argentaplc.com

Full Name	Richard Mark Brewster
Year of Birth	1956
Professional Qualifications	Information not available

PROFESSIONAL INFORMATION

CURRENT MAJOR POSITIONS/APPOINTMENTS

| Non-Executive Director | Argenta Syndicate Management Limited | 2002 - |
| Executive Director | Equity Direct Broking Limited | 2009 - |

PREVIOUS MAJOR POSITIONS/APPOINTMENTS

| Executive Director | Equity Syndicate Management Limited | 2001 - 2002 |
| Chairman | Argenta Syndicate Management Limited | 2005 - 2009 |

Stuart J Bridges

Position	Executive Director
Company	Hiscox Syndicates Limited
Address (Office)	1 Great St Helen's
	London EC3A 6HX
Telephone	+44 (0)20 7448 6000
Fax	+44 (0)20 7448 6900
Email	stuart.bridges@hiscox.com
Website	www.hiscox.com
PERSONAL PROFILE	A profile can be found in the People at Lloyd's, Personal section.

Ian Brimecome

Position	Non-Executive Director
Company	R J Kiln & Co Limited
Address (Office)	106 Fenchurch Street
	London EC3M 5NR
Telephone	+44 (0)20 7886 9000
Fax	+44 (0)20 7488 1848
Email	See R J Kiln & Co Ltd Company Profile
Website	www.kilnplc.com
Full Name	Ian Brimecome
Year of Birth	1953
Professional Qualifications	Information not available

PROFESSIONAL INFORMATION

CURRENT MAJOR POSITIONS/APPOINTMENTS

Non-Executive Director	AXA Sun Life Plc	2007 -
Non-Executive Director	AXA Insurance Plc	2007 -
Non-Executive Director	AXA PPP Healthcare Limited	2007 -
Non-Executive Director	AXA Annuity Company Limited	2007 -
Non-Executive Director	Winterthur Pension Funds UK Limited	2007 -
Non-Executive Director	AXA Insurance UK Plc	2007 -
Non-Executive Director	AXA General Insurance Limited	2007 -
Non-Executive Director	The Equitable Life Assurance Society	2007 -
Non-Executive Director	Sun Life Assurance Society Plc	2007 -
Non-Executive Director	Winterthur Life UK Limited	2007 -
Executive Director	R J Kiln & Co Limited	2008 -
Non-Executive Director	Independent Sales Force Solutions Limited	2008 -
Non-Executive Director	Stuart Alexander Limited	2008 -
Non-Executive Director	LBBS Ltd	2008 -
Non-Executive Director	Layton Blackham Underwriting Ltd	2008 -
Non-Executive Director	Davis Underwriting Ltd	2008 -
Non-Executive Director	Smart & Cook Financial Services Limited	2008 -
Non-Executive Director	Layton Blackham Insurance Brokers Ltd	2008 -
Non-Executive Director	Smart & Cook Ltd	2008 -
Non-Executive Director	Davis Corporate Risks Ltd	2008 -
Non-Executive Director	Layton Blackham Financial Services Limited	2008 -

PREVIOUS MAJOR POSITIONS/APPOINTMENTS

Chief Executive	Putnam Lovell NBF Securities Inc	2002 - 2004
Non-Executive Director	Winterthur Life UK Limited	2003 - 2006
Non-Executive Director	Winterthur Pension Funds UK Limited	2003 - 2006
Non-Executive Director	NBC Financial (UK) Limited	2004 - 2004
Non-Executive Director	Sun Life Pensions Management Limited	2007 - 2007
Non-Executive Director	Sun Life Unit Assurance Limited	2007 - 2007
Non-Executive Director	PPP Lifetime Care Plc	2007 - 2007

Andrew L Brooks

Position	Chief Executive Officer & Active Underwriter Syndicate 1414
Company	Ascot Underwriting Limited
Address (Office)	Plantation Place
	30 Fenchurch Street
	London EC3M 3BD
Telephone	+44 (0)20 7743 9600
Fax	+44 (0)20 7743 9601
Email	andrew.brooks@ascotuw.com
Website	www.ascotuw.com

Full Name	Andrew Lewis Brooks
Year of Birth	1965
Professional Qualifications	Information not available

PROFESSIONAL INFORMATION

CURRENT MAJOR POSITIONS/APPOINTMENTS

Executive Director	Ascot Underwriting Limited	2004 -
Executive Director	Ascot Insurance Services Ltd	2008 -
Chief Executive	Ascot Underwriting Limited	2008 -

PREVIOUS MAJOR POSITIONS/APPOINTMENTS

Information not available

Christopher D Brown

Position	Executive Director
Company	Pembroke Managing Agency Ltd
Address (Office)	2nd Floor
	3 Minster Court
	Mincing Lane
	London EC3R 7DD
Telephone	+44 (0)20 7337 4400
Fax	+44 (0)20 7337 4401
Email	christopher.brown@pembrokeunderwriting.com
Website	www.pembrokeunderwriting.com

Full Name	Christopher David Brown
Year of Birth	1964
Professional Qualifications	ACII

PROFESSIONAL INFORMATION

CURRENT MAJOR POSITIONS/APPOINTMENTS

Executive Director	Pembroke Managing Agency Ltd	2007 -

PREVIOUS MAJOR POSITIONS/APPOINTMENTS

Information not available

David JW Bruce

Position	Executive Director
Company	Hiscox Syndicates Limited
Address (Office)	1 Great St Helen's
	London EC3A 6HX
Telephone	+44 (0)20 7448 6000
Fax	+44 (0)20 7448 6900
Email	david.bruce@hiscox.com
Website	www.hiscox.com

Full Name	David John William Bruce
Year of Birth	1951
Professional Qualifications	Information not available

PROFESSIONAL INFORMATION

CURRENT MAJOR POSITIONS/APPOINTMENTS

Executive Director	Hiscox Syndicates Limited	2002 -

PREVIOUS MAJOR POSITIONS/APPOINTMENTS

Information not available

Peter J Bruin

Position	Risk Management Director, Compliance Director & Company Secretary
Company	Argenta Syndicate Management Limited
Address (Office)	Fountain House
	130 Fenchurch Street
	London EC3M 5DJ
Telephone	+44 (0)20 7825 7272
Fax	+44 (0)20 7825 7155
Email	peter.bruin@argentaplc.com
Website	www.argentaplc.com

Full Name	Peter James Bruin
Year of Birth	1958
Professional Qualifications	Information not available

PROFESSIONAL INFORMATION

CURRENT MAJOR POSITIONS/APPOINTMENTS

Executive Director	Argenta Syndicate Management Limited	2001 -

PREVIOUS MAJOR POSITIONS/APPOINTMENTS

Information not available

Jorg W Bruniecki

Position	Non-Executive Director
Company	Beaufort Underwriting Agency Limited
Address (Office)	Third Floor
	One Minster Court
	Mincing Lane
	London EC3R 7AA
Telephone	+44 (0)20 7220 8200
Fax	+44 (0)20 7220 8290
Email	info@beaufort-group.com
Website	www.beaufort-group.com
Full Name	Jorg Wolfgang Bruniecki
Year of Birth	1978
Professional Qualifications	Information not available

PROFESSIONAL INFORMATION

CURRENT MAJOR POSITIONS/APPOINTMENTS

Non-Executive Director	Beaufort Underwriting Agency Limited	2007 -

PREVIOUS MAJOR POSITIONS/APPOINTMENTS

Information not available

Nigel JC Buchanan

Position	Non-Executive Director
Company	Amlin Underwriting Limited
Address (Office)	St Helen's
	1 Undershaft
	London EC3A 8ND
Telephone	+44 (0)20 7746 1000
Fax	+44 (0)20 7746 1696
Email	amlinreception@amlin.co.uk
Website	www.amlin.com
Full Name	Nigel James Cubitt Buchanan
Year of Birth	1943
Professional Qualifications	ACA

PROFESSIONAL INFORMATION

CURRENT MAJOR POSITIONS/APPOINTMENTS

Non-Executive Director	Butterfield Bank (UK) Limited	2001 -
Chairman	Amlin Group Plc Audit Committee	2005 -
Non-Executive Director	Amlin Underwriting Limited	2006 -

PREVIOUS MAJOR POSITIONS/APPOINTMENTS

Senior Client Partner	PricewaterhouseCoopers	Unknown - 2001
Member	Accounting Foundation, Ethics Standards Board	Unknown - 2002

Richard JS Bucknall

Position	Non-Executive Director
Company	Aspen Managing Agency Limited
Address (Office)	30 Fenchurch Street
	London EC3M 3BD
Telephone	+44 (0)20 7184 8000
Fax	+44 (0)20 7184 8500
Email	richardbucknall.theboard@aspen.bm
Website	www.aspen-re.com

Full Name	Richard John Stafford Bucknall
Year of Birth	1948
Professional Qualifications	Information not available

PROFESSIONAL INFORMATION

CURRENT MAJOR POSITIONS/APPOINTMENTS

Non-Executive Director	FIM Services Limited	2007 -
Non-Executive Director	Aspen Insurance UK Limited	2008 -
Non-Executive Director	Aspen Managing Agency Limited	2008 -
Non-Executive Director	Kron AS	Unknown -

PREVIOUS MAJOR POSITIONS/APPOINTMENTS

Vice Chairman	Willis Group Holdings Limited	2004 - 2007
Chief Executive	Willis Limited	2005 - 2007

Ralph Bull

Position	Chief Operating Officer
Company	Starr Managing Agents Limited
Address (Office)	3rd Floor
	140 Leadenhall Street
	London EC3V 4QT
Telephone	+44 (0)20 7337 3550
Fax	+44 (0)20 7337 3551
Email	ralph.bull@cvstarrco.com
Website	www.cvstarrco.com

Full Name	Ralph Bull
Year of Birth	1951
Professional Qualifications	Information not available

PROFESSIONAL INFORMATION

CURRENT MAJOR POSITIONS/APPOINTMENTS

Executive Director	Starr Managing Agents Ltd	2007 -

PREVIOUS MAJOR POSITIONS/APPOINTMENTS

Executive Director	Starr Underwriting Agents Limited	2006 - 2008

Nicolas J Burkinshaw

Position	Underwriting Director & Active Underwriter Syndicate 2003
Company	Catlin Underwriting Agencies Ltd
Address (Office)	6th Floor
	3 Minster Court
	Mincing Lane
	London EC3R 7DD
Telephone	+44 (0)20 7626 0486
Fax	+44 (0)20 7623 9101
Email	nicolas.burkinshaw@catlin.com
Website	www.catlin.com

Full Name	Nicolas John Burkinshaw
Year of Birth	1964
Professional Qualifications	Information not available

PROFESSIONAL INFORMATION

CURRENT MAJOR POSITIONS/APPOINTMENTS

Executive Director	Catlin Insurance Company (UK) Ltd	2006 -
Executive Director	Catlin Underwriting Agencies Ltd	2006 -

PREVIOUS MAJOR POSITIONS/APPOINTMENTS

Information not available

Steven P Burns

Position	Chief Executive Officer
Company	QBE Underwriting Limited
Address (Office)	Plantation Place
	30 Fenchurch Street
	London EC3M 3BD
Telephone	+44 (0)20 7105 4000
Fax	+44 (0)20 7105 4019
Email	enquiries@uk.qbe.com
Website	www.qbeeurope.com

PERSONAL PROFILE	A profile can be found in the People at Lloyd's, Personal section.

Timothy W Burrows

Position	Non-Executive Director
Company	Catlin Underwriting Agencies Ltd
Address (Office)	6th Floor
	3 Minster Court
	Mincing Lane
	London EC3R 7DD
Telephone	+44 (0)20 7626 0486
Fax	+44 (0)20 7623 9101
Email	catlininfo@catlin.com
Website	www.catlin.com

Full Name	Timothy William Burrows
Year of Birth	1953
Professional Qualifications	Information not available

PROFESSIONAL INFORMATION

CURRENT MAJOR POSITIONS/APPOINTMENTS

Non-Executive Director	Catlin Underwriting Agencies Ltd	2008 -
Non-Executive Director	Catlin Insurance Company (UK) Ltd	2008 -

PREVIOUS MAJOR POSITIONS/APPOINTMENTS

Executive Director	Catlin (Wellington) Underwriting Agencies Ltd	2001 - 2005

Thomas GS Busher

Position	Chairman
Company	Montpelier Underwriting Agencies Ltd
Address (Office)	7th Floor
	85 Gracechurch Street
	London EC3V 0AA
Telephone	+44 (0)20 7648 4500
Fax	+44 (0)20 7648 4501
Email	tom.busher@montpelier.bm
Website	www.montpelierre.com

Full Name	Thomas George Story Busher
Year of Birth	1955
Professional Qualifications	Information not available

PROFESSIONAL INFORMATION

CURRENT MAJOR POSITIONS/APPOINTMENTS

Executive Director	Montpelier Marketing Services (UK) Limited	2005 -
Executive Director	Montpelier Underwriting Agencies Ltd	2008 -

PREVIOUS MAJOR POSITIONS/APPOINTMENTS

Non-Executive Director	Spectrum Syndicate Management Limited	2007 - 2008

Jonathan LJ Butcher

Position	Executive Director & Active Underwriter Syndicate 2007
Company	Novae Syndicates Limited
Address (Office)	71 Fenchurch Street
	London EC3M 4HH
Telephone	+44 (0)20 7903 7300
Fax	+44 (0)20 7903 7333
Email	jbutcher@novae.com
Website	www.novae.com

Full Name	Jonathan Louis James Butcher
Year of Birth	1963
Professional Qualifications	ACII

PROFESSIONAL INFORMATION

CURRENT MAJOR POSITIONS/APPOINTMENTS

Executive Director	Novae Syndicates Limited	2002 -

PREVIOUS MAJOR POSITIONS/APPOINTMENTS

Non-Executive Director	Novae Underwriting Limited	2005 - 2005

Gina C Butterworth

Position	Risk Officer
Company	Chaucer Syndicates Limited
Address (Office)	Plantation Place
	30 Fenchurch Street
	London EC3M 3AD
Telephone	+44 (0)20 7397 9700
Fax	+44 (0)20 7397 9710
Email	gina.butterworth@chaucerplc.com
Website	www.chaucerplc.com
Full Name	Gina Claire Butterworth
Year of Birth	1973
Professional Qualifications	ACA

PROFESSIONAL INFORMATION

CURRENT MAJOR POSITIONS/APPOINTMENTS

Executive Director	Chaucer Syndicates Limited	2005 -

PREVIOUS MAJOR POSITIONS/APPOINTMENTS

	Pembroke Managing Agency Ltd	2007 - 2008

Mark C Butterworth

Position	Managing Director
Company	Pembroke Managing Agency Ltd
Address (Office)	2nd Floor
	3 Minster Court
	Mincing Lane
	London EC3R 7DD
Telephone	+44 (0)20 7337 4400
Fax	+44 (0)20 7337 4401
Email	mark.butterworth@pembrokeunderwriting.com
Website	www.pembrokeunderwriting.com
Full Name	Mark Condie Butterworth
Year of Birth	1952
Professional Qualifications	BA, MBA, FCII, FIRM

PROFESSIONAL INFORMATION

CURRENT MAJOR POSITIONS/APPOINTMENTS

Chief Executive	Pembroke Managing Agency Ltd	2007 -

PREVIOUS MAJOR POSITIONS/APPOINTMENTS

Executive Director	Liberty Syndicate Management Limited	2003 - 2007

Mark J Byrne

Position	Chairman
Company	Marlborough Underwriting Agency Ltd
Address (Office)	Birchin Court
	20 Birchin Lane
	London EC3V 9DU
Telephone	+44 (0)20 7456 1800
Fax	+44 (0)20 7456 1810
Email	compliance@marlborough.co.uk
Website	www.marlborough.co.uk
Full Name	Mark James Byrne
Year of Birth	1961
Professional Qualifications	Information not available

PROFESSIONAL INFORMATION

CURRENT MAJOR POSITIONS/APPOINTMENTS

Executive Director	Flagstone Representatives Ltd	2006 -
Non-Executive Director	Marlborough Underwriting Agency Ltd	2009 -

PREVIOUS MAJOR POSITIONS/APPOINTMENTS

Executive Director	Gen Re Securities Limited	2001 - 2002
Chief Executive	West End Capital Management Limited	2002 - 2003

Stephen P Cane

Position	Chief Executive Officer
Company	Whittington Capital Management Limited
Address (Office)	33 Creechurch Lane
	London EC3A 5EB
Telephone	+44 (0)20 7743 0900
Fax	+44 (0)20 7743 0901
Email	stephen.cane@whittingtoninsurance.com
Website	www.whittingtoninsurance.com
Full Name	Stephen Paul Cane
Year of Birth	1953
Professional Qualifications	Information not available

PROFESSIONAL INFORMATION

CURRENT MAJOR POSITIONS/APPOINTMENTS

Chief Executive	Whittington Capital Management Limited	2007 -
Executive Director	Reliance National Insurance Company (Europe) Ltd	2008 -

PREVIOUS MAJOR POSITIONS/APPOINTMENTS

Executive Director	Alea Financial UK Limited	2001 - 2006
Chief Executive	Alea London Limited	2001 - 2006

Paul CF Caprez

Position	Chief Financial Officer
Company	ARK Syndicate Management Limited
Address (Office)	8th Floor
	St Helen's
	1 Undershaft
	London EC3A 8EE
Telephone	+44 (0)20 3023 4020
Fax	+44 (0)20 3023 4000
Email	paul.caprez@arkunderwriting.com
Website	www.arkunderwriting.com

Full Name	Paul Charles Felix Caprez
Year of Birth	1962
Professional Qualifications	Information not available

PROFESSIONAL INFORMATION

CURRENT MAJOR POSITIONS/APPOINTMENTS

Executive Director	ARK Syndicate Management Limited	2008 -

PREVIOUS MAJOR POSITIONS/APPOINTMENTS

Information not available

Brian D Carpenter

Position	Underwriting Director, UK Commercial & Joint Active Underwriter Syndicate 2001
Company	Amlin Underwriting Limited
Address (Office)	St Helen's
	1 Undershaft
	London EC3A 8ND
Telephone	+44 (0)1245 214 875
Fax	+44 (0)20 7746 1696
Email	brian.carpenter@amlin.co.uk
Website	www.amlin.com

PERSONAL PROFILE	A profile can be found in the People at Lloyd's, Personal section.

Michael EA Carpenter

Position	Chairman
Company	Talbot Underwriting Ltd
Address (Office)	Gracechurch House
	55 Gracechurch Street
	London EC3V 0JP
Telephone	+44 (0)20 7550 3500
Fax	+44 (0)20 7550 3555
Email	michael.carpenter@talbotuw.com
Website	www.talbotuw.com

PERSONAL PROFILE	A profile can be found in the People at Lloyd's, Personal section.

Andrew J Carrier

Position	Non-Executive Director
Company	Argo Managing Agency Ltd
Address (Office)	47 Mark Lane
	London EC3R 7QQ
Telephone	+44 (0)20 7712 7600
Fax	+44 (0)20 7712 7601
Email	katie.gales@argo-int.com
Website	www.argo-int.com
Full Name	Andrew John Carrier
Year of Birth	1961
Professional Qualifications	Information not available

PROFESSIONAL INFORMATION

CURRENT MAJOR POSITIONS/APPOINTMENTS

Non-Executive Director	Argo Managing Agency Ltd	2008 -

PREVIOUS MAJOR POSITIONS/APPOINTMENTS

Executive Director	R J Kiln & Co Limited	2001 - 2007

Stephen (Steve) M Carroll

Position	Executive Director
Company	Markel Syndicate Management Limited
Address (Office)	The Markel Building
	49 Leadenhall Street
	London EC3A 2EA
Telephone	+44 (0)20 7953 6000
Fax	+44 (0)20 7953 6001
Email	steve.carroll@markelintl.com
Website	www.markelintl.com
Full Name	Stephen Michael Carroll
Year of Birth	Information not available
Professional Qualifications	Information not available

PROFESSIONAL INFORMATION

CURRENT MAJOR POSITIONS/APPOINTMENTS

Executive Director	Markel (UK) Limited	2005 -
Executive Director	Markel International Insurance Company Limited	2008 -
Executive Director	Markel Syndicate Management Limited	2008 -

PREVIOUS MAJOR POSITIONS/APPOINTMENTS

	Information not available

Richard G Carter

Position	Chairman
Company	Beaufort Underwriting Agency Limited

Address (Office)	Third Floor	
	One Minster Court	
	Mincing Lane	
	London EC3R 7AA	
Telephone	+44 (0)20 7220 8200	
Fax	+44 (0)20 7220 8290	
Email	info@beaufort-group.com	
Website	www.beaufort-group.com	

Full Name	Richard Graham Carter	
Year of Birth	1948	
Professional Qualifications	Information not available	

PROFESSIONAL INFORMATION

CURRENT MAJOR POSITIONS/APPOINTMENTS

Non-Executive Director	Beaufort Underwriting Agency Limited	2002 -

PREVIOUS MAJOR POSITIONS/APPOINTMENTS

Executive Director	Beaufort Underwriting Agency Limited	2001 - 2002

Stephen JO Catlin

Position	Chairman	
Company	Catlin Underwriting Agencies Ltd	
Address (Office)	6th Floor	
	3 Minster Court	
	Mincing Lane	
	London EC3R 7DD	
Telephone	+44 (0)20 7626 0486	
Fax	+44 (0)20 7623 9101	
Email	stephen.catlin@catlin.com	
Website	www.catlin.com	

Full Name	Stephen John Oakley Catlin	
Year of Birth	1954	
Professional Qualifications	Information not available	

PROFESSIONAL INFORMATION

CURRENT MAJOR POSITIONS/APPOINTMENTS

Executive Director	Catlin Underwriting Agencies Ltd	1991 -
Executive Director	Catlin Insurance Company (UK) Ltd	2005 -

PREVIOUS MAJOR POSITIONS/APPOINTMENTS

Director	Equitas Holdings Limited	1996 - 2002
Chairman	Lloyd's Market Association	2000 - 2003
Non-Executive Director	Equitas Limited	2001 - 2002
Non-Executive Director	Equitas Reinsurance Limited	2001 - 2002
Working Member	Council of Lloyd's	2002 - 2005
Non-Executive Director	Lloyd's Franchise Board	2003 - 2007

Simon N Catt

Position	Claims Director
Company	Travelers Syndicate Management Ltd
Address (Office)	Exchequer Court
	33 St Mary Axe
	London EC3A 8AG
Telephone	+44 (0)20 3207 6217
Fax	+44 (0)20 7621 0975
Email	scatt@travelers.com
Website	www.travelers.co.uk/lloyds
Full Name	Simon Nicholas Catt
Year of Birth	1965
Professional Qualifications	Information not available

PROFESSIONAL INFORMATION

CURRENT MAJOR POSITIONS/APPOINTMENTS

Executive Director	Travelers Syndicate Management Limited	2006 -

PREVIOUS MAJOR POSITIONS/APPOINTMENTS

Information not available

Paul NE Ceurvorst

Position	Joint Chief Underwriting Officer & Active Underwriter Syndicate 435
Company	Faraday Underwriting Limited
Address (Office)	5th Floor
	Corn Exchange
	55 Mark Lane
	London EC3R 7NE
Telephone	+44 (0)20 7264 4611
Fax	+44 (0)20 7680 4369
Email	paul.ceurvorst@faraday.com
Secretary/PA	Jill Clark
Email	jill.clark@faraday.com
Telephone	+44 (0)20 7680 4222
Website	www.faraday.com
Full Name	Paul Norman Edward Ceurvorst
Year of Birth	1960
Professional Qualifications	ACII

PROFESSIONAL INFORMATION

CURRENT MAJOR POSITIONS/APPOINTMENTS

Executive Director	Faraday Reinsurance Co Limited	2001 -
Executive Director	Faraday Underwriting Limited	2003 -
Member	ABI Liability Committee	Unknown -
Member	ABI GIC Members Forum	Unknown -

PREVIOUS MAJOR POSITIONS/APPOINTMENTS

Chief Executive	Faraday Reinsurance Co Limited	2001 - 2002

Gareth A Challingsworth

Position	Operations & IT Director
Company	Ascot Underwriting Limited
Address (Office)	Plantation Place
	30 Fenchurch Street
	London EC3M 3BD
Telephone	+44 (0)20 7743 9600
Fax	+44 (0)20 7743 9601
Email	gareth.challingsworth@ascotuw.com
Website	www.ascotuw.com
Full Name	Gareth Ashley Challingsworth
Year of Birth	1967
Professional Qualifications	Information not available

PROFESSIONAL INFORMATION

CURRENT MAJOR POSITIONS/APPOINTMENTS

Executive Director	Ascot Underwriting Limited	2008 -

PREVIOUS MAJOR POSITIONS/APPOINTMENTS

Information not available

John E Chambers

Position	Executive Director
Company	AEGIS Managing Agency Ltd
Address (Office)	110 Fenchurch Street
	London EC3M 5JT
Telephone	+44 (0)20 7265 2129
Fax	+44 (0)20 7265 2101
Email	jchambers@aegislondon.co.uk
Website	www.aegislink.com
Full Name	John Edmond Chambers
Year of Birth	1965
Professional Qualifications	ACII

PROFESSIONAL INFORMATION

CURRENT MAJOR POSITIONS/APPOINTMENTS

Executive Director	AEGIS Managing Agency Ltd	2000 -

PREVIOUS MAJOR POSITIONS/APPOINTMENTS

Information not available

Neil R Chapman

Position	Executive Director & Joint Active Underwriter,
	Property Division Syndicate 1200
Company	Argo Managing Agency Ltd
Address (Office)	47 Mark Lane
	London EC3R 7QQ

Telephone	+44 (0)20 7712 7600
Fax	+44 (0)20 7712 7601
Email	neil.chapman@argo-int.com
Website	www.argo-int.com

Full Name	Neil Richard Chapman
Year of Birth	1958
Professional Qualifications	Information not available

PROFESSIONAL INFORMATION

CURRENT MAJOR POSITIONS/APPOINTMENTS

Executive Director	Argo Managing Agency Ltd	2008 -

PREVIOUS MAJOR POSITIONS/APPOINTMENTS

Executive Director	Catlin (Wellington) Underwriting Agencies Limited	2001 - 2006

Colin D Charles

Position	Financial Director
Company	Mitsui Sumitomo Insurance Underwriting at Lloyd's Ltd
Address (Office)	25 Fenchurch Avenue
	London EC3M 5AD
Telephone	+44 (0)20 7977 8374
Fax	+44 (0)20 7977 8300
Email	ccharles@msilm.com
Website	www.msilm.com

Full Name	Colin David Charles
Year of Birth	1959
Professional Qualifications	ACA

PROFESSIONAL INFORMATION

CURRENT MAJOR POSITIONS/APPOINTMENTS

Executive Director	Mitsui Sumitomo Insurance (London) Limited	2005 -
Executive Director	Mitsui Sumitomo Insurance Underwriting at Lloyd's Ltd	2006 -

PREVIOUS MAJOR POSITIONS/APPOINTMENTS

Information not available

Richard MM Chattock

Position	Executive Director & Active Underwriter Syndicate 5151
Company	Montpelier Underwriting Agencies Ltd
Address (Office)	7th Floor
	85 Gracechurch Street
	London EC3V 0AA
Telephone	+44 (0)20 7648 4500
Fax	+44 (0)20 7648 4501
Email	richard.chattock@montpelierua.com
Website	www.montpelierre.com

Full Name	Richard Michael Maguire Chattock	
Year of Birth	1963	
Professional Qualifications	Information not available	

PROFESSIONAL INFORMATION

CURRENT MAJOR POSITIONS/APPOINTMENTS

Executive Director	Montpelier Underwriting Agencies Ltd	2008 -

PREVIOUS MAJOR POSITIONS/APPOINTMENTS

Executive Director	Spectrum Syndicate Management Limited	2007 - 2008

Paul A Chubb

Position	Finance Director
Company	Marlborough Underwriting Agency Ltd
Address (Office)	Birchin Court
	20 Birchin Lane
	London EC3V 9DU
Telephone	+44 (0)20 7456 1800
Fax	+44 (0)20 7456 1810
Email	paul.chubb@marlborough.co.uk
Website	www.marlborough.co.uk

Position	Non-Executive Director
Company	Starr Managing Agents Limited
Address (Office)	3rd Floor
	140 Leadenhall Street
	London EC3V 4QT
Telephone	+44 (0)20 7337 3550
Fax	+44 (0)20 7337 3551
Email	paul.chubb@cvstarrco.com
Website	www.cvstarrco.com

Full Name	Paul Alan Chubb
Year of Birth	1961
Professional Qualifications	Information not available

PROFESSIONAL INFORMATION

CURRENT MAJOR POSITIONS/APPOINTMENTS

Executive Director	Marlborough Underwriting Agency Ltd	2001 -
Non-Executive Director	Starr Managing Agents Ltd	2007 -

PREVIOUS MAJOR POSITIONS/APPOINTMENTS

	Information not available

Richard M Clapham

Position	Executive Director
Company	Catlin Underwriting Agencies Ltd

Address (Office)	6th Floor
	3 Minster Court
	Mincing Lane
	London EC3R 7DD
Telephone	+44 (0)20 7626 0486
Fax	+44 (0)20 7623 9101
Email	richard.clapham@catlin.com
Website	www.catlin.com
Full Name	Richard Malcolm Clapham
Year of Birth	1964
Professional Qualifications	Information not available

PROFESSIONAL INFORMATION

CURRENT MAJOR POSITIONS/APPOINTMENTS

Executive Director	Catlin Insurance Company (UK) Ltd	2005 -
Executive Director	Catlin Underwriting Agencies Ltd	2005 -

PREVIOUS MAJOR POSITIONS/APPOINTMENTS

Executive Director	BRIT Insurance (UK) Ltd	2002 - 2003

Robert JI Clark

Position	Executive Director & Compliance Officer
Company	Aspen Managing Agency Limited
Address (Office)	30 Fenchurch Street
	London EC3M 3BD
Telephone	+44 (0)20 7184 8000
Fax	+44 (0)20 7184 8500
Email	c/o robert.long@aspen-re.com
Website	www.aspen-re.com
Full Name	Robert James Ingham Clark
Year of Birth	1959
Professional Qualifications	Information not available

PROFESSIONAL INFORMATION

CURRENT MAJOR POSITIONS/APPOINTMENTS

Executive Director	Aspen Managing Agency Limited	2008 -

PREVIOUS MAJOR POSITIONS/APPOINTMENTS

Information not available

Harold E Clarke

Position	Independent Review Director
Company	Equity Syndicate Management Limited
Address (Office)	Library House
	New Road
	Brentwood
	Essex CM14 4GD

Telephone	+44 (0)1277 200 100
Fax	+44 (0)1206 777 223
Email	info@equitygroup.co.uk
Website	www.equitygroup.co.uk

Full Name	Harold Edward Clarke
Year of Birth	1951
Professional Qualifications	Information not available

PROFESSIONAL INFORMATION

CURRENT MAJOR POSITIONS/APPOINTMENTS

Non-Executive Director	Equity Syndicate Management Limited	2008 -
Non-Executive Director	MDU Services Limited	2008 -

PREVIOUS MAJOR POSITIONS/APPOINTMENTS

Information not available

Jane S Clouting

Position	Compliance Director & Company Secretary
Company	Talbot Underwriting Ltd
Address (Office)	Gracechurch House
	55 Gracechurch Street
	London EC3V 0JP
Telephone	+44 (0)20 7550 3500
Fax	+44 (0)20 7550 3555
Email	jane.clouting@talbotuw.com
Website	www.talbotuw.com

Full Name	Jane Sarah Clouting
Year of Birth	1957
Professional Qualifications	Information not available

PROFESSIONAL INFORMATION

CURRENT MAJOR POSITIONS/APPOINTMENTS

Executive Director	Talbot Underwriting Ltd	1996 -
Executive Director	Underwriting Risk Services Ltd	2005 -

PREVIOUS MAJOR POSITIONS/APPOINTMENTS

Information not available

Henry NA Colthurst

Position	Executive Director
Company	Equity Syndicate Management Limited
Address (Office)	Library House
	New Road
	Brentwood
	Essex CM14 4GD
Telephone	+44 (0)1277 200 100
Fax	+44 (0)1206 777 223

Email	info@equitygroup.co.uk
Website	www.equitygroup.co.uk

Full Name	Henry Nicholas Almroth Colthurst
Year of Birth	1959
Professional Qualifications	Information not available

PROFESSIONAL INFORMATION

CURRENT MAJOR POSITIONS/APPOINTMENTS

Non-Executive Director	MV Reinsurance Advisors Ltd	2006 -
Executive Director	Equity Syndicate Management Limited	2008 -

PREVIOUS MAJOR POSITIONS/APPOINTMENTS
Information not available

Joseph E Consolino

Position	Non-Executive Director
Company	Talbot Underwriting Ltd
Address (Office)	Gracechurch House
	55 Gracechurch Street
	London EC3V 0JP
Telephone	+44 (0)20 7550 3500
Fax	+44 (0)20 7550 3555
Email	central@talbotuw.com
Website	www.talbotuw.com

Full Name	Joseph Evans Consolino
Year of Birth	1966
Professional Qualifications	Information not available

PROFESSIONAL INFORMATION

CURRENT MAJOR POSITIONS/APPOINTMENTS

Non-Executive Director	Talbot Underwriting Ltd	2007 -

PREVIOUS MAJOR POSITIONS/APPOINTMENTS
Information not available

David A Constable

Position	Underwriting Director & Active Underwriter Syndicate 386
Company	QBE Underwriting Limited
Address (Office)	Plantation Place
	30 Fenchurch Street
	London EC3M 3BD
Telephone	+44 (0)20 7105 4000
Fax	+44 (0)20 7105 4019
Email	enquiries@uk.qbe.com
Website	www.qbeeurope.com

PERSONAL PROFILE	A profile can be found in the People at Lloyd's, Personal section.

Histasp A Contractor

Position	Chief Financial Officer
Company	Sagicor at Lloyd's Limited
Address (Office)	1 Great Tower Street
	London EC3R 5AA
Telephone	+44 (0)20 3003 6800
Fax	+44 (0)20 3003 6999
Email	histasp.contractor@sagicor.eu
Website	www.sagicor.com

Full Name	Histasp Aspi Contractor
Year of Birth	1962
Professional Qualifications	ACA

PROFESSIONAL INFORMATION

CURRENT MAJOR POSITIONS/APPOINTMENTS

Executive Director	Sagicor at Lloyd's Limited	2001 -
Executive Director	Sagicor Syndicate Services Ltd	2005 -
Executive Director	Byrne and Stacey Underwriting Limited	2007 -

PREVIOUS MAJOR POSITIONS/APPOINTMENTS

Information not available

Alison C Cook

Position	Claims Director
Company	Munich Re Underwriting Limited
Address (Office)	St Helen's
	1 Undershaft
	London EC3A 8EE
Telephone	+44 (0)20 7886 3900
Fax	+44 (0)20 7886 3901
Email	alison.cook@mrunderwriting.com
Website	www.watkins-syndicate.co.uk

Full Name	Alison Clare Cook
Year of Birth	1964
Professional Qualifications	Information not available

PROFESSIONAL INFORMATION

CURRENT MAJOR POSITIONS/APPOINTMENTS

Executive Director	Munich Re Underwriting Limited	2006 -

PREVIOUS MAJOR POSITIONS/APPOINTMENTS

Information not available

Steven J Cook

Position	Chief Executive Officer
Company	Atrium Underwriters Limited

Address (Office)	Room 790
	Lloyd's
	One Lime Street
	London EC3M 7DQ
Telephone	+44 (0)20 7327 4877
Fax	+44 (0)20 7327 4878
Email	info@atrium-uw.com
Website	www.atrium-uw.com
Full Name	Steven James Cook
Year of Birth	1964
Professional Qualifications	BSc (Hons), ACA

PROFESSIONAL INFORMATION

CURRENT MAJOR POSITIONS/APPOINTMENTS

Executive Director	Atrium Underwriters Limited	1997 -
Chief Executive	Atrium Underwriters Limited	1997 -
Executive Director	Atrium Insurance Agency Limited	2007 -
Member	Lloyd's Market Association, Capital Committee	Unknown -

PREVIOUS MAJOR POSITIONS/APPOINTMENTS

Partner	M H Cockell & Partners	1996 - 1997
Managing Director	Atrium Underwriting plc	2003 - 2005

John A Cooper

Position	Non-Executive Director
Company	Munich Re Underwriting Limited
Address (Office)	St Helen's
	1 Undershaft
	London EC3A 8EE
Telephone	+44 (0)20 7886 3900
Fax	+44 (0)20 7886 3901
Email	central@mrunderwriting.com
Website	www.watkins-syndicate.co.uk
Full Name	John Anthony Cooper
Year of Birth	1943
Professional Qualifications	ACII

PROFESSIONAL INFORMATION

CURRENT MAJOR POSITIONS/APPOINTMENTS

Non-Executive Director	Munich Re Underwriting Limited	2007 -

PREVIOUS MAJOR POSITIONS/APPOINTMENTS

Executive Director	Navigators Insurance Company	2001 - 2002
Executive Director	Navigators Underwriting Agency Ltd	2001 - 2002
Non-Executive Director	SSL Insurance Brokers Limited	2005 - 2007

Simon D Cooper

Position	Chief Operating Officer
Company	Atrium Underwriters Limited
Address (Office)	Room 790
	Lloyd's
	One Lime Street
	London EC3M 7DQ
Telephone	+44 (0)20 7327 4877
Fax	+44 (0)20 7327 4878
Email	info@atrium-uw.com
Website	www.atrium-uw.com

Full Name	Simon David Cooper
Year of Birth	1964
Professional Qualifications	ACII

PROFESSIONAL INFORMATION

CURRENT MAJOR POSITIONS/APPOINTMENTS

Executive Director	Atrium Underwriters Limited	2004 -
Executive Director	Atrium Insurance Agency Limited	2007 -

PREVIOUS MAJOR POSITIONS/APPOINTMENTS

Deputy Chairman	Joint Hull Committee

Oliver RP Corbett

Position	Non-Executive Director
Company	Novae Syndicates Limited
Address (Office)	71 Fenchurch Street
	London EC3M 4HH
Telephone	+44 (0)20 7903 7300
Fax	+44 (0)20 7903 7333
Email	ocorbett@novae.com
Website	www.novae.com

Full Name	Oliver Roebling Panton Corbett
Year of Birth	1965
Professional Qualifications	ACA

PROFESSIONAL INFORMATION

CURRENT MAJOR POSITIONS/APPOINTMENTS

Non-Executive Director	Novae Syndicates Limited	2003 -
Non-Executive Director	Rathbone Brothers plc	Unknown -
Chairman	Rathbone Brothers plc, Investment Committee	Unknown -
Member	Rathbone Brothers plc, Risk Committee	Unknown -

PREVIOUS MAJOR POSITIONS/APPOINTMENTS

Partner	Phoenix Securities	1999 - 2000
Non-Executive Director	Fusion Insurance Services Ltd	2005 - 2005
Managing Director	Dresdner Kleinwort Wasserstein	Unknown - 2003

Thomas RC Corfield

Position	Underwriting Director & Active Underwriter Syndicate 4472
Company	Liberty Syndicate Management Limited
Address (Office)	5th Floor
	Plantation Place South
	60 Great Tower Street
	London EC3R 5AZ
Telephone	+44 (0)20 7070 4472
Fax	+44 (0)20 7863 1001
Email	tom.corfield@libertygroup.co.uk
Website	www.libertysyndicates.com
Full Name	Thomas Rokeby Conyngham Corfield
Year of Birth	1962
Professional Qualifications	Information not available

PROFESSIONAL INFORMATION

CURRENT MAJOR POSITIONS/APPOINTMENTS

Executive Director	Liberty Syndicate Management Limited	1998 -
Member	Lloyd's Market Association Board	Unknown -

PREVIOUS MAJOR POSITIONS/APPOINTMENTS

External Member	Council of Lloyd's	2006 - 2007

Timur (Tim) Coskun

Position	Compliance Director & Company Secretary
Company	Munich Re Underwriting Limited
Address (Office)	St Helen's
	1 Undershaft
	London EC3A 8EE
Telephone	+44 (0)20 7886 3900
Fax	+44 (0)20 7886 3901
Email	tim.coskun@mrunderwriting.com
Website	www.watkins-syndicate.co.uk
Full Name	Timur Coskun
Year of Birth	1959
Professional Qualifications	MSc, ACA

PROFESSIONAL INFORMATION

CURRENT MAJOR POSITIONS/APPOINTMENTS

Executive Director	Munich Re Underwriting Limited	2001 -
Non-Executive Director	Northern Marine Underwriters Ltd	2005 -

PREVIOUS MAJOR POSITIONS/APPOINTMENTS

Information not available

Stephen R Coward

Position	Chief Operating Officer
Company	Navigators Underwriting Agency Ltd
Address (Office)	7th Floor
	2 Minster Court
	Mincing Lane
	London EC3R 7BB
Telephone	+44 (0)20 7220 6900
Fax	+44 (0)20 7220 6901
Email	scoward@navg.com
Website	www.navg.com
Full Name	Stephen Richard Coward
Year of Birth	1954
Professional Qualifications	Information not available

PROFESSIONAL INFORMATION

CURRENT MAJOR POSITIONS/APPOINTMENTS

Executive Director	Navigators Underwriting Agency Ltd	2005 -
Chief Executive	Navigators Underwriting Agency Ltd	2006 -

PREVIOUS MAJOR POSITIONS/APPOINTMENTS

Information not available

Adrian P Cox

Position	Executive Director & Head of Specialty Lines
Company	Beazley Furlonge Ltd
Address (Office)	Plantation Place South
	60 Great Tower Street
	London EC3R 5AD
Telephone	+44 (0)20 7667 0623
Fax	+44 (0)20 7674 7100
Email	adrian.cox@beazley.com
Website	www.beazley.com
Full Name	Adrian Peter Cox
Year of Birth	1971
Professional Qualifications	Information not available

PROFESSIONAL INFORMATION

CURRENT MAJOR POSITIONS/APPOINTMENTS

Executive Director	Beazley Furlonge Ltd	2008 -
Executive Director	Beazley Solutions Limited	2009 -

PREVIOUS MAJOR POSITIONS/APPOINTMENTS

Information not available

Malcolm J Cox

Position	Independent Review Director
Company	Beaufort Underwriting Agency Limited
Address (Office)	Third Floor
	One Minster Court
	Mincing Lane
	London EC3R 7AA
Telephone	+44 (0)20 7220 8200
Fax	+44 (0)20 7220 8290
Email	info@beaufort-group.com
Website	www.beaufort-group.com

Position	Non-Executive Director
Company	Chaucer Syndicates Limited
Address (Office)	Plantation Place
	30 Fenchurch Street
	London EC3M 3AD
Telephone	+44 (0)20 7397 9700
Fax	+44 (0)20 7397 9710
Email	malcolm.cox@chaucerplc.com
Website	www.chaucerplc.com

Full Name	Malcolm John Cox
Year of Birth	1949
Professional Qualifications	Information not available

PROFESSIONAL INFORMATION

CURRENT MAJOR POSITIONS/APPOINTMENTS

Non-Executive Director	Chaucer Syndicates Limited	2001 -
Non-Executive Director	Beaufort Underwriting Agency Limited	2001 -

PREVIOUS MAJOR POSITIONS/APPOINTMENTS

Executive Director	Denham Syndicate Management Ltd	2001 - 2002
Non-Executive Director	AE Grant (Underwriting Agencies) Ltd	2001 - 2003
Chief Executive	Morgan, Fentiman and Barber	2001 - 2003

Oliver J Crabtree

Position	Executive Director & Joint Active Underwriter Syndicate 457
Company	Munich Re Underwriting Limited
Address (Office)	St Helen's
	1 Undershaft
	London EC3A 8EE
Telephone	+44 (0)20 7886 3900
Fax	+44 (0)20 7886 3901
Email	oliver.crabtree@mrunderwriting.com
Website	www.watkins-syndicate.co.uk

Full Name	Oliver John Crabtree
Year of Birth	1960
Professional Qualifications	ACII

PROFESSIONAL INFORMATION

CURRENT MAJOR POSITIONS/APPOINTMENTS

Executive Director	Munich Re Underwriting Limited	2001 -
Non-Executive Director	Groves, John and Westrup Ltd	2005 -

PREVIOUS MAJOR POSITIONS/APPOINTMENTS

Information not available

Matthew F Crane

Position	Underwriting Director
Company	QBE Underwriting Limited
Address (Office)	Plantation Place
	30 Fenchurch Street
	London EC3M 3BD
Telephone	+44 (0)20 7105 4000
Fax	+44 (0)20 7105 4019
Email	enquiries@uk.qbe.com
Website	www.qbeeurope.com

Full Name	Matthew Francis Crane
Year of Birth	1972
Professional Qualifications	Information not available

PROFESSIONAL INFORMATION

CURRENT MAJOR POSITIONS/APPOINTMENTS

Executive Director	QBE Insurance (Europe) Limited	2005 -
Executive Director	QBE Underwriting Limited	2008 -

PREVIOUS MAJOR POSITIONS/APPOINTMENTS

Executive Director	QBE Insurance Company (UK) Limited	2005 - 2006

Edward G Creasy

Position	Chairman
Company	R J Kiln & Co Limited
Address (Office)	106 Fenchurch Street
	London EC3M 5NR
Telephone	+44 (0)20 7886 9000
Fax	+44 (0)20 7488 1848
Email	edward.creasey@kilngroup.com
Website	www.kilnplc.com

PERSONAL PROFILE	A profile can be found in the People at Lloyd's, Personal section.

Peter WJ Cresswell

Position	Chairman
Company	Advent Underwriting Limited

Address (Office)	10th Floor
	One Minster Court
	Mincing Lane
	London EC3R 7AA
Telephone	+44 (0)20 7743 8200
Fax	+44 (0)20 7743 8299
Email	head.office@adventgroup.co.uk
Website	www.adventgroup.co.uk

Full Name	Peter William John Cresswell
Year of Birth	1944
Professional Qualifications	Information not available

PROFESSIONAL INFORMATION

CURRENT MAJOR POSITIONS/APPOINTMENTS

Non-Executive Director	Advent Underwriting Limited	1999 -

PREVIOUS MAJOR POSITIONS/APPOINTMENTS
Information not available

David P Croom-Johnson

Position	Underwriting Director & Active Underwriter Syndicate 1225
Company	AEGIS Managing Agency Ltd
Address (Office)	110 Fenchurch Street
	London EC3M 5JT
Telephone	+44 (0)20 7265 2130
Fax	+44 (0)20 7265 2101
Email	dcroom-johnson@aegislondon.co.uk
Website	www.aegislink.com

Full Name	David Patrick Croom-Johnson
Year of Birth	1963
Professional Qualifications	ACII

PROFESSIONAL INFORMATION

CURRENT MAJOR POSITIONS/APPOINTMENTS

Executive Director	AEGIS Managing Agency Ltd	2000 -

PREVIOUS MAJOR POSITIONS/APPOINTMENTS
Information not available

Paul M Culham

Position	Executive Director
Company	R J Kiln & Co Limited
Address (Office)	106 Fenchurch Street
	London EC3M 5NR
Telephone	+44 (0)20 7886 9000
Fax	+44 (0)20 7488 1848

Email	paul.culham@kilngroup.com	
Website	www.kilnplc.com	

Full Name	Paul Michael Culham	
Year of Birth	1965	
Professional Qualifications	ACII	

PROFESSIONAL INFORMATION

CURRENT MAJOR POSITIONS/APPOINTMENTS

Executive Director	R J Kiln & Co Limited	2007 -

PREVIOUS MAJOR POSITIONS/APPOINTMENTS

Information not available

Kenneth Culley, CBE

Position	Non-Executive Director
Company	Brit Syndicates Limited
Address (Office)	2nd Floor
	55 Bishopsgate
	London EC2N 3AS
Telephone	+44 (0)20 7984 8500
Fax	+44 (0)20 7984 8501
Email	kenneth.culley@britinsurance.com
Website	www.britinsurance.com

Full Name	Kenneth Culley, CBE
Year of Birth	1942
Professional Qualifications	FCIB

PROFESSIONAL INFORMATION

CURRENT MAJOR POSITIONS/APPOINTMENTS

Non-Executive Director	BRIT Insurance Limited	2001 -
Non-Executive Director	Marks & Spencer Financial Services Plc	2001 -
Non-Executive Director	Brit Syndicates Limited	2004 -

PREVIOUS MAJOR POSITIONS/APPOINTMENTS

Non-Executive Director	JP Morgan Fleming Managed Income plc	2000 - 2002
Non-Executive Director	Marks & Spencer Savings and Investments Ltd	2001 - 2004
Non-Executive Director	Marks & Spencer Unit Trust Management Limited	2001 - 2004
Non-Executive Director	Marks and Spencer Life Assurance Limited	2001 - 2004
Director	Financial Services Compensation Scheme	2002 - 2005
Non-Executive Director	BRIT Insurance (UK) Ltd	2003 - 2007
Deputy President	International Union for Housing Finance Institutions	Unknown - 1999
Chairman	Building Societies Association	Unknown

Kenneth (Ken) D Curtis

Position	Financial Director
Company	Chaucer Syndicates Limited

Address (Office)	Plantation Place
	30 Fenchurch Street
	London EC3M 3AD
Telephone	+44 (0)20 7397 9700
Fax	+44 (0)20 7397 9710
Email	ken.curtis@chaucerplc.com
Website	www.chaucerplc.com
Full Name	Kenneth Douglas Curtis
Year of Birth	1961
Professional Qualifications	BA (Econ), ACA

PROFESSIONAL INFORMATION

CURRENT MAJOR POSITIONS/APPOINTMENTS

Executive Director	Chaucer Syndicates Limited	2003 -

PREVIOUS MAJOR POSITIONS/APPOINTMENTS

Executive Director	Pembroke Managing Agency Ltd	2007 - 2008

Philippa M Curtis

Position	Chief Financial Officer
Company	Ace Underwriting Agencies Limited
Address (Office)	100 Leadenhall Street
	London EC3A 3BP
Telephone	+44 (0)20 7173 7711
Fax	+44 (0)20 7173 7800
Email	philippa.curtis@ace-ina.com
Website	www.acelimited.com
Full Name	Philippa Mary Curtis
Year of Birth	1960
Professional Qualifications	Information not available

PROFESSIONAL INFORMATION

CURRENT MAJOR POSITIONS/APPOINTMENTS

Executive Director	Ace Underwriting Agencies Limited	1998 -
Executive Director	Ridge Underwriting Agencies Limited	2000 -
Executive Director	ACE European Group Limited	2001 -
Executive Director	ACE Europe Life Limited	2007 -

PREVIOUS MAJOR POSITIONS/APPOINTMENTS

Executive Director	ACE London Aviation Limited	2001 - 2003
Executive Director	ACE London Underwriting Limited	2001 - 2003
Executive Director	R&Q Reinsurance Company (UK) Limited	2001 - 2005

Paul M Cusition

Position	Ceded Reinsurance & Independent Review Director
Company	Travelers Syndicate Management Ltd

Address (Office)	Exchequer Court	
	33 St Mary Axe	
	London EC3A 8AG	
Telephone	+44 (0)20 3207 6870	
Fax	+44 (0)20 7645 4526	
Email	pcusition@travelers.com	
Website	www.travelers.co.uk/lloyds	

Full Name	Paul Michael Cusition	
Year of Birth	1956	
Professional Qualifications	Information not available	

PROFESSIONAL INFORMATION

CURRENT MAJOR POSITIONS/APPOINTMENTS

Executive Director	Solicitors Professional Indemnity Ltd	2005 -
Executive Director	St Paul Travelers Professional Risks Ltd	2005 -
Executive Director	Travelers Syndicate Management Limited	2006 -

PREVIOUS MAJOR POSITIONS/APPOINTMENTS

Information not available

William RP Dalton

Position	Non-Executive Director	
Company	AEGIS Managing Agency Ltd	
Address (Office)	110 Fenchurch Street	
	London EC3M 5JT	
Telephone	+44 (0)20 7265 2100	
Fax	+44 (0)20 7265 2101	
Email	enquiries@aegislink.com	
Website	www.aegislink.com	

Full Name	William Robert Patrick Dalton	
Year of Birth	1943	
Professional Qualifications	Information not available	

PROFESSIONAL INFORMATION

CURRENT MAJOR POSITIONS/APPOINTMENTS

Non-Executive Director	AEGIS Managing Agency Ltd	2005 -

PREVIOUS MAJOR POSITIONS/APPOINTMENTS

Non-Executive Director	Merrill Lynch HSBC Limited	2001 - 2002
Chief Executive	HSBC Bank Plc	2001 - 2004
Non-Executive Director	Swiss Re Life & Health Limited	2005 - 2006
Non-Executive Director	Swiss Reinsurance Company UK Limited	2005 - 2006
Non-Executive Director	The Mercantile & General Reinsurance	
	Company Ltd	2005 - 2006

Mark I Daly

Position	Chief Operating Officer	
Company	Omega Underwriting Agents Ltd	

Address (Office)	4th Floor
	New London House
	6 London Street
	London EC3R 7LP
Telephone	+44 (0)20 7767 3000
Fax	+44 (0)20 7488 9639
Email	mark.daly@omegauw.com
Website	www.omegauw.com

Full Name	Mark Ian Daly
Year of Birth	1965
Professional Qualifications	Information not available

PROFESSIONAL INFORMATION

CURRENT MAJOR POSITIONS/APPOINTMENTS

Executive Director	Omega Underwriting Agents Ltd	2000 -

PREVIOUS MAJOR POSITIONS/APPOINTMENTS

Information not available

Rodney G Dampier

Position	Head of Aviation
Company	Amlin Underwriting Limited
Address (Office)	St Helen's
	1 Undershaft
	London EC3A 8ND
Telephone	+44 (0)20 7746 1000
Fax	+44 (0)20 7746 1696
Email	rodney.dampier@amlin.co.uk
Website	www.amlin.com

Full Name	Rodney Guy Dampier
Year of Birth	1949
Professional Qualifications	ACA, FCII

PROFESSIONAL INFORMATION

CURRENT MAJOR POSITIONS/APPOINTMENTS

Executive Director	Amlin Underwriting Limited	1998 -
Member	Royal Aeronautical Society	Unknown -
Member	Lloyd's Market Association Board	Unknown -
Member	Lloyd's Aviation Committee	Unknown -

PREVIOUS MAJOR POSITIONS/APPOINTMENTS

Senior Underwriter	BAIG	1991 - 1997

Christine E Dandridge

Position	Non-Executive Director
Company	Managing Agency Partners Limited

Address (Office)	1st Floor
	110 Fenchurch Street
	London EC3M 5JT
Telephone	+44 (0)20 7709 3860
Fax	+44 (0)20 7709 3861
Email	map@mapunderwriting.co.uk
Website	www.mapunderwriting.co.uk
PERSONAL PROFILE	A profile can be found in the People at Lloyd's, Personal section.

Andrew J Davies

Position	Finance Director
Company	Markel Syndicate Management Limited
Address (Office)	The Markel Building
	49 Leadenhall Street
	London EC3A 2EA
Telephone	+44 (0)20 7953 6000
Fax	+44 (0)20 7953 6001
Email	andy.davies@markelintl.com
Website	www.markelintl.com
PERSONAL PROFILE	A profile can be found in the People at Lloyd's, Personal section.

Sarah A Davies

Position	Operations Director
Company	AEGIS Managing Agency Ltd
Address (Office)	110 Fenchurch Street
	London EC3M 5JT
Telephone	+44 (0)20 7265 2110
Fax	+44 (0)20 7265 2101
Email	sdavies@aegislondon.co.uk
Website	www.aegislink.com
Full Name	Sarah Ann Davies
Year of Birth	1964
Professional Qualifications	MBA, FCII

PROFESSIONAL INFORMATION

CURRENT MAJOR POSITIONS/APPOINTMENTS

Executive Director	AEGIS Managing Agency Ltd	2007 -

PREVIOUS MAJOR POSITIONS/APPOINTMENTS

Executive Director	Catlin (Wellington) Underwriting Agencies Limited	2001 - 2002
Executive Director	Aspen Insurance UK Limited	2002 - 2006

Stuart R Davies

Position	Managing Director
Company	AEGIS Managing Agency Ltd
Address (Office)	110 Fenchurch Street
	London EC3M 5JT
Telephone	+44 (0)20 7265 2152
Fax	+44 (0)20 7265 2101
Email	sdavies@aegislondon.co.uk
Website	www.aegislink.com

Full Name	Stuart Robert Davies
Year of Birth	1967
Professional Qualifications	ACA

PROFESSIONAL INFORMATION

CURRENT MAJOR POSITIONS/APPOINTMENTS

Executive Director	AEGIS Managing Agency Ltd	2005 -
Chief Executive	AEGIS Managing Agency Ltd	2004 -

PREVIOUS MAJOR POSITIONS/APPOINTMENTS

Executive Director	Highway Insurance Agency Limited	2001 - 2004
Executive Director	Highway Insurance Company Limited	2001 - 2004

William (Bill) J Davis

Position	Non-Executive Director
Company	Novae Syndicates Limited
Address (Office)	71 Fenchurch Street
	London EC3M 4HH
Telephone	+44 (0)20 7903 7300
Fax	+44 (0)20 7903 7333
Email	bdavis@novae.com
Website	www.novae.com

PERSONAL PROFILE	A profile can be found in the People at Lloyd's, Personal section.

Andrew S Dawe

Position	Chief Executive Officer
Company	Beaufort Underwriting Agency Limited
Address (Office)	Third Floor
	One Minster Court
	Mincing Lane
	London EC3R 7AA
Telephone	+44 (0)20 7220 8200
Fax	+44 (0)20 7220 8290
Email	andrew.dawe@beaufort-group.com
Website	www.beaufort-group.com

Full Name	Andrew Steven Dawe
Year of Birth	1966
Professional Qualifications	Information not available

PROFESSIONAL INFORMATION

CURRENT MAJOR POSITIONS/APPOINTMENTS

Executive Director	Beaufort Underwriting Agency Limited	2000 -

PREVIOUS MAJOR POSITIONS/APPOINTMENTS

Information not available

Sir Richard B Dearlove

Position	Chairman
Company	Ascot Underwriting Limited
Address (Office)	Plantation Place
	30 Fenchurch Street
	London EC3M 3BD
Telephone	+44 (0)20 7743 9600
Fax	+44 (0)20 7743 9601
Email	enquiries@ascotuw.com
Website	www.ascotuw.com

Full Name	Sir Richard Billing Dearlove
Year of Birth	1945
Professional Qualifications	Information not available

PROFESSIONAL INFORMATION

CURRENT MAJOR POSITIONS/APPOINTMENTS

Non-Executive Director	Ascot Underwriting Limited	2006 -

PREVIOUS MAJOR POSITIONS/APPOINTMENTS

Information not available

Nicholas GA Denniston

Position	Chief Financial Officer
Company	Argo Managing Agency Ltd
Address (Office)	47 Mark Lane
	London EC3R 7QQ
Telephone	+44 (0)20 7712 7600
Fax	+44 (0)20 7712 7601
Email	nick.denniston@argo-int.com
Website	www.argo-int.com

PERSONAL PROFILE	A profile can be found in the People at Lloyd's, Personal section.

Aneil (Neil) P Deshpande

Position	Operations Director
Company	ARK Syndicate Management Limited

Address (Office)	8th Floor
	St Helen's
	1 Undershaft
	London EC3A 8EE
Telephone	+44 (0)20 3023 4004
Fax	+44 (0)20 3023 4000
Email	aneil.deshpande@arkunderwriting.com
Website	www.arkunderwriting.com

Full Name	Aneil Paul Deshpande
Year of Birth	1956
Professional Qualifications	Information not available

PROFESSIONAL INFORMATION

CURRENT MAJOR POSITIONS/APPOINTMENTS

Executive Director	ARK Syndicate Management Limited	2007 -

PREVIOUS MAJOR POSITIONS/APPOINTMENTS

Executive Director	Travelers Syndicate Management Limited	2001 - 2002
Executive Director	Whittington Capital Management Limited	2004 - 2007
Chief Executive	Whittington Capital Management Limited	2004 - 2007

Bernard G Devereese

Position	Independent Review Director
Company	Hardy (Underwriting Agencies) Ltd
Address (Office)	4th Floor
	40 Lime Street
	London EC3M 7AW
Telephone	+44 (0)20 7626 0382
Fax	+44 (0)20 7283 4677
Email	bernard.devereese@hardygroup.co.uk
Website	www.hardygroup.co.uk

Full Name	Bernard George Devereese
Year of Birth	1949
Professional Qualifications	Information not available

PROFESSIONAL INFORMATION

CURRENT MAJOR POSITIONS/APPOINTMENTS

Non-Executive Director	Hardy (Underwriting Agencies) Ltd	2001 -
Chief Executive	Generic Underwriting Solutions Limited	2005 -

PREVIOUS MAJOR POSITIONS/APPOINTMENTS

Information not available

Emilio A Di Silvio

Position	Underwriting Director & Managing Director Syndicate 5555
Company	QBE Underwriting Limited

Address (Office)	Plantation Place
	30 Fenchurch Street
	London EC3M 3BD
Telephone	+44 (0)20 7105 4000
Fax	+44 (0)20 7105 4019
Email	enquiries@uk.qbe.com
Website	www.qbeeurope.com
PERSONAL PROFILE	A profile can be found in the People at Lloyd's, Personal section.

Anthony (Tony) J Dilley

Position	Chief Operating Officer & Compliance Officer
Company	Travelers Syndicate Management Ltd
Address (Office)	Exchequer Court
	33 St Mary Axe
	London EC3A 8AG
Telephone	+44 (0)20 3207 6851
Fax	+44 (0)20 7645 4526
Email	tdilley@travelers.com
Website	www.travelers.co.uk/lloyds
Full Name	Anthony John Dilley
Year of Birth	1954
Professional Qualifications	Information not available

PROFESSIONAL INFORMATION

CURRENT MAJOR POSITIONS/APPOINTMENTS

Executive Director	Travelers Insurance Company Limited	2001 -
Executive Director	Travelers Syndicate Management Limited	2004 -
Executive Director	Galatea Underwriting Agencies Ltd	2007 -

PREVIOUS MAJOR POSITIONS/APPOINTMENTS

Information not available

Robert WE Dimsey

Position	Finance Director
Company	Ascot Underwriting Limited
Address (Office)	Plantation Place
	30 Fenchurch Street
	London EC3M 3BD
Telephone	+44 (0)20 7743 9600
Fax	+44 (0)20 7743 9601
Email	rob.dimsey@ascotuw.com
Website	www.ascotuw.com
Full Name	Robert William Edward Dimsey
Year of Birth	1969
Professional Qualifications	Information not available

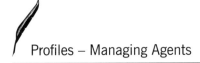

PROFESSIONAL INFORMATION

CURRENT MAJOR POSITIONS/APPOINTMENTS

Executive Director	Ascot Insurance Services Ltd	2004 -
Executive Director	Ascot Underwriting Limited	2008 -

PREVIOUS MAJOR POSITIONS/APPOINTMENTS
Information not available

Philip A Dodridge

Position	Chief Actuarial Officer
Company	QBE Underwriting Limited
Address (Office)	Plantation Place
	30 Fenchurch Street
	London EC3M 3BD
Telephone	+44 (0)20 7105 4000
Fax	+44 (0)20 7105 4019
Email	enquiries@uk.qbe.com
Website	www.qbeeurope.com

Full Name	Philip Andrew Dodridge
Year of Birth	1968
Professional Qualifications	Information not available

PROFESSIONAL INFORMATION

CURRENT MAJOR POSITIONS/APPOINTMENTS

Executive Director	QBE Insurance (Europe) Limited	2005 -
Executive Director	QBE Underwriting Limited	2006 -

PREVIOUS MAJOR POSITIONS/APPOINTMENTS

Executive Director	QBE Insurance Company (UK) Limited	2005 - 2006

Richard S Donovan

Position	Non-Executive Director
Company	Newline Underwriting Management Ltd
Address (Office)	Suite 5/4
	London Underwriting Centre
	3 Minster Court
	Mincing Lane
	London EC3R 7DD
Telephone	+44 (0)20 7090 1700
Fax	+44 (0)20 7090 1701
Email	rdonovan@odysseyre.com
Website	www.newlineuml.com

Full Name	Richard Scott Donovan
Year of Birth	1957
Professional Qualifications	Certified Public Accountant, BSc

PROFESSIONAL INFORMATION

CURRENT MAJOR POSITIONS/APPOINTMENTS

Non-Executive Director	Newline Insurance Company Limited	2006 -
Non-Executive Director	Newline Underwriting Management Ltd	2006 -
Chief Financial Officer	Odyssey Re Holdings Corp	Unknown -

PREVIOUS MAJOR POSITIONS/APPOINTMENTS

Chief Operating Officer	TIG Specialty Insurance Solutions	2002 - 2006
Chief Financial Officer	Coregis Insurance Group	Unknown - 2002

Roger A Doubtfire

Position	Chief Financial Officer
Company	Marketform Managing Agency Limited
Address (Office)	8 Lloyd's Avenue
	London EC3N 3EL
Telephone	+44 (0)20 7488 7730
Fax	+44 (0)20 7488 7800
Email	roger.doubtfire@marketform.com
Website	www.marketform.com

Full Name	Roger Alan Doubtfire
Year of Birth	1949
Professional Qualifications	Information not available

PROFESSIONAL INFORMATION

CURRENT MAJOR POSITIONS/APPOINTMENTS

Executive Director	Marketform Managing Agency Limited	2002 -
Executive Director	Marketform Limited	2005 -

PREVIOUS MAJOR POSITIONS/APPOINTMENTS

Information not available

Dane J Douetil, CBE

Position	Chief Executive Officer
Company	Brit Syndicates Limited
Address (Office)	2nd Floor
	55 Bishopsgate
	London EC2N 3AS
Telephone	+44 (0)20 7984 8500
Fax	+44 (0)20 7984 8501
Email	dane.douetil@britinsurance.com
Website	www.britinsurance.com

PERSONAL PROFILE	A profile can be found in the People at Lloyd's, Personal section.

James W Dover

Position	Finance Director
Company	R J Kiln & Co Limited

Address (Office)	106 Fenchurch Street
	London EC3M 5NR
Telephone	+44 (0)20 7886 9000
Fax	+44 (0)20 7488 1848
Email	james.dover@kilngroup.com
Website	www.kilnplc.com

Full Name	James William Dover
Year of Birth	1973
Professional Qualifications	Information not available

PROFESSIONAL INFORMATION

CURRENT MAJOR POSITIONS/APPOINTMENTS

Executive Director	R J Kiln & Co Limited	2006 -

PREVIOUS MAJOR POSITIONS/APPOINTMENTS

Information not available

Toby D Drysdale

Position	Executive Director & Deputy Underwriter Syndicate 609
Company	Atrium Underwriters Limited
Address (Office)	Room 790
	Lloyd's
	One Lime Street
	London EC3M 7DQ
Telephone	+44 (0)20 7327 4877
Fax	+44 (0)20 7327 4878
Email	info@atrium-uw.com
Website	www.atrium-uw.com

Full Name	Toby Douglas Drysdale
Year of Birth	1970
Professional Qualifications	Information not available

PROFESSIONAL INFORMATION

CURRENT MAJOR POSITIONS/APPOINTMENTS

Executive Director	Atrium Underwriters Limited	2008 -

PREVIOUS MAJOR POSITIONS/APPOINTMENTS

Information not available

Christopher Duca

Position	Non-Executive Director
Company	Navigators Underwriting Agency Ltd
Address (Office)	7th Floor
	2 Minster Court
	Mincing Lane
	London EC3R 7BB
Telephone	+44 (0)20 7220 6900

Fax	+44 (0)20 7220 6901	
Email	cduca@navg.com	
Website	www.navg.com	

Full Name	Christopher Duca	
Year of Birth	1966	
Professional Qualifications	BSc, MBA, MA	

PROFESSIONAL INFORMATION

CURRENT MAJOR POSITIONS/APPOINTMENTS

Executive Director	Navigators Insurance Company	2001 -
Non-Executive Director	Navigators Underwriting Agency Ltd	2006 -

PREVIOUS MAJOR POSITIONS/APPOINTMENTS

	Harvard Business School Executive Education	
	Leadership Program, Participant	Unknown

H Raymond Dumas

Position	Non-Executive Director
Company	Managing Agency Partners Limited
Address (Office)	1st Floor
	110 Fenchurch Street
	London EC3M 5JT
Telephone	+44 (0)20 7709 3860
Fax	+44 (0)20 7709 3861
Email	map@mapunderwriting.co.uk
Website	www.mapunderwriting.co.uk

Full Name	Henry Raymond Dumas
Year of Birth	1952
Professional Qualifications	Information not available

PROFESSIONAL INFORMATION

CURRENT MAJOR POSITIONS/APPOINTMENTS

Non-Executive Director	Managing Agency Partners Ltd	2000 -

PREVIOUS MAJOR POSITIONS/APPOINTMENTS

Non-Executive Director	Atrium Underwriters Limited	2006 - 2007

James D Denoon Duncan

Position	Managing Director
Company	Managing Agency Partners Limited
Address (Office)	1st Floor
	110 Fenchurch Street
	London EC3M 5JT
Telephone	+44 (0)20 7709 3862
Fax	+44 (0)20 7709 3861
Email	jdenoonduncan@mapunderwriting.co.uk
Website	www.mapunderwriting.co.uk

Full Name	James Douglas Denoon Duncan
Year of Birth	1957
Professional Qualifications	Information not available

PROFESSIONAL INFORMATION

CURRENT MAJOR POSITIONS/APPOINTMENTS

Chief Executive	Managing Agency Partners Ltd	2000 -

PREVIOUS MAJOR POSITIONS/APPOINTMENTS

Information not available

John AR Dunn

Position	Director of Operations & Director of Finance
Company	Liberty Syndicate Management Limited
Address (Office)	5th Floor
	Plantation Place South
	60 Great Tower Street
	London EC3R 5AZ
Telephone	+44 (0)20 7070 4472
Fax	+44 (0)20 7863 1001
Email	info@libertysyndicates.com
Website	www.libertysyndicates.com

Full Name	John Anthony Roberts Dunn
Year of Birth	1967
Professional Qualifications	Information not available

PROFESSIONAL INFORMATION

CURRENT MAJOR POSITIONS/APPOINTMENTS

Executive Director	Liberty Syndicate Management Limited	1999 -

PREVIOUS MAJOR POSITIONS/APPOINTMENTS

Information not available

Derek C Eales

Position	Executive Director & Deputy Underwriter Syndicate 318
Company	Beaufort Underwriting Agency Limited
Address (Office)	Third Floor
	One Minster Court
	Mincing Lane
	London EC3R 7AA
Telephone	+44 (0)20 7220 8200
Fax	+44 (0)20 7220 8290
Email	derek.eales@beaufort-group.com
Website	www.beaufort-group.com

Full Name	Derek Christopher Eales
Year of Birth	1965
Professional Qualifications	Information not available

PROFESSIONAL INFORMATION

CURRENT MAJOR POSITIONS/APPOINTMENTS

| Executive Director | Beaufort Underwriting Agency Limited | 2004 - |

PREVIOUS MAJOR POSITIONS/APPOINTMENTS

Information not available

Steve G Eccles

Position	Underwriting Director & Active Underwriter Syndicate 5000
Company	Travelers Syndicate Management Ltd
Address (Office)	Exchequer Court
	33 St Mary Axe
	London EC3A 8AG
Telephone	+44 (0)20 3207 6246
Fax	+44 (0)20 7645 4526
Email	seccles@travelers.com
Website	www.travelers.co.uk/lloyds

Full Name	Stephen Gordon Eccles
Year of Birth	1964
Professional Qualifications	Information not available

PROFESSIONAL INFORMATION

CURRENT MAJOR POSITIONS/APPOINTMENTS

| Executive Director | Travelers Syndicate Management Limited | 2006 - |
| Executive Director | Galatea Underwriting Agencies Ltd | 2007 - |

PREVIOUS MAJOR POSITIONS/APPOINTMENTS

Information not available

Julian AP Enoizi

Position	Chief Executive Officer
Company	Argo Managing Agency Ltd
Address (Office)	47 Mark Lane
	London EC3R 7QQ
Telephone	+44 (0)20 7712 7600
Fax	+44 (0)20 7712 7601
Email	julian.enoizi@argo-int.com
Website	www.argo-int.com

Full Name	Julian Antony Peter Enoizi
Year of Birth	1967
Professional Qualifications	LLB (Hons)

PROFESSIONAL INFORMATION

CURRENT MAJOR POSITIONS/APPOINTMENTS

Chief Executive Officer	Argo Managing Agency Ltd	2009 -

PREVIOUS MAJOR POSITIONS/APPOINTMENTS

Non-Executive Director	CNA Insurance Company	2002 - 2003
Non-Executive Director	CNA Insurance Company	2002 - 2005
Chief Executive	Global Resource Managers Limited	2005 - 2006
Chief Executive	KX Reinsurance Company Ltd	2005 - 2006
Chief Executive	The Continental Insurance	2005 - 2006
Chief Executive	CNA Insurance Company	2005 - 2009

Martin D Feinstein

Position	Non-Executive Director
Company	Amlin Underwriting Limited
Address (Office)	St Helen's
	1 Undershaft
	London EC3A 8ND
Telephone	+44 (0)20 7746 1000
Fax	+44 (0)20 7746 1696
Email	amlinreception@amlin.co.uk
Website	www.amlin.com
Full Name	Martin Douglas Feinstein
Year of Birth	1948
Professional Qualifications	Information not available

PROFESSIONAL INFORMATION

CURRENT MAJOR POSITIONS/APPOINTMENTS

Non-Executive Director	Amlin Underwriting Limited	2007 -
Non-Executive Director	Reynolds American Inc	Unknown -
Non-Executive Director	GeoVera Insurance Ltd	Unknown -

PREVIOUS MAJOR POSITIONS/APPOINTMENTS

Executive Director	BAT Industries Plc	1997 - 1998
Chairman and Chief Executive Officer	Farmers Group Inc	1997 - 2005
Executive Director	Zurich Advice Network Limited	2004 - 2004

Walter M Fiederowicz

Position	Non-Executive Director
Company	Omega Underwriting Agents Ltd
Address (Office)	4th Floor
	New London House
	6 London Street
	London EC3R 7LP
Telephone	+44 (0)20 7767 3000
Fax	+44 (0)20 7488 9639

Email	info@omegauw.com	
Website	www.omegauw.com	

Full Name	Walter Michael Fiederowicz	
Year of Birth	1946	
Professional Qualifications	Information not available	

PROFESSIONAL INFORMATION

CURRENT MAJOR POSITIONS/APPOINTMENTS

Non-Executive Director	Omega Underwriting Agents Ltd	2008 -

PREVIOUS MAJOR POSITIONS/APPOINTMENTS

Information not available

Richard GM Finn

Position	Independent Review Director
Company	Advent Underwriting Limited
Address (Office)	10th Floor
	One Minster Court
	Mincing Lane
	London EC3R 7AA
Telephone	+44 (0)20 7743 8200
Fax	+44 (0)20 7743 8299
Email	head.office@adventgroup.co.uk
Website	www.adventgroup.co.uk

PERSONAL PROFILE   A profile can be found in the People at Lloyd's, Personal section.

J Dudley Fishburn

Position	Non-Executive Director
Company	Beazley Furlonge Ltd
Address (Office)	Plantation Place South
	60 Great Tower Street
	London EC3R 5AD
Telephone	+44 (0)20 7667 0623
Fax	+44 (0)20 7674 7100
Email	john.fishburn@beazley.com
Website	www.beazley.com

Full Name	John Dudley Fishburn
Year of Birth	1946
Professional Qualifications	Information not available

PROFESSIONAL INFORMATION

CURRENT MAJOR POSITIONS/APPOINTMENTS

Non-Executive Director	HSBC Bank Plc	2003 -
Non-Executive Director	Beazley Furlonge Ltd	2006 -
Non-Executive Director	Household International Inc	Unknown -
Non-Executive Director	Altria Inc	Unknown -

PREVIOUS MAJOR POSITIONS/APPOINTMENTS

Non-Executive Director   HFC Bank Limited   2001 - 2008

Brian A Fitzgerald

Position	Chairman
Company	Liberty Syndicate Management Limited
Address (Office)	5th Floor
	Plantation Place South
	60 Great Tower Street
	London EC3R 5AZ
Telephone	+44 (0)20 7070 4472
Fax	+44 (0)20 7863 1001
Email	info@libertysyndicates.com
Website	www.libertysyndicates.com

Full Name	Brian Anthony Fitzgerald
Year of Birth	1943
Professional Qualifications	Information not available

PROFESSIONAL INFORMATION

CURRENT MAJOR POSITIONS/APPOINTMENTS

Non-Executive Director   Liberty Syndicate Management Limited   2002 -

PREVIOUS MAJOR POSITIONS/APPOINTMENTS

Non-Executive Director	Riggs & Company International Limited	2001 - 2002
Chief Executive	Riggs & Company International Limited	2002 - 2005
Non-Executive Director	Riggs Bank Europe Ltd	2003 - 2005
Chief Executive	Riggs Bank NA	2003 - 2005
Chief Executive	Liberty Syndicate Management Limited	2006 - 2007

Andrew S Foote

Position	Non-Executive Director
Company	Managing Agency Partners Limited
Address (Office)	1st Floor
	110 Fenchurch Street
	London EC3M 5JT
Telephone	+44 (0)20 7709 3860
Fax	+44 (0)20 7709 3861
Email	map@mapunderwriting.co.uk
Website	www.mapunderwriting.co.uk

Full Name	Andrew Swift Foote
Year of Birth	1968
Professional Qualifications	Information not available

PROFESSIONAL INFORMATION

CURRENT MAJOR POSITIONS/APPOINTMENTS

Non-Executive Director   Managing Agency Partners Ltd   2001 -

PREVIOUS MAJOR POSITIONS/APPOINTMENTS

Information not available

Christopher D Forbes

Position	Non-Executive Director
Company	AEGIS Managing Agency Ltd
Address (Office)	110 Fenchurch Street
	London EC3M 5JT
Telephone	+44 (0)20 7265 2100
Fax	+44 (0)20 7265 2101
Email	enquiries@aegislink.com
Website	www.aegislink.com

Full Name	Christopher David Forbes
Year of Birth	1954
Professional Qualifications	LLB, FCA

PROFESSIONAL INFORMATION

CURRENT MAJOR POSITIONS/APPOINTMENTS

Non-Executive Director	AEGIS Managing Agency Ltd	2007 -

PREVIOUS MAJOR POSITIONS/APPOINTMENTS

Chairman (Non-Executive)	Chaucer Syndicates Limited	2001 - 2009
Non-Executive Director	Faraday Underwriting Limited	2001 - 2002
Finance Director	Charman Underwriting	1991 - Unknown
Board Member	Additional Securities Limited	Unknown
Chairman	Chaucer Remuneration Committee	Unknown
Member	Lloyd's North American Board	Unknown

Nicholas NS Ford

Position	Chief Financial Officer
Company	SA Meacock & Company Limited
Address (Office)	4th Floor
	15 St Helen's Place
	London EC3A 6DE
Telephone	+44 (0)20 7374 6727
Fax	+44 (0)20 7374 4727
Email	nicholas.ford@sameacock.com
Website	None at present

Full Name	Nicholas Noel Sebastian Ford
Year of Birth	1957
Professional Qualifications	Information not available

PROFESSIONAL INFORMATION

CURRENT MAJOR POSITIONS/APPOINTMENTS

Executive Director	SA Meacock & Company Limited	1996 -

PREVIOUS MAJOR POSITIONS/APPOINTMENTS
Information not available

David P Foreman

Position	Group Director of Underwriting
Company	ARK Syndicate Management Limited
Address (Office)	8th Floor
	St Helen's
	1 Undershaft
	London EC3A 8EE
Telephone	+44 (0)20 3023 4002
Fax	+44 (0)20 3023 4000
Email	david.foreman@arkunderwriting.com
Website	www.arkunderwriting.com

PERSONAL PROFILE   A profile can be found in the People at Lloyd's, Personal section.

Daniel TN Forsythe

Position	Non-Executive Director
Company	Liberty Syndicate Management Limited
Address (Office)	5th Floor
	Plantation Place South
	60 Great Tower Street
	London EC3R 5AZ
Telephone	+44 (0)20 7070 4472
Fax	+44 (0)20 7863 1001
Email	info@libertysyndicates.com
Website	www.libertysyndicates.com

Full Name	Daniel Terence Niall Forsythe
Year of Birth	1958
Professional Qualifications	Information not available

PROFESSIONAL INFORMATION
CURRENT MAJOR POSITIONS/APPOINTMENTS

Non-Executive Director	Liberty Syndicate Management Limited	2001 -
Non-Executive Director	Liberty Mutual Insurance Europe Limited	2002 -

PREVIOUS MAJOR POSITIONS/APPOINTMENTS
Information not available

Matthew K Fosh

Position	Non-Executive Director
Company	Novae Syndicates Limited
Address (Office)	71 Fenchurch Street
	London EC3M 4HH
Telephone	+44 (0)20 7903 7300
Fax	+44 (0)20 7903 7333

Email	mfosh@novae.com
Website	www.novae.com

PERSONAL PROFILE	A profile can be found in the People at Lloyd's, Personal section.

Kim T Fox

Position	Chief Operating Officer
Company	Spectrum Syndicate Management Limited
Address (Office)	2nd Floor
	6 Bevis Marks
	London EC3A 7HL
Telephone	+44 (0)20 7283 2646
Fax	+44 (0)20 7621 0975
Email	kim.fox@spectrumins.com
Website	www.spectrumins.com

Full Name	Kim Theresa Fox
Year of Birth	1965
Professional Qualifications	Information not available

PROFESSIONAL INFORMATION

CURRENT MAJOR POSITIONS/APPOINTMENTS

Executive Director	Spectrum Syndicate Management Limited	2001 -

PREVIOUS MAJOR POSITIONS/APPOINTMENTS

Executive Director	Crowe Syndicate Management Ltd	2001 - 2006

Simon T Fradd

Position	Independent Review Director
Company	Newline Underwriting Management Ltd
Address (Office)	Suite 5/4
	London Underwriting Centre
	3 Minster Court
	Mincing Lane
	London EC3R 7DD
Telephone	+44 (0)20 7090 1700
Fax	+44 (0)20 7090 1701
Email	sfradd@newlineuml.com
Website	www.newlineuml.com

Full Name	Simon Timothy Fradd
Year of Birth	1944
Professional Qualifications	Information not available

PROFESSIONAL INFORMATION

CURRENT MAJOR POSITIONS/APPOINTMENTS

Non-Executive Director	Newline Underwriting Management Ltd	2001 -
Non-Executive Director	Newline Insurance Company Limited	2006 -

PREVIOUS MAJOR POSITIONS/APPOINTMENTS
Information not available

Charles AS Franks

Position	Chief Executive Officer
Company	R J Kiln & Co Limited
Address (Office)	106 Fenchurch Street
	London EC3M 5NR
Telephone	+44 (0)20 7886 9000
Fax	+44 (0)20 7488 1848
Email	charles.franks@kilngroup.com
Website	www.kilnplc.com

Full Name	Charles Anthony Stapleton Franks
Year of Birth	1962
Professional Qualifications	Information not available

PROFESSIONAL INFORMATION

CURRENT MAJOR POSITIONS/APPOINTMENTS

Executive Director	R J Kiln & Co Limited	2001 -
Non-Executive Director	International Marine (Underwriting Agency) Ltd	2005 -
Chief Executive	R J Kiln & Co Limited	2007 -
Member	Lloyd's Market Association	2009 -

PREVIOUS MAJOR POSITIONS/APPOINTMENTS
Information not available

David S French

Position	Non-Executive Director
Company	Starr Managing Agents Limited
Address (Office)	3rd Floor
	140 Leadenhall Street
	London EC3V 4QT
Telephone	+44 (0)20 7337 3550
Fax	+44 (0)20 7337 3551
Email	david.french@cvstarrco.com
Website	www.cvstarrco.com

Full Name	David Scott French
Year of Birth	1953
Professional Qualifications	Information not available

PROFESSIONAL INFORMATION

CURRENT MAJOR POSITIONS/APPOINTMENTS

Non-Executive Director	Starr Underwriting Agents Limited	2007 -
Non-Executive Director	Starr Managing Agents Ltd	2007 -

PREVIOUS MAJOR POSITIONS/APPOINTMENTS

Executive Director	Starr Underwriting Agents Limited	2006 - 2008

Neil A Freshwater

Position	Chief Financial Officer
Company	Catlin Underwriting Agencies Ltd
Address (Office)	6th Floor
	3 Minster Court
	Mincing Lane
	London EC3R 7DD
Telephone	+44 (0)20 7626 0486
Fax	+44 (0)20 7623 9101
Email	neil.freshwater@catlin.com
Website	www.catlin.com

Full Name	Neil Andrew Freshwater
Year of Birth	1969
Professional Qualifications	Information not available

PROFESSIONAL INFORMATION

CURRENT MAJOR POSITIONS/APPOINTMENTS

Executive Director	Catlin Underwriting Agencies Ltd	2007 -
Executive Director	Catlin Insurance Company (UK) Ltd	2007 -
Executive Director	Catlin (Wellington) Underwriting Agencies Limited	2008 -
Executive Director	Brighter Business Limited	2009 -

PREVIOUS MAJOR POSITIONS/APPOINTMENTS

Information not available

Nicholas (Nick) H Furlonge

Position	Executive Director & Head of Risk Management
Company	Beazley Furlonge Ltd
Address (Office)	Plantation Place South
	60 Great Tower Street
	London EC3R 5AD
Telephone	+44 (0)20 7667 0623
Fax	+44 (0)20 7674 7100
Email	nicholas.furlonge@beazley.com
Website	www.beazley.com

PERSONAL PROFILE	A profile can be found in the People at Lloyd's, Personal section.

Patrick J Gage

Position	Executive Director & Deputy Underwriter Syndicate 382
Company	Hardy (Underwriting Agencies) Ltd
Address (Office)	4th Floor
	40 Lime Street
	London EC3M 7AW
Telephone	+44 (0)20 7626 0382
Fax	+44 (0)20 7283 4677
Email	patrick.gage@hardygroup.co.uk
Website	www.hardygroup.co.uk

Full Name	Patrick James Gage
Year of Birth	1959
Professional Qualifications	Information not available

PROFESSIONAL INFORMATION

CURRENT MAJOR POSITIONS/APPOINTMENTS

Executive Director	Hardy (Underwriting Agencies) Ltd	2006 -

PREVIOUS MAJOR POSITIONS/APPOINTMENTS

Information not available

Stanley A Galanski

Position	Non-Executive Director
Company	Navigators Underwriting Agency Ltd
Address (Office)	7th Floor
	2 Minster Court
	Mincing Lane
	London EC3R 7BB
Telephone	+44 (0)20 7220 6900
Fax	+44 (0)20 7220 6901
Email	sgalanski@navg.com
Website	www.navg.com

Full Name	Stanley Adam Galanski
Year of Birth	1958
Professional Qualifications	Information not available

PROFESSIONAL INFORMATION

CURRENT MAJOR POSITIONS/APPOINTMENTS

Executive Director	Navigators Insurance Company	2001 -
Non-Executive Director	Navigators Underwriting Agency Ltd	2001 -

PREVIOUS MAJOR POSITIONS/APPOINTMENTS

President	New Hampshire Insurance Company	1995 - 1997
President	XL Specialty Insurance Company	1997 - 2001
President	XL Insurance Company	2000 - 2001

Michael G Gardiner

Position	Technical Director
Company	Mitsui Sumitomo Insurance Underwriting at Lloyd's Ltd
Address (Office)	25 Fenchurch Avenue
	London EC3M 5AD
Telephone	+44 (0)20 7977 8340
Fax	+44 (0)20 7977 8300
Email	mgardiner@msilm.com
Website	www.msilm.com

Full Name	Michael Geoffrey Gardiner
Year of Birth	1962
Professional Qualifications	FCII, FCILA, FIRM

PROFESSIONAL INFORMATION

CURRENT MAJOR POSITIONS/APPOINTMENTS

Executive Director	Mitsui Sumitomo Insurance (London) Limited	2005 -
Executive Director	Mitsui Sumitomo Insurance Underwriting at Lloyd's Ltd	2006 -

PREVIOUS MAJOR POSITIONS/APPOINTMENTS

Executive Director	Mitsui Sumitomo Insurance Company Limited	2003 - 2005

Michael J Gent

Position	Chief Financial Officer
Company	Travelers Syndicate Management Ltd
Address (Office)	Exchequer Court
	33 St Mary Axe
	London EC3A 8AG
Telephone	+44 (0)20 3207 6330
Fax	+44 (0)20 7645 4526
Email	mgent@travelers.com
Website	www.travelers.co.uk/lloyds

Full Name	Michael John Gent
Year of Birth	1964
Professional Qualifications	Information not available

PROFESSIONAL INFORMATION

CURRENT MAJOR POSITIONS/APPOINTMENTS

Executive Director	Travelers Insurance Company Limited	2001 -
Executive Director	Travelers Syndicate Management Limited	2003 -
Executive Director	Solicitors Professional Indemnity Ltd	2005 -
Executive Director	St Paul Travelers Professional Risks Ltd	2005 -

PREVIOUS MAJOR POSITIONS/APPOINTMENTS

Executive Director	Cassidy Davis Insurance Services Ltd	2005 - 2005

Lance J Gibbins

Position	Chief Financial Officer
Company	Max at Lloyd's Ltd
Address (Office)	4th Floor
	70 Gracechurch Street
	London EC3V 0XL
Telephone	+44 (0)20 3102 3100
Fax	+44 (0)20 3102 3200
Email	lance.gibbins@maxatlloyds.com
Website	www.maxatlloyds.com

Full Name	Lance John Gibbins	
Year of Birth	1964	
Professional Qualifications	Information not available	

PROFESSIONAL INFORMATION

CURRENT MAJOR POSITIONS/APPOINTMENTS

Executive Director	Max at Lloyd's Ltd	2007 -
Member	Securities & Investment Institute	Unknown -

PREVIOUS MAJOR POSITIONS/APPOINTMENTS

Chief Executive	Max at Lloyd's Ltd	2001 - 2002

Ewen H Gilmour

Position	Chairman
Company	Chaucer Syndicates Limited
Address (Office)	Plantation Place
	30 Fenchurch Street
	London EC3M 3AD
Telephone	+44 (0)20 7397 9700
Fax	+44 (0)20 7397 9710
Email	ewen.gilmour@chaucerplc.com
Website	www.chaucerplc.com

Full Name	Ewen Hamilton Gilmour
Year of Birth	1953
Professional Qualifications	MA, FCA

PROFESSIONAL INFORMATION

CURRENT MAJOR POSITIONS/APPOINTMENTS

Working Member & Deputy Chairman	Council of Lloyd's	2006 -
Executive Director	Chaucer Syndicates Limited	2009 -

PREVIOUS MAJOR POSITIONS/APPOINTMENTS

Corporate Financier	Charterhouse Bank	1980 - 1993
Chief Executive	Chaucer Syndicates Limited	1998 - 2009
Executive Director	Aberdeen Underwriting Advisers Ltd	2001 - 2003
Chairman	Lloyd's Market Association,	
	Market Processes Committee	2005 - 2007

James (Jim) A Giordano

Position	Group Chief Underwriting Officer & Active Underwriter Syndicate 4444
Company	Canopius Managing Agents Limited
Address (Office)	Gallery 9
	One Lime Street
	London EC3M 7HA
Telephone	+44 (0)20 7337 3710
Fax	+44 (0)20 7337 3999
Email	jim.giordano@canopius.com
Website	www.canopius.com

Full Name	James Andrew Giordano
Year of Birth	1952
Professional Qualifications	Information not available

PROFESSIONAL INFORMATION

CURRENT MAJOR POSITIONS/APPOINTMENTS

Executive Director	Canopius Managing Agents Limited	2001 -

PREVIOUS MAJOR POSITIONS/APPOINTMENTS

Executive Director	Bestpark International Limited	2001 - 2003

Timothy ABH Glover

Position	Executive Director
Company	Pembroke Managing Agency Ltd
Address (Office)	2nd Floor
	3 Minster Court
	Mincing Lane
	London EC3R 7DD
Telephone	+44 (0)20 7337 4400
Fax	+44 (0)20 7337 4401
Email	tim.glover@pembrokeunderwriting.com
Website	www.pembrokeunderwriting.com

Full Name	Timothy Anthony Brian Harvey Glover
Year of Birth	1967
Professional Qualifications	ACII

PROFESSIONAL INFORMATION

CURRENT MAJOR POSITIONS/APPOINTMENTS

Executive Director	Pembroke Managing Agency Ltd	2007 -

PREVIOUS MAJOR POSITIONS/APPOINTMENTS

Information not available

Ann F Godbehere

Position	Non-Executive Director
Company	Atrium Underwriters Limited
Address (Office)	Room 790
	Lloyd's
	One Lime Street
	London EC3M 7DQ
Telephone	+44 (0)20 7327 4877
Fax	+44 (0)20 7327 4878
Email	info@atrium-uw.com
Website	www.atrium-uw.com

Full Name	Ann Frances Godbehere
Year of Birth	1955
Professional Qualifications	Information not available

PROFESSIONAL INFORMATION

CURRENT MAJOR POSITIONS/APPOINTMENTS

Non-Executive Director	Atrium Underwriters Limited	2008 -
Non-Executive Director	UBS	2009 -

PREVIOUS MAJOR POSITIONS/APPOINTMENTS

Non-Executive Director	Swiss Re Life & Health Limited	2003 - 2006
Non-Executive Director	Swiss Reinsurance Company UK Limited	2003 - 2006
Non-Executive Director	The Mercantile & General Reinsurance Company Ltd	2003 - 2006
Non-Executive Director	Reassure UK Life Assurance Company Limited	2003 - 2006
Non-Executive Director	Windsor Life Assurance Company Limited	2004 - 2006
Non-Executive Director	XSMA Limited	2004 - 2006
Chief Financial Officer	Northern Rock Plc	2008 - 2009

John S Goldsmith

Position	Non-Executive Director
Company	AEGIS Managing Agency Ltd
Address (Office)	110 Fenchurch Street
	London EC3M 5JT
Telephone	+44 (0)20 7265 2100
Fax	+44 (0)20 7265 2101
Email	enquiries@aegislink.com
Website	www.aegislink.com

Position	Non-Executive Director
Company	Cathedral Underwriting Limited
Address (Office)	5th Floor
	Fitzwilliam House
	10 St Mary Axe
	London EC3A 8EN
Telephone	+44 (0)20 7170 9000
Fax	+44 (0)20 7170 9001
Email	info@cathedralcapital.com
Website	www.cathedralcapital.com

Position	Independent Non-Executive Director
Company	Montpelier Underwriting Agencies Ltd
Address (Office)	7th Floor
	85 Gracechurch Street
	London EC3V 0AA
Telephone	+44 (0)20 7648 4500
Fax	+44 (0)20 7648 4501
Email	–
Website	www.montpelierre.com

Full Name	John Stanley Goldsmith
Year of Birth	1947
Professional Qualifications	Information not available

PROFESSIONAL INFORMATION

CURRENT MAJOR POSITIONS/APPOINTMENTS

Non-Executive Director	Cathedral Underwriting Limited	2008 -
Non-Executive Director	Montpelier Underwriting Agencies Ltd	2008 -
Non-Executive Director	AEGIS Managing Agency Ltd	2008 -

PREVIOUS MAJOR POSITIONS/APPOINTMENTS

Non-Executive Director	The Griffin Insurance Association Limited	2002 - 2007
Chief Executive	Denis M Clayton & Co Ltd	2005 - 2006
Executive Director	Denis M Clayton & Co Ltd	2005 - 2007

Anthony JR Gordon

Position	Chief Financial Officer
Company	Whittington Capital Management Limited
Address (Office)	33 Creechurch Lane
	London EC3A 5EB
Telephone	+44 (0)20 7743 0900
Fax	+44 (0)20 7743 0901
Email	anthony.gordon@whittingtoninsurance.com
Website	www.whittingtoninsurance.com

Full Name	Anthony John Ramsay Gordon
Year of Birth	1951
Professional Qualifications	Information not available

PROFESSIONAL INFORMATION

CURRENT MAJOR POSITIONS/APPOINTMENTS

Executive Director	Whittington Capital Management Limited	2004 -

PREVIOUS MAJOR POSITIONS/APPOINTMENTS

Executive Director	Syndicate 138 Agency Limited	2001 - 2002

Derek C Grainger

Position	Compliance Director
Company	Cathedral Underwriting Limited
Address (Office)	5th Floor
	Fitzwilliam House
	10 St Mary Axe
	London EC3A 8EN
Telephone	+44 (0)20 7170 9023
Fax	+44 (0)20 7170 9001
Email	derek.grainger@cathedralcapital.com
Website	www.cathedralcapital.com

Full Name	Derek Charles Grainger	
Year of Birth	1951	
Professional Qualifications	Information not available	

PROFESSIONAL INFORMATION

CURRENT MAJOR POSITIONS/APPOINTMENTS

Executive Director	Cathedral Underwriting Limited	2000 -
Member	Lloyd's Market Association, Regulatory Committee	2002 -

PREVIOUS MAJOR POSITIONS/APPOINTMENTS

Executive Director	Cathedral Capital Management Limited	2001 - 2007

Roderic WR Grande

Position	Managing Director
Company	Munich Re Underwriting Limited
Address (Office)	St Helen's
	1 Undershaft
	London EC3A 8EE
Telephone	+44 (0)20 7886 3900
Fax	+44 (0)20 7886 3901
Email	rod.grande@mrunderwriting.com
Website	www.watkins-syndicate.co.uk

Full Name	Roderic William Ricardo Grande
Year of Birth	1957
Professional Qualifications	BSc, ACA, MBA, ACII

PROFESSIONAL INFORMATION

CURRENT MAJOR POSITIONS/APPOINTMENTS

Chief Executive	Munich Re Underwriting Limited	1993 -
Non-Executive Director	Groves, John and Westrup Ltd	2005 -
Non-Executive Director	Northern Marine Underwriters Ltd	2005 -

PREVIOUS MAJOR POSITIONS/APPOINTMENTS

Information not available

Keith N Grant

Position	Compliance Officer & Company Secretary
Company	R J Kiln & Co Limited
Address (Office)	106 Fenchurch Street
	London EC3M 5NR
Telephone	+44 (0)20 7886 9000
Fax	+44 (0)20 7488 1848
Email	keith.grant@kilngroup.com
Website	www.kilnplc.com

Full Name	Keith Nigel Grant
Year of Birth	1954
Professional Qualifications	Information not available

PROFESSIONAL INFORMATION

CURRENT MAJOR POSITIONS/APPOINTMENTS

Executive Director	R J Kiln & Co Limited	2000 -

PREVIOUS MAJOR POSITIONS/APPOINTMENTS

Information not available

Jonathan G Gray

Position	Executive Director & Head of Property Group
Company	Beazley Furlonge Ltd
Address (Office)	Plantation Place South
	60 Great Tower Street
	London EC3R 5AD
Telephone	+44 (0)20 7667 0623
Fax	+44 (0)20 7674 7100
Email	jonathan.gray@beazley.com
Website	www.beazley.com

Full Name	Jonathan George Gray
Year of Birth	1953
Professional Qualifications	Information not available

PROFESSIONAL INFORMATION

CURRENT MAJOR POSITIONS/APPOINTMENTS

Executive Director	Beazley Furlonge Ltd	1993 -

PREVIOUS MAJOR POSITIONS/APPOINTMENTS

Information not available

Nicholas JT Gray

Position	Chief Financial Officer
Company	Munich Re Underwriting Limited
Address (Office)	St Helen's
	1 Undershaft
	London EC3A 8EE
Telephone	+44 (0)20 7886 3900
Fax	+44 (0)20 7886 3901
Email	nick.gray@mrunderwriting.com
Website	www.watkins-syndicate.co.uk

Full Name	Nicholas John Talbot Gray
Year of Birth	1965
Professional Qualifications	BSc, ACA

PROFESSIONAL INFORMATION

CURRENT MAJOR POSITIONS/APPOINTMENTS

Executive Director	Munich Re Underwriting Limited	1996 -

PREVIOUS MAJOR POSITIONS/APPOINTMENTS
Information not available

Karen A Green

Position	Managing Director
Company	Aspen Managing Agency Limited
Address (Office)	30 Fenchurch Street
	London EC3M 3BD
Telephone	+44 (0)20 7184 8000
Fax	+44 (0)20 7184 8500
Email	c/o robert.long@aspen-re.com
Website	www.aspen-re.com

Full Name	Karen Ann Green
Year of Birth	1967
Professional Qualifications	Information not available

PROFESSIONAL INFORMATION

CURRENT MAJOR POSITIONS/APPOINTMENTS

Executive Director	Aspen Managing Agency Limited	2008 -
Chief Executive	Aspen Managing Agency Limited	2008 -

PREVIOUS MAJOR POSITIONS/APPOINTMENTS

Executive Director	GE Capital in London	1997 - 2001
Non-Executive Director	Danish Re Syndicates Ltd	2001 - 2004

Philip J Green

Position	Finance Director
Company	Advent Underwriting Limited
Address (Office)	10th Floor
	One Minster Court
	Mincing Lane
	London EC3R 7AA
Telephone	+44 (0)20 7743 8234
Fax	+44 (0)20 7743 8299
Email	phil.green@adventgroup.co.uk
Website	www.adventgroup.co.uk

Full Name	Philip James Green
Year of Birth	1967
Professional Qualifications	ACA

PROFESSIONAL INFORMATION

CURRENT MAJOR POSITIONS/APPOINTMENTS

Executive Director	Advent Underwriting Limited	2006 -

PREVIOUS MAJOR POSITIONS/APPOINTMENTS
Information not available

Donald J Greene

Position	Non-Executive Director
Company	AEGIS Managing Agency Ltd
Address (Office)	110 Fenchurch Street
	London EC3M 5JT
Telephone	+44 (0)20 7265 2100
Fax	+44 (0)20 7265 2101
Email	enquiries@aegislink.com
Website	www.aegislink.com
Full Name	Donald John Greene
Year of Birth	1933
Professional Qualifications	Information not available

PROFESSIONAL INFORMATION

CURRENT MAJOR POSITIONS/APPOINTMENTS

Non-Executive Director	AEGIS Managing Agency Ltd	2003 -

PREVIOUS MAJOR POSITIONS/APPOINTMENTS

Information not available

Timothy P Griffin

Position	Executive Director & Compliance Officer
Company	Hardy (Underwriting Agencies) Ltd
Address (Office)	4th Floor
	40 Lime Street
	London EC3M 7AW
Telephone	+44 (0)20 7626 0382
Fax	+44 (0)20 7283 4677
Email	timothy.griffin@hardygroup.co.uk
Website	www.hardygroup.co.uk
Full Name	Timothy Paul Griffin
Year of Birth	1967
Professional Qualifications	LLB (Hons), ACII

PROFESSIONAL INFORMATION

CURRENT MAJOR POSITIONS/APPOINTMENTS

Executive Director	Hardy (Underwriting Agencies) Ltd	2001 -

PREVIOUS MAJOR POSITIONS/APPOINTMENTS

Information not available

Gary L Griffiths

Position	Claims Director
Company	Whittington Capital Management Limited
Address (Office)	33 Creechurch Lane
	London EC3A 5EB
Telephone	+44 (0)20 7743 0900

Fax	+44 (0)20 7743 0901
Email	gary.griffiths@whittingtoninsurance.com
Website	www.whittingtoninsurance.com

Full Name	Gary Leonard Griffiths
Year of Birth	1953
Professional Qualifications	Information not available

PROFESSIONAL INFORMATION

CURRENT MAJOR POSITIONS/APPOINTMENTS

| Executive Director | Whittington Capital Management Limited | 2003 - |
| Chief Executive | Whittington Capital Management Limited | 2007 - |

PREVIOUS MAJOR POSITIONS/APPOINTMENTS

| Non-Executive Director | Whittington Capital Management Limited | 2001 - 2003 |

William H Grigg

Position	Non-Executive Director
Company	AEGIS Managing Agency Ltd
Address (Office)	110 Fenchurch Street
	London EC3M 5JT
Telephone	+44 (0)20 7265 2100
Fax	+44 (0)20 7265 2101
Email	enquiries@aegislink.com
Website	www.aegislink.com

Full Name	William Humphrey Grigg
Year of Birth	1932
Professional Qualifications	Information not available

PROFESSIONAL INFORMATION

CURRENT MAJOR POSITIONS/APPOINTMENTS

| Non-Executive Director | AEGIS Managing Agency Ltd | 2000 - |

PREVIOUS MAJOR POSITIONS/APPOINTMENTS

Information not available

Doron Grossman

Position	Underwriting Director
Company	QBE Underwriting Limited
Address (Office)	Plantation Place
	30 Fenchurch Street
	London EC3M 3BD
Telephone	+44 (0)20 7105 4000
Fax	+44 (0)20 7105 4019
Email	enquiries@uk.qbe.com
Website	www.qbeeurope.com

Full Name	Doron Grossman
Year of Birth	1962
Professional Qualifications	Information not available

PROFESSIONAL INFORMATION

CURRENT MAJOR POSITIONS/APPOINTMENTS

Executive Director	QBE Insurance (Europe) Limited	2007 -
Executive Director	QBE Underwriting Limited	2008 -

PREVIOUS MAJOR POSITIONS/APPOINTMENTS
Information not available

Peter E Grove

Position	Chief Underwriting Officer
Company	QBE Underwriting Limited
Address (Office)	Plantation Place
	30 Fenchurch Street
	London EC3M 3BD
Telephone	+44 (0)20 7105 4000
Fax	+44 (0)20 7105 4019
Email	enquiries@uk.qbe.com
Website	www.qbeeurope.com

PERSONAL PROFILE   A profile can be found in the People at Lloyd's, Personal section.

Paul P Guiry

Position	Finance Director
Company	AEGIS Managing Agency Ltd
Address (Office)	110 Fenchurch Street
	London EC3M 5JT
Telephone	+44 (0)20 7265 2108
Fax	+44 (0)20 7265 2101
Email	pguiry@aegislondon.co.uk
Website	www.aegislink.com

Full Name	Paul Philip Guiry
Year of Birth	1963
Professional Qualifications	FCA

PROFESSIONAL INFORMATION

CURRENT MAJOR POSITIONS/APPOINTMENTS

Executive Director	AEGIS Managing Agency Ltd	2005 -

PREVIOUS MAJOR POSITIONS/APPOINTMENTS
Information not available

Diana Guy

Position	Non-Executive Director
Company	Catlin Underwriting Agencies Ltd
Address (Office)	6th Floor
	3 Minster Court
	Mincing Lane
	London EC3R 7DD
Telephone	+44 (0)20 7626 0486
Fax	+44 (0)20 7623 9101
Email	catlininfo@catlin.com
Website	www.catlin.com

Full Name	Diana Guy
Year of Birth	1943
Professional Qualifications	Information not available

PROFESSIONAL INFORMATION

CURRENT MAJOR POSITIONS/APPOINTMENTS

Non-Executive Director	Catlin Underwriting Agencies Ltd	1996 -
Non-Executive Director	Catlin Insurance Company (UK) Ltd	2005 -

PREVIOUS MAJOR POSITIONS/APPOINTMENTS

Information not available

Geoffrey M Halpin

Position	Chief Executive Officer, Underwriting Director &
	Active Underwriter Syndicate 1206
Company	Sagicor at Lloyd's Limited
Address (Office)	1 Great Tower Street
	London EC3R 5AA
Telephone	+44 (0)20 3003 6800
Fax	+44 (0)20 3003 6999
Email	geoffrey.halpin@sagicor.eu
Website	www.sagicor.com

Full Name	Geoffrey Michael Halpin
Year of Birth	1962
Professional Qualifications	Information not available

PROFESSIONAL INFORMATION

CURRENT MAJOR POSITIONS/APPOINTMENTS

Chief Executive	Sagicor at Lloyd's Limited	2004 -
Executive Director	Sagicor Syndicate Services Ltd	2005 -
Chief Executive	Byrne and Stacey Underwriting Limited	2007 -

PREVIOUS MAJOR POSITIONS/APPOINTMENTS

Information not available

John C Hamblin

Position	Executive Director & Active Underwriter Syndicates 2010 & 3010
Company	Cathedral Underwriting Limited
Address (Office)	5th Floor
	Fitzwilliam House
	10 St Mary Axe
	London EC3A 8EN
Telephone	+44 (0)20 7170 9062
Fax	+44 (0)20 7170 9001
Email	john.hamblin@cathedralcapital.com
Website	www.cathedralcapital.com
Full Name	John Charles Hamblin
Year of Birth	1957
Professional Qualifications	Information not available

PROFESSIONAL INFORMATION

CURRENT MAJOR POSITIONS/APPOINTMENTS

Executive Director	Cathedral Underwriting Limited	2001 -

PREVIOUS MAJOR POSITIONS/APPOINTMENTS

Active underwriter	Syndicate 566	1998 - 2000
Member	Lloyd's Aviation Underwriters' Association	1998 - 2005
Director	Bankside Underwriting Agencies	Unknown
Director	LIMIT plc	Unknown

Christopher E Hancock

Position	Executive Director & Active Underwriter Syndicate 1919
Company	Starr Managing Agents Limited
Address (Office)	3rd Floor
	140 Leadenhall Street
	London EC3V 4QT
Telephone	+44 (0)20 7337 3550
Fax	+44 (0)20 7337 3551
Email	christopher.hancock@cvstarrco.com
Website	www.cvstarrco.com
Full Name	Christopher Ernest Hancock
Year of Birth	1960
Professional Qualifications	Information not available

PROFESSIONAL INFORMATION

CURRENT MAJOR POSITIONS/APPOINTMENTS

Executive Director	Starr Underwriting Agents Limited	2007 -
Executive Director	Starr Managing Agents Ltd	2007 -

PREVIOUS MAJOR POSITIONS/APPOINTMENTS

Executive Director	Marlborough Underwriting Agency Limited	2006 - 2008

Martyn J Hardy

Position	Claims Director
Company	KGM Underwriting Agencies Limited
Address (Office)	KGM House
	George Lane
	South Woodford
	London E18 1RZ
Telephone	+44 (0)20 8530 1837
Fax	+44 (0)20 8530 7037
Email	martyn.hardy@kgminsurance.co.uk
Website	www.kgminsurance.co.uk
Full Name	Martyn James Hardy
Year of Birth	1956
Professional Qualifications	Information not available

PROFESSIONAL INFORMATION

CURRENT MAJOR POSITIONS/APPOINTMENTS

Executive Director	KGM Underwriting Agencies Limited	2004 -

PREVIOUS MAJOR POSITIONS/APPOINTMENTS

Information not available

Robin G Hargreaves

Position	Executive Director
Company	R J Kiln & Co Limited
Address (Office)	106 Fenchurch Street
	London EC3M 5NR
Telephone	+44 (0)20 7886 9000
Fax	+44 (0)20 7488 1848
Email	robin.hargreaves@kilngroup.com
Website	www.kilnplc.com
Full Name	Robin Graham Hargreaves
Year of Birth	1959
Professional Qualifications	FCII

PROFESSIONAL INFORMATION

CURRENT MAJOR POSITIONS/APPOINTMENTS

Executive Director	R J Kiln & Co Limited	1995 -

PREVIOUS MAJOR POSITIONS/APPOINTMENTS

Information not available

Richard de WW Harries

Position	Executive Director & Active Underwriter Syndicate 609
Company	Atrium Underwriters Limited

Address (Office)	Room 790
	Lloyd's
	One Lime Street
	London EC3M 7DQ
Telephone	+44 (0)20 7327 4877
Fax	+44 (0)20 7327 4878
Email	info@atrium-uw.com
Website	www.atrium-uw.com
Full Name	Richard de Winton Wilkin Harries
Year of Birth	1965
Professional Qualifications	Information not available

PROFESSIONAL INFORMATION

CURRENT MAJOR POSITIONS/APPOINTMENTS

Executive Director	Atrium Insurance Agency Limited	2008 -
Executive Director	Atrium Underwriters Limited	2008 -

PREVIOUS MAJOR POSITIONS/APPOINTMENTS

Information not available

Christopher L Harris

Position	Non-Executive Director
Company	Montpelier Underwriting Agencies Ltd
Address (Office)	7th Floor
	85 Gracechurch Street
	London EC3V 0AA
Telephone	+44 (0)20 7648 4500
Fax	+44 (0)20 7648 4501
Email	chris.harris@montpelierre.com
Website	www.montpelierre.com
Full Name	Christopher L Harris
Year of Birth	1969
Professional Qualifications	Information not available

PROFESSIONAL INFORMATION

CURRENT MAJOR POSITIONS/APPOINTMENTS

Non-Executive Director	Montpelier Underwriting Agencies Ltd	2008 -

PREVIOUS MAJOR POSITIONS/APPOINTMENTS

Information not available

David J Harris

Position	Managing Director
Company	Amlin Underwriting Limited
Address (Office)	St Helen's
	1 Undershaft
	London EC3A 8ND

Telephone	+44 (0)20 7746 1000
Fax	+44 (0)20 7746 1696
Email	david.harris@amlin.co.uk
Website	www.amlin.com

Full Name	David Jonathan Harris
Year of Birth	1963
Professional Qualifications	LLB, FCII

PROFESSIONAL INFORMATION

CURRENT MAJOR POSITIONS/APPOINTMENTS

Executive Director	Amlin Underwriting Limited	2005 -
Executive Director	Amlin Underwriting Services Limited	2005 -
Chief Executive	Amlin Underwriting Limited	2008 -

PREVIOUS MAJOR POSITIONS/APPOINTMENTS

Executive Director	Amlin Credit Limited	2005 - 2007

Colin Hart

Position	Chief Executive Officer, Underwriting Director & Active Underwriter Syndicate 260
Company	KGM Underwriting Agencies Limited
Address (Office)	KGM House
	George Lane
	South Woodford
	London E18 1RZ
Telephone	+44 (0)20 8530 1816
Fax	+44 (0)20 8530 7037
Email	colin.hart@kgminsurance.co.uk
Website	www.kgminsurance.co.uk

Full Name	Colin Hart
Year of Birth	1964
Professional Qualifications	Information not available

PROFESSIONAL INFORMATION

CURRENT MAJOR POSITIONS/APPOINTMENTS

Executive Director	KGM Underwriting Agencies Limited	2001 -
Chief Executive	KGM Underwriting Agencies Limited	2004 -
Non-Executive Director	1 Answer Network Limited	2006 -

PREVIOUS MAJOR POSITIONS/APPOINTMENTS

	Information not available

Terence (Terry) G Hebden

Position	Non-Executive Director
Company	Marketform Managing Agency Limited
Address (Office)	8 Lloyd's Avenue
	London EC3N 3EL

Telephone	+44 (0)20 7488 7761
Fax	+44 (0)20 7488 7800
Email	terence.hebden@marketform.com
Website	www.marketform.com

Full Name	Terence George Hebden
Year of Birth	1944
Professional Qualifications	Information not available

PROFESSIONAL INFORMATION

CURRENT MAJOR POSITIONS/APPOINTMENTS

| Non-Executive Director | Marketform Managing Agency Limited | 2002 - |
| Non-Executive Director | Preferential Direct Limited | 2005 - |

PREVIOUS MAJOR POSITIONS/APPOINTMENTS

Information not available

S Janet Helson

Position	Executive Director, Third Party Syndicates
Company	Chaucer Syndicates Limited
Address (Office)	Plantation Place
	30 Fenchurch Street
	London EC3M 3AD
Telephone	+44 (0)20 7397 9700
Fax	+44 (0)20 7397 9710
Email	janet.helson@chaucerplc.com
Website	www.chaucerplc.com

Full Name	Susan Janet Helson
Year of Birth	1959
Professional Qualifications	Information not available

PROFESSIONAL INFORMATION

CURRENT MAJOR POSITIONS/APPOINTMENTS

| Executive Director | Chaucer Syndicates Limited | 2005 - |

PREVIOUS MAJOR POSITIONS/APPOINTMENTS

| Executive Director | R J Kiln & Co Limited | 2001 - 2003 |
| Executive Director | Pembroke Managing Agency Ltd | 2007 - 2008 |

Stephen J Heming

Position	Compliance Director
Company	Novae Syndicates Limited
Address (Office)	71 Fenchurch Street
	London EC3M 4HH
Telephone	+44 (0)20 7903 7300
Fax	+44 (0)20 7903 7333
Email	sheming@novae.com
Website	www.novae.com

Full Name	Stephen John Heming	
Year of Birth	1963	
Professional Qualifications	ACII, IPFA	

PROFESSIONAL INFORMATION

CURRENT MAJOR POSITIONS/APPOINTMENTS

Executive Director	Novae Underwriting Limited	2006 -
Executive Director	Novae Syndicates Limited	2006 -
Executive Director	Novae Insurance Company Ltd	2006 -

PREVIOUS MAJOR POSITIONS/APPOINTMENTS

Executive Director	BRIT Insurance (UK) Ltd	2002 - 2003

Paul V Hennessy

Position	Chief Executive Officer
Company	Navigators Underwriting Agency Ltd
Address (Office)	7th Floor
	2 Minster Court
	Mincing Lane
	London EC3R 7BB
Telephone	+44 (0)20 7220 6900
Fax	+44 (0)20 7220 6901
Email	phennessy@navg.com
Website	www.navg.com

Full Name	Paul Vladimir Hennessy
Year of Birth	1948
Professional Qualifications	Information not available

PROFESSIONAL INFORMATION

CURRENT MAJOR POSITIONS/APPOINTMENTS

Executive Director	Navigators Underwriting Agency Ltd	2008 -

PREVIOUS MAJOR POSITIONS/APPOINTMENTS

Executive Director	CNA Insurance Company Limited	2001 - 2005
Executive Director	CNA Insurance Company (Europe) Limited	2001 - 2003

Ian M Hewitt

Position	Independent Non-Executive Director
Company	Advent Underwriting Limited
Address (Office)	10th Floor
	One Minster Court
	Mincing Lane
	London EC3R 7AA
Telephone	+44 (0)20 7743 8245
Fax	+44 (0)20 7743 8299
Email	ian.hewitt@adventgroup.co.uk
Website	www.adventgroup.co.uk

Full Name	Ian Malcolm Hewitt
Year of Birth	1962
Professional Qualifications	BA (Hons), FCII, MIRM

PROFESSIONAL INFORMATION

CURRENT MAJOR POSITIONS/APPOINTMENTS

| Executive Director | Advent Underwriting Limited | 2008 - |

PREVIOUS MAJOR POSITIONS/APPOINTMENTS
| | Information not available |

Paul W Hewitt

Position	Independent Non-Executive Director
Company	R J Kiln & Co Limited
Address (Office)	106 Fenchurch Street
	London EC3M 5NR
Telephone	+44 (0)20 7886 9000
Fax	+44 (0)20 7488 1848
Email	See R J Kiln & Co Ltd Company Profile
Website	www.kilnplc.com

Full Name	Paul William Hewitt
Year of Birth	1956
Professional Qualifications	Information not available

PROFESSIONAL INFORMATION

CURRENT MAJOR POSITIONS/APPOINTMENTS

Non-Executive Director	The Co-Operative Bank Plc	2005 -
Non-Executive Director	Co-operative Insurance Society Limited	2005 -
Non-Executive Director	CIS General Insurance Limited	2006 -
Non-Executive Director	R J Kiln & Co Limited	2007 -

PREVIOUS MAJOR POSITIONS/APPOINTMENTS

Executive Director	RAC Insurance Limited	2001 - 2003
Non-Executive Director	The Co-Operative Bank Plc	2003 - 2005
Non-Executive Director	Co-operative Insurance Society Limited	2003 - 2005
Chief Executive	The Co-Operative Bank Plc	2005 - 2005
Chief Executive	Co-operative Insurance Society Limited	2005 - 2005
Executive Director	The Co-Operative Bank Plc	2006 - 2006

Richard A Hextall

Position	Non-Executive Director
Company	Amlin Underwriting Limited
Address (Office)	St Helen's
	1 Undershaft
	London EC3A 8ND
Telephone	+44 (0)20 7746 1000
Fax	+44 (0)20 7746 1696

Email	richard.hextall@amlin.co.uk	
Website	www.amlin.com	

Full Name	Richard Anthony Hextall
Year of Birth	1968
Professional Qualifications	ACA

PROFESSIONAL INFORMATION

CURRENT MAJOR POSITIONS/APPOINTMENTS

Member	Lloyd's Market Association, Finance Committee	2002 -
Member	Lloyd's Investment Committee	2003 -
Chairman	Lloyd's Market Association, Finance Committee	2005 -
Non-Executive Director	City of London Investment Trust PLC	2007 -
Director	Lloyd's Market Association	2007 -
Non-Executive Director	Amlin Underwriting Limited	2008 -

PREVIOUS MAJOR POSITIONS/APPOINTMENTS

Executive Director	Amlin Underwriting Limited	1999 - 2008
Member	Lloyd's Investment Committee	2003 - 2007
Executive Director	Amlin Credit Limited	2005 - 2005

Michael E Hildesley

Position	Non-Executive Director
Company	KGM Underwriting Agencies Limited
Address (Office)	KGM House
	George Lane
	South Woodford
	London E18 1RZ
Telephone	+44 (0)20 8530 1813
Fax	+44 (0)20 8530 7037
Email	enquires@kgminsurance.co.uk
Website	www.kgminsurance.co.uk

Full Name	Michael Edmund Hildesley
Year of Birth	1948
Professional Qualifications	Information not available

PROFESSIONAL INFORMATION

CURRENT MAJOR POSITIONS/APPOINTMENTS

Non-Executive Director	KGM Underwriting Agencies Limited	2006 -

PREVIOUS MAJOR POSITIONS/APPOINTMENTS

	Information not available

Robert RS Hiscox

Position	Chairman
Company	Hiscox Syndicates Limited
Address (Office)	1 Great St Helen's
	London EC3A 6HX

Telephone	+44 (0)20 7448 6000
Fax	+44 (0)20 7448 6900
Email	robert.hiscox@hiscox.com
Website	www.hiscox.com

PERSONAL PROFILE	A profile can be found in the People at Lloyd's, Personal section.

Andrew N Hitchcox

Position	Executive Director
Company	R J Kiln & Co Limited
Address (Office)	106 Fenchurch Street
	London EC3M 5NR
Telephone	+44 (0)20 7886 9000
Fax	+44 (0)20 7488 1848
Email	andrew.hitchcox@kilngroup.com
Website	www.kilnplc.com

Full Name	Andrew Nelson Hitchcox
Year of Birth	1954
Professional Qualifications	Information not available

PROFESSIONAL INFORMATION

CURRENT MAJOR POSITIONS/APPOINTMENTS

Executive Director	R J Kiln & Co Limited	2006 -

PREVIOUS MAJOR POSITIONS/APPOINTMENTS

Executive Director	ERC Frankona Reinsurance (III) Limited	2001 - 2001

Dominick JR Hoare

Position	Executive Director & Joint Active Underwriter Syndicate 457
Company	Munich Re Underwriting Limited
Address (Office)	St Helen's
	1 Undershaft
	London EC3A 8EE
Telephone	+44 (0)20 7886 3900
Fax	+44 (0)20 7886 3901
Email	dominick.hoare@mrunderwriting.com
Website	www.watkins-syndicate.co.uk

Full Name	Dominick James Rolls Hoare
Year of Birth	1963
Professional Qualifications	BA, ACII

PROFESSIONAL INFORMATION

CURRENT MAJOR POSITIONS/APPOINTMENTS

Executive Director	Munich Re Underwriting Limited	1996 -

PREVIOUS MAJOR POSITIONS/APPOINTMENTS

Information not available

John F Hobbs

Position	Non-Executive Director
Company	Aspen Managing Agency Limited
Address (Office)	30 Fenchurch Street
	London EC3M 3BD
Telephone	+44 (0)20 7184 8000
Fax	+44 (0)20 7184 8500
Email	c/o robert.long@aspen-re.com
Website	www.aspen-re.com
Full Name	John Frederick Hobbs
Year of Birth	1952
Professional Qualifications	Information not available

PROFESSIONAL INFORMATION

CURRENT MAJOR POSITIONS/APPOINTMENTS

Non-Executive Director	Aspen Managing Agency Limited	2008 -

PREVIOUS MAJOR POSITIONS/APPOINTMENTS

Information not available

Darren J Hogg

Position	Finance Director
Company	Jubilee Managing Agency Limited
Address (Office)	4th Floor
	50 Fenchurch Street
	London EC3M 3JY
Telephone	+44 (0)20 7220 8728
Fax	+44 (0)20 7220 8732
Email	darren.hogg@jubilee-insurance.com
Website	www.jubilee-insurance.com
Full Name	Darren James Hogg
Year of Birth	1972
Professional Qualifications	Information not available

PROFESSIONAL INFORMATION

CURRENT MAJOR POSITIONS/APPOINTMENTS

Executive Director	Jubilee Managing Agency Limited	2009 -

PREVIOUS MAJOR POSITIONS/APPOINTMENTS

Information not available

Lawrence A Holder

Position	Managing Director
Company	Cathedral Underwriting Limited

Address (Office)	5th Floor
	Fitzwilliam House
	10 St Mary Axe
	London EC3A 8EN
Telephone	+44 (0)20 7170 9022
Fax	+44 (0)20 7170 9001
Email	lawrence.holder@cathedralcapital.com
Website	www.cathedralcapital.com

Full Name	Lawrence Albert Holder
Year of Birth	1959
Professional Qualifications	Information not available

PROFESSIONAL INFORMATION

CURRENT MAJOR POSITIONS/APPOINTMENTS

Chief Executive	Cathedral Underwriting Limited	2000 -
Trustee	Lloyd's Charities Trust	Unknown -

PREVIOUS MAJOR POSITIONS/APPOINTMENTS

Managing Director	Bankside Syndicates Limited	1990 - 1999
Non-Executive Director	Beaufort Underwriting Agency Limited	2001 - 2007
Deputy Managing Director	LIMIT Underwriting Limited	Unknown - 2000
Chairman	Lloyd's Market Association,	
	Risk Management Committee	2003 - 2008

Anthony (Tony) W Holt

Position	Non-Executive Director
Company	Amlin Underwriting Limited
Address (Office)	St Helen's
	1 Undershaft
	London EC3A 8ND
Telephone	+44 (0)20 7746 1000
Fax	+44 (0)20 7746 1696
Email	amlinreception@amlin.co.uk
Website	www.amlin.com

Full Name	Anthony Wareham Holt
Year of Birth	1951
Professional Qualifications	ACII

PROFESSIONAL INFORMATION

CURRENT MAJOR POSITIONS/APPOINTMENTS

Non-Executive Director	Amlin Underwriting Limited	2009 -

PREVIOUS MAJOR POSITIONS/APPOINTMENTS

Executive Director	Amlin Underwriting Limited	1992 - 2008
Member	Amlin Underwriting Advisory Committee	2003 - 2006
Executive Director	Amlin Credit Limited	2005 - 2007

David A Horton

Position	Chief Executive Officer
Company	Beazley Furlonge Ltd
Address (Office)	Plantation Place South
	60 Great Tower Street
	London EC3R 5AD
Telephone	+44 (0)20 7667 0623
Fax	+44 (0)20 7674 7100
Email	andrew.horton@beazley.com
Website	www.beazley.com

Full Name	David Andrew Horton
Year of Birth	1962
Professional Qualifications	ACA

PROFESSIONAL INFORMATION

CURRENT MAJOR POSITIONS/APPOINTMENTS

Executive Director	Beazley Solutions Limited	2004 -
Executive Director	Beazley Furlonge Ltd	2004 -
Chief Executive	Momentum Underwriting Management Ltd	2008 -
Chief Executive	Beazley Furlonge Ltd	2008 -

PREVIOUS MAJOR POSITIONS/APPOINTMENTS

Executive Director	Matterley Limited	2001 - 2002
Executive Director	Charterhouse Securities Limited	2001 - 2003
Executive Director	ING Barings Limited	2001 - 2003

Anthony GC Howland-Jackson

Position	Non-Executive Director
Company	Hiscox Syndicates Limited
Address (Office)	1 Great St Helen's
	London EC3A 6HX
Telephone	+44 (0)20 7448 6000
Fax	+44 (0)20 7448 6900
Email	enquiry@hiscox.com
Website	www.hiscox.com

Full Name	Anthony Geoffrey Clive Howland-Jackson
Year of Birth	1941
Professional Qualifications	Information not available

PROFESSIONAL INFORMATION

CURRENT MAJOR POSITIONS/APPOINTMENTS

Non-Executive Director	Hiscox Syndicates Limited	2001 -
Non-Executive Director	Hiscox Insurance Company Limited	2006 -

PREVIOUS MAJOR POSITIONS/APPOINTMENTS

Member	Lloyd's Regulatory Board	2001 - 2003
Non-Executive Director	Troika Insurance Company Limited	2001 - 2004

David J Huckstepp

Position	Executive Director & Active Underwriter Syndicate 557
Company	R J Kiln & Co Limited
Address (Office)	106 Fenchurch Street
	London EC3M 5NR
Telephone	+44 (0)20 7886 9000
Fax	+44 (0)20 7488 1848
Email	david.huckstepp@kilngroup.com
Website	www.kilnplc.com

Full Name	David John Huckstepp
Year of Birth	1967
Professional Qualifications	ACII

PROFESSIONAL INFORMATION

CURRENT MAJOR POSITIONS/APPOINTMENTS

Executive Director	R J Kiln & Co Limited	2007 -

PREVIOUS MAJOR POSITIONS/APPOINTMENTS

Information not available

Mark A Hudson

Position	Finance Director
Company	Novae Syndicates Limited
Address (Office)	71 Fenchurch Street
	London EC3M 4HH
Telephone	+44 (0)20 7903 7300
Fax	+44 (0)20 7903 7333
Email	mhudson@novae.com
Website	www.novae.com

Full Name	Mark Andrew Hudson
Year of Birth	1967
Professional Qualifications	ACA

PROFESSIONAL INFORMATION

CURRENT MAJOR POSITIONS/APPOINTMENTS

Executive Director	Novae Syndicates Limited	1999 -

PREVIOUS MAJOR POSITIONS/APPOINTMENTS

Executive Director	Novae Underwriting Limited	2005 - 2005
Member	Novae Group Investment Committee	Unknown
Chairman of Trustees	Novae Group Retirement Benefit Scheme	Unknown

Martin Peter Hudson

Position	Chief Executive Officer
Company	Travelers Syndicate Management Ltd

Address (Office)	Exchequer Court
	33 St Mary Axe
	London EC3A 8AG
Telephone	+44 (0)20 3207 6000
Fax	+44 (0)20 7645 4526
Email	mphudson@travelers.com
Website	www.travelers.co.uk/lloyds

Full Name	Martin Peter Hudson
Year of Birth	1959
Professional Qualifications	Information not available

PROFESSIONAL INFORMATION

CURRENT MAJOR POSITIONS/APPOINTMENTS

Executive Director	Travelers Insurance Company Limited	2001 -
Chief Executive	Travelers Syndicate Management Limited	2003 -
Chief Executive	Travelers Insurance Company Limited	2004 -
Executive Director	Galatea Underwriting Agencies Ltd	2007 -

PREVIOUS MAJOR POSITIONS/APPOINTMENTS

Information not available

Paul Hunt

Position	Underwriting Director & Active Underwriter Syndicate 2121
Company	Argenta Syndicate Management Limited
Address (Office)	Fountain House
	130 Fenchurch Street
	London EC3M 5DJ
Telephone	+44 (0)20 7825 7200
Fax	+44 (0)20 7825 7155
Email	paul.hunt@argentaplc.com
Website	www.argentaplc.com

PERSONAL PROFILE   A profile can be found in the People at Lloyd's, Personal section.

Barnabas J Hurst-Bannister

Position	Chairman
Company	Travelers Syndicate Management Ltd
Address (Office)	Exchequer Court
	33 St Mary Axe
	London EC3A 8AG
Telephone	+44 (0)20 3207 6000
Fax	+44 (0)20 7645 4526
Email	bhurstba@travelers.com
Website	www.travelers.co.uk/lloyds

Full Name	Barnabas John Hurst-Bannister
Year of Birth	1952
Professional Qualifications	Information not available

PROFESSIONAL INFORMATION

CURRENT MAJOR POSITIONS/APPOINTMENTS

Executive Director	Travelers Syndicate Management Limited	2003 -
Executive Director	Galatea Underwriting Agencies Ltd	2007 -
Deputy Chairman	Lloyd's Market Association Board	2007 -

PREVIOUS MAJOR POSITIONS/APPOINTMENTS

Non-Executive Director	Travelers Syndicate Management Limited	2001 - 2003

John R Hustler

Position	Chairman
Company	Spectrum Syndicate Management Limited
Address (Office)	2nd Floor
	6 Bevis Marks
	London EC3A 7HL
Telephone	+44 (0)20 7283 2646
Fax	+44 (0)20 7621 0975
Email	john.hustler@btconnect.com
Website	www.spectrumins.com

Full Name	John Randolph Hustler
Year of Birth	1946
Professional Qualifications	Information not available

PROFESSIONAL INFORMATION

CURRENT MAJOR POSITIONS/APPOINTMENTS

Non-Executive Director	Spectrum Syndicate Management Limited	2007 -

PREVIOUS MAJOR POSITIONS/APPOINTMENTS

Non-Executive Director	Crowe Syndicate Management Ltd	2001 - 2002

Theresa Hutchings

Position	Executive Director & Company Secretary
Company	Hardy (Underwriting Agencies) Ltd
Address (Office)	4th Floor
	40 Lime Street
	London EC3M 7AW
Telephone	+44 (0)20 7626 0382
Fax	+44 (0)20 7283 4677
Email	theresa.hutchings@hardygroup.co.uk
Website	www.hardygroup.co.uk

Full Name	Theresa Hutchings
Year of Birth	1947
Professional Qualifications	Information not available

PROFESSIONAL INFORMATION

CURRENT MAJOR POSITIONS/APPOINTMENTS

Executive Director	Hardy (Underwriting Agencies) Ltd	1992 -

PREVIOUS MAJOR POSITIONS/APPOINTMENTS
Information not available

Heidi E Hutter

Position	Chairman
Company	Aspen Managing Agency Limited
Address (Office)	30 Fenchurch Street
	London EC3M 3BD
Telephone	+44 (0)20 7184 8000
Fax	+44 (0)20 7184 8500
Email	heidihutter.theboard@aspen.bm
Website	www.aspen-re.com

Full Name	Heidi Elisabeth Hutter
Year of Birth	1957
Professional Qualifications	Information not available

PROFESSIONAL INFORMATION

CURRENT MAJOR POSITIONS/APPOINTMENTS

Non-Executive Director	Aspen Insurance UK Limited	2002 -
Non-Executive Director	Aspen Managing Agency Limited	2008 -

PREVIOUS MAJOR POSITIONS/APPOINTMENTS

Project Director	Lloyd's Reconstruction & Renewal	1993 - 1995
Chief Executive Officer	Swiss Re America	1996 - 1999
Chief Executive Officer	Black Diamond Group, LLC	2001 - Unknown
Non-Executive Director	Talbot Underwriting Ltd	2002 - 2007

Nicholas I Hutton-Penman

Position	Chief Executive Officer
Company	HCC Underwriting Agency Ltd
Address (Office)	Walsingham House
	35 Seething Lane
	London EC3N 4AH
Telephone	+44 (0)20 7680 3000
Fax	+44 (0)20 7977 7350
Email	info@hccual.com
Website	www.hccual.com

Full Name	Nicholas Ian Hutton-Penman
Year of Birth	1966
Professional Qualifications	Information not available

PROFESSIONAL INFORMATION

CURRENT MAJOR POSITIONS/APPOINTMENTS

Executive Director	HCC International Insurance Company Plc	2006 -
Chief Executive	HCC Underwriting Agency Ltd	2008 -

PREVIOUS MAJOR POSITIONS/APPOINTMENTS

Executive Director	St Paul Reinsurance Company Limited	2001 - 2002
Chief Executive	Houston Casualty Company	2002 - 2006
Non-Executive Director	Credance Limited	2005 - 2005

David CB Ibeson

Position	Chief Executive Officer
Company	Catlin Underwriting Agencies Ltd
Address (Office)	6th Floor
	3 Minster Court
	Mincing Lane
	London EC3R 7DD
Telephone	+44 (0)20 7626 0486
Fax	+44 (0)20 7623 9101
Email	david.ibeson@catlin.com
Website	www.catlin.com

Full Name	David Christopher Ben Ibeson
Year of Birth	1965
Professional Qualifications	Information not available

PROFESSIONAL INFORMATION

CURRENT MAJOR POSITIONS/APPOINTMENTS

Chief Executive	Catlin (Wellington) Underwriting Agencies Limited	2001 -
Chief Executive	Catlin Underwriting Agencies Ltd	2007 -
Executive Director	Catlin Insurance Company (UK) Ltd	2007 -
Executive Director	Brighter Business Limited	2008 -
Chief Executive	Catlin Insurance Company (UK) Ltd	2008 -

PREVIOUS MAJOR POSITIONS/APPOINTMENTS

| Executive Director | Wellington Syndicate Services Limited | 2005 - 2007 |

Hiroyuki Iioka

Position	Non-Executive Director
Company	Mitsui Sumitomo Insurance Underwriting at Lloyd's Ltd
Address (Office)	25 Fenchurch Avenue
	London EC3M 5AD
Telephone	+44 (0)20 7977 8321
Fax	+44 (0)20 7977 8300
Email	enquiries@msilm.com
Website	www.msilm.com

Full Name	Hiroyuki Iioka
Year of Birth	Information not available
Professional Qualifications	Information not available

PROFESSIONAL INFORMATION

CURRENT MAJOR POSITIONS/APPOINTMENTS

| Non-Executive Director | Mitsui Sumitomo Insurance Underwriting at Lloyd's Ltd |

PREVIOUS MAJOR POSITIONS/APPOINTMENTS
Information not available

James Le Tall Illingworth

Position	Chief Risk Officer
Company	Amlin Underwriting Limited
Address (Office)	St Helen's
	1 Undershaft
	London EC3A 8ND
Telephone	+44 (0)20 7746 1060
Fax	+44 (0)20 7746 1696
Email	james.illingworth@amlin.co.uk
Website	www.amlin.com

PERSONAL PROFILE   A profile can be found in the People at Lloyd's, Personal section.

Ian E Ivory

Position	Non-Executive Director
Company	Hardy (Underwriting Agencies) Ltd
Address (Office)	4th Floor
	40 Lime Street
	London EC3M 7AW
Telephone	+44 (0)20 7626 0382
Fax	+44 (0)20 7283 4677
Email	ian.ivory@hardygroup.co.uk
Website	www.hardygroup.co.uk

Full Name	Ian Eric Ivory
Year of Birth	1944
Professional Qualifications	Information not available

PROFESSIONAL INFORMATION

CURRENT MAJOR POSITIONS/APPOINTMENTS

Non-Executive Director	Hardy (Underwriting Agencies) Ltd	2007 -

PREVIOUS MAJOR POSITIONS/APPOINTMENTS
Information not available

Robin AG Jackson

Position	Chairman
Company	Marketform Managing Agency Limited
Address (Office)	8 Lloyd's Avenue
	London EC3N 3EL
Telephone	+44 (0)20 7488 7762
Fax	+44 (0)20 7488 7800
Email	robin.jackson@marketform.com
Website	www.marketform.com

PERSONAL PROFILE   A profile can be found in the People at Lloyd's, Personal section.

Bjorn Jansli

Position	Non-Executive Director
Company	Sagicor at Lloyd's Limited
Address (Office)	1 Great Tower Street
	London EC3R 5AA
Telephone	+44 (0)20 3003 6800
Fax	+44 (0)20 3003 6999
Email	duncan.reed@sagicor.eu
Website	www.sagicor.com
Full Name	1946
Year of Birth	Information not available
Professional Qualifications	Information not available

PROFESSIONAL INFORMATION

CURRENT MAJOR POSITIONS/APPOINTMENTS

Non-Executive Director	Sagicor at Lloyd's Limited	2008 -

PREVIOUS MAJOR POSITIONS/APPOINTMENTS

Information not available

Paul A Jardine

Position	Deputy Chairman
Company	Catlin Underwriting Agencies Ltd
Address (Office)	6th Floor
	3 Minster Court
	Mincing Lane
	London EC3R 7DD
Telephone	+44 (0)20 7626 0486
Fax	+44 (0)20 7623 9101
Email	paul.jardine@catlin.com
Website	www.catlin.com
Full Name	Paul Andrew Jardine
Year of Birth	1961
Professional Qualifications	ACA

PROFESSIONAL INFORMATION

CURRENT MAJOR POSITIONS/APPOINTMENTS

Executive Director	Catlin Underwriting Agencies Ltd	2001 -
Non-Executive Director	CX Reinsurance Company Limited	2003 -
Executive Director	Catlin Insurance Company (UK) Ltd	2005 -
Executive Director	Catlin (Wellington) Underwriting Agencies Limited	2007 -
Chairman	Lloyd's Market Association Board	2007 -
Non-Executive Director	Brighter Business Limited	2008 -
External Member	Council of Lloyd's	2008 -
Member	Institute of Actuaries	Unknown -
Associate	Casualty Actuarial Society	Unknown -

PREVIOUS MAJOR POSITIONS/APPOINTMENTS

Chief Actuary & Commutations Director	Equitas Limited	1996 - 2001
Chief Executive	Catlin Underwriting Agencies Ltd	2003 - 2007
Non-Executive Director	Brighter Business Limited	2006 - 2008

Karl W Jarvis

Position	Chief Operating Officer, Compliance Officer & Company Secretary
Company	SA Meacock & Company Limited
Address (Office)	4th Floor
	15 St Helen's Place
	London EC3A 6DE
Telephone	+44 (0)20 7374 6727
Fax	+44 (0)20 7374 4727
Email	karl.jarvis@sameacock.com
Website	None at present
Full Name	Karl William Jarvis
Year of Birth	1961
Professional Qualifications	MBA, ACIS, ACII

PROFESSIONAL INFORMATION

CURRENT MAJOR POSITIONS/APPOINTMENTS

Executive Director	SA Meacock & Company Limited	1996 -

PREVIOUS MAJOR POSITIONS/APPOINTMENTS

Information not available

Mark S Johnson

Position	Executive Director
Company	Talbot Underwriting Ltd
Address (Office)	Gracechurch House
	55 Gracechurch Street
	London EC3V 0JP
Telephone	+44 (0)20 7550 3500
Fax	+44 (0)20 7550 3555
Email	mark.johnsonr@talbotuw.com
Website	www.talbotuw.com
Full Name	Mark Sutherland Johnson
Year of Birth	1958
Professional Qualifications	Information not available

PROFESSIONAL INFORMATION

CURRENT MAJOR POSITIONS/APPOINTMENTS

Executive Director	Talbot Underwriting Ltd	2001 -

PREVIOUS MAJOR POSITIONS/APPOINTMENTS

Information not available

John E Josiah

Position	Executive Director & Active Underwriter Syndicate 218
Company	Equity Syndicate Management Limited
Address (Office)	Library House
	New Road
	Brentwood
	Essex CM14 4GD
Telephone	+44 (0)1277 200 100
Fax	+44 (0)1206 777 223
Email	john.josiah@equitygroup.co.uk
Website	www.equitygroup.co.uk
Full Name	John Edward Josiah
Year of Birth	1953
Professional Qualifications	Information not available

PROFESSIONAL INFORMATION

CURRENT MAJOR POSITIONS/APPOINTMENTS

Executive Director	Equity Syndicate Management Limited	2005 -
Executive Director	Arista Insurance Ltd	2005 -
Executive Director	Equity Red Star Services Limited	2005 -

PREVIOUS MAJOR POSITIONS/APPOINTMENTS

Information not available

Lady Barbara S Judge

Position	Non-Executive Director
Company	Hardy (Underwriting Agencies) Ltd
Address (Office)	4th Floor
	40 Lime Street
	London EC3M 7AW
Telephone	+44 (0)20 7626 0382
Fax	+44 (0)20 7283 4677
Email	info@hardygroup.co.uk
Website	www.hardygroup.co.uk
Full Name	Barbara Singer Judge
Year of Birth	1946
Professional Qualifications	Information not available

PROFESSIONAL INFORMATION

CURRENT MAJOR POSITIONS/APPOINTMENTS

Non-Executive Director	Friends Provident Life and Pensions Limited	2001 -
Non-Executive Director	Friends Provident Pensions Limited	2001 -
Non-Executive Director	Friends Provident Life Assurance Limited	2001 -
Chairman	UK Atomic Energy Authority	2004 -
Non-Executive Director	Hardy (Underwriting Agencies) Ltd	2008 -

PREVIOUS MAJOR POSITIONS/APPOINTMENTS

Executive Director	Friends Provident Life Office	2001 - 2002

Non-Executive Director	Friends Provident Administration Services Limited	2001 - 2003
Non-Executive Director	DSGVC Limited	2005 - 2006
Director	News International plc	Unknown
Director	Samuel Montagu & Company Limited	Unknown
Commissioner	US Securities and Exchange Commission	Unknown

Yohichi Kamagai

Position	Non-Executive Director
Company	Mitsui Sumitomo Insurance Underwriting at Lloyd's Ltd
Address (Office)	25 Fenchurch Avenue
	London EC3M 5AD
Telephone	+44 (0)20 7977 8321
Fax	+44 (0)20 7977 8300
Email	enquiries@msilm.com
Website	www.msilm.com

Full Name	Yohichi Kamagai
Year of Birth	Information not available
Professional Qualifications	Information not available

PROFESSIONAL INFORMATION

CURRENT MAJOR POSITIONS/APPOINTMENTS

Non-Executive Director	Mitsui Sumitomo Insurance Underwriting at Lloyd's Ltd

PREVIOUS MAJOR POSITIONS/APPOINTMENTS

Information not available

Sonny Kapur

Position	Finance Director
Company	Travelers Syndicate Management Ltd
Address (Office)	Exchequer Court
	33 St Mary Axe
	London EC3A 8AG
Telephone	+44 (0)20 3207 6101
Fax	+44 (0)20 7645 4526
Email	skapur@travelers.com
Website	www.travelers.co.uk/lloyds

Full Name	Sonny Kapur
Year of Birth	1960
Professional Qualifications	Information not available

PROFESSIONAL INFORMATION

CURRENT MAJOR POSITIONS/APPOINTMENTS

Executive Director	Travelers Syndicate Management Limited	2000 -

PREVIOUS MAJOR POSITIONS/APPOINTMENTS

Information not available

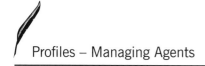

Robert B Kastner

Position	Claims Director
Company	Newline Underwriting Management Ltd
Address (Office)	Suite 5/4
	London Underwriting Centre
	3 Minster Court
	Mincing Lane
	London EC3R 7DD
Telephone	+44 (0)20 7090 1700
Fax	+44 (0)20 7090 1701
Email	rkastner@newlineuml.com
Website	www.newlineuml.com

Full Name	Robert Bernhard Kastner
Year of Birth	1968
Professional Qualifications	Information not available

PROFESSIONAL INFORMATION

CURRENT MAJOR POSITIONS/APPOINTMENTS

Executive Director	Newline Insurance Company Limited	2007 -
Executive Director	Newline Underwriting Management Ltd	2007 -

PREVIOUS MAJOR POSITIONS/APPOINTMENTS

Information not available

Allan Kaufman

Position	Non-Executive Director
Company	Pembroke Managing Agency Ltd
Address (Office)	2nd Floor
	3 Minster Court
	Mincing Lane
	London EC3R 7DD
Telephone	+44 (0)20 7337 4400
Fax	+44 (0)20 7337 4401
Email	hq@pembrokeunderwriting.com
Website	www.pembrokeunderwriting.com

Full Name	Allan Kaufman
Year of Birth	1948
Professional Qualifications	Information not available

PROFESSIONAL INFORMATION

CURRENT MAJOR POSITIONS/APPOINTMENTS

Non-Executive Director	Pembroke Managing Agency Ltd	2008 -

PREVIOUS MAJOR POSITIONS/APPOINTMENTS

Information not available

Dr Paul Kelly

Position	Non-Executive Director
Company	Navigators Underwriting Agency Ltd
Address (Office)	7th Floor
	2 Minster Court
	Mincing Lane
	London EC3R 7BB
Telephone	+44 (0)20 7220 6900
Fax	+44 (0)20 7220 6901
Email	pkelly@navg.com
Website	www.navg.com
Full Name	Dr Paul Kelly
Year of Birth	1943
Professional Qualifications	Information not available

PROFESSIONAL INFORMATION

CURRENT MAJOR POSITIONS/APPOINTMENTS

Non-Executive Director	Navigators Underwriting Agency Ltd	1993 -

PREVIOUS MAJOR POSITIONS/APPOINTMENTS
Information not available

Andrew J Kendrick

Position	Chairman & Chief Executive Officer
Company	ACE Underwriting Agencies Limited
Address (Office)	100 Leadenhall Street
	London EC3A 3BP
Telephone	+44 (0)20 7173 7000
Fax	+44 (0)20 7173 7800
Email	andrew.kendrick@ace-ina.com
Website	www.acelimited.com
Full Name	Andrew James Kendrick
Year of Birth	1957
Professional Qualifications	Information not available

PROFESSIONAL INFORMATION

CURRENT MAJOR POSITIONS/APPOINTMENTS

Chief Executive	ACE European Group Limited	2004 -
Chief Executive	ACE Underwriting Agencies Limited	2004 -
Executive Director	ACE Europe Life Limited	2007 -
Non-Executive Director	Lloyd's Franchise Board	2007 -
Member	Lloyd's Market Association Board	2006 -

PREVIOUS MAJOR POSITIONS/APPOINTMENTS

Executive Director	ACE London Underwriting Limited	2001 - 2002
Executive Director	ACE Underwriting Agencies Limited	2001 - 2003
Executive Director	ACE European Group Limited	2002 - 2003

Executive Director	Ridge Underwriting Agencies Limited	2002 - 2003
Non-Executive Director	Lloyd's Franchise Board	2003 - 2003

Anthony J Keys

Position	Independent Review Director
Company	Talbot Underwriting Ltd
Address (Office)	Gracechurch House
	55 Gracechurch Street
	London EC3V 0JP
Telephone	+44 (0)20 7550 3500
Fax	+44 (0)20 7550 3555
Email	central@talbotuw.com
Website	www.talbotuw.com

Full Name	Anthony James Keys
Year of Birth	1941
Professional Qualifications	Information not available

PROFESSIONAL INFORMATION

CURRENT MAJOR POSITIONS/APPOINTMENTS

Non-Executive Director	Talbot Underwriting Ltd	2003 -
Non-Executive Director	Underwriting Risk Services Ltd	2005 -
Non-Executive Director	RiverStone Managing Agency Limited	2005 -

PREVIOUS MAJOR POSITIONS/APPOINTMENTS

Non-Executive Director	Admiral Syndicate Management Limited	2001 - 2006
Non-Executive Director	Danish Re Syndicates Ltd	2001 - 2005
Non-Executive Director	Newmarket Underwriting Ltd	2001 - 2004

Derek Kingston

Position	Non-Executive Director
Company	Mitsui Sumitomo Insurance Underwriting at Lloyd's Ltd
Address (Office)	25 Fenchurch Avenue
	London EC3M 5AD
Telephone	+44 (0)20 7977 8321
Fax	+44 (0)20 7977 8300
Email	enquiries@msilm.com
Website	www.msilm.com

Full Name	Derek Kingston
Year of Birth	1937
Professional Qualifications	Information not available

PROFESSIONAL INFORMATION

CURRENT MAJOR POSITIONS/APPOINTMENTS

Non-Executive Director	Mitsui Sumitomo Insurance (London) Limited	2004 -
Non-Executive Director	Mitsui Sumitomo Insurance	
	Underwriting at Lloyd's Ltd	2006 -

PREVIOUS MAJOR POSITIONS/APPOINTMENTS
Information not available

Dominic J Kirby

Position	Deputy Managing Director
Company	Marlborough Underwriting Agency Ltd
Address (Office)	Birchin Court
	20 Birchin Lane
	London EC3V 9DU
Telephone	+44 (0)20 7456 1800
Fax	+44 (0)20 7456 1810
Email	dominic.kirby@marlborough.co.uk
Website	www.marlborough.co.uk

Full Name	Dominic James Kirby
Year of Birth	1970
Professional Qualifications	Information not available

PROFESSIONAL INFORMATION

CURRENT MAJOR POSITIONS/APPOINTMENTS

Executive Director	Flagstone Representatives Ltd	2008 -
Executive Director	Marlborough Underwriting Agency Ltd	2009 -

PREVIOUS MAJOR POSITIONS/APPOINTMENTS

Executive Director	Navigators Underwriting Agency Ltd	2002 - 2007

Aidan Kong

Position	Executive Director & Deputy Underwriter Syndicates 2791 & 6103
Company	Managing Agency Partners Limited
Address (Office)	1st Floor
	110 Fenchurch Street
	London EC3M 5JT
Telephone	+44 (0)20 7709 3860
Fax	+44 (0)20 7709 3861
Email	map@mapunderwriting.co.uk
Website	www.mapunderwriting.co.uk

Full Name	Aidan Kong
Year of Birth	1965
Professional Qualifications	Information not available

PROFESSIONAL INFORMATION

CURRENT MAJOR POSITIONS/APPOINTMENTS

Executive Director	Managing Agency Partners Ltd	2000 -

PREVIOUS MAJOR POSITIONS/APPOINTMENTS
Information not available

Don Kramer

Position	Non-Executive Director
Company	Atrium Underwriters Limited
Address (Office)	Room 790
	Lloyd's
	One Lime Street
	London EC3M 7DQ
Telephone	+44 (0)20 7327 4877
Fax	+44 (0)20 7327 4878
Email	info@atrium-uw.com
Website	www.atrium-uw.com

Full Name	Donald Kramer
Year of Birth	1937
Professional Qualifications	Information not available

PROFESSIONAL INFORMATION

CURRENT MAJOR POSITIONS/APPOINTMENTS

Non-Executive Director	Atrium Underwriters Limited	2007 -

PREVIOUS MAJOR POSITIONS/APPOINTMENTS

Information not available

Stewart K Laderman

Position	Underwriting Director
Company	Whittington Capital Management Limited
Address (Office)	33 Creechurch Lane
	London EC3A 5EB
Telephone	+44 (0)20 7743 0900
Fax	+44 (0)20 7743 0901
Email	stewart.laderman@whittingtoninsurance.com
Website	www.whittingtoninsurance.com

Full Name	Stewart Keith Laderman
Year of Birth	1956
Professional Qualifications	Information not available

PROFESSIONAL INFORMATION

CURRENT MAJOR POSITIONS/APPOINTMENTS

Executive Director	Whittington Capital Management Limited	2007 -

PREVIOUS MAJOR POSITIONS/APPOINTMENTS

Executive Director	Alea London Limited	2001 - 2005

Anthony PD Lancaster

Position	Non-Executive Director
Company	Jubilee Managing Agency Limited

Address (Office)	4th Floor
	50 Fenchurch Street
	London EC3M 3JY
Telephone	+44 (0)20 7220 8728
Fax	+44 (0)20 7220 8732
Email	jubilee@jubilee-insurance.com
Website	www.jubilee-insurance.com

Full Name	Antony Philip Dawson Lancaster
Year of Birth	1942
Professional Qualifications	Information not available

PROFESSIONAL INFORMATION

CURRENT MAJOR POSITIONS/APPOINTMENTS

Non-Executive Director	Platinum Re (UK) Limited	2002 -
Non-Executive Director	Jubilee Managing Agency Limited	2004 -
Non-Executive Director	Mondial Assistance (UK) Ltd	2005 -
Non-Executive Director	Interglobal Insurance Company Limited	2007 -

PREVIOUS MAJOR POSITIONS/APPOINTMENTS

Executive Director	Contingency Insurance Company Limited	2001 - 2002
Executive Director	Groupama Insurance Company Limited	2001 - 2002
Executive Director	Malvern Insurance Company Limited	2001 - 2002
Executive Director	Minster Insurance Company Limited	2001 - 2002
Executive Director	Minster Trust Ltd	2001 - 2002
Executive Director	The National Motor and Accident Insurance Union Limited	2001 - 2002
Chief Executive	Groupama Insurance Company Limited	2001 - 2002
Chief Executive	Minster Insurance Company Limited	2001 - 2002
Non-Executive Director	Co-operative Insurance Society Limited	2004 - 2007
Non-Executive Director	The Co-Operative Bank Plc	2004 - 2007
Non-Executive Director	CIS General Insurance Limited	2006 - 2007

Gillian S Langford

Position	Claims Director
Company	Talbot Underwriting Ltd
Address (Office)	Gracechurch House
	55 Gracechurch Street
	London EC3V 0JP
Telephone	+44 (0)20 7550 3500
Fax	+44 (0)20 7550 3555
Email	gill.langford@talbotuw.com
Website	www.talbotuw.com

Full Name	Gillian Susan Langford
Year of Birth	1959
Professional Qualifications	Information not available

PROFESSIONAL INFORMATION

CURRENT MAJOR POSITIONS/APPOINTMENTS

Executive Director	Talbot Underwriting Ltd	2003 -

PREVIOUS MAJOR POSITIONS/APPOINTMENTS

Information not available

Robert D Law

Position	Non-Executive Director
Company	Canopius Managing Agents Limited
Address (Office)	Gallery 9
	One Lime Street
	London EC3M 7HA
Telephone	+44 (0)20 7337 3700
Fax	+44 (0)20 7337 3999
Email	robert.law@canopius.com
Website	www.canopius.com

Full Name	Robert David Law
Year of Birth	1960
Professional Qualifications	FCA

PROFESSIONAL INFORMATION

CURRENT MAJOR POSITIONS/APPOINTMENTS

Executive Director	Creechurch Services Limited	2007 -
Non-Executive Director	Canopius Managing Agents Limited	2007 -
Executive Director	Canopius Underwriting Limited	2008 -

PREVIOUS MAJOR POSITIONS/APPOINTMENTS

Executive Director	Canopius Managing Agents Limited	2001 - 2007

Mark W Lawrence

Position	Executive Director & Joint Active Underwriter,
	Liability Division Syndicate 1200
Company	Argo Managing Agency Ltd
Address (Office)	47 Mark Lane
	London EC3R 7QQ
Telephone	+44 (0)20 7712 7600
Fax	+44 (0)20 7712 7601
Email	mark.lawrence@argo-int.com
Website	www.argo-int.com

Full Name	Mark William Lawrence
Year of Birth	1962
Professional Qualifications	Information not available

PROFESSIONAL INFORMATION

CURRENT MAJOR POSITIONS/APPOINTMENTS

Executive Director	Argo Managing Agency Ltd	2000 -
Executive Director	Heritage Direct Ltd	2006 -

PREVIOUS MAJOR POSITIONS/APPOINTMENTS

Information not available

James RF Lee

Position	Compliance Director
Company	Atrium Underwriters Limited
Address (Office)	Room 790
	Lloyd's
	One Lime Street
	London EC3M 7DQ
Telephone	+44 (0)20 7327 4877
Fax	+44 (0)20 7327 4878
Email	info@atrium-uw.com
Website	www.atrium-uw.com
Full Name	James Robert Francis Lee
Year of Birth	1962
Professional Qualifications	BSc (Hons)

PROFESSIONAL INFORMATION

CURRENT MAJOR POSITIONS/APPOINTMENTS

Executive Director	Atrium Underwriters Limited	2002 -
Executive Director	Atrium Insurance Agency Limited	2007 -
Deputy Chairman	Lloyd's Market Association Board,	
	Regulatory Committee	Unknown -

PREVIOUS MAJOR POSITIONS/APPOINTMENTS

Executive Director	Denham Syndicate Management Ltd	2001 - 2002
Partner	Morgan, Fentiman and Barber	2001 - 2003

Paul M Letherbarrow

Position	Executive Director
Company	R J Kiln & Co Limited
Address (Office)	106 Fenchurch Street
	London EC3M 5NR
Telephone	+44 (0)20 7886 9000
Fax	+44 (0)20 7488 1848
Email	paul.letherbarrow@kilngroup.com
Website	www.kilnplc.com
Full Name	Paul Michael Letherbarrow
Year of Birth	1967
Professional Qualifications	ACII

PROFESSIONAL INFORMATION

CURRENT MAJOR POSITIONS/APPOINTMENTS

Executive Director	R J Kiln & Co Limited	1999 -

PREVIOUS MAJOR POSITIONS/APPOINTMENTS
Information not available

Kathryn J Lewis

Position	Managing Director
Company	Jubilee Managing Agency Limited
Address (Office)	4th Floor
	50 Fenchurch Street
	London EC3M 3JY
Telephone	+44 (0)20 7220 8728
Fax	+44 (0)20 7220 8732
Email	kate.lewis@jubilee-insurance.com
Website	www.jubilee-insurance.com
Full Name	Kathryn Jane Lewis
Year of Birth	1971
Professional Qualifications	Information not available

PROFESSIONAL INFORMATION

CURRENT MAJOR POSITIONS/APPOINTMENTS

Executive Director	Jubilee Managing Agency Limited	2005 -
Executive Director	Lutine Assurance Services Limited	2008 -
Executive Director	Cassidy Davis Insurance Services Ltd	2008 -

PREVIOUS MAJOR POSITIONS/APPOINTMENTS
Information not available

Richard CW Lewis

Position	Director of Underwriting & Active Underwriter Syndicate 510
Company	R J Kiln & Co Limited
Address (Office)	106 Fenchurch Street
	London EC3M 5NR
Telephone	+44 (0)20 7886 9000
Fax	+44 (0)20 7488 1848
Email	richard.lewis@kilngroup.com
Website	www.kilnplc.com
Full Name	Richard Charles William Lewis
Year of Birth	1963
Professional Qualifications	Information not available

PROFESSIONAL INFORMATION

CURRENT MAJOR POSITIONS/APPOINTMENTS

Executive Director	R J Kiln & Co Limited	2007 -

PREVIOUS MAJOR POSITIONS/APPOINTMENTS
Information not available

Tracey O Lillington

Position	Chief Financial Officer
Company	Navigators Underwriting Agency Ltd
Address (Office)	7th Floor
	2 Minster Court
	Mincing Lane
	London EC3R 7BB
Telephone	+44 (0)20 7220 6900
Fax	+44 (0)20 7220 6901
Email	communications@navg.com
Website	www.navg.com

Full Name	Tracey Olivia Lillington
Year of Birth	1968
Professional Qualifications	Information not available

PROFESSIONAL INFORMATION

CURRENT MAJOR POSITIONS/APPOINTMENTS

Executive Director	Navigators Insurance Company	2008 -
Executive Director	Navigators Underwriting Agency Ltd	2008 -

PREVIOUS MAJOR POSITIONS/APPOINTMENTS

Executive Director	Newline Underwriting Management Ltd	2001 - 2007
Executive Director	Newline Insurance Company Limited	2006 - 2007

Nicholas JS Line

Position	Chief Actuary Director
Company	Markel Syndicate Management Limited
Address (Office)	The Markel Building
	49 Leadenhall Street
	London EC3A 2EA
Telephone	+44 (0)20 7953 6000
Fax	+44 (0)20 7953 6800
Email	underwriters@marketform.com
Website	www.markelintl.com

Full Name	Nicholas James Stephen Line
Year of Birth	1972
Professional Qualifications	MA, FIA

PROFESSIONAL INFORMATION

CURRENT MAJOR POSITIONS/APPOINTMENTS

Executive Director	Markel Syndicate Management Limited	2008 -
Executive Director	Markel International Insurance Company Limited	2008 -

PREVIOUS MAJOR POSITIONS/APPOINTMENTS
                          Information not available

Chris M London

Position	Non-Executive Director
Company	Beazley Furlonge Ltd
Address (Office)	Plantation Place South
	60 Great Tower Street
	London EC3R 5AD
Telephone	+44 (0)20 7667 0623
Fax	+44 (0)20 7674 7100
Email	chris.london@beazley.com
Website	www.beazley.com

Full Name	Christopher Michael London
Year of Birth	1948
Professional Qualifications	Information not available

PROFESSIONAL INFORMATION

CURRENT MAJOR POSITIONS/APPOINTMENTS

Non-Executive Director	Beazley Furlonge Ltd	2008 -

PREVIOUS MAJOR POSITIONS/APPOINTMENTS
                          Information not available

Robert J Long

Position	Syndicate Operations Director
Company	Aspen Managing Agency Limited
Address (Office)	30 Fenchurch Street
	London EC3M 3BD
Telephone	+44 (0)20 7184 8000
Fax	+44 (0)20 7184 8500
Email	c/o robert.long@aspen-re.com
Website	www.aspen-re.com

Full Name	Robert James Long
Year of Birth	1964
Professional Qualifications	Information not available

PROFESSIONAL INFORMATION

CURRENT MAJOR POSITIONS/APPOINTMENTS

Executive Director	Aspen Managing Agency Limited	2008 -

PREVIOUS MAJOR POSITIONS/APPOINTMENTS
                          Information not available

Simon P Lotter

Position	Underwriting Director & Active Underwriter Syndicate 2468
Company	Marketform Managing Agency Limited

Address (Office)	8 Lloyd's Avenue
	London EC3N 3EL
Telephone	+44 (0)20 7488 7700
Fax	+44 (0)20 7488 7800
Email	simon.lotter@marketform.com
Website	www.marketform.com

Full Name	Simon Peter Lotter
Year of Birth	1958
Professional Qualifications	ACII

PROFESSIONAL INFORMATION

CURRENT MAJOR POSITIONS/APPOINTMENTS

Executive Director	Marketform Managing Agency Limited	1998 -

PREVIOUS MAJOR POSITIONS/APPOINTMENTS

Information not available

Andreas C Loucaides

Position	Group Chief Executive Officer
Company	Jubilee Managing Agency Limited
Address (Office)	4th Floor
	50 Fenchurch Street
	London EC3M 3JY
Telephone	+44 (0)20 7220 8728
Fax	+44 (0)20 7220 8732
Email	andreas.loucaides@jubilee-insurance.com
Website	www.jubilee-insurance.com

Full Name	Andreas Costas Loucaides
Year of Birth	1952
Professional Qualifications	Information not available

PROFESSIONAL INFORMATION

CURRENT MAJOR POSITIONS/APPOINTMENTS

Executive Director	Jubilee Managing Agency Limited	2008 -
Executive Director	Cassidy Davis Insurance Services Ltd	2008 -
Executive Director	Lutine Assurance Services Limited	2008 -

PREVIOUS MAJOR POSITIONS/APPOINTMENTS

Chief Executive	BRIT Insurance (UK) Ltd	2002 - 2003
Chief Executive	Catlin Insurance Company Ltd	2004 - 2006
Executive Director	Catlin Underwriting Agencies Ltd	2005 - 2008
Chief Executive	Catlin Insurance Company (UK) Ltd	2005 - 2008

Rupert JG Lowe

Position	Non-Executive Director
Company	Jubilee Managing Agency Limited
Address (Office)	4th Floor

50 Fenchurch Street
London EC3M 3JY

Telephone	+44 (0)20 7220 8728
Fax	+44 (0)20 7220 8732
Email	jubilee@jubilee-insurance.com
Website	www.jubilee-insurance.com

Full Name	Rupert James Graham Lowe
Year of Birth	1957
Professional Qualifications	Information not available

PROFESSIONAL INFORMATION

CURRENT MAJOR POSITIONS/APPOINTMENTS

Non-Executive Director	Jubilee Managing Agency Limited	2004 -
Non-Executive Director	W H Ireland Limited	2008 -

PREVIOUS MAJOR POSITIONS/APPOINTMENTS

Executive Director	Southampton Insurance Services Ltd	2005 - 2006

Mark Lowton

Position	Chief Financial Officer
Company	Faraday Underwriting Limited
Address (Office)	5th Floor
	Corn Exchange
	55 Mark Lane
	London EC3R 7NE
Telephone	+44 (0)20 7426 6010
Fax	+44 (0)20 7680 4369
Email	mark.lowton@genre.com
Website	www.faraday.com

Full Name	Mark Lowton
Year of Birth	1962
Professional Qualifications	FCMA

PROFESSIONAL INFORMATION

CURRENT MAJOR POSITIONS/APPOINTMENTS

Executive Director	General Reinsurance UK Limited	2008 -
Executive Director	Faraday Underwriting Limited	2008 -
Executive Director	General Star International Indemnity Ltd	2008 -
Executive Director	Faraday Reinsurance Co Limited	2008 -

PREVIOUS MAJOR POSITIONS/APPOINTMENTS

Executive Director	Unionamerica Insurance Company Limited	2005 - 2008
Executive Director	St Paul Reinsurance Company Limited	2005 - 2008

Duncan P Lummis

Position	Chief Underwriting Officer
Company	Advent Underwriting Limited

Address (Office)	10th Floor
	One Minster Court
	Mincing Lane
	London EC3R 7AA
Telephone	+44 (0)20 7743 8233
Fax	+44 (0)20 7743 8299
Email	duncan.lummis@adventgroup.co.uk
Website	www.adventgroup.co.uk

Full Name	Duncan Paul Lummis
Year of Birth	1964
Professional Qualifications	BSc (Hons)

PROFESSIONAL INFORMATION

CURRENT MAJOR POSITIONS/APPOINTMENTS

Executive Director	Advent Underwriting Limited	2008 -

PREVIOUS MAJOR POSITIONS/APPOINTMENTS
Information not available

Peter Lütke-Bornefeld

Position	Non-Executive Director
Company	Faraday Underwriting Limited
Address (Office)	5th Floor
	Corn Exchange
	55 Mark Lane
	London EC3R 7NE
Telephone	+44 (0)20 7702 3333
Fax	+44 (0)20 7680 4369
Email	liz.richardson@faraday.com
Website	www.faraday.com

Full Name	Peter Lutke-Bornefeld
Year of Birth	1946
Professional Qualifications	Information not available

PROFESSIONAL INFORMATION

CURRENT MAJOR POSITIONS/APPOINTMENTS

Non-Executive Director	Faraday Reinsurance Co Limited	2003 -
Non-Executive Director	Faraday Underwriting Limited	2008 -

PREVIOUS MAJOR POSITIONS/APPOINTMENTS
Information not available

John A Lynch

Position	Finance Director & Company Secretary
Company	Cathedral Underwriting Limited

Address (Office)	5th Floor	
	Fitzwilliam House	
	10 St Mary Axe	
	London EC3A 8EN	
Telephone	+44 (0)20 7170 9024	
Fax	+44 (0)20 7170 9001	
Email	john.lynch@cathedralcapital.com	
Website	www.cathedralcapital.com	

Full Name	John Anthony Lynch	
Year of Birth	1965	
Professional Qualifications	ACA	

PROFESSIONAL INFORMATION

CURRENT MAJOR POSITIONS/APPOINTMENTS

Executive Director	Cathedral Underwriting Limited	2000 -

PREVIOUS MAJOR POSITIONS/APPOINTMENTS

Executive Director	Cathedral Capital Management Limited	2001 - 2007
Finance Director	Wren Underwriting Agencies Limited	Unknown
Finance Director	Wren Capital Management Limited	Unknown

James D MacDiarmid

Position	Chief Financial Officer
Company	Hardy (Underwriting Agencies) Ltd
Address (Office)	4th Floor
	40 Lime Street
	London EC3M 7AW
Telephone	+44 (0)20 7626 0382
Fax	+44 (0)20 7283 4677
Email	jamie.macdiarmid@hardygroup.co.uk
Website	www.hardygroup.co.uk

Full Name	James David MacDiarmid
Year of Birth	1971
Professional Qualifications	BA (Hons), ACA

PROFESSIONAL INFORMATION

CURRENT MAJOR POSITIONS/APPOINTMENTS

Executive Director	Hardy (Underwriting Agencies) Ltd	2003 -

PREVIOUS MAJOR POSITIONS/APPOINTMENTS

Information not available

Iain F MacDowall

Position	Compliance Director & Company Secretary
Company	Marlborough Underwriting Agency Ltd
Address (Office)	Birchin Court
	20 Birchin Lane
	London EC3V 9DU

Telephone	+44 (0)20 7456 1800
Fax	+44 (0)20 7456 1810
Email	iain.macdowall@marlborough.co.uk
Website	www.marlborough.co.uk

Full Name	Iain Falconer MacDowall
Year of Birth	1962
Professional Qualifications	Information not available

PROFESSIONAL INFORMATION

CURRENT MAJOR POSITIONS/APPOINTMENTS

Executive Director	Marlborough Underwriting Agency Ltd	2004 -

PREVIOUS MAJOR POSITIONS/APPOINTMENTS

Information not available

Bernard Mageean

Position	Underwriting Director & Managing Director Syndicate 2000
Company	QBE Underwriting Limited
Address (Office)	Plantation Place
	30 Fenchurch Street
	London EC3M 3BD
Telephone	+44 (0)20 7105 4000
Fax	+44 (0)20 7105 4019
Email	enquiries@uk.qbe.com
Website	www.qbeeurope.com

Full Name	Bernard Mageean
Year of Birth	1956
Professional Qualifications	Information not available

PROFESSIONAL INFORMATION

CURRENT MAJOR POSITIONS/APPOINTMENTS

Executive Director	QBE Insurance (Europe) Limited	2008 -
Executive Director	QBE Underwriting Limited	2008 -

PREVIOUS MAJOR POSITIONS/APPOINTMENTS

Information not available

Alan J Maguire

Position	Chairman
Company	AEGIS Managing Agency Ltd
Address (Office)	110 Fenchurch Street
	London EC3M 5JT
Telephone	+44 (0)20 7265 2100
Fax	+44 (0)20 7265 2101
Email	amaguire@aegislondon.co.uk
Website	www.aegislink.com

Full Name	Alan Joseph Maguire	
Year of Birth	1951	
Professional Qualifications	Information not available	

PROFESSIONAL INFORMATION

CURRENT MAJOR POSITIONS/APPOINTMENTS

Non-Executive Director	AEGIS Managing Agency Ltd	1998 -

PREVIOUS MAJOR POSITIONS/APPOINTMENTS

Information not available

Thomas J Mahoney

Position	Non-Executive Director
Company	AEGIS Managing Agency Ltd
Address (Office)	110 Fenchurch Street
	London EC3M 5JT
Telephone	+44 (0)20 7265 2100
Fax	+44 (0)20 7265 2101
Email	enquiries@aegislink.com
Website	www.aegislink.com

Full Name	Thomas Joseph Mahoney
Year of Birth	1948
Professional Qualifications	Information not available

PROFESSIONAL INFORMATION

CURRENT MAJOR POSITIONS/APPOINTMENTS

Non-Executive Director	AEGIS Managing Agency Ltd	2005 -

PREVIOUS MAJOR POSITIONS/APPOINTMENTS

Executive Director	St Paul Reinsurance Company Limited	2001 - 2002
Executive Director	Platinum Re (UK) Limited	2002 - 2003
Chief Executive	Platinum Re (UK) Limited	2002 - 2003

Neil P Maidment

Position	Chairman of the Underwriting Committee, Head of Reinsurance & Active Underwriter Syndicates 623, 2623, 3622 & 3623
Company	Beazley Furlonge Ltd
Address (Office)	Plantation Place South
	60 Great Tower Street
	London EC3R 5AD
Telephone	+44 (0)20 7667 0623
Fax	+44 (0)20 7674 7100
Email	neil.maidment@beazley.com
Website	www.beazley.com

Full Name	Neil Patrick Maidment
Year of Birth	1962
Professional Qualifications	FCII

PROFESSIONAL INFORMATION

CURRENT MAJOR POSITIONS/APPOINTMENTS

Executive Director	Beazley Furlonge Ltd	1993 -

PREVIOUS MAJOR POSITIONS/APPOINTMENTS

Information not available

Ian R Mallery

Position	Claims & RI Recoveries Director
Company	Marlborough Underwriting Agency Ltd
Address (Office)	Birchin Court
	20 Birchin Lane
	London EC3V 9DU
Telephone	+44 (0)20 7456 1800
Fax	+44 (0)20 7456 1810
Email	ian.mallery@marlborough.co.uk
Website	www.marlborough.co.uk
Full Name	Ian Richard Mallery
Year of Birth	1959
Professional Qualifications	Information not available

PROFESSIONAL INFORMATION

CURRENT MAJOR POSITIONS/APPOINTMENTS

Executive Director	Marlborough Underwriting Agency Ltd	2001 -

PREVIOUS MAJOR POSITIONS/APPOINTMENTS

Information not available

William A Malloy

Position	Chairman
Company	ARK Syndicate Management Limited
Address (Office)	8th Floor
	St Helen's
	1 Undershaft
	London EC3A 8EE
Telephone	+44 (0)20 3023 4020
Fax	+44 (0)20 3023 4000
Email	enquiries@arkunderwriting.com
Website	www.arkunderwriting.com
Full Name	William Arthur Malloy
Year of Birth	1958
Professional Qualifications	Information not available

PROFESSIONAL INFORMATION

CURRENT MAJOR POSITIONS/APPOINTMENTS

Non-Executive Director	ARK Syndicate Management Limited	2007 -

PREVIOUS MAJOR POSITIONS/APPOINTMENTS

Executive Director	Marsh Ltd	2005 - 2006

David P Mann

Position	Chairman
Company	Hardy (Underwriting Agencies) Ltd
Address (Office)	4th Floor
	40 Lime Street
	London EC3M 7AW
Telephone	+44 (0)20 7626 0382
Fax	+44 (0)20 7283 4677
Email	david.mann@hardygroup.co.uk
Website	www.hardygroup.co.uk

Full Name	David Preston Mann
Year of Birth	1949
Professional Qualifications	Information not available

PROFESSIONAL INFORMATION

CURRENT MAJOR POSITIONS/APPOINTMENTS

Non-Executive Director	Hardy (Underwriting Agencies) Ltd	2004 -

PREVIOUS MAJOR POSITIONS/APPOINTMENTS

Executive Director	Faraday Underwriting Limited	2001 - 2002
Executive Director	Faraday Reinsurance Co Limited	2001 - 2002
Non-Executive Director	Faraday Underwriting Limited	2002 - 2008

James W Mann

Position	Director of Underwriting
Company	Spectrum Syndicate Management Limited
Address (Office)	2nd Floor
	6 Bevis Marks
	London EC3A 7HL
Telephone	+44 (0)20 7283 2646
Fax	+44 (0)20 7621 0975
Email	jim.mann@spectrumins.com
Website	www.spectrumins.com

Full Name	James William Mann
Year of Birth	1969
Professional Qualifications	Information not available

PROFESSIONAL INFORMATION

CURRENT MAJOR POSITIONS/APPOINTMENTS

Executive Director	Spectrum Syndicate Management Limited	2007 -

PREVIOUS MAJOR POSITIONS/APPOINTMENTS

	Information not available

Arthur R Manners

Position	Executive Director & Company Secretary
Company	Beazley Furlonge Ltd
Address (Office)	Plantation Place South
	60 Great Tower Street
	London EC3R 5AD
Telephone	+44 (0)20 7667 0623
Fax	+44 (0)20 7674 7100
Email	arthur.manners@beazley.com
Website	www.beazley.com
Secretary/PA	Jannine Bosman
Email	jannine.bosman@beazley.com
Telephone	+44 (0)20 7674 7004

Full Name	Arthur Roger Manners
Year of Birth	1959
Professional Qualifications	Information not available

PROFESSIONAL INFORMATION

CURRENT MAJOR POSITIONS/APPOINTMENTS

Executive Director	Beazley Furlonge Ltd	1993 -
Executive Director	Beazley Solutions Limited	2004 -
Executive Director	Momentum Underwriting Management Ltd	2008 -

PREVIOUS MAJOR POSITIONS/APPOINTMENTS
Information not available

Stephen T Manning

Position	Chief Risk Officer, Chief Operating Officer & Compliance Officer
Company	Canopius Managing Agents Limited
Address (Office)	Gallery 9
	One Lime Street
	London EC3M 7HA
Telephone	+44 (0)20 7337 3732
Fax	+44 (0)20 7337 3999
Email	stephen.manning@canopius.com
Website	www.canopius.com

Full Name	Stephen Trevor Manning
Year of Birth	1963
Professional Qualifications	Information not available

PROFESSIONAL INFORMATION

CURRENT MAJOR POSITIONS/APPOINTMENTS

Executive Director	Canopius Managing Agents Limited	2005 -
Non-Executive Director	Creechurch Underwriting Limited	2006 -

PREVIOUS MAJOR POSITIONS/APPOINTMENTS
Information not available

John M Mantz

Position	Non-Executive Director
Company	Sagicor at Lloyd's Limited
Address (Office)	1 Great Tower Street
	London EC3R 5AA
Telephone	+44 (0)20 3003 6800
Fax	+44 (0)20 3003 6999
Email	duncan.reed@sagicor.eu
Website	www.sagicor.com

Full Name	John Martin Mantz
Year of Birth	1948
Professional Qualifications	FCA

PROFESSIONAL INFORMATION

CURRENT MAJOR POSITIONS/APPOINTMENTS

Non-Executive Director	Sagicor at Lloyd's Limited	2006 -

PREVIOUS MAJOR POSITIONS/APPOINTMENTS

Executive Director	Sagicor at Lloyd's Limited	2003 - 2006

Lord Marland of Odstock

Position	Chairman
Company	Jubilee Managing Agency Limited
Address (Office)	4th Floor
	50 Fenchurch Street
	London EC3M 3JY
Telephone	+44 (0)20 7220 8728
Fax	+44 (0)20 7220 8732
Email	jubilee@jubilee-insurance.com
Website	www.jubilee-insurance.com

PERSONAL PROFILE	A profile can be found in the People at Lloyd's, Personal section.

David Marock

Position	Chief Operating Officer
Company	Beazley Furlonge Ltd
Address (Office)	Plantation Place South
	60 Great Tower Street
	London EC3R 5AD
Telephone	+44 (0)20 7667 0623
Fax	+44 (0)20 7674 7100
Email	david.marock@beazley.com
Website	www.beazley.com

Full Name	David Marock
Year of Birth	1970
Professional Qualifications	Information not available

PROFESSIONAL INFORMATION

CURRENT MAJOR POSITIONS/APPOINTMENTS

Executive Director	Beazley Furlonge Ltd	2009 -

PREVIOUS MAJOR POSITIONS/APPOINTMENTS

Information not available

Nicholas (Nick) C Marsh

Position	Executive Director
Company	Atrium Underwriters Limited
Address (Office)	Room 790
	Lloyd's
	One Lime Street
	London EC3M 7DQ
Telephone	+44 (0)20 7327 4877
Fax	+44 (0)20 7327 4878
Email	info@atrium-uw.com
Website	www.atrium-uw.com

Full Name	Nicholas Carl Marsh
Year of Birth	1955
Professional Qualifications	Information not available

PROFESSIONAL INFORMATION

CURRENT MAJOR POSITIONS/APPOINTMENTS

Executive Director	Atrium Underwriters Limited	1996 -
Working Member	Council of Lloyd's	2008 -
Member	Lloyd's Market Association Board	2007 -

PREVIOUS MAJOR POSITIONS/APPOINTMENTS

Non-Executive Director	Imagine Syndicate Management Limited	2001 - 2003

Ian Marshall

Position	Non-Executive Director
Company	Markel Syndicate Management Limited
Address (Office)	The Markel Building
	49 Leadenhall Street
	London EC3A 2EA
Telephone	+44 (0)20 7953 6000
Fax	+44 (0)20 7953 6001
Email	ian.marshall@markelintl.com
Website	www.markelintl.com

Full Name	Ian Marshall
Year of Birth	1947
Professional Qualifications	FCA

PROFESSIONAL INFORMATION

CURRENT MAJOR POSITIONS/APPOINTMENTS

Non-Executive Director	Leeds Building Society	2004 -
Non-Executive Director	Markel Syndicate Management Limited	2005 -
Non-Executive Director	Markel International Insurance Company Limited	2005 -

PREVIOUS MAJOR POSITIONS/APPOINTMENTS

Executive Director	Markel Asset Management Limited	2001 - 2006
Executive Director	Markel Syndicate Management Limited	2001 - 2005
Executive Director	Markel International Insurance Company Limited	2001 - 2005
Chief Executive	Markel Asset Management Limited	2002 - 2006

Ian P Martin

Position	Non-Executive Director
Company	Ascot Underwriting Limited
Address (Office)	Plantation Place
	30 Fenchurch Street
	London EC3M 3BD
Telephone	+44 (0)20 7743 9600
Fax	+44 (0)20 7743 9601
Email	enquiries@ascotuw.com
Website	www.ascotuw.com

Full Name	Ian Paul Martin
Year of Birth	1960
Professional Qualifications	Information not available

PROFESSIONAL INFORMATION

CURRENT MAJOR POSITIONS/APPOINTMENTS

Non-Executive Director	Ascot Underwriting Limited	2005 -

PREVIOUS MAJOR POSITIONS/APPOINTMENTS

Non-Executive Director	Chelverton Asset Management Limited	2001 - 2008

Stavros Martis

Position	Chief Actuary
Company	Spectrum Syndicate Management Limited
Address (Office)	2nd Floor
	6 Bevis Marks
	London EC3A 7HL
Telephone	+44 (0)20 7283 2646
Fax	+44 (0)20 7621 0975
Email	stavros.martis@spectrumins.com
Website	www.spectrumins.com
Full Name	Stavros Martis
Year of Birth	1973
Professional Qualifications	Information not available

PROFESSIONAL INFORMATION

CURRENT MAJOR POSITIONS/APPOINTMENTS

Executive Director	Spectrum Syndicate Management Limited	2002 -

PREVIOUS MAJOR POSITIONS/APPOINTMENTS
Information not available

Bronek Masojada

Position	Chief Executive Officer
Company	Hiscox Syndicates Limited
Address (Office)	1 Great St Helen's
	London EC3A 6HX
Telephone	+44 (0)20 7448 6000
Fax	+44 (0)20 7448 6900
Email	bronek.masojada@hiscox.com
Website	www.hiscox.com

PERSONAL PROFILE	A profile can be found in the People at Lloyd's, Personal section.

John M Massey

Position	Non-Executive Director
Company	Novae Syndicates Limited
Address (Office)	71 Fenchurch Street
	London EC3M 4HH
Telephone	+44 (0)20 7903 7300
Fax	+44 (0)20 7903 7333
Email	jmassey@novae.com
Website	www.novae.com

Full Name	John Michael Massey
Year of Birth	1937
Professional Qualifications	FCA, ATII

PROFESSIONAL INFORMATION

CURRENT MAJOR POSITIONS/APPOINTMENTS

Non-Executive Director	Novae Syndicates Limited	1997 -
Non-Executive Director	Stronghold Insurance Company Limited	2001 -

PREVIOUS MAJOR POSITIONS/APPOINTMENTS
Information not available

Stephen D Mathers

Position	Executive Director & Active Underwriter Syndicate 1880
Company	R J Kiln & Co Limited
Address (Office)	106 Fenchurch Street
	London EC3M 5NR
Telephone	+44 (0)20 7886 9000
Fax	+44 (0)20 7488 1848
Email	stephen.mathers@kilngroup.com

Website	www.kilnplc.com

Full Name	Stephen Dale Mathers
Year of Birth	1953
Professional Qualifications	Information not available

PROFESSIONAL INFORMATION

CURRENT MAJOR POSITIONS/APPOINTMENTS

Executive Director	R J Kiln & Co Limited	1992 -

PREVIOUS MAJOR POSITIONS/APPOINTMENTS

Information not available

Peter C Matson

Position	Group Chief Underwriting Officer
Company	Novae Syndicates Limited
Address (Office)	71 Fenchurch Street
	London EC3M 4HH
Telephone	+44 (0)20 7903 7300
Fax	+44 (0)20 7903 7333
Email	pmatson@novae.com
Website	www.novae.com

Full Name	Peter Colin Matson
Year of Birth	1954
Professional Qualifications	Information not available

PROFESSIONAL INFORMATION

CURRENT MAJOR POSITIONS/APPOINTMENTS

Executive Director	Novae Syndicates Limited	2004 -
Non-Executive Director	Novae Underwriting Limited	2005 -
Chief Executive	Novae Insurance Company Ltd	2006 -

PREVIOUS MAJOR POSITIONS/APPOINTMENTS

Executive Director	Denham Syndicate Management Ltd	2001 - 2002
Executive Director	XL London Market Limited	2001 - 2002
Executive Director	BRIT Insurance (UK) Ltd	2002 - 2003
Executive Director	Novae Underwriting Limited	2005 - 2005

C David May

Position	Head of Casualty Reinsurance
Company	ARK Syndicate Management Limited
Address (Office)	8th Floor
	St Helen's
	1 Undershaft
	London EC3A 8EE
Telephone	+44 (0)20 3023 4042
Fax	+44 (0)20 3023 4000

Email	david.may@arkunderwriting.com
Website	www.arkunderwriting.com

Full Name	Christopher David May
Year of Birth	1946
Professional Qualifications	Information not available

PROFESSIONAL INFORMATION

CURRENT MAJOR POSITIONS/APPOINTMENTS

Executive Director	ARK Syndicate Management Limited	2007 -

PREVIOUS MAJOR POSITIONS/APPOINTMENTS

Executive Director	Catlin (Wellington) Underwriting Agencies Limited	2001 - 2002
Executive Director	Aspen Insurance UK Limited	2002 - 2006

B Siobhan McAuley

Position	Compliance Director & Company Secretary
Company	Managing Agency Partners Limited
Address (Office)	1st Floor
	110 Fenchurch Street
	London EC3M 5JT
Telephone	+44 (0)20 7709 3867
Fax	+44 (0)20 7709 3861
Email	smcauley@mapunderwriting.co.uk
Website	www.mapunderwriting.co.uk

Full Name	Brighd Siobhan McAuley
Year of Birth	1961
Professional Qualifications	Information not available

PROFESSIONAL INFORMATION

CURRENT MAJOR POSITIONS/APPOINTMENTS

Executive Director	Managing Agency Partners Ltd	2000 -

PREVIOUS MAJOR POSITIONS/APPOINTMENTS

Information not available

Gordon J McBurney

Position	Non-Executive Director
Company	Liberty Syndicate Management Limited
Address (Office)	5th Floor
	Plantation Place South
	60 Great Tower Street
	London EC3R 5AZ
Telephone	+44 (0)20 7070 4472
Fax	+44 (0)20 7863 1001
Email	info@libertysyndicates.com
Website	www.libertysyndicates.com

Full Name	Gordon James McBurney
Year of Birth	1957
Professional Qualifications	Information not available

PROFESSIONAL INFORMATION

CURRENT MAJOR POSITIONS/APPOINTMENTS

Non-Executive Director	Liberty Syndicate Management Limited	1997 -
Non-Executive Director	Liberty Mutual Insurance Europe Limited	2002 -

PREVIOUS MAJOR POSITIONS/APPOINTMENTS

Information not available

Eileen E McCusker

Position	Chief Operating Officer, UK & Ireland
Company	XL London Market Limited
Address (Office)	XL House
	70 Gracechurch Street
	London EC3V 0XL
Telephone	+44 (0)20 7933 7000
Fax	+44 (0)20 7469 1071
Email	eileen.mccusker@xlgroup.com
Website	www.xlinsurance.co.uk

Full Name	Eileen Elizabeth McCusker
Year of Birth	1953
Professional Qualifications	Information not available

PROFESSIONAL INFORMATION

CURRENT MAJOR POSITIONS/APPOINTMENTS

Executive Director	XL London Market Limited	2006 -
Executive Director	XL Insurance Company Limited	2006 -
External Member	Council of Lloyd's	2009 -

PREVIOUS MAJOR POSITIONS/APPOINTMENTS

Executive Director	XL Insurance Company Limited	2006 - 2008

Ian McIsaac

Position	Non-Executive Director
Company	Jubilee Managing Agency Limited
Address (Office)	4th Floor
	50 Fenchurch Street
	London EC3M 3JY
Telephone	+44 (0)20 7220 8728
Fax	+44 (0)20 7220 8732
Email	jubilee@jubilee-insurance.com
Website	www.jubilee-insurance.com

Full Name	Ian McIsaac
Year of Birth	1945
Professional Qualifications	Information not available

PROFESSIONAL INFORMATION

CURRENT MAJOR POSITIONS/APPOINTMENTS

Non-Executive Director	Jubilee Managing Agency Limited	2007 -

PREVIOUS MAJOR POSITIONS/APPOINTMENTS

Information not available

Graham J McKean

Position	Non-Executive Director
Company	Travelers Syndicate Management Ltd
Address (Office)	Exchequer Court
	33 St Mary Axe
	London EC3A 8AG
Telephone	+44 (0)20 3207 6000
Fax	+44 (0)20 7645 4526
Email	trv5000@travelers.com
Website	www.travelers.co.uk/lloyds

Full Name	Graham John McKean
Year of Birth	1941
Professional Qualifications	Information not available

PROFESSIONAL INFORMATION

CURRENT MAJOR POSITIONS/APPOINTMENTS

Non-Executive Director	Travelers Syndicate Management Limited	2007 -
Non-Executive Director	Media Insurance Brokers Ltd	2007 -

PREVIOUS MAJOR POSITIONS/APPOINTMENTS

Executive Director	BMS Greenstock Limited	2001 - 2003
Working Member	Council of Lloyd's	2001 - 2003
Member	Lloyd's Market Board	2001 - 2003
Non-Executive Director	The Griffin Insurance Association Limited	2001 - 2006
Executive Director	BMS Group Ltd	2005 - 2006
Executive Director	BMS Intermediaries Ltd	2005 - 2006
Executive Director	Bankserve Insurance Services Limited	2005 - 2006
Executive Director	BMS Facultative Limited	2005 - 2006
Executive Director	BMS Vision Re Limited	2005 - 2006
Non-Executive Director	Unionamerica Insurance Company Limited	2008 - 2008

Andrew McKee

Position	Chief Executive Officer
Company	Mitsui Sumitomo Insurance Underwriting at Lloyd's Ltd
Address (Office)	25 Fenchurch Avenue
	London EC3M 5AD
Telephone	+44 (0)20 7977 8330

Fax	+44 (0)20 7977 8300
Email	enquiries@msilm.com
Website	www.msilm.com

Full Name	Andrew McKee
Year of Birth	Information not available
Professional Qualifications	Information not available

PROFESSIONAL INFORMATION

CURRENT MAJOR POSITIONS/APPOINTMENTS

Chief Executive Officer	Mitsui Sumitomo Insurance Underwriting at Lloyd's Ltd

PREVIOUS MAJOR POSITIONS/APPOINTMENTS
Information not available

Steven R McMurray

Position	Finance Director
Company	Amlin Underwriting Limited
Address (Office)	St Helen's
	1 Undershaft
	London EC3A 8ND
Telephone	+44 (0)20 7746 1000
Fax	+44 (0)20 7746 1696
Email	steven.mcmurray@amlin.co.uk
Website	www.amlin.com

Full Name	Steven Roy McMurray
Year of Birth	Information not available
Professional Qualifications	Information not available

PROFESSIONAL INFORMATION

CURRENT MAJOR POSITIONS/APPOINTMENTS

Executive Director	Amlin Underwriting Services Limited	2007 -
Executive Director	Amlin Underwriting Limited	2008 -

PREVIOUS MAJOR POSITIONS/APPOINTMENTS
Information not available

James M Meacock

Position	Non-Executive Director
Company	SA Meacock & Company Limited
Address (Office)	4th Floor
	15 St Helen's Place
	London EC3A 6DE
Telephone	+44 (0)20 7374 6727
Fax	+44 (0)20 7374 4727
Email	linda.mailoudi@sameacock.com
Website	None at present

Full Name	James Michael Meacock	
Year of Birth	1968	
Professional Qualifications	Information not available	

PROFESSIONAL INFORMATION

CURRENT MAJOR POSITIONS/APPOINTMENTS

Non-Executive Director	SA Meacock & Company Limited	2006 -

PREVIOUS MAJOR POSITIONS/APPOINTMENTS

Information not available

Michael J Meacock

Position	Underwriting Director & Active Underwriter Syndicate 727
Company	SA Meacock & Company Limited
Address (Office)	4th Floor
	15 St Helen's Place
	London EC3A 6DE
Telephone	+44 (0)20 7374 6727
Fax	+44 (0)20 7374 4727
Email	michael.meacock@sameacock.com
Website	None at present

PERSONAL PROFILE	A profile can be found in the People at Lloyd's, Personal section.

Ian W Mercer

Position	Non-Executive Director
Company	Omega Underwriting Agents Ltd
Address (Office)	4th Floor
	New London House
	6 London Street
	London EC3R 7LP
Telephone	+44 (0)20 7767 3000
Fax	+44 (0)20 7488 9639
Email	info@omegauw.com
Website	www.omegauw.com

Full Name	Ian William Mercer
Year of Birth	1948
Professional Qualifications	Information not available

PROFESSIONAL INFORMATION

CURRENT MAJOR POSITIONS/APPOINTMENTS

Non-Executive Director	Omega Underwriting Agents Ltd	2008 -

PREVIOUS MAJOR POSITIONS/APPOINTMENTS

Information not available

Peter FS Merrett

Position	Compliance Officer
Company	Equity Syndicate Management Limited
Address (Office)	Library House
	New Road
	Brentwood
	Essex CM14 4GD
Telephone	+44 (0)1277 200 100
Fax	+44 (0)1206 777 223
Email	peter.merrett@equitygroup.co.uk
Website	www.equitygroup.co.uk
Full Name	Peter Frank Snell Merrett
Year of Birth	1958
Professional Qualifications	Information not available

PROFESSIONAL INFORMATION

CURRENT MAJOR POSITIONS/APPOINTMENTS

Executive Director	Equity Syndicate Management Limited	2003 -
Executive Director	Equity Claims Limited	2005 -

PREVIOUS MAJOR POSITIONS/APPOINTMENTS

Executive Director	KGM Underwriting Agencies Limited	2001 - 2002

Joanne Merrick

Position	UK General Counsel
Company	Faraday Underwriting Limited
Address (Office)	5th Floor
	Corn Exchange
	55 Mark Lane
	London EC3R 7NE
Telephone	+44 (0)20 7426 6012
Fax	+44 (0)20 7767 0315
Secretary/PA	Gretchen Hines
Email	gretchen.hines@faraday.com
Telephone	+44 (0)20 7426 6011
Website	www.faraday.com
Email	joanne.merrick@faraday.com
Full Name	Joanne Merrick
Year of Birth	1964
Professional Qualifications	LLB, Solicitor of the Supreme Court

PROFESSIONAL INFORMATION

CURRENT MAJOR POSITIONS/APPOINTMENTS

Executive Director	Faraday Underwriting Limited	2005 -
Executive Director	Faraday Reinsurance Co Limited	2005 -
Executive Director	General Star International Indemnity Ltd	2005 -
Executive Director	General Reinsurance UK Limited	2005 -

PREVIOUS MAJOR POSITIONS/APPOINTMENTS

Executive Director	Bestpark International Limited	2001 - 2002
Non-Executive Director	Bestpark International Limited	2001 - 2002
Executive Director	General Reinsurance Life UK Limited	2005 - 2008

Barbara J Merry

Position	Chief Executive Officer
Company	Hardy (Underwriting Agencies) Ltd
Address (Office)	4th Floor
	40 Lime Street
	London EC3M 7AW
Telephone	+44 (0)20 7626 0382
Fax	+44 (0)20 7283 4677
Email	barbara.merry@hardygroup.co.uk
Website	www.hardygroup.co.uk

PERSONAL PROFILE	A profile can be found in the People at Lloyd's, Personal section.

Nicholas J Metcalf

Position	Chief Executive Officer
Company	Liberty Syndicate Management Limited
Address (Office)	5th Floor
	Plantation Place South
	60 Great Tower Street
	London EC3R 5AZ
Telephone	+44 (0)20 7070 4472
Fax	+44 (0)20 7863 1001
Email	info@libertysyndicates.com
Website	www.libertysyndicates.com

Full Name	Nicholas John Metcalf
Year of Birth	1956
Professional Qualifications	Information not available

PROFESSIONAL INFORMATION

CURRENT MAJOR POSITIONS/APPOINTMENTS

Chief Executive	Liberty Syndicate Management Limited	2007 -

PREVIOUS MAJOR POSITIONS/APPOINTMENTS

Executive Director	Brockbank Personal Lines Limited	2001 - 2004
Executive Director	XL London Market Limited	2001 - 2004
Executive Director	Denham Syndicate Management Ltd	2001 - 2004
Executive Director	Arch Insurance Company (Europe) Ltd	2005 - 2007

James (Dick) RF Micklem

Position	Chief Operating Officer, Compliance Officer & Company Secretary
Company	Newline Underwriting Management Ltd

Address (Office)	Suite 5/4
	London Underwriting Centre
	3 Minster Court
	Mincing Lane
	London EC3R 7DD
Telephone	+44 (0)20 7090 1700
Fax	+44 (0)20 7090 1701
Email	dickmicklem@newlineuml.com
Website	www.newlineuml.com
Full Name	James Richard Fenwick Micklem
Year of Birth	1956
Professional Qualifications	Information not available

PROFESSIONAL INFORMATION

CURRENT MAJOR POSITIONS/APPOINTMENTS

Executive Director	Newline Underwriting Management Ltd	1996 -
Executive Director	Newline Underwriting Limited	2005 -
Executive Director	Newline Insurance Company Limited	2006 -

PREVIOUS MAJOR POSITIONS/APPOINTMENTS

Information not available

Dodridge D Miller

Position	Chairman
Company	Sagicor at Lloyd's Limited
Address (Office)	1 Great Tower Street
	London EC3R 5AA
Telephone	+44 (0)20 3003 6800
Fax	+44 (0)20 3003 6999
Email	duncan.reed@sagicor.eu
Website	www.sagicor.com
Full Name	Dodridge Denton Miller
Year of Birth	1957
Professional Qualifications	ACCA

PROFESSIONAL INFORMATION

CURRENT MAJOR POSITIONS/APPOINTMENTS

Non-Executive Director	Byrne and Stacey Underwriting Limited	2007 -
Non-Executive Director	Sagicor at Lloyd's Limited	2007 -

PREVIOUS MAJOR POSITIONS/APPOINTMENTS

Executive Director	Sagicor Capital Life Insurance Company Limited	2007 - 2008

Peter A Minton

Position	Executive Director
Company	Max at Lloyd's Ltd

Address (Office)	4th Floor
	70 Gracechurch Street
	London EC3V 0XL
Telephone	+44 (0)20 3102 3100
Fax	+44 (0)20 3102 3200
Email	peter.minton@maxatlloyds.com
Website	www.maxatlloyds.com

Full Name	Peter Andrew Minton
Year of Birth	1958
Professional Qualifications	Information not available

PROFESSIONAL INFORMATION

CURRENT MAJOR POSITIONS/APPOINTMENTS

Executive Director	Max at Lloyd's Ltd	2008 -
Executive Director	Max UK Underwriting Services Ltd	2008 -

PREVIOUS MAJOR POSITIONS/APPOINTMENTS

Information not available

Douglas M Morgan

Position	Chief Financial Officer
Company	Equity Syndicate Management Limited
Address (Office)	Library House
	New Road
	Brentwood
	Essex CM14 4GD
Telephone	+44 (0)1277 200 100
Fax	+44 (0)1206 777 223
Email	douglas.morgan@equitygroup.co.uk
Website	www.equitygroup.co.uk

Full Name	Douglas Michael Morgan
Year of Birth	1968
Professional Qualifications	FCMA

PROFESSIONAL INFORMATION

CURRENT MAJOR POSITIONS/APPOINTMENTS

Executive Director	Equity Claims Limited	2005 -
Executive Director	Equity Red Star (Accident & Health) Limited	2005 -
Executive Director	Equity Red Star Services Limited	2005 -
Executive Director	E Red Ltd	2005 -
Executive Director	Arista Insurance Ltd	2005 -
Executive Director	Equity Syndicate Management Limited	2006 -

PREVIOUS MAJOR POSITIONS/APPOINTMENTS

Information not available

Roger B Morgan

Position	Chairman
Company	Omega Underwriting Agents Ltd
Address (Office)	4th Floor
	New London House
	6 London Street
	London EC3R 7LP
Telephone	+44 (0)20 7767 3000
Fax	+44 (0)20 7488 9639
Email	info@omegauw.com
Website	www.omegauw.com
Full Name	Roger Bramall Morgan
Year of Birth	1941
Professional Qualifications	Information not available

PROFESSIONAL INFORMATION

CURRENT MAJOR POSITIONS/APPOINTMENTS

Non-Executive Director	Omega Underwriting Agents Ltd	1998 -

PREVIOUS MAJOR POSITIONS/APPOINTMENTS

Non-Executive Director	Harman Wicks & Swayne Ltd	2005 - 2008
Non-Executive Director	AEGIS Managing Agency Ltd	2005 - 2006

Gregory EA Morrison

Position	Executive Director
Company	Max at Lloyd's Ltd
Address (Office)	4th Floor
	70 Gracechurch Street
	London EC3V 0XL
Telephone	+44 (0)20 3102 3100
Fax	+44 (0)20 3102 3200
Email	gregory.morrison@maxatlloyds.com
Website	www.maxatlloyds.com
Full Name	Gregory Ernest Alexander Morrison
Year of Birth	1957
Professional Qualifications	Information not available

PROFESSIONAL INFORMATION

CURRENT MAJOR POSITIONS/APPOINTMENTS

Executive Director	Max at Lloyd's Ltd	2006 -

PREVIOUS MAJOR POSITIONS/APPOINTMENTS

Chief Executive Officer	London Reinsurance Group Inc	1989 - 1998
President	Unum Reinsurance	1999 - 2000
Chief Executive Officer	London Reinsurance Group Inc	2000 - 2003
Executive Director	Platinum Re (UK) Limited	2003 - 2006
Executive Director	Danish Re Syndicates Ltd	2006 - 2006
Executive Director	Imagine Underwriting Limited	2006 - 2007

Scott P Moser

Position	Non-Executive Director
Company	Atrium Underwriters Limited
Address (Office)	Room 790
	Lloyd's
	One Lime Street
	London EC3M 7DQ
Telephone	+44 (0)20 7327 4877
Fax	+44 (0)20 7327 4878
Email	info@atrium-uw.com
Website	www.atrium-uw.com

PERSONAL PROFILE   A profile can be found in the People at Lloyd's, Personal section.

Stephen J Muggeridge

Position	Chief Financial Officer
Company	Canopius Managing Agents Limited
Address (Office)	Gallery 9
	One Lime Street
	London EC3M 7HA
Telephone	+44 (0)20 7337 3770
Fax	+44 (0)20 7337 3999
Email	stephen.muggeridge@canopius.com
Website	www.canopius.com

Full Name	Stephen John Muggeridge
Year of Birth	1956
Professional Qualifications	ACA

PROFESSIONAL INFORMATION

CURRENT MAJOR POSITIONS/APPOINTMENTS

Executive Director	Canopius Managing Agents Limited	2006 -

PREVIOUS MAJOR POSITIONS/APPOINTMENTS

Executive Director	QBE Underwriting Services (UK) Limited	2004 - 2006

Adam Mullan

Position	Executive Director
Company	Max at Lloyd's Ltd
Address (Office)	4th Floor
	70 Gracechurch Street
	London EC3V 0XL
Telephone	+44 (0)20 3102 3100
Fax	+44 (0)20 3102 3200
Email	adam.mullan@maxatlloyds.com
Website	www.maxatlloyds.com

Full Name	Adam Mullan	
Year of Birth	1965	
Professional Qualifications	Information not available	

PROFESSIONAL INFORMATION

CURRENT MAJOR POSITIONS/APPOINTMENTS

Executive Director	Max at Lloyd's Ltd	2008 -
Executive Director	Max UK Underwriting Services Ltd	2008 -

PREVIOUS MAJOR POSITIONS/APPOINTMENTS

Information not available

Homi PR Mullan

Position	Non-Executive Director
Company	Ascot Underwriting Limited
Address (Office)	Plantation Place
	30 Fenchurch Street
	London EC3M 3BD
Telephone	+44 (0)20 7743 9600
Fax	+44 (0)20 7743 9601
Email	enquiries@ascotuw.com
Website	www.ascotuw.com

Full Name	Homi Phiroz Rustom Mullan
Year of Birth	1948
Professional Qualifications	Information not available

PROFESSIONAL INFORMATION

CURRENT MAJOR POSITIONS/APPOINTMENTS

Non-Executive Director	Ascot Underwriting Limited	2001 -

PREVIOUS MAJOR POSITIONS/APPOINTMENTS

Vice Chairman of Investment Banking	JP Morgan Chase & Co	Unknown

John E Mumford

Position	Non-Executive Director
Company	Argenta Syndicate Management Limited
Address (Office)	Fountain House
	130 Fenchurch Street
	London EC3M 5DJ
Telephone	+44 (0)20 7825 7200
Fax	+44 (0)20 7825 7155
Email	john.mumford@argentaplc.com
Website	www.argentaplc.com

Position	Non-Executive Director
Company	Marketform Managing Agency Limited
Address (Office)	8 Lloyd's Avenue
	London EC3N 3EL

Telephone	+44 (0)20 7488 7700
Fax	+44 (0)20 7488 7800
Email	john.mumford@marketform.com
Website	www.marketform.com

Full Name	John Edward Mumford
Year of Birth	1951
Professional Qualifications	FCA

PROFESSIONAL INFORMATION

CURRENT MAJOR POSITIONS/APPOINTMENTS

Non-Executive Director	Syndicate 138 Agency Limited	2003 -
Non-Executive Director	Marketform Managing Agency Limited	2004 -
Non-Executive Director	Argenta Syndicate Management Limited	2006 -

PREVIOUS MAJOR POSITIONS/APPOINTMENTS

Non-Executive Director	RITC Syndicate Management Ltd	2007 - 2008

Digby FC Murphy

Position	Non-Executive Director
Company	Whittington Capital Management Limited
Address (Office)	33 Creechurch Lane
	London EC3A 5EB
Telephone	+44 (0)20 7743 0900
Fax	+44 (0)20 7743 0901
Email	jon.francis@whittingtoninsurance.com
Website	www.whittingtoninsurance.com

Full Name	Digby Francis Considine Murphy
Year of Birth	1942
Professional Qualifications	Information not available

PROFESSIONAL INFORMATION

CURRENT MAJOR POSITIONS/APPOINTMENTS

Chief Executive	World Marine & General Insurances Pty Limited	2001 -
Chief Executive	FAI Insurances Limited	2004 -
Chief Executive	HIH Casualty and General Insurance Limited	2004 -
Non-Executive Director	Whittington Capital Management Limited	2005 -

PREVIOUS MAJOR POSITIONS/APPOINTMENTS

Information not available

Richard J Murphy

Position	Chief Executive Officer
Company	Spectrum Syndicate Management Limited
Address (Office)	2nd Floor
	6 Bevis Marks
	London EC3A 7HL
Telephone	+44 (0)20 7283 2646

Fax	+44 (0)20 7621 0975	
Email	richard.murphy@spectrumins.com	
Website	www.spectrumins.com	

Full Name	Richard John Murphy
Year of Birth	1956
Professional Qualifications	Information not available

PROFESSIONAL INFORMATION

CURRENT MAJOR POSITIONS/APPOINTMENTS

Chief Executive	Spectrum Syndicate Management Limited	2001 -
Chief Executive	Aviation & General Insurance Company Limited	2003 -
Chief Executive	Amalfi Underwriting (PA) Ltd	2006 -

PREVIOUS MAJOR POSITIONS/APPOINTMENTS

Chief Executive	Crowe Syndicate Management Ltd	2001 - 2006
Executive Director	City General Insurance Company Limited	2003 - 2006

Clive L Murray

Position	Chief Information Officer
Company	Novae Syndicates Limited
Address (Office)	71 Fenchurch Street
	London EC3M 4HH
Telephone	+44 (0)20 7903 7300
Fax	+44 (0)20 7903 7333
Email	cmurray@novae.com
Website	www.novae.com

Full Name	Clive Lee Murray
Year of Birth	1962
Professional Qualifications	ACII

PROFESSIONAL INFORMATION

CURRENT MAJOR POSITIONS/APPOINTMENTS

Executive Director	Novae Syndicates Limited	1997 -
Non-Executive Director	Novae Insurance Company Ltd	2006 -

PREVIOUS MAJOR POSITIONS/APPOINTMENTS

	Information not available

R Peter Murray

Position	Claims Director
Company	Ace Underwriting Agencies Limited
Address (Office)	100 Leadenhall Street
	London EC3A 3BP
Telephone	+44 (0)20 7173 7000
Fax	+44 (0)20 7173 7800
Email	peter.murray@ace-ina.com
Website	www.acelimited.com

Full Name	Roland Peter Murray
Year of Birth	1956
Professional Qualifications	Information not available

PROFESSIONAL INFORMATION

CURRENT MAJOR POSITIONS/APPOINTMENTS

Executive Director	Ace Underwriting Agencies Limited	2000 -
Executive Director	ACE European Group Limited	2002 -

PREVIOUS MAJOR POSITIONS/APPOINTMENTS

Information not available

Harinderjit (Harry) S Nagra

Position	Compliance Director
Company	Marketform Managing Agency Limited
Address (Office)	8 Lloyd's Avenue
	London EC3N 3EL
Telephone	+44 (0)20 7488 7700
Fax	+44 (0)20 7488 7800
Email	harry.nagra@marketform.com
Website	www.marketform.com

Full Name	Harinderjit Singh Nagra
Year of Birth	1956
Professional Qualifications	FCA, FCII

PROFESSIONAL INFORMATION

CURRENT MAJOR POSITIONS/APPOINTMENTS

Executive Director	Marketform Limited	2005 -
Executive Director	Marketform Managing Agency Limited	2001 -

PREVIOUS MAJOR POSITIONS/APPOINTMENTS

Information not available

Christopher P Nash

Position	Executive Director & Active Underwriter Syndicate 3334
Company	Sportscover Underwriting Ltd
Address (Office)	3 Minster Court
	Mincing Lane
	London EC3R 7DD
Telephone	+44 (0)20 7398 4080
Fax	+44 (0)20 7398 4090
Email	chris.nash@sportscover.com
Website	www.sportscoverunderwriting.com

Full Name	Christopher Peter Nash
Year of Birth	1971
Professional Qualifications	Information not available

PROFESSIONAL INFORMATION

CURRENT MAJOR POSITIONS/APPOINTMENTS

Chief Executive	Active Underwriting Specialists Ltd	2006 -
Chief Executive	Sportscover Europe Limited	2006 -
Executive Director	Sportscover Underwriting Ltd	2008 -

PREVIOUS MAJOR POSITIONS/APPOINTMENTS

Non-Executive Director	Sportscover Europe Limited	2006 - 2006

Peter JR Nash

Position	Director of Underwriting & Director of Claims
Company	Sportscover Underwriting Ltd
Address (Office)	3 Minster Court
	Mincing Lane
	London EC3R 7DD
Telephone	+44 (0)20 7398 4080
Fax	+44 (0)20 7398 4090
Email	peter.nash@sportscover.com
Website	www.sportscoverunderwriting.com
Full Name	Peter John Robert Nash
Year of Birth	1952
Professional Qualifications	Information not available

PROFESSIONAL INFORMATION

CURRENT MAJOR POSITIONS/APPOINTMENTS

Non-Executive Director	Sportscover Europe Limited	2006 -
Executive Director	Sportscover Underwriting Ltd	2008 -

PREVIOUS MAJOR POSITIONS/APPOINTMENTS

Executive Director	Argenta Syndicate Management Limited	2006 - 2008

John D Neal

Position	Chief Operating Officer & Managing Director
	Syndicate 1886
Company	QBE Underwriting Limited
Address (Office)	Plantation Place
	30 Fenchurch Street
	London EC3M 3BD
Telephone	+44 (0)20 7105 4000
Fax	+44 (0)20 7105 4019
Email	enquiries@uk.qbe.com
Website	www.qbeeurope.com
Full Name	John David Neal
Year of Birth	1964
Professional Qualifications	Information not available

PROFESSIONAL INFORMATION

CURRENT MAJOR POSITIONS/APPOINTMENTS

Executive Director	QBE Underwriting Limited	2004 -
Executive Director	The Minibus and Coach Club Ltd	2005 -
Executive Director	QBE Insurance (Europe) Limited	2005 -
Executive Director	QBE (Stafford) Limited	2005 -
Executive Director	Greenhill Underwriting Espana Ltd	2005 -
Executive Director	Greenhill Sturge Underwriting Ltd	2005 -
Executive Director	Greenhill International Ins Holdings Ltd	2005 -
Executive Director	QBE Management Services (UK) Limited	2005 -

PREVIOUS MAJOR POSITIONS/APPOINTMENTS

Executive Director	Beaufort Underwriting Agency Limited	2001 - 2004
Chief Executive	Beaufort Underwriting Agency Limited	2001 - 2002
Executive Director	QBE Insurance Company (UK) Limited	2005 - 2006
Executive Director	QBE Reinsurance (UK) Ltd	2005 - 2005

Nicholas J Newman-Young

Position	Independent Non-Executive Director
Company	Montpelier Underwriting Agencies Ltd
Address (Office)	7th Floor
	85 Gracechurch Street
	London EC3V 0AA
Telephone	+44 (0)20 7648 4500
Fax	+44 (0)20 7648 4501
Email	-
Website	www.montpelierre.com

Full Name	Nicholas John Newman-Young
Year of Birth	1952
Professional Qualifications	Information not available

PROFESSIONAL INFORMATION

CURRENT MAJOR POSITIONS/APPOINTMENTS

Executive Director	Montpelier Marketing Services (UK) Limited	2005 -
Non-Executive Director	Montpelier Underwriting Agencies Ltd	2008 -

PREVIOUS MAJOR POSITIONS/APPOINTMENTS

	Information not available

M Fraser Newton

Position	Non-Executive Director
Company	Travelers Syndicate Management Ltd
Address (Office)	Exchequer Court
	33 St Mary Axe
	London EC3A 8AG
Telephone	+44 (0)20 3207 6000
Fax	+44 (0)20 7645 4526
Email	trv5000@travelers.com

Website	www.travelers.co.uk/lloyds

Full Name	Matthew Fraser Newton
Year of Birth	1948
Professional Qualifications	Information not available

PROFESSIONAL INFORMATION

CURRENT MAJOR POSITIONS/APPOINTMENTS

Non-Executive Director	Travelers Syndicate Management Limited	2004 -

PREVIOUS MAJOR POSITIONS/APPOINTMENTS

Executive Director	Cotterell and Maguire Limited	2001 - 2005

Jerome B Nice

Position	Non-Executive Director
Company	Sagicor at Lloyd's Limited
Address (Office)	1 Great Tower Street
	London EC3R 5AA
Telephone	+44 (0)20 3003 6800
Fax	+44 (0)20 3003 6999
Email	duncan.reed@sagicor.eu
Website	www.sagicor.com

Full Name	Jerome Baskerville Nice
Year of Birth	1940
Professional Qualifications	Information not available

PROFESSIONAL INFORMATION

CURRENT MAJOR POSITIONS/APPOINTMENTS

Non-Executive Director	Sagicor at Lloyd's Limited	2000 -

PREVIOUS MAJOR POSITIONS/APPOINTMENTS

Information not available

Allan M Nichols

Position	Chairman
Company	Novae Syndicates Limited
Address (Office)	71 Fenchurch Street
	London EC3M 4HH
Telephone	+44 (0)20 7903 7300
Fax	+44 (0)20 7903 7333
Email	anichols@novae.com
Website	www.novae.com

PERSONAL PROFILE	A profile can be found in the People at Lloyd's, Personal section.

Jane M Nicholson

Position	Executive Director
Company	Jubilee Managing Agency Limited

Address (Office)	4th Floor
	50 Fenchurch Street
	London EC3M 3JY
Telephone	+44 (0)20 7220 8728
Fax	+44 (0)20 7220 8732
Email	jane.nicholson@cassidydavis.com
Website	www.jubilee-insurance.com

Full Name	Jane Marga Nicholson
Year of Birth	1964
Professional Qualifications	Information not available

PROFESSIONAL INFORMATION

CURRENT MAJOR POSITIONS/APPOINTMENTS

Chief Executive	Cassidy Davis Insurance Services Ltd	2005 -
Executive Director	Jubilee Managing Agency Limited	2006 -

PREVIOUS MAJOR POSITIONS/APPOINTMENTS

Information not available

Edward N Noble

Position	Non-Executive Director
Company	Munich Re Underwriting Limited
Address (Office)	St Helen's
	1 Undershaft
	London EC3A 8EE
Telephone	+44 (0)20 7886 3900
Fax	+44 (0)20 7886 3901
Email	central@mrunderwriting.com
Website	www.watkins-syndicate.co.uk

Full Name	Edward Nelson Noble
Year of Birth	1948
Professional Qualifications	Information not available

PROFESSIONAL INFORMATION

CURRENT MAJOR POSITIONS/APPOINTMENTS

Non-Executive Director	Munich Re Underwriting Limited	2008 -

PREVIOUS MAJOR POSITIONS/APPOINTMENTS

Executive Director	Chaucer Syndicates Limited	2001 - 2007
Executive Director	Aberdeen Underwriting Advisers Ltd	2001 - 2003

Edward J Noonan

Position	Non-Executive Director
Company	Talbot Underwriting Ltd
Address (Office)	Gracechurch House
	55 Gracechurch Street
	London EC3V 0JP

Telephone	+44 (0)20 7550 3500
Fax	+44 (0)20 7550 3555
Email	central@talbotuw.com
Website	www.talbotuw.com

Full Name	Edward Joseph Noonan
Year of Birth	1958
Professional Qualifications	Information not available

PROFESSIONAL INFORMATION

CURRENT MAJOR POSITIONS/APPOINTMENTS

Non-Executive Director	Talbot Underwriting Ltd	2007 -

PREVIOUS MAJOR POSITIONS/APPOINTMENTS

Information not available

Robin Oakes

Position	Non-Executive Director
Company	ARK Syndicate Management Limited
Address (Office)	8th Floor
	St Helen's
	1 Undershaft
	London EC3A 8EE
Telephone	+44 (0)20 3023 4020
Fax	+44 (0)20 3023 4000
Email	enquiries@arkunderwriting.com
Website	www.arkunderwriting.com

Full Name	Robin Oakes
Year of Birth	1946
Professional Qualifications	Information not available

PROFESSIONAL INFORMATION

CURRENT MAJOR POSITIONS/APPOINTMENTS

Executive Director	Benfield Limited	2007 -
Non-Executive Director	ARK Syndicate Management Limited	2007 -

PREVIOUS MAJOR POSITIONS/APPOINTMENTS

Executive Director	Mazars Corporate Finance Limited	2001 - 2002

Christopher PJ O'Brien

Position	Finance Director
Company	Aspen Managing Agency Limited
Address (Office)	30 Fenchurch Street
	London EC3M 3BD
Telephone	+44 (0)20 7184 8000
Fax	+44 (0)20 7184 8500
Email	c/o robert.long@aspen-re.com
Website	www.aspen-re.com

Full Name	Christopher Patrick James O'Brien
Year of Birth	1965
Professional Qualifications	Information not available

PROFESSIONAL INFORMATION

CURRENT MAJOR POSITIONS/APPOINTMENTS

Executive Director	Aspen Managing Agency Limited	2008 -

PREVIOUS MAJOR POSITIONS/APPOINTMENTS

Executive Director	Amlin Underwriting Services Limited	2005 - 2006
Executive Director	Amlin Credit Limited	2005 - 2006

Mike P O'Dea

Position	Executive Director
Company	Faraday Underwriting Limited
Address (Office)	5th Floor
	Corn Exchange
	55 Mark Lane
	London EC3R 7NE
Telephone	+44 (0)20 7680 4326
Fax	+44 (0)20 7680 4369
Email	mike.odea@genre.com
Website	www.faraday.com

Full Name	Michael Patrick O'Dea
Year of Birth	1964
Professional Qualifications	BSc, ACA

PROFESSIONAL INFORMATION

CURRENT MAJOR POSITIONS/APPOINTMENTS

Executive Director	Faraday Underwriting Limited	2001 -
Executive Director	Faraday Reinsurance Co Limited	2002 -
Executive Director	General Star International Indemnity Ltd	2006 -
Chief Executive	General Reinsurance UK Limited	2006 -

PREVIOUS MAJOR POSITIONS/APPOINTMENTS

Executive Director	General Reinsurance UK Limited	2002 - 2006

Colin R O'Farrell

Position	Underwriting Director & Managing Director Syndicate 1036
Company	QBE Underwriting Limited
Address (Office)	Plantation Place
	30 Fenchurch Street
	London EC3M 3BD
Telephone	+44 (0)20 7105 4000
Fax	+44 (0)20 7105 4019
Email	enquiries@uk.qbe.com
Website	www.qbeeurope.com

Full Name	Colin Raymond O'Farrell
Year of Birth	1964
Professional Qualifications	Information not available

PROFESSIONAL INFORMATION

CURRENT MAJOR POSITIONS/APPOINTMENTS

Executive Director	QBE Underwriting Limited	2002 -
Executive Director	QBE Underwriting Services Ltd	2007 -
Executive Director	QBE Insurance (Europe) Limited	2008 -

PREVIOUS MAJOR POSITIONS/APPOINTMENTS

Information not available

Francis (Frank) M O'Halloran

Position	Chairman
Company	QBE Underwriting Limited
Address (Office)	Plantation Place
	30 Fenchurch Street
	London EC3M 3BD
Telephone	+44 (0)20 7105 4000
Fax	+44 (0)20 7105 4019
Email	enquiries@uk.qbe.com
Website	www.qbeeurope.com

Full Name	Francis Michael O'Halloran
Year of Birth	1946
Professional Qualifications	ACA

PROFESSIONAL INFORMATION

CURRENT MAJOR POSITIONS/APPOINTMENTS

Non-Executive Director	QBE Underwriting Limited	2000 -
Executive Director	QBE Insurance (Europe) Limited	2001 -
Non-Executive Director	QBE Insurance (Europe) Limited	2003 -

PREVIOUS MAJOR POSITIONS/APPOINTMENTS

President	Insurance Council of Australia	1999 - 2000
Executive Director	QBE Reinsurance (UK) Ltd	2001 - 2006
Executive Director	QBE Insurance Company (UK) Limited	2001 - 2006
Executive Director	Minster Court Asset Management (UK) Limited	2003 - 2005
Non-Executive Director	QBE Reinsurance (UK) Ltd	2003 - 2006
Non-Executive Director	QBE Insurance Company (UK) Limited	2003 - 2006

Gary M Oliver

Position	Risk Management & Compliance Director
Company	ARK Syndicate Management Limited
Address (Office)	8th Floor
	St Helen's
	1 Undershaft
	London EC3A 8EE

Telephone	+44 (0)20 3023 4006
Fax	+44 (0)20 3023 4000
Email	gary.oliver@arkunderwriting.com
Website	www.arkunderwriting.com

Full Name	Gary Michael Oliver
Year of Birth	1964
Professional Qualifications	Information not available

PROFESSIONAL INFORMATION

CURRENT MAJOR POSITIONS/APPOINTMENTS

Executive Director	ARK Syndicate Management Limited	2007 -

PREVIOUS MAJOR POSITIONS/APPOINTMENTS

Information not available

Philip V Olsen

Position	Independent Non-Executive Director
Company	QBE Underwriting Limited
Address (Office)	Plantation Place
	30 Fenchurch Street
	London EC3M 3BD
Telephone	+44 (0)20 7105 4000
Fax	+44 (0)20 7105 4019
Email	enquiries@uk.qbe.com
Website	www.qbeeurope.com

Full Name	Philip Vernon Olsen
Year of Birth	1945
Professional Qualifications	Information not available

PROFESSIONAL INFORMATION

CURRENT MAJOR POSITIONS/APPOINTMENTS

Non-Executive Director	Syndicate 138 Agency Limited	1991 -
Non-Executive Director	QBE Underwriting Limited	1991 -
Non-Executive Director	QBE Insurance (Europe) Limited	2005 -

PREVIOUS MAJOR POSITIONS/APPOINTMENTS

Non-Executive Director	QBE Insurance Company (UK) Limited	2005 - 2006

P Terry O'Neill

Position	Independent Non-Executive Director
Company	Montpelier Underwriting Agencies Ltd
Address (Office)	7th Floor
	85 Gracechurch Street
	London EC3V 0AA
Telephone	+44 (0)20 7648 4500
Fax	+44 (0)20 7648 4501

Email	–
Website	www.montpelierre.com

Full Name	Peter Terence O'Neill
Year of Birth	1944
Professional Qualifications	Information not available

PROFESSIONAL INFORMATION

CURRENT MAJOR POSITIONS/APPOINTMENTS

Non-Executive Director	Arthur J Gallagher (UK) Ltd	2006 -
Non-Executive Director	Montpelier Underwriting Agencies Ltd	2008 -
Non-Executive Director	OIM Underwriting Limited	2008 -

PREVIOUS MAJOR POSITIONS/APPOINTMENTS

Information not available

Michael L Onslow

Position	Executive Director & Active Underwriter Syndicates 4040 & 4141
Company	HCC Underwriting Agency Ltd
Address (Office)	Walsingham House
	35 Seething Lane
	London EC3N 4AH
Telephone	+44 (0)20 7680 3000
Fax	+44 (0)20 7977 7350
Email	monslow@hccint.com
Website	www.hccual.com

Full Name	Michael Leonard Onslow
Year of Birth	1959
Professional Qualifications	Information not available

PROFESSIONAL INFORMATION

CURRENT MAJOR POSITIONS/APPOINTMENTS

Executive Director	HCC International Insurance Company Plc	2006 -
Executive Director	HCC Underwriting Agency Ltd	2009 -

PREVIOUS MAJOR POSITIONS/APPOINTMENTS

Information not available

Philip NW Osborne

Position	Non-Executive Director
Company	Sagicor at Lloyd's Limited
Address (Office)	1 Great Tower Street
	London EC3R 5AA
Telephone	+44 (0)20 3003 6800
Fax	+44 (0)20 3003 6999
Email	duncan.reed@sagicor.eu
Website	www.sagicor.com

Full Name	Philip Neville Wayne Osborne
Year of Birth	1956
Professional Qualifications	ACA

PROFESSIONAL INFORMATION

CURRENT MAJOR POSITIONS/APPOINTMENTS

Non-Executive Director	Byrne and Stacey Underwriting Limited	2007 -
Non-Executive Director	Sagicor at Lloyd's Limited	2007 -

PREVIOUS MAJOR POSITIONS/APPOINTMENTS

Information not available

Carl A Overy

Position	Chief Executive Officer
Company	Newline Underwriting Management Ltd
Address (Office)	Suite 5/4
	London Underwriting Centre
	3 Minster Court
	Mincing Lane
	London EC3R 7DD
Telephone	+44 (0)20 7090 1700
Fax	+44 (0)20 7090 1701
Email	covery@newlineuml.com
Website	www.newlineuml.com

Full Name	Carl Anthony Overy
Year of Birth	1968
Professional Qualifications	Information not available

PROFESSIONAL INFORMATION

CURRENT MAJOR POSITIONS/APPOINTMENTS

Executive Director	Newline Insurance Company Limited	2007 -
Executive Director	Newline Underwriting Management Ltd	2007 -
Chief Executive	Newline Underwriting Management Ltd	2008 -
Chief Executive	Newline Insurance Company Limited	2008 -
Chief Executive	Odyssey America Reinsurance Corporation	2008 -

PREVIOUS MAJOR POSITIONS/APPOINTMENTS

Information not available

Dr Ian B Owen

Position	Non-Executive Director
Company	Canopius Managing Agents Limited
Address (Office)	Gallery 9
	One Lime Street
	London EC3M 7HA
Telephone	+44 (0)20 7337 3700
Fax	+44 (0)20 7337 3999
Email	ian.owen@canopius.com

Website	www.canopius.com

Full Name	Ian Bruce Owen
Year of Birth	1953
Professional Qualifications	Information not available

PROFESSIONAL INFORMATION

CURRENT MAJOR POSITIONS/APPOINTMENTS

Non-Executive Director	Scout Insurance Services Limited	2005 -
Non-Executive Director	Canopius Managing Agents Limited	2006 -
Non-Executive Director	Phoenix & London Assurance Limited	2007 -
Non-Executive Director	Creechurch Underwriting Limited	2007 -
Non-Executive Director	Phoenix Pensions Limited	2007 -
Non-Executive Director	Scottish Provident Limited	2007 -
Non-Executive Director	Phoenix Life Limited	2007 -
Non-Executive Director	Annuity Direct Limited	2007 -
Non-Executive Director	Scottish Mutual Assurance Limited	2007 -
Non-Executive Director	Partnership Home Loans Limited	2008 -
Non-Executive Director	Partnership Life Assurance Company Limited	2008 -

PREVIOUS MAJOR POSITIONS/APPOINTMENTS

Executive Director	Preferred Assurance Company Limited	2001 - 2002
Executive Director	Eagle Star Insurance Company Limited	2001 - 2004
Executive Director	Navigators and General Insurance Company Limited	2002 - 2004
Executive Director	Zurich GSG Limited	2002 - 2004
Executive Director	Zurich International (UK) Ltd	2002 - 2004
Non-Executive Director	Partnership Life Assurance Company Limited	2005 - 2007
Non-Executive Director	Partnership Home Loans Limited	2006 - 2007
Executive Director	Partnership Life Assurance Company Limited	2007 - 2008
Executive Director	Partnership Home Loans Limited	2007 - 2008
Non-Executive Director	Phoenix Life Assurance Limited	2007 - 2008
Non-Executive Director	Phoenix Life Assurance Limited	2008 - 2008

Michael S Paquette

Position	Chief Financial Officer
Company	Montpelier Underwriting Agencies Ltd
Address (Office)	7th Floor
	85 Gracechurch Street
	London EC3V 0AA
Telephone	+44 (0)20 7648 4500
Fax	+44 (0)20 7648 4501
Email	mike.paquette@montpeliertr.com
Website	www.montpelierre.com

Full Name	Michael S Paquette
Year of Birth	1963
Professional Qualifications	Information not available

PROFESSIONAL INFORMATION

CURRENT MAJOR POSITIONS/APPOINTMENTS

Executive Director	Montpelier Underwriting Agencies Ltd	2008 -

PREVIOUS MAJOR POSITIONS/APPOINTMENTS

Information not available

Jonathan W Parry

Position	Underwriting Director & Managing Director Syndicate 566
Company	QBE Underwriting Limited
Address (Office)	Plantation Place
	30 Fenchurch Street
	London EC3M 3BD
Telephone	+44 (0)20 7105 4000
Fax	+44 (0)20 7105 4019
Email	enquiries@uk.qbe.com
Website	www.qbeeurope.com
PERSONAL PROFILE	A profile can be found in the People at Lloyd's, Personal section.

Elvin E Patrick

Position	Non-Executive Director
Company	Cathedral Underwriting Limited
Address (Office)	5th Floor
	Fitzwilliam House
	10 St Mary Axe
	London EC3A 8EN
Telephone	+44 (0)20 7170 9000
Fax	+44 (0)20 7170 9001
Email	info@cathedralcapital.com
Website	www.cathedralcapital.com
Full Name	Elvin Ensor Patrick
Year of Birth	1944
Professional Qualifications	MBA

PROFESSIONAL INFORMATION

CURRENT MAJOR POSITIONS/APPOINTMENTS

Non-Executive Director	Cathedral Underwriting Limited	2000 -

PREVIOUS MAJOR POSITIONS/APPOINTMENTS

Chairman	Bankside Underwriting Agencies Limited	1989 - 1999
Chief Executive	LIMIT plc	1998 - 1999
Member	Lloyd's Rowland Task Force	1991 - 1991
Member	Lloyd's Regulatory Review Board	1997 - Unknown
Working Member & Deputy Chairman	Council of Lloyd's	1998 - Unknown

Mark Patterson

Position	Chief Underwriting Officer
Company	Starr Managing Agents Limited
Address (Office)	3rd Floor
	140 Leadenhall Street
	London EC3V 4QT
Telephone	+44 (0)20 7337 3550
Fax	+44 (0)20 7337 3551
Email	mark.patterson@cvstarrco.com
Website	www.cvstarrco.com

Full Name	Mark Patterson
Year of Birth	1956
Professional Qualifications	Information not available

PROFESSIONAL INFORMATION

CURRENT MAJOR POSITIONS/APPOINTMENTS

Executive Director	Starr Managing Agents Ltd	2007 -

PREVIOUS MAJOR POSITIONS/APPOINTMENTS

Executive Director	Starr Underwriting Agents Limited	2007 - 2008

Nicholas CT Pawson

Position	Non-Executive Director
Company	Marlborough Underwriting Agency Ltd
Address (Office)	Birchin Court
	20 Birchin Lane
	London EC3V 9DU
Telephone	+44 (0)20 7456 1800
Fax	+44 (0)20 7456 1810
Email	nicholas.pawson@marlborough.co.uk
Website	www.marlborough.co.uk

Position	Chairman
Company	Starr Managing Agents Limited
Address (Office)	3rd Floor
	140 Leadenhall Street
	London EC3V 4QT
Telephone	+44 (0)20 7337 3550
Fax	+44 (0)20 7337 3551
Email	nicholas.pawson@cvstarrco.com
Website	www.cvstarrco.com

PERSONAL PROFILE	A profile can be found in the People at Lloyd's, Personal section.

Philip R Pearce

Position	Risk Director & Compliance Director
Company	Mitsui Sumitomo Insurance Underwriting at Lloyd's Ltd

Address (Office)	25 Fenchurch Avenue
	London EC3M 5AD
Telephone	+44 (0)20 7702 6329
Fax	+44 (0)20 7977 8300
Email	ppearce@msilm.com
Website	www.msilm.com

Full Name	Philip Richard Pearce
Year of Birth	1964
Professional Qualifications	Information not available

PROFESSIONAL INFORMATION

CURRENT MAJOR POSITIONS/APPOINTMENTS

Executive Director	Mitsui Sumitomo Insurance	
	Underwriting at Lloyd's Ltd	2006 -
Executive Director	Mitsui Sumitomo Insurance (London) Limited	2007 -

PREVIOUS MAJOR POSITIONS/APPOINTMENTS

Executive Director	Catlin (Wellington) Underwriting Agencies Limited	2003 - 2005

Giuseppe (Joe) Perdoni

Position	Managing Director
Company	Montpelier Underwriting Agencies Ltd
Address (Office)	7th Floor
	85 Gracechurch Street
	London EC3V 0AA
Telephone	+44 (0)20 7648 4517
Fax	+44 (0)20 7648 4501
Email	joe.perdoni@montpelierua.com
Website	www.montpelierre.com

Full Name	Giuseppe Perdoni
Year of Birth	1964
Professional Qualifications	Information not available

PROFESSIONAL INFORMATION

CURRENT MAJOR POSITIONS/APPOINTMENTS

Chief Executive	Montpelier Underwriting Agencies Ltd	2008 -

PREVIOUS MAJOR POSITIONS/APPOINTMENTS

Executive Director	RiverStone Managing Agency Limited	2001 - 2003
Executive Director	Advent Underwriting Limited	2001 - 2008

Jonathan D Perkins

Position	Group Actuary
Company	Chaucer Syndicates Limited
Address (Office)	Plantation Place
	30 Fenchurch Street
	London EC3M 3AD

Telephone	+44 (0)20 7397 9700
Fax	+44 (0)20 7397 9710
Email	jonathan.perkins@chaucerplc.com
Website	www.chaucerplc.com

Full Name	Jonathan David Perkins
Year of Birth	1970
Professional Qualifications	BSc, FIA

PROFESSIONAL INFORMATION

CURRENT MAJOR POSITIONS/APPOINTMENTS

Executive Director	Chaucer Syndicates Limited	2006 -

PREVIOUS MAJOR POSITIONS/APPOINTMENTS

Information not available

Matthew A Petzold

Position	Underwriting Director & Active Underwriter Syndicate 1400
Company	Max at Lloyd's Ltd
Address (Office)	4th Floor
	70 Gracechurch Street
	London EC3V 0XL
Telephone	+44 (0)20 3102 3100
Fax	+44 (0)20 3102 3200
Email	matthew.petzold@maxatlloyds.com
Website	www.maxatlloyds.com

Full Name	Matthew Andrew Petzold
Year of Birth	1952
Professional Qualifications	Information not available

PROFESSIONAL INFORMATION

CURRENT MAJOR POSITIONS/APPOINTMENTS

Executive Director	Max at Lloyd's Ltd	2006 -
Executive Director	Max UK Underwriting Services Ltd	2006 -

PREVIOUS MAJOR POSITIONS/APPOINTMENTS

Underwriter	Copenhagen Re UK	1975 - 1998
Executive Director	Danish Re Syndicates Ltd	2001 - 2005
Executive Director	Danish Re Syndicates Ltd	2006 - 2006
Executive Director	Imagine Underwriting Limited	2006 - 2007

Charles EL Philipps

Position	Non-Executive Director
Company	Amlin Underwriting Limited
Address (Office)	St Helen's
	1 Undershaft
	London EC3A 8ND
Telephone	+44 (0)20 7746 1000

Fax	+44 (0)20 7746 1696
Email	charles.philipps@amlin.co.uk
Website	www.amlin.com

Full Name	Charles Edward Laurence Philipps
Year of Birth	1959
Professional Qualifications	Information not available

PROFESSIONAL INFORMATION

CURRENT MAJOR POSITIONS/APPOINTMENTS

| Non-Executive Director | Amlin Underwriting Limited | 2008 - |
| President | The Insurance Institute of London | 2008 - |

PREVIOUS MAJOR POSITIONS/APPOINTMENTS

Executive Director	NatWest Markets Corporate Finance Limited	1983 - 1997
Chief Executive	Amlin Underwriting Limited	1998 - 2008
Member	Lloyd's Market Board	2001 - 2002
Executive Director	Angerstein Underwriting Limited	2001 - 2003
External Member	Council of Lloyd's	2001 - 2007
Chairman	Lloyd's Market Association, Capital Committee	2002 - 2003
Non-Executive Director	Lloyd's Market Association	2003 - 2007
Vice Chairman	Lloyd's Market Association	2004 - 2007
Member	Council of The Insurance Institute of London	2004 - 2008

Lord Phillips Of Sudbury

Position	Non-Executive Director
Company	Faraday Underwriting Limited
Address (Office)	5th Floor
	Corn Exchange
	55 Mark Lane
	London EC3R 7NE
Telephone	+44 (0)20 7702 3333
Fax	+44 (0)20 7680 4369
Email	liz.richardson@faraday.com
Website	www.faraday.com

Full Name	Lord Andrew Wyndham Phillips Of Sudbury
Year of Birth	1939
Professional Qualifications	Information not available

PROFESSIONAL INFORMATION

CURRENT MAJOR POSITIONS/APPOINTMENTS

| Non-Executive Director | Faraday Underwriting Limited | 1999 - |
| Non-Executive Director | Faraday Reinsurance Co Limited | 2003 - |

PREVIOUS MAJOR POSITIONS/APPOINTMENTS

Information not available

Brian W Pomeroy, CBE

Position	Independent Non-Executive Director
Company	QBE Underwriting Limited
Address (Office)	Plantation Place
	30 Fenchurch Street
	London EC3M 3BD
Telephone	+44 (0)20 7105 4000
Fax	+44 (0)20 7105 4019
Email	enquiries@uk.qbe.com
Website	www.qbeeurope.com

PERSONAL PROFILE   A profile can be found in the People at Lloyd's, Personal section.

Andrew D Pomfret

Position	Non-Executive Director
Company	Beazley Furlonge Ltd
Address (Office)	Plantation Place South
	60 Great Tower Street
	London EC3R 5AD
Telephone	+44 (0)20 7667 0623
Fax	+44 (0)20 7674 7100
Email	andrew.pomfret@beazley.com
Website	www.beazley.com

Full Name	Andrew David Pomfret
Year of Birth	1960
Professional Qualifications	Information not available

PROFESSIONAL INFORMATION

CURRENT MAJOR POSITIONS/APPOINTMENTS

Executive Director	Rathbone Investment Management Limited	2001 -
Non-Executive Director	Beazley Furlonge Ltd	2004 -
Chief Executive	Rathbone Investment Management Limited	2004 -
Executive Director	Rathbone Unit Trust Management Limited	2005 -
Executive Director	Rathbone Pension & Advisory Services Ltd	2006 -

PREVIOUS MAJOR POSITIONS/APPOINTMENTS

Information not available

Nicolas G Poole

Position	Chairman
Company	KGM Underwriting Agencies Limited
Address (Office)	KGM House
	George Lane
	South Woodford
	London E18 1RZ
Telephone	+44 (0)20 8530 1813
Fax	+44 (0)20 8530 7037

Email	nic.poole@kgminsurance.co.uk
Website	www.kgminsurance.co.uk

Full Name	Nicolas George Poole
Year of Birth	1970
Professional Qualifications	Information not available

PROFESSIONAL INFORMATION

CURRENT MAJOR POSITIONS/APPOINTMENTS

Non-Executive Director	KGM Underwriting Agencies Limited	2006 -
Non-Executive Director	Premium Choice Ltd	2009 -

PREVIOUS MAJOR POSITIONS/APPOINTMENTS

Executive Director	Camomille Associates Limited	2001 - 2006
Non-Executive Director	Roadsure Ltd	2006 - 2007

Howard M Posner

Position	Independent Non-Executive Director
Company	QBE Underwriting Limited
Address (Office)	Plantation Place
	30 Fenchurch Street
	London EC3M 3BD
Telephone	+44 (0)20 7105 4000
Fax	+44 (0)20 7105 4019
Email	enquiries@uk.qbe.com
Website	www.qbeeurope.com

Full Name	Howard Michael Posner
Year of Birth	1956
Professional Qualifications	Information not available

PROFESSIONAL INFORMATION

CURRENT MAJOR POSITIONS/APPOINTMENTS

Non-Executive Director	QBE Insurance (Europe) Limited	2006 -
Non-Executive Director	QBE Underwriting Limited	2006 -
Non-Executive Director	UK Underwriting Limited	2006 -
Non-Executive Director	TPS (Insurance Admin Services) Ltd	2007 -
Non-Executive Director	Acumus Insurance Solutions Limited	2007 -

PREVIOUS MAJOR POSITIONS/APPOINTMENTS

Non-Executive Director	esure Insurance Limited	2001 - 2005
Non-Executive Director	RAC Insurance Limited	2001 - 2005
Executive Director	Capital Bank Insurance Services Limited	2002 - 2003
Non-Executive Director	Clerical Medical Investment Group Limited	2002 - 2003
Non-Executive Director	Clerical Medical Managed Funds Limited	2002 - 2003
Non-Executive Director	Halifax Life Limited	2002 - 2003
Chief Executive	St Andrew's Life Assurance Plc	2003 - 2004
Non-Executive Director	First Alternative Insurance Company Limited	2003 - 2005
Chief Executive	St Andrew's Insurance Plc	2003 - 2005
Non-Executive Director	RAC Motoring Services	2005 - 2005

Chief Executive	Halifax General Insurance Services Limited	2005 - 2005
Executive Director	St Andrew's Membership Services Limited	2005 - 2005
Non-Executive Director	Paymentshield Ltd	2005 - 2006
Non-Executive Director	Dallas Kirkland (Professions) Limited	2006 - 2008
Non-Executive Director	Giles Insurance Brokers Ltd	2006 - 2008

Gary A Powell

Position	Non-Executive Director
Company	Argenta Syndicate Management Limited
Address (Office)	Fountain House
	130 Fenchurch Street
	London EC3M 5DJ
Telephone	+44 (0)20 7825 7200
Fax	+44 (0)20 7825 7155
Email	gary.powell@argentaplc.com
Website	www.argentaplc.com
Full Name	Gary Alan Powell
Year of Birth	Information not available
Professional Qualifications	Information not available

PROFESSIONAL INFORMATION

CURRENT MAJOR POSITIONS/APPOINTMENTS

Executive Director	Rothschild Private Management Limited	2006 -
Non-Executive Director	Argenta Syndicate Management Limited	2008 -

PREVIOUS MAJOR POSITIONS/APPOINTMENTS

Information not available

John F Powell

Position	Non-Executive Director
Company	Omega Underwriting Agents Ltd
Address (Office)	4th Floor
	New London House
	6 London Street
	London EC3R 7LP
Telephone	+44 (0)20 7767 3000
Fax	+44 (0)20 7488 9639
Email	info@omegauw.com
Website	www.omegauw.com
Full Name	John Francis Powell
Year of Birth	1953
Professional Qualifications	Information not available

PROFESSIONAL INFORMATION

CURRENT MAJOR POSITIONS/APPOINTMENTS

Non-Executive Director	Omega Underwriting Agents Ltd	2005 -

PREVIOUS MAJOR POSITIONS/APPOINTMENTS

Executive Director	Axiom Consulting Ltd	2005 - 2005

Timothy P Prifti

Position	Executive Director
Company	R J Kiln & Co Limited
Address (Office)	106 Fenchurch Street
	London EC3M 5NR
Telephone	+44 (0)20 7886 9000
Fax	+44 (0)20 7488 1848
Email	timothy.prifti@kilngroup.com
Website	www.kilnplc.com

Full Name	Timothy Peter Prifti
Year of Birth	1968
Professional Qualifications	ACII

PROFESSIONAL INFORMATION

CURRENT MAJOR POSITIONS/APPOINTMENTS

Executive Director	R J Kiln & Co Limited	2003 -

PREVIOUS MAJOR POSITIONS/APPOINTMENTS

Information not available

Michael SF Pritchard

Position	Executive Director & Active Underwriter Syndicate 318
Company	Beaufort Underwriting Agency Limited
Address (Office)	Third Floor
	One Minster Court
	Mincing Lane
	London EC3R 7AA
Telephone	+44 (0)20 7220 8200
Fax	+44 (0)20 7220 8290
Email	michael.pritchard@beaufort-group.com
Website	www.beaufort-group.com

Full Name	Michael Stephen Francis Pritchard
Year of Birth	1955
Professional Qualifications	Information not available

PROFESSIONAL INFORMATION

CURRENT MAJOR POSITIONS/APPOINTMENTS

Executive Director	Beaufort Underwriting Agency Limited	2000 -

PREVIOUS MAJOR POSITIONS/APPOINTMENTS

Information not available

Richard V Pryce

Position	Underwriting Director & Active Underwriter Syndicate 2488
Company	Ace Underwriting Agencies Limited
Address (Office)	100 Leadenhall Street
	London EC3A 3BP
Telephone	+44 (0)20 7173 7396
Fax	+44 (0)20 7173 7800
Email	richard.pryce@ace-ina.com
Website	www.acelimited.com
Full Name	Richard Vaughan Pryce
Year of Birth	1959
Professional Qualifications	Information not available

PROFESSIONAL INFORMATION

CURRENT MAJOR POSITIONS/APPOINTMENTS

Executive Director	ACE European Group Limited	2003 -
Executive Director	Ace Underwriting Agencies Limited	2003 -
Executive Director	Ridge Underwriting Agencies Limited	2003 -

PREVIOUS MAJOR POSITIONS/APPOINTMENTS

Information not available

David J Pye

Position	Chairman
Company	Equity Syndicate Management Limited
Address (Office)	Library House
	New Road
	Brentwood
	Essex CM14 4GD
Telephone	+44 (0)1277 200 100
Fax	+44 (0)1206 777 223
Email	info@equitygroup.co.uk
Website	www.equitygroup.co.uk
Full Name	David John Pye
Year of Birth	1947
Professional Qualifications	Information not available

PROFESSIONAL INFORMATION

CURRENT MAJOR POSITIONS/APPOINTMENTS

Executive Director	A To B Mobility Ltd	2006 -
Non-Executive Director	Equity Syndicate Management Limited	2007 -
Non-Executive Director	Creechurch Underwriting Limited	2007 -
Executive Director	Canopius Underwriting Limited	2008 -

PREVIOUS MAJOR POSITIONS/APPOINTMENTS

Executive Director	Creechurch Underwriting Limited	2001 - 2007
Non-Executive Director	Hastings Insurance Services Ltd	2005 - 2007
Executive Director	Creechurch Services Limited	2005 - 2007

| Chief Executive | Creechurch Underwriting Limited | 2006 - 2007 |
| Non-Executive Director | Canopius Managing Agents Limited | 2007 - 2007 |

Stephen J Quick

Position	Executive Director
Company	Hiscox Syndicates Limited
Address (Office)	1 Great St Helen's
	London EC3A 6HX
Telephone	+44 (0)20 7448 6000
Fax	+44 (0)20 7448 6900
Email	stephen.quick@hiscox.com
Website	www.hiscox.com

Full Name	Stephen John Quick
Year of Birth	1952
Professional Qualifications	Information not available

PROFESSIONAL INFORMATION

CURRENT MAJOR POSITIONS/APPOINTMENTS

| Executive Director | Hiscox Syndicates Limited | 2002 - |

PREVIOUS MAJOR POSITIONS/APPOINTMENTS

Information not available

Jeremy B Raishbrook

Position	Chief Financial Officer
Company	Omega Underwriting Agents Ltd
Address (Office)	4th Floor
	New London House
	6 London Street
	London EC3R 7LP
Telephone	+44 (0)20 7767 3000
Fax	+44 (0)20 7488 9639
Email	jeremy.raishbrook@omegauw.com
Website	www.omegauw.com

Full Name	Jeremy Benton Raishbrook
Year of Birth	1967
Professional Qualifications	Information not available

PROFESSIONAL INFORMATION

CURRENT MAJOR POSITIONS/APPOINTMENTS

| Executive Director | Omega Underwriting Agents Ltd | 2000 - |

PREVIOUS MAJOR POSITIONS/APPOINTMENTS

Information not available

Arabella Ramage

Position	Executive Director
Company	XL London Market Limited
Address (Office)	XL House
	70 Gracechurch Street
	London EC3V 0XL
Telephone	+44 (0)20 7933 7000
Fax	+44 (0)20 7469 1071
Email	arabella.ramage@xlgroup.com
Website	www.xlinsurance.co.uk

Full Name	Arabella Ramage
Year of Birth	1966
Professional Qualifications	Information not available

PROFESSIONAL INFORMATION

CURRENT MAJOR POSITIONS/APPOINTMENTS

Executive Director	XL London Market Limited	2005 -

PREVIOUS MAJOR POSITIONS/APPOINTMENTS

Information not available

Ravi C Rambarran

Position	Non-Executive Director
Company	Sagicor at Lloyd's Limited
Address (Office)	1 Great Tower Street
	London EC3R 5AA
Telephone	+44 (0)20 3003 6800
Fax	+44 (0)20 3003 6999
Email	duncan.reed@sagicor.eu
Website	www.sagicor.com

Full Name	Ravi Clifton Rambarran
Year of Birth	1965
Professional Qualifications	BSc, MSc, FIA

PROFESSIONAL INFORMATION

CURRENT MAJOR POSITIONS/APPOINTMENTS

Non-Executive Director	Sagicor at Lloyd's Limited	2007 -
Non-Executive Director	Byrne and Stacey Underwriting Limited	2007 -

PREVIOUS MAJOR POSITIONS/APPOINTMENTS

Information not available

Peter J Rand

Position	Independent Review Director and Director of Underwriting
Company	Montpelier Underwriting Agencies Ltd

Address (Office)	7th Floor
	85 Gracechurch Street
	London EC3V 0AA
Telephone	+44 (0)20 7648 4500
Fax	+44 (0)20 7648 4501
Email	peter.rand@montpelierua.com
Website	www.montpelierre.com

Full Name	Peter John Rand
Year of Birth	1951
Professional Qualifications	Information not available

PROFESSIONAL INFORMATION

CURRENT MAJOR POSITIONS/APPOINTMENTS

| Executive Director | Montpelier Underwriting Agencies Ltd | 2008 - |

PREVIOUS MAJOR POSITIONS/APPOINTMENTS

| Non-Executive Director | Argenta Syndicate Management Limited | 2001 - 2005 |

Graeme S Rayner

Position	Underwriting Director
Company	QBE Underwriting Limited
Address (Office)	Plantation Place
	30 Fenchurch Street
	London EC3M 3BD
Telephone	+44 (0)20 7105 4000
Fax	+44 (0)20 7105 4019
Email	enquiries@uk.qbe.com
Website	www.qbeeurope.com

Full Name	Graeme Scott Rayner
Year of Birth	1969
Professional Qualifications	Information not available

PROFESSIONAL INFORMATION

CURRENT MAJOR POSITIONS/APPOINTMENTS

| Executive Director | QBE Insurance (Europe) Limited | 2006 - |
| Executive Director | QBE Underwriting Limited | 2008 - |

PREVIOUS MAJOR POSITIONS/APPOINTMENTS

| | Information not available |

Mark J Rayner

Position	Joint Chief Underwriting Officer & Active Underwriter Syndicate 435
Company	Faraday Underwriting Limited
Address (Office)	5th Floor
	Corn Exchange
	55 Mark Lane
	London EC3R 7NE
Telephone	+44 (0)20 7702 3333

Fax	+44 (0)20 7680 4369
Email	mark.rayner@faraday.com
Website	www.faraday.com

PERSONAL PROFILE	A profile can be found in the People at Lloyd's, Personal section.

Duncan J Reed

Position	Executive Director, Company Secretary & Compliance Officer
Company	Sagicor at Lloyd's Limited
Address (Office)	1 Great Tower Street
	London EC3R 5AA
Telephone	+44 (0)20 3003 6800
Fax	+44 (0)20 3003 6999
Email	duncan.reed@sagicor.eu
Website	www.sagicor.com

Full Name	Duncan James Reed
Year of Birth	1970
Professional Qualifications	Information not available

PROFESSIONAL INFORMATION

CURRENT MAJOR POSITIONS/APPOINTMENTS

Executive Director	Sagicor at Lloyd's Limited	2007 -
Executive Director	Byrne and Stacey Underwriting Limited	2007 -
Executive Director	Sagicor Syndicate Services Ltd	2007 -

PREVIOUS MAJOR POSITIONS/APPOINTMENTS

Executive Director	Newline Underwriting Management Ltd	2002 - 2004

George P Reeth

Position	Non-Executive Director
Company	Talbot Underwriting Ltd
Address (Office)	Gracechurch House
	55 Gracechurch Street
	London EC3V 0JP
Telephone	+44 (0)20 7550 3500
Fax	+44 (0)20 7550 3555
Email	central@talbotuw.com
Website	www.talbotuw.com

Full Name	George Peter Reeth
Year of Birth	1956
Professional Qualifications	Information not available

PROFESSIONAL INFORMATION

CURRENT MAJOR POSITIONS/APPOINTMENTS

Non-Executive Director	Talbot Underwriting Ltd	2007 -
Non-Executive Director	Underwriting Risk Services Ltd	2007 -

PREVIOUS MAJOR POSITIONS/APPOINTMENTS
Information not available

Martin RD Reith

Position	Non-Executive Director
Company	Ascot Underwriting Limited
Address (Office)	Plantation Place
	30 Fenchurch Street
	London EC3M 3BD
Telephone	+44 (0)20 7743 9600
Fax	+44 (0)20 7743 9601
Email	enquiries@ascotuw.com
Website	www.ascotuw.com

PERSONAL PROFILE   A profile can be found in the People at Lloyd's, Personal section.

Thomas A Riddell

Position	Chairman
Company	Whittington Capital Management Limited
Address (Office)	33 Creechurch Lane
	London EC3A 5EB
Telephone	+44 (0)20 7743 0900
Fax	+44 (0)20 7743 0901
Email	jon.francis@whittingtoninsurance.com
Website	www.whittingtoninsurance.com

Full Name	Thomas Alexander Riddell
Year of Birth	1952
Professional Qualifications	Information not available

PROFESSIONAL INFORMATION

CURRENT MAJOR POSITIONS/APPOINTMENTS

Chief Executive	World Marine & General Insurances Pty Limited	2001 -
Chief Executive	HIH Casualty and General Insurance Limited	2004 -
Chief Executive	FAI Insurances Limited	2004 -
Non-Executive Director	Whittington Capital Management Limited	2008 -

PREVIOUS MAJOR POSITIONS/APPOINTMENTS
Information not available

Matthew S Riley

Position	Chief Executive Officer
Company	Sportscover Underwriting Ltd
Address (Office)	3 Minster Court
	Mincing Lane
	London EC3R 7DD
Telephone	+44 (0)20 7398 4080
Fax	+44 (0)20 7398 4090

Email	matthew.riley@sportscover.com
Website	www.sportscoverunderwriting.com

Full Name	Matthew Saxon Riley
Year of Birth	1966
Professional Qualifications	Information not available

PROFESSIONAL INFORMATION

CURRENT MAJOR POSITIONS/APPOINTMENTS

Chief Executive	Active Underwriting Specialists Ltd	2007 -
Chief Executive	Sportscover Europe Limited	2007 -
Chief Executive	Sportscover Underwriting Ltd	2008 -

PREVIOUS MAJOR POSITIONS/APPOINTMENTS

Information not available

Andrew (Andy) G Ripley

Position	Non-Executive Director
Company	Sportscover Underwriting Ltd
Address (Office)	3 Minster Court
	Mincing Lane
	London EC3R 7DD
Telephone	+44 (0)20 7398 4080
Fax	+44 (0)20 7398 4090
Email	dominic.ford@sportscover.com
Website	www.sportscoverunderwriting.com

Full Name	Andrew George Ripley
Year of Birth	1947
Professional Qualifications	Information not available

PROFESSIONAL INFORMATION

CURRENT MAJOR POSITIONS/APPOINTMENTS

Finance Director	Duncanson & Holt Syndicate Management Ltd	2009 -
Non-Executive Director	Sportscover Underwriting Ltd	2008 -

PREVIOUS MAJOR POSITIONS/APPOINTMENTS

Non-Executive Director	Duncanson & Holt Syndicate Management Ltd	2001 - 2009

Bruno C Ritchie

Position	Executive Director
Company	Hiscox Syndicates Limited
Address (Office)	1 Great St Helen's
	London EC3A 6HX
Telephone	+44 (0)20 7448 6000
Fax	+44 (0)20 7448 6900
Email	bruno.ritchie@hiscox.com
Website	www.hiscox.com

Full Name	Bruno Christopher Ritchie
Year of Birth	1964
Professional Qualifications	Information not available

PROFESSIONAL INFORMATION

CURRENT MAJOR POSITIONS/APPOINTMENTS

Executive Director	Hiscox Syndicates Limited	2002 -

PREVIOUS MAJOR POSITIONS/APPOINTMENTS

Information not available

George F Rivaz

Position	Chairman
Company	Atrium Underwriters Limited
Address (Office)	Room 790
	Lloyd's
	One Lime Street
	London EC3M 7DQ
Telephone	+44 (0)20 7327 4877
Fax	+44 (0)20 7327 4878
Email	info@atrium-uw.com
Website	www.atrium-uw.com

Full Name	George Farnworth Rivaz
Year of Birth	1963
Professional Qualifications	Information not available

PROFESSIONAL INFORMATION

CURRENT MAJOR POSITIONS/APPOINTMENTS

Chairman	Atrium Underwriters Limited	2007 -

PREVIOUS MAJOR POSITIONS/APPOINTMENTS

Non-Executive Director	Atrium Underwriters Limited	2003 - 2006

Joseph W Roberts

Position	Executive Director
Company	Max at Lloyd's Ltd
Address (Office)	4th Floor
	70 Gracechurch Street
	London EC3V 0XL
Telephone	+44 (0)20 3102 3100
Fax	+44 (0)20 3102 3200
Email	joseph.roberts@maxatlloyds.com
Website	www.maxatlloyds.com

Full Name	Joseph William Roberts
Year of Birth	1970
Professional Qualifications	Information not available

PROFESSIONAL INFORMATION

CURRENT MAJOR POSITIONS/APPOINTMENTS

Executive Director	Max at Lloyd's Ltd	2008 -

PREVIOUS MAJOR POSITIONS/APPOINTMENTS

Information not available

Colin G Robinson

Position	Non-Executive Director
Company	Catlin Underwriting Agencies Ltd
Address (Office)	6th Floor
	3 Minster Court
	Mincing Lane
	London EC3R 7DD
Telephone	+44 (0)20 7626 0486
Fax	+44 (0)20 7623 9101
Email	catlininfo@catlin.com
Website	www.catlin.com

Full Name	Colin Graham Robinson
Year of Birth	1947
Professional Qualifications	Information not available

PROFESSIONAL INFORMATION

CURRENT MAJOR POSITIONS/APPOINTMENTS

Non-Executive Director	Catlin Underwriting Agencies Ltd	2004 -
Non-Executive Director	Catlin Insurance Company (UK) Ltd	2005 -

PREVIOUS MAJOR POSITIONS/APPOINTMENTS

Information not available

John D Robinson

Position	Underwriting Director & Active Underwriter Syndicate 958
Company	Omega Underwriting Agents Ltd
Address (Office)	4th Floor
	New London House
	6 London Street
	London EC3R 7LP
Telephone	+44 (0)20 7767 3000
Fax	+44 (0)20 7488 9639
Email	john.robinson@omegauw.com
Website	www.omegauw.com

PERSONAL PROFILE	A profile can be found in the People at Lloyd's, Personal section.

John H Rochman

Position	Chairman
Company	Munich Re Underwriting Limited

Address (Office)	St Helen's
	1 Undershaft
	London EC3A 8EE
Telephone	+44 (0)20 7886 3900
Fax	+44 (0)20 7886 3901
Email	john.rochman@mrunderwriting.com
Website	www.watkins-syndicate.co.uk

Full Name	John Howard Rochman
Year of Birth	1946
Professional Qualifications	Information not available

PROFESSIONAL INFORMATION

CURRENT MAJOR POSITIONS/APPOINTMENTS

Non-Executive Director	Munich Re Underwriting Limited	1999 -

PREVIOUS MAJOR POSITIONS/APPOINTMENTS

Information not available

Richard P Rosenbaum

Position	Non-Executive Director
Company	ARK Syndicate Management Limited
Address (Office)	8th Floor
	St Helen's
	1 Undershaft
	London EC3A 8EE
Telephone	+44 (0)20 3023 4020
Fax	+44 (0)20 3023 4000
Email	enquiries@arkunderwriting.com
Website	www.arkunderwriting.com

Full Name	Richard Paul Rosenbaum
Year of Birth	1971
Professional Qualifications	Information not available

PROFESSIONAL INFORMATION

CURRENT MAJOR POSITIONS/APPOINTMENTS

Non-Executive Director	ARK Syndicate Management Limited	2007 -

PREVIOUS MAJOR POSITIONS/APPOINTMENTS

Information not available

Gary L Ross

Position	Chief Operating Officer & Claims Director
Company	Sagicor at Lloyd's Limited
Address (Office)	1 Great Tower Street
	London EC3R 5AA
Telephone	+44 (0)20 3003 6800
Fax	+44 (0)20 3003 6999

Email	gary.ross@sagicor.eu
Website	www.sagicor.com

Full Name	Gary Leonard Ross
Year of Birth	1967
Professional Qualifications	ACII

PROFESSIONAL INFORMATION

CURRENT MAJOR POSITIONS/APPOINTMENTS

Executive Director	Sagicor at Lloyd's Limited	2004 -
Executive Director	Byrne and Stacey Underwriting Limited	2007 -
Executive Director	Sagicor Syndicate Services Ltd	2007 -

PREVIOUS MAJOR POSITIONS/APPOINTMENTS

Information not available

Julian G Ross

Position	Executive Director
Company	Talbot Underwriting Ltd
Address (Office)	Gracechurch House
	55 Gracechurch Street
	London EC3V 0JP
Telephone	+44 (0)20 7550 3500
Fax	+44 (0)20 7550 3555
Email	julian.ross@talbotuw.com
Website	www.talbotuw.com

Full Name	Julian Graeme Ross
Year of Birth	1965
Professional Qualifications	Information not available

PROFESSIONAL INFORMATION

CURRENT MAJOR POSITIONS/APPOINTMENTS

Executive Director	Talbot Underwriting Ltd	2001 -

PREVIOUS MAJOR POSITIONS/APPOINTMENTS

Information not available

Brian W Rowbotham

Position	Non-Executive Director
Company	Advent Underwriting Limited
Address (Office)	10th Floor
	One Minster Court
	Mincing Lane
	London EC3R 7AA
Telephone	+44 (0)20 7743 8200
Fax	+44 (0)20 7743 8299
Email	head.office@adventgroup.co.uk
Website	www.adventgroup.co.uk

Full Name	Brian William Rowbotham
Year of Birth	1931
Professional Qualifications	FCA

PROFESSIONAL INFORMATION

CURRENT MAJOR POSITIONS/APPOINTMENTS

| Non-Executive Director | Advent Underwriting Limited | 2003 - |

PREVIOUS MAJOR POSITIONS/APPOINTMENTS

| Chairman | Adscene Group PLC | 1987 - 1994 |

James C Sardeson

Position	Underwriting Director
Company	Argo Managing Agency Ltd
Address (Office)	47 Mark Lane
	London EC3R 7QQ
Telephone	+44 (0)20 7712 7600
Fax	+44 (0)20 7712 7601
Email	james.sardeson@argo-int.com
Website	www.argo-int.com

Full Name	James Christopher Sardeson
Year of Birth	1964
Professional Qualifications	Information not available

PROFESSIONAL INFORMATION

CURRENT MAJOR POSITIONS/APPOINTMENTS

| Executive Director | Heritage Direct Ltd | 2007 - |
| Executive Director | Argo Managing Agency Ltd | 2007 - |

PREVIOUS MAJOR POSITIONS/APPOINTMENTS

| Chief Executive | Benfield Limited | 2005 - 2005 |

Matthew Scales

Position	Finance Director
Company	Brit Syndicates Limited
Address (Office)	2nd Floor
	55 Bishopsgate
	London EC2N 3AS
Telephone	+44 (0)20 7984 8500
Fax	+44 (0)20 7984 8501
Email	matthew.scales@britinsurance.com
Website	www.britinsurance.com

Full Name	Matthew Scales
Year of Birth	1954
Professional Qualifications	FCA

PROFESSIONAL INFORMATION

CURRENT MAJOR POSITIONS/APPOINTMENTS

Executive Director	BRIT Insurance Limited	2001 -
Executive Director	BRIT Syndicates Limited	2004 -
Member	Finance Committee of the Lloyd's Market Association	Unknown -

PREVIOUS MAJOR POSITIONS/APPOINTMENTS

Finance Director	English & American Group plc	1991 - 1993
Group Financial Controller	Benfield Group plc	1996 - 1999
Executive Director	BRIT Insurance (UK) Ltd	2003 - 2007
Executive Director	EPIC Asset Management Limited	2004 - 2007
Executive Director	EPIC Private Equity Limited	2004 - 2007

Peter D Scales

Position	Executive Director
Company	Cathedral Underwriting Limited
Address (Office)	5th Floor
	Fitzwilliam House
	10 St Mary Axe
	London EC3A 8EN
Telephone	+44 (0)20 7170 9025
Fax	+44 (0)20 7170 9001
Email	peter.scales@cathedralcapital.com
Website	www.cathedralcapital.com

Full Name	Peter David Scales
Year of Birth	1964
Professional Qualifications	Information not available

PROFESSIONAL INFORMATION

CURRENT MAJOR POSITIONS/APPOINTMENTS

Director	BRIT Syndicates Limited	1993 -
Managing Director	BRIT Syndicates Limited	1994 -
Executive Director	Cathedral Underwriting Limited	2000 -

PREVIOUS MAJOR POSITIONS/APPOINTMENTS

Director	Wren Underwriting Agencies Limited	1993 - Unknown
Chief Executive	Cathedral Capital Management Limited	2001 - 2007
Managing Director	Wren Underwriting Agencies Limited	Unknown

Richard T Scholes

Position	Non-Executive Director
Company	Chaucer Syndicates Limited
Address (Office)	Plantation Place
	30 Fenchurch Street
	London EC3M 3AD
Telephone	+44 (0)20 7397 9700
Fax	+44 (0)20 7397 9710

Email	richard.scholes@chaucerplc.com
Website	www.chaucerplc.com

Full Name	Richard Thomas Scholes
Year of Birth	1945
Professional Qualifications	ACA

PROFESSIONAL INFORMATION

CURRENT MAJOR POSITIONS/APPOINTMENTS

Non-Executive Director	Chaucer Syndicates Limited	2003 -
Non-Executive Director	Bodycote International plc	Unknown -
Non-Executive Director	Crest Nicholson PLC	Unknown -
Non-Executive Director	Keller Group plc	Unknown -
Non-Executive Director	Marshalls PLC	Unknown -
Chairman	Bodycote International plc, Audit Committee	Unknown -
Chairman	Crest Nicholson PLC, Audit Committee	Unknown -
Chairman	Marshalls PLC, Audit Committee	Unknown -
Member	Chaucer Plc, Audit Remuneration and Nomination Committee	Unknown -

PREVIOUS MAJOR POSITIONS/APPOINTMENTS

Executive Director	Dresdner Kleinwort Limited	1986 - 2001
Non-Executive Director	British Vita PLC	Unknown
Non-Executive Director	RCO Holdings PLC	Unknown

Dr Cornelius ACM Schrauwers

Position	Non-Executive Director
Company	Brit Syndicates Limited
Address (Office)	2nd Floor
	55 Bishopsgate
	London EC2N 3AS
Telephone	+44 (0)20 7984 8500
Fax	+44 (0)20 7984 8501
Email	cornelis.schrauwers@britinsurance.com
Website	www.britinsurance.com

Full Name	Dr Cornelius Antonius Carolus Maria Schrauwers
Year of Birth	1947
Professional Qualifications	Information not available

PROFESSIONAL INFORMATION

CURRENT MAJOR POSITIONS/APPOINTMENTS

Non-Executive Director	Record Currency Management Limited	2007 -
Non-Executive Director	BRIT Insurance Limited	2007 -
Non-Executive Director	Brit Syndicates Limited	2007 -
Chairman	Drive Assist Holdings Limited	Unknown -
Senior Independent Director	Record PLC	Unknown -
Member	Audit and Remuneration Committees	Unknown -

PREVIOUS MAJOR POSITIONS/APPOINTMENTS

Non-Executive Director	The British Aviation Insurance Company Limited	2001 - 2004
Non-Executive Director	Canopius Managing Agents Limited	2004 - 2005
Non-Executive Director	Capita Commercial Insurance Services Limited	2005 - 2006

Derek J Scott

Position	Non-Executive Director
Company	Liberty Syndicate Management Limited
Address (Office)	5th Floor
	Plantation Place South
	60 Great Tower Street
	London EC3R 5AZ
Telephone	+44 (0)20 7070 4472
Fax	+44 (0)20 7863 1001
Email	info@libertysyndicates.com
Website	www.libertysyndicates.com

Full Name	Derek John Scott
Year of Birth	1947
Professional Qualifications	Information not available

PROFESSIONAL INFORMATION

CURRENT MAJOR POSITIONS/APPOINTMENTS

Non-Executive Director	Liberty Syndicate Management Limited	2008 -

PREVIOUS MAJOR POSITIONS/APPOINTMENTS

Non-Executive Director	Bradford Insurance Company Limited	2005 - 2005
Non-Executive Director	PA (GI) Limited	2005 - 2005
Non-Executive Director	Phoenix & London Assurance Limited	2005 - 2005
Non-Executive Director	Phoenix Life & Pensions Limited	2005 - 2005
Non-Executive Director	Phoenix Life Limited	2005 - 2005
Non-Executive Director	SL Liverpool Plc	2005 - 2005

Adam C Seager

Position	Risk Director, Compliance Director & Company Secretary
Company	KGM Underwriting Agencies Limited
Address (Office)	KGM House
	George Lane
	South Woodford
	London E18 1RZ
Telephone	+44 (0)20 8530 1813
Fax	+44 (0)20 8530 7037
Email	adam.seager@kgminsurance.co.uk
Website	www.kgminsurance.co.uk

Full Name	Adam Clive Seager
Year of Birth	1963
Professional Qualifications	Information not available

PROFESSIONAL INFORMATION

CURRENT MAJOR POSITIONS/APPOINTMENTS

Executive Director	KGM Underwriting Agencies Limited	2006 -

PREVIOUS MAJOR POSITIONS/APPOINTMENTS
Information not available

Richard N Shaak

Position	Non-Executive Director
Company	Starr Managing Agents Limited
Address (Office)	3rd Floor
	140 Leadenhall Street
	London EC3V 4QT
Telephone	+44 (0)20 7337 3550
Fax	+44 (0)20 7337 3551
Email	richard.shaak@cvstarrco.com
Website	www.cvstarrco.com
Full Name	Richard Nathan Shaak
Year of Birth	1964
Professional Qualifications	Information not available

PROFESSIONAL INFORMATION

CURRENT MAJOR POSITIONS/APPOINTMENTS

Non-Executive Director	Starr Underwriting Agents Limited	2007 -
Non-Executive Director	Starr Managing Agents Ltd	2007 -

PREVIOUS MAJOR POSITIONS/APPOINTMENTS

Executive Director	Starr Underwriting Agents Limited	2006 - 2008

Wesley W von Schack

Position	Non-Executive Director
Company	AEGIS Managing Agency Ltd
Address (Office)	110 Fenchurch Street
	London EC3M 5JT
Telephone	+44 (0)20 7265 2100
Fax	+44 (0)20 7265 2101
Email	enquiries@aegislink.com
Website	www.aegislink.com
Full Name	Wesley William von Schack
Year of Birth	1944
Professional Qualifications	Information not available

PROFESSIONAL INFORMATION

CURRENT MAJOR POSITIONS/APPOINTMENTS

Non-Executive Director	AEGIS Managing Agency Ltd	2007 -

                            Information not available

Bruce D Shepherd

Position	Executive Director
Company	R J Kiln & Co Limited
Address (Office)	106 Fenchurch Street
	London EC3M 5NR
Telephone	+44 (0)20 7886 9000
Fax	+44 (0)20 7488 1848
Email	bruce.shepherd@kilngroup.com
Website	www.kilnplc.com

PERSONAL PROFILE   A profile can be found in the People at Lloyd's, Personal section.

Philip O Sheridan

Position	Non-Executive Director
Company	XL London Market Limited
Address (Office)	XL House
	70 Gracechurch Street
	London EC3V 0XL
Telephone	+44 (0)20 7933 7000
Fax	+44 (0)20 7469 1071
Email	graham.brady@xlgroup.com
Website	www.xlinsurance.co.uk

Full Name	Philip Ogilvie Sheridan
Year of Birth	1934
Professional Qualifications	Information not available

PROFESSIONAL INFORMATION

CURRENT MAJOR POSITIONS/APPOINTMENTS

Non-Executive Director	XL Insurance Company Limited	2001 -
Non-Executive Director	XL London Market Limited	2007 -

PREVIOUS MAJOR POSITIONS/APPOINTMENTS
                            Information not available

David ES Shipley

Position	Chairman
Company	Managing Agency Partners Limited
Address (Office)	1st Floor
	110 Fenchurch Street
	London EC3M 5JT
Telephone	+44 (0)20 7709 3860
Fax	+44 (0)20 7709 3861
Email	dshipley@mapunderwriting.co.uk
Website	www.mapunderwriting.co.uk

PERSONAL PROFILE   A profile can be found in the People at Lloyd's, Personal section.

Matthew J Simpson

Position	Executive Director
Company	Hardy (Underwriting Agencies) Ltd
Address (Office)	4th Floor
	40 Lime Street
	London EC3M 7AW
Telephone	+44 (0)20 7626 0382
Fax	+44 (0)20 7283 4677
Email	matthew.simpson@hardygroup.co.uk
Website	www.hardygroup.co.uk
Full Name	Matthew John Simpson
Year of Birth	1962
Professional Qualifications	BSc (Hons), FCII

PROFESSIONAL INFORMATION

CURRENT MAJOR POSITIONS/APPOINTMENTS

Executive Director	Hardy (Underwriting Agencies) Ltd	1995 -

PREVIOUS MAJOR POSITIONS/APPOINTMENTS

Information not available

Karen Sinden

Position	Managing Director
Company	Marketform Managing Agency Limited
Address (Office)	8 Lloyd's Avenue
	London EC3N 3EL
Telephone	+44 (0)20 7488 7700
Fax	+44 (0)20 7488 7800
Email	karen.sinden@marketform.com
Website	www.marketform.com

PERSONAL PROFILE   A profile can be found in the People at Lloyd's, Personal section.

Nicholas C Sinfield

Position	Claims Director
Company	Catlin Underwriting Agencies Ltd
Address (Office)	6th Floor
	3 Minster Court
	Mincing Lane
	London EC3R 7DD
Telephone	+44 (0)20 7626 0486
Fax	+44 (0)20 7623 9101
Email	nicholas.sinfield@catlin.com
Website	www.catlin.com
Full Name	Nicholas Christopher Sinfield
Year of Birth	1959
Professional Qualifications	Information not available

PROFESSIONAL INFORMATION

CURRENT MAJOR POSITIONS/APPOINTMENTS

Executive Director	Catlin Insurance Company (UK) Ltd	2006 -
Executive Director	Catlin Underwriting Agencies Ltd	2006 -

PREVIOUS MAJOR POSITIONS/APPOINTMENTS

Managing Director	Davies Arnold Cooper	1987 - 2001

Christopher J Smelt

Position	Executive Director
Company	Managing Agency Partners Limited
Address (Office)	1st Floor
	110 Fenchurch Street
	London EC3M 5JT
Telephone	+44 (0)20 7709 3860
Fax	+44 (0)20 7709 3861
Email	map@mapunderwriting.co.uk
Website	www.mapunderwriting.co.uk

Full Name	Christopher James Smelt
Year of Birth	1974
Professional Qualifications	Information not available

PROFESSIONAL INFORMATION

CURRENT MAJOR POSITIONS/APPOINTMENTS

Executive Director	Managing Agency Partners Ltd	2007 -

PREVIOUS MAJOR POSITIONS/APPOINTMENTS

	Information not available

Daniel AW Smith

Position	Claims Director
Company	Marketform Managing Agency Limited
Address (Office)	8 Lloyd's Avenue
	London EC3N 3EL
Telephone	+44 (0)20 7488 7700
Fax	+44 (0)20 7488 7800
Email	daniel.smith@marketform.com
Website	www.marketform.com

Full Name	Daniel Arthur William Smith
Year of Birth	1960
Professional Qualifications	Information not available

PROFESSIONAL INFORMATION

CURRENT MAJOR POSITIONS/APPOINTMENTS

Executive Director	Marketform Managing Agency Limited	2004 -

Profiles – Managing Agents

Information not available

Neil M Smith

Position	Finance Director
Company	ARK Syndicate Management Limited
Address (Office)	8th Floor
	St Helen's
	1 Undershaft
	London EC3A 8EE
Telephone	+44 (0)20 3023 4020
Fax	+44 (0)20 3023 4000
Email	neil.smith@arkunderwriting.com
Website	www.arkunderwriting.com

Full Name	Neil Martin Smith
Year of Birth	1971
Professional Qualifications	Information not available

PROFESSIONAL INFORMATION

CURRENT MAJOR POSITIONS/APPOINTMENTS

Executive Director	ARK Syndicate Management Limited	2007 -

PREVIOUS MAJOR POSITIONS/APPOINTMENTS

Executive Director	Goshawk Syndicate Management Limited	2001 - 2004
Executive Director	Euclidian Underwriting Limited	2004 - 2005

Anthony (Tony) IG South

Position	Chairman
Company	Cathedral Underwriting Limited
Address (Office)	5th Floor
	Fitzwilliam House
	10 St Mary Axe
	London EC3A 8EN
Telephone	+44 (0)20 7170 9021
Fax	+44 (0)20 7170 9001
Email	tony.south@cathedralcapital.com
Website	www.cathedralcapital.com

Full Name	Anthony Ian Godfrey South
Year of Birth	1943
Professional Qualifications	Information not available

PROFESSIONAL INFORMATION

CURRENT MAJOR POSITIONS/APPOINTMENTS

Non-Executive Director	Cathedral Underwriting Limited	2000 -

PREVIOUS MAJOR POSITIONS/APPOINTMENTS

Executive Director	Wren Underwriting Limited	1989 - Unknown

Non-Executive Director	Anton Members Agency Ltd	2001 - 2002
Non-Executive Director	The Stop Loss Mutual Insurance Association Ltd	2001 - 2003
Non-Executive Director	Anton Private Capital Limited	2001 - 2004
Executive Director	Cathedral Capital Management Limited	2001 - 2007

Verner G Southey

Position	Non-Executive Director
Company	ARK Syndicate Management Limited
Address (Office)	8th Floor
	St Helen's
	1 Undershaft
	London EC3A 8EE
Telephone	+44 (0)20 3023 4020
Fax	+44 (0)20 3023 4000
Email	enquiries@arkunderwriting.com
Website	www.arkunderwriting.com

Position	Non-Executive Director
Company	Talbot Underwriting Ltd
Address (Office)	Gracechurch House
	55 Gracechurch Street
	London EC3V 0JP
Telephone	+44 (0)20 7550 3500
Fax	+44 (0)20 7550 3555
Email	central@talbotuw.com
Website	www.talbotuw.com

Full Name	Verner George Southey
Year of Birth	1942
Professional Qualifications	Information not available

PROFESSIONAL INFORMATION

CURRENT MAJOR POSITIONS/APPOINTMENTS

| Non-Executive Director | Talbot Underwriting Ltd | 1996 - |
| Non-Executive Director | ARK Syndicate Management Limited | 2007 - |

PREVIOUS MAJOR POSITIONS/APPOINTMENTS

| Non-Executive Director | Jago Managing Agency Ltd | 2001 - 2002 |
| Non-Executive Director | Capita Syndicate Management Limited | 2002 - 2008 |

John WJ Spencer

Position	Non-Executive Director
Company	Argo Managing Agency Ltd
Address (Office)	47 Mark Lane
	London EC3R 7QQ
Telephone	+44 (0)20 7712 7600
Fax	+44 (0)20 7712 7601
Email	belinda.rose@argo-int.com
Website	www.argo-int.com

Full Name	John William James Spencer
Year of Birth	1957
Professional Qualifications	Information not available

PROFESSIONAL INFORMATION

CURRENT MAJOR POSITIONS/APPOINTMENTS

| Non-Executive Director | Argo Managing Agency Ltd | 2008 - |
| Trustee | Lloyd's Charities Trust | Unknown |

PREVIOUS MAJOR POSITIONS/APPOINTMENTS

Executive Director	BMS Greenstock Limited	2001 - 2003
Executive Director	Underwriting Facilities Limited	2005 - 2005
Chief Executive	BMS Group Ltd	2005 - 2007
Executive Director	Bankserve Insurance Services Limited	2005 - 2007
Executive Director	BMS Harris & Dixon Insurance Brokers Limited	2005 - 2007
Executive Director	BMS Harris & Dixon Limited	2005 - 2007
Executive Director	BMS Harris & Dixon Marine Limited	2005 - 2007
Executive Director	BMS Harris & Dixon Reinsurance Brokers Limited	2005 - 2007
Executive Director	BMS Intermediaries Ltd	2005 - 2007
Executive Director	BMS International Intermediaries Limited	2005 - 2007
Executive Director	BMS Management Services Limited	2005 - 2007
Executive Director	BMS Re Limited	2005 - 2007
Executive Director	BMS Special Risk Services Limited	2005 - 2007
Executive Director	Jansen & Hastings Intermediaries Limited	2005 - 2007
Executive Director	BMS Facultative Limited	2006 - 2007
Executive Director	International Reinsurance Brokers Limited	2006 - 2008

David H Spiller

Position	Chairman
Company	Argo Managing Agency Ltd
Address (Office)	47 Mark Lane
	London EC3R 7QQ
Telephone	+44 (0)20 7712 7600
Fax	+44 (0)20 7712 7601
Email	belinda.rose@argo-int.com
Website	www.argo-int.com

Full Name	David Hutchinson Spiller
Year of Birth	1956
Professional Qualifications	Information not available

PROFESSIONAL INFORMATION

CURRENT MAJOR POSITIONS/APPOINTMENTS

| Non-Executive Director | Argo Managing Agency Ltd | 2008 - |

PREVIOUS MAJOR POSITIONS/APPOINTMENTS

| Chief Executive | Benfield Limited | 2005 - 2005 |

David Stewart

Position	Executive Director & Active Underwriter Syndicate 2243
Company	Starr Managing Agents Limited
Address (Office)	3rd Floor
	140 Leadenhall Street
	London EC3V 4QT
Telephone	+44 (0)20 7337 3550
Fax	+44 (0)20 7337 3551
Email	david.stewart@cvstarrco.com
Website	www.cvstarrco.com

Full Name	David Stewart
Year of Birth	1956
Professional Qualifications	Information not available

PROFESSIONAL INFORMATION

CURRENT MAJOR POSITIONS/APPOINTMENTS

Executive Director	Starr Managing Agents Ltd	2008 -

PREVIOUS MAJOR POSITIONS/APPOINTMENTS

Information not available

Darren J Stockman

Position	Executive Director & Active Underwriter Syndicate 780
Company	Advent Underwriting Limited
Address (Office)	10th Floor
	One Minster Court
	Mincing Lane
	London EC3R 7AA
Telephone	+44 (0)20 7743 8200
Fax	+44 (0)20 7743 8299
Email	darren.stockman@adventgroup.co.uk
Website	www.adventgroup.co.uk

Full Name	Darren John Stockman
Year of Birth	1967
Professional Qualifications	Information not available

PROFESSIONAL INFORMATION

CURRENT MAJOR POSITIONS/APPOINTMENTS

Executive Director	Advent Underwriting Limited	2008 -

PREVIOUS MAJOR POSITIONS/APPOINTMENTS

Information not available

William D Stovin

Position	Chief Executive Officer
Company	Markel Syndicate Management Limited

Address (Office)	The Markel Building
	49 Leadenhall Street
	London EC3A 2EA
Telephone	+44 (0)20 7953 6000
Fax	+44 (0)20 7953 6001
Email	william.stovin@markelintl.com
Website	www.markelintl.com

Full Name	William David Stovin
Year of Birth	1961
Professional Qualifications	LLB

PROFESSIONAL INFORMATION

CURRENT MAJOR POSITIONS/APPOINTMENTS

Executive Director	Markel Syndicate Management Limited	2001 -
Executive Director	Markel International Insurance Company Limited	2005 -
Executive Director	Markel Asset Management Limited	2005 -

PREVIOUS MAJOR POSITIONS/APPOINTMENTS

Information not available

Robert (Bob) A Stuchbery

Position	Chief Underwriting Officer
Company	Chaucer Syndicates Limited
Address (Office)	Plantation Place
	30 Fenchurch Street
	London EC3M 3AD
Telephone	+44 (0)20 7397 9700
Fax	+44 (0)20 7397 9710
Email	robert.stuchbery@chaucerplc.com
Website	www.chaucerplc.com

Full Name	Robert Arthur Stuchbery
Year of Birth	1957
Professional Qualifications	FCII

PROFESSIONAL INFORMATION

CURRENT MAJOR POSITIONS/APPOINTMENTS

Chief Executive Officer	Chaucer Syndicates Limited	2009 -
Non-Executive Director	Chaucer Insurance Services Ltd	2007 -
Member	Lloyd's Market Association Board	Unknown -
Chairman	Lloyd's Market Association, Underwriting Committee	2009 -

PREVIOUS MAJOR POSITIONS/APPOINTMENTS

Executive Director	Chaucer Syndicates Limited	1993 - 2009
Chairman	Lloyd's Market Association, Underwriting and	
	Claims Committee	2005 - 2008
Non-Executive Director	Nuclear Risk Insurers Ltd	2005 - 2006
Executive Director	Pembroke Managing Agency Ltd	2007 - 2008

Mervyn TA Sugden

Position	Executive Director
Company	Hardy (Underwriting Agencies) Ltd
Address (Office)	4th Floor
	40 Lime Street
	London EC3M 7AW
Telephone	+44 (0)20 7626 0382
Fax	+44 (0)20 7283 4677
Email	mervyn.sugden@hardygroup.co.uk
Website	www.hardygroup.co.uk
Full Name	Mervyn Terence Arthur Sugden
Year of Birth	1952
Professional Qualifications	Information not available

PROFESSIONAL INFORMATION

CURRENT MAJOR POSITIONS/APPOINTMENTS

Executive Director	Hardy (Underwriting Agencies) Ltd	1992 -

PREVIOUS MAJOR POSITIONS/APPOINTMENTS

Information not available

Richard J Sumner

Position	Finance Director
Company	Managing Agency Partners Limited
Address (Office)	1st Floor
	110 Fenchurch Street
	London EC3M 5JT
Telephone	+44 (0)20 7709 3866
Fax	+44 (0)20 7709 3861
Email	rsumner@mapunderwriting.co.uk
Website	www.mapunderwriting.co.uk
Full Name	Richard John Sumner
Year of Birth	1964
Professional Qualifications	Information not available

PROFESSIONAL INFORMATION

CURRENT MAJOR POSITIONS/APPOINTMENTS

Executive Director	Managing Agency Partners Ltd	2000 -

PREVIOUS MAJOR POSITIONS/APPOINTMENTS

Information not available

George Sweatman

Position	Executive Director
Company	Sagicor at Lloyd's Limited
Address (Office)	1 Great Tower Street
	London EC3R 5AA

Telephone	+44 (0)20 3003 6800
Fax	+44 (0)20 3003 6999
Email	george.sweatman@sagicor.eu
Website	www.sagicor.com

Full Name	George Sweatman
Year of Birth	1957
Professional Qualifications	Information not available

PROFESSIONAL INFORMATION

CURRENT MAJOR POSITIONS/APPOINTMENTS

Executive Director	Sagicor at Lloyd's Limited	2007 -
Executive Director	Byrne and Stacey Underwriting Limited	2007 -
Executive Director	Sagicor Syndicate Services Ltd	2007 -

PREVIOUS MAJOR POSITIONS/APPOINTMENTS
Information not available

Brandon Swim

Position	Non-Executive Director
Company	KGM Underwriting Agencies Limited
Address (Office)	KGM House
	George Lane
	South Woodford
	London E18 1RZ
Telephone	+44 (0)20 8530 1813
Fax	+44 (0)20 8530 7037
Email	brandon.swim@kgminsurance.co.uk
Website	www.kgminsurance.co.uk

Full Name	Brandon Swim
Year of Birth	1972
Professional Qualifications	Information not available

PROFESSIONAL INFORMATION

CURRENT MAJOR POSITIONS/APPOINTMENTS

Non-Executive Director	KGM Underwriting Agencies Limited	2002 -

PREVIOUS MAJOR POSITIONS/APPOINTMENTS
Information not available

Alec Taylor

Position	Executive Director & Deputy Underwriter Syndicate 727
Company	SA Meacock & Company Limited
Address (Office)	4th Floor
	15 St Helen's Place
	London EC3A 6DE
Telephone	+44 (0)20 7374 6727
Fax	+44 (0)20 7374 4727

Email	alec.taylor@sameacock.com
Website	None at present

Full Name	Alec Taylor
Year of Birth	1952
Professional Qualifications	Information not available

PROFESSIONAL INFORMATION

CURRENT MAJOR POSITIONS/APPOINTMENTS

Executive Director	SA Meacock & Company Limited	1996 -

PREVIOUS MAJOR POSITIONS/APPOINTMENTS

Information not available

Belinda J Taylor

Position	Finance Director
Company	Sportscover Underwriting Ltd
Address (Office)	3 Minster Court
	Mincing Lane
	London EC3R 7DD
Telephone	+44 (0)20 7398 4080
Fax	+44 (0)20 7398 4090
Email	belinda.taylor@sportscover.com
Website	www.sportscoverunderwriting.com

Full Name	Belinda Julie Taylor
Year of Birth	1965
Professional Qualifications	Information not available

PROFESSIONAL INFORMATION

CURRENT MAJOR POSITIONS/APPOINTMENTS

Executive Director	Sportscover Underwriting Ltd	2008 -

PREVIOUS MAJOR POSITIONS/APPOINTMENTS

Information not available

J Maxwell (Max) P Taylor

Position	Chairman
Company	Mitsui Sumitomo Insurance Underwriting at Lloyd's Ltd
Address (Office)	25 Fenchurch Avenue
	London EC3M 5AD
Telephone	+44 (0)20 7977 8321
Fax	+44 (0)20 7977 8300
Email	enquiries@msilm.com
Website	www.msilm.com

Full Name	John Maxwell Percy Taylor
Year of Birth	1948
Professional Qualifications	Information not available

PROFESSIONAL INFORMATION

CURRENT MAJOR POSITIONS/APPOINTMENTS

| Non-Executive Director | Mitsui Sumitomo Insurance Underwriting at Lloyd's Ltd | 2006 - |
| Non-Executive Director | Mitsui Sumitomo Insurance (London) Limited | 2006 - |

PREVIOUS MAJOR POSITIONS/APPOINTMENTS

Chairman	Lloyd's	1998 - 2000
Executive Director	Aon Limited	2005 - 2005
Executive Director	SLE Worldwide Ltd	2005 - 2006

Roger J Taylor

Position	Chairman
Company	Amlin Underwriting Limited
Address (Office)	St Helen's
	1 Undershaft
	London EC3A 8ND
Telephone	+44 (0)20 7746 1000
Fax	+44 (0)20 7746 1696
Email	roger.taylor@amlin.co.uk
Website	www.amlin.com

Full Name	Roger John Taylor
Year of Birth	1941
Professional Qualifications	Information not available

PROFESSIONAL INFORMATION

CURRENT MAJOR POSITIONS/APPOINTMENTS

Non-Executive Director	Amlin Underwriting Limited	2006 -
Non-Executive President	Yura International Holding BV	Unknown -
Non-Executive Director	White Ensign Association Limited	Unknown -

PREVIOUS MAJOR POSITIONS/APPOINTMENTS

Chairman	Association of British Insurers	1997 - 1998
Deputy Chairman	Royal & Sun Alliance Insurance Group plc	Unknown - 1998
Non-Executive Deputy Chairman	Helphire Group plc	Unknown - 2008
Chief Executive	Sun Alliance Group plc	Unknown

William J Taylor

Position	Finance Director
Company	HCC Underwriting Agency Ltd
Address (Office)	Walsingham House
	35 Seething Lane
	London EC3N 4AH
Telephone	+44 (0)20 7680 3000
Fax	+44 (0)20 7977 7350

Email	wtaylor@hccual.com	
Website	www.hccual.com	

Full Name	William John Taylor	
Year of Birth	1955	
Professional Qualifications	BCom, ACA	

PROFESSIONAL INFORMATION

CURRENT MAJOR POSITIONS/APPOINTMENTS

Executive Director	HCC Underwriting Agency Ltd	2003 -

PREVIOUS MAJOR POSITIONS/APPOINTMENTS

Executive Director	Whittington Capital Management Limited	2001 - 2003
Executive Director	Lewar Ltd	2001 - 2002

Elisabetta Tenenti

Position	Executive Director
Company	Sagicor at Lloyd's Limited
Address (Office)	1 Great Tower Street
	London EC3R 5AA
Telephone	+44 (0)20 3003 6800
Fax	+44 (0)20 3003 6999
Email	elisabetta.tenenti@sagicor.eu
Website	www.sagicor.com

Full Name	Elisabetta Tenenti
Year of Birth	1964
Professional Qualifications	Information not available

PROFESSIONAL INFORMATION

CURRENT MAJOR POSITIONS/APPOINTMENTS

Executive Director	Byrne and Stacey Underwriting Limited	2007 -
Executive Director	Sagicor at Lloyd's Limited	2007 -
Executive Director	Sagicor Syndicate Services Ltd	2007 -

PREVIOUS MAJOR POSITIONS/APPOINTMENTS

Information not available

John RW Thirlwell

Position	Non-Executive Director
Company	Novae Syndicates Limited
Address (Office)	71 Fenchurch Street
	London EC3M 4HH
Telephone	+44 (0)20 7903 7300
Fax	+44 (0)20 7903 7333
Email	jthirlwell@novae.com
Website	www.novae.com

Full Name	John Robert William Thirlwell
Year of Birth	1948
Professional Qualifications	MA Oxon

PROFESSIONAL INFORMATION

CURRENT MAJOR POSITIONS/APPOINTMENTS

Non-Executive Director	Novae Syndicates Limited	2003 -
Non-Executive Director	CX Reinsurance Company Limited	2008 -

PREVIOUS MAJOR POSITIONS/APPOINTMENTS

Information not available

Ian N Thomson

Position	Non-Executive Director
Company	Hiscox Syndicates Limited
Address (Office)	1 Great St Helen's
	London EC3A 6HX
Telephone	+44 (0)20 7448 6000
Fax	+44 (0)20 7448 6900
Email	enquiry@hiscox.com
Website	www.hiscox.com

Full Name	Ian Nicholas Thomson
Year of Birth	1943
Professional Qualifications	Information not available

PROFESSIONAL INFORMATION

CURRENT MAJOR POSITIONS/APPOINTMENTS

Non-Executive Director	Hiscox Insurance Company Limited	2006 -
Non-Executive Director	Hiscox Syndicates Limited	2006 -

PREVIOUS MAJOR POSITIONS/APPOINTMENTS

Executive Director	Hiscox Syndicates Limited	2001 - 2006
Executive Director	Hiscox Insurance Company Limited	2001 - 2006

Keith D Thompson

Position	Managing Director
Company	Advent Underwriting Limited
Address (Office)	10th Floor
	One Minster Court
	Mincing Lane
	London EC3R 7AA
Telephone	+44 (0)20 7743 8200
Fax	+44 (0)20 7743 8299
Email	keith.thompson@adventgroup.co.uk
Website	www.adventgroup.co.uk

PERSONAL PROFILE	A profile can be found in the People at Lloyd's, Personal section.

Sir David Thomson Bt

Position	Chairman
Company	SA Meacock & Company Limited
Address (Office)	4th Floor
	15 St Helen's Place
	London EC3A 6DE
Telephone	+44 (0)20 7374 6727
Fax	+44 (0)20 7374 4727
Email	linda.mailoudi@sameacock.com
Website	None at present
Full Name	Sir Frederick Douglas David Thomson
Year of Birth	1940
Professional Qualifications	Information not available

PROFESSIONAL INFORMATION

CURRENT MAJOR POSITIONS/APPOINTMENTS

Non-Executive Director	SA Meacock & Company Limited	1996 -

PREVIOUS MAJOR POSITIONS/APPOINTMENTS

Executive Director	The West of England Ship Owners Mutual	
	Insurance Association (Luxembourg)	2001 - 2001
Non-Executive Director	The Britannia Steam Ship Insurance Association Ltd	2001 - 2008
Non-Executive Director	TT Club Mutual Insurance Limited	2001 - 2008

David A Thorp

Position	Chief Executive Officer
Company	SA Meacock & Company Limited
Address (Office)	4th Floor
	15 St Helen's Place
	London EC3A 6DE
Telephone	+44 (0)20 7374 6727
Fax	+44 (0)20 7374 4727
Email	david.thorp@sameacock.com
Website	None at present
Full Name	David Allan Thorp
Year of Birth	1944
Professional Qualifications	FCA

PROFESSIONAL INFORMATION

CURRENT MAJOR POSITIONS/APPOINTMENTS

Chief Executive	SA Meacock & Company Limited	1996 -

PREVIOUS MAJOR POSITIONS/APPOINTMENTS

Information not available

John P Tilling

Position	Independent Review Director
Company	Cathedral Underwriting Limited
Address (Office)	5th Floor
	Fitzwilliam House
	10 St Mary Axe
	London EC3A 8EN
Telephone	+44 (0)20 7170 9000
Fax	+44 (0)20 7170 9001
Email	info@cathedralcapital.com
Website	www.cathedralcapital.com
Full Name	John Peter Tilling
Year of Birth	1947
Professional Qualifications	Information not available

PROFESSIONAL INFORMATION

CURRENT MAJOR POSITIONS/APPOINTMENTS

Non-Executive Director	Cavell Managing Agency Ltd	2000 -
Non-Executive Director	Cathedral Underwriting Limited	2004 -

PREVIOUS MAJOR POSITIONS/APPOINTMENTS

Active Underwriter	Syndicate 340	1981 - 2000
Director	Gravett & Tilling Syndicate Management Limited	Unknown
Director	St Paul Syndicate Management Limited	Unknown

Richard JW Titley

Position	Non-Executive Director
Company	XL London Market Limited
Address (Office)	XL House
	70 Gracechurch Street
	London EC3V 0XL
Telephone	+44 (0)20 7933 7000
Fax	+44 (0)20 7469 1071
Email	graham.brady@xlgroup.com
Website	www.xlinsurance.co.uk
Full Name	Richard John Wolseley Titley
Year of Birth	1939
Professional Qualifications	Information not available

PROFESSIONAL INFORMATION

CURRENT MAJOR POSITIONS/APPOINTMENTS

Non-Executive Director	Glencairn Limited	2005 -
Non-Executive Director	XL London Market Limited	2007 -

PREVIOUS MAJOR POSITIONS/APPOINTMENTS

Non-Executive Director	Charles Taylor Consulting Plc	2005 - 2008

Norman H Topche

Position	Group Director of Underwriting and Reinsurance
Company	Jubilee Managing Agency Limited
Address (Office)	4th Floor
	50 Fenchurch Street
	London EC3M 3JY
Telephone	+44 (0)20 7220 8728
Fax	+44 (0)20 7220 8732
Email	norman.topche@jubilee-insurance.com
Website	www.jubilee-insurance.com

Full Name	Norman Harvey Topche
Year of Birth	1958
Professional Qualifications	Information not available

PROFESSIONAL INFORMATION

CURRENT MAJOR POSITIONS/APPOINTMENTS

Executive Director	Jubilee Managing Agency Limited	2008 -

PREVIOUS MAJOR POSITIONS/APPOINTMENTS

Information not available

Mike Toran

Position	Chief Financial Officer
Company	Starr Managing Agents Limited
Address (Office)	3rd Floor
	140 Leadenhall Street
	London EC3V 4QT
Telephone	+44 (0)20 7337 3550
Fax	+44 (0)20 7337 3551
Email	michael.toran@cvstarrco.com
Website	www.cvstarrco.com

Full Name	Michael Toran
Year of Birth	1972
Professional Qualifications	Information not available

PROFESSIONAL INFORMATION

CURRENT MAJOR POSITIONS/APPOINTMENTS

Executive Director	Starr Underwriting Agents Limited	2006 -
Executive Director	Starr Managing Agents Ltd	2007 -

PREVIOUS MAJOR POSITIONS/APPOINTMENTS

Information not available

Simon GH Tovey

Position	Compliance Director
Company	Faraday Underwriting Limited

Address (Office)	5th Floor
	Corn Exchange
	55 Mark Lane
	London EC3R 7NE
Telephone	+44 (0)20 7680 4203
Fax	+44 (0)20 7680 4369
Secretary/PA	Corinne Brooks
Email	simon.tovey@faraday.com
Telephone	+44 (0)20 7680 4213
Website	www.faraday.com
Full Name	Simon George Houghton Tovey
Year of Birth	1948
Professional Qualifications	MA, FCA

PROFESSIONAL INFORMATION

CURRENT MAJOR POSITIONS/APPOINTMENTS

Executive Director	Faraday Underwriting Limited	2001 -
Executive Director	Faraday Reinsurance Co Limited	2006 -

PREVIOUS MAJOR POSITIONS/APPOINTMENTS

Non-Executive Director	AE Grant (Underwriting Agencies) Ltd	2001 - 2001

John C Towers

Position	Director of Operations
Company	Advent Underwriting Limited
Address (Office)	10th Floor
	One Minster Court
	Mincing Lane
	London EC3R 7AA
Telephone	+44 (0)20 7743 8205
Fax	+44 (0)20 7743 8299
Email	john.towers@adventgroup.co.uk
Website	www.adventgroup.co.uk
Full Name	John Charles Towers
Year of Birth	1954
Professional Qualifications	Information not available

PROFESSIONAL INFORMATION

CURRENT MAJOR POSITIONS/APPOINTMENTS

Executive Director	Advent Underwriting Limited	2001 -

PREVIOUS MAJOR POSITIONS/APPOINTMENTS

Information not available

W Raymond Treen

Position	Non-Executive Director
Company	HCC Underwriting Agency Ltd

Address (Office)	Walsingham House
	35 Seething Lane
	London EC3N 4AH
Telephone	+44 (0)20 7680 3000
Fax	+44 (0)20 7977 7350
Email	info@hccual.com
Website	www.hccual.com

Full Name	William Raymond Treen
Year of Birth	1940
Professional Qualifications	Information not available

PROFESSIONAL INFORMATION

CURRENT MAJOR POSITIONS/APPOINTMENTS

Non-Executive Director	HCC Underwriting Agency Ltd	2003 -
Non-Executive Director	London Life Limited	2005 -
Non-Executive Director	NPI Limited	2005 -
Non-Executive Director	Pearl Assurance Public Limited Company	2005 -
Non-Executive Director	National Provident Life Limited	2005 -
Non-Executive Director	Taylor Price Insurance Services Ltd	2006 -
Non-Executive Director	Drakefield Insurance Services Limited	2007 -
Non-Executive Director	Saga Services Limited	2008 -
Non-Executive Director	Ignis Investment Services Limited	2008 -
Non-Executive Director	Axial Investment Management Limited	2008 -
Non-Executive Director	Automobile Association Underwriting Services Ltd	2008 -
Non-Executive Director	Automobile Association Insurance Services Ltd	2008 -
Non-Executive Director	Ignis Fund Managers Limited	2008 -

PREVIOUS MAJOR POSITIONS/APPOINTMENTS

Executive Director	British Reserve Insurance Company Limited	2001 - 2003
Executive Director	DBI Insurance Company Limited	2001 - 2003
Non-Executive Director	Merchant Investors Assurance Company Limited	2001 - 2003
Chief Executive	Allianz Insurance Plc	2001 - 2003
Chief Executive	Trafalgar Insurance Public Limited Company	2001 - 2003
Executive Director	AGF Insurance Limited	2001 - 2003
Non-Executive Director	Automobile Association Underwriting Services Ltd	2005 - 2008
Non-Executive Director	Automobile Association Insurance Services Ltd	2005 - 2008

Richard K Trubshaw

Position	Executive Director & Active Underwriter Syndicates 2791 & 6103
Company	Managing Agency Partners Limited
Address (Office)	1st Floor
	110 Fenchurch Street
	London EC3M 5JT
Telephone	+44 (0)20 7709 3860
Fax	+44 (0)20 7709 3861
Email	map@mapunderwriting.co.uk
Website	www.mapunderwriting.co.uk

Full Name	Richard Kevin Trubshaw
Year of Birth	1964
Professional Qualifications	Information not available

PROFESSIONAL INFORMATION

CURRENT MAJOR POSITIONS/APPOINTMENTS

Executive Director	Managing Agency Partners Ltd	2000 -

PREVIOUS MAJOR POSITIONS/APPOINTMENTS

Information not available

Graham M Tuck

Position	Financial Director
Company	Beaufort Underwriting Agency Limited
Address (Office)	Third Floor
	One Minster Court
	Mincing Lane
	London EC3R 7AA
Telephone	+44 (0)20 7220 8200
Fax	+44 (0)20 7220 8290
Email	graham.tuck@beaufort-group.com
Website	www.beaufort-group.com

Full Name	Graham Matthew Tuck
Year of Birth	1975
Professional Qualifications	Information not available

PROFESSIONAL INFORMATION

CURRENT MAJOR POSITIONS/APPOINTMENTS

Executive Director	Beaufort Underwriting Agency Limited	2004 -

PREVIOUS MAJOR POSITIONS/APPOINTMENTS

Information not available

Alan W Tucker

Position	Non-Executive Director
Company	Argenta Syndicate Management Limited
Address (Office)	Fountain House
	130 Fenchurch Street
	London EC3M 5DJ
Telephone	+44 (0)20 7825 7135
Fax	+44 (0)20 7825 7155
Email	alan.tucker@argentaplc.com
Website	www.argentaplc.com

Full Name	Alan William Tucker
Year of Birth	1948
Professional Qualifications	Information not available

PROFESSIONAL INFORMATION

CURRENT MAJOR POSITIONS/APPOINTMENTS

Executive Director	Argenta Private Capital Limited	2001 -
Non-Executive Director	Argenta Syndicate Management Limited	2004 -
Executive Director	SLP (Management) Limited	2008 -

PREVIOUS MAJOR POSITIONS/APPOINTMENTS

Information not available

Martin D Turner

Position	Claims Director
Company	XL London Market Limited
Address (Office)	XL House
	70 Gracechurch Street
	London EC3V 0XL
Telephone	+44 (0)20 7933 7000
Fax	+44 (0)20 7469 1071
Email	martin.turner@xlgroup.com
Website	www.xlinsurance.co.uk

Full Name	Martin David Turner
Year of Birth	1967
Professional Qualifications	Information not available

PROFESSIONAL INFORMATION

CURRENT MAJOR POSITIONS/APPOINTMENTS

Executive Director	XL London Market Limited	2001 -

PREVIOUS MAJOR POSITIONS/APPOINTMENTS

Information not available

Simon G Turner

Position	Executive Director
Company	Marketform Managing Agency Limited
Address (Office)	8 Lloyd's Avenue
	London EC3N 3EL
Telephone	+44 (0)20 7488 7700
Fax	+44 (0)20 7488 7800
Email	simon.turner@marketform.com
Website	www.marketform.com

Full Name	Simon George Turner
Year of Birth	1967
Professional Qualifications	Information not available

PROFESSIONAL INFORMATION

CURRENT MAJOR POSITIONS/APPOINTMENTS

Executive Director	Marketform Managing Agency Limited	2000 -
Executive Director	Marketform Limited	2005 -

PREVIOUS MAJOR POSITIONS/APPOINTMENTS
Information not available

Nigel B Tyler

Position	Executive Director
Company	Hiscox Syndicates Limited
Address (Office)	1 Great St Helen's
	London EC3A 6HX
Telephone	+44 (0)20 7448 6000
Fax	+44 (0)20 7448 6900
Email	nigel.tyler@hiscox.com
Website	www.hiscox.com

Full Name	Nigel Barlow Tyler
Year of Birth	1952
Professional Qualifications	Information not available

PROFESSIONAL INFORMATION

CURRENT MAJOR POSITIONS/APPOINTMENTS

Executive Director	Hiscox Syndicates Limited	2003 -

PREVIOUS MAJOR POSITIONS/APPOINTMENTS
Information not available

Neil A Utley

Position	Chief Executive Officer
Company	Equity Syndicate Management Limited
Address (Office)	Library House
	New Road
	Brentwood
	Essex CM14 4GD
Telephone	+44 (0)1277 200 100
Fax	+44 (0)1206 777 223
Email	neil.utley@equitygroup.co.uk
Website	www.equitygroup.co.uk

Full Name	Neil Alan Utley
Year of Birth	1962
Professional Qualifications	Information not available

PROFESSIONAL INFORMATION

CURRENT MAJOR POSITIONS/APPOINTMENTS

Non-Executive Director	Insurancewide.com Services Limited	2005 -
Chief Executive	Equity Syndicate Management Limited	2005 -
Executive Director	Equity Insurance Brokers Limited	2006 -
Executive Director	Hastings Insurance Services Ltd	2008 -

PREVIOUS MAJOR POSITIONS/APPOINTMENTS

Chief Executive	Equity Syndicate Management Limited	2004 - 2004

Executive Director	Arista Insurance Ltd	2006 - 2007
Executive Director	Equity Insurance Brokers Limited	2006 - 2009
Executive Director	Open + Direct Insurance Services Ltd	2007 - 2008

Damon N Vocke

Position	Non-Executive Director
Company	Faraday Underwriting Limited
Address (Office)	5th Floor
	Corn Exchange
	55 Mark Lane
	London EC3R 7NE
Telephone	+44 (0)20 7702 3333
Fax	+44 (0)20 7680 4369
Email	liz.richardson@faraday.com
Website	www.faraday.com
Full Name	Damon Nicholas Vocke
Year of Birth	1963
Professional Qualifications	Information not available

PROFESSIONAL INFORMATION

CURRENT MAJOR POSITIONS/APPOINTMENTS

Non-Executive Director	Faraday Underwriting Limited	2005 -

PREVIOUS MAJOR POSITIONS/APPOINTMENTS

Non-Executive Director	General Reinsurance UK Limited	2005 - 2008

Nigel D Wachman

Position	Chief Financial Officer
Company	Talbot Underwriting Ltd
Address (Office)	Gracechurch House
	55 Gracechurch Street
	London EC3V 0JP
Telephone	+44 (0)20 7550 3500
Fax	+44 (0)20 7550 3555
Email	nigel.wachman@talbotuw.com
Website	www.talbotuw.com
Full Name	Nigel David Wachman
Year of Birth	1958
Professional Qualifications	Information not available

PROFESSIONAL INFORMATION

CURRENT MAJOR POSITIONS/APPOINTMENTS

Executive Director	Talbot Underwriting Ltd	2000 -
Executive Director	Underwriting Risk Services Ltd	2005 -

PREVIOUS MAJOR POSITIONS/APPOINTMENTS

	Information not available

Adrian J Walker

Position	Underwriting Director & Active Underwriter Syndicate 382
Company	Hardy (Underwriting Agencies) Ltd
Address (Office)	4th Floor
	40 Lime Street
	London EC3M 7AW
Telephone	+44 (0)20 7626 0382
Fax	+44 (0)20 7283 4677
Email	adrian.walker@hardygroup.co.uk
Website	www.hardygroup.co.uk
Full Name	Adrian Jeremy Walker
Year of Birth	1956
Professional Qualifications	BA (Hons), ACII

PROFESSIONAL INFORMATION

CURRENT MAJOR POSITIONS/APPOINTMENTS

Executive Director	Hardy (Underwriting Agencies) Ltd	2000 -

PREVIOUS MAJOR POSITIONS/APPOINTMENTS

Information not available

Robert (Bob) J Wallace

Position	Chairman
Company	Pembroke Managing Agency Ltd
Address (Office)	2nd Floor
	3 Minster Court
	Mincing Lane
	London EC3R 7DD
Telephone	+44 (0)20 7337 4400
Fax	+44 (0)20 7337 4401
Email	hq@pembrokeunderwriting.com
Website	www.pembrokeunderwriting.com
Position	Chairman
Company	Sportscover Underwriting Ltd
Address (Office)	3 Minster Court
	Mincing Lane
	London EC3R 7DD
Telephone	+44 (0)20 7398 4080
Fax	+44 (0)20 7398 4090
Email	dominic.ford@sportscover.com
Website	www.sportscoverunderwriting.com
Full Name	Robert Jeffrey Wallace
Year of Birth	1942
Professional Qualifications	Information not available

PROFESSIONAL INFORMATION

CURRENT MAJOR POSITIONS/APPOINTMENTS

Non-Executive Director	Pembroke Managing Agency Ltd	2008 -
Non-Executive Director	Sportscover Underwriting Ltd	2008 -

PREVIOUS MAJOR POSITIONS/APPOINTMENTS

Executive Director	QBE Underwriting Limited	2001 - 2005
Non-Executive Director	BRIT Insurance (UK) Ltd	2002 - 2003
Executive Director	Max at Lloyd's Ltd	2003 - 2007
Executive Director	Max at Lloyd's Services Ltd	2006 - 2007
Executive Director (AR)	Danish Re Syndicates Ltd	2006 - 2006

Elizabeth M Walsh

Position	Chief Operating Officer
Company	R J Kiln & Co Limited
Address (Office)	106 Fenchurch Street
	London EC3M 5NR
Telephone	+44 (0)20 7886 9000
Fax	+44 (0)20 7488 1848
Email	elizabeth.walsh@kilngroup.com
Website	www.kilnplc.com
Full Name	Elizabeth Mary Flux Walsh
Year of Birth	1973
Professional Qualifications	Information not available

PROFESSIONAL INFORMATION

CURRENT MAJOR POSITIONS/APPOINTMENTS

Executive Director	R J Kiln & Co Limited	2007 -

PREVIOUS MAJOR POSITIONS/APPOINTMENTS

Information not available

Nicholas C Walsh

Position	Non-Executive Director
Company	Ascot Underwriting Limited
Address (Office)	Plantation Place
	30 Fenchurch Street
	London EC3M 3BD
Telephone	+44 (0)20 7743 9600
Fax	+44 (0)20 7743 9601
Email	enquiries@ascotuw.com
Website	www.ascotuw.com
Full Name	Nicholas Charles Walsh
Year of Birth	1950
Professional Qualifications	Information not available

PROFESSIONAL INFORMATION

CURRENT MAJOR POSITIONS/APPOINTMENTS

Non-Executive Director	Ascot Underwriting Limited	2005 -
Non-Executive Director	AIG UK Limited	2007 -

PREVIOUS MAJOR POSITIONS/APPOINTMENTS

Executive Director	AIG UK Limited	2001 - 2002
Executive Director	Samsung Insurance Company of Europe Limited	2001 - 2002
Chief Executive	Hanover Insurance Company	2001 - 2002
Chief Executive	AIG UK Limited	2001 - 2002
Chief Executive	American Home Assurance Company	2001 - 2002
Chief Executive	Uzbekinvest International Insurance Company Ltd	2001 - 2002
Chief Executive	New Hampshire Insurance Company	2001 - 2002

David C Wardle

Position	Finance Director
Company	KGM Underwriting Agencies Limited
Address (Office)	KGM House
	George Lane
	South Woodford
	London E18 1RZ
Telephone	+44 (0)20 8530 1831
Fax	+44 (0)20 8530 7037
Email	david.wardle@kgminsurance.co.uk
Website	www.kgminsurance.co.uk

Full Name	David Charles Wardle
Year of Birth	1967
Professional Qualifications	Information not available

PROFESSIONAL INFORMATION

CURRENT MAJOR POSITIONS/APPOINTMENTS

Executive Director	KGM Underwriting Agencies Limited	2006 -

PREVIOUS MAJOR POSITIONS/APPOINTMENTS

Information not available

Dipak Warren

Position	Executive Director & Active Underwriter Syndicate 3210
Company	Mitsui Sumitomo Insurance Underwriting at Lloyd's Ltd
Address (Office)	25 Fenchurch Avenue
	London EC3M 5AD
Telephone	+44 (0)20 7977 8333
Fax	+44 (0)20 7977 8300
Email	dwarren@msilm.com
Website	www.msilm.com

Full Name	Dipak Warren
Year of Birth	1951
Professional Qualifications	FCII

PROFESSIONAL INFORMATION

CURRENT MAJOR POSITIONS/APPOINTMENTS

Executive Director   Mitsui Sumitomo Insurance Underwriting at Lloyd's Ltd   2006 -

PREVIOUS MAJOR POSITIONS/APPOINTMENTS

Information not available

Justin AS Wash

Position	Finance Director
Company	Pembroke Managing Agency Ltd
Address (Office)	2nd Floor
	3 Minster Court
	Mincing Lane
	London EC3R 7DD
Telephone	+44 (0)20 7337 4400
Fax	+44 (0)20 7337 4401
Email	justin.wash@pembrokeunderwriting.com
Website	www.pembrokeunderwriting.com

Full Name	Justin Andrew Spencer Wash
Year of Birth	1965
Professional Qualifications	Information not available

PROFESSIONAL INFORMATION

CURRENT MAJOR POSITIONS/APPOINTMENTS

Executive Director	Pembroke Managing Agency Ltd	2008 -

PREVIOUS MAJOR POSITIONS/APPOINTMENTS

Executive Director	Argo Managing Agency Ltd	2001 - 2006
Executive Director	Heritage Direct Ltd	2005 - 2006

Clive A Washbourn

Position	Executive Director & Head of Marine
Company	Beazley Furlonge Ltd
Address (Office)	Plantation Place South
	60 Great Tower Street
	London EC3R 5AD
Telephone	+44 (0)20 7667 0623
Fax	+44 (0)20 7674 7100
Email	clive.washbourn@beazley.com
Website	www.beazley.com

Full Name	Clive Andrew Washbourn
Year of Birth	1960
Professional Qualifications	Information not available

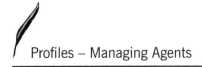

PROFESSIONAL INFORMATION
CURRENT MAJOR POSITIONS/APPOINTMENTS

Executive Director	Beazley Furlonge Ltd	2005 -
Member	Lloyd's Market Association Board, Marine Committee	Unknown -
Chairman	Joint War Committee	Unknown -

PREVIOUS MAJOR POSITIONS/APPOINTMENTS
Information not available

Mark C Watkins

Position	Executive Director
Company	Munich Re Underwriting Limited
Address (Office)	St Helen's
	1 Undershaft
	London EC3A 8EE
Telephone	+44 (0)20 7886 3900
Fax	+44 (0)20 7886 3901
Email	mark.watkins@mrunderwriting.com
Website	www.watkins-syndicate.co.uk
Full Name	Mark Christopher Watkins
Year of Birth	1951
Professional Qualifications	FCII

PROFESSIONAL INFORMATION
CURRENT MAJOR POSITIONS/APPOINTMENTS

Executive Director	Munich Re Underwriting Limited	1992 -
Non-Executive Director	Northern Marine Underwriters Ltd	2005 -
Non-Executive Director	Groves, John and Westrup Ltd	2005 -

PREVIOUS MAJOR POSITIONS/APPOINTMENTS
Information not available

Christopher E Watson

Position	Non-Executive Director
Company	ARK Syndicate Management Limited
Address (Office)	8th Floor
	St Helen's
	1 Undershaft
	London EC3A 8EE
Telephone	+44 (0)20 3023 4020
Fax	+44 (0)20 3023 4000
Email	enquiries@arkunderwriting.com
Website	www.arkunderwriting.com
Full Name	Christopher Eric Watson
Year of Birth	1950
Professional Qualifications	Information not available

PROFESSIONAL INFORMATION

CURRENT MAJOR POSITIONS/APPOINTMENTS

Non-Executive Director	ARK Syndicate Management Limited	2007 -

PREVIOUS MAJOR POSITIONS/APPOINTMENTS

Information not available

Clive A Watson

Position	Chief Executive Officer & Claims Director
Company	Canopius Managing Agents Limited
Address (Office)	Gallery 9
	One Lime Street
	London EC3M 7HA
Telephone	+44 (0)20 7337 3720
Fax	+44 (0)20 7337 3999
Email	clive.watson@canopius.com
Website	www.canopius.com

Full Name	Clive Anthony Watson
Year of Birth	1958
Professional Qualifications	Information not available

PROFESSIONAL INFORMATION

CURRENT MAJOR POSITIONS/APPOINTMENTS

Director	Canopius Managing Agents Limited	2004 -
Chief Executive	Canopius Managing Agents Limited	2007 -
Executive Director	Canopius Underwriting Limited	2009 -

PREVIOUS MAJOR POSITIONS/APPOINTMENTS

Non-Executive Director	Aviation & General Insurance Company Limited	2003	- 2003
Executive Director	Canopius Underwriting Limited	2006	- 2007
Non-Executive Director	Creechurch Underwriting Limited	2006	- 2007

Michael C Watson

Position	Chairman
Company	Canopius Managing Agents Limited
Address (Office)	Gallery 9
	One Lime Street
	London EC3M 7HA
Telephone	+44 (0)20 7337 3730
Fax	+44 (0)20 7337 3999
Email	michael.watson@canopius.com
Website	www.canopius.com

Full Name	Michael Clive Watson
Year of Birth	1954
Professional Qualifications	Chartered Accountant

PROFESSIONAL INFORMATION

CURRENT MAJOR POSITIONS/APPOINTMENTS

Non-Executive Director	Creechurch Underwriting Limited	2006 -
Non-Executive Director	Canopius Managing Agents Limited	2007 -
Non-Executive Director	Arista Insurance Ltd	2007 -
Executive Director	Canopius Underwriting Limited	2008 -

PREVIOUS MAJOR POSITIONS/APPOINTMENTS

Chief Executive	Bestpark International Limited	2001 - 2003
Executive Director	Canopius Managing Agents Limited	2001 - 2007
Chief Executive	Canopius Managing Agents Limited	2001 - 2007

Richard C Watson

Position	Executive Director & Active Underwriter Syndicates 33 & 6104
Company	Hiscox Syndicates Limited
Address (Office)	1 Great St Helen's
	London EC3A 6HX
Telephone	+44 (0)20 7448 6000
Fax	+44 (0)20 7448 6900
Email	richard.watson@hiscox.com
Website	www.hiscox.com

Full Name	Richard Colin Watson
Year of Birth	1963
Professional Qualifications	Information not available

PROFESSIONAL INFORMATION

CURRENT MAJOR POSITIONS/APPOINTMENTS

Executive Director	Hiscox Syndicates Limited	2000 -

PREVIOUS MAJOR POSITIONS/APPOINTMENTS

Information not available

Iain T Webb-Wilson

Position	Non-Executive Director
Company	Hiscox Syndicates Limited
Address (Office)	1 Great St Helen's
	London EC3A 6HX
Telephone	+44 (0)20 7448 6000
Fax	+44 (0)20 7448 6900
Email	enquiry@hiscox.com
Website	www.hiscox.com
Full Name	Iain Thomas Webb-Wilson
Year of Birth	1948
Professional Qualifications	Information not available

PROFESSIONAL INFORMATION

CURRENT MAJOR POSITIONS/APPOINTMENTS

Non-Executive Director	Hiscox Syndicates Limited	2008 -
Trustee	Lloyd's Charities Trust	Unknown

PREVIOUS MAJOR POSITIONS/APPOINTMENTS

Executive Director	Miller Insurance Services Limited	2005 - 2008

Michael J Wells

Position	Deputy Chairman
Company	Spectrum Syndicate Management Limited
Address (Office)	2nd Floor
	6 Bevis Marks
	London EC3A 7HL
Telephone	+44 (0)20 7283 2646
Fax	+44 (0)20 7621 0975
Email	mike.wells@spectrumins.com
Website	www.spectrumins.com
Full Name	Michael John Wells
Year of Birth	1956
Professional Qualifications	Information not available

PROFESSIONAL INFORMATION

CURRENT MAJOR POSITIONS/APPOINTMENTS

Executive Director	Spectrum Syndicate Management Limited	2001 -

PREVIOUS MAJOR POSITIONS/APPOINTMENTS

Executive Director	Crowe Syndicate Management Ltd	2001 - 2006

Andrew T West

Position	Non-Executive Director
Company	Max at Lloyd's Ltd
Address (Office)	4th Floor
	70 Gracechurch Street
	London EC3V 0XL
Telephone	+44 (0)20 3102 3100
Fax	+44 (0)20 3102 3200
Email	andrew.west@maxatlloyds.com
Website	www.maxatlloyds.com
Full Name	Andrew Thomas West
Year of Birth	1957
Professional Qualifications	Information not available

PROFESSIONAL INFORMATION

CURRENT MAJOR POSITIONS/APPOINTMENTS

Non-Executive Director	Max at Lloyd's Ltd	2006 -

| Non-Executive Director | FirstCity Partnership Limited | 2006 - |
| Non-Executive Director | Tri-Artisan Partners Advisors Europe LLP | 2008 - |

PREVIOUS MAJOR POSITIONS/APPOINTMENTS

| Non-Executive Director | Imagine Underwriting Limited | 2001 - 2007 |
| Non-Executive Director | Danish Re Syndicates Ltd | 2006 - 2006 |

Helen M Westcott

Position	Executive Director
Company	Whittington Capital Management Limited
Address (Office)	33 Creechurch Lane
	London EC3A 5EB
Telephone	+44 (0)20 7743 0900
Fax	+44 (0)20 7743 0901
Email	helen.westcott@whittingtoninsurance.com
Website	www.whittingtoninsurance.com

Full Name	Helen Margaret Westcott
Year of Birth	1953
Professional Qualifications	Information not available

PROFESSIONAL INFORMATION

CURRENT MAJOR POSITIONS/APPOINTMENTS

Executive Director	Reliance National Insurance	
	Company (Europe) Ltd	2007 -
Executive Director	Whittington Capital Management Limited	2007 -

PREVIOUS MAJOR POSITIONS/APPOINTMENTS

| Executive Director | Alea London Limited | 2006 - 2007 |

Mark H Wheeler

Position	Underwriting Director & Active Underwriter Syndicate 4000
Company	Pembroke Managing Agency Ltd
Address (Office)	2nd Floor
	3 Minster Court
	Mincing Lane
	London EC3R 7DD
Telephone	+44 (0)20 7337 4400
Fax	+44 (0)20 7337 4401
Email	mark.wheeler@pembrokeunderwriting.com
Website	www.pembrokeunderwriting.com

PERSONAL PROFILE A profile can be found in the People at Lloyd's, Personal section.

David KL White

Position	Independent Review Director
Company	SA Meacock & Company Limited

Address (Office)	4th Floor
	15 St Helen's Place
	London EC3A 6DE
Telephone	+44 (0)20 7374 6727
Fax	+44 (0)20 7374 4727
Email	linda.mailoudi@sameacock.com
Website	None at present

Position	Non-Executive Director
Company	Whittington Capital Management Limited
Address (Office)	33 Creechurch Lane
	London EC3A 5EB
Telephone	+44 (0)20 7743 0900
Fax	+44 (0)20 7743 0901
Email	jon.francis@whittingtoninsurance.com
Website	www.whittingtoninsurance.com

Full Name	David Kenneth Leoline White
Year of Birth	1938
Professional Qualifications	Information not available

PROFESSIONAL INFORMATION

CURRENT MAJOR POSITIONS/APPOINTMENTS

Non-Executive Director	Whittington Capital Management Limited	1996 -
Executive Director	Atlantic Mutual International Limited	2001 -
Non-Executive Director	SA Meacock & Company Limited	2004 -

PREVIOUS MAJOR POSITIONS/APPOINTMENTS

Executive Director	Guarantee Protection Insurance Limited	2002 - 2002

Graham J White

Position	Deputy Chairman
Company	Argenta Syndicate Management Limited
Address (Office)	Fountain House
	130 Fenchurch Street
	London EC3M 5DJ
Telephone	+44 (0)20 7825 7182
Fax	+44 (0)20 7825 7155
Email	graham.white@argentaplc.com
Website	www.argentaplc.com

PERSONAL PROFILE	A profile can be found in the People at Lloyd's, Personal section.

Graham RA White

Position	Executive Director
Company	Marketform Managing Agency Limited
Address (Office)	8 Lloyd's Avenue
	London EC3N 3EL
Telephone	+44 (0)20 7488 7700

Fax	+44 (0)20 7488 7800
Email	underwriters@marketform.com
Website	www.marketform.com

Full Name	Graham Richard Austen White
Year of Birth	1968
Professional Qualifications	Information not available

PROFESSIONAL INFORMATION

CURRENT MAJOR POSITIONS/APPOINTMENTS

Executive Director	Marketform Managing Agency Limited	2006 -
Chairman	Lloyd's Charities Trust	Unknown

PREVIOUS MAJOR POSITIONS/APPOINTMENTS

Information not available

John LP Whiter

Position	Chairman
Company	Argenta Syndicate Management Limited
Address (Office)	Fountain House
	130 Fenchurch Street
	London EC3M 5DJ
Telephone	+44 (0)20 7825 7200
Fax	+44 (0)20 7825 7155
Email	john.whiter@argentaplc.com
Website	www.argentaplc.com

Full Name	John Lindsay Pearce Whiter
Year of Birth	Information not available
Professional Qualifications	Information not available

PROFESSIONAL INFORMATION

CURRENT MAJOR POSITIONS/APPOINTMENTS

Non-Executive Director	Argenta Syndicate Management Limited	2009 -

PREVIOUS MAJOR POSITIONS/APPOINTMENTS

Executive Director	Benfield Capital Limited	2001 - 2006
Executive Director	Aon Benfield Securities Limited	2001 - 2006
Executive Director	Bluesure Ltd	2005 - 2005
Executive Director	Benfield Limited	2005 - 2009

Terence J Whittaker

Position	Underwriting Director
Company	QBE Underwriting Limited
Address (Office)	Plantation Place
	30 Fenchurch Street
	London EC3M 3BD
Telephone	+44 (0)20 7105 4000
Fax	+44 (0)20 7105 4019

Email	enquiries@uk.qbe.com
Website	www.qbeeurope.com

Full Name	Terence James Whittaker
Year of Birth	1961
Professional Qualifications	Information not available

PROFESSIONAL INFORMATION

CURRENT MAJOR POSITIONS/APPOINTMENTS

Executive Director	QBE Underwriting Services (UK) Limited	2007 -
Executive Director	QBE Insurance (Europe) Limited	2008 -
Executive Director	QBE Underwriting Limited	2008 -

PREVIOUS MAJOR POSITIONS/APPOINTMENTS

Information not available

Kevin W Wilkins

Position	Executive Director & Active Underwriter Syndicate 570
Company	Atrium Underwriters Limited
Address (Office)	Room 790
	Lloyd's
	One Lime Street
	London EC3M 7DQ
Telephone	+44 (0)20 7327 4877
Fax	+44 (0)20 7327 4878
Email	info@atrium-uw.com
Website	www.atrium-uw.com

PERSONAL PROFILE	A profile can be found in the People at Lloyd's, Personal section.

Anthony D Williams

Position	Executive Director
Company	Hardy (Underwriting Agencies) Ltd
Address (Office)	4th Floor
	40 Lime Street
	London EC3M 7AW
Telephone	+44 (0)20 7626 0382
Fax	+44 (0)20 7283 4677
Email	anthony.williams@hardygroup.co.uk
Website	www.hardygroup.co.uk

Full Name	Anthony David Williams
Year of Birth	1974
Professional Qualifications	BSc, FIA, FIAA

PROFESSIONAL INFORMATION

CURRENT MAJOR POSITIONS/APPOINTMENTS

Executive Director	Hardy (Underwriting Agencies) Ltd	2006 -

PREVIOUS MAJOR POSITIONS/APPOINTMENTS
Information not available

David G Williams

Position	Operations Director & Claims Director
Company	Argenta Syndicate Management Limited
Address (Office)	Fountain House
	130 Fenchurch Street
	London EC3M 5DJ
Telephone	+44 (0)20 7825 7211
Fax	+44 (0)20 7825 7155
Email	david.williams@argentaplc.com
Website	www.argentaplc.com

Full Name	David Gareth Williams
Year of Birth	1957
Professional Qualifications	Information not available

PROFESSIONAL INFORMATION

CURRENT MAJOR POSITIONS/APPOINTMENTS

Executive Director	Argenta Syndicate Management Limited	2008 -

PREVIOUS MAJOR POSITIONS/APPOINTMENTS

Claims Director	RM Pateman (Underwriting) Agencies	1985 - Unknown
Member	Lloyd's Claims Handling Business Committee	1997 - 2000

Graham D Williams

Position	Non-Executive Director
Company	Ace Underwriting Agencies Limited
Address (Office)	100 Leadenhall Street
	London EC3A 3BP
Telephone	+44 (0)20 7173 7000
Fax	+44 (0)20 7173 7800
Email	info.uk@ace-ina.com
Website	www.acelimited.com

Full Name	Graham David Williams
Year of Birth	1942
Professional Qualifications	Information not available

PROFESSIONAL INFORMATION

CURRENT MAJOR POSITIONS/APPOINTMENTS

Non-Executive Director	Ace Underwriting Agencies Limited	1999 -
Non-Executive Director	ACE European Group Limited	2003 -

PREVIOUS MAJOR POSITIONS/APPOINTMENTS
Information not available

Paul Wilson

Position	Independent Non-Executive Director
Company	R J Kiln & Co Limited
Address (Office)	106 Fenchurch Street
	London EC3M 5NR
Telephone	+44 (0)20 7886 9000
Fax	+44 (0)20 7488 1848
Email	See R J Kiln & Co Ltd Company Profile
Website	www.kilnplc.com
Full Name	Paul Wilson
Year of Birth	1951
Professional Qualifications	Information not available

PROFESSIONAL INFORMATION

CURRENT MAJOR POSITIONS/APPOINTMENTS

Non-Executive Director	R J Kiln & Co Limited	2007 -

PREVIOUS MAJOR POSITIONS/APPOINTMENTS

Information not available

David J Winkett

Position	Chief Financial Officer
Company	QBE Underwriting Limited
Address (Office)	Plantation Place
	30 Fenchurch Street
	London EC3M 3BD
Telephone	+44 (0)20 7105 4000
Fax	+44 (0)20 7105 4019
Email	enquiries@uk.qbe.com
Website	www.qbeeurope.com
Full Name	David James Winkett
Year of Birth	1969
Professional Qualifications	ACA

PROFESSIONAL INFORMATION

CURRENT MAJOR POSITIONS/APPOINTMENTS

Executive Director	QBE Underwriting Limited	2000 -
Executive Director	QBE Reinsurance (UK) Ltd	2004 -
Executive Director	QBE Insurance (Europe) Limited	2004 -
Executive Director	QBE Underwriting Services Ltd	2005 -
Executive Director	Greenhill Sturge Underwriting Ltd	2005 -
Executive Director	Greenhill International Ins Holdings Ltd	2005 -
Executive Director	Greenhill Underwriting Espana Ltd	2005 -

| Executive Director | QBE (Stafford) Limited | 2005 - |
| Executive Director | The Minibus and Coach Club Ltd | 2005 - |

PREVIOUS MAJOR POSITIONS/APPOINTMENTS

Executive Director	Bates Cunningham Underwriting Limited	2001 - 2003
Executive Director	QBE Insurance Company (UK) Limited	2004 - 2006
Executive Director	Energy Insurance Services Limited	2005 - 2005
Executive Director	Icon (Schemes) Ltd	2005 - 2006

Andrew D Winyard

Position	Executive Director & Deputy Underwriter Syndicate 570
Company	Atrium Underwriters Limited
Address (Office)	Room 790
	Lloyd's
	One Lime Street
	London EC3M 7DQ
Telephone	+44 (0)20 7327 4877
Fax	+44 (0)20 7327 4878
Email	info@atrium-uw.com
Website	www.atrium-uw.com

Full Name	Andrew Dennis Winyard
Year of Birth	1965
Professional Qualifications	Information not available

PROFESSIONAL INFORMATION

CURRENT MAJOR POSITIONS/APPOINTMENTS

| Executive Director | Atrium Underwriters Limited | 2008 - |

PREVIOUS MAJOR POSITIONS/APPOINTMENTS

Information not available

Kazuo Yamada

Position	Non-Executive Director
Company	Mitsui Sumitomo Insurance Underwriting at Lloyd's Ltd
Address (Office)	25 Fenchurch Avenue
	London EC3M 5AD
Telephone	+44 (0)20 7977 8321
Fax	+44 (0)20 7977 8300
Email	enquiries@msilm.com
Website	www.msilm.com

Full Name	Kazuo Yamada
Year of Birth	1946
Professional Qualifications	Information not available

PROFESSIONAL INFORMATION

CURRENT MAJOR POSITIONS/APPOINTMENTS

Non-Executive Director	Mitsui Sumitomo Insurance Underwriting at Lloyd's Ltd	2006 -
Non-Executive Director	Mitsui Sumitomo Insurance (London) Limited	2006 -
Non-Executive Director	Mitsui Sumitomo Insurance Company (Europe) Ltd	2006 -

PREVIOUS MAJOR POSITIONS/APPOINTMENTS

Executive Director	Mitsui Sumitomo Insurance Company Limited	2001 - 2002

Tadashi Yamada

Position	Non-Executive Director
Company	Mitsui Sumitomo Insurance Underwriting at Lloyd's Ltd
Address (Office)	25 Fenchurch Avenue
	London EC3M 5AD
Telephone	+44 (0)20 7977 8321
Fax	+44 (0)20 7977 8300
Email	enquiries@msilm.com
Website	www.msilm.com
Full Name	Tadashi Yamada
Year of Birth	1969
Professional Qualifications	Information not available

PROFESSIONAL INFORMATION

CURRENT MAJOR POSITIONS/APPOINTMENTS

Non-Executive Director	Mitsui Sumitomo Insurance Underwriting at Lloyd's Ltd

PREVIOUS MAJOR POSITIONS/APPOINTMENTS

Information not available

David B Yandell

Position	Finance Director
Company	Spectrum Syndicate Management Limited
Address (Office)	2nd Floor
	6 Bevis Marks
	London EC3A 7HL
Telephone	+44 (0)20 7283 2646
Fax	+44 (0)20 7621 0975
Email	david.yandell@spectrumins.com
Website	www.spectrumins.com
Full Name	David Bawden Yandell
Year of Birth	1947
Professional Qualifications	Information not available

PROFESSIONAL INFORMATION

CURRENT MAJOR POSITIONS/APPOINTMENTS

Executive Director	Spectrum Syndicate Management Limited	2004 -

PREVIOUS MAJOR POSITIONS/APPOINTMENTS

Information not available

Matthew C Yeldham

Position	Executive Director & Active Underwriter Syndicate 4711
Company	Aspen Managing Agency Limited
Address (Office)	30 Fenchurch Street
	London EC3M 3BD
Telephone	+44 (0)20 7184 8000
Fax	+44 (0)20 7184 8500
Email	c/o robert.long@aspen-re.com
Website	www.aspen-re.com

Full Name	Matthew Charles Yeldham
Year of Birth	1969
Professional Qualifications	Information not available

PROFESSIONAL INFORMATION

CURRENT MAJOR POSITIONS/APPOINTMENTS

Executive Director	Aspen Managing Agency Limited	2008 -

PREVIOUS MAJOR POSITIONS/APPOINTMENTS

Executive Director	Catlin (Wellington) Underwriting Agencies Limited	2002 - 2007
Executive Director	Wellington Syndicate Services Limited	2005 - 2007

J Richard L Youell

Position	Non-Executive Director
Company	Liberty Syndicate Management Limited
Address (Office)	5th Floor
	Plantation Place South
	60 Great Tower Street
	London EC3R 5AZ
Telephone	+44 (0)20 7070 4472
Fax	+44 (0)20 7863 1001
Email	info@libertysyndicates.com
Website	www.libertysyndicates.com

Full Name	John Richard Ludbrooke Youell
Year of Birth	1942
Professional Qualifications	Information not available

PROFESSIONAL INFORMATION

CURRENT MAJOR POSITIONS/APPOINTMENTS

Non-Executive Director	The Britannia Steam Ship Insurance Association Ltd	2001 -
Non-Executive Director	Liberty Syndicate Management Limited	2008 -

PREVIOUS MAJOR POSITIONS/APPOINTMENTS
Information not available

Brian D Young

Position	Executive Director
Company	Newline Underwriting Management Ltd
Address (Office)	Suite 5/4
	London Underwriting Centre
	3 Minster Court
	Mincing Lane
	London EC3R 7DD
Telephone	+44 (0)20 7090 1700
Fax	+44 (0)20 7090 1701
Email	byoung@newlineuml.com
Website	www.newlineuml.com

Full Name	Brian David Young
Year of Birth	1964
Professional Qualifications	Information not available

PROFESSIONAL INFORMATION

CURRENT MAJOR POSITIONS/APPOINTMENTS

Chief Executive	Odyssey America Reinsurance Corporation	2001 -
Executive Director	Newline Underwriting Management Ltd	2002 -
Executive Director	Newline Insurance Company Limited	2008 -

PREVIOUS MAJOR POSITIONS/APPOINTMENTS

Non-Executive Director	Newline Underwriting Management Ltd	2001 - 2008
Chief Executive	Newline Underwriting Management Ltd	2002 - 2008
Chief Executive	Newline Insurance Company Limited	2006 - 2008

David T Young

Position	Non-Executive Director
Company	Marlborough Underwriting Agency Ltd
Address (Office)	Birchin Court
	20 Birchin Lane
	London EC3V 9DU
Telephone	+44 (0)20 7456 1800
Fax	+44 (0)20 7456 1810
Email	david.young@marlborough.co.uk
Website	www.marlborough.co.uk

PERSONAL PROFILE	A profile can be found in the People at Lloyd's, Personal section.

Profiles – Run-Off Agents

Simon P Amies

Position	Executive Director
Company	Cavell Managing Agency Ltd
Address (Office)	9–13 Fenchurch Buildings
	London EC3M 5HR
Telephone	+44 (0)20 7780 5850
Fax	+44 (0)20 7780 5851
Email	compliance@cavell.co.uk
Website	www.rqih.co.uk
Full Name	Simon Peter Amies
Year of Birth	1965
Professional Qualifications	Information not available

PROFESSIONAL INFORMATION

CURRENT MAJOR POSITIONS/APPOINTMENTS

Executive Director	Cavell Managing Agency Ltd	2007 –

PREVIOUS MAJOR POSITIONS/APPOINTMENTS

Information not available

Michael Bell

Position	Executive Director
Company	Cavell Managing Agency Ltd
Address (Office)	9–13 Fenchurch Buildings
	London EC3M 5HR
Telephone	+44 (0)20 7780 5850
Fax	+44 (0)20 7780 5851
Email	compliance@cavell.co.uk
Website	www.rqih.co.uk
Full Name	Michael Bell
Year of Birth	1962
Professional Qualifications	ACA

PROFESSIONAL INFORMATION

CURRENT MAJOR POSITIONS/APPOINTMENTS

Executive Director	Cavell Managing Agency Ltd	2005 –

PREVIOUS MAJOR POSITIONS/APPOINTMENTS

Executive Director	RiverStone Managing Agency Limited	2001 – 2002
Executive Director	Imagine Syndicate Management Limited	2002 – 2005

Nicholas C Bentley

Position	Chief Executive Officer
Company	RiverStone Managing Agency Limited

Address (Office)	2nd Floor	
	Mint House	
	77 Mansell Street	
	London E1 8AF	
Telephone	+44 (0)20 7977 1600	
Fax	+44 (0)20 7977 1687	
Email	nick.bentley@rsml.co.uk	
Website	www.rsml.co.uk	

Full Name	Nicholas Craig Bentley
Year of Birth	1960
Professional Qualifications	Information not available

PROFESSIONAL INFORMATION

CURRENT MAJOR POSITIONS/APPOINTMENTS

Executive Director	RiverStone Insurance (UK) Limited	2001 –
Executive Director	Sphere Drake Insurance Limited	2001 –
Executive Director	RiverStone Managing Agency Limited	2002 –
Chief Executive	RiverStone Managing Agency Limited	2003 –
Chief Executive	Sphere Drake Insurance Limited	2003 –
Chief Executive	RiverStone Insurance (UK) Limited	2003 –

PREVIOUS MAJOR POSITIONS/APPOINTMENTS

Executive Director	ORG Re (UK) Limited	2001 – 2005
Chief Executive	ORG Re (UK) Limited	2003 – 2005

George N Cochran

Position	Chairman
Company	Shelbourne Syndicate Services Limited
Address (Office)	4 Royal Mint Court
	London EC3N 4HJ
Telephone	+44 (0)20 7961 0810
Fax	+44 (0)20 7481 6801
Email	–
Website	None at present

Full Name	George Newcomb Cochran
Year of Birth	1954
Professional Qualifications	Information not available

PROFESSIONAL INFORMATION

CURRENT MAJOR POSITIONS/APPOINTMENTS

Executive Director	Fox-Pitt, Kelton Limited	2007 –
Non–Executive Director	Shelbourne Syndicate Services Limited	2008 –

PREVIOUS MAJOR POSITIONS/APPOINTMENTS

	Information not available

Philippa M Curtis

Position	Chief Financial Officer
Company	Ridge Underwriting Agencies Limited
Address (Office)	100 Leadenhall Street
	London EC3A 3BP
Telephone	+44 (0)20 7173 7711
Fax	+44 (0)20 7173 7800
Email	philippa.curtis@ace–ina.com
Website	–

Full Name	Philippa Mary Curtis
Year of Birth	1960
Professional Qualifications	Information not available

PROFESSIONAL INFORMATION

CURRENT MAJOR POSITIONS/APPOINTMENTS

Executive Director	Ace Underwriting Agencies Limited	2001 –
Executive Director	ACE European Group Limited	2001 –
Executive Director	Ridge Underwriting Agencies Limited	2001 –
Executive Director	ACE Europe Life Limited	2007 –

PREVIOUS MAJOR POSITIONS/APPOINTMENTS

Executive Director	R&Q Reinsurance Company (UK) Limited	2001 – 2005
Executive Director	ACE London Aviation Limited	2001 – 2003
Executive Director	ACE London Underwriting Limited	2001 – 2003

Sean J Dalton

Position	Chief Executive Officer
Company	Shelbourne Syndicate Services Limited
Address (Office)	4 Royal Mint Court
	London EC3N 4HJ
Telephone	+44 (0)20 7961 0810
Fax	+44 (0)20 7481 6801
Email	–
Website	None at present

Full Name	Sean James Dalton
Year of Birth	1965
Professional Qualifications	Information not available

PROFESSIONAL INFORMATION

CURRENT MAJOR POSITIONS/APPOINTMENTS

Chief Executive	Shelbourne Syndicate Services Limited	2008 –

PREVIOUS MAJOR POSITIONS/APPOINTMENTS

Information not available

Philip Dietz

Position	Executive Director & Run–Off Manager Syndicates 1688, 1900 & 5500
Company	Capita Managing Agency Limited
Address (Office)	40 Dukes Place
	London EC3A 7NH
Telephone	+44 (0)870 402 7658
Fax	+44 (0)870 162 4566
Email	philip.dietz@capita.co.uk
Website	www.capitainsuranceservices.co.uk

Full Name	Philip Dietz
Year of Birth	1966
Professional Qualifications	Information not available

PROFESSIONAL INFORMATION

CURRENT MAJOR POSITIONS/APPOINTMENTS

Executive Director	Capita Syndicate Management Limited	2003 –
Chief Executive	Capita Syndicate Management Limited	2007 –
Executive Director	Capita Managing Agency Limited	2008 –

PREVIOUS MAJOR POSITIONS/APPOINTMENTS

Information not available

Peter L Doyle

Position	Non–Executive Director
Company	Duncanson & Holt Syndicate Management Ltd
Address (Office)	40 Dukes Place
	London EC3A 7NH
Telephone	+44 (0)870 402 7278
Fax	+44 (0)870 162 4541
Email	–
Website	–

Full Name	Peter Lawrence Doyle
Year of Birth	1952
Professional Qualifications	Information not available

PROFESSIONAL INFORMATION

CURRENT MAJOR POSITIONS/APPOINTMENTS

Non–Executive Director	Duncanson & Holt Syndicate Management Ltd	2008 –

PREVIOUS MAJOR POSITIONS/APPOINTMENTS

Executive Director	Duncanson & Holt Syndicate Management Ltd	2004 – 2008

Andrew D Elliott

Position	Executive Director & Run–Off Manager Syndicates 529 & 2008
Company	Shelbourne Syndicate Services Limited
Address (Office)	4 Royal Mint Court
	London EC3N 4HJ

Telephone	+44 (0)20 7961 0810
Fax	+44 (0)20 7481 6801
Email	andrew.elliott@shelbournegroup.com
Website	None at present

Full Name	Andrew Duncan Elliott
Year of Birth	1959
Professional Qualifications	Information not available

PROFESSIONAL INFORMATION

CURRENT MAJOR POSITIONS/APPOINTMENTS

Executive Director	Shelbourne Syndicate Services Limited	2008 –

PREVIOUS MAJOR POSITIONS/APPOINTMENTS

Executive Director	Liberty Syndicate Management Limited	2001 – 2006

Steven Fass

Position	Independent Non–Executive Director
Company	RITC Syndicate Management Ltd
Address (Office)	3rd Floor
	117 Fenchurch Street
	London EC3M 5DY
Telephone	+44 (0)20 7220 8899
Fax	+44 (0)20 7220 8898
Email	ritcwebenquiry@ritcsm.com
Website	www.ritcsm.com

Full Name	Steven Fass
Year of Birth	1946
Professional Qualifications	Information not available

PROFESSIONAL INFORMATION

CURRENT MAJOR POSITIONS/APPOINTMENTS

Non–Executive Director	RITC Syndicate Management Ltd	2007 –

PREVIOUS MAJOR POSITIONS/APPOINTMENTS

	Information not available

Joseph R Foley

Position	Chief Executive Officer
Company	Duncanson & Holt Syndicate Management Ltd
Address (Office)	40 Dukes Place
	London EC3A 7NH
Telephone	+44 (0)870 402 7278
Fax	+44 (0)870 162 4541
Email	–
Website	–

Full Name	Joseph Richard Foley
Year of Birth	1955
Professional Qualifications	Information not available

PROFESSIONAL INFORMATION

CURRENT MAJOR POSITIONS/APPOINTMENTS

Chief Executive	UNUM Life Insurance Company of America	2001 –
Chief Executive	Trafalgar Underwriting Agencies Limited	2001 –
Chief Executive	Duncanson & Holt Syndicate Management Ltd	2001 –

PREVIOUS MAJOR POSITIONS/APPOINTMENTS

Information not available

Dinah J Gately

Position	Claims Director
Company	RITC Syndicate Management Ltd
Address (Office)	3rd Floor
	117 Fenchurch Street
	London EC3M 5DY
Telephone	+44 (0)20 7220 8899
Fax	+44 (0)20 7220 8898
Email	ritcwebenquiry@ritcsm.com
Website	www.ritcsm.com

Full Name	Dinah Janine Gately
Year of Birth	1964
Professional Qualifications	Information not available

PROFESSIONAL INFORMATION

CURRENT MAJOR POSITIONS/APPOINTMENTS

Executive Director	The Underwriter Insurance Company Limited	2003 –
Executive Director	RITC Syndicate Management Ltd	2007 –

PREVIOUS MAJOR POSITIONS/APPOINTMENTS

Information not available

Dennis C Gibbs

Position	Non–Executive Director
Company	RiverStone Managing Agency Limited
Address (Office)	2nd Floor
	Mint House
	77 Mansell Street
	London E1 8AF
Telephone	+44 (0)20 7977 1600
Fax	+44 (0)20 7977 1687
Email	–
Website	www.rsml.co.uk

Full Name	Dennis Coyle Gibbs
Year of Birth	1952
Professional Qualifications	Information not available

PROFESSIONAL INFORMATION

CURRENT MAJOR POSITIONS/APPOINTMENTS

Non–Executive Director	RiverStone Managing Agency Limited	2003 –

PREVIOUS MAJOR POSITIONS/APPOINTMENTS

Non–Executive Director	RiverStone Insurance (UK) Limited	2001 – 2005
Non–Executive Director	ORG Re (UK) Limited	2001 – 2005
Non–Executive Director	Sphere Drake Insurance Limited	2001 – 2005

William F Goodier

Position	Non–Executive Director
Company	RiverStone Managing Agency Limited
Address (Office)	2nd Floor
	Mint House
	77 Mansell Street
	London E1 8AF
Telephone	+44 (0)20 7977 1600
Fax	+44 (0)20 7977 1687
Email	–
Website	www.rsml.co.uk

Full Name	William Frank Goodier
Year of Birth	1940
Professional Qualifications	Information not available

PROFESSIONAL INFORMATION

CURRENT MAJOR POSITIONS/APPOINTMENTS

Executive Director	Additional Underwriting Agencies (No 5) Limited	2001 –
Executive Director	Additional Underwriting Agencies (No 2) Limited	2001 –
Non–Executive Director	RiverStone Managing Agency Limited	2003 –

PREVIOUS MAJOR POSITIONS/APPOINTMENTS

Non–Executive Director	Munich Re Underwriting Limited	2001 – 2008
Non–Executive Director	El Paso Insurance Company Limited	2001 – 2006
Non–Executive Director	Kingscroft Insurance Company Limited	2001 – 2006
Non–Executive Director	Lime Street Insurance Company Limited	2001 – 2006
Non–Executive Director	Mutual Reinsurance Company Limited	2001 – 2006
Non–Executive Director	Walbrook Insurance Company Limited	2001 – 2006
Non–Executive Director	Kwelm Holdings Limited	2005 – 2006
Non–Executive Director	Continuum Holdings Limited	2006 – 2008

Peter AG Green

Position	Executive Director
Company	Cavell Managing Agency Ltd

Address (Office)	9–13 Fenchurch Buildings
	London EC3M 5HR
Telephone	+44 (0)20 7780 5850
Fax	+44 (0)20 7780 5851
Email	compliance@cavell.co.uk
Website	www.rqih.co.uk

Full Name	Peter Alexander George Green
Year of Birth	1949
Professional Qualifications	FIA

PROFESSIONAL INFORMATION

CURRENT MAJOR POSITIONS/APPOINTMENTS

Executive Director	Cavell Managing Agency Ltd	2006 –

PREVIOUS MAJOR POSITIONS/APPOINTMENTS

Executive Director	Cavell Insurance Company Limited	2001 – 2006

John S Hale

Position	Executive Director & Compliance Officer
Company	Capita Managing Agency Limited
Address (Office)	40 Dukes Place
	London EC3A 7NH
Telephone	+44 (0)870 402 7591
Fax	+44 (0)870 162 4566
Email	john.hale@capita.co.uk
Website	www.capitainsuranceservices.co.uk

Full Name	John Selwyn Hale
Year of Birth	1959
Professional Qualifications	Information not available

PROFESSIONAL INFORMATION

CURRENT MAJOR POSITIONS/APPOINTMENTS

Executive Director	Capita Managing Agency Limited	2007 –
Executive Director	Capita Commercial Insurance Services Limited	2007 –

PREVIOUS MAJOR POSITIONS/APPOINTMENTS

	Information not available

Timothy J Hanford

Position	Non–Executive Director
Company	Shelbourne Syndicate Services Limited
Address (Office)	4 Royal Mint Court
	London EC3N 4HJ
Telephone	+44 (0)20 7961 0810
Fax	+44 (0)20 7481 6801
Email	–
Website	None at present

Full Name	Timothy John Hanford
Year of Birth	1964
Professional Qualifications	Information not available

PROFESSIONAL INFORMATION

CURRENT MAJOR POSITIONS/APPOINTMENTS

Non–Executive Director	Shelbourne Syndicate Services Limited	2008 –

PREVIOUS MAJOR POSITIONS/APPOINTMENTS

Executive Director	Dresdner Kleinwort Limited	2003 – 2006
Non–Executive Director	August Equity Limited	2004 – 2006

Christopher P Hare

Position	Business Development
Company	RITC Syndicate Management Ltd
Address (Office)	3rd Floor
	117 Fenchurch Street
	London EC3M 5DY
Telephone	+44 (0)20 7220 8878
Fax	+44 (0)20 7220 8898
Email	ritcwebenquiry@ritcsm.com
Website	www.ritcsm.com

Full Name	Christopher Peter Hare
Year of Birth	1947
Professional Qualifications	Information not available

PROFESSIONAL INFORMATION

CURRENT MAJOR POSITIONS/APPOINTMENTS

Non–Executive Director	Lloyd's Members Agency Services Ltd	2001 –
Executive Director	RITC Syndicate Management Ltd	2007 –

PREVIOUS MAJOR POSITIONS/APPOINTMENTS

Executive Director	PRO Syndicate Management Limited	2001 – 2005

Richard J Harris

Position	Non–Executive Director
Company	Shelbourne Syndicate Services Limited
Address (Office)	4 Royal Mint Court
	London EC3N 4HJ
Telephone	+44 (0)20 7961 0810
Fax	+44 (0)20 7481 6801
Email	–
Website	None at present

Full Name	Richard John Harris
Year of Birth	1961
Professional Qualifications	Information not available

PROFESSIONAL INFORMATION

CURRENT MAJOR POSITIONS/APPOINTMENTS

Non–Executive Director	Shelbourne Syndicate Services Limited	2008 –

PREVIOUS MAJOR POSITIONS/APPOINTMENTS

Executive Director	ORG Re (UK) Limited	2001 – 2003
Executive Director	RiverStone Insurance (UK) Limited	2001 – 2003
Executive Director	Sphere Drake Insurance Limited	2001 – 2003
Executive Director	RiverStone Managing Agency Limited	2002 – 2003
Chief Executive	ORG Re (UK) Limited	2002 – 2003
Chief Executive	RiverStone Insurance (UK) Limited	2002 – 2003
Chief Executive	Sphere Drake Insurance Limited	2002 – 2003

Lorna A Hemsley

Position	Chief Financial Officer
Company	RiverStone Managing Agency Limited
Address (Office)	2nd Floor
	Mint House
	77 Mansell Street
	London E1 8AF
Telephone	+44 (0)20 7977 1600
Fax	+44 (0)20 7977 1687
Email	lorna.hemsley@rsml.co.uk
Website	www.rsml.co.uk

Full Name	Lorna Anne Hemsley
Year of Birth	1967
Professional Qualifications	Information not available

PROFESSIONAL INFORMATION

CURRENT MAJOR POSITIONS/APPOINTMENTS

Executive Director	RiverStone Insurance (UK) Limited	2008 –
Executive Director	Sphere Drake Insurance Limited	2008 –
Executive Director	RiverStone Managing Agency Limited	2008 –

PREVIOUS MAJOR POSITIONS/APPOINTMENTS

Information not available

Anthony G Hines

Position	Chairman
Company	RITC Syndicate Management Ltd
Address (Office)	3rd Floor
	117 Fenchurch Street
	London EC3M 5DY
Telephone	+44 (0)20 7220 8899
Fax	+44 (0)20 7220 8898
Email	ritcwebenquiry@ritcsm.com
Website	www.ritcsm.com

Full Name	Anthony Gordon Hines
Year of Birth	1935
Professional Qualifications	Information not available

PROFESSIONAL INFORMATION

CURRENT MAJOR POSITIONS/APPOINTMENTS

Non–Executive Director	The Underwriter Insurance Company Limited	2004 –
Non–Executive Director	RITC Syndicate Management Ltd	2007 –

PREVIOUS MAJOR POSITIONS/APPOINTMENTS

Information not available

Roy Katzenberg

Position	Chief Financial Officer
Company	RITC Syndicate Management Ltd
Address (Office)	3rd Floor
	117 Fenchurch Street
	London EC3M 5DY
Telephone	+44 (0)20 7220 8899
Fax	+44 (0)20 7220 8898
Email	ritcwebenquiry@ritcsm.com
Website	www.ritcsm.com

Full Name	Roy Katzenberg
Year of Birth	1952
Professional Qualifications	CAS, CA(SA), CFE

PROFESSIONAL INFORMATION

CURRENT MAJOR POSITIONS/APPOINTMENTS

Honorary Treasurer	British Insurance Law Association	1999 -
Executive Director	RITC Syndicate Management Ltd	2007 -
Executive Director	Underwriter Insurance Company Limited	2008 -

PREVIOUS MAJOR POSITIONS/APPOINTMENTS

Information not available

Anthony J Keys

Position	Non–Executive Director
Company	RiverStone Managing Agency Limited
Address (Office)	2nd Floor
	Mint House
	77 Mansell Street
	London E1 8AF
Telephone	+44 (0)20 7977 1600
Fax	+44 (0)20 7977 1687
Email	stephen.osborne@rsml.co.uk
Website	www.rsml.co.uk

Full Name	Anthony James Keys
Year of Birth	1941
Professional Qualifications	Information not available

PROFESSIONAL INFORMATION

CURRENT MAJOR POSITIONS/APPOINTMENTS

Non–Executive Director	Talbot Underwriting Ltd	2003 –
Non–Executive Director	RiverStone Managing Agency Limited	2005 –
Non–Executive Director	Underwriting Risk Services Ltd	2005 –

PREVIOUS MAJOR POSITIONS/APPOINTMENTS

Non–Executive Director	Admiral Syndicate Management Limited	2001 – 2006
Non–Executive Director	Danish Re Syndicates Ltd	2001 – 2005
Non–Executive Director	Newmarket Underwriting Ltd	2001 – 2004

John B King

Position	Managing Director
Company	Capita Managing Agency Limited
Address (Office)	40 Dukes Place
	London EC3A 7NH
Telephone	+44 (0)870 402 7614
Fax	+44 (0)870 162 4566
Email	john.king@capita.co.uk
Website	www.capitainsuranceservices.co.uk

Full Name	John Bryan King
Year of Birth	1964
Professional Qualifications	Information not available

PROFESSIONAL INFORMATION

CURRENT MAJOR POSITIONS/APPOINTMENTS

Executive Director	Capita Syndicate Management Limited	2001 –
Executive Director	Capita London Market Services Limited	2005 –
Executive Director	Capita Commercial Insurance Services Limited	2007 –
Executive Director	Lambourn Insurance Services Limited	2007 –
Chief Executive	Capita Managing Agency Limited	2008 –
Executive Director	City International Insurance Company Limited	2008 –

PREVIOUS MAJOR POSITIONS/APPOINTMENTS

Executive Director	P & B (Run–Off) Limited	2004 – 2005

George E Lloyd-Roberts

Position	Non–Executive Director
Company	Duncanson & Holt Syndicate Management Ltd
Address (Office)	40 Dukes Place
	London EC3A 7NH
Telephone	+44 (0)870 402 7278
Fax	+44 (0)870 162 4541

| Email | – |
| Website | – |

Full Name	George Edward Lloyd–Roberts
Year of Birth	1948
Professional Qualifications	Information not available

PROFESSIONAL INFORMATION

CURRENT MAJOR POSITIONS/APPOINTMENTS

Non–Executive Director	Liberty Syndicate Management Limited	2001 –
Non–Executive Director	Duncanson & Holt Syndicate Management Ltd	2001 –
Executive Director	European Brokers Associated Ltd	2007 –

PREVIOUS MAJOR POSITIONS/APPOINTMENTS

Non–Executive Director	Commodore Underwriting Agency Limited	2001 – 2006
Executive Director	Capita Syndicate Management Limited	2002 – 2004
Executive Director	Capita London Market Services Limited	2005 – 2007

Phillip C Martin

Position	Non–Executive Director
Company	Shelbourne Syndicate Services Limited
Address (Office)	4 Royal Mint Court
	London EC3N 4HJ
Telephone	+44 (0)20 7961 0810
Fax	+44 (0)20 7481 6801
Email	–
Website	None at present

Full Name	Phillip Charles Martin
Year of Birth	1962
Professional Qualifications	Information not available

PROFESSIONAL INFORMATION

CURRENT MAJOR POSITIONS/APPOINTMENTS

| Non–Executive Director | Shelbourne Syndicate Services Limited | 2008 – |

PREVIOUS MAJOR POSITIONS/APPOINTMENTS

| Executive Director | GC Securities Limited | 2001 – 2007 |

Robin E McCoy

Position	Chief Executive Officer & Run–Off Manager Syndicate 102
Company	Cavell Managing Agency Ltd
Address (Office)	9–13 Fenchurch Buildings
	London EC3M 5HR
Telephone	+44 (0)20 7780 5850
Fax	+44 (0)20 7780 5851
Email	compliance@cavell.co.uk
Website	www.rqih.co.uk

Full Name	Robin Edward McCoy
Year of Birth	1966
Professional Qualifications	ACA

PROFESSIONAL INFORMATION

CURRENT MAJOR POSITIONS/APPOINTMENTS

Executive Director	Cavell Managing Agency Ltd	2004 –
Chief Executive	Cavell Managing Agency Ltd	2005 –
Chief Executive	Cavell Management Services Limited	2005 –
Chief Executive	R&Q Broking Services Ltd	2007 –
Executive Director	Continuum Holdings Limited	2008 –

PREVIOUS MAJOR POSITIONS/APPOINTMENTS

Chief Executive	Capita Syndicate Management Limited	2001 – 2003

Donald C McCrickard

Position	Non–Executive Director
Company	RITC Syndicate Management Ltd
Address (Office)	3rd Floor
	117 Fenchurch Street
	London EC3M 5DY
Telephone	+44 (0)20 7220 8899
Fax	+44 (0)20 7220 8898
Email	ritcwebenquiry@ritcsm.com
Website	www.ritcsm.com

Full Name	Donald Cecil McCrickard
Year of Birth	1936
Professional Qualifications	Information not available

PROFESSIONAL INFORMATION

CURRENT MAJOR POSITIONS/APPOINTMENTS

Non–Executive Director	Hampshire Trust Plc	2006 –
Non–Executive Director	RITC Syndicate Management Ltd	2007 –

PREVIOUS MAJOR POSITIONS/APPOINTMENTS

Information not available

Richard TA Morgan

Position	Executive Director
Company	Capita Managing Agency Limited
Address (Office)	40 Dukes Place
	London EC3A 7NH
Telephone	+44 (0)870 402 7278
Fax	+44 (0)870 162 4566
Email	rick.morgan@capita.co.uk
Website	www.capitainsuranceservices.co.uk

Full Name	Richard Trevor Antony Morgan
Year of Birth	1951
Professional Qualifications	Information not available

PROFESSIONAL INFORMATION

CURRENT MAJOR POSITIONS/APPOINTMENTS

Executive Director	Capita Managing Agency Limited	2001 –

PREVIOUS MAJOR POSITIONS/APPOINTMENTS

Information not available

Clifford E Murphy

Position	Chief Financial Officer
Company	Shelbourne Syndicate Services Limited
Address (Office)	4 Royal Mint Court
	London EC3N 4HJ
Telephone	+44 (0)20 7961 0810
Fax	+44 (0)20 7481 6801
Email	–
Website	None at present

Full Name	Clifford Edward Murphy
Year of Birth	1959
Professional Qualifications	Information not available

PROFESSIONAL INFORMATION

CURRENT MAJOR POSITIONS/APPOINTMENTS

Executive Director	Shelbourne Syndicate Services Limited	2008 –

PREVIOUS MAJOR POSITIONS/APPOINTMENTS

Executive Director	Advent Underwriting Limited	2001 – 2006

R Peter Murray

Position	Claims Director
Company	Ridge Underwriting Agencies Limited
Address (Office)	100 Leadenhall Street
	London EC3A 3BP
Telephone	+44 (0)20 7173 7709
Fax	+44 (0)20 7173 7800
Email	peter.murray@ace–ina.com
Website	–

Full Name	Roland Peter Murray
Year of Birth	1956
Professional Qualifications	Information not available

PROFESSIONAL INFORMATION

CURRENT MAJOR POSITIONS/APPOINTMENTS

Executive Director	Ace Underwriting Agencies Limited	2001 –
Executive Director	ACE European Group Limited	2002 –

PREVIOUS MAJOR POSITIONS/APPOINTMENTS
Information not available

John GF O'Neill

Position	Chief Operating Officer
Company	Cavell Managing Agency Ltd
Address (Office)	9–13 Fenchurch Buildings
	London EC3M 5HR
Telephone	+44 (0)20 7780 5850
Fax	+44 (0)20 7780 5851
Email	compliance@cavell.co.uk
Website	www.rqih.co.uk

Full Name	John Gerard Francis O'Neill
Year of Birth	1962
Professional Qualifications	Information not available

PROFESSIONAL INFORMATION

CURRENT MAJOR POSITIONS/APPOINTMENTS

Executive Director	R&Q Broking Services Ltd	2008 –
Executive Director	Cavell Management Services Limited	2008 –
Executive Director	Continuum Holdings Limited	2008 –
Executive Director	Cavell Managing Agency Ltd	2009 –

PREVIOUS MAJOR POSITIONS/APPOINTMENTS

Executive Director	Catlin (Wellington) Underwriting Agencies Limited	2003 – 2003

Alan C Pollard, MBE

Position	Non–Executive Director
Company	Cavell Managing Agency Ltd
Address (Office)	9–13 Fenchurch Buildings
	London EC3M 5HR
Telephone	+44 (0)20 7780 5850
Fax	+44 (0)20 7780 5851
Email	compliance@cavell.co.uk
Website	www.rqih.co.uk

Full Name	Alan Craig Pollard, MBE
Year of Birth	1934
Professional Qualifications	Information not available

PROFESSIONAL INFORMATION

CURRENT MAJOR POSITIONS/APPOINTMENTS

Non–Executive Director	Cavell Managing Agency Ltd	2003 –

PREVIOUS MAJOR POSITIONS/APPOINTMENTS

Information not available

Richard V Pryce

Position	Executive Director
Company	Ridge Underwriting Agencies Limited
Address (Office)	100 Leadenhall Street
	London EC3A 3BP
Telephone	+44 (0)20 7173 7396
Fax	+44 (0)20 7173 7800
Email	richard.pryce@ace-ina.com
Website	–

Full Name	Richard Vaughan Pryce
Year of Birth	1959
Professional Qualifications	Information not available

PROFESSIONAL INFORMATION

CURRENT MAJOR POSITIONS/APPOINTMENTS

Executive Director	ACE European Group Limited	2003 –
Executive Director	Ridge Underwriting Agencies Limited	2003 –
Executive Director	Ace Underwriting Agencies Limited	2003 –

PREVIOUS MAJOR POSITIONS/APPOINTMENTS

Information not available

Ken E Randall

Position	Executive Director
Company	Cavell Managing Agency Ltd
Address (Office)	9–13 Fenchurch Buildings
	London EC3M 5HR
Telephone	+44 (0)20 7780 5850
Fax	+44 (0)20 7780 5851
Email	compliance@cavell.co.uk
Website	www.rqih.co.uk

Full Name	Kenneth Edward Randall
Year of Birth	1948
Professional Qualifications	FCCA

PROFESSIONAL INFORMATION

CURRENT MAJOR POSITIONS/APPOINTMENTS

Executive Director	Cavell Managing Agency Ltd	2003 –
Executive Director	Arran Insurance Company Limited	2006 –
Executive Director	Chevanstell Limited	2006 –
Executive Director	R&Q Reinsurance Company (UK) Limited	2006 –

PREVIOUS MAJOR POSITIONS/APPOINTMENTS

Chief Executive	Ludgate Insurance Company Limited	2001 – 2007

Chief Executive	Renaissance Capital Partners Limited	2001 – 2007
Executive Director	Unione Italiana (UK) Reinsurance Company Limited	2001 – 2006
Non–Executive Director	Newmarket Underwriting Ltd	2001 – 2004
Executive Director	Cavell Insurance Company Limited	2002 – 2006
Chief Executive	Cavell Managing Agency Ltd	2003 – 2005
Chief Executive	Arran Insurance Company Limited	2006 – 2007

Andrew (Andy) G Ripley

Position	Non–Executive Director
Company	Duncanson & Holt Syndicate Management Ltd
Address (Office)	40 Dukes Place
	London EC3A 7NH
Telephone	+44 (0)870 402 7278
Fax	+44 (0)870 162 4541
Email	–
Website	–

Full Name	Andrew George Ripley
Year of Birth	1947
Professional Qualifications	Information not available

PROFESSIONAL INFORMATION

CURRENT MAJOR POSITIONS/APPOINTMENTS

| Non–Executive Director | Sportscover Underwriting Ltd | 2008 – |
| Finance Director | Duncanson & Holt Syndicate Management Ltd | 2009 – |

PREVIOUS MAJOR POSITIONS/APPOINTMENTS

| Non–Executive Director | Duncanson & Holt Syndicate Management Ltd | 2001 – 2009 |

Nigel HJ Rogers

Position	Chief Executive Officer
Company	RITC Syndicate Management Ltd
Address (Office)	3rd Floor
	117 Fenchurch Street
	London EC3M 5DY
Telephone	+44 (0)20 7220 8899
Fax	+44 (0)20 7220 8898
Email	ritcwebenquiry@ritcsm.com
Website	www.ritcsm.com

Full Name	Nigel Harold John Rogers
Year of Birth	1949
Professional Qualifications	Information not available

PROFESSIONAL INFORMATION

CURRENT MAJOR POSITIONS/APPOINTMENTS

| Chief Executive | The Underwriter Insurance Company Limited | 2003 – |
| Chief Executive | RITC Syndicate Management Ltd | 2007 – |

PREVIOUS MAJOR POSITIONS/APPOINTMENTS

Non–Executive Director	The Underwriter Insurance Company Limited	2002 – 2003

William Scott

Position	Chief Financial Officer
Company	Capita Managing Agency Limited
Address (Office)	40 Dukes Place
	London EC3A 7NH
Telephone	+44 (0)870 402 7575
Fax	+44 (0)870 162 4566
Email	william.scott@capita.co.uk
Website	www.capitainsuranceservices.co.uk

Full Name	William Scott
Year of Birth	1958
Professional Qualifications	Information not available

PROFESSIONAL INFORMATION

CURRENT MAJOR POSITIONS/APPOINTMENTS

Executive Director	Capita Syndicate Management Limited	2001 –
Executive Director	Capita London Market Services Limited	2006 –
Executive Director	Capita Managing Agency Limited	2008 –

PREVIOUS MAJOR POSITIONS/APPOINTMENTS

Information not available

Timothy Shenton

Position	Executive Director
Company	Capita Managing Agency Limited
Address (Office)	40 Dukes Place
	London EC3A 7NH
Telephone	+44 (0)870 402 7900
Fax	+44 (0)870 162 4566
Email	tim.shenton@capita.co.uk
Website	www.capitainsuranceservices.co.uk

Full Name	Timothy Shenton
Year of Birth	1954
Professional Qualifications	Information not available

PROFESSIONAL INFORMATION

CURRENT MAJOR POSITIONS/APPOINTMENTS

Executive Director	Capita Managing Agency Limited	2004 –
Executive Director	AE Grant (Underwriting Agencies) Ltd	2007 –

PREVIOUS MAJOR POSITIONS/APPOINTMENTS

Information not available

Angus M Sladen

Position	Executive Director
Company	Duncanson & Holt Syndicate Management Ltd
Address (Office)	40 Dukes Place
	London EC3A 7NH
Telephone	+44 (0)870 402 7278
Fax	+44 (0)870 162 4541
Email	–
Website	–

Full Name	Angus Murray Sladen
Year of Birth	1950
Professional Qualifications	Information not available

PROFESSIONAL INFORMATION

CURRENT MAJOR POSITIONS/APPOINTMENTS

Executive Director	Duncanson & Holt Syndicate Management Ltd	2007 –

PREVIOUS MAJOR POSITIONS/APPOINTMENTS

Non–Executive Director	Duncanson & Holt Syndicate Management Ltd	2001 – 2007

Michael G Smith

Position	Non–Executive Director
Company	Cavell Managing Agency Ltd
Address (Office)	9–13 Fenchurch Buildings
	London EC3M 5HR
Telephone	+44 (0)20 7780 5850
Fax	+44 (0)20 7780 5851
Email	compliance@cavell.co.uk
Website	www.rqih.co.uk

Full Name	Michael Gordon Smith
Year of Birth	1945
Professional Qualifications	Information not available

PROFESSIONAL INFORMATION

CURRENT MAJOR POSITIONS/APPOINTMENTS

Non–Executive Director	Cavell Managing Agency Ltd	2004 –
Non–Executive Director	CFC Underwriting Ltd	2005 –

PREVIOUS MAJOR POSITIONS/APPOINTMENTS

Non–Executive Director	Ace Underwriting Agencies Limited	2001 – 2004
Non–Executive Director	ACE London Aviation Limited	2001 – 2002
Non–Executive Director	ACE London Underwriting Limited	2001 – 2002
Non–Executive Director	Heath Lambert Financial Resolutions Limited	2003 – 2004

William L Spiegel

Position	Non–Executive Director
Company	RITC Syndicate Management Ltd
Address (Office)	3rd Floor
	117 Fenchurch Street
	London EC3M 5DY
Telephone	+44 (0)20 7220 8899
Fax	+44 (0)20 7220 8898
Email	ritcwebenquiry@ritcsm.com
Website	www.ritcsm.com
Full Name	William Larry Spiegel
Year of Birth	1962
Professional Qualifications	Information not available

PROFESSIONAL INFORMATION

CURRENT MAJOR POSITIONS/APPOINTMENTS

Non–Executive Director	RITC Syndicate Management Ltd	2007 –

PREVIOUS MAJOR POSITIONS/APPOINTMENTS
Information not available

Eric SC Stobart

Position	Chairman
Company	Capita Managing Agency Limited
Address (Office)	40 Dukes Place
	London EC3A 7NH
Telephone	+44 (0)870 523 4567
Fax	+44 (0)870 162 4566
Email	insurance@capita.co.uk
Website	www.capitainsuranceservices.co.uk
Full Name	Eric St Clair Stobart
Year of Birth	1954
Professional Qualifications	Information not available

PROFESSIONAL INFORMATION

CURRENT MAJOR POSITIONS/APPOINTMENTS

Non–Executive Director	AE Grant (Underwriting Agencies) Ltd	2002 –
Non–Executive Director	Capita Managing Agency Limited	2004 –
Executive Director	Falcon Managers Ltd	2006 –

PREVIOUS MAJOR POSITIONS/APPOINTMENTS
Information not available

Luke R Tanzer

Position	Operations Director
Company	RiverStone Managing Agency Limited

Address (Office)	2nd Floor
	Mint House
	77 Mansell Street
	London E1 8AF
Telephone	+44 (0)20 7977 1600
Fax	+44 (0)20 7977 1687
Email	–
Website	www.rsml.co.uk

Full Name	Luke Robert Tanzer
Year of Birth	1965
Professional Qualifications	Information not available

PROFESSIONAL INFORMATION

CURRENT MAJOR POSITIONS/APPOINTMENTS

Executive Director	Sphere Drake Insurance Limited	2005 –
Executive Director	RiverStone Insurance (UK) Limited	2005 –
Executive Director	RiverStone Managing Agency Limited	2008 –

PREVIOUS MAJOR POSITIONS/APPOINTMENTS
Information not available

John P Tilling

Position	Chairman
Company	Cavell Managing Agency Ltd
Address (Office)	9–13 Fenchurch Buildings
	London EC3M 5HR
Telephone	+44 (0)20 7780 5850
Fax	+44 (0)20 7780 5851
Email	compliance@cavell.co.uk
Website	www.rqih.co.uk

Full Name	John Peter Tilling
Year of Birth	1947
Professional Qualifications	Information not available

PROFESSIONAL INFORMATION

CURRENT MAJOR POSITIONS/APPOINTMENTS

Non–Executive Director	Cathedral Underwriting Limited	2001 –
Non–Executive Director	Cavell Managing Agency Ltd	2004 –

PREVIOUS MAJOR POSITIONS/APPOINTMENTS
Information not available

James A Willsher

Position	Executive Director, Compliance Officer & Company Secretary
Company	Cavell Managing Agency Ltd
Address (Office)	9–13 Fenchurch Buildings
	London EC3M 5HR

Telephone	+44 (0)20 7780 5850
Fax	+44 (0)20 7780 5851
Email	compliance@cavell.co.uk
Website	www.rqih.co.uk

Full Name	James Andrew Willsher
Year of Birth	1973
Professional Qualifications	ACII

PROFESSIONAL INFORMATION

CURRENT MAJOR POSITIONS/APPOINTMENTS

Executive Director	Cavell Management Services Limited	2006 –
Executive Director	Cavell Managing Agency Ltd	2006 –

PREVIOUS MAJOR POSITIONS/APPOINTMENTS

Information not available

Sarah M Wilton

Position	Non–Executive Director
Company	Capita Managing Agency Limited
Address (Office)	40 Dukes Place
	London EC3A 7NH
Telephone	+44 (0)870 523 4567
Fax	+44 (0)870 162 4566
Email	insurance@capita.co.uk
Website	www.capitainsuranceservices.co.uk

Full Name	Sarah Margaret Wilton
Year of Birth	1959
Professional Qualifications	Information not available

PROFESSIONAL INFORMATION

CURRENT MAJOR POSITIONS/APPOINTMENTS

Non–Executive Director	Capita Managing Agency Limited	2004 –
Non–Executive Director	Hampden Agencies Ltd	2008 –

PREVIOUS MAJOR POSITIONS/APPOINTMENTS

Executive Director	Additional Underwriting Agencies (No 2) Limited	2001 – 2003
Executive Director	Lioncover Insurance Company Limited	2002 – 2003

J Nicholas C Wooldridge

Position	Underwriting Director & Run–Off Manager Syndicate 5678
Company	RITC Syndicate Management Ltd
Address (Office)	3rd Floor
	117 Fenchurch Street
	London EC3M 5DY
Telephone	+44 (0)20 7220 8899
Fax	+44 (0)20 7220 8898

Email	ritcwebenquiry@ritcsm.com	
Website	www.ritcsm.com	

Full Name	John Nicholas Copleston Wooldridge	
Year of Birth	1956	
Professional Qualifications	Information not available	

PROFESSIONAL INFORMATION

CURRENT MAJOR POSITIONS/APPOINTMENTS

Executive Director	RITC Syndicate Management Ltd	2007 –

PREVIOUS MAJOR POSITIONS/APPOINTMENTS

Executive Director	Whittington Capital Management Limited	2004 – 2006

Ravi P Yadav

Position	Non–Executive Director
Company	RITC Syndicate Management Ltd
Address (Office)	3rd Floor
	117 Fenchurch Street
	London EC3M 5DY
Telephone	+44 (0)20 7220 8899
Fax	+44 (0)20 7220 8898
Email	ritcwebenquiry@ritcsm.com
Website	www.ritcsm.com

Full Name	Ravi Prakash Yadav
Year of Birth	1968
Professional Qualifications	Information not available

PROFESSIONAL INFORMATION

CURRENT MAJOR POSITIONS/APPOINTMENTS

Non–Executive Director	RITC Syndicate Management Ltd	2007 –

PREVIOUS MAJOR POSITIONS/APPOINTMENTS

	Information not available

Profiles – Members' Agents

Robert FM Adair

Position	Non-Executive Director
Company	ICP General Partner Limited
Address (Office)	Unit C25
	Jack's Place
	6 Corbet Place
	London E1 6NN
Telephone	+44 (0)20 7392 8480
Fax	+44 (0)20 7392 8481
Email	info@inscap.co.uk
Website	www.inscap.co.uk
Full Name	Robert Fredrick Martin Adair
Year of Birth	Information not available
Professional Qualifications	Information not available

PROFESSIONAL INFORMATION

CURRENT MAJOR POSITIONS/APPOINTMENTS

Non-Executive Director	Revera Asset Management Ltd	2005 -
Non-Executive Director	ICP General Partner Limited	2007 -

PREVIOUS MAJOR POSITIONS/APPOINTMENTS

Information not available

Andrew J Annandale

Position	Non-Executive Director
Company	Argenta Private Capital Limited
Address (Office)	Fountain House
	130 Fenchurch Street
	London EC3M 5DJ
Telephone	+44 (0)20 7825 7239
Fax	+44 (0)20 7825 7212
Email	andrew.annandale@argentaplc.com
Website	www.argentaplc.com
Full Name	Andrew John Annandale
Year of Birth	1963
Professional Qualifications	Information not available

PROFESSIONAL INFORMATION

CURRENT MAJOR POSITIONS/APPOINTMENTS

Non-Executive Director	Argenta Private Capital Limited	2008 -
Chief Executive	Argenta Syndicate Management Limited	2008 -

PREVIOUS MAJOR POSITIONS/APPOINTMENTS

Executive Director	Richmond Underwriting Limited	2001 - 2006
Chief Executive	Argenta Private Capital Limited	2001 - 2008
Non-Executive Director	The Stop Loss Mutual Insurance Association Ltd	2002 - 2004

Emily L Apple

Position	Executive Director & Analyst
Company	Alpha Insurance Analysts Ltd
Address (Office)	150 Minories
	London EC3N 1LS
Telephone	+44 (0)20 7264 2146
Fax	+44 (0)20 7264 2134
Email	emily@aianalysts.com
Website	www.aianalysts.com
Full Name	Emily Lisa Apple
Year of Birth	1978
Professional Qualifications	BA

PROFESSIONAL INFORMATION

CURRENT MAJOR POSITIONS/APPOINTMENTS

Executive Director	Alpha Insurance Analysts Ltd	2008 -

PREVIOUS MAJOR POSITIONS/APPOINTMENTS

Information not available

Trevor R Bird

Position	Client Services Director
Company	Argenta Private Capital Limited
Address (Office)	Fountain House
	130 Fenchurch Street
	London EC3M 5DJ
Telephone	+44 (0)20 7825 7131
Fax	+44 (0)20 7825 7212
Email	trevor.bird@argentaplc.com
Website	www.argentaplc.com
Full Name	Trevor Robert Bird
Year of Birth	1955
Professional Qualifications	Information not available

PROFESSIONAL INFORMATION

CURRENT MAJOR POSITIONS/APPOINTMENTS

Executive Director	Argenta Private Capital Limited	2001 -
Executive Director	SLP (Management) Limited	2008 -

PREVIOUS MAJOR POSITIONS/APPOINTMENTS

Executive Director	Richmond Underwriting Limited	2001 - 2006
	Alpha Insurance Analysts Ltd	

Paul E Box

Position	Managing Director
Company	Lloyd's Members Agency Services Limited

Address (Office)	Fidentia House	
	Walter Burke Way	
	Chatham	
	Kent ME4 4RN	
Telephone	+44 (0)1634 392 082	
Fax	+44 (0)1634 392 081	
Email	paul.box@lloyds.com	
Website	www.lmas.co.uk	

Full Name	Paul Ernest Box
Year of Birth	1953
Professional Qualifications	Information not available

PROFESSIONAL INFORMATION

CURRENT MAJOR POSITIONS/APPOINTMENTS

Executive Director	Lloyd's Members Agency Services Limited	2003 -

PREVIOUS MAJOR POSITIONS/APPOINTMENTS

Names Director	Lloyd's Members Agency Services Limited	2000 - 2003

Lord Brabourne

Position	Chairman
Company	Argenta Private Capital Limited
Address (Office)	Fountain House
	130 Fenchurch Street
	London EC3M 5DJ
Telephone	+44 (0)20 7825 7200
Fax	+44 (0)20 7825 7212
Email	privatecapital@argentaplc.com
Website	www.argentaplc.com

Full Name	Lord Norton Louis Philip Brabourne
Year of Birth	1947
Professional Qualifications	BA

PROFESSIONAL INFORMATION

CURRENT MAJOR POSITIONS/APPOINTMENTS

Non-Executive Director	Argenta Private Capital Limited	2001 -
Non-Executive Director	Smartfund Administration Limited	2007 -

PREVIOUS MAJOR POSITIONS/APPOINTMENTS
Information not available

James RV Brandon

Position	Finance Director
Company	ICP General Partner Limited

Address (Office)	Unit C25
	Jack's Place
	6 Corbet Place
	London E1 6NN
Telephone	+44 (0)20 7392 8480
Fax	+44 (0)20 7392 8481
Email	james.brandon@inscap.co.uk
Website	www.inscap.co.uk
PERSONAL PROFILE	A profile can be found in the People at Lloyd's, Personal section.

Jeremy M Bray

Position	Head of Research
Company	Argenta Private Capital Limited
Address (Office)	Fountain House
	130 Fenchurch Street
	London EC3M 5DJ
Telephone	+44 (0)20 7825 7174
Fax	+44 (0)20 7825 7212
Email	jeremy.bray@argentaplc.com
Website	www.argentaplc.com
Full Name	Jeremy Mark Bray
Year of Birth	1957
Professional Qualifications	MA (Hons), ACII, IMC

PROFESSIONAL INFORMATION

CURRENT MAJOR POSITIONS/APPOINTMENTS

Non-Executive Director	The Stop Loss Mutual Insurance Association Ltd	2001 -
Executive Director	Argenta Private Capital Limited	2005 -

PREVIOUS MAJOR POSITIONS/APPOINTMENTS

Executive Director	Anton Members Agency Ltd	2001 - 2002
Executive Director	Anton Private Capital Limited	2001 - 2008

David A Cant

Position	Executive Director & Compliance Officer
Company	Hampden Agencies Ltd
Address (Office)	85 Gracechurch Street
	London EC3V 0AA
Telephone	+44 (0)20 7863 6573
Fax	+44 (0)20 7863 6555
Email	david.cant@hampden.co.uk
Website	www.hampden.co.uk
Full Name	David Anthony Cant
Year of Birth	1954
Professional Qualifications	Information not available

PROFESSIONAL INFORMATION

CURRENT MAJOR POSITIONS/APPOINTMENTS

Executive Director	Hampden Agencies Ltd	2007 -

PREVIOUS MAJOR POSITIONS/APPOINTMENTS

Executive Director	Origen Investment Services Limited	2001 - 2005

Nicholas HD Carrick

Position	Executive Director
Company	Hampden Agencies Ltd
Address (Office)	85 Gracechurch Street
	London EC3V 0AA
Telephone	+44 (0)20 7863 6526
Fax	+44 (0)20 7863 6555
Email	nick.carrick@hampden.co.uk
Website	www.hampden.co.uk

Full Name	Nicholas Henry Debenham Carrick
Year of Birth	1958
Professional Qualifications	Information not available

PROFESSIONAL INFORMATION

CURRENT MAJOR POSITIONS/APPOINTMENTS

Executive Director	Hampden Agencies Ltd	2002 -
Non-Executive Director	Hampden Agencies Ltd	2006 -

PREVIOUS MAJOR POSITIONS/APPOINTMENTS

	Information not available

Christopher JR Fairs

Position	Compliance Director & Company Secretary
Company	Argenta Private Capital Limited
Address (Office)	Fountain House
	130 Fenchurch Street
	London EC3M 5DJ
Telephone	+44 (0)20 7825 7100
Fax	+44 (0)20 7825 7212
Email	chris.fairs@argentaplc.com
Website	www.argentaplc.com

Full Name	Christopher John Rupert Fairs
Year of Birth	1969
Professional Qualifications	Information not available

PROFESSIONAL INFORMATION

CURRENT MAJOR POSITIONS/APPOINTMENTS

Executive Director	Argenta Private Capital Limited	2001 -
Executive Director	SLP (Management) Limited	2005 -

PREVIOUS MAJOR POSITIONS/APPOINTMENTS

Executive Director	Richmond Underwriting Limited	2001 - 2006
Executive Director	Anton Private Capital Limited	2005 - 2008

Robert P Flach

Position	Technical Director
Company	Argenta Private Capital Limited
Address (Office)	Fountain House
	130 Fenchurch Street
	London EC3M 5DJ
Telephone	+44 (0)20 7825 7179
Fax	+44 (0)20 7825 7212
Email	robert.flach@argentaplc.com
Website	www.argentaplc.com

Full Name	Robert Paul Flach
Year of Birth	1967
Professional Qualifications	MBA

PROFESSIONAL INFORMATION

CURRENT MAJOR POSITIONS/APPOINTMENTS

Executive Director	Argenta Private Capital Limited	2005 -

PREVIOUS MAJOR POSITIONS/APPOINTMENTS

Executive Director	Anton Private Capital Limited	2002 - 2008

Nigel J Hanbury

Position	Chairman
Company	Hampden Agencies Ltd
Address (Office)	85 Gracechurch Street
	London EC3V 0AA
Telephone	+44 (0)20 7863 6502
Fax	+44 (0)20 7863 6555
Email	nigel.hanbury@hampden.co.uk
Website	www.hampden.co.uk

PERSONAL PROFILE   A profile can be found in the People at Lloyd's, Personal section.

The Hon Charles AA Harbord-Hamond

Position	Chief Executive Officer
Company	ICP General Partner Limited
Address (Office)	Unit 25
	Jack's Place
	6 Corbet Place
	London E1 6NN
Telephone	+44 (0)20 7392 8480
Fax	+44 (0)20 7392 8481

Email	charles.hh@inscap.co.uk
Website	www.inscap.co.uk

Full Name	Charles Anthony Asheton Harbord-Hamond
Year of Birth	1953
Professional Qualifications	Information not available

PROFESSIONAL INFORMATION

CURRENT MAJOR POSITIONS/APPOINTMENTS

Chief Executive	CBS Private Capital Limited	2001 -
Chief Executive	ICP General Partner Limited	2007 -

PREVIOUS MAJOR POSITIONS/APPOINTMENTS

Chief Executive	ICP General Partner Limited	2001 - 2005
Non-Executive Director	Centrewrite Limited	2001 - 2006
Chief Executive	CBS Services Number 1 Limited	2001 - 2007
Chief Executive	BMA Members Agency Limited	2001 - 2007
Chief Executive	Christie Brockbank Shipton Limited	2001 - 2007
Non-Executive Director	Imagine Syndicate Management Limited	2002 - 2005
Non-Executive Director	Catlin (Wellington) Underwriting Agencies Limited	2002 - 2006

Christopher Hare

Position	Non-Executive Director
Company	Lloyd's Members Agency Services Limited
Address (Office)	Fidentia House
	Walter Burke Way
	Chatham
	Kent ME4 4RN
Telephone	+44 (0)1634 392 090
Fax	+44 (0)1634 392 081
Email	lloyds-lmas@lloyds.com
Website	www.lmas.co.uk

Full Name	Christopher Peter Hare
Year of Birth	1947
Professional Qualifications	Information not available

PROFESSIONAL INFORMATION

CURRENT MAJOR POSITIONS/APPOINTMENTS

Non-Executive Director	Lloyd's Members Agency Services Limited	1998 -
Executive Director	RITC Syndicate Management Ltd	2007 -

PREVIOUS MAJOR POSITIONS/APPOINTMENTS

Members Agent	Hampton Private Capital Ltd.	1985 - 2001
Executive Director	Shelbourne Syndicate Services Ltd	2001 - 2005

David BK Harrison

Position	Non-Executive Director
Company	Argenta Private Capital Limited

Address (Office)	Fountain House
	130 Fenchurch Street
	London EC3M 5DJ
Telephone	+44 (0)20 7825 7200
Fax	+44 (0)20 7825 7212
Email	privatecapital@argentaplc.com
Website	www.argentaplc.com

Full Name	David Bernard Kosta Harrison
Year of Birth	1938
Professional Qualifications	MA, FCA

PROFESSIONAL INFORMATION

CURRENT MAJOR POSITIONS/APPOINTMENTS

Executive Director	Argenta Private Capital Limited	2001 -
Non-Executive Director	Argenta Private Capital Limited	2001 -
Non-Executive Director	Insurancewide.com Services Limited	2005 -
Non-Executive Director	Smartfund Administration Limited	2007 -

PREVIOUS MAJOR POSITIONS/APPOINTMENTS

Information not available

Guy B Hudson

Position	Client Director
Company	Argenta Private Capital Limited
Address (Office)	Fountain House
	130 Fenchurch Street
	London EC3M 5DJ
Telephone	+44 (0)20 7825 7241
Fax	+44 (0)20 7825 7212
Email	guy.hudson@argentaplc.com
Website	www.argentaplc.com

Full Name	Guy Bentley Hudson
Year of Birth	1960
Professional Qualifications	BA (Hons), MSc, ACII, IMC

PROFESSIONAL INFORMATION

CURRENT MAJOR POSITIONS/APPOINTMENTS

Executive Director	Argenta Private Capital Limited	2001 -

PREVIOUS MAJOR POSITIONS/APPOINTMENTS

Executive Director	Richmond Underwriting Limited	2001 - 2006

Angela Kerr

Position	Names Director, Compliance Officer & Company Secretary
Company	Lloyd's Members Agency Services Limited

Address (Office)	Fidentia House
	Walter Burke Way
	Chatham
	Kent ME4 4RN
Telephone	+44 (0)1634 392 083
Fax	+44 (0)1634 392 081
Email	angela.kerr@lloyds.com
Website	www.lmas.co.uk

Full Name	Angela Jeanette Kerr
Year of Birth	1963
Professional Qualifications	Information not available

PROFESSIONAL INFORMATION

CURRENT MAJOR POSITIONS/APPOINTMENTS

Executive Director	Lloyd's Members Agency Services Limited	2003 -

PREVIOUS MAJOR POSITIONS/APPOINTMENTS
Information not available

Nicholas D Lewis

Position	Chief Financial Officer
Company	Hampden Agencies Ltd
Address (Office)	85 Gracechurch Street
	London EC3V 0AA
Telephone	+44 (0)20 7863 6507
Fax	+44 (0)20 7863 6555
Email	nicholas.lewis@hampden.co.uk
Website	www.hampden.co.uk

Full Name	Nicholas David Lewis
Year of Birth	1942
Professional Qualifications	Information not available

PROFESSIONAL INFORMATION

CURRENT MAJOR POSITIONS/APPOINTMENTS

Executive Director	Hampden Agencies Ltd	2001 -

PREVIOUS MAJOR POSITIONS/APPOINTMENTS
Information not available

Alan C Lovell

Position	Non-Executive Director
Company	Alpha Insurance Analysts Ltd
Address (Office)	150 Minories
	London EC3N 1LS
Telephone	+44 (0)20 7264 2133
Fax	+44 (0)20 7264 2134

Email	alan.lovell@aianalysts.com
Website	www.aianalysts.com

Full Name	Alan Charles Lovell
Year of Birth	1953
Professional Qualifications	MA, FCA

PROFESSIONAL INFORMATION

CURRENT MAJOR POSITIONS/APPOINTMENTS

Chairman	Mary Rose Trust Appeal Committee	2006 -
Director	Association of Lloyd's Members	2006 -
External Member	Council of Lloyd's	2007 -
Non-Executive Director	Alpha Insurance Analysts Ltd	2007 -

PREVIOUS MAJOR POSITIONS/APPOINTMENTS

Chief Executive	Conder Group Plc	1989 - 1992
Finance Director	Costain Group Plc	1992 - 1995
Chief Executive	Costain Group Plc	1995 - 1997
Finance Director	Dunlop Slazenger Group Ltd	1997 - 2004
Chief Executive	Dunlop Slazenger Group Ltd	2004 - 2004
Chief Executive	Jarvis Plc	2004 - 2006
Chief Executive	Infinis Limited	2006 - 2009

James A Mackay

Position	New Business Director
Company	Argenta Private Capital Limited
Address (Office)	Fountain House
	130 Fenchurch Street
	London EC3M 5DJ
Telephone	+44 (0)20 7825 7288
Fax	+44 (0)20 7825 7212
Email	james.mackay@argentaplc.com
Website	www.argentaplc.com
PERSONAL PROFILE	A profile can be found in the People at Lloyd's, Personal section.

Lord Marland of Odstock

Position	Non-Executive Director
Company	ICP General Partner Limited
Address (Office)	Unit C25
	Jack's Place
	6 Corbet Place
	London E1 6NN
Telephone	+44 (0)20 7392 8480
Fax	+44 (0)20 7392 8481
Email	info@inscap.co.uk
Website	www.inscap.co.uk
PERSONAL PROFILE	A profile can be found in the People at Lloyd's, Personal section.

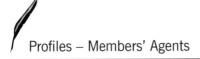

Michael J Meacock

Position	Non-Executive Director
Company	Alpha Insurance Analysts Ltd
Address (Office)	150 Minories
	London EC3N 1LS
Telephone	+44 (0)20 7264 2133
Fax	+44 (0)20 7264 2134
Email	michael.meacock@sameacock.com
Website	www.aianalysts.com
PERSONAL PROFILE	A profile can be found in the People at Lloyd's, Personal section.

David Monksfield

Position	Head of Client Management
Company	Argenta Private Capital Limited
Address (Office)	Fountain House
	130 Fenchurch Street
	London EC3M 5DJ
Telephone	+44 (0)20 7825 7139
Fax	+44 (0)20 7825 7212
Email	david.monksfield@argentaplc.com
Website	www.argentaplc.com
Full Name	David Monksfield
Year of Birth	1952
Professional Qualifications	Information not available

PROFESSIONAL INFORMATION

CURRENT MAJOR POSITIONS/APPOINTMENTS

Executive Director	Argenta Private Capital Limited	2001 -
Non-Executive Director	The Stop Loss Mutual Insurance Association Ltd	2004 -

PREVIOUS MAJOR POSITIONS/APPOINTMENTS

Executive Director	Richmond Underwriting Limited	2001 - 2006

Charles GC Oliver

Position	Executive Director
Company	Hampden Agencies Ltd
Address (Office)	85 Gracechurch Street
	London EC3V 0AA
Telephone	+44 (0)20 7863 6621
Fax	+44 (0)20 7863 6555
Email	charles.oliver@hampden.co.uk
Website	www.hampden.co.uk
Full Name	Charles Guy Camroux Oliver
Year of Birth	1970
Professional Qualifications	Information not available

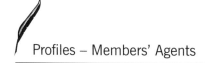

PROFESSIONAL INFORMATION

CURRENT MAJOR POSITIONS/APPOINTMENTS

Executive Director	Hampden Agencies Ltd	2008 -

PREVIOUS MAJOR POSITIONS/APPOINTMENTS

Information not available

WS Clive Richards, OBE

Position	Chairman
Company	Alpha Insurance Analysts Ltd
Address (Office)	150 Minories
	London EC3N 1LS
Telephone	+44 (0)20 7264 2133
Fax	+44 (0)20 7264 2134
Email	cr@crco.co.uk
Website	www.aianalysts.com

Full Name	William Samuel Clive Richards, OBE
Year of Birth	1937
Professional Qualifications	FCA

PROFESSIONAL INFORMATION

CURRENT MAJOR POSITIONS/APPOINTMENTS

Non-Executive Director	Alpha Insurance Analysts Ltd	2007 -

PREVIOUS MAJOR POSITIONS/APPOINTMENTS

Information not available

Sir Adam N Ridley

Position	Non-Executive Director
Company	Hampden Agencies Ltd
Address (Office)	85 Gracechurch Street
	London EC3V 0AA
Telephone	+44 (0)20 7863 6500
Fax	+44 (0)20 7863 6555
Email	adam.ridley@hampden.co.uk
Website	www.hampden.co.uk

PERSONAL PROFILE	A profile can be found in the People at Lloyd's, Personal section.

W David Robson

Position	Client Director
Company	Argenta Private Capital Limited
Address (Office)	Fountain House
	130 Fenchurch Street
	London EC3M 5DJ
Telephone	+44 (0)20 7825 7139
Fax	+44 (0)20 7825 7212

| Email | david.robson@argentaplc.com |
| Website | www.argentaplc.com |

Full Name	William David Robson
Year of Birth	1944
Professional Qualifications	Information not available

PROFESSIONAL INFORMATION

CURRENT MAJOR POSITIONS/APPOINTMENTS

| Chief Executive | SLP (Management) Limited | 2001 - |
| Executive Director | Argenta Private Capital Limited | 2005 - |

PREVIOUS MAJOR POSITIONS/APPOINTMENTS

Executive Director	Anton Members Agency Ltd	2001 - 2002
External Member	Council of Lloyd's	2001 - 2004
Chief Executive	Anton Private Capital Limited	2001 - 2008

Emma Royds

Position	Executive Director
Company	Alpha Insurance Analysts Ltd
Address (Office)	150 Minories
	London EC3N 1LS
Telephone	+44 (0)20 7264 2132
Fax	+44 (0)20 7264 2134
Email	emma@aianalysts.com
Website	www.aianalysts.com

Full Name	Emma Royds
Year of Birth	1961
Professional Qualifications	BA, ACII

PROFESSIONAL INFORMATION

CURRENT MAJOR POSITIONS/APPOINTMENTS

| Executive Director | Alpha Insurance Analysts Ltd | 2007 - |

PREVIOUS MAJOR POSITIONS/APPOINTMENTS

Non-Executive Director	Imagine Syndicate Management Limited	2001 - 2005
Executive Director	CBS Private Capital Limited	2001 - 2006
Executive Director	ICP General Partner Limited	2005 - 2007

Paul F Sandilands

Position	Non-Executive Director
Company	Argenta Private Capital Limited
Address (Office)	Fountain House
	130 Fenchurch Street
	London EC3M 5DJ
Telephone	+44 (0)20 7825 7200
Fax	+44 (0)20 7825 7212

Email	paul.sandilands@argentaplc.com
Website	www.argentaplc.com

PERSONAL PROFILE   A profile can be found in the People at Lloyd's, Personal section.

Luke Savage

Position	Non-Executive Director
Company	Lloyd's Members Agency Services Limited
Address (Office)	Fidentia House
	Walter Burke Way
	Chatham
	Kent ME4 4RN
Telephone	+44 (0)1634 392 082
Fax	+44 (0)1634 392 081
Email	lloyds-lmas@lloyds.com
Website	www.lmas.co.uk

PERSONAL PROFILE   A profile can be found in the Corporation section.

A James Sparrow

Position	Managing Director
Company	Alpha Insurance Analysts Ltd
Address (Office)	150 Minories
	London EC3N 1LS
Telephone	+44 (0)20 7264 2148
Fax	+44 (0)20 7264 2134
Email	james@aianalysts.com
Website	www.aianalysts.com

Full Name	Andrew James Sparrow
Year of Birth	1954
Professional Qualifications	ACII

PROFESSIONAL INFORMATION

CURRENT MAJOR POSITIONS/APPOINTMENTS

Managing Director	Alpha Insurance Analysts Ltd	2007 -
Chief Executive	Alpha Insurance Analysts Ltd	2007 -

PREVIOUS MAJOR POSITIONS/APPOINTMENTS

Executive Director	CBS Private Capital Limited	2001 - 2006
Executive Director	ICP General Partner Limited	2005 - 2006

Neil LC Smith

Position	Chief Executive Officer
Company	Hampden Agencies Ltd
Address (Office)	85 Gracechurch Street
	London EC3V 0AA
Telephone	+44 (0)20 7863 6562

Fax	+44 (0)20 7863 6555
Email	neil.smith@hampden.co.uk
Website	www.hampden.co.uk

Full Name	Neil Leslie Crawford Smith
Year of Birth	1960
Professional Qualifications	Information not available

PROFESSIONAL INFORMATION

CURRENT MAJOR POSITIONS/APPOINTMENTS

Chief Executive	Hampden Agencies Ltd	2008 -

PREVIOUS MAJOR POSITIONS/APPOINTMENTS

Executive Director	CBS Private Capital Limited	2001 - 2006
Non-Executive Director	Lloyd's Members Agency Services Ltd	2002 - 2002

Lord Strathclyde

Position	Non-Executive Director
Company	Hampden Agencies Ltd
Address (Office)	85 Gracechurch Street
	London EC3V 0AA
Telephone	+44 (0)20 7863 6500
Fax	+44 (0)20 7863 6555
Email	hal@hampden.co.uk
Website	www.hampden.co.uk

Full Name	Lord Thomas Dunlop Galloway De Roy De Blicquy Galbraith Strathclyde
Year of Birth	1960
Professional Qualifications	Information not available

PROFESSIONAL INFORMATION

CURRENT MAJOR POSITIONS/APPOINTMENTS

Non-Executive Director	Galena Asset Management Limited	2004 -
Non-Executive Director	Hampden Agencies Ltd	2008 -

PREVIOUS MAJOR POSITIONS/APPOINTMENTS

Non-Executive Director	Trafalgar Capital Management Limited	2001 - 2005

Mark J Tottman

Position	Chief Operating Officer
Company	Hampden Agencies Ltd
Address (Office)	85 Gracechurch Street
	London EC3V 0AA
Telephone	+44 (0)20 7863 6504
Fax	+44 (0)20 7863 6555
Email	mark.tottman@hampden.co.uk
Website	www.hampden.co.uk

Full Name	Mark John Tottman
Year of Birth	1964
Professional Qualifications	Information not available

PROFESSIONAL INFORMATION

CURRENT MAJOR POSITIONS/APPOINTMENTS

Executive Director	Hampden Agencies Ltd	2001 -

PREVIOUS MAJOR POSITIONS/APPOINTMENTS

Information not available

Alan W Tucker

Position	Client Director
Company	Argenta Private Capital Limited
Address (Office)	Fountain House
	130 Fenchurch Street
	London EC3M 5DJ
Telephone	+44 (0)20 7825 7135
Fax	+44 (0)20 7825 7212
Email	alan.tucker@argentaplc.com
Website	www.argentaplc.com

Full Name	Alan William Tucker
Year of Birth	1948
Professional Qualifications	Information not available

PROFESSIONAL INFORMATION

CURRENT MAJOR POSITIONS/APPOINTMENTS

Executive Director	Argenta Private Capital Limited	2001 -
Non-Executive Director	Argenta Syndicate Management Limited	2004 -
Executive Director	SLP (Management) Limited	2008 -

PREVIOUS MAJOR POSITIONS/APPOINTMENTS

Information not available

Marcus G Warner

Position	Finance Director
Company	Argenta Private Capital Limited
Address (Office)	Fountain House
	130 Fenchurch Street
	London EC3M 5DJ
Telephone	+44 (0)20 7825 7262
Fax	+44 (0)20 7825 7212
Email	marcus.warner@argentaplc.com
Website	www.argentaplc.com

Full Name	Marcus Gary Warner
Year of Birth	1973
Professional Qualifications	BA (Hons), ACMA, IMC

PROFESSIONAL INFORMATION

CURRENT MAJOR POSITIONS/APPOINTMENTS

Executive Director	Argenta Private Capital Limited	2003 -

PREVIOUS MAJOR POSITIONS/APPOINTMENTS
Information not available

Graham J White

Position	Managing Director
Company	Argenta Private Capital Limited
Address (Office)	Fountain House
	130 Fenchurch Street
	London EC3M 5DJ
Telephone	+44 (0)20 7825 7182
Fax	+44 (0)20 7825 7212
Email	graham.white@argentaplc.com
Website	www.argentaplc.com

Position	Non-Executive Director
Company	Lloyd's Members Agency Services Limited
Address (Office)	Fidentia House
	Walter Burke Way
	Chatham
	Kent ME4 4RN
Telephone	+44 (0)1634 392 082
Fax	+44 (0)1634 392 081
Email	lloyds-lmas@lloyds.com
Website	www.lmas.co.uk

PERSONAL PROFILE	A profile can be found in the People at Lloyd's, Personal section.

Stephen M Wilcox

Position	Executive Director
Company	Hampden Agencies Ltd
Address (Office)	85 Gracechurch Street
	London EC3V 0AA
Telephone	+44 (0)20 7863 6530
Fax	+44 (0)20 7863 6555
Email	stephen.wilcox@hampden.co.uk
Website	www.hampden.co.uk

Full Name	Stephen Mark Wilcox
Year of Birth	1954
Professional Qualifications	Information not available

PROFESSIONAL INFORMATION

CURRENT MAJOR POSITIONS/APPOINTMENTS

Non-Executive Director	The Stop Loss Mutual Insurance Association Ltd	2001 -
Executive Director	Hampden Agencies Ltd	2002 -

Information not available

Sarah M Wilton

Position	Non-Executive Director
Company	Hampden Agencies Ltd
Address (Office)	85 Gracechurch Street
	London EC3V 0AA
Telephone	+44 (0)20 7863 6500
Fax	+44 (0)20 7863 6555
Email	sarah.wilton@hampden.co.uk
Website	www.hampden.co.uk

Full Name	Sarah Margaret Wilton
Year of Birth	1959
Professional Qualifications	Information not available

PROFESSIONAL INFORMATION

CURRENT MAJOR POSITIONS/APPOINTMENTS

Non-Executive Director	Capita Managing Agency Limited	2004 -
Non-Executive Director	Hampden Agencies Ltd	2008 -

PREVIOUS MAJOR POSITIONS/APPOINTMENTS

Executive Director	Additional Underwriting Agencies (No 2) Limited	2001 - 2003
Executive Director	Lioncover Insurance Company Limited	2002 - 2003

Francis Edward (Jock) Worsley, OBE

Position	Chairman
Company	Lloyd's Members Agency Services Limited
Address (Office)	Fidentia House
	Walter Burke Way
	Chatham
	Kent ME4 4RN
Telephone	+44 (0)1634 392 090
Fax	+44 (0)1634 392 081
Email	lloyds-lmas@lloyds.com
Website	www.lmas.co.uk

Full Name	Francis Edward Worsley, OBE
Year of Birth	1941
Professional Qualifications	FCA

PROFESSIONAL INFORMATION

CURRENT MAJOR POSITIONS/APPOINTMENTS

Non-Executive Director	Lloyd's Members Agency Services Limited	1994 -
Non-Executive Director	Brewin Dolphin Ltd	2007 -

PREVIOUS MAJOR POSITIONS/APPOINTMENTS

Founder & Chairman	Financial Training Company Ltd	1972 - 1993

President	Institute of Chartered Accountants in England and Wales	1989 - 1989
Non-Executive Director	Court Holdings Ltd	1989 - 1994
Independent Complaints Commisioner	Financial Services Authorities	Unknown - 2001
Member	Building Societies Commission	Unknown - 2001
Deputy Chairman	LAUTRO	Unknown
Non-Executive Director	Cleveland Trust Plc	Unknown
Chairman	Cancer Research Campaign	1998 - 2002

Listings – Managing Agents

Chairmen & Deputy Chairmen

Ace Underwriting Agencies Ltd	Andrew J Kendrick	+44 (0)20 7173 7000	andrew.kendrick@ace-ina.com
Advent Underwriting Ltd	Peter WJ Cresswell	+44 (0)20 7743 8200	head.office@adventgroup.co.uk
AEGIS Managing Agency Ltd	Alan J Maguire	+44 (0)20 7265 2100	amaguire@aegislondon.co.uk
Amlin Underwriting Ltd	Roger J Taylor	+44 (0)20 7746 1000	roger.taylor@amlin.co.uk
Argenta Syndicate Management Ltd	John LP Whiter	+44 (0)20 7825 7200	john.whiter@argentaplc.com
Argo Managing Agency Ltd	David H Spiller	+44 (0)20 7712 7600	belinda.rose@argo-int.com
Ark Syndicate Management Ltd	William A Malloy	+44 (0)20 3023 4020	enquiries@arkunderwriting.com
Ascot Underwriting Ltd	Sir Richard B Dearlove	+44 (0)20 7743 9600	enquiries@ascotuw.com
Aspen Managing Agency Ltd	Heidi E Hutter	+44 (0)20 7184 8000	heidihutter.theboard@aspen.bm
Atrium Underwriters Ltd	George F Rivaz	+44 (0)20 7327 4877	info@atrium-uw.com
Beaufort Underwriting Agency Ltd	Richard G Carter	+44 (0)20 7220 8200	info@beaufort-group.com
Beazley Furlonge Ltd	Jonathan GW Agnew	+44 (0)20 7667 0623	jonathan.agnew@beazley.com
Brit Syndicates Ltd	R John O Barton	+44 (0)20 7984 8500	john.barton@britinsurance.com
Canopius Managing Agents Ltd	Michael C Watson	+44 (0)20 7337 3730	michael.watson@canopius.com
Cathedral Underwriting Ltd	Anthony IG South	+44 (0)20 7170 9021	tony.south@cathedralcapital.com
Catlin Underwriting Agencies Ltd	Stephen JO Catlin	+44 (0)20 7626 0486	stephen.catlin@catlin.com
Chaucer Syndicates Ltd	Ewen H Gilmour	+44 (0)20 7397 9700	ewen.gilmour@chaucerplc.com
Equity Syndicate Management Ltd	David J Pye	+44 (0)1277 200 100	info@equitygroup.co.uk
Faraday Underwriting Ltd	Lord Ashton of Hyde	+44 (0)20 7680 4239	henry.ashton@faraday.com
Hardy (Underwriting Agencies) Ltd	David P Mann	+44 (0)20 7626 0382	david.mann@hardygroup.co.uk
HCC Underwriting Agency Ltd	John H Bishop	+44 (0)20 7680 3000	info@hccual.com
Hiscox Syndicates Ltd	Robert RS Hiscox	+44 (0)20 7448 6000	robert.hiscox@hiscox.com
Jubilee Managing Agency Ltd	Lord Marland of Odstock	+44 (0)20 7220 8728	jubilee@jubilee-insurance.com
KGM Underwriting Agencies Ltd	Nicolas G Poole	+44 (0)20 8530 1813	nic.poole@kgminsurance.co.uk
Liberty Syndicate Management Ltd	Brian A FitzGerald	+44 (0)20 7070 4472	info@libertysyndicates.com
Managing Agency Partners Ltd	David ES Shipley	+44 (0)20 7709 3860	dshipley@mapunderwriting.co.uk
Markel Syndicate Management Ltd	Simon R Arnold	+44 (0)20 7953 6000	simon.arnold@markelintl.com
Marketform Managing Agency Ltd	Robin AG Jackson	+44 (0)20 7488 7762	robin.jackson@marketform.com
Marlborough Underwriting Agency Ltd	Mark J Byrne	+44 (0)20 7456 1800	compliance@marlborough.co.uk
Max at Lloyd's Ltd	W Marston Becker	+44 (0)20 3102 3100	william.becker@maxatlloyds.com
Mitsui Sumitomo Insurance Underwriting at Lloyd's Ltd	J Maxwell P Taylor	+44 (0)20 7977 8321	enquiries@msilm.com
Montpelier Underwriting Agencies Ltd	Thomas GS Busher	+44 (0)20 7648 4500	tom.busher@montpelierre.bm
Munich Re Underwriting Ltd	John H Rochman	+44 (0)20 7886 3900	john.rochman@mrunderwriting.com
Navigators Underwriting Agency Ltd	Henry JM Blakeney	+44 (0)20 7220 6900	hblakeney@navg.com
Newline Underwriting Management Ltd	Andrew A Barnard	+44 (0)20 7090 1700	abarnard@odysseyre.com
Novae Syndicates Ltd	Allan M Nichols	+44 (0)20 7903 7300	anichols@novae.com
Omega Underwriting Agents Ltd	Roger B Morgan	+44 (0)20 7767 3000	info@omegauw.com
Pembroke Managing Agency Ltd	Robert J Wallace	+44 (0)20 7337 4400	hq@pembrokeunderwriting.com
QBE Underwriting Ltd	Francis M O'Halloran	+44 (0)20 7105 4000	enquiries@uk.qbe.com
R J Kiln & Co Limited	Edward G Creasy	+44 (0)20 7886 9000	See R J Kiln & Co Ltd Company Profile
SA Meacock & Company Ltd	Sir David Thomson	+44 (0)20 7374 6727	linda.mailoudi@sameacock.com
Sagicor at Lloyd's Ltd	Dodridge D Miller	+44 (0)20 3003 6800	duncan.reed@sagicor.eu
Spectrum Syndicate Management Ltd	John R Hustler	+44 (0)20 7283 2646	john.hustler@btconnect.com
Sportscover Underwriting Ltd	Robert J Wallace	+44 (0)20 7398 4080	dominic.ford@sportscover.com
Starr Managing Agents Ltd	Nicholas CT Pawson	+44 (0)20 7337 3550	nicholas.pawson@cvstarrco.com
Talbot Underwriting Ltd	Michael EA Carpenter	+44 (0)20 7550 3500	michael.carpenter@talbotuw.com
Travelers Syndicate Management Ltd	Barnabas J Hurst-Bannister	+44 (0)20 3207 6000	bhurstba@travelers.com
Whittington Capital Management Ltd	Thomas A Riddell	+44 (0)20 7743 0900	jon.francis@whittingtoninsurance.com
XL London Market Ltd	Philip O Sheridan	+44 (0)20 7933 7000	info@xlgroup.com

Deputy Chairmen

Argenta Syndicate Management Ltd	Graham J White	+44 (0)20 7825 7182	graham.white@argentaplc.com
Beazley Furlonge Ltd	Andrew F Beazley	+44 (0)20 7667 0623	andrew.beazley@beazley.com
Catlin Underwriting Agencies Ltd	Paul A Jardine	+44 (0)20 7626 0486	paul.jardine@catlin.com
Jubilee Managing Agency Ltd	Theodore TM Agnew	+44 (0)20 7220 8728	theodore.agnew@jubilee-insurance.com
QBE Underwriting Ltd	Vincent McLenaghan	+44 (0)20 7105 4000	enquiries@uk.qbe.com
Spectrum Syndicate Management Ltd	Michael J Wells	+44 (0)20 7283 2646	mike.wells@spectrumins.com

Chief Executive Officers/Managing Directors & Deputy Managing Directors

Ace Underwriting Agencies Ltd	Andrew J Kendrick	+44 (0)20 7173 7000	andrew.kendrick@ace-ina.com
Advent Underwriting Ltd	Keith D Thompson	+44 (0)20 7743 8200	keith.thompson@adventgroup.co.uk
AEGIS Managing Agency Ltd	Stuart R Davies	+44 (0)20 7265 2152	sdavies@aegislondon.co.uk
Amlin Underwriting Ltd	David J Harris	+44 (0)20 7746 1000	david.harris@amlin.co.uk
Argenta Syndicate Management Ltd	Andrew J Annandale	+44 (0)20 7825 7239	andrew.annandale@argentaplc.com
Argo Managing Agency Ltd	Julian Enoizi	+44 (0)20 7712 7600	julian.enoizi@argo-int.com
Ark Syndicate Management Ltd	Ian E Beaton	+44 (0)20 3023 4001	ian.beaton@arkunderwriting.com
Ascot Underwriting Ltd	Andrew L Brooks	+44 (0)20 7743 9600	enquiries@ascotuw.com
Aspen Managing Agency Ltd	Karen A Green	+44 (0)20 7184 8000	robert.long@aspen-re.com
Atrium Underwriters Ltd	Steven J Cook	+44 (0)20 7327 4877	info@atrium-uw.com
Beaufort Underwriting Agency Ltd	Andrew S Dawe	+44 (0)20 7220 8200	andrew.dawe@beaufort-group.com
Beazley Furlonge Ltd	David A Horton	+44 (0)20 7667 0623	andrew.horton@beazley.com
Brit Syndicates Ltd	Dane J Douetil	+44 (0)20 7984 8500	dane.douetil@britinsurance.com
Canopius Managing Agents Ltd	Clive A Watson	+44 (0)20 7337 3720	clive.watson@canopius.com
Cathedral Underwriting Ltd	Lawrence A Holder	+44 (0)20 7170 9022	lawrence.holder@cathedralcapital.com
Catlin Underwriting Agencies Ltd	David CB Ibeson	+44 (0)20 7626 0486	david.ibeson@catlin.com
Chaucer Syndicates Ltd	Robert Stuchbery	+44 (0)20 7397 9700	robert.stuchbery@chaucerplc.com
Equity Syndicate Management Ltd	Neil A Utley	+44 (0)1277 200 100	neil.utley@equitygroup.co.uk
Faraday Underwriting Ltd	Lord Ashton of Hyde	+44 (0)20 7680 4239	henry.ashton@faraday.com
Hardy (Underwriting Agencies) Ltd	Barbara J Merry	+44 (0)20 7626 0382	barbara.merry@hardygroup.co.uk
HCC Underwriting Agency Ltd	Nicholas I Hutton-Penman	+44 (0)20 7680 3000	info@hccual.com
Hiscox Syndicates Ltd	Bronislaw E Masojada	+44 (0)20 7448 6000	bronek.masojada@hiscox.com
Jubilee Managing Agency Ltd	Andreas C Loucaides	+44 (0)20 7220 8728	andreas.loucaides@jubilee-insurance.com
Jubilee Managing Agency Ltd	Kathryn J Lewis	+44 (0)20 7220 8728	kate.lewis@jubilee-insurance.com
KGM Underwriting Agencies Ltd	Colin Hart	+44 (0)20 8530 1816	colin.hart@kgminsurance.co.uk
Liberty Syndicate Management Ltd	Nicholas J Metcalf	+44 (0)20 7070 4472	info@libertysyndicates.com
Managing Agency Partners Ltd	James D Denoon Duncan	+44 (0)20 7709 3862	jdenoonduncan@mapunderwriting.co.uk
Markel Syndicate Management Ltd	William D Stovin	+44 (0)20 7953 6000	william.stovin@markelintl.com
Marketform Managing Agency Ltd	Karen Sinden	+44 (0)20 7488 7700	karen.sinden@marketform.com
Marlborough Underwriting Agency Ltd	Thomas A Bolt	+44 (0)20 7456 1800	thomas.bolt@marlborough.co.uk
Max at Lloyd's Ltd	Iain J Bremner	+44 (0)20 3102 3100	iain.bremner@maxatlloyds.com
Mitsui Sumitomo Insurance Underwriting at Lloyd's Ltd	Andrew McKee	+44 (0)20 7977 8330	amckee@msilm.com
Montpelier Underwriting Agencies Ltd	Giuseppe Perdoni	+44 (0)20 7648 4517	joe.perdoni@montpelierua.com
Munich Re Underwriting Ltd	Roderic WR Grande	+44 (0)20 7886 3900	rod.grande@mrunderwriting.com
Navigators Underwriting Agency Ltd	Paul V Hennessy	+44 (0)20 7220 6900	phennessy@navg.com
Newline Underwriting Management Ltd	Carl A Overy	+44 (0)20 7090 1700	covery@newlineuml.com
Novae Syndicates Ltd	Jeremy R Adams	+44 (0)20 7903 7300	jadams@novae.com
Omega Underwriting Agents Ltd	Andrew J Adie	+44 (0)20 7767 3000	andrew.adie@omegauw.com
Pembroke Managing Agency Ltd	Mark C Butterworth	+44 (0)20 7337 4400	mark.butterworth@pembrokeunderwriting.com
QBE Underwriting Ltd	Steven P Burns	+44 (0)20 7105 4000	enquiries@uk.qbe.com
R J Kiln & Co Limited	Charles AS Franks	+44 (0)20 7886 9000	See R J Kiln & Co Ltd Company Profile
SA Meacock & Company Ltd	David A Thorp	+44 (0)20 7374 6727	david.thorp@sameacock.com
Sagicor at Lloyd's Ltd	Geoffrey M Halpin	+44 (0)20 3003 6800	geoffrey.halpin@sagicor.eu
Spectrum Syndicate Management Ltd	Richard J Murphy	+44 (0)20 7283 2646	richard.murphy@spectrumins.com
Sportscover Underwriting Ltd	Matthew S Riley	+44 (0)20 7398 4080	matthew.riley@sportscover.com
Starr Managing Agents Ltd	Steven G Blakey	+44 (0)20 7337 3550	steven.blakey@cvstarrco.com
Talbot Underwriting Ltd	CN Rupert Atkin	+44 (0)20 7550 3500	rupert.atkin@talbotuw.com
Travelers Syndicate Management Ltd	Martin P Hudson	+44 (0)20 3207 6000	mphudson@travelers.com
Whittington Capital Management Ltd	Stephen P Cane	+44 (0)20 7743 0900	stephen.cane@whittingtoninsurance.com
XL London Market Ltd	tba	+44 (0)20 7933 7000	info@xlgroup.com

Deputy Managing Directors

Marlborough Underwriting Agency Ltd	Dominic J Kirby	+44 (0)20 7456 1800	dominic.kirby@marlborough.co.uk

Chief Financial Officers/Finance Directors

Ace Underwriting Agencies Ltd	Philippa M Curtis	+44 (0)20 7173 7711	philippa.curtis@ace-ina.com
Advent Underwriting Ltd	Philip J Green	+44 (0)20 7743 8234	phil.green@adventgroup.co.uk
AEGIS Managing Agency Ltd	Paul P Guiry	+44 (0)20 7265 2108	pguiry@aegislondon.co.uk
Amlin Underwriting Ltd	Steven R McMurray	+44 (0)20 7746 1000	steven.mcmurray@amlin.co.uk
Argenta Syndicate Management Ltd	Graham K Allen	+44 (0)20 7825 7243	graham.allen@argentaplc.com
Argo Managing Agency Ltd	Nicholas GA Denniston	+44 (0)20 7712 7600	nick.denniston@argo-int.com
Ark Syndicate Management Ltd	Neil M Smith	+44 (0)20 3023 4020	neil.smith@arkunderwriting.com
	Paul CF Caprez	+44 (0)20 3023 4020	paul.caprez@arkunderwriting.com
Ascot Underwriting Ltd	Robert WE Dimsey	+44 (0)20 7743 9600	enquiries@ascotuw.com
Aspen Managing Agency Ltd	Christopher PJ O'Brien	+44 (0)20 7184 8000	robert.long@aspen-re.com
Atrium Underwriters Ltd	Andrew M Baddeley	+44 (0)20 7327 4877	info@atrium-uw.com
Beaufort Underwriting Agency Ltd	Graham M Tuck	+44 (0)20 7220 8200	graham.tuck@beaufort-group.com
Beazley Furlonge Ltd	Martin Bride	+44 (0)20 7667 0623	martin.bride@beazley.com
Brit Syndicates Ltd	Matthew Scales	+44 (0)20 7984 8500	matthew.scales@britinsurance.com
Canopius Managing Agents Ltd	Stephen J Muggeridge	+44 (0)20 7337 3770	stephen.muggeridge@canopius.com
Cathedral Underwriting Ltd	John A Lynch	+44 (0)20 7170 9024	john.lynch@cathedralcapital.com
Catlin Underwriting Agencies Ltd	Neil A Freshwater	+44 (0)20 7626 0486	neil.freshwater@catlin.com
Chaucer Syndicates Ltd	Kenneth D Curtis	+44 (0)20 7397 9700	ken.curtis@chaucerplc.com
Equity Syndicate Management Ltd	Douglas M Morgan	+44 (0)1277 200 100	douglas.morgan@equitygroup.co.uk
Faraday Underwriting Ltd	Mark Lowton	+44 (0)20 7426 6010	mark.lowton@genre.com
Hardy (Underwriting Agencies) Ltd	James D MacDiarmid	+44 (0)20 7626 0382	jamie.macdiarmid@hardygroup.co.uk
HCC Underwriting Agency Ltd	William J Taylor	+44 (0)20 7680 3000	wtaylor@hccual.com
Hiscox Syndicates Ltd	Ian J Martin	+44 (0)20 7448 6000	ian.martin@hiscox.com
Jubilee Managing Agency Ltd	Darren James Hogg	+44 (0)20 7220 8728	jubilee@jubilee-insurance.com
KGM Underwriting Agencies Ltd	David C Wardle	+44 (0)20 8530 1831	david.wardle@kgminsurance.co.uk
Liberty Syndicate Management Ltd	John AR Dunn	+44 (0)20 7070 4472	info@libertysyndicates.com
Managing Agency Partners Ltd	Richard J Sumner	+44 (0)20 7709 3866	rsumner@mapunderwriting.co.uk
Markel Syndicate Management Ltd	Andrew J Davies	+44 (0)20 7953 6000	andy.davies@markelintl.com
Marketform Managing Agency Ltd	Roger A Doubtfire	+44 (0)20 7488 7730	roger.doubtfire@marketform.com
Marlborough Underwriting Agency Ltd	Paul A Chubb	+44 (0)20 7456 1800	paul.chubb@marlborough.co.uk
Max at Lloyd's Ltd	Lance J Gibbins	+44 (0)20 3102 3100	lance.gibbins@maxatlloyds.com
Mitsui Sumitomo Insurance Underwriting at Lloyd's Ltd	Colin D Charles	+44 (0)20 7977 8374	ccharles@msilm.com
Montpelier Underwriting Agencies Ltd	Michael S Paquette	+44 (0)20 7648 4500	mike.paquette@montpeliertr.com
Munich Re Underwriting Ltd	Nicholas JT Gray	+44 (0)20 7886 3900	nick.gray@mrunderwriting.com
Navigators Underwriting Agency Ltd	Tracey O Lillington	+44 (0)20 7220 6900	tlillington@navg.com
Newline Underwriting Management Ltd	Paul Clayden	+44 (0)20 7090 1700	pclayden@newlineuml.com
Novae Syndicates Ltd	Mark A Hudson	+44 (0)20 7903 7300	mhudson@novae.com
Omega Underwriting Agents Ltd	Jeremy B Raishbrook	+44 (0)20 7767 3000	jeremy.raishbrook@omegauw.com
Pembroke Managing Agency Ltd	Justin AS Wash	+44 (0)20 7337 4400	justin.wash@pembrokeunderwriting.com
QBE Underwriting Ltd	David J Winkett	+44 (0)20 7105 4000	enquiries@uk.qbe.com
R J Kiln & Co Limited	James W Dover	+44 (0)20 7886 9000	See R J Kiln & Co Ltd Company Profile
SA Meacock & Company Ltd	Nicholas NS Ford	+44 (0)20 7374 6727	nicholas.ford@sameacock.com
Sagicor at Lloyd's Ltd	Histasp A Contractor	+44 (0)20 3003 6800	histasp.contractor@sagicor.eu
Spectrum Syndicate Management Ltd	David B Yandell	+44 (0)20 7283 2646	david.yandell@spectrumins.com
Sportscover Underwriting Ltd	Belinda J Taylor	+44 (0)20 7398 4080	belinda.taylor@sportscover.com
Starr Managing Agents Ltd	Michael Toran	+44 (0)20 7337 3550	michael.toran@cvstarrco.com
Talbot Underwriting Ltd	Nigel D Wachman	+44 (0)20 7550 3500	nigel.wachman@talbotuw.com
Travelers Syndicate Management Ltd	Michael J Gent	+44 (0)20 3207 6330	mgent@travelers.com
	Sonny Kapur	+44 (0)20 3207 6101	skapur@travelers.com
Whittington Capital Management Ltd	Anthony JR Gordon	+44 (0)20 7743 0900	anthony.gordon@whittingtoninsurance.com
XL London Market Ltd	Simon C Barrett	+44 (0)20 7933 7000	simon.barrett@xlgroup.com

Other Executive Directors

Advent Underwriting Ltd	Darren J Stockman	+44 (0)20 7743 8219	darren.stockman@adventgroup.co.uk
AEGIS Managing Agency Ltd	John E Chambers	+44 (0)20 7265 2129	jchambers@aegislondon.co.uk
Argo Managing Agency Ltd	Neil R Chapman	+44 (0)20 7712 7600	neil.chapman@argo-int.com
	Mark W Lawrence	+44 (0)20 7712 7600	mark.lawrence@argo-int.com
Aspen Managing Agency Ltd	R James Ingham Clark	+44 (0)20 7184 8000	robert.long@aspen-re.com
	Matthew C Yeldham	+44 (0)20 7184 8000	robert.long@aspen-re.com
Atrium Underwriters Ltd	Toby D Drysdale	+44 (0)20 7327 4877	info@atrium-uw.com
	Richard de WW Harries	+44 (0)20 7327 4877	info@atrium-uw.com
	Nicholas C Marsh	+44 (0)20 7327 4877	info@atrium-uw.com
	Kevin W Wilkins	+44 (0)20 7327 4877	info@atrium-uw.com
	Andrew D Winyard	+44 (0)20 7327 4877	info@atrium-uw.com
Beaufort Underwriting Agency Ltd	Derek C Eales	+44 (0)20 7220 8200	derek.eales@beaufort-group.com
	Michael SF Pritchard	+44 (0)20 7220 8200	michael.pritchard@beaufort-group.com
Beazley Furlonge Ltd	Arthur R Manners	+44 (0)20 7667 0623	arthur.manners@beazley.com
Cathedral Underwriting Ltd	John C Hamblin	+44 (0)20 7170 9062	john.hamblin@cathedralcapital.com
	Elvin E Patrick	+44 (0)20 7170 9000	info@cathedralcapital.com
	Peter D Scales	+44 (0)20 7170 9025	peter.scales@cathedralcapital.com
Catlin Underwriting Agencies Ltd	Richard M Clapham	+44 (0)20 7626 0486	richard.clapham@catlin.com
Chaucer Syndicates Ltd	Bruce P Bartell	+44 (0)20 7397 9700	bruce.bartell@chaucerplc.com
	Ashley R Bissett	+44 (0)20 7397 9700	ashley.bissett@chaucerplc.com
Equity Syndicate Management Ltd	Henry NA Colthurst	+44 (0)1277 200 100	info@equitygroup.co.uk
	John E Josiah	+44 (0)1277 200 100	john.josiah@equitygroup.co.uk
Faraday Underwriting Ltd	Michael P O'Dea	+44 (0)20 7680 4326	mike.odea@genre.com
Hardy (Underwriting Agencies) Ltd	Patrick J Gage	+44 (0)20 7626 0382	patrick.gage@hardygroup.co.uk
	Timothy P Griffin	+44 (0)20 7626 0382	timothy.griffin@hardygroup.co.uk
	Theresa Hutchings	+44 (0)20 7626 0382	theresa.hutchings@hardygroup.co.uk
	Matthew J Simpson	+44 (0)20 7626 0382	matthew.simpson@hardygroup.co.uk
	Mervyn TA Sugden	+44 (0)20 7626 0382	mervyn.sugden@hardygroup.co.uk
	Anthony D Williams	+44 (0)20 7626 0382	anthony.williams@hardygroup.co.uk
HCC Underwriting Agency Ltd	Michael L Onslow	+44 (0)20 7680 3000	monslow@hccint.com
Hiscox Syndicates Ltd	Stuart J Bridges	+44 (0)20 7448 6000	stuart.bridges@hiscox.com
	David JW Bruce	+44 (0)20 7448 6000	david.bruce@hiscox.com
	Stephen J Quick	+44 (0)20 7448 6000	stephen.quick@hiscox.com
	Bruno C Ritchie	+44 (0)20 7448 6000	bruno.ritchie@hiscox.com
	Nigel B Tyler	+44 (0)20 7448 6000	nigel.tyler@hiscox.com
	Richard C Watson	+44 (0)20 7448 6000	richard.watson@hiscox.com
Managing Agency Partners Ltd	Aidan Kong	+44 (0)20 7709 3860	map@mapunderwriting.co.uk
	Christopher J Smelt	+44 (0)20 7709 3860	map@mapunderwriting.co.uk
	Richard K Trubshaw	+44 (0)20 7709 3860	map@mapunderwriting.co.uk
Markel Syndicate Management Ltd	Stephen M Carroll	+44 (0)20 7953 6000	steve.carroll@markelintl.com
Marketform Managing Agency Ltd	Simon G Turner	+44 (0)20 7488 7700	simon.turner@marketform.com
	Graham RA White	+44 (0)20 7488 7700	underwriters@marketform.com
Max at Lloyd's Ltd	John M Boylan	+44 (0)20 3102 3100	john.boylan@maxatlloyds.com
	Peter A Minton	+44 (0)20 3102 3100	peter.minton@maxatlloyds.com
	Gregory EA Morrison	+44 (0)20 3102 3100	gregory.morrison@maxatlloyds.com
	Adam Mullan	+44 (0)20 3102 3100	adam.mullan@maxatlloyds.com
	Joseph W Roberts	+44 (0)20 3102 3100	jospeh.roberts@maxatlloyds.com
Mitsui Sumitomo Insurance Underwriting at Lloyd's Ltd	Dipak Warren	+44 (0)20 7977 8333	dwarren@msilm.com
Montpelier Underwriting Agencies Ltd	Richard MM Chattock	+44 (0)20 7648 4500	richard.chattock@montpelierua.com
Munich Re Underwriting Ltd	Oliver J Crabtree	+44 (0)20 7886 3900	oliver.crabtree@mrunderwriting.com
	Dominick JR Hoare	+44 (0)20 7886 3900	dominick.hoare@mrunderwriting.com
	Mark C Watkins	+44 (0)20 7886 3900	mark.watkins@mrunderwriting.com

Newline Underwriting Management Ltd	James RF Micklem	+44 (0)20 7090 1700	dickmicklem@newlineuml.com
	Brian D Young	+44 (0)20 7090 1700	byoung@newlineuml.com
Novae Syndicates Ltd	Jonathan LJ Butcher	+44 (0)20 7903 7300	jbutcher@novae.com
Pembroke Managing Agency Ltd	Christopher D Brown	+44 (0)20 7337 4400	christopher.brown@pembrokeunderwriting.com
	Timothy ABH Glover	+44 (0)20 7337 4400	tim.glover@pembrokeunderwriting.com
R J Kiln & Co Limited	Shingo Batori	+44 (0)20 7886 9000	See R J Kiln & Co Ltd Company Profile
	Roger A Bickmore	+44 (0)20 7886 9000	See R J Kiln & Co Ltd Company Profile
	Paul M Culham	+44 (0)20 7886 9000	See R J Kiln & Co Ltd Company Profile
	Robin G Hargreaves	+44 (0)20 7886 9000	See R J Kiln & Co Ltd Company Profile
	Andrew N Hitchcox	+44 (0)20 7886 9000	See R J Kiln & Co Ltd Company Profile
	David J Huckstepp	+44 (0)20 7886 9000	See R J Kiln & Co Ltd Company Profile
	Paul M Letherbarrow	+44 (0)20 7886 9000	See R J Kiln & Co Ltd Company Profile
	Stephen D Mathers	+44 (0)20 7886 9000	See R J Kiln & Co Ltd Company Profile
	Timothy P Prifti	+44 (0)20 7886 9000	See R J Kiln & Co Ltd Company Profile
	Bruce D Shepherd	+44 (0)20 7886 9000	See R J Kiln & Co Ltd Company Profile
SA Meacock & Company Ltd	Karl W Jarvis	+44 (0)20 7374 6727	karl.jarvis@sameacock.com
	Alec Taylor	+44 (0)20 7374 6727	alec.taylor@sameacock.com
Sagicor at Lloyd's Ltd	George Sweatman	+44 (0)20 3003 6800	george.sweatman@sagicor.eu
	Elisabetta Tenenti	+44 (0)20 3003 6800	elisabetta.tenenti@sagicor.eu
Sportscover Underwriting Ltd	Christopher P Nash	+44 (0)20 7398 4080	chris.nash@sportscover.com
Starr Managing Agents Ltd	Christopher E Hancock	+44 (0)20 7337 3550	christopher.hancock@cvstarrco.com
	David Stewart	+44 (0)20 7337 3550	david.stewart@cvstarrco.com
Talbot Underwriting Ltd	Mark S Johnson	+44 (0)20 7550 3500	mark.johnsonr@talbotuw.com
	Julian G Ross	+44 (0)20 7550 3500	julian.ross@talbotuw.com
Whittington Capital Management Ltd	Helen M Westcott	+44 (0)20 7743 0900	helen.westcott@whittingtoninsurance.com
XL London Market Ltd	Jonathan F Ibbott	+44 (0)20 7933 7000	jonathan.ibbott@xlgroup.com
	Arabella Ramage	+44 (0)20 7933 7000	arabella.ramage@xlgroup.com
	Neil Robertson	+44 (0)20 7933 7000	neil.robertson@xlgroup.com

Non-Executive Directors

Ace Underwriting Agencies Ltd	Graham D Williams	+44 (0)20 7173 7000	info.uk@ace-ina.com
Advent Underwriting Ltd	Brian W Rowbotham	+44 (0)20 7743 8200	head.office@adventgroup.co.uk
AEGIS Managing Agency Ltd	William RP Dalton	+44 (0)20 7265 2100	enquiries@aegislink.com
	Christopher D Forbes	+44 (0)20 7265 2100	enquiries@aegislink.com
	John S Goldsmith	+44 (0)20 7265 2100	enquiries@aegislink.com
	Donald J Greene	+44 (0)20 7265 2100	enquiries@aegislink.com
	William H Grigg	+44 (0)20 7265 2100	enquiries@aegislink.com
	Thomas J Mahoney	+44 (0)20 7265 2100	enquiries@aegislink.com
	Wesley W von Schack	+44 (0)20 7265 2100	enquiries@aegislink.com
Amlin Underwriting Ltd	Nigel JC Buchanan	+44 (0)20 7746 1000	amlinreception@amlin.co.uk
	Martin D Feinstein	+44 (0)20 7746 1000	amlinreception@amlin.co.uk
	Richard A Hextall	+44 (0)20 7746 1000	richard.hextall@amlin.co.uk
	Anthony W Holt	+44 (0)20 7746 1000	amlinreception@amlin.co.uk
	Charles EL Philipps	+44 (0)20 7746 1000	charles.philipps@amlin.co.uk
Argenta Syndicate Management Ltd	Richard M Brewster	+44 (0)20 7825 7200	richard.brewster@argentaplc.com
	John E Mumford	+44 (0)20 7825 7200	john.mumford@argentaplc.com
	Gary A Powell	+44 (0)20 7825 7200	gary.powell@argentaplc.com
	Alan W Tucker	+44 (0)20 7825 7135	alan.tucker@argentaplc.com
Argo Managing Agency Ltd	Andrew J Carrier	+44 (0)20 7712 7600	katie.gales@argo-int.com
	John WJ Spencer	+44 (0)20 7712 7600	belinda.rose@argo-int.com
Ark Syndicate Management Ltd	Robin Oakes	+44 (0)20 3023 4020	enquiries@arkunderwriting.com
	Richard P Rosenbaum	+44 (0)20 3023 4020	enquiries@arkunderwriting.com
	Verner G Southey	+44 (0)20 3023 4020	enquiries@arkunderwriting.com
	Christopher E Watson	+44 (0)20 3023 4020	enquiries@arkunderwriting.com
Ascot Underwriting Ltd	Alexander R Baugh	+44 (0)20 7743 9600	enquiries@ascotuw.com
	Ian P Martin	+44 (0)20 7743 9600	enquiries@ascotuw.com
	Homi PR Mullan	+44 (0)20 7743 9600	enquiries@ascotuw.com
	Martin RD Reith	+44 (0)20 7743 9600	enquiries@ascotuw.com

	Nicholas C Walsh	+44 (0)20 7743 9600	enquiries@ascotuw.com
Aspen Managing Agency Ltd	Richard JS Bucknall	+44 (0)20 7184 8000	richardbucknall.theboard@aspen.bm
	John F Hobbs	+44 (0)20 7184 8000	robert.long@aspen-re.com
Atrium Underwriters Ltd	Ann F Godbehere	+44 (0)20 7327 4877	info@atrium-uw.com
	Don Kramer	+44 (0)20 7327 4877	info@atrium-uw.com
	Scott P Moser	+44 (0)20 7327 4877	info@atrium-uw.com
Beaufort Underwriting Agency Ltd	Jorg W Bruniecki	+44 (0)20 7220 8200	info@beaufort-group.com
Beazley Furlonge Ltd	George P Blunden	+44 (0)20 7667 0623	george.blunden@beazley.com
	J Dudley Fishburn	+44 (0)20 7667 0623	john.fishburn@beazley.com
	Chris M London	+44 (0)20 7667 0623	chris.london@beazley.com
	Andrew D Pomfret	+44 (0)20 7667 0623	andrew.pomfret@beazley.com
Brit Syndicates Ltd	Kenneth Culley	+44 (0)20 7984 8500	kenneth.culley@britinsurance.com
	Dr Cornelius Schrauwers	+44 (0)20 7984 8500	cornelis.schrauwers@britinsurance.com
Canopius Managing Agents Ltd	Adam J Barron	+44 (0)20 7337 3700	adam.barron@canopius.com
	Robert D Law	+44 (0)20 7337 3700	robert.law@canopius.com
	Dr Ian B Owen	+44 (0)20 7337 3700	ian.owen@canopius.com
Cathedral Underwriting Ltd	J Michael G Andrews	+44 (0)20 7170 9000	info@cathedralcapital.com
	John S Goldsmith	+44 (0)20 7170 9000	info@cathedralcapital.com
Catlin Underwriting Agencies Ltd	Timothy W Burrows	+44 (0)20 7626 0486	catlininfo@catlin.com
	Diana Guy	+44 (0)20 7626 0486	catlininfo@catlin.com
	Colin G Robinson	+44 (0)20 7626 0486	catlininfo@catlin.com
Chaucer Syndicates Ltd	Malcolm J Cox	+44 (0)20 7397 9700	malcolm.cox@chaucerplc.com
	Richard T Scholes	+44 (0)20 7397 9700	richard.scholes@chaucerplc.com
Faraday Underwriting Ltd	Peter Lutke-Bornefeld	+44 (0)20 7702 3333	liz.richardson@faraday.com
	Lord Phillips of Sudbury	+44 (0)20 7702 3333	liz.richardson@faraday.com
	Damon N Vocke	+44 (0)20 7702 3333	liz.richardson@faraday.com
Hardy (Underwriting Agencies) Ltd	Richard D Abbott	+44 (0)20 7626 0382	info@hardygroup.co.uk
	Ian E Ivory	+44 (0)20 7626 0382	ian.ivory@hardygroup.co.uk
	Lady Barbara S Judge	+44 (0)20 7626 0382	info@hardygroup.co.uk
HCC Underwriting Agency Ltd	W Raymond Treen	+44 (0)20 7680 3000	info@hccual.com
Hiscox Syndicates Ltd	Anthony Howland-Jackson	+44 (0)20 7448 6000	enquiry@hiscox.com
	Ian N Thomson	+44 (0)20 7448 6000	enquiry@hiscox.com
	Iain T Webb-Wilson	+44 (0)20 7448 6000	enquiry@hiscox.com
Jubilee Managing Agency Ltd	Anthony PD Lancaster	+44 (0)20 7220 8728	jubilee@jubilee-insurance.com
	Rupert JG Lowe	+44 (0)20 7220 8728	jubilee@jubilee-insurance.com
	Ian McIsaac	+44 (0)20 7220 8728	jubilee@jubilee-insurance.com
KGM Underwriting Agencies Ltd	Michael E Hildesley	+44 (0)20 8530 1813	michael.hildesley@kgminsurance.co.uk
	Brandon Swim	+44 (0)20 8530 1813	brandon.swim@kgminsurance.co.uk
Liberty Syndicate Management Ltd	Daniel TN Forsythe	+44 (0)20 7070 4472	info@libertysyndicates.com
	David H Long	+44 (0)20 7070 4472	info@libertysyndicates.com
	Gordon J McBurney	+44 (0)20 7070 4472	info@libertysyndicates.com
	Derek J Scott	+44 (0)20 7070 4472	info@libertysyndicates.com
	J Richard L Youell	+44 (0)20 7070 4472	info@libertysyndicates.com
Managing Agency Partners Ltd	Christine E Dandridge	+44 (0)20 7709 3860	map@mapunderwriting.co.uk
	H Raymond Dumas	+44 (0)20 7709 3860	map@mapunderwriting.co.uk
	Andrew S Foote	+44 (0)20 7709 3860	map@mapunderwriting.co.uk
Markel Syndicate Management Ltd	Ian Marshall	+44 (0)20 7953 6000	ian.marshall@markelintl.com
Marketform Managing Agency Ltd	Terence G Hebden	+44 (0)20 7488 7761	terence.hebden@marketform.com
	John E Mumford	+44 (0)20 7488 7700	john.mumford@marketform.com
Marlborough Underwriting Agency Ltd	David A Brown	+44 (0)20 7456 1800	compliance@marlborough.co.uk
	Howard J Cheetham	+44 (0)20 7456 1800	compliance@marlborough.co.uk
	Karl G Grieves	+44 (0)20 7456 1800	compliance@marlborough.co.uk
	Nicholas CT Pawson	+44 (0)20 7456 1800	nicholas.pawson@marlborough.co.uk
	David T Young	+44 (0)20 7456 1800	david.young@marlborough.co.uk
Max at Lloyd's Ltd	Baron Clemens ATW von Bechtolsheim	+44 (0)20 3102 3100	clemens.vonbechtolsheim@maxatlloyds.com
	Andrew T West	+44 (0)20 3102 3100	andrew.west@maxatlloyds.com
Mitsui Sumitomo Insurance Underwriting at Lloyd's Ltd	Hiroyuki Iioka	+44 (0)20 7977 8321	enquiries@msilm.com

	Yohichi Kamagai	+44 (0)20 7977 8321	enquiries@msilm.com
	Derek Kingston	+44 (0)20 7977 8321	enquiries@msilm.com
	Kazuo Yamada	+44 (0)20 7977 8321	enquiries@msilm.com
	Tadashi Yamada	+44 (0)20 7977 8321	enquiries@msilm.com
Montpelier Underwriting Agencies Ltd	John S Goldsmith	+44 (0)20 7648 4500	-
	Christopher L Harris	+44 (0)20 7648 4500	chris.harris@montpelierre.bm
	Nicholas J Newman-Young	+44 (0)20 7648 4500	-
	P Terry O'Neill	+44 (0)20 7648 4500	-
Munich Re Underwriting Ltd	Thomas E Artmann	+44 (0)20 7886 3900	central@mrunderwriting.com
	John A Cooper	+44 (0)20 7886 3900	central@mrunderwriting.com
	Edward N Noble	+44 (0)20 7886 3900	central@mrunderwriting.com
Navigators Underwriting Agency Ltd	H Clay Bassett JR	+44 (0)20 7220 6900	cbassett@navg.com
	Christopher Duca	+44 (0)20 7220 6900	cduca@navg.com
	Stanley A Galanski	+44 (0)20 7220 6900	sgalanski@navg.com
	Dr Paul Kelly	+44 (0)20 7220 6900	pkelly@navg.com
Newline Underwriting Management Ltd	Richard S Donovan	+44 (0)20 7090 1700	rdonovan@odysseyre.com
Novae Syndicates Ltd	Oliver RP Corbett	+44 (0)20 7903 7300	ocorbett@novae.com
	William J Davis	+44 (0)20 7903 7300	bdavis@novae.com
	Matthew K Fosh	+44 (0)20 7903 7300	mfosh@novae.com
	John M Massey	+44 (0)20 7903 7300	jmassey@novae.com
	John RW Thirlwell	+44 (0)20 7903 7300	jthirlwell@novae.com
Omega Underwriting Agents Ltd	Walter M Fiederowicz	+44 (0)20 7767 3000	info@omegauw.com
	Ian W Mercer	+44 (0)20 7767 3000	info@omegauw.com
	John F Powell	+44 (0)20 7767 3000	info@omegauw.com
Pembroke Managing Agency Ltd	Allan Kaufman	+44 (0)20 7337 4400	hq@pembrokeunderwriting.com
QBE Underwriting Ltd	Philip V Olsen (Independent)	+44 (0)20 7105 4000	enquiries@uk.qbe.com
	Brian W Pomeroy (Independent)	+44 (0)20 7105 4000	enquiries@uk.qbe.com
	Howard M Posner (Independent)	+44 (0)20 7105 4000	enquiries@uk.qbe.com
R J Kiln & Co Limited	Ian Brimecome	+44 (0)20 7886 9000	See R J Kiln & Co Ltd Company Profile
	Paul W Hewitt (Independent)	+44 (0)20 7886 9000	See R J Kiln & Co Ltd Company Profile
	Paul Wilson (Independent)	+44 (0)20 7886 9000	See R J Kiln & Co Ltd Company Profile
SA Meacock & Company Ltd	James M Meacock	+44 (0)20 7374 6727	linda.mailoudi@sameacock.com
Sagicor at Lloyd's Ltd	Bjorn Jansli	+44 (0)20 3003 6800	duncan.reed@sagicor.eu
	John M Mantz	+44 (0)20 3003 6800	duncan.reed@sagicor.eu
	Jerome B Nice	+44 (0)20 3003 6800	duncan.reed@sagicor.eu
	Philip NW Osborne	+44 (0)20 3003 6800	duncan.reed@sagicor.eu
	Ravi C Rambarran	+44 (0)20 3003 6800	duncan.reed@sagicor.eu
Spectrum Syndicate Management Ltd	Jerome Breslin	+44 (0)20 7283 2646	newbusiness@spectrumins.com
Sportscover Underwriting Ltd	Andrew G Ripley	+44 (0)20 7398 4080	dominic.ford@sportscover.com
Starr Managing Agents Ltd	Paul A Chubb	+44 (0)20 7337 3550	paul.chubb@cvstarrco.com
	David S French	+44 (0)20 7337 3550	david.french@cvstarrco.com
	Richard N Shaak	+44 (0)20 7337 3550	richard.shaak@cvstarrco.com
Talbot Underwriting Ltd	Joseph E Consolino	+44 (0)20 7550 3500	central@talbotuw.com
	Edward J Noonan	+44 (0)20 7550 3500	central@talbotuw.com
	George P Reeth	+44 (0)20 7550 3500	central@talbotuw.com
	Verner G Southey	+44 (0)20 7550 3500	central@talbotuw.com
Travelers Syndicate Management Ltd	Graham J McKean	+44 (0)20 3207 6000	trv5000@travelers.com
	M Fraser Newton	+44 (0)20 3207 6000	trv5000@travelers.com
Whittington Capital Management Ltd	Digby FC Murphy	+44 (0)20 7743 0900	jon.francis@whittingtoninsurance.com
	David KL White	+44 (0)20 7743 0900	jon.francis@whittingtoninsurance.com
XL London Market Ltd	Philip O Sheridan	+44 (0)20 7933 7000	graham.brady@xlgroup.com
	Richard JW Titley	+44 (0)20 7933 7000	graham.brady@xlgroup.com

Chief Underwriting Officers & Underwriting Directors

Ace Underwriting Agencies Ltd	AW Matthew Shaw	+44 (0)20 7173 7000	matthew.shaw@ace-ina.com
	Richard V Pryce	+44 (0)20 7173 7396	richard.pryce@ace-ina.com
Advent Underwriting Ltd	Duncan P Lummis	+44 (0)20 7743 8233	duncan.lummis@adventgroup.co.uk
AEGIS Managing Agency Ltd	David P Croom-Johnson	+44 (0)20 7265 2130	dcroom-johnson@aegislondon.co.uk
Amlin Underwriting Ltd	Simon CW Beale	+44 (0)20 7746 1000	simon.beale@amlin.co.uk
	Brian D Carpenter	+44 (0)1245 214 875	brian.carpenter@amlin.co.uk
	Rodney G Dampier	+44 (0)20 7746 1000	rodney.dampier@amlin.co.uk
Argenta Syndicate Management Ltd	Paul Hunt	+44 (0)20 7825 7200	paul.hunt@argentaplc.com
Argo Managing Agency Ltd	James C Sardeson	+44 (0)20 7712 7600	james.sardeson@argo-int.com
Ark Syndicate Management Ltd	Nicholas K Bonnar	+44 (0)20 3023 4003	nick.bonnar@arkunderwriting.com
	David P Foreman	+44 (0)20 3023 4002	david.foreman@arkunderwriting.com
	C David May	+44 (0)20 3023 4042	david.may@arkunderwriting.com
Ascot Underwriting Ltd	Mark Pepper	+44 (0)20 7743 9617	mark.pepper@ascotuw.com
Aspen Managing Agency Ltd	Robert J Long	+44 (0)20 7184 8000	robert.long@aspen-re.com
Beazley Furlonge Ltd	Adrian P Cox	+44 (0)20 7667 0623	adrian.cox@beazley.com
	Nicholas H Furlonge	+44 (0)20 7667 0623	nicholas.furlonge@beazley.com
	Jonathan G Gray	+44 (0)20 7667 0623	jonathan.gray@beazley.com
	Neil P Maidment	+44 (0)20 7667 0623	neil.maidment@beazley.com
	Clive A Washbourn	+44 (0)20 7667 0623	clive.washbourn@beazley.com
Brit Syndicates Ltd	Kevin R Huttly	+44 (0)20 7984 8500	enquiries@britinsurance.com
Canopius Managing Agents Ltd	Timothy J Carroll	+44 (0)20 7337 3700	info@canopius.com
	James A Giordano	+44 (0)20 7337 3710	jim.giordano@canopius.com
Catlin Underwriting Agencies Ltd	Nicolas J Burkinshaw	+44 (0)20 7626 0486	nicolas.burkinshaw@catlin.com
Chaucer Syndicates Ltd	Kim Barber	+44 (0)1227 284 700	kim.barber@chaucerplc.com
	S Janet Helson	+44 (0)20 7397 9700	janet.helson@chaucerplc.com
	Robert A Stuchbery	+44 (0)20 7397 9700	robert.stuchbery@chaucerplc.com
Faraday Underwriting Ltd	Paul NE Ceurvorst	+44 (0)20 7264 4611	paul.ceurvorst@faraday.com
	Mark J Rayner	+44 (0)20 7702 3333	mark.rayner@faraday.com
Hardy (Underwriting Agencies) Ltd	Adrian J Walker	+44 (0)20 7626 0382	adrian.walker@hardygroup.co.uk
HCC Underwriting Agency Ltd	Paul Baynham	+44 (0)20 7680 3009	pbaynham@hccual.com
Hiscox Syndicates Ltd	Robert S Childs	+44 (0)20 7448 6000	robert.childs@hiscox.com
Jubilee Managing Agency Ltd	Norman H Topche	+44 (0)20 7220 8728	norman.topche@jubilee-insurance.com
KGM Underwriting Agencies Ltd	Colin Hart	+44 (0)20 8530 1816	colin.hart@kgminsurance.co.uk
Liberty Syndicate Management Ltd	Thomas RC Corfield	+44 (0)20 7070 4472	info@libertysyndicates.com
Markel Syndicate Management Ltd	Jeremy W Brazil	+44 (0)20 7953 6000	jeremy.brazil@markelintl.com
Marketform Managing Agency Ltd	Simon P Lotter	+44 (0)20 7488 7700	simon.lotter@marketform.com
Marlborough Underwriting Agency Ltd	Leslie F Allen	+44 (0)20 7456 1800	leslie.allen@marlborough.co.uk
Max at Lloyd's Ltd	Matthew A Petzold	+44 (0)20 3102 3100	matthew.petzold@maxatlloyds.com
Montpelier Underwriting Agencies Ltd	Peter J Rand	+44 (0)20 7648 4500	peter.rand@montpelierua.com
Navigators Underwriting Agency Ltd	Richard P Bardwell	+44 (0)20 7220 6900	rbardwell@navg.com
Newline Underwriting Management Ltd	Philip T Foley	+44 (0)20 7090 1700	pfoley@newlineuml.com
Novae Syndicates Ltd	Peter C Matson	+44 (0)20 7903 7300	pmatson@novae.com
Omega Underwriting Agents Ltd	John D Robinson	+44 (0)20 7767 3000	john.robinson@omegauw.com
Pembroke Managing Agency Ltd	Mark H Wheeler	+44 (0)20 7337 4400	mark.wheeler@pembrokeunderwriting.com
QBE Underwriting Ltd	Ashis M Bathia	+44 (0)20 7105 4000	enquiries@uk.qbe.com
	David A Constable	+44 (0)20 7105 4000	enquiries@uk.qbe.com
	Matthew F Crane	+44 (0)20 7105 4000	enquiries@uk.qbe.com
	Emilio A Di Silvio	+44 (0)20 7105 4000	enquiries@uk.qbe.com
	Doron Grossman	+44 (0)20 7105 4000	enquiries@uk.qbe.com
	Peter E Grove	+44 (0)20 7105 4000	enquiries@uk.qbe.com
	Robert BM Johnston	+44 (0)20 7105 4000	enquiries@uk.qbe.com
	Bernard Mageean	+44 (0)20 7105 4000	enquiries@uk.qbe.com
	Colin R O'Farrell	+44 (0)20 7105 4000	enquiries@uk.qbe.com
	Jonathan W Parry	+44 (0)20 7105 4000	enquiries@uk.qbe.com
	Graham S Rayner	+44 (0)20 7105 4000	enquiries@uk.qbe.com
	Terence J Whittaker	+44 (0)20 7105 4000	enquiries@uk.qbe.com

R J Kiln & Co Limited	Robert D Chase	+44 (0)20 7886 9000	See R J Kiln & Co Ltd Company Profile
	Richard CW Lewis	+44 (0)20 7886 9000	See R J Kiln & Co Ltd Company Profile
SA Meacock & Company Ltd	Michael J Meacock	+44 (0)20 7374 6727	michael.meacock@sameacock.com
Sagicor at Lloyd's Ltd	Geoffrey M Halpin	+44 (0)20 3003 6800	geoffrey.halpin@sagicor.eu
Spectrum Syndicate Management Ltd	James W Mann	+44 (0)20 7283 2646	jim.mann@spectrumins.com
Sportscover Underwriting Ltd	Peter JR Nash	+44 (0)20 7398 4080	peter.nash@sportscover.com
Starr Managing Agents Ltd	Mark Patterson	+44 (0)20 7337 3550	mark.patterson@cvstarrco.com
Travelers Syndicate Management Ltd	Steve G Eccles	+44 (0)20 3207 6246	seccles@travelers.com
Whittington Capital Management Ltd	Stewart K Laderman	+44 (0)20 7743 0900	stewart.laderman@whittingtoninsurance.com

Risk Officers

Amlin Underwriting Ltd	James Le Tall Illingworth	+44 (0)20 7746 1060	james.illingworth@amlin.co.uk
Argenta Syndicate Management Ltd	Peter J Bruin	+44 (0)20 7825 7272	peter.bruin@argentaplc.com
Ark Syndicate Management Ltd	Gary M Oliver	+44 (0)20 3023 4006	gary.oliver@arkunderwriting.com
Canopius Managing Agents Ltd	Stephen T Manning	+44 (0)20 7337 3732	stephen.manning@canopius.com
Chaucer Syndicates Ltd	Gina C Butterworth	+44 (0)20 7397 9700	gina.butterworth@chaucerplc.com
Jubilee Managing Agency Ltd	Pauline A Cockburn	+44 (0)20 7220 8728	pauline.cockburn@jubilee-insurance.com
KGM Underwriting Agencies Ltd	Adam C Seager	+44 (0)20 8530 1813	adam.seager@kgminsurance.co.uk
Mitsui Sumitomo Insurance Underwriting at Lloyd's Ltd	Philip R Pearce	+44 (0)20 7702 6329	ppearce@msilm.com
Pembroke Managing Agency Ltd	Philip Hicks	+44 (0)20 7337 4400	philip.hicks@pembrokeunderwriting.com
QBE Underwriting Ltd	Ian D Beckerson	+44 (0)20 7105 4000	enquiries@uk.qbe.com
Travelers Syndicate Management Ltd	Paul M Cusition	+44 (0)20 3207 6870	pcusition@travelers.com

Actuarial Officers

Chaucer Syndicates Ltd	Jonathan D Perkins	+44 (0)20 7397 9700	jonathan.perkins@chaucerplc.com
Faraday Underwriting Ltd	Nigel J Finlay	+44 (0)20 7680 4322	nigel.finlay@faraday.com
Markel Syndicate Management Ltd	Nicholas JS Line	+44 (0)20 7953 6000	underwriters@marketform.com
Newline Underwriting Management Ltd	Neil Duncan	+44 (0)20 7090 1700	nduncan@newlineuml.com
QBE Underwriting Ltd	Philip A Dodridge	+44 (0)20 7105 4000	enquiries@uk.qbe.com
Spectrum Syndicate Management Ltd	Stavros Martis	+44 (0)20 7283 2646	stavros.martis@spectrumins.com

Senior Claims Officers

Ace Underwriting Agencies Ltd	R Peter Murray	+44 (0)20 7173 7000	peter.murray@ace-ina.com
AEGIS Managing Agency Ltd	Richard Foulger	+44 (0)20 7265 2127	rfoulger@aegislondon.co.uk
Argenta Syndicate Management Ltd	David G Williams	+44 (0)20 7825 7211	david.williams@argentaplc.com
Ark Syndicate Management Ltd	James D Masson	+44 (0)20 3023 4020	james.masson@arkunderwriting.com
Ascot Underwriting Ltd	Neil Dalton	+44 (0)20 7743 9600	enquiries@ascotuw.com
Brit Syndicates Ltd	Robert Foster	+44 (0)20 7984 8500	enquiries@britinsurance.com
Canopius Managing Agents Ltd	Clive A Watson	+44 (0)20 7337 3720	clive.watson@canopius.com
Catlin Underwriting Agencies Ltd	Nicholas C Sinfield	+44 (0)20 7626 0486	nicholas.sinfield@catlin.com
Chaucer Syndicates Ltd	Martin Francis	+44 (0)20 7397 9723	martin.francis@chaucerplc.com
	Tony Gates	+44 (0)20 7105 8205	tony.gates@chaucerplc.com
Faraday Underwriting Ltd	Charles F Glaisher	+44 (0)20 7680 4283	charles.glaisher@faraday.com
HCC Underwriting Agency Ltd	Nick Woodward	+44 (0)20 7680 3000	info@hccual.com
Hiscox Syndicates Ltd	Jeremy Pinchin	+44 (0)20 7448 6000	jeremy.pinchin@hiscox.com
KGM Underwriting Agencies Ltd	Martyn J Hardy	+44 (0)20 8530 1837	martyn.hardy@kgminsurance.co.uk
Liberty Syndicate Management Ltd	Mike Gillett	+44 (0)20 7070 4472	info@libertysyndicates.com
Markel Syndicate Management Ltd	Stuart C Willoughby	+44 (0)20 7953 6000	stuart.willoughby@markelintl.com
Marketform Managing Agency Ltd	Daniel AW Smith	+44 (0)20 7488 7700	daniel.smith@marketform.com
Marlborough Underwriting Agency Ltd	Ian R Mallery	+44 (0)20 7456 1800	ian.mallery@marlborough.co.uk
Montpelier Underwriting Agencies Ltd	Paul Moss	+44 (0)20 7648 4500	paul.moss@montpelierua.com
Munich Re Underwriting Ltd	Alison C Cook	+44 (0)20 7886 3900	alison.cook@mrunderwriting.com
Navigators Underwriting Agency Ltd	David Paveling	+44 (0)20 7220 6900	dpaveling@navg.com
Newline Underwriting Management Ltd	Robert B Kastner	+44 (0)20 7090 1700	rkastner@newlineuml.com

Novae Syndicates Ltd	Jonathan A Boyns	+44 (0)20 7903 7300	jboyns@novae.com
Pembroke Managing Agency Ltd	Gillian E Barnes	+44 (0)20 7337 4400	gillian.barnes@pembrokeunderwriting.com
SA Meacock & Company Ltd	Sean Farrelly	+44 (0)20 7374 6727	sean.farrelly@sameacock.com
Sagicor at Lloyd's Ltd	Gary L Ross	+44 (0)20 3003 6800	gary.ross@sagicor.eu
Sportscover Underwriting Ltd	Peter JR Nash	+44 (0)20 7398 4080	peter.nash@sportscover.com
Talbot Underwriting Ltd	Gillian S Langford	+44 (0)20 7550 3500	gill.langford@talbotuw.com
Travelers Syndicate Management Ltd	Simon N Catt	+44 (0)20 3207 6217	scatt@travelers.com
Whittington Capital Management Ltd	Gary L Griffiths	+44 (0)20 7743 0900	gary.griffiths@whittingtoninsurance.com
XL London Market Ltd	Martin D Turner	+44 (0)20 7933 7000	martin.turner@xlgroup.com

Chief Operating Officers

Advent Underwriting Ltd	John C Towers	+44 (0)20 7743 8205	john.towers@adventgroup.co.uk
AEGIS Managing Agency Ltd	Sarah A Davies	+44 (0)20 7265 2110	sdavies@aegislondon.co.uk
Argenta Syndicate Management Ltd	David G Williams	+44 (0)20 7825 7211	david.williams@argentaplc.com
Argo Managing Agency Ltd	Paul D Battagliola	+44 (0)20 7712 7600	paul.battagliola@argo-int.com
Ark Syndicate Management Ltd	Aneil P Deshpande	+44 (0)20 3023 4004	neil.deshpande@arkunderwriting.com
Atrium Underwriters Ltd	Simon D Cooper	+44 (0)20 7327 4877	info@atrium-uw.com
Beazley Furlonge Ltd	David Marock	+44 (0)20 7667 0623	david.marock@beazley.com
Brit Syndicates Ltd	Kathy M Lisson	+44 (0)20 7984 8500	enquiries@britinsurance.com
Canopius Managing Agents Ltd	Stephen T Manning	+44 (0)20 7337 3732	stephen.manning@canopius.com
Chaucer Syndicates Ltd	David C Bendle	+44 (0)20 7397 9700	david.bendle@chaucerplc.com
Hardy (Underwriting Agencies) Ltd	Stuart Blakeborough	+44 (0)20 7626 0382	stuart.blakeborough@hardygroup.co.uk
Hiscox Syndicates Ltd	Michael D Gould	+44 (0)20 7448 6000	michael.gould@hiscox.com
Liberty Syndicate Management Ltd	John AR Dunn	+44 (0)20 7070 4472	info@libertysyndicates.com
Mitsui Sumitomo Insurance Underwriting at Lloyd's Ltd	Michael G Gardiner	+44 (0)20 7977 8340	mgardiner@msilm.com
Navigators Underwriting Agency Ltd	Stephen R Coward	+44 (0)20 7220 6900	scoward@navg.com
Newline Underwriting Management Ltd	James RF Micklem	+44 (0)20 7090 1700	dickmicklem@newlineuml.com
Omega Underwriting Agents Ltd	Mark I Daly	+44 (0)20 7767 3000	mark.daly@omegauw.com
QBE Underwriting Ltd	John D Neal	+44 (0)20 7105 4000	enquiries@uk.qbe.com
R J Kiln & Co Limited	Elizabeth M Walsh	+44 (0)20 7886 9000	See R J Kiln & Co Ltd Company Profile
SA Meacock & Company Ltd	Karl W Jarvis	+44 (0)20 7374 6727	karl.jarvis@sameacock.com
Sagicor at Lloyd's Ltd	Gary L Ross	+44 (0)20 3003 6800	gary.ross@sagicor.eu
Spectrum Syndicate Management Ltd	Kim T Fox	+44 (0)20 7283 2646	kim.fox@spectrumins.com
Starr Managing Agents Ltd	Ralph Bull	+44 (0)20 7337 3550	ralph.bull@cvstarrco.com
Travelers Syndicate Management Ltd	Anthony J Dilley	+44 (0)20 3207 6851	tdilley@travelers.com
Whittington Capital Management Ltd	Luke N Barnett	+44 (0)20 7743 0900	luke.barnett@whittingtoninsurance.com
XL London Market Ltd	Eileen E McCusker	+44 (0)20 7933 7000	eileen.mccusker@xlgroup.com

Compliance Officers

Ace Underwriting Agencies Ltd	Adrian W Missen	+44 (0)20 7173 7709	adrian.missen@ace-ina.com
Advent Underwriting Ltd	Ian M Hewitt	+44 (0)20 7743 8245	ian.hewitt@adventgroup.co.uk
AEGIS Managing Agency Ltd	Darren Wells	+44 (0)20 7265 2169	dwells@aegislondon.co.uk
Amlin Underwriting Ltd	Allan Rayner	+44 (0)20 7746 1000	allan.rayner@amlin.co.uk
Argenta Syndicate Management Ltd	Peter J Bruin	+44 (0)20 7825 7272	peter.bruin@argentaplc.com
Argo Managing Agency Ltd	John Gill	+44 (0)20 7712 7600	john.gill@argo-int.com
Ark Syndicate Management Ltd	Gary M Oliver	+44 (0)20 3023 4006	gary.oliver@arkunderwriting.com
Ascot Underwriting Ltd	Yvonne Keyes	+44 (0)20 7743 9600	enquiries@ascotuw.com
Aspen Managing Agency Ltd	R James Ingham Clark	+44 (0)20 7184 8000	robert.long@aspen-re.com
Atrium Underwriters Ltd	James RF Lee	+44 (0)20 7327 4877	info@atrium-uw.com
Beaufort Underwriting Agency Ltd	Paul Langridge	+44 (0)20 7220 8200	paul.langridge@beaufort-group.com
Beazley Furlonge Ltd	Sian A Coope	+44 (0)20 7667 0623	sian.coope@beazley.com
Brit Syndicates Ltd	Michael D Jackson	+44 (0)20 7984 8500	michael.jackson@britinsurance.com
Canopius Managing Agents Ltd	Stephen T Manning	+44 (0)20 7337 3732	stephen.manning@canopius.com
Cathedral Underwriting Ltd	Derek C Grainger	+44 (0)20 7170 9023	derek.grainger@cathedralcapital.com
Catlin Underwriting Agencies Ltd	Andrew J Gray	+44 (0)20 7626 0486	andrew.gray@catlin.com

...es Ltd	Lorraine Webb	+44 (0)20 7397 9700	lorraine.webb@chaucerplc.com
...Management Ltd	Peter FS Merrett	+44 (0)1277 200 100	peter.merrett@equitygroup.co.uk
...writing Ltd	Simon GH Tovey	+44 (0)20 7680 4203	simon.tovey@faraday.com
...writing Agencies) Ltd	Timothy P Griffin	+44 (0)20 7626 0382	timothy.griffin@hardygroup.co.uk
Hcc...writing Agency Ltd	David R Feldman	+44 (0)20 7680 3000	dfeldman@hccual.com
Hiscox Syndicates Ltd	Jason S Jones	+44 (0)20 7448 6000	jason.jones@hiscox.com
Jubilee Managing Agency Ltd	Donal JL Barrett	+44 (0)20 7220 8728	donal.barrett@jubilee-insurance.com
KGM Underwriting Agencies Ltd	Adam C Seager	+44 (0)20 8530 1813	adam.seager@kgminsurance.co.uk
Liberty Syndicate Management Ltd	Andrew Hall	+44 (0)20 7070 4472	info@libertysyndicates.com
Managing Agency Partners Ltd	B Siobhan McAuley	+44 (0)20 7709 3867	smcauley@mapunderwriting.co.uk
Markel Syndicate Management Ltd	Andrew J Bailey	+44 (0)20 7953 6000	andrew.bailey@markelintl.com
Marketform Managing Agency Ltd	Harinderjit S Nagra	+44 (0)20 7488 7700	harry.nagra@marketform.com
Marlborough Underwriting Agency Ltd	Iain F MacDowall	+44 (0)20 7456 1800	iain.macdowall@marlborough.co.uk
Max at Lloyd's Ltd	Marion Jewry	+44 (0)20 3102 3100	marion.jewry@maxatlloyds.com
Mitsui Sumitomo Insurance Underwriting at Lloyd's Ltd	Philip R Pearce	+44 (0)20 7702 6329	ppearce@msilm.com
Montpelier Underwriting Agencies Ltd	Gillian Phillips	+44 (0)20 7648 4500	gillian.phillips@montpelierua.com
Munich Re Underwriting Ltd	Timur Coskun	+44 (0)20 7886 3900	tim.coskun@mrunderwriting.com
Navigators Underwriting Agency Ltd	Kate Hillery	+44 (0)20 7220 6900	khillery@navg.com
Newline Underwriting Management Ltd	James RF Micklem	+44 (0)20 7090 1700	dickmicklem@newlineuml.com
Novae Syndicates Ltd	Stephen J Heming	+44 (0)20 7903 7300	sheming@novae.com
Omega Underwriting Agents Ltd	Andrew D Smith	+44 (0)20 7767 3000	andrew.smith@omegauw.com
Pembroke Managing Agency Ltd	Lorraine Webb	+44 (0)20 7337 4400	lorraine.webb@chaucerplc.com
QBE Underwriting Ltd	Ian D Beckerson	+44 (0)20 7105 4000	enquiries@uk.qbe.com
R J Kiln & Co Limited	Keith N Grant	+44 (0)20 7886 9000	keith.grant@kilngroup.com
SA Meacock & Company Ltd	Karl W Jarvis	+44 (0)20 7374 6727	karl.jarvis@sameacock.com
Sagicor at Lloyd's Ltd	Duncan J Reed	+44 (0)20 3003 6800	duncan.reed@sagicor.eu
Spectrum Syndicate Management Ltd	Kim Fox	+44 (0)20 7283 2646	kim.fox@spectrumins.com
Sportscover Underwriting Ltd	Dominic VT Ford	+44 (0)20 7398 4080	dominic.ford@sportscover.com
Starr Managing Agents Ltd	John S Moffat	+44 (0)20 7337 3550	john.moffatt@cvstarrco.com
Talbot Underwriting Ltd	Jane S Clouting	+44 (0)20 7550 3500	jane.clouting@talbotuw.com
Travelers Syndicate Management Ltd	Anthony J Dilley	+44 (0)20 3207 6851	tdilley@travelers.com
Whittington Capital Management Ltd	Luke N Barnett	+44 (0)20 7743 0900	luke.barnett@whittingtoninsurance.com
XL London Market Ltd	Graham L Brady	+44 (0)20 7933 7306	graham.brady@xlgroup.com

Independent Review Directors

Advent Underwriting Ltd	Richard GM Finn	+44 (0)20 7743 8200	head.office@adventgroup.co.uk
Beaufort Underwriting Agency Ltd	Malcolm J Cox	+44 (0)20 7220 8200	info@beaufort-group.com
Canopius Managing Agents Ltd	John D Birney	+44 (0)20 7337 3700	john.birney@canopius.com
Cathedral Underwriting Ltd	John P Tilling	+44 (0)20 7170 9000	info@cathedralcapital.com
Equity Syndicate Management Ltd	Harold E Clarke	+44 (0)1277 200 100	info@equitygroup.co.uk
Hardy (Underwriting Agencies) Ltd	Bernard G Devereese	+44 (0)20 7626 0382	bernard.devereese@hardygroup.co.uk
Liberty Syndicate Management Ltd	Geoffrey Lynch, OBE	+44 (0)20 7070 4472	info@libertysyndicates.com
Newline Underwriting Management Ltd	Simon T Fradd	+44 (0)20 7090 1700	sfradd@newlineuml.com
SA Meacock & Company Ltd	David KL White	+44 (0)20 7374 6727	linda.mailoudi@sameacock.com
Talbot Underwriting Ltd	Anthony J Keys	+44 (0)20 7550 3500	central@talbotuw.com

Company Secretaries

Ace Underwriting Agencies Ltd	Adrian W Missen	+44 (0)20 7173 7309	adrian.missen@ace-ina.com
Advent Underwriting Ltd	Neil M Ewing	+44 (0)20 7743 8250	neil.ewing@adventgroup.co.uk
AEGIS Managing Agency Ltd	Hayley J Connell	+44 (0)20 7265 2100	hconnell@aegislondon.co.uk
Amlin Underwriting Ltd	Charles CT Pender	+44 (0)20 7746 1000	charles.pender@amlin.co.uk
	Jeanette M Mansell	+44 (0)20 7746 1000	jeanette.mansell@amlin.co.uk
Argenta Syndicate Management Ltd	Peter J Bruin	+44 (0)20 7825 7272	peter.bruin@argentaplc.com
Argo Managing Agency Ltd	Belinda Rose	+44 (0)20 7712 7600	belinda.rose@argo-int.com
Ark Syndicate Management Ltd	James D Masson	+44 (0)20 3023 4020	james.masson@arkunderwriting.com

Ascot Underwriting Ltd	Yvonne Keyes	+44 (0)20 7743 9600	enquiries@ascotuw.com
Aspen Managing Agency Ltd	Alastair GC McKay	+44 (0)20 7184 8000	alastair.mckay@aspen-re.com
Atrium Underwriters Ltd	Martha BW Bruce	+44 (0)20 7327 4877	info@atrium-uw.com
Beaufort Underwriting Agency Ltd	Paul Langridge	+44 (0)20 7220 8200	paul.langridge@beaufort-group.com
Beazley Furlonge Ltd	Arthur R Manners	+44 (0)20 7667 0623	arthur.manners@beazley.com
Brit Syndicates Ltd	Michael D Jackson	+44 (0)20 7984 8500	michael.jackson@britinsurance.com
Canopius Managing Agents Ltd	Philip Osman	+44 (0)20 7337 3700	philip.osman@canopius.com
Cathedral Underwriting Ltd	John A Lynch	+44 (0)20 7170 9024	john.lynch@cathedralcapital.com
Catlin Underwriting Agencies Ltd	Andrew J Gray	+44 (0)20 7626 0486	andrew.gray@catlin.com
Chaucer Syndicates Ltd	David C Turner	+44 (0)20 7397 9700	david.turner@chaucerplc.com
Equity Syndicate Management Ltd	Victoria L Cuggy	+44 (0)1277 200 100	victoria.cuggy@equitygroup.co.uk
Faraday Underwriting Ltd	Elisabeth A Richardson	+44 (0)20 7680 7206	liz.richardson@faraday.com
Hardy (Underwriting Agencies) Ltd	Theresa Hutchings	+44 (0)20 7626 0382	theresa.hutchings@hardygroup.co.uk
HCC Underwriting Agency Ltd	David R Feldman	+44 (0)20 7680 3000	dfeldman@hccual.com
Hiscox Syndicates Ltd	Jason S Jones	+44 (0)20 7448 6000	jason.jones@hiscox.com
Jubilee Managing Agency Ltd	Pauline A Cockburn	+44 (0)20 7220 8728	pauline.cockburn@jubilee-insurance.com
Liberty Syndicate Management Ltd	Liam O'Connell (Acting)	+44 (0)20 7070 4472	info@libertysyndicates.com
KGM Underwriting Agencies Ltd	Adam C Seager	+44 (0)20 8530 1813	adam.seager@kgminsurance.co.uk
Managing Agency Partners Ltd	B Siobhan McAuley	+44 (0)20 7709 3867	smcauley@mapunderwriting.co.uk
Markel Syndicate Management Ltd	Andrew J Bailey	+44 (0)20 7953 6000	andrew.bailey@markelintl.com
Marketform Managing Agency Ltd	Anne C Durkin	+44 (0)20 7488 7716	anne.durkin@marketform.com
Marlborough Underwriting Agency Ltd	Iain F MacDowall	+44 (0)20 7456 1800	iain.macdowall@marlborough.co.uk
Max at Lloyd's Ltd	Paul M Armfield	+44 (0)20 3102 3100	paul.armfield@maxatlloyds.com
Mitsui Sumitomo Insurance Underwriting at Lloyd's Ltd	Christopher J Ringrose	+44 (0)20 7977 8346	cringrose@msilm.com
Montpelier Underwriting Agencies Ltd	Gillian Phillips	+44 (0)20 7648 4500	gillian.phillips@montpelierua.com
Munich Re Underwriting Ltd	Timur Coskun	+44 (0)20 7886 3900	tim.coskun@mrunderwriting.com
Navigators Underwriting Agency Ltd	Steven Luck	+44 (0)20 7220 6900	sluck@navg.com
Newline Underwriting Management Ltd	James RF Micklem	+44 (0)20 7090 1700	dickmicklem@newlineuml.com
Novae Syndicates Ltd	Mark J Turvey	+44 (0)20 7903 7300	mturvey@novae.com
Omega Underwriting Agents Ltd	Andrew D Smith	+44 (0)20 7767 3000	andrew.smith@omegauw.com
Pembroke Managing Agency Ltd	Philip Hicks	+44 (0)20 7337 4400	philip.hicks@pembrokeunderwriting.com
QBE Underwriting Ltd	Sharon M Boland	+44 (0)20 7105 4000	enquiries@uk.qbe.com
R J Kiln & Co Limited	Keith N Grant	+44 (0)20 7886 9000	See R J Kiln & Co Ltd Company Profile
SA Meacock & Company Ltd	Karl W Jarvis	+44 (0)20 7374 6727	karl.jarvis@sameacock.com
Sagicor at Lloyd's Ltd	Duncan J Reed	+44 (0)20 3003 6800	duncan.reed@sagicor.eu
Spectrum Syndicate Management Ltd	Julie J Marshall	+44 (0)20 7283 2646	julie.marshall@spectrumins.com
Sportscover Underwriting Ltd	Dominic VT Ford	+44 (0)20 7398 4080	dominic.ford@sportscover.com
Starr Managing Agents Ltd	John S Moffat	+44 (0)20 7337 3550	john.moffatt@cvstarrco.com
Talbot Underwriting Ltd	Jane S Clouting	+44 (0)20 7550 3500	jane.clouting@talbotuw.com
Travelers Syndicate Management Ltd	Graham K Jones	+44 (0)20 3207 6263	gjones2@travelers.com
	Michael DL Vernon	+44 (0)20 3207 6231	mvernon@travelers.com
Whittington Capital Management Ltd	Julie M Wilson	+44 (0)20 7743 0900	julie.wilson@whittingtoninsurance.com
XL London Market Ltd	Graham L Brady	+44 (0)20 7933 7306	graham.brady@xlgroup.com

Other (Chief Information Officers, Operations & IT, Legal)

Ascot Underwriting Ltd	Gareth A Challingsworth Operations & IT Director	+44 (0)20 7743 9600	enquiries@ascotuw.com
Faraday Underwriting Ltd	Joanne Merrick UK General Councel	+44 (0)20 7426 6012	joanne.merrick@faraday.com
Newline Underwriting Management Ltd	James RF Micklem Chief Information Officer	+44 (0)20 7090 1700	dickmicklem@newlineuml.com
Novae Syndicates Ltd	Clive L Murray Chief Information Officer	+44 (0)20 7903 7300	cmurray@novae.com
Spectrum Syndicate Management Ltd	C Mark Everest Legal Councel	+44 (0)20 7283 2646	mark.everest@spectrumins.com

Listings – Run-Off Agents

Chairmen

Capita Managing Agency Ltd	Eric SC Stobart	+44 (0)870 523 4568	insurance@capita.co.uk
Cavell Managing Agency Ltd	John P Tilling	+44 (0)20 7780 5850	compliance@cavell.co.uk
RITC Syndicate Management Ltd	Anthony G Hines	+44 (0)20 7220 8899	ritcwebenquiry@ritcsm.com
Shelbourne Syndicate Services Ltd	George N Cochran	+44 (0)20 7961 0810	–

Chief Executive Officers/Managing Directors

Capita Managing Agency Ltd	John B King	+44 (0)870 402 7614	john.king@capita.co.uk
Cavell Managing Agency Ltd	Robin E McCoy	+44 (0)20 7780 5850	compliance@cavell.co.uk
Duncanson & Holt Syndicate Management Ltd	Joseph R Foley	+44 (0)870 402 7278	–
RITC Syndicate Management Ltd	Nigel HJ Rogers	+44 (0)20 7220 8899	ritcwebenquiry@ritcsm.com
RiverStone Managing Agency Ltd	Nicholas C Bentley	+44 (0)20 7977 1600	nick.bentley@rsml.co.uk
Shelbourne Syndicate Services Ltd	Sean J Dalton	+44 (0)20 7961 0810	–

Chief Financial Officers

Capita Managing Agency Ltd	William Scott	+44 (0)870 402 7575	william.scott@capita.co.uk
Duncanson & Holt Syndicate Management Ltd	Andrew G Ripley	+44 (0)20 8704 7278	rick.morgan@capita.co.uk
Ridge Underwriting Agencies Ltd	Philippa M Curtis	+44 (0)20 7173 7711	philippa.curtis@ace-ina.com
RITC Syndicate Management Ltd	Roy Katzenberg	+44 (0)20 7220 8899	ritcwebenquiry@ritcsm.com
RiverStone Managing Agency Ltd	Lorna A Hemsley	+44 (0)20 7977 1600	lorna.hemsley@rsml.co.uk
Shelbourne Syndicate Services Ltd	Clifford E Murphy	+44 (0)20 7961 0810	roger.durowse@shelbournegroup.com

Executive Directors

Capita Managing Agency Ltd	Philip Dietz	+44 (0)870 402 7658	philip.dietz@capita.co.uk
	John S Hale	+44 (0)870 402 7591	john.hale@capita.co.uk
	Richard TA Morgan	+44 (0)870 402 7278	rick.morgan@capita.co.uk
	Timothy Shenton	+44 (0)870 402 7900	tim.shenton@capita.co.uk
Cavell Managing Agency Ltd	Simon P Amies	+44 (0)20 7780 5850	compliance@cavell.co.uk
	Michael Bell	+44 (0)20 7780 5850	compliance@cavell.co.uk
	Peter AG Green	+44 (0)20 7780 5850	compliance@cavell.co.uk
	Ken E Randall	+44 (0)20 7780 5850	compliance@cavell.co.uk
	James A Willsher	+44 (0)20 7780 5850	compliance@cavell.co.uk
Duncanson & Holt Syndicate Management Ltd	Angus M Sladen	+44 (0)870 402 7278	–
Ridge Underwriting Agencies Ltd	Richard V Pryce	+44 (0)20 7173 7396	richard.pryce@ace-ina.com
Shelbourne Syndicate Services Ltd	Andrew D Elliott	+44 (0)20 7961 0810	–

Non-Executive Directors

Capita Managing Agency Ltd	Sarah M Wilton	+44 (0)870 523 4568	insurance@capita.co.uk
Cavell Managing Agency Ltd	Alan C Pollard, MBE	+44 (0)20 7780 5850	compliance@cavell.co.uk
	Michael G Smith	+44 (0)20 7780 5850	compliance@cavell.co.uk
Duncanson & Holt Syndicate Management Ltd	Peter L Doyle	+44 (0)870 402 7278	–
	George E Lloyd-Roberts	+44 (0)870 402 7278	–
RITC Syndicate Management Ltd	Steven Fass (Independent)	+44 (0)20 7220 8899	ritcwebenquiry@ritcsm.com
	Donald C McCrickard (Independent)	+44 (0)20 7220 8899	ritcwebenquiry@ritcsm.com
	William L Spiegel	+44 (0)20 7220 8899	ritcwebenquiry@ritcsm.com
	Ravi P Yadav	+44 (0)20 7220 8899	ritcwebenquiry@ritcsm.com
RiverStone Managing Agency Ltd	Dennis C Gibbs	+44 (0)20 7977 1600	–
	William F Goodier	+44 (0)20 7977 1600	–
	Anthony J Keys	+44 (0)20 7977 1600	stephen.osborne@rsml.co.uk
Shelbourne Syndicate Services Ltd	Timothy J Hanford	+44 (0)20 7961 0810	–
	Richard J Harris	+44 (0)20 7961 0810	–
	Phillip C Martin	+44 (0)20 7961 0810	–

Chief Operating Officers/Operations Directors

Cavell Managing Agency Ltd	John GF O'Neill	+44 (0)20 7780 5850	compliance@cavell.co.uk
RiverStone Managing Agency Ltd	Luke R Tanzer	+44 (0)20 7977 1600	luke.tanzer@rsml.co.uk
Shelbourne Syndicate Services Ltd	Clifford E Murphy	+44 (0)20 7961 0810	roger.durowse@shelbournegroup.com

Business Development Director

RITC Syndicate Management Ltd	Christopher P Hare	+44 (0)20 7220 8878	ritcwebenquiry@ritcsm.com

Claims Directors

Cavell Managing Agency Ltd	Stephen T Clarke	+44 (0)20 7780 5850	compliance@cavell.co.uk
Ridge Underwriting Agencies Ltd	R Peter Murray	+44 (0)20 7173 7709	peter.murray@ace-ina.com
RITC Syndicate Management Ltd	Dinah J Gately	+44 (0)20 7220 8899	ritcwebenquiry@ritcsm.com

Underwriting Director(s), Head of Assurance

RiverStone Managing Agency Ltd	Stephen Osborne Head of Assurance	+44 (0)20 7977 1600	–
RITC Syndicate Management Ltd	J Nicholas C Wooldridge Underwriting Director	+44 (0)20 7220 8899	ritcwebenquiry@ritcsm.com

Compliance Directors & Officers

Capita Managing Agency Ltd	John S Hale	+44 (0)870 402 7591	john.hale@capita.co.uk
Cavell Managing Agency Ltd	James A Willsher	+44 (0)20 7780 5850	compliance@cavell.co.uk
Duncanson & Holt Syndicate Management Ltd	Richard (Rick) TA Morgan	+44 (0)870 402 7278	rick.morgan@capita.co.uk
Ridge Underwriting Agencies Ltd	Adrian W Missen	+44 (0)20 7173 7000	adrian.missen@ace-ina.com
RITC Syndicate Management Ltd	Roy Katzenberg	+44 (0)20 7220 8899	ritcwebenquiry@ritcsm.com
Shelbourne Syndicate Services Ltd	Roger H Durowse	+44 (0)20 7961 0810	roger.durowse@shelbournegroup.com

Company Secretaries

Capita Managing Agency Ltd	Capita Company Secretarial Services Limited		
Cavell Managing Agency Ltd	James A Willsher	+44 (0)20 7780 5850	compliance@cavell.co.uk
Duncanson & Holt Syndicate Management Ltd	Richard (Rick) TA Morgan	+44 (0)870 402 7278	rick.morgan@capita.co.uk
Ridge Underwriting Agencies Ltd	Adrian W Missen	+44 (0)20 7173 7000	adrian.missen@ace-ina.com
RITC Syndicate Management Ltd	Shirley L Blakelock	+44 (0)20 7220 8899	ritcwebenquiry@ritcsm.com
RiverStone Managing Agency Ltd	Fraser Henry	+44 (0)1273 792 104	fraser.henry@rsml.co.uk
Shelbourne Syndicate Services Ltd	Roger H Durowse	+44 (0)20 7961 0810	roger.durowse@shelbournegroup.com

Listings – Members' Agents

Chairmen

Alpha Insurance Analysts Limited	WS Clive Richards	+44 (0)20 7264 2133	cr@crco.co.uk
Argenta Private Capital Limited	Lord Brabourne	+44 (0)20 7825 7200	privatecapital@argentaplc.com
Hampden Agencies Ltd	Nigel J Hanbury	+44 (0)20 7863 6502	nigel.hanbury@hampden.co.uk
ICP General Partner Limited	tba		
Lloyd's Members Agency Services Ltd	Jock Worsley	+44 (0)1634 392 090	lloyds-lmas@lloyds.com

Chief Executive Officers/Managing Directors

Alpha Insurance Analysts Limited	A James Sparrow	+44 (0)20 7264 2148	james@aianalysts.com
Argenta Private Capital Limited	Graham J White	+44 (0)20 7825 7182	graham.white@argentaplc.com
Hampden Agencies Ltd	Neil LC Smith	+44 (0)20 7863 6562	neil.smith@hampden.co.uk
ICP General Partner Limited	The Hon Charles AA Harbord-Hamond	+44 (0)20 7392 8480	charles.hh@inscap.co.uk
Lloyd's Members Agency Services Ltd	Paul Box	+44 (0)1634 392 082	paul.box@lloyds.com

Chief Financial Officers/Finance Directors

Alpha Insurance Analysts Limited	Appointment not made - outsourced		
Argenta Private Capital Limited	Marcus G Warner	+44 (0)20 7825 7262	marcus.warner@argentaplc.com
Hampden Agencies Ltd	Nicholas D Lewis	+44 (0)20 7863 6507	nicholas.lewis@hampden.co.uk
ICP General Partner Limited	James RV Brandon	+44 (0)20 7392 8480	james.brandon@inscap.co.uk
Lloyd's Members Agency Services Ltd	Handled by the Corporation of Lloyd's		

Chief Operating Officers/Agency Managers

Hampden Agencies Ltd	Mark J Tottman	+44 (0)20 7863 6504	mark.tottman@hampden.co.uk

Executive Directors

Alpha Insurance Analysts Limited	Emma Royds	+44 (0)20 7264 2132	emma@aianalysts.com
Argenta Private Capital Limited	Jeremy M Bray	+44 (0)20 7825 7174	jeremy.bray@argentaplc.com
	Trevor R Bird	+44 (0)20 7825 7131	trevor.bird@argentaplc.com
	Robert P Flach	+44 (0)20 7825 7179	robert.flach@argentaplc.com
	Guy B Hudson	+44 (0)20 7825 7241	guy.hudson@argentaplc.com
	James A Mackay	+44 (0)20 7825 7288	james.mackay@argentaplc.com
	David Monksfield	+44 (0)20 7825 7139	david.monksfield@argentaplc.com
	W David Robson	+44 (0)20 7825 7139	david.robson@argentaplc.com
Hampden Agencies Ltd	David A Cant	+44 (0)20 7863 6573	david.cant@hampden.co.uk
	Nicholas HD Carrick	+44 (0)20 7863 6526	nick.carrick@hampden.co.uk
	Charles GC Oliver	+44 (0)20 7863 6621	charles.oliver@hampden.co.uk
	Stephen M Wilcox	+44 (0)20 7863 6530	stephen.wilcox@hampden.co.uk
	Alistair T Wood	+44 (0)20 7863 6570	alistair.wood@hampden.co.uk

Non-Executive Directors

Alpha Insurance Analysts Limited	Alan C Lovell	+44 (0)20 7264 2133	alan.lovell@aianalysts.com
	Michael J Meacock	+44 (0)20 7264 2133	michael.meacock@sameacock.com
Argenta Private Capital Limited	Andrew J Annandale	+44 (0)20 7825 7239	andrew.annandale@argentaplc.com
	David BK Harrison	+44 (0)20 7825 7200	privatecapital@argentaplc.com
	Paul F Sandilands	+44 (0)20 7825 7200	paul.sandilands@argentaplc.com
Hampden Agencies Ltd	Sir Adam N Ridley	+44 (0)20 7863 6500	adam.ridley@hampden.co.uk
	Lord Strathclyde	+44 (0)20 7863 6500	hal@hampden.co.uk
	Sarah M Wilton	+44 (0)20 7863 6500	sarah.wilton@hampden.co.uk
ICP General Partner Limited	Robert FM Adair	+44 (0)20 7392 8480	info@inscap.co.uk
	Lord JP Marland of Odstock	+44 (0)20 7392 8480	info@inscap.co.uk
Lloyd's Members Agency Services Ltd	Christopher Hare	+44 (0)1634 392 090	lloyds-lmas@lloyds.com
	Luke Savage	+44 (0)1634 392 090	lloyds-lmas@lloyds.com
	Graham White	+44 (0)1634 392 090	lloyds-lmas@lloyds.com

Executive Directors – Research

Alpha Insurance Analysts Limited	Emily L Apple	+44 (0)20 7264 2146	emily@aianalysts.com
Argenta Private Capital Limited	Jeremy M Bray	+44 (0)20 7825 7174	jeremy.bray@argentaplc.com
Hampden Agencies Ltd	Alistair T Wood	+44 (0)20 7863 6570	alistair.wood@hampden.co.uk

Research Team

Alpha Insurance Analysts Limited	Chandon Bleackley	+44 (0)20 7264 2147	chandon@aianalysts.com
Argenta Private Capital	Andrew Brooks	+44 (0)20 7825 7132	andrew.brooks@argentaplc.com
	Andrew M Colcomb	+44 (0)20 7825 7176	andrew.colcomb@argentaplc.com
Hampden Agencies Ltd	John EH Francis	+44 (0)20 7863 6548	john.francis@hampden.co.uk
	Mark Isaacs	+44 (0)20 7863 6500	mark.isaacs@hampden.co.uk
	William W Lewis	+44 (0)20 7863 6572	william.lewis@hampden.co.uk
	Nicholas WL Nops	+44 (0)20 7863 6543	nicholas.nops@hampden.co.uk
	Michael J Wake-Walker	+44 (0)20 7863 6564	michael.walker@hampden.co.uk

Client Management – Executive Directors

Argenta Private Capital Limited	Trevor R Bird	+44 (0)20 7825 7131	trevor.bird@argentaplc.com
	Guy B Hudson	+44 (0)20 7825 7241	guy.hudson@argentaplc.com
	James A Mackay	+44 (0)20 7825 7288	james.mackay@argentaplc.com
	David Monksfield	+44 (0)20 7825 7139	david.monksfield@argentaplc.com
	Alan W Tucker	+44 (0)20 7825 7135	alan.tucker@argentaplc.com
Lloyd's Members Agency Services Ltd	Angela Kerr	+44 (0)1634 392 083	angela.kerr@lloyds.com

Client Services Team

Argenta Private Capital Limited	Fiona A Blood	+44 (0)20 7825 7178	fiona.blood@argentaplc.com
	Michael RP Doughty	+44 (0)20 7825 7237	michael.doughty@argentaplc.com
	Peter T Fletcher	+44 (0)20 7825 7232	peter.fletcher@argentaplc.com
	Neil L Geisa	+44 (0)20 7825 7200	neil.geisa@argentaplc.com
	Milka Jacoby	+44 (0)20 7825 7180	milka.jacoby@argentaplc.com
	Jacquie A Phillips	+44 (0)20 7825 7230	jacquie.a.phillips@argentaplc.com
	John R Robson	+44 (0)20 7825 7177	john.robson@argentaplc.com
	Robin CG Taylor	+44 (0)20 7825 7291	robin.taylor@argentaplc.com
Hampden Agencies Ltd	Timothy CJ Andrews	+44 (0)20 7863 6586	tim.andrews@hampden.co.uk
	Andrew NC Bengough	+44 (0)20 7863 6500	andrew.bengough@hampden.co.uk
	Giles R Berkeley	+44 (0)20 7863 6524	giles.berkeley@hampden.co.uk
	Timothy C Bruce	+44 (0)20 7863 6566	tim.bruce@hampden.co.uk
	Stuart H Buchanan-Smith	+44 (0)20 7863 6535	stuart.buchanan-smith@hampden.co.uk
Hampden Agencies Ltd (Continued)	David J de M Coulthard	+44 (0)20 7938 4321	david.coulthard@hampden.co.uk
	Nicholas J D'Ambrumenil	+44 (0)20 7863 6546	nicholas.dambrumenil@hampden.co.uk
	Stuart M Elswood	+44 (0)20 7863 6595	stuart.elswood@hampden.co.uk
	Jonathan N Green	+44 (0)20 7863 6577	jonathan.gre4n@hampden.co.uk
	John W Hayter	+44 (0)20 7863 6500	john.hayter@hampden.co.uk
	Charles GL Hulbert-Powell	+44 (0)20 7863 6537	charles.hulbert-powell@hampden.co.uk
	Christopher AG Keeling	+44 (0)20 7863 6542	christopher.keeling@hampden.co.uk
	Stephen Lumley	+44 (0)20 7863 6551	stephen.lumley@hampden.co.uk
	John SM Mocatta	+44 (0)20 7863 6534	john.mocatta@hampden.co.uk
	Richard A Page	+44 (0)20 7863 6515	richard.page@hampden.co.uk
	Alexander CM Raven	+44 (0)20 7863 6559	alexander.raven@hampden.co.uk
	W Roger P Sedgwick Rough	+44 (0)20 7863 6547	roger.sr@hampden.co.uk
	Richard MA Watson	+44 (0)133 287 3332	richard.watson@hampden.co.uk
	Gregory C White	+44 (0)20 7863 6553	gregory.white@hampden.co.uk
	Nigel ER Wood	+44 (0)20 7863 6571	nigel.wood@hampden.co.uk
Lloyd's Members Agency Services Ltd	Chomps Kaeowsri	+44 (0)1634 392 087	chomps.kaeowsri@lloyds.com
	Jenny Inkpen	+44 (0)1634 392 084	jennifer.inkpen@lloyds.com
	Tony Skelt	+44 (0)1634 392 088	anthony.skelt@lloyds.com
	Cliff Talbot	+44 (0)1634 392 085	clifford.talbot@lloyds.com

Compliance Directors & Officers

Alpha Insurance Analysts Limited	Jennifer SC Doyle	+44 (0)20 7264 2151	jenny@aianalysts.com
Argenta Private Capital Limited	Christopher JR Fairs	+44 (0)20 7825 7100	chris.fairs@argentaplc.com
Hampden Agencies Ltd	David A Cant	+44 (0)20 7863 6573	david.cant@hampden.co.uk
ICP General Partner Limited	Andrew S Fox	+44 (0)20 7392 8480	andrew.fox@inscap.co.uk
Lloyd's Members Agency Services Ltd	Angela Kerr	+44 (0)1634 392 083	angela.kerr@lloyds.com

Company Secretaries

Alpha Insurance Analysts Limited	Andrew S Fox	+44 (0)20 7264 2133	foxyharding@btinternet.com
Argenta Private Capital Limited	Christopher JR Fairs	+44 (0)20 7825 7100	chris.fairs@argentaplc.com
Hampden Agencies Ltd	Hampden Legal plc		
ICP General Partner Limited	Andrew S Fox	+44 (0)20 7392 8480	andrew.fox@inscap.co.uk
Lloyd's Members Agency Services Ltd	Angela Kerr	+44 (0)1634 392 083	angela.kerr@lloyds.com

Listings – Active & Run-Off Syndicates 2009

Syndicates 2009 – Active Underwriters with Contact Details

No	Managing Agency	Active Underwriter	Telephone	Email
33	Hiscox Syndicates Ltd	Richard C Watson	+44 (0)20 7448 6000	richard.watson@hiscox.com
44	Sagicor at Lloyd's Ltd	Christopher J Ray	+44 (0)20 3003 6800	duncan.reed@sagicor.eu
218	Equity Syndicate Management Ltd	John E Josiah	+44 (0)1277 200 100	john.josiah@equitygroup.co.uk
260	KGM Underwriting Agencies Ltd	Colin Hart	+44 (0)20 8530 1816	colin.hart@kgminsurance.co.uk
308	R J Kiln & Co Limited	Catharine J Toomey	+44 (0)20 7886 9000	cathy.toomey@kilngroup.com
318	Beaufort Underwriting Agency Ltd	Michael SF Pritchard	+44 (0)20 7220 8200	michael.pritchard@beaufort-group.com
382	Hardy (Underwriting Agencies) Ltd*	Adrian J Walker	+44 (0)20 7626 0382	adrian.walker@hardygroup.co.uk
386	QBE Underwriting Ltd	David A Constable	+44 (0)20 7105 4000	enquiries@uk.qbe.com
435	Faraday Underwriting Ltd	Paul NE Ceurvorst	+44 (0)20 7264 4611	paul.ceurvorst@faraday.com
		Mark J Rayner	+44 (0)20 7702 3333	mark.rayner@faraday.com
457	Munich Re Underwriting Ltd	Dominick JR Hoare	+44 (0)20 7886 3900	dominick.hoare@mrunderwriting.com
		Oliver J Crabtree	+44 (0)20 7886 3900	oliver.crabtree@mrunderwriting.com
510	R J Kiln & Co Limited			
	Accident & Health	Tim Prifti	+44 (0)20 7886 9000	tim.prifti@kilngroup.com
	Aviation	Paul Letherbarrow	+44 (0)20 7886 9000	paul.letherbarrow@kilngroup.com
	Marine & Special Risks	Paul Culham	+44 (0)20 7886 9000	paul.culham@kilngroup.com
	Property & Special Lines	Robin Hargreaves	+44 (0)20 7886 9000	robin.hargreaves@kilngroup.com
	Reinsurance	David Huckstepp	+44 (0)20 7886 9000	david.huckstepp@kilngroup.com
	Risk Solutions	Dan Trueman	+44 (0)20 7886 9000	dan.trueman@kilngroup.com
557	R J Kiln & Co Limited	David J Huckstepp	+44 (0)20 7886 9000	david.huckstepp@kilngroup.com
570	Atrium Underwriters Ltd	Kevin W Wilkins	+44 (0)20 7327 4877	kevin.wilkins@atrium-uw.com
609	Atrium Underwriters Ltd	Richard de WW Harries	+44 (0)20 7327 4877	richard.harries@atrium-uw.com
623	Beazley Furlonge Ltd	Neil P Maidment	+44 (0)20 7667 0623	neil.maidment@beazley.com
727	SA Meacock & Company Ltd	Michael J Meacock	+44 (0)20 7374 6727	michael.meacock@sameacock.com
779	Jubilee Managing Agency Ltd	Brian J Jackson	+44 (0)20 7220 8728	brian.jackson@jubilee-insurance.co.uk
780	Advent Underwriting Ltd	Darren J Stockman	+44 (0)20 7743 8200	darren.stockman@adventgroup.co.uk
807	R J Kiln & Co Limited	Lloyd Tunnicliffe	+44 (0)20 7886 9000	lloyd.tunnicliffe@kilngroup.com
958	Omega Underwriting Agents Ltd	John D Robinson	+44 (0)20 7767 3000	john.robinson@omegauw.com
1084	Chaucer Syndicates Ltd	Bruce P Bartell	+44 (0)20 7397 9700	bruce.bartell@chaucerplc.com
1176	Chaucer Syndicates Ltd	Michael G Dawson	+44 (0)20 7397 9700	michael.dawson@chaucerplc.com
1183	Talbot Underwriting Ltd	James E Skinner	+44 (0)20 7550 3500	central@talbotuw.com
1200	Argo Managing Agency Ltd	Mark W Lawrence	+44 (0)20 7712 7600	mark.lawrence@argo-int.com
		Neil R Chapman	+44 (0)20 7712 7600	neil.chapman@argo-int.com
1206	Sagicor at Lloyd's Ltd	Geoffrey M Halpin	+44 (0)20 3003 6800	geoffrey.halpin@sagicor.eu
1209	XL London Market Ltd	Neil D Robertson	+44 (0)20 7933 7000	neil.robertson@xlgroup.com
1218	Newline Underwriting Management Ltd	Philip T Foley	+44 (0)20 7090 1700	pfoley@newlineuml.com
1221	Navigators Underwriting Agency Ltd	Richard P Bardwell	+44 (0)20 7220 6900	rbardwell@navg.com
1225	AEGIS Managing Agency Ltd	David P Croom-Johnson	+44 (0)20 7265 2130	dcroom-johnson@aegislondon.co.uk
1231	Jubilee Managing Agency Ltd	Julian R Cashen	+44 (0)20 7220 8728	jubilee@jubilee-insurance.com
1274	Chaucer Syndicates Ltd	Stephen D Redmond	+44 (0)20 7959 1900	info@antaresunderwriting.com
1301	Chaucer Syndicates Ltd	Robert AG Katzaros	+44 (0)20 7397 9700	info@broadgate-uwg.co.uk
1318	Beaufort Underwriting Agency Ltd	Gordon J Breslin	+44 (0)20 7220 8200	gordon.breslin@beaufort-group.com
1400	Max at Lloyd's Ltd	Matthew A Petzold	+44 (0)20 3102 3100	matthew.petzold@maxalllloyds.com
1414	Ascot Underwriting Ltd	Andrew L Brooks	+44 (0)20 7743 9600	andrew.brooks@ascotuw.com
1458	Spectrum Syndicate Management Ltd	J James Lewis	+44(0)20 7283 2646	newbusiness@spectrumins.com

* 3820 merged into 382.

Syndicates 2009 – Active Underwriters with Contact Details

No	Managing Agency	Active Underwriter	Telephone	Email
1861	Marlborough Underwriting Agency Ltd	Leslie F Allen	+44 (0)20 7456 1800	leslie.allen@marlborough.co.uk
1880	R J Kiln & Co Limited	Stephen D Mathers	+44 (0)20 7886 9000	stephen.mathers@kilngroup.com
1910	Whittington Capital Management Ltd	AJ Tom Milligan	+44 (0)20 7743 0900	tom.milligan@gs.com
1919	Starr Managing Agents Ltd	Christopher Hancock	+44 (0)20 7337 3550	christopher.hancock@cvstarrco.com
1955	Whittington Capital Management Ltd	Mark J Harrington	+44 (0)20 7743 0900	mark.harrington@whittingtoninsurance.com
1965	Argenta Syndicate Management Ltd	Paul Hunt	+44 (0)20 7825 7200	paul.hunt@argentaplc.com
1967	Whittington Capital Management Ltd	Michael Sibthorpe	+44 (0)20 7743 0900	msibthorpe@wrbsyndicate.com
2001	Amlin Underwriting Ltd	Simon CW Beale	+44 (0)20 7746 1000	simon.beale@amlin.co.uk
		Brian D Carpenter	+44 (0)1245 214 875	brian.carpenter@amlin.co.uk
2003	Catlin Underwriting Agencies Ltd	Nicolas J Burkinshaw	+44 (0)20 7626 0486	nicolas.burkinshaw@catlin.com
2007	Novae Syndicates Ltd	Jonathan LJ Butcher	+44 (0)20 7903 7300	jbutcher@novae.com
2010	Cathedral Underwriting Ltd	John C Hamblin	+44 (0)20 7170 9062	john.hamblin@cathedralcapital.com
2012	Arch Underwriting at Lloyd's Ltd	William E Beveridge	+44 (0)20 7621 4525	wbeveridge@archinsurance.co.uk
2112	Spectrum Syndicate Management Ltd	Randolph Roppelt	+44 (0)20 7283 2646	newbusiness@spectrumins.com
2121	Argenta Syndicate Management Ltd	Paul Hunt	+44 (0)20 7825 7200	paul.hunt@argentaplc.com
2243	Starr Managing Agents Ltd	David Stewart	+44 (0)20 7337 3550	david.stewart@cvstarrco.com
2468	Marketform Managing Agency Ltd	Simon P Lotter	+44 (0)20 7488 7700	simon.lotter@marketform.com
2488	Ace Underwriting Agencies Ltd	Richard V Pryce	+44 (0)20 7173 7396	richard.pryce@ace-ina.com
2525	Max at Lloyd's Ltd	David L Dale	+44 (0)20 3102 3100	david.dale@maxatlloyds.com
2526	Max at Lloyd's Ltd	Andrew G Dore	+44 (0)20 3102 3100	andrew.dore@maxatlloyds.com
2623	Beazley Furlonge Ltd	Neil P Maidment	+44 (0)20 7667 0623	neil.maidment@beazley.com
2791	Managing Agency Partners Ltd	Richard K Trubshaw	+44 (0)20 7709 3860	map@mapunderwriting.co.uk
2987	Brit Syndicates Ltd	Johnathan R Turner	+44 (0)20 7984 8500	enquiries@britinsurance.com
2999	QBE Underwriting Ltd	John Neal	+44 (0)20 7105 4000	enquiries@uk.qbe.com

Business Units of Syndicate 2999

No	Managing Agency	Active Underwriter	Telephone	Email
566	*QBE Underwriting Ltd*	*Jonathan W Parry*	*+44 (0)20 7105 4000*	*enquiries@uk.qbe.com*
1036	*QBE Underwriting Ltd*	*Colin R O'Farrell*	*+44 (0)20 7105 4000*	*enquiries@uk.qbe.com*
1886	*QBE Underwriting Ltd*	*John D Neal*	*+44 (0)20 7105 4000*	*enquiries@uk.qbe.com*
2000	*QBE Underwriting Ltd*	*Bernard Mageean*	*+44 (0)20 7105 4000*	*enquiries@uk.qbe.com*
5555	*QBE Underwriting Ltd*	*Emilio A Di Silvio*	*+44 (0)20 7105 4000*	*emilio.disilvio@uk.qbe.com*
3000	Markel Syndicate Management Ltd	Jeremy Brazil	+44 (0)20 7953 6000	jeremy.brazil@markelintl.com
3010	Cathedral Underwriting Ltd	John C Hamblin	+44 (0)20 7170 9062	john.hamblin@cathedralcapital.com
3210	Mitsui Sumitomo Insurance Underwriting at Lloyd's Ltd	Dipak Warren	+44 (0)20 7977 8333	dwarren@msilm.com
3334	Sportscover Underwriting Ltd	Christopher P Nash	+44 (0)20 7398 4080	chris.nash@sportscover.com
3622	Beazley Furlonge Ltd	Neil P Maidment	+44 (0)20 7667 0623	neil.maidment@beazley.com
3623	Beazley Furlonge Ltd	Neil P Maidment	+44 (0)20 7667 0623	neil.maidment@beazley.com
3624	Hiscox Syndicates Ltd	Robert S Childs	+44 (0)20 7448 6000	robert.childs@hiscox.com
4000	Pembroke Managing Agency Ltd	Mark H Wheeler	+44 (0)20 7105 8480	mark.wheeler@pembrokeunderwriting.com
4020	Ark Syndicate Management Ltd	Nicholas K Bonnar	+44 (0)20 3023 4003	nick.bonnar@arkunderwriting.com
4040	HCC Underwriting Agency Ltd	Michael L Onslow	+44 (0)20 7680 3000	monslow@hccint.com
4141	HCC Underwriting Agency Ltd	Michael L Onslow	+44 (0)20 7680 3000	monslow@hccint.com
4242	Chaucer Syndicates Ltd	Gregory Butler	+44 (0)20 7397 9700	enquiries@chaucerplc.com
4444	Canopius Managing Agents Ltd	James A Giordano	+44 (0)20 7337 3710	jim.giordano@canopius.com
4472	Liberty Syndicate Management Ltd	Thomas RC Corfield	+44 (0)20 7070 4472	tom.corfield@libertygroup.co.uk
4711	Aspen Managing Agency Ltd	Matthew Yeldham	+44 (0)20 7184 8000	robert.long@aspen-re.com
5000	Travelers Syndicate Management Ltd	Stephen Eccles	+44 (0)20 3207 6000	seccles@travelers.com

Syndicates 2009 – Active Underwriters with Contact Details

No	Managing Agency	Active Underwriter	Telephone	Email
5151	Montpelier Underwriting Agencies Ltd	Richard MM Chattock	+44 (0)20 7648 4500	richard.chattock@montpelier5151.co.uk
5820	Jubilee Managing Agency Ltd	Christopher H Biles	+44 (0)20 7220 8728	chris.biles@jubilee-insurance.com
6103	Managing Agency Partners Ltd	Richard K Trubshaw	+44 (0)20 7709 3860	map@mapunderwriting.co.uk
6104	Hiscox Syndicates Ltd	Richard C Watson	+44 (0)20 7448 6000	richard.watson@hiscox.com
6105	Ark Syndicate Management Ltd	Nicholas K Bonnar	+44 (0)20 3023 4003	nick.bonnar@arkunderwriting.com
6106	Amlin Underwriting Ltd	Simon CW Beale	+44 (0)20 7746 1000	simon.beale@amlin.co.uk

Run-Off Syndicates 2009 – Run-Off Managers with Contact Details

No	Managing Agency	Run-Off Manager	Telephone	Email
102	Cavell Managing Agency Ltd	Robin E McCoy	+44 (0)20 7780 5850	compliance@cavell.co.uk
529	Shelbourne Syndicate Services Ltd	Andrew D Elliott	+44 (0)20 7961 0810	–
839	Canopius Managing Agents Ltd	Michael East	+44 (0)20 7337 3700	mike.east@canopius.com
957	Duncanson & Holt Syndicate Management Limited	David F McElhiney	+44 (0)870 402 7278	–
991	Capita Managing Agency Ltd	Harvey Simons	+44 (0)870 523 4567	harvey.simons@capita.co.uk
1101	Duncanson & Holt Syndicate Management Limited	David F McElhiney	+44 (0)870 402 7278	–
1171	Ridge Underwriting Agencies Ltd	Russell Burgess	+44 (0)20 7173 7000	info.uk@ace-ina.com
1688	Capita Managing Agency Ltd	Philip Dietz	+44 (0)870 402 7658	philip.dietz@capita.co.uk
1900	Capita Managing Agency Ltd	Philip Dietz	+44 (0)870 402 7658	philip.dietz@capita.co.uk
2008	Shelbourne Syndicate Services Ltd	Andrew D Elliott	+44 (0)20 7961 0810	–
2020	Catlin Underwriting Agencies Ltd	David CB Ibeson	+44 (0)20 7626 0486	david.ibeson@catlin.com
3330	Cavell Managing Agency Ltd	John GF O'Neill	+44 (0)20 7780 5850	compliance@cavell.co.uk
3500	RiverStone Managing Agency Ltd	Appointment not made	+44 (0)20 7977 1600	–
5500	Capita Managing Agency Ltd	Philip Dietz	+44 (0)870 402 7658	philip.dietz@capita.co.uk
5678	RITC Syndicate Management Ltd	J Nicholas Wooldridge	+44 (0)20 7220 8899	ritcwebenquiry@ritcsm.com

Other Syndicates in Run-Off 2009

No	Managing Agency	Run-Off Manager	Telephone	Email	Open Year(s)
53	Spectrum Syndicate Management Ltd	R John Murphy	+44 (0)20 7283 2646	newbusiness@spectrumins.com	1998, 1999, 2000
340	Travelers Syndicate Management Ltd	Stephen Gordon Eccles	+44 (0)20 3207 6000	trv5000@travelers.com	2002, 2001
376	Whittington Capital Management Ltd	Gary Leonard Griffiths	+44 (0)20 7743 0900	jon.francis@whittingtoninsurance.com	2003
389	Brit Syndicates Limited	Nigel David Hartley	+44 (0)20 7984 8500	enquiries@britinsurance.com	2003
994	Max at Lloyd's Ltd	Matthew A Petzold	+44 (0)20 3102 3100	info@maxatlloyds.com	2006
1007	Novae Syndicates Ltd	Information not available	+44 (0)20 7903 7300	novae@mconsulting.co.uk	2002
1010	Novae Syndicates Ltd	Information not available	+44 (0)20 7903 7300	novae@mconsulting.co.uk	2002
1115	Novae Syndicates Ltd	Information not available	+44 (0)20 7903 7300	novae@mconsulting.co.uk	2002
1203	Novae Syndicates Ltd	Information not available	+44 (0)20 7903 7300	novae@mconsulting.co.uk	2002
1241	Novae Syndicates Ltd	Jeremy Richard Adam	+44 (0)20 7903 7300	novae@mconsulting.co.uk	2002
1243	Marlborough Underwriting Agency Ltd	John Collyear	+44 (0)20 7456 1800	compliance@marlborough.co.uk	2002/3
		Raymond Spicer	+44 (0)20 7456 1800	compliance@marlborough.co.uk	2004
4455	Equity Syndicate Management Ltd	Information not available	+44 (0)1277 200 100	info@equitygroup.co.uk	2006

Lloyd's Market

Governance

Governance

Council

Title	Name	Telephone	Email
Chairman	Lord Levene of Portsoken, KBE	+44 (0)20 7327 6556	peter.levene@lloyds.com
Chief Executive Officer	Dr Richard Ward	+44 (0)20 7226 6930	richard.ward@lloyds.com
Deputy Chairman of Lloyd's	Ewen Gilmour	+44 (0)20 7105 8080	gavin.steele@lloyds.com
Deputy Chairman of Lloyd's	Dr Andreas Prindl, CBE	+44 (0)20 7638 9382	gavin.steele@lloyds.com
Deputy Chairman of Lloyd's	Graham White	+44 (0)20 7825 7182	gavin.steele@lloyds.com
Working Member	Rupert Atkin	+44 (0)20 7327 6032	gavin.steele@lloyds.com
External Member	Michael Deeny	+44 (0)20 7327 6032	gavin.steele@lloyds.com
Nominated Member	Celia Denton	+44 (0)20 7327 6032	gavin.steele@lloyds.com
Nominated Member	Sir Robert Finch	+44 (0)20 7327 6032	gavin.steele@lloyds.com
Working Member	Christopher Harman	+44 (0)20 7327 6032	gavin.steele@lloyds.com
Nominated Member	Dr Reg Hinkley	+44 (0)20 7327 6032	gavin.steele@lloyds.com
Representative of Aprilgrange Limited	Martin Hudson	+44 (0)20 7327 6032	gavin.steele@lloyds.com
Representative of Catlin Syndicates Ltd	Paul Jardine	+44 (0)20 7327 6032	gavin.steele@lloyds.com
Nominated Member	The Hon Philip Lader	+44 (0)20 7327 6032	gavin.steele@lloyds.com
External Member	Alan Lovell	+44 (0)20 7327 6032	gavin.steele@lloyds.com
Working member	Nick Marsh	+44 (0)20 7327 6032	gavin.steele@lloyds.com
External member	Barbara Merry	+44 (0)20 7327 6032	gavin.steele@lloyds.com
External member (resigned May 2009)	Dermot O'Donohoe	+44 (0)20 7327 6032	gavin.steele@lloyds.com
Secretary to the Council	Gavin Steele	+44 (0)20 7327 6032	gavin.steele@lloyds.com

Franchise Board

Title	Name	Telephone	Email
Chairman	Lord Levene of Portsoken, KBE	+44 (0)20 7327 6556	peter.levene@lloyds.com
Executive Director	Dr Richard Ward	+44 (0)20 7226 6930	richard.ward@lloyds.com
Non-Executive Director	Nicholas Furlonge	+44 (0)20 7327 6032	gavin.steele@lloyds.com
Non-Executive Director	Claire Ighodaro, CBE	+44 (0)20 7327 6032	gavin.steele@lloyds.com
Non-Executive Director	Andrew Kendrick	+44 (0)20 7327 6032	gavin.steele@lloyds.com
Executive Director	Luke Savage	+44 (0)20 7327 6032	luke.savage@lloyds.com
Non-Executive Director	Dipesh Shah, OBE	+44 (0)20 7327 6032	gavin.steele@lloyds.com
Non-Executive Director	David Shipley	+44 (0)20 7327 6032	gavin.steele@lloyds.com
Non-Executive Director	James Stretton	+44 (0)20 7327 6032	gavin.steele@lloyds.com
Executive Director	Rolf Tolle	+44 (0)20 7327 6032	rolf.tolle@lloyds.com
Secretary to the Franchise Board	Gavin Steele	+44 (0)20 7327 6032	gavin.steele@lloyds.com

Corporation

Corporation

Title	Name	Telephone	Email
Chairman	Lord Levene of Portsoken, KBE	+44 (0)20 7327 6556	peter.levene@lloyds.com
Chief Executive Officer	Dr Richard Ward	+44 (0)20 7327 6930	richard.ward@lloyds.com
Deputy Chairman of Lloyd's	Ewen Gilmour	+44 (0)20 7105 8080	ewen.gilmour@chaucerplc.com
Deputy Chairman of Lloyd's	Dr Andreas Prindl	+44 (0)20 7638 9382	andreas.prindl@lloyds.com
Deputy Chairmen of Lloyd's	Graham White	+44 (0)20 7825 7182	graham.white@lloyds.com
Director of Finance, Risk Management, and Operations	Luke Savage	+44 (0)20 7327 6711	luke.savage@lloyds.com
Franchise Performance Director	Rolf Tolle	+44 (0)20 7327 6743	rolf.tolle@lloyds.com
Executive Director & General Counsel	Sean McGovern	+44 (0)20 7327 6142	sean.mcgovern@lloyds.com
Director of International Markets and Business Development	Jose Ribeiro	+44 (0)20 7327 6179	jose.ribeiro@lloyds.com
Director of Market Operations and North America	Susan Langley	+44 (0)20 7327 6200	sue.langley@lloyds.com

Corporation Departments

Corporate Services

Head of the Department	Dr Richard Ward	+44 (0)20 7327 6930	richard.ward@lloyds.com
Communications	Louise Shield	+44 (0)20 7327 5793	louise.shield@lloyds.com
Human Resources	Suzy Black	+44 (0)20 7327 6025	suzy.black@lloyds.com
Internal Audit	Hilary Weaver	+44 (0)20 7327 5545	hilary.weaver@lloyds.com
Secretary to Council and Franchise Board	Gavin Steele	+44 (0)20 7327 6032	gavin.steele@lloyds.com

Finance, Risk Management & Operations

Head of the Department	Luke Savage	+44 (0)20 7327 6711	luke.savage@lloyds.com
Chief Information Officer	Peter Hambling	+44 (0)20 7327 6660	peter.hambling@lloyds.com
Financial Control	Jonathan May	+44 (0)20 7327 5314	jonathan.may@lloyds.com
Investor Relations & Ratings	Christina Nallaiah	+44 (0)20 7327 6456	christina.nallaiah@lloyds.com
Market Finance	John Parry	+44 (0)20 7327 5129	john.parry@lloyds.com
Market Risk and Reserving Unit & Lloyd's Actuary	Henry Johnson	+44 (0)20 7327 5235	henry.johnson@lloyds.com
Market Services	Steve Robertson	+44 (0)20 7327 2111	steven.robertson@lloyds.com
Property Services	John Mitchell	+44 (0)20 7327 6548	john.mitchell@lloyds.com
Risk Management	Olly Reeves	+44 (0)20 7327 6229	olly.reeves@lloyds.com
Treasury	Stuart Simpson	+44 (0)20 7327 5760	stuart.simpson@lloyds.com

Corporation

Franchise Performance

Head of the Department	Rolf AW Tolle	+44 (0)20 7327 6743	rolf.tolle@lloyds.com
Agency	Karen Bizon	+44 (0)20 7327 5735	karen.bizon@lloyds.com
Claims	Kent Chaplin	+44 (0)20 7327 5552	kent.chaplin@lloyds.com
Underwriting Performance	David Indge	+44 (0)20 7327 5716	david.indge@lloyds.com
Delegated Authorities	Peter Montanaro	+44 (0)20 7327 5971	peter.montanaro@lloyds.com
Exposure Management & Reinsurance	Paul Nunn	+44 (0)20 7327 6402	paul.nunn@lloyds.com
Analysis	Markus Gesmann	+44 (0)20 7327 5694	markus.gesmann@lloyds.com
Open Years	Steve McCann	+44 (0)20 7327 5984	steve.mccann@lloyds.com
FPD Operations	Robert Humphreys	+44 (0)20 7327 5985	robert.humphreys@lloyds.com
Underwriting Standards	Kieran Flynn	+44 (0)20 7327 5739	kieran.flynn@lloyds.com
Information Management	Eamon Brown	+44 (0)20 7327 6266	eamon.brown@lloyds.com

General Counsel's Division

Head of the Department	Sean G McGovern	+44 (0)20 7327 6142	sean.mcgovern@lloyds.com
Counsel to Lloyd's	Julian Burling	+44 (0)20 7327 5601	julian.burling@lloyds.com
Government Policy & Affairs	Alastair Evans	+44 (0)20 7327 6682	alastair.evans@lloyds.com
International Regulatory Affairs	Rosemary Beaver	+44 (0)20 7327 5208	rosemary.beaver@lloyds.com
Legal & Compliance	Peter Spires	+44 (0)20 7327 6170	peter.spires@lloyds.com
Relationship Management	Robert Stevenson	+44 (0)20 7327 5541	robert.stevenson@lloyds.com

International Markets

Head of the Department	Jose Ribeiro	+44 (0)20 7327 6179	jose.ribeiro@lloyds.com
Operations	Kevin Reeves	+44 (0)20 7327 6264	kevin.reeves@lloyds.com
Market Development	Matthew Chandler	+44 (0)20 7327 5743	matthew.chandler@lloyds.com
Asia Pasific	Keith Stern	+61 2 9223 1433	keith.stern@lloyds.com
China	Eric Gao	+44 (0)20 7327 7801	eric.gao@lloyds.com
Europe	Enrico Bertagna	+44 (0)20 7327 7920	enrico.bertagna@lloyds.com
Japan	Iain Ferguson	+81 3 3215 5297	iain.ferguson@lloyds.com

Market Operations & North America

Head of the Department	Susan C Langley	+44 (0)20 7327 6200	sue.langley@lloyds.com
Head of Market Operations	Carl Phillips	+44 (0)20 7327 5665	carl.phillips@lloyds.com
Lloyd's America Inc, President	tba	+44 (0)20 7327 7290	c/o sue.langley@lloyds.com
Lloyd's Illinois, President	Maryanne Swaim	+44 (0)20 7327 7201	maryanne.swaim@lloyds.com
Lloyd's Kentucky, President	Pat Talley	+44 (0)20 7327 7241	pat.talley@lloyds.com
Lloyd's Canada, Attorney in Fact	Deborah Moor	+1 514 864 5046	deborah.moor@lloyds.com
Lloyd's USVI, General Representative	Hank Feuerzeig	+1 340 715 4443	hank.feuerzeig@lloyds.com
Market Reform Office	Christopher Croft	+44 (0)20 7327 5278	christopher.croft@lloyds.com

Companies – Managing Agents

Ace Underwriting Agencies Limited

Address	100 Leadenhall Street
	London EC3A 3BP
Telephone	+44 (0)20 7173 7000
Fax	+44 (0)20 7173 7800
Contact Email	info.uk@ace-ina.com
Website	www.acelimited.com

SENIOR MANAGEMENT

Title	Name	Telephone	Email
Chairman (Executive) & Chief Executive Officer	Andrew J Kendrick	+44 (0)20 7173 7000	andrew.kendrick@ace-ina.com
Chief Financial Officer	Philippa M Curtis	+44 (0)20 7173 7711	philippa.curtis@ace-ina.com
Underwriting Director	Richard V Pryce	+44 (0)20 7173 7396	richard.pryce@ace-ina.com
Chief Underwriting Officer	AW Matthew Shaw	+44 (0)20 7173 7000	matthew.shaw@ace-ina.com
Claims Director	R Peter Murray	+44 (0)20 7173 7000	peter.murray@ace-ina.com
Non-Executive Director	Graham D Williams	+44 (0)20 7173 7000	info.uk@ace-ina.com
Compliance Officer	Adrian W Missen	+44 (0)20 7173 7709	adrian.missen@ace-ina.com
Company Secretary	Adrian W Missen	+44 (0)20 7173 7309	adrian.missen@ace-ina.com

SYNDICATES MANAGED IN 2009

SYNDICATE NUMBER	**2488 Ace Global Markets**		
Active Underwriter	Richard V Pryce	+44 (0)20 7173 7396	richard.pryce@ace-ina.com
Appointed	2003		
Main Areas of Underwriting	UK & European Property; Accident & Health		
YEAR	CAPACITY £m		
2009	285		
2008	330		
2007	400		

BACKGROUND INFORMATION

Ownership	Ace Underwriting Agencies Ltd is controlled by ACE Ltd, part of the ACE Group of Companies of Zurich, Switzerland
Date of Incorporation	1985
Former Names	Simbridge Limited to 1989
	Charman Underwriting Agencies Ltd to 1999
Syndicates merged into 2488	47, 48, 112, 122, 204, 219, 322, 375, 483, 484, 490, 545, 732, 925, 960, 998, 2322, 2490

Advent Underwriting Limited

Address	10th Floor
	1 Minster Court
	Mincing Lane
	London EC3R 7AA
Telephone	+44 (0)20 7743 8200
Fax	+44 (0)20 7743 8299

Contact Email	head.office@adventgroup.co.uk
Website	www.adventgroup.co.uk

SENIOR MANAGEMENT

Title	Name	Telephone	Email
Chairman (Non-Executive)	Peter WJ Cresswell	+44 (0)20 7743 8200	head.office@adventgroup.co.uk
Managing Director	Keith D Thompson	+44 (0)20 7743 8200	keith.thompson@adventgroup.co.uk
Finance Director	Philip J Green	+44 (0)20 7743 8234	phil.green@adventgroup.co.uk
Director of Operations	John C Towers	+44 (0)20 7743 8205	john.towers@adventgroup.co.uk
Chief Underwriting Officer	Duncan P Lummis	+44 (0)20 7743 8233	duncan.lummis@adventgroup.co.uk
Executive Director & Active Underwriter	Darren J Stockman	+44 (0)20 7743 8219	darren.stockman@adventgroup.co.uk
Independent Review Director	Richard GM Finn	+44 (0)20 7743 8200	head.office@adventgroup.co.uk
Non-Executive Director	Brian W Rowbotham	+44 (0)20 7743 8200	head.office@adventgroup.co.uk
Compliance Officer	Ian M Hewitt	+44 (0)20 7743 8245	ian.hewitt@adventgroup.co.uk
Company Secretary	Neil M Ewing	+44 (0)20 7743 8250	neil.ewing@adventgroup.co.uk

SYNDICATES MANAGED IN 2009

SYNDICATE NUMBER	**Advent Syndicate 780**		
Active Underwriter	Darren J Stockman	+44 (0)20 7743 8219	darren.stockman@adventgroup.co.uk
Appointed	2008		
Main Areas of Underwriting	Property Reinsurance & Insurance; Energy; Marine Reinsurance		
YEAR	CAPACITY £m		
2009	135		
2008	135		
2007	151		

BACKGROUND INFORMATION

Ownership	Advent Underwriting Ltd is controlled by Advent Capital (Holdings) PLC, listed on the London AIM market and whose majority shareholder is the Fairfax Financial Holdings Limited, a Company incorporated and registered in Canada
Date of Incorporation	1975
Former Names	BF Caudle Agencies Limited to 2002
Syndicates merged into 780	None

AEGIS Managing Agency Ltd

Address	110 Fenchurch Street
	London EC3M 5JT
Telephone	+44 (0)20 7265 2100
Fax	+44 (0)20 7265 2101
Contact Email	aegislondon@aegislimited.co.uk
Website	www.aegislink.com

SENIOR MANAGEMENT

Title	Name	Telephone	Email
Chairman (Non-Executive)	Alan J Maguire	+44 (0)20 7265 2100	amaguire@aegislondon.co.uk
Managing Director	Stuart R Davies	+44 (0)20 7265 2152	sdavies@aegislondon.co.uk
Finance Director	Paul P Guiry	+44 (0)20 7265 2108	pguiry@aegislondon.co.uk

AEGIS Managing Agency Ltd (continued)

Operations Director	Sarah A Davies	+44 (0)20 7265 2110	sdavies@aegislondon.co.uk
Underwriting Director	David P Croom-Johnson	+44 (0)20 7265 2130	dcroom-johnson@aegislondon.co.uk
Claims Manager	Richard Foulger	+44 (0)20 7265 2127	rfoulger@aegislondon.co.uk
Compliance Officer	Darren Wells	+44 (0)20 7265 2169	dwells@aegislondon.co.uk
Other Executive Director(s)	John E Chambers	+44 (0)20 7265 2129	jchambers@aegislondon.co.uk
Non-Executive Director(s)	William RP Dalton	+44 (0)20 7265 2100	enquiries@aegislink.com
	Christopher D Forbes	+44 (0)20 7265 2100	enquiries@aegislink.com
	John S Goldsmith	+44 (0)20 7265 2100	enquiries@aegislink.com
	Donald J Greene	+44 (0)20 7265 2100	enquiries@aegislink.com
	William H Grigg	+44 (0)20 7265 2100	enquiries@aegislink.com
	Thomas J Mahoney	+44 (0)20 7265 2100	enquiries@aegislink.com
	Wesley W von Schack	+44 (0)20 7265 2100	enquiries@aegislink.com
Company Secretary	Hayley J Connell	+44 (0)20 7265 2100	hconnell@aegislondon.co.uk

SYNDICATES MANAGED IN 2009

SYNDICATE NUMBER	**Aegis Syndicate 1225**		
Active Underwriter	David P Croom-Johnson	+44 (0)20 7265 2130	dcroom-johnson@aegislondon.co.uk
Appointed	2007		
Main Areas of Underwriting	Energy		
YEAR	CAPACITY £m		
2009	200		
2008	183		
2007	221		

BACKGROUND INFORMATION

Ownership	AEGIS Managing Agency Ltd is controlled by Associated Electric & Gas Insurance Services Inc of New Jersey, USA, which is a subsidiary of AEGIS Ltd of Hamilton, Bermuda
Date of Incorporation	1997
Former Names	None in past 20 years
Syndicates merged into 1225	None

Amlin Underwriting Ltd

Address	St Helen's
	1 Undershaft
	London EC3A 8ND
Telephone	+44 (0)20 7746 1000
Fax	+44 (0)20 7746 1696
Contact Email	info@amlin.co.uk
Website	www.amlin.com

SENIOR MANAGEMENT

Title	Name	Telephone	Email
Chairman (Non-Executive)	Roger J Taylor	+44 (0)20 7746 1000	roger.taylor@amlin.co.uk
Managing Director	David J Harris	+44 (0)20 7746 1000	david.harris@amlin.co.uk

Finance Director	Steven R McMurray	+44 (0)20 7746 1000	steven.mcmurray@amlin.co.uk
Underwriting Director, Amlin London	Simon CW Beale	+44 (0)20 7746 1000	simon.beale@amlin.co.uk
Underwriting Director, UK Commercial	Brian D Carpenter	+44 (0)1245 214 875	brian.carpenter@amlin.co.uk
Head of Aviation	Rodney G Dampier	+44 (0)20 7746 1000	rodney.dampier@amlin.co.uk
Chief Risk Officer	James LeT Illingworth	+44 (0)20 7746 1060	james.illingworth@amlin.co.uk
Compliance Officer	Allan Rayner	+44 (0)20 7746 1000	allan.rayner@amlin.co.uk
Non-Executive Director(s)	Nigel JC Buchanan	+44 (0)20 7746 1000	amlinreception@amlin.co.uk
	Martin D Feinstein	+44 (0)20 7746 1000	amlinreception@amlin.co.uk
	Richard A Hextall	+44 (0)20 7746 1000	richard.hextall@amlin.co.uk
	Anthony W Holt	+44 (0)20 7746 1000	amlinreception@amlin.co.uk
	Charles EL Philipps	+44 (0)20 7746 1000	charles.philipps@amlin.co.uk
Company Secretary ⅄	Jeanette M Mansell	+44 (0)20 7746 1000	jeanette.mansell@amlin.co.uk
Group Company Secretary	Charles CT Pender	+44 (0)20 7746 1000	charles.pender@amlin.co.uk

SYNDICATES MANAGED IN 2009

SYNDICATE NUMBER	**Syndicate 2001**		
Active Underwriter (Joint)	Simon CW Beale	+44 (0)20 7746 1000	simon.beale@amlin.co.uk
Appointed	2008		
Active Underwriter (Joint)	Brian D Carpenter	+44 (0)1245 214 875	brian.carpenter@amlin.co.uk
Appointed	2008		
Main Areas of Underwriting	Aviation; International Property & Casualty; Marine; UK Commercial; Reinsurance		
YEAR	CAPACITY £m		
2009	825		
2008	825		
2007	1000		

SYNDICATE NUMBER	**6106 Amlin s.2001 R/i A/c SPS**		
Active Underwriter	Simon CW Beale	+44 (0)20 7746 1000	simon.beale@amlin.co.uk
Appointed	2009		
Main Areas of Underwriting	Reinsurance of Non-Marine, Marine & Aviation		
YEAR	CAPACITY £m		
2009	50		
2008	–		
2007	–		

BACKGROUND INFORMATION

Ownership	Amlin Underwriting Ltd is controlled by Amlin plc of London, a FTSE100 company listed on the London Stock Exchange
Date of Incorporation	1988
Former Names	Taskhawk Limited to 1989
	Murray Lawrence & Partners Limited to 1998
Syndicates merged into 2001	28, 40, 173, 362, 820, 824, 887, 902, 913, 919, 920, 1141
Syndicates merged into 6106	None

Arch Underwriting at Lloyd's Ltd

Address	6th Floor
	Plantation Place South
	60 Great Tower Street
	London EC3R 5AZ
Telephone	+44 20 7621 4500
Fax	+44 20 7451 4501
Contact Email	info@archinsurance.co.uk
Website	www.archinsurance.co.uk

Arch Underwriting at Lloyd's Ltd is a recently approved managing agency at Lloyd's. Further details are not available.

Argenta Syndicate Management Limited

Address	Fountain House
	130 Fenchurch Street
	London EC3M 5DJ
Telephone	+44 (0)20 7825 7200
Fax	+44 (0)20 7825 7155
Contact Email	syndicate@argentaplc.com
Website	www.argentaplc.com

SENIOR MANAGEMENT

Title	Name	Telephone	Email
Chairman (Non-Executive)	John LP Whiter	+44 (0)20 7825 7200	john.whiter@argentaplc.com
Deputy Chairman (Non-Executive)	Graham J White	+44 (0)20 7825 7182	graham.white@argentaplc.com
Managing Director	Andrew J Annandale	+44 (0)20 7825 7239	andrew.annandale@argentaplc.com
Finance Director	Graham K Allen	+44 (0)20 7825 7243	graham.allen@argentaplc.com
Operations Director	David G Williams	+44 (0)20 7825 7211	david.williams@argentaplc.com
Underwriting Director	Paul Hunt	+44 (0)20 7825 7200	paul.hunt@argentaplc.com
Risk Management Director	Peter J Bruin	+44 (0)20 7825 7272	peter.bruin@argentaplc.com
Claims Director	David G Williams	+44 (0)20 7825 7211	david.williams@argentaplc.com
Compliance Director	Peter J Bruin	+44 (0)20 7825 7272	peter.bruin@argentaplc.com
Non-Executive Director(s)	Richard M Brewster	+44 (0)20 7825 7200	richard.brewster@argentaplc.com
	John E Mumford	+44 (0)20 7825 7200	john.mumford@argentaplc.com
	Gary A Powell	+44 (0)20 7825 7200	gary.powell@argentaplc.com
	Alan W Tucker	+44 (0)20 7825 7135	alan.tucker@argentaplc.com
Company Secretary	Peter J Bruin	+44 (0)20 7825 7272	peter.bruin@argentaplc.com

SYNDICATES MANAGED IN 2009

SYNDICATE NUMBER	1965 Asian Marine Syndicate		
Active Underwriter	Paul Hunt	+44 (0)20 7825 7200	enquiries@argentaplc.com
Appointed	2009		
Main Areas of Underwriting	Marine; Energy		
YEAR	CAPACITY £m		
2009	30		
2008	30		
2007	15		

SYNDICATE NUMBER	**2121 Argenta Syndicate**		
Active Underwriter	Paul Hunt	+44 (0)20 7825 7200	paul.hunt@argentaplc.com
Appointed	2006		
Main Areas of Underwriting	Non-marine Property; Marine; Energy		
YEAR	CAPACITY £m		
2009	130		
2008	113		
2007	89		

BACKGROUND INFORMATION

Ownership	Argenta Syndicate Management Ltd is controlled by Argenta Holdings plc, an unlisted holding company based in London
Date of Incorporation	1998
Former Names	Capital Syndicates Limited to 1999
	Sackville Syndicate Management Limited to 2004
Syndicates merged into 1965	None
Syndicates merged into 2121	None

Argo Managing Agency Ltd

Address	47 Mark Lane
	London EC3R 7QQ
Telephone	+44 (0)20 7712 7600
Fax	+44 (0)20 7712 7601
Contact Email	katie.gales@argo-int.com
Website	www.argo-int.com

SENIOR MANAGEMENT

Title	Name	Telephone	Email
Chairman (Non-Executive)	David Spiller	+44 (0)20 7712 7600	belinda.rose@argo-int.com
Chief Executive Officer	Julian Enoizi	+44 (0)20 7712 7600	julian.enoizi@argo-int.com
Chief Financial Officer	Nicholas GA Denniston	+44 (0)20 7712 7600	nick.denniston@argo-int.com
Chief Operating Officer	Paul D Battagliola	+44 (0)20 7712 7600	paul.battagliola@argo-int.com
Underwriting Director	James C Sardeson	+44 (0)20 7712 7600	james.sardeson@argo-int.com
Compliance Officer	John Gill	+44 (0)20 7712 7600	john.gill@argo-int.com
Other Executive Director(s)	Neil R Chapman	+44 (0)20 7712 7600	neil.chapman@argo-int.com
	Mark W Lawrence	+44 (0)20 7712 7600	mark.lawrence@argo-int.com
Non-Executive Director(s)	Andrew J Carrier	+44 (0)20 7712 7600	katie.gales@argo-int.com
	John WJ Spencer	+44 (0)20 7712 7600	belinda.rose@argo-int.com
Company Secretary	Belinda Rose	+44 (0)20 7712 7600	belinda.rose@argo-int.com

Argo Managing Agency Ltd (continued)

SYNDICATES MANAGED IN 2009

SYNDICATE NUMBER	**Argo Syndicate 1200**

Active Underwriter (Joint), Liability Division

	Mark W Lawrence	+44 (0)20 7712 7600	mark.lawrence@argo-int.com
Appointed	2006		

Active Underwriter (Joint), Property Division

	Neil R Chapman	+44 (0)20 7712 7600	neil.chapman@argo-int.com
Appointed	2009		
Main Areas of Underwriting	Property; Liability		

YEAR	CAPACITY £m
2009	326
2008	326
2007	314

BACKGROUND INFORMATION

Ownership	Argo Managing Agency Ltd is controlled by Argo Group International Holdings Ltd of Hamilton, Bermuda
Date of Incorporation	1999
Former Names	Heritage Syndicate Management Limited to 1999
	Heritage Managing Agency Limited to 2009
Syndicates merged into 1200	3245

Ark Syndicate Management Limited

No

Address	8th Floor
	St Helen's
	1 Undershaft
	London EC3A 8EE
Telephone	+44 (0)20 3023 4020
Fax	+44 (0)20 3023 4000
Contact Email	enquiries@arkunderwriting.com
Website	www.arkunderwriting.com

SENIOR MANAGEMENT

Title	Name	Telephone	Email
Chairman (Non-Executive)	William A Malloy	+44 (0)20 3023 4020	enquiries@arkunderwriting.com
Chief Executive Officer	Ian E Beaton	+44 (0)20 3023 4001	ian.beaton@arkunderwriting.com
Finance Director	Neil M Smith	+44 (0)20 3023 4020	neil.smith@arkunderwriting.com
Chief Financial Officer	Paul CF Caprez	+44 (0)20 3023 4020	paul.caprez@arkunderwriting.com
Operations Director	Aneil (Neil) P Deshpande	+44 (0)20 3023 4004	neil.deshpande@arkunderwriting.com
Group Director of Underwriting	David P Foreman	+44 (0)20 3023 4002	david.foreman@arkunderwriting.com
Chief Underwriting Officer	Nicholas (Nick) K Bonnar	+44 (0)20 3023 4003	nick.bonnar@arkunderwriting.com
Head of Casualty Reinsurance	C David May	+44 (0)20 3023 4042	david.may@arkunderwriting.com
Head of Claims & Legal	James D Masson	+44 (0)20 3023 4020	james.masson@arkunderwriting.com
Risk Management & Compliance Director	Gary M Oliver	+44 (0)20 3023 4006	gary.oliver@arkunderwriting.com
Non-Executive Director(s)	Robin Oakes	+44 (0)20 3023 4020	enquiries@arkunderwriting.com
	Richard P Rosenbaum	+44 (0)20 3023 4020	enquiries@arkunderwriting.com

	Verner G Southey	+44 (0)20 3023 4020	enquiries@arkunderwriting.com
	Christopher E Watson	+44 (0)20 3023 4020	enquiries@arkunderwriting.com
Company Secretary	James D Masson	+44 (0)20 3023 4020	james.masson@arkunderwriting.com

SYNDICATES MANAGED IN 2009

SYNDICATE NUMBER	**Ark Syndicate 4020**		
Active Underwriter	Nicholas (Nick) K Bonnar	+44 (0)20 3023 4003	nick.bonnar@arkunderwriting.com
Appointed	2009		
Main Areas of Underwriting	Marine; Energy; Property; Casualty		
YEAR	CAPACITY £m		
2009	250		
2008	190		
2007	114		

SYNDICATE NUMBER	**Ark Special Purpose Syndicate 6105**		
Active Underwriter	Nicholas (Nick) K Bonnar	+44 (0)20 3023 4003	nick.bonnar@arkunderwriting.com
Appointed	2008		
Main Areas of Underwriting	Marine; Energy; Property; Casualty		
YEAR	CAPACITY £m		
2009	30		
2008	20		
2007	–		

BACKGROUND INFORMATION

Ownership	Ark Syndicate Management Ltd is wholly owned by Group Ark Insurance Holdings Ltd based in Hamilton, Bermuda
Date of Incorporation	2006
Former Names	Darner Nymph Limited to 2007
Syndicates merged into 4020	None
Syndicates merged into 6105	None

Ascot Underwriting Ltd

Address	Plantation Place
	30 Fenchurch Street
	London EC3M 3BD
Telephone	+44 (0)20 7743 9600
Fax	+44 (0)20 7743 9601
Contact Email	enquiries@ascotuw.com
Website	www.ascotuw.com

SENIOR MANAGEMENT

Title	Name	Telephone	Email
Chairman (Non-Executive)	Sir Richard B Dearlove	+44 (0)20 7743 9600	enquiries@ascotuw.com
Chief Executive Officer	Andrew L Brooks	+44 (0)20 7743 9600	andrew.brooks@ascotuw.com
Finance Director	Robert (Rob) WE Dimsey	+44 (0)20 7743 9600	rob.dimsey@ascotuw.com
Chief Operating Officer	tba		
Chief Underwriting Officer	Mark Pepper	+44 (0)20 7743 9600	mark.pepper@ascotuw.com
Head of Claims	Neil Dalton	+44 (0)20 7743 9600	neil.dalton@ascotuw.com

Ascot Underwriting Ltd (continued)

Compliance Officer	Yvonne Keyes	+44 (0)20 7743 9600	yvonne.keyes@ascotuw.com
Operations & IT Director	Gareth A Challingsworth	+44 (0)20 7743 9600	gareth.challingsworth@ascotuw.com
Non-Executive Director(s)	Alexander R Baugh	+44 (0)20 7743 9600	enquiries@ascotuw.com
	Ian P Martin	+44 (0)20 7743 9600	enquiries@ascotuw.com
	Homi PR Mullan	+44 (0)20 7743 9600	enquiries@ascotuw.com
	Martin RD Reith	+44 (0)20 7743 9600	enquiries@ascotuw.com
	Nicholas C Walsh	+44 (0)20 7743 9600	enquiries@ascotuw.com
Company Secretary	Yvonne Keyes	+44 (0)20 7743 9600	yvonne.keyes@ascotuw.com

SYNDICATES MANAGED IN 2009

SYNDICATE NUMBER	**1414**		
Active Underwriter	Andrew L Brooks	+44 (0)20 7743 9600	andrew.brooks@ascotuw.com
Appointed	2008		
Main Areas of Underwriting	Property; Energy; Cargo; Terrorism & Political Risk; Marine Hull/Liability; Excess of Loss; Specie & Fine Art; Renewable Energy; Accident & Health		

YEAR	CAPACITY £m
2009	470
2008	450
2007	625

BACKGROUND INFORMATION

Ownership	Ascot Underwriting Ltd is controlled by American International Group of New York, USA
Date of Incorporation	2001
Former Names	None
Syndicates merged into 1414	None

Aspen Managing Agency Limited

Address	30 Fenchurch Street
	London EC3M 3BD
Telephone	+44 (0)20 7184 8000
Fax	+44 (0)20 7184 8500
Contact Email	robert.long@aspen-re.com
Website	www.aspen-re.com

SENIOR MANAGEMENT

Title	Name	Telephone	Email
Chairman (Non-Executive)	Heidi E Hutter	+44 (0)20 7184 8000	heidihutter.theboard@aspen.bm
Managing Director	Karen A Green	+44 (0)20 7184 8000	robert.long@aspen-re.com
Finance Director	Christopher PJ O'Brien	+44 (0)20 7184 8000	robert.long@aspen-re.com
Compliance Director	R James Ingham Clark	+44 (0)20 7184 8000	robert.long@aspen-re.com
Syndicate Operations Director	Robert J Long	+44 (0)20 7184 8000	robert.long@aspen-re.com
Other Executive Director(s)	Matthew C Yeldham	+44 (0)20 7184 8000	robert.long@aspen-re.com

Non-Executive Director(s)	Richard JS Bucknall	+44 (0)20 7184 8000	richardbucknall.theboard@aspen.bm
	John F Hobbs	+44 (0)20 7184 8000	robert.long@aspen-re.com
Company Secretary	Alastair GC McKay	+44 (0)20 7184 8000	alastair.mckay@aspen-re.com

SYNDICATES MANAGED IN 2009

SYNDICATE NUMBER	**4711**		
Active Underwriter	Matthew Yeldham	+44 (0)20 7184 8000	robert.long@aspen-re.com
Appointed	2008		
Main Areas of Underwriting	Energy; Hull; Marine Liability; Transportation related Liability; Aviation		
YEAR	CAPACITY £m		
2009	160		
2008	88		
2007	–		

BACKGROUND INFORMATION

Ownership	Aspen Managing Agency Ltd is controlled by Aspen Insurance Holdings Ltd of Hamilton, Bermuda
Date of Incorporation	2007
Former Names	Whistler Managing Agency Limited to 2008
Syndicates merged into 4711	None

Atrium Underwriters Ltd

Address	Room 790
	Lloyd's
	One Lime Street
	London EC3M 7DQ
Telephone	+44 (0)20 7327 4877
Fax	+44 (0)20 7327 4878
Contact Email	info@atrium-uw.com
Website	www.atrium-uw.com

SENIOR MANAGEMENT

Title	Name	Telephone	Email
Chairman (Non-Executive)	George F Rivaz	+44 (0)20 7327 4877	info@atrium-uw.com
Chief Executive Officer	Steven J Cook	+44 (0)20 7327 4877	info@atrium-uw.com
Chief Financial Officer	Andrew M Baddeley	+44 (0)20 7327 4877	info@atrium-uw.com
Chief Operating Officer	Simon D Cooper	+44 (0)20 7327 4877	info@atrium-uw.com
Compliance Director	James RF Lee	+44 (0)20 7327 4877	info@atrium-uw.com
Other Executive Director(s)	Toby D Drysdale	+44 (0)20 7327 4877	info@atrium-uw.com
	Richard de WW Harries	+44 (0)20 7327 4877	info@atrium-uw.com
	Nicholas (Nick) C Marsh	+44 (0)20 7327 4877	info@atrium-uw.com
	Kevin W Wilkins	+44 (0)20 7327 4877	info@atrium-uw.com
	Andrew D Winyard	+44 (0)20 7327 4877	info@atrium-uw.com
Non-Executive Director(s)	Ann F Godbehere	+44 (0)20 7327 4877	info@atrium-uw.com
	Don Kramer	+44 (0)20 7327 4877	info@atrium-uw.com
	Scott P Moser	+44 (0)20 7327 4877	info@atrium-uw.com
Company Secretary	Martha BW Bruce	+44 (0)20 7327 4877	info@atrium-uw.com

Atrium Underwriters Ltd (continued)

SYNDICATES MANAGED IN 2009

SYNDICATE NUMBER	**Atrium Syndicate 570**		
Active Underwriter	Kevin W Wilkins	+44 (0)20 7327 4877	info@atrium-uw.com
Appointed	2005		
Main Areas of Underwriting	Non-Marine		
YEAR	CAPACITY £m		
2009	125		
2008	125		
2007	125		

SYNDICATE NUMBER	**Atrium Syndicate 609**		
Active Underwriter	Richard de WW Harries	+44 (0)20 7327 4877	info@atrium-uw.com
Appointed	2008		
Main Areas of Underwriting	Marine; Energy; Aviation; Non-Marine Property; Liabilities; War & Terrorism		
YEAR	CAPACITY £m		
2009	200		
2008	215		
2007	215		

BACKGROUND INFORMATION

Ownership	Atrium Underwriters Ltd is controlled by Ariel Holdings Ltd of Hamilton, Bermuda
Date of Incorporation	1985
Former Names	Atrium Underwriting Limited to 1997
	Atrium Cockell Underwriting Limited to 1999
Syndicates merged into 570	269
Syndicates merged into 609	None

Beaufort Underwriting Agency Limited

Address	Third Floor
	One Minster Court
	Mincing Lane
	London EC3R 7AA
Telephone	+44 (0)20 7220 8200
Fax	+44 (0)20 7220 8290
Contact Email	info@beaufort-group.com
Website	www.beaufort-group.com

SENIOR MANAGEMENT

Title	Name	Telephone	Email
Chairman (Non-Executive)	Richard G Carter	+44 (0)20 7220 8200	info@beaufort-group.com
Chief Executive Officer	Andrew S Dawe	+44 (0)20 7220 8200	andrew.dawe@beaufort-group.com
Financial Director	Graham M Tuck	+44 (0)20 7220 8200	graham.tuck@beaufort-group.com
Independent Review Director	Malcolm J Cox	+44 (0)20 7220 8200	info@beaufort-group.com
Compliance Officer	Paul Langridge	+44 (0)20 7220 8200	paul.langridge@beaufort-group.com
Other Executive Director(s)	Derek C Eales	+44 (0)20 7220 8200	derek.eales@beaufort-group.com

	Michael SF Pritchard	+44 (0)20 7220 8200	michael.pritchard@beaufort-group.com
Non-Executive Director(s)	Jorg W Bruniecki	+44 (0)20 7220 8200	info@beaufort-group.com
Company Secretary	Paul Langridge	+44 (0)20 7220 8200	paul.langridge@beaufort-group.com

SYNDICATES MANAGED IN 2009

SYNDICATE NUMBER	**318**		
Active Underwriter	Michael SF Pritchard	+44 (0)20 7220 8200	michael.pritchard@beaufort-group.com
Appointed	1985		
Main Areas of Underwriting	International Property; Aviation; UK Commercial		
YEAR	CAPACITY £m		
2009	201		
2008	201		
2007	201		

SYNDICATE NUMBER	**1318 Beaufort Aligned Binders Syndicate**		
Active Underwriter	Gordon J Breslin	+44 (0)20 7220 8200	gordon.breslin@beaufort-group.com
Appointed	2009		
Main Areas of Underwriting	North American SME & Residential		
YEAR	CAPACITY £m		
2009	35		
2008	–		
2007	–		

BACKGROUND INFORMATION

Ownership	Beaufort Underwriting Agency Ltd is controlled by the Munich Re Group of Bavaria, Germany
Date of Incorporation	2000
Former Names	Minimar (525) Limited to 2000
	Ensign Managing Agency Limited to 2004
Syndicates merged into 318	None
Syndicates merged into 1318	None

Beazley Furlonge Limited

Address	Plantation Place South
	60 Great Tower Street
	London EC3R 5AD
Telephone	+44 (0)20 7667 0623
Fax	+44 (0)20 7674 7100
Contact Email	info@beazley.com
Website	www.beazley.com

SENIOR MANAGEMENT

Title	Name	Telephone	Email
Chairman (Non-Executive)	Jonathan GW Agnew	+44 (0)20 7667 0623	jonathan.agnew@beazley.com
Deputy Chairman (& Group Chairman)	Andrew F Beazley	+44 (0)20 7667 0623	andrew.beazley@beazley.com
Chief Executive Officer	David A Horton	+44 (0)20 7667 0623	andrew.horton@beazley.com
Group Finance Director	Martin Bride	+44 (0)20 7667 0623	martin.bride@beazley.com
Chief Operating Officer	David Marock	+44 (0)20 7667 0623	david.marock@beazley.com
Executive Director & Head of Marine	Clive A Washbourn	+44 (0)20 7667 0623	clive.washbourn@beazley.com

Beazley Furlonge Limited (continued)

Executive Director & Head of Property Group	Jonathan G Gray	+44 (0)20 7667 0623	jonathan.gray@beazley.com
Executive Director & Head of Reinsurance	Neil P Maidment	+44 (0)20 7667 0623	neil.maidment@beazley.com
Executive Director & Head of Risk Management	Nicholas H Furlonge	+44 (0)20 7667 0623	nicholas.furlonge@beazley.com
Executive Director & Head of Specialty Lines	Adrian P Cox	+44 (0)20 7667 0623	adrian.cox@beazley.com
Chairman of the Underwriting Committee	Neil P Maidment	+44 (0)20 7667 0623	neil.maidment@beazley.com
Compliance Officer	Sian A Coope	+44 (0)20 7667 0623	sian.coope@beazley.com
Other Executive Director(s)	Arthur R Manners	+44 (0)20 7667 0623	arthur.manners@beazley.com
Non-Executive Director(s)	George P Blunden	+44 (0)20 7667 0623	george.blunden@beazley.com
	J Dudley Fishburn	+44 (0)20 7667 0623	john.fishburn@beazley.com
	Chris M London	+44 (0)20 7667 0623	chris.london@beazley.com
	Andrew D Pomfret	+44 (0)20 7667 0623	andrew.pomfret@beazley.com
Company Secretary	Arthur R Manners	+44 (0)20 7667 0623	arthur.manners@beazley.com

SYNDICATES MANAGED IN 2009

SYNDICATE NUMBER	**623 AF Beazley & Ors**		
Active Underwriter	Neil P Maidment	+44 (0)20 7667 0623	neil.maidment@beazley.com
Appointed	1985		
Main Areas of Underwriting	Professional Indemnity; Commercial Property; Marine; Reinsurance; Personal Lines		
YEAR	CAPACITY £m		
2009	150		
2008	158		
2007	164		

SYNDICATE NUMBER	**2623 AF Beazley & Ors**		
Active Underwriter	Neil P Maidment	+44 (0)20 7667 0623	neil.maidment@beazley.com
Appointed	2002		
Main Areas of Underwriting	Non-Marine		
YEAR	CAPACITY £m		
2009	624		
2008	656		
2007	697		

SYNDICATE NUMBER	**3622 Beazley Aligned Life Syndicate**		
Active Underwriter	Neil P Maidment	+44 (0)20 7667 0623	neil.maidment@beazley.com
Appointed	2009		
Main Areas of Underwriting	Dedicated Life Assurance		
YEAR	CAPACITY £m		
2009	7		
2008	–		
2007	–		

SYNDICATE NUMBER	**3623 Beazley A&H - Non-Life**		
Active Underwriter	Neil P Maidment	+44 (0)20 7667 0623	neil.maidment@beazley.com
Appointed	2008		
Main Areas of Underwriting	Personal Accident; Sports		
YEAR	CAPACITY £m		
2009	33		
2008	Information not disclosed		
2007	–		

BACKGROUND INFORMATION

Ownership	Beazley Furlonge Ltd is controlled by Beazley Group plc of London, listed on the London Stock Exchange
Date of Incorporation	1985
Former Names	Hellebore Limited to 1985
	Beazley Furlonge & Hiscox Limited to 1993
Syndicates merged into 623	None
Syndicates merged into 2623	None
Syndicates merged into 3622	None
Syndicates merged into 3623	None

Brit Syndicates Limited

Address	2nd Floor
	55 Bishopsgate
	London EC2N 3AS
Telephone	+44 (0)20 7984 8500
Fax	+44 (0)20 7984 8501
Contact Email	enquiries@britinsurance.com
Website	www.britinsurance.com

SENIOR MANAGEMENT

Title	Name	Telephone	Email
Chairman (Non-Executive)	R John O Barton	+44 (0)20 7984 8500	john.barton@britinsurance.com
Chief Executive Officer	Dane J Douetil, CBE	+44 (0)20 7984 8500	dane.douetil@britinsurance.com
Finance Director	Matthew Scales	+44 (0)20 7984 8500	matthew.scales@britinsurance.com
Chief Operating Officer	Kathy M Lisson	+44 (0)20 7984 8500	enquiries@britinsurance.com
Underwriting Director	Kevin R Huttly	+44 (0)20 7984 8500	enquiries@britinsurance.com
Claims Director	Robert (Bob) Foster	+44 (0)20 7984 8500	enquiries@britinsurance.com
Compliance Officer	Michael D Jackson	+44 (0)20 7984 8500	michael.jackson@britinsurance.com
Non-Executive Director(s)	Kenneth Culley	+44 (0)20 7984 8500	kenneth.culley@britinsurance.com
	Dr Cornelius ACM Schrauwers	+44 (0)20 7984 8500	cornelis.schrauwers@britinsurance.com
Company Secretary	Michael D Jackson	+44 (0)20 7984 8500	michael.jackson@britinsurance.com

Brit Syndicates Limited (continued)

SYNDICATES MANAGED IN 2009

SYNDICATE NUMBER	**Brit Syndicate 2987**
Active Underwriter	Johnathan R Turner +44 (0)20 7984 8500 enquiries@britinsurance.com
Appointed	2008
Main Areas of Underwriting	Accident & Health; Professional Risks; Aerospace; Reinsurance; Financial Risks; Specialty Lines; Legal Expenses; UK Liability; Marine; UK Property; Motor; US & International Property; Personal Lines; War & Terrorism

YEAR	CAPACITY £m
2009	525
2008	600
2007	525

Syndicate 389 Wren Life in Run-Off (open year: 2003)

Run-Off Manager	Nigel David Hartley

BACKGROUND INFORMATION

Ownership	Brit Syndicates Ltd is controlled by Brit Insurance Holdings plc listed on the London Stock Exchange
Date of Incorporation	1964
Former Names	Savill Gough & Hay Limited to 1991
	Wren Syndicates Management Limited to 2001
Syndicates merged into 2987	250, 431, 735, 800, 1202

Canopius Managing Agents Limited

Address	Gallery 9
	One Lime Street
	London EC3M 7HA
Telephone	+44 (0)20 7337 3700
Fax	+44 (0)20 7337 3999
Contact Email	info@canopius.com
Website	www.canopius.com

SENIOR MANAGEMENT

Title	Name	Telephone	Email
Chairman (Executive)	Michael C Watson	+44 (0)20 7337 3730	michael.watson@canopius.com
Chief Executive Officer	Clive A Watson	+44 (0)20 7337 3720	clive.watson@canopius.com
Chief Financial Officer	Stephen J Muggeridge	+44 (0)20 7337 3770	stephen.muggeridge@canopius.com
Chief Operating Officer	Stephen T Manning	+44 (0)20 7337 3732	stephen.manning@canopius.com
Group Chief Underwriting Officer	James (Jim) A Giordano	+44 (0)20 7337 3710	jim.giordano@canopius.com
Underwriting Director	Timothy (Tim) J Carroll	+44 (0)20 7337 3700	info@canopius.com
Chief Risk Officer	Stephen T Manning	+44 (0)20 7337 3732	stephen.manning@canopius.com
Claims Director	Clive A Watson	+44 (0)20 7337 3720	clive.watson@canopius.com
Independent Review Director	John D Birney	+44 (0)20 7337 3700	john.birney@canopius.com
Compliance Officer	Stephen T Manning	+44 (0)20 7337 3732	stephen.manning@canopius.com
Non-Executive Director(s)	Adam J Barron	+44 (0)20 7337 3700	adam.barron@canopius.com
	Robert D Law	+44 (0)20 7337 3700	robert.law@canopius.com

| | Dr Ian B Owen | +44 (0)20 7337 3700 | ian.owen@canopius.com |
| Company Secretary | Philip Osman | +44 (0)20 7337 3700 | philip.osman@canopius.com |

SYNDICATES MANAGED IN 2009

SYNDICATE NUMBER	**4444 Canopius**		
Active Underwriter	James (Jim) A Giordano	+44 (0)20 7337 3710	jim.giordano@canopius.com
Appointed	2001		
Main Areas of Underwriting	UK Property; North American Facilities; Marine & Energy; Global Property; Casualty & Treaty Reinsurance; Financial Institutions		

YEAR	CAPACITY £m
2009	450
2008	410
2007	450

SYNDICATE NUMBER	**RITC Syndicate 839** (in Run-off)		
Run-off Manager	Michael (Mike) East	+44 (0)20 7337 3700	mike.east@canopius.com
Appointed	2008		

BACKGROUND INFORMATION

Ownership	Canopius Managing Agents Ltd is controlled by Canopius Group Ltd, a holding company incorporated in Guernsey, Channel Islands. Recently acquired Creechurch Underwriting Limited and its subsidiaries
Date of Incorporation	1980
Former Names	Castle Underwriting Agents Limited to 1994
	Tower Managing Agents Limited to 1996
	Archer Managing Agents to 1998
	Chartwell Managing Agents Limited to 2002
	Trenwick Managing Agents Limited to 2003
Syndicates merged into 4444	270, 463, 544, 657, 741, 839, 962, 1087, 1154, 1607, 2607, 2741, 2962, 3786

Cathedral Underwriting Limited

Address	5th Floor
	Fitzwilliam House
	10 St Mary Axe
	London EC3A 8EN
Telephone	+44 (0)20 7170 9000
Fax	+44 (0)20 7170 9001
Contact Email	info@cathedralcapital.com
Website	www.cathedralcapital.com

SENIOR MANAGEMENT

Title	Name	Telephone	Email
Chairman (Non-Executive)	Anthony (Tony) IG South	+44 (0)20 7170 9021	tony.south@cathedralcapital.com
Managing Director	Lawrence A Holder	+44 (0)20 7170 9022	lawrence.holder@cathedralcapital.com
Finance Director	John A Lynch	+44 (0)20 7170 9024	john.lynch@cathedralcapital.com
Independent Review Director	John P Tilling	+44 (0)20 7170 9000	info@cathedralcapital.com
Compliance Director	Derek C Grainger	+44 (0)20 7170 9023	derek.grainger@cathedralcapital.com
Other Executive Director(s)	John C Hamblin	+44 (0)20 7170 9062	john.hamblin@cathedralcapital.com
	Elvin E Patrick	+44 (0)20 7170 9000	info@cathedralcapital.com

Cathedral Underwriting Limited (continued)

Other Executive Director(s)	Peter D Scales	+44 (0)20 7170 9025	peter.scales@cathedralcapital.com
Non-Executive Director(s)	J Michael G Andrews	+44 (0)20 7170 9000	info@cathedralcapital.com
	John S Goldsmith	+44 (0)20 7170 9000	info@cathedralcapital.com
Company Secretary	John A Lynch	+44 (0)20 7170 9024	info@cathedralcapital.com

SYNDICATES MANAGED IN 2009

SYNDICATE NUMBER	**2010 Cathedral**		
Active Underwriter	John C Hamblin	+44 (0)20 7170 9062	john.hamblin@cathedralcapital.com
Appointed	2001		
Main Areas of Underwriting	Property & Aviation Treaty Reinsurance; Direct & Facultative Property Insurance & Reinsurance, Satellite & Contingency Business.		

YEAR	CAPACITY £m
2009	300
2008	300
2007	300

SYNDICATE NUMBER	**3010 Cathedral**		
Active Underwriter	John C Hamblin	+44 (0)20 7170 9062	john.hamblin@cathedralcapital.com
Appointed	2007		
Main Areas of Underwriting	Marine Cargo		

YEAR	CAPACITY £m
2009	30
2008	30
2007	20

BACKGROUND INFORMATION

Ownership	Cathedral Underwriting Ltd is controlled by Cathedral Capital Ltd, a company controlled by Alchemy Investment Plan and the Cathedral management
Date of Incorporation	1934
Former Names	Sisson & Parker Limited to 1987
	Warren Barber Underwriting Agencies limited to 1989
	London Wall Managing Agencies Limited to 1994
	Highgate Managing Agencies Limited to 1998
	MMO Underwriting Agency Limited to 2000
	Cathedral Underwriting Limited from 2000
Syndicates merged into 2010	None
Syndicates merged into 3010	None

Catlin Underwriting Agencies Limited

Address	6th Floor
	3 Minster Court
	Mincing Lane
	London EC3R 7DD
Telephone	+44 (0)20 7626 0486
Fax	+44 (0)20 7623 9101

Contact Email   catlininfo@catlin.com
Website   www.catlin.com

SENIOR MANAGEMENT

Title	Name	Telephone	Email
Chairman (Executive)	Stephen JO Catlin	+44 (0)20 7626 0486	stephen.catlin@catlin.com
Deputy Chairman (Executive)	Paul A Jardine	+44 (0)20 7626 0486	paul.jardine@catlin.com
Chief Executive Officer	David CB Ibeson	+44 (0)20 7626 0486	david.ibeson@catlin.com
Chief Financial Officer	Neil A Freshwater	+44 (0)20 7626 0486	neil.freshwater@catlin.com
Underwriting Director	Nicolas J Burkinshaw	+44 (0)20 7626 0486	nicolas.burkinshaw@catlin.com
Claims Director	Nicholas C Sinfield	+44 (0)20 7626 0486	nicholas.sinfield@catlin.com
Compliance Officer	Andrew J Gray	+44 (0)20 7626 0486	andrew.gray@catlin.com
Other Executive Director(s)	Richard M Clapham	+44 (0)20 7626 0486	richard.clapham@catlin.com
Non-Executive Director(s)	Timothy W Burrows	+44 (0)20 7626 0486	catlininfo@catlin.com
	Diana Guy	+44 (0)20 7626 0486	catlininfo@catlin.com
	Colin G Robinson	+44 (0)20 7626 0486	catlininfo@catlin.com
Company Secretary	Andrew J Gray	+44 (0)20 7626 0486	andrew.gray@catlin.com

SYNDICATES MANAGED IN 2009

SYNDICATE NUMBER	**2003 Catlin Syndicate**		
Active Underwriter	Nicolas J Burkinshaw	+44 (0)20 7626 0486	nicolas.burkinshaw@catlin.com
Appointed	2006		
Main Areas of Underwriting	Reinsurance; Property Damage; Accident & Health; Aviation; Marine; Energy; War & Political Risk; Professional Risks & Casualty		

YEAR	CAPACITY £m
2009	1094
2008	1094
2007	1094

SYNDICATE NUMBER	**2020 Wellington** (in Run-off)		
Active Underwriter	David CB Ibeson	+44 (0)20 7626 0486	david.ibeson@catlin.com
Appointed	Information not disclosed		

BACKGROUND INFORMATION

Ownership	Catlin Underwriting Agencies Ltd is controlled by Catlin Group Ltd of Hamilton, Bermuda
Date of Incorporation	1984
Former Names	SJO Catlin Underwriting Agencies Limited to 1992
Syndicates merged into 2003	51, 179, 1003, 1028, 1095, 1251

Chaucer Syndicates Limited

Address	Plantation Place
	30 Fenchurch Street
	London EC3M 3AD
Telephone	+44 (0)20 7397 9700
Fax	+44 (0)20 7397 9710
Contact Email	enquiries@chaucerplc.com
Website	www.chaucerplc.com

Chaucer Syndicates Limited (continued)

SENIOR MANAGEMENT

Title	Name	Telephone	Email
Chairman	Ewen H Gilmour	+44 (0)20 7397 9700	ewen.gilmour@chaucerplc.com
Chief Executive Officer	Robert (Bob) A Stuchbery	+44 (0)20 7397 9700	robert.stuchbery@chaucerplc.com
Chief Financial Officer	tba		
Financial Director	Kenneth D Curtis	+44 (0)20 7397 9700	ken.curtis@chaucerplc.com
Operations Director	David C Bendle	+44 (0)20 7397 9700	david.bendle@chaucerplc.com
Chief Underwriting Officer	Robert A Stuchbery	+44 (0)20 7397 9700	robert.stuchbery@chaucerplc.com
Executive Director & Head of Motor Division	Kim Barber	+44 (0)1227 284 700	kim.barber@chaucerplc.com
Executive Director, Third Party Syndicates	S Janet Helson	+44 (0)20 7397 9700	janet.helson@chaucerplc.com
Group Actuary	Jonathan D Perkins	+44 (0)20 7397 9700	jonathan.perkins@chaucerplc.com
Risk Officer	Gina C Butterworth	+44 (0)20 7397 9700	gina.butterworth@chaucerplc.com
Claims Manager, Marine	Tony Gates	+44 (0)20 7105 8205	tony.gates@chaucerplc.com
Claims Manager, Non-Marine	Martin Francis	+44 (0)20 7397 9723	martin.francis@chaucerplc.com
Compliance Officer	Lorraine Webb	+44 (0)20 7397 9700	lorraine.webb@chaucerplc.com
Other Executive Director(s)	Bruce P Bartell	+44 (0)20 7397 9700	bruce.bartell@chaucerplc.com
	Ashley R Bissett	+44 (0)20 7397 9700	ashley.bissett@chaucerplc.com
Non-Executive Director(s)	Malcolm J Cox	+44 (0)20 7397 9700	malcolm.cox@chaucerplc.com
	Richard T Scholes	+44 (0)20 7397 9700	richard.scholes@chaucerplc.com
Company Secretary	David C Turner	+44 (0)20 7397 9700	david.turner@chaucerplc.com

SYNDICATES MANAGED IN 2009

SYNDICATE NUMBER	**Chaucer Syndicate 1084**		
Active Underwriter	Bruce P Bartell	+44 (0)20 7397 9700	bruce.bartell@chaucerplc.com
Appointed	2006		
Main Areas of Underwriting	International Aviation; Marine; Property & Specialist Lines; Motor		
YEAR	CAPACITY £m		
2009	545		
2008	445		
2007	485		

SYNDICATE NUMBER	**Nuclear Syndicate 1176**		
Active Underwriter	Michael G Dawson	+44 (0)20 7397 9700	michael.dawson@chaucerplc.com
Appointed	1991		
Main Areas of Underwriting	Nuclear		
YEAR	CAPACITY £m		
2009	32		
2008	28		
2007	28		

SYNDICATE NUMBER	**1274 Antares**		
Active Underwriter	Stephen D Redmond	+44 (0)20 7959 1900	info@antaresunderwriting.com
Appointed	2008		
Main Areas of Underwriting	Property; Casualty; Marine; Aviation		
YEAR	CAPACITY £m		
2009	135		
2008	135		
2007	–		

SYNDICATE NUMBER	**Broadgate Syndicate 1301**		
Active Underwriter	Robert (Bob) AG Katzaros	+44 (0)20 7397 9700	info@broadgate-uwg.co.uk
Appointed	2006		
Main Areas of Underwriting	International Property; Accident & Health; Personal Accident Treaty; Property Special Risks		
YEAR	CAPACITY £m		
2009	75		
2008	75		
2007	72		

SYNDICATE NUMBER	**ICM Syndicate 4242**		
Active Underwriter	Gregory (Greg) Butler	+44 (0)20 7397 9700	enquiries@chaucerplc.com
Appointed	2007		
Main Areas of Underwriting	Property Catastrophe		
YEAR	CAPACITY £m		
2009	84		
2008	84		
2007	84		

BACKGROUND INFORMATION

Ownership	Chaucer Syndicates Ltd is controlled by Chaucer Holdings PLC, listed on the London Stock Exchange
Date of Incorporation	1922
Former Names	Stewart & Hughman Limited to 1994
	Stewart Syndicates Limited to 1996
Syndicates merged into 1084	396, 587, 1096, 1204, 1229
Syndicates merged into 1176	None
Syndicates merged into 1274	None
Syndicates merged into 1301	None
Syndicates merged into 4242	None

Equity Syndicate Management Limited

Address	Library House
	New Road
	Brentwood
	Essex CM14 4GD
Telephone	+44 (0)1277 200 100
Fax	+44 (0)1206 777 223

Equity Syndicate Management Limited (continued)

Contact Email	info@equitygroup.co.uk
Website	www.equitygroup.co.uk

SENIOR MANAGEMENT

Title	Name	Telephone	Email
Chairman (Non-Executive)	David J Pye	+44 (0)1277 200 100	info@equitygroup.co.uk
Chief Executive Officer	Neil A Utley	+44 (0)1277 200 100	neil.utley@equitygroup.co.uk
Chief Financial Officer	Douglas M Morgan	+44 (0)1277 200 100	douglas.morgan@equitygroup.co.uk
Independent Review Director	Harold E Clarke	+44 (0)1277 200 100	info@equitygroup.co.uk
Compliance Officer	Peter FS Merrett	+44 (0)1277 200 100	peter.merrett@equitygroup.co.uk
Other Executive Director(s)	Henry NA Colthurst	+44 (0)1277 200 100	info@equitygroup.co.uk
	John E Josiah	+44 (0)1277 200 100	john.josiah@equitygroup.co.uk
Company Secretary	Victoria L Cuggy	+44 (0)1277 200 100	victoria.cuggy@equitygroup.co.uk

SYNDICATES MANAGED IN 2009

SYNDICATE NUMBER	**218 Equity Red Star**		
Active Underwriter	John E Josiah	+44 (0)1277 200 100	john.josiah@equitygroup.co.uk
Appointed	2006		
Main Areas of Underwriting	Motor		
YEAR	CAPACITY £m		
2009	452		
2008	420		
2007	420		

Syndicate 4455 Alba in Run-off (open year: 2006)

Run-Off Manager	Information not available

BACKGROUND INFORMATION

Ownership	Equity Syndicate Management Ltd is controlled by Insurance Australia Group of Sydney, Australia
Date of Incorporation	1946
Former Names	Equity Underwriting Agencies Limited to 1986
	Christopherson Heath Limited to 1999
	Cox Syndicate Management Limted to 2006
Syndicates merged into 218	866
Syndicates merged into 1208	None
Syndicates merged into 4455	None

Faraday Underwriting Limited

Address	5th Floor
	Corn Exchange
	55 Mark Lane
	London EC3R 7NE
Telephone	+44 (0)20 7702 3333
Fax	+44 (0)20 7680 4369

Contact Email	liz.richardson@faraday.com
Website	www.faraday.com

SENIOR MANAGEMENT

Title	Name	Telephone	Email
Chairman (Executive) & Chief Executive Officer	Lord Ashton of Hyde	+44 (0)20 7680 4239	henry.ashton@faraday.com
Chief Financial Officer	Mark Lowton	+44 (0)20 7426 6010	mark.lowton@genre.com
Joint Chief Underwriting Officer	Paul NE Ceurvorst	+44 (0)20 7264 4611	paul.ceurvorst@faraday.com
Joint Chief Underwriting Officer	Mark J Rayner	+44 (0)20 7702 3333	mark.rayner@faraday.com
Actuarial Officer	Nigel J Finlay	+44 (0)20 7680 4322	nigel.finlay@faraday.com
Head of Claims	Charles F Glaisher	+44 (0)20 7680 4283	charles.glaisher@faraday.com
UK General Counsel	Joanne Merrick	+44 (0)20 7426 6012	joanne.merrick@faraday.com
Compliance Director	Simon GH Tovey	+44 (0)20 7680 4203	simon.tovey@faraday.com
Other Executive Director(s)	Michael P O'Dea	+44 (0)20 7680 4326	mike.odea@genre.com
Non-Executive Director(s)	Peter Lütke-Bornefeld	+44 (0)20 7702 3333	liz.richardson@faraday.com
	Lord Phillips of Sudbury	+44 (0)20 7702 3333	liz.richardson@faraday.com
	Damon N Vocke	+44 (0)20 7702 3333	liz.richardson@faraday.com
Company Secretary	Elisabeth A Richardson	+44 (0)20 7680 7206	liz.richardson@faraday.com

SYNDICATES MANAGED IN 2009

SYNDICATE NUMBER	**435 Faraday**		
Active Underwriter (Joint)	Paul NE Ceurvorst	+44 (0)20 7264 4611	paul.ceurvorst@faraday.com
Appointed	2003		
Active Underwriter (Joint)	Mark J Rayner	+44 (0)20 7702 3333	mark.rayner@faraday.com
Appointed	2003		
Main Areas of Underwriting	Aviation; Casualty; Property		
YEAR	CAPACITY £m		
2009	250		
2008	250		
2007	325		

BACKGROUND INFORMATION

Ownership	Faraday Underwriting Ltd is controlled by General Re Corporation, a subsidiary of Berkshire Hathaway Inc of the USA
Date of Incorporation	1982
Former Names	DP Mann Underwriting Agency Limited to 1997
	DP Mann Limited to 2001
Syndicates merged into 435	None

Hardy (Underwriting Agencies) Ltd

Address	4th Floor
	40 Lime Street
	London EC3M 7AW
Telephone	+44 (0)20 7626 0382
Fax	+44 (0)20 7283 4677
Contact Email	info@hardygroup.co.uk
Website	www.hardygroup.co.uk

SENIOR MANAGEMENT

Title	Name	Telephone	Email
Chairman (Non-Executive)	David P Mann	+44 (0)20 7626 0382	david.mann@hardygroup.co.uk
Chief Executive Officer	Barbara J Merry	+44 (0)20 7626 0382	barbara.merry@hardygroup.co.uk
Chief Financial Officer	James D MacDiarmid	+44 (0)20 7626 0382	jamie.macdiarmid@hardygroup.co.uk
Chief Operating Officer	Stuart Blakeborough	+44 (0)20 7626 0382	stuart.blakeborough@hardygroup.co.uk
Underwriting Director	Adrian J Walker	+44 (0)20 7626 0382	adrian.walker@hardygroup.co.uk
Independent Review Director	Bernard G Devereese	+44 (0)20 7626 0382	bernard.devereese@hardygroup.co.uk
Compliance Officer	Timothy P Griffin	+44 (0)20 7626 0382	timothy.griffin@hardygroup.co.uk
Other Executive Director(s)	Patrick J Gage	+44 (0)20 7626 0382	patrick.gage@hardygroup.co.uk
	Timothy P Griffin	+44 (0)20 7626 0382	timothy.griffin@hardygroup.co.uk
	Theresa Hutchings	+44 (0)20 7626 0382	theresa.hutchings@hardygroup.co.uk
	Matthew J Simpson	+44 (0)20 7626 0382	matthew.simpson@hardygroup.co.uk
	Mervyn TA Sugden	+44 (0)20 7626 0382	mervyn.sugden@hardygroup.co.uk
	Anthony D Williams	+44 (0)20 7626 0382	anthony.williams@hardygroup.co.uk
Non-Executive Director(s)	Richard D Abbott	+44 (0)20 7626 0382	info@hardygroup.co.uk
	Ian E Ivory	+44 (0)20 7626 0382	ian.ivory@hardygroup.co.uk
	Lady Barbara S Judge	+44 (0)20 7626 0382	info@hardygroup.co.uk
Company Secretary	Theresa Hutchings	+44 (0)20 7626 0382	theresa.hutchings@hardygroup.co.uk

SYNDICATES MANAGED IN 2009

SYNDICATE NUMBER	**382 Hardy Underwriting Ltd**		
Active Underwriter	Adrian J Walker	+44 (0)20 7626 0382	adrian.walker@hardygroup.co.uk
Appointed	2001		
Main Areas of Underwriting	Aviation; Marine Hull; Cargo & Specie; D&F Property; Property Treaty; Financial Institutions; Political Risk; Conveyancing; Terrorism; Non-Marine Property; Specialty lines		

YEAR	CAPACITY £m
2009	250
2008	110 (+75 - Syndicate 3820)
2007	110 (+65 - Syndicate 3820)

BACKGROUND INFORMATION

Ownership	Hardy (Underwriting Agencies) Ltd is controlled by Hardy Underwriting Bermuda Ltd of Hamilton, Bermuda, a company listed on the London Stock Exchange
Date of Incorporation	1976
Former Names	None in past 20 years
Syndicates merged into 382	3820

HCC Underwriting Agency Ltd

Address	Walsingham House
	35 Seething Lane
	London EC3N 4AH
Telephone	+44 (0)20 7680 3000
Fax	+44 (0)20 7977 7350

Contact Email	info@hccual.com
Website	www.hccual.com

SENIOR MANAGEMENT

Title	Name	Telephone	Email
Chairman (Non-Executive)	John H Bishop	+44 (0)20 7680 3000	info@hccual.com
Chief Executive Officer	Nicholas I Hutton-Penman	+44 (0)20 7680 3000	info@hccual.com
Finance Director	William J Taylor	+44 (0)20 7680 3000	wtaylor@hccual.com
Executive Director & Active Underwriter	Michael L Onslow	+44 (0)20 7680 3000	monslow@hccint.com
Underwriting Director, Liability & CAR	Paul Baynham	+44 (0)20 7680 3009	pbaynham@hccual.com
Head of Liability Claims	Nick Woodward	+44 (0)20 7680 3000	info@hccual.com
Compliance Officer	David R Feldman	+44 (0)20 7680 3000	dfeldman@hccual.com
Non-Executive Director(s)	W Raymond Treen	+44 (0)20 7680 3000	info@hccual.com
Company Secretary	David R Feldman	+44 (0)20 7680 3000	dfeldman@hccual.com

SYNDICATES MANAGED IN 2009

SYNDICATE NUMBER	**ILM 4040**		
Active Underwriter	Michael L Onslow	+44 (0)20 7680 3000	monslow@hccint.com
Appointed	2009		
Main Areas of Underwriting	Employers' Liability; Public Liability; Products Liability; Contractors' All Risks; Contingency; Accident & Health		
YEAR	CAPACITY £m		
2009	54		
2008	54		
2007	54		

SYNDICATE NUMBER	**HCC 4141**		
Active Underwriter	Michael L Onslow	+44 (0)20 7680 3000	monslow@hccint.com
Appointed	2009		
Main Areas of Underwriting	Travel & Medical; E&O		
YEAR	CAPACITY £m		
2009	16		
2008	12		
2007	–		

BACKGROUND INFORMATION

Ownership	HCC Underwriting Agency Ltd is controlled by Houston Insurance Holdings Inc. of Houston, Texas, listed on the New York Stock Exchange
Date of Incorporation	2003
Former Names	Minmar (644) Limited to 2003
	Illium Insurance Limited to 2003
	Illium Capital Limited to 2003
	Illium Managing Agency Limited to 2007
Syndicates merged into 4040	None
Syndicates merged into 4141	None

Heritage Managing Agency Limited

Please see Argo Managing Agency Ltd

Hiscox Syndicates Limited

Address	1 Great St Helen's
	London EC3A 6HX
Telephone	+44 (0)20 7448 6000
Fax	+44 (0)20 7448 6900
Contact Email	enquiry@hiscox.com
Website	www.hiscox.com

SENIOR MANAGEMENT

Title	Name	Telephone	Email
Chairman (Executive)	Robert RS Hiscox	+44 (0)20 7448 6000	robert.hiscox@hiscox.com
Chief Executive Officer	Bronek E Masojada	+44 (0)20 7448 6000	bronek.masojada@hiscox.com
Finance Director	Ian J Martin	+44 (0)20 7448 6000	ian.martin@hiscox.com
Group Chief Operating Officer	Michael D Gould	+44 (0)20 7448 6000	michael.gould@hiscox.com
Chief Underwriting Officer	Robert S Childs	+44 (0)20 7448 6000	robert.childs@hiscox.com
Group Claims Director	Jeremy Pinchin	+44 (0)20 7448 6000	jeremy.pinchin@hiscox.com
Group Compliance Director	Jason S Jones	+44 (0)20 7448 6000	jason.jones@hiscox.com
Other Executive Director(s)	Stuart J Bridges	+44 (0)20 7448 6000	stuart.bridges@hiscox.com
	David JW Bruce	+44 (0)20 7448 6000	david.bruce@hiscox.com
	Stephen J Quick	+44 (0)20 7448 6000	stephen.quick@hiscox.com
	Bruno C Ritchie	+44 (0)20 7448 6000	bruno.ritchie@hiscox.com
	Nigel B Tyler	+44 (0)20 7448 6000	nigel.tyler@hiscox.com
	Richard C Watson	+44 (0)20 7448 6000	richard.watson@hiscox.com
Non-Executive Director(s)	Anthony Howland-Jackson	+44 (0)20 7448 6000	enquiry@hiscox.com
	Ian N Thomson	+44 (0)20 7448 6000	enquiry@hiscox.com
	Iain T Webb-Wilson	+44 (0)20 7448 6000	enquiry@hiscox.com
Company Secretary	Jason S Jones	+44 (0)20 7448 6000	jason.jones@hiscox.com

SYNDICATES MANAGED IN 2009

SYNDICATE NUMBER	**Hiscox Syndicate 33**		
Active Underwriter	Richard C Watson	+44 (0)20 7448 6000	richard.watson@hiscox.com
Appointed	2006		
Main Areas of Underwriting	Reinsurance; Major Property; Art; Private Client		
YEAR	CAPACITY £m		
2009	750		
2008	700		
2007	875		

SYNDICATE NUMBER	**3624 Hiscox US E&O aligned syndicate**		
Active Underwriter	Robert S Childs	+44 (0)20 7448 6000	robert.childs@hiscox.com
Appointed	2009		
Main Areas of Underwriting	Special Purpose Vehicle		
YEAR	CAPACITY £m		
2009	80		
2008	–		
2007	–		

SYNDICATE NUMBER	**6104 Hiscox SPS**		
Active Underwriter	Richard C Watson	+44 (0)20 7448 6000	richard.watson@hiscox.com
Appointed	2008		
Main Areas of Underwriting	Catastrophe Reinsurance		
YEAR	CAPACITY £m		
2009	52		
2008	35		
2007	–		

BACKGROUND INFORMATION

Ownership	Hiscox Syndicates Ltd is controlled by Hiscox Ltd of Hamilton, Bermuda, listed on the London Stock Exchange
Date of Incorporation	1991
Former Names	Minimar (154) to 1991
Syndicates merged into 33	52, 624, 625
Syndicates merged into 3624	None
Syndicates merged into 6104	None

Jubilee Managing Agency Limited

Address	4th Floor
	50 Fenchurch Street
	London EC3M 3JY
Telephone	+44 (0)20 7220 8728
Fax	+44 (0)20 7220 8732
Contact Email	jubilee@jubilee-insurance.com
Website	www.jubilee-insurance.com

SENIOR MANAGEMENT

Title	Name	Telephone	Email
Chairman (Non-Executive)	Lord Marland of Odstock	+44 (0)20 7220 8728	jubilee@jubilee-insurance.com
Deputy Chairman	Theodore TM Agnew	+44 (0)20 7220 8728	theodore.agnew@jubilee-insurance.com
Group Chief Executive Officer	Andreas C Loucaides	+44 (0)20 7220 8728	andreas.loucaides@jubilee-insurance.com
Managing Director	Kathryn J Lewis	+44 (0)20 7220 8728	kate.lewis@jubilee-insurance.com
Finance Director	Darren J Hogg	+44 (0)20 7220 8728	jubilee@jubilee-insurance.com
Group Director of Underwriting & Reinsurance	Norman H Topche	+44 (0)20 7220 8728	norman.topche@jubilee-insurance.com
Risk Manager	Pauline A Cockburn	+44 (0)20 7220 8728	pauline.cockburn@jubilee-insurance.com
Non-Executive Director(s)	Anthony PD Lancaster	+44 (0)20 7220 8728	jubilee@jubilee-insurance.com
	Rupert JG Lowe	+44 (0)20 7220 8728	jubilee@jubilee-insurance.com
	Ian McIsaac	+44 (0)20 7220 8728	jubilee@jubilee-insurance.com
Compliance Officer	Donal JL Barrett	+44 (0)20 7220 8728	donal.barrett@jubilee-insurance.com
Company Secretary	Pauline A Cockburn	+44 (0)20 7220 8728	pauline.cockburn@jubilee-insurance.com

Jubilee Managing Agency Limited (continued)

SYNDICATES MANAGED IN 2009

SYNDICATE NUMBER	**779 Cassidy Davis Life**		
Active Underwriter	Brian J Jackson	+44 (0)20 7220 8728	brian.jackson@cassidydavis.com
Appointed	1986		
Main Areas of Underwriting	Life		
YEAR	CAPACITY £m		
2009	30		
2008	30		
2007	38		

SYNDICATE NUMBER	**1231 Jubilee Motor Policies**		
Active Underwriter	Julian R Cashen	+44 (0)20 7220 8728	jubilee@jubilee-insurance.com
Appointed	2007		
Main Areas of Underwriting	Motor		
YEAR	CAPACITY £m		
2009	45		
2008	54		
2007	46		

SYNDICATE NUMBER	**5820 Cassidy Davis General**		
Active Underwriter	Christopher H Biles	+44 (0)20 7220 8728	chris.biles@jubilee-insurance.com
Appointed	2008		
Main Areas of Underwriting	Personal Lines		
YEAR	CAPACITY £m		
2009	63		
2008	42		
2007	44		

BACKGROUND INFORMATION

Ownership	Jubilee Managing Agency Ltd is controlled by the Appleclaim Group
Date of Incorporation	2002
Former Names	Hivegold Limited to 2002
Syndicates merged into 779	None
Syndicates merged into 1231	None
Syndicates merged into 5820	None

KGM Underwriting Agencies Limited

Address	KGM House
	George Lane
	South Woodford
	London E18 1RZ
Telephone	+44 (0)20 8530 7351
Fax	+44 (0)20 8530 7037
Contact Email	enquiries@kgminsurance.co.uk
Website	www.kgminsurance.co.uk

SENIOR MANAGEMENT

Title	Name	Telephone	Email
Chairman (Non-Executive)	Nicolas G Poole	+44 (0)20 8530 1813	nic.poole@kgminsurance.co.uk
Chief Executive Officer	Colin Hart	+44 (0)20 8530 1816	colin.hart@kgminsurance.co.uk
Finance Director	David C Wardle	+44 (0)20 8530 1831	david.wardle@kgminsurance.co.uk
Underwriting Director	Colin Hart	+44 (0)20 8530 1816	colin.hart@kgminsurance.co.uk
Risk Director	Adam C Seager	+44 (0)20 8530 1813	adam.seager@kgminsurance.co.uk
Claims Director	Martyn J Hardy	+44 (0)20 8530 1837	martyn.hardy@kgminsurance.co.uk
Compliance Director	Adam C Seager	+44 (0)20 8530 1813	adam.seager@kgminsurance.co.uk
Non-Executive Director(s)	Michael E Hildesley	+44 (0)20 8530 1813	michael.hildesley@kgminsurance.co.uk
	Brandon Swim	+44 (0)20 8530 1813	brandon.swim@kgminsurance.co.uk
Company Secretary	Adam C Seager	+44 (0)20 8530 1813	adam.seager@kgminsurance.co.uk

SYNDICATES MANAGED IN 2009

SYNDICATE NUMBER	260 KGM Motor Policies at Lloyd's		
Active Underwriter	Colin Hart	+44 (0)20 8530 1816	colin.hart@kgminsurance.co.uk
Appointed	2002		
Main Areas of Underwriting	Motor		
YEAR	CAPACITY £m		
2009	73		
2008	54		
2007	50		

BACKGROUND INFORMATION

Ownership	KGM Underwriting Agencies Ltd is controlled by Perserverance Ltd of Gibraltar
Date of Incorporation	1983
Former Names	None in past 20 years
Syndicates merged into 260	None

Liberty Syndicate Management Limited

Address	5th Floor
	Plantation Place South
	60 Great Tower Street
	London EC3R 5AZ
Telephone	+44 (0)20 7070 4472
Fax	+44 (0)20 7863 1001
Contact Email	info@libertysyndicates.com
Website	www.libertysyndicates.com

SENIOR MANAGEMENT

Title	Name	Telephone	Email
Chairman (Non-Executive)	Brian A FitzGerald	+44 (0)20 7070 4472	info@libertysyndicates.com
Chief Executive Officer	Nicholas J Metcalf	+44 (0)20 7070 4472	info@libertysyndicates.com
Director of Finance	John AR Dunn	+44 (0)20 7070 4472	info@libertysyndicates.com
Director of Operations	John AR Dunn	+44 (0)20 7070 4472	info@libertysyndicates.com
Underwriting Director	Thomas RC Corfield	+44 (0)20 7070 4472	info@libertysyndicates.com
Head of Claims	Mike Gillett	+44 (0)20 7070 4472	info@libertysyndicates.com

Liberty Syndicate Management Limited (continued)

Global Peer Reviewer	Geoffrey Lynch, OBE	+44 (0)20 7070 4472	info@libertysyndicates.com
Compliance Officer	Andrew Hall	+44 (0)20 7070 4472	info@libertysyndicates.com
Non-Executive Director(s)	Daniel TN Forsythe	+44 (0)20 7070 4472	info@libertysyndicates.com
	David H Long	+44 (0)20 7070 4472	info@libertysyndicates.com
	Gordon J McBurney	+44 (0)20 7070 4472	info@libertysyndicates.com
	Derek J Scott	+44 (0)20 7070 4472	info@libertysyndicates.com
	J Richard L Youell	+44 (0)20 7070 4472	info@libertysyndicates.com
Company Secretary	Liam O'Connell (Acting)	+44 (0)20 7070 4472	info@libertysyndicates.com

SYNDICATES MANAGED IN 2009

SYNDICATE NUMBER	**4472 Liberty**		
Active Underwriter	Thomas RC Corfield	+44 (0)20 7070 4472	info@libertysyndicates.com
Appointed	1998		
Main Areas of Underwriting	WW Reinsurance; London Market Reinsurance; Casualty; Contingent Lines; Property; Marine		

YEAR	CAPACITY £m
2009	715
2008	830
2007	917

BACKGROUND INFORMATION

Ownership	Liberty Syndicate Management Ltd is controlled by Liberty Mutual Group Inc of Boston, USA
Date of Incorporation	1994
Former Names	None in past 20 years
Syndicates merged into 4472	190, 282

Managing Agency Partners Limited

Address	1st Floor
	110 Fenchurch Street
	London EC3M 5JT
Telephone	+44 (0)20 7709 3860
Fax	+44 (0)20 7709 3861
Contact Email	map@mapunderwriting.co.uk
Website	www.mapunderwriting.co.uk

SENIOR MANAGEMENT

Title	Name	Telephone	Email
Chairman (Non-Executive)	David ES Shipley	+44 (0)20 7709 3860	dshipley@mapunderwriting.co.uk
Managing Director	James D Denoon Duncan	+44 (0)20 7709 3862	jdenoonduncan@mapunderwriting.co.uk
Finance Director	Richard J Sumner	+44 (0)20 7709 3866	rsumner@mapunderwriting.co.uk
Compliance Director	Siobhan McAuley	+44 (0)20 7709 3867	smcauley@mapunderwriting.co.uk
Other Executive Director(s)	Aidan Kong	+44 (0)20 7709 3860	map@mapunderwriting.co.uk
	Christopher J Smelt	+44 (0)20 7709 3860	map@mapunderwriting.co.uk
	Richard K Trubshaw	+44 (0)20 7709 3860	map@mapunderwriting.co.uk

Non-Executive Director(s)	Christine E Dandridge	+44 (0)20 7709 3860	map@mapunderwriting.co.uk
	H Raymond Dumas	+44 (0)20 7709 3860	map@mapunderwriting.co.uk
	Andrew S Foote	+44 (0)20 7709 3860	map@mapunderwriting.co.uk
Company Secretary	Siobhan McAuley	+44 (0)20 7709 3867	smcauley@mapunderwriting.co.uk

SYNDICATES MANAGED IN 2009

SYNDICATE NUMBER	**MAP 2791**		
Active Underwriter	Richard K Trubshaw	+44 (0)20 7709 3860	map@mapunderwriting.co.uk
Appointed	2007		
Main Areas of Underwriting	Marine; Property Insurance; Property Reinsurance; War & Political Risk; Casualty; Specialty Lines; Auto		
YEAR	CAPACITY £m		
2009	401		
2008	401		
2007	459		

SYNDICATE NUMBER	**MAP 6103**		
Active Underwriter	Richard K Trubshaw	+44 (0)20 7709 3860	map@mapunderwriting.co.uk
Appointed	2007		
Main Areas of Underwriting	Special Purpose Syndicate		
YEAR	CAPACITY £m		
2009	40		
2008	40		
2007	43		

BACKGROUND INFORMATION

Ownership	Managing Agency Partners Ltd is controlled by MAP Equity Ltd, a company owned by the underwriting and management team
Date of Incorporation	2000
Former Names	Branchgrove Limited to 2000
Syndicates merged into 2791	None
Syndicates merged into 6103	None

Markel Syndicate Management Limited

Address	The Markel Building
	49 Leadenhall Street
	London EC3A 2EA
Telephone	+44 (0)20 7953 6000
Fax	+44 (0)20 7953 6001
Contact Email	derah.mccall@markelintl.com
Website	www.markelintl.com

SENIOR MANAGEMENT

Title	Name	Telephone	Email
Chairman (Non-Executive)	Simon R Arnold	+44 (0)20 7953 6000	simon.arnold@markelintl.com
Chief Executive Officer	William D Stovin	+44 (0)20 7953 6000	william.stovin@markelintl.com
Finance Director	Andrew J Davies	+44 (0)20 7953 6000	andy.davies@markelintl.com
Director of London Underwriting	Jeremy W Brazil	+44 (0)20 7953 6000	jeremy.brazil@markelintl.com

Markel Syndicate Management Limited (continued)

Chief Actuary Director	Nicholas JS Line	+44 (0)20 7953 6000	nicholas.line@markelintl.com
Director of Claims	Stuart C Willoughby	+44 (0)20 7953 6000	stuart.willoughby@markelintl.com
Compliance Officer	Andrew J Bailey	+44 (0)20 7953 6000	andrew.bailey@markelintl.com
Other Executive Director(s)	Stephen (Steve) M Carroll	+44 (0)20 7953 6000	steve.carroll@markelintl.com
Non-Executive Director(s)	Ian Marshall	+44 (0)20 7953 6000	ian.marshall@markelintl.com
Company Secretary	Andrew J Bailey	+44 (0)20 7953 6000	andrew.bailey@markelintl.com

SYNDICATES MANAGED IN 2009

SYNDICATE NUMBER	**Markel Syndicate 3000**		
Active Underwriter	Jeremy Brazil	+44 (0)20 7953 6000	jeremy.brazil@markelintl.com
Appointed	2008		
Main Areas of Underwriting	Marine; Professional Lines; Property		
YEAR	CAPACITY £m		
2009	170		
2008	170		
2007	175		

BACKGROUND INFORMATION

Ownership	Markel Syndicate Management Ltd is controlled by the Markel Corporation of Virginia, USA
Date of Incorporation	1995
Former Names	Saffronplace Limited to 1996
	Octavian Syndicate Management Limited to 2000
Syndicates merged into 3000	329, 554, 702, 959, 1009, 1227, 1228, 1239

Marketform Managing Agency Limited

Address	8 Lloyd's Avenue
	London EC3N 3EL
Telephone	+44 (0)20 7488 7700
Fax	+44 (0)20 7488 7800
Contact Email	underwriters@marketform.com
Website	www.marketform.com

SENIOR MANAGEMENT

Title	Name	Telephone	Email
Chairman (Non-Executive)	Robin AG Jackson	+44 (0)20 7488 7762	robin.jackson@marketform.com
Managing Director	Karen Sinden	+44 (0)20 7488 7700	karen.sinden@marketform.com
Chief Financial Officer	Roger A Doubtfire	+44 (0)20 7488 7730	roger.doubtfire@marketform.com
Underwriting Director	Simon P Lotter	+44 (0)20 7488 7700	simon.lotter@marketform.com
Claims Director	Daniel AW Smith	+44 (0)20 7488 7700	daniel.smith@marketform.com
Compliance Director	Harinderjit (Harry) Nagra	+44 (0)20 7488 7700	harry.nagra@marketform.com
Other Executive Director(s)	Simon G Turner	+44 (0)20 7488 7700	simon.turner@marketform.com
	Graham RA White	+44 (0)20 7488 7700	underwriters@marketform.com

Non-Executive Director(s)	Terence G Hebden	+44 (0)20 7488 7761	terence.hebden@marketform.com
	John E Mumford	+44 (0)20 7488 7700	john.mumford@marketform.com
Company Secretary	Anne C Durkin	+44 (0)20 7488 7716	anne.durkin@marketform.com

SYNDICATES MANAGED IN 2009

SYNDICATE NUMBER	**2468**		
Active Underwriter	Simon P Lotter	+44 (0)20 7488 7700	simon.lotter@marketform.com
Appointed	1999		
Main Areas of Underwriting	Non-US Medical Liabilities; PI; Product Recall; D&O; Specialist PA Classes		
YEAR	CAPACITY £m		
2009	120		
2008	100		
2007	100		

BACKGROUND INFORMATION

Ownership	Marketform Managing Agency Ltd is controlled by American Financial Group of Cincinnatti, Ohio through GAI Holding Bermuda Ltd
Date of Incorporation	1998
Former Names	None in past 20 years
Syndicates merged into 2468	None

Marlborough Underwriting Agency Limited

Address	Birchin Court
	20 Birchin Lane
	London EC3V 9DU
Telephone	+44 (0)20 7456 1800
Fax	+44 (0)20 7456 1810
Contact Email	compliance@marlborough.co.uk
Website	www.marlborough.co.uk

SENIOR MANAGEMENT

Title	Name	Telephone	Email
Chairman (Non-Executive)	Mark J Byrne	+44 (0)20 7456 1800	compliance@marlborough.co.uk
Managing Director	Thomas A Bolt	+44 (0)20 7456 1800	thomas.bolt@marlborough.co.uk
Deputy Managing Director	Dominic J Kirby	+44 (0)20 7456 1800	dominic.kirby@marlborough.co.uk
Finance Director	Paul A Chubb	+44 (0)20 7456 1800	paul.chubb@marlborough.co.uk
Underwriting Director	Leslie F Allen	+44 (0)20 7456 1800	leslie.allen@marlborough.co.uk
Claims & RI Recoveries Director	Ian R Mallery	+44 (0)20 7456 1800	ian.mallery@marlborough.co.uk
Compliance Director	Iain F MacDowall	+44 (0)20 7456 1800	iain.macdowall@marlborough.co.uk
Non-Executive Director(s)	David A Brown	+44 (0)20 7456 1800	compliance@marlborough.co.uk
	Howard J Cheetham	+44 (0)20 7456 1800	compliance@marlborough.co.uk
	Karl G Grieves	+44 (0)20 7456 1800	compliance@marlborough.co.uk
	Nicholas CT Pawson	+44 (0)20 7456 1800	compliance@marlborough.co.uk
	David T Young	+44 (0)20 7456 1800	compliance@marlborough.co.uk
Company Secretary	Iain F MacDowall	+44 (0)20 7456 1800	iain.macdowall@marlborough.co.uk

Marlborough Underwriting Agency Limited (continued)

SYNDICATES MANAGED IN 2009

SYNDICATE NUMBER	**BRM 1861**		
Active Underwriter	Leslie F Allen	+44 (0)20 7456 1800	leslie.allen@marlborough.co.uk
Appointed	2004		
Main Areas of Underwriting	Reinsurance; Marine; Aviation; Energy		
YEAR	CAPACITY £m		
2009	100		
2008	82		
2007	120		

Syndicate 1243 Euclidian in Run-off (open years: 2002, 2003, 2004)

Run-Off Manager 2002 & 2003	John Robert Newman Collyear
Run-Off Manager 2004	Raymond John Spicer

BACKGROUND INFORMATION

Ownership	Marlborough Underwriting Agency Ltd is controlled by Flagstone Re of Hamilton, Bermuda
Date of Incorporation	1963
Former Names	Barder & Marsh Services Limited to 1991
	Barder & Marsh Limited to 1995
Syndicates merged into 1861	None

Max at Lloyd's Ltd

Address	4th Floor
	70 Gracechurch Street
	London EC3V 0XL
Telephone	+44 (0)20 3102 3100
Fax	+44 (0)20 3102 3200
Contact Email	info@maxatlloyds.com
Website	www.maxatlloyds.com

SENIOR MANAGEMENT

Title	Name	Telephone	Email
Chairman (Executive)	William M Becker	+44 (0)20 3102 3100	william.becker@maxatlloyds.com
Managing Director	Iain J Bremner	+44 (0)20 3102 3100	iain.bremner@maxatlloyds.com
Chief Financial Officer	Lance J Gibbins	+44 (0)20 3102 3100	lance.gibbins@maxatlloyds.com
Underwriting Director	Matthew A Petzold	+44 (0)20 3102 3100	matthew.petzold@maxatlloyds.com
Other Executive Director(s)	John M Boylan	+44 (0)20 3102 3100	john.boylan@maxatlloyds.com
	Peter A Minton	+44 (0)20 3102 3100	peter.minton@maxatlloyds.com
	Gregory EA Morrison	+44 (0)20 3102 3100	gregory.morrison@maxatlloyds.com
	Adam Mullan	+44 (0)20 3102 3100	adam.mullan@maxatlloyds.com
	Joseph W Roberts	+44 (0)20 3102 3100	joseph.roberts@maxatlloyds.com
Non-Executive Director(s)	Baron Clemens ATW von Bechtolsheim	+44 (0)20 3102 3100	clemens.vonbechtolsheim@ maxatlloyds.com
	Andrew T West	+44 (0)20 3102 3100	andrew.west@maxatlloyds.com

Compliance Officer	Marion Jewry	+44 (0)20 3102 3100	marion.jewry@maxatlloyds.com
Company Secretary	Paul M Armfield	+44 (0)20 3102 3100	paul.armfield@maxatlloyds.com

SYNDICATES MANAGED IN 2009

SYNDICATE NUMBER	**Syndicate 1400**		
Active Underwriter	Matthew A Petzold	+44 (0)20 3102 3100	matthew.petzold@maxatlloyds.com
Appointed	1999		
Main Areas of Underwriting	Property Reinsurance; Accident & Health; Financial Institutions; Reinsurance to Close; Custom Risks		
YEAR	CAPACITY £m		
2009	125		
2008	125		
2007	125		

SYNDICATE NUMBER	**2525 DL Pratt & Ors**		
Active Underwriter	David L Dale	+44 (0)20 3102 3100	david.dale@maxatlloyds.com
Appointed	2003		
Main Areas of Underwriting	Public Liability; Employers' Liability		
YEAR	CAPACITY £m		
2009	42		
2008	42		
2007	42		

SYNDICATE NUMBER	**2526 Andy Doré & Ors**		
Active Underwriter	Andrew G Doré	+44 (0)20 3102 3100	andrew.dore@maxatlloyds.com
Appointed	2004		
Main Areas of Underwriting	Professional Indemnity; Medical Malpractice		
YEAR	CAPACITY £m		
2009	32		
2008	32		
2007	32		

Syndicate 994 MIC Simmonds & Ors in Run-off (open year: 2006)

Run-Off Manager	Matthew A Petzold

BACKGROUND INFORMATION

Ownership	Max at Lloyd's is controlled by the Max Capital Group Ltd of Hamilton, Bermuda
Date of Incorporation	2001
Former Names	Imagine Syndicate Management Limited to 2008
	Batch Properties Limited to 1997
	Trinity Syndicates Limited to 2000
	Abacus Syndicates Limited to 2006
Syndicates merged into 1400	1923
Syndicates merged into 2525	None
Syndicates merged into 2526	None

Mitsui Sumitomo Insurance Underwriting at Lloyd's Ltd

Address	25 Fenchurch Avenue
	London EC3M 5AD
Telephone	+44 (0)20 7977 8321
Fax	+44 (0)20 7977 8300
Contact Email	enquiries@msilm.com
Website	www.msilm.com

SENIOR MANAGEMENT

Title	Name	Telephone	Email
Chairman (Non-Executive)	J Maxwell (Max) P Taylor	+44 (0)20 7977 8321	enquiries@msilm.com
Chief Executive Officer	Andrew McKee	+44 (0)20 7977 8330	amckee@msilm.com
Financial Director	Colin D Charles	+44 (0)20 7977 8374	ccharles@msilm.com
Risk Director	Philip R Pearce	+44 (0)20 7702 6329	ppearce@msilm.com
Compliance Director	Philip R Pearce	+44 (0)20 7702 6329	ppearce@msilm.com
Technical Director	Michael G Gardiner	+44 (0)20 7977 8340	mgardiner@msilm.com
Other Executive Director(s)	Dipak Warren	+44 (0)20 7977 8333	dwarren@msilm.com
Non-Executive Director(s)	Hiroyuki Iioka	+44 (0)20 7977 8321	enquiries@msilm.com
	Yohichi Kamagai	+44 (0)20 7977 8321	enquiries@msilm.com
	Derek Kingston	+44 (0)20 7977 8321	enquiries@msilm.com
	Kazuo Yamada	+44 (0)20 7977 8321	enquiries@msilm.com
	Tadashi Yamada	+44 (0)20 7977 8321	enquiries@msilm.com
Company Secretary	Christopher J Ringrose	+44 (0)20 7977 8346	cringrose@msilm.com

SYNDICATES MANAGED IN 2009

SYNDICATE NUMBER	**3210 Mitsui Sumitomo Insurance**		
Active Underwriter	Dipak Warren	+44 (0)20 7977 8333	dwarren@msilm.com
Appointed	2003		
Main Areas of Underwriting	Property; Construction; Casualty; Motor (Fleet); Marine; Aviation; Professional Indemnity		
YEAR	CAPACITY £m		
2009	340		
2008	340		
2007	340		

BACKGROUND INFORMATION

Ownership	MSIUL is ultimately controlled by Mitsui Sumitomo insurance Group Holdings Inc., of Japan
Date of Incorporation	2006
Former Names	None
Syndicates merged into 3210	None

Montpelier Underwriting Agencies Ltd

Address	7th Floor
	85 Gracechurch Street
	London EC3V 0AA
Telephone	+44 (0)20 7648 4500
Fax	+44 (0)20 7648 4501
Contact Email	info@montpelierua.com
Website	www.montpelierre.com

SENIOR MANAGEMENT

Title	Name	Telephone	Email
Chairman (Executive)	Thomas GS Busher	+44 (0)20 7648 4500	tom.busher@montpelierre.bm
Managing Director	Giuseppe (Joe) Perdoni	+44 (0)20 7648 4517	joe.perdoni@montpelierua.com
Chief Financial Officer	Michael S Paquette	+44 (0)20 7648 4500	mike.paquette@montpeliertr.com
Director of Underwriting	Peter J Rand	+44 (0)20 7648 4500	peter.rand@montpelierua.com
Claims Manager	Paul Moss	+44 (0)20 7648 4500	paul.moss@montpelierua.com
Compliance Officer	Gillian Phillips	+44 (0)20 7648 4500	gillian.phillips@montpelierua.com
Other Executive Director(s)	Richard MM Chattock	+44 (0)20 7648 4500	richard.chattock@montpelierua.com
Non-Executive Director(s)	Christopher L Harris	+44 (0)20 7648 4500	chris.harris@montpelierre.bm
(Independent)	John S Goldsmith	+44 (0)20 7648 4500	–
(Independent)	P Terry O'Neill	+44 (0)20 7648 4500	–
(Independent)	Nicholas J Newman-Young	+44 (0)20 7648 4500	–
Company Secretary	Gillian Phillips	+44 (0)20 7648 4500	gillian.phillips@montpelierua.com

SYNDICATES MANAGED IN 2009

SYNDICATE NUMBER	Montpelier Syndicate 5151		
Active Underwriter	Richard MM Chattock	+44 (0)20 7648 4500	richard.chattock@montpelierua.com
Appointed	2007		
Main Areas of Underwriting	Non-Marine Property; Engineering Classes; Specialty Casualty		
YEAR	CAPACITY £m		
2009	143		
2008	143		
2007	47		

BACKGROUND INFORMATION

Ownership	Montpelier Underwriting Agencies Ltd is controlled by the Montpelier Group of Bermuda, listed on the New York Stock Exchange
Date of Incorporation	2008
Former Names	None
Syndicates merged into 5151	None

Munich Re Underwriting Limited

Address	St Helens
	1 Undershaft
	London EC3A 8EE
Telephone	+44 (0)20 7886 3900
Fax	+44 (0)20 7886 3901
Contact Email	info@mrunderwriting.com
Website	www.munichre.com

SENIOR MANAGEMENT

Title	Name	Telephone	Email
Chairman (Non-Executive)	John H Rochman	+44 (0)20 7886 3900	john.rochman@mrunderwriting.com
Managing Director	Roderic WR Grande	+44 (0)20 7886 3900	rod.grande@mrunderwriting.com
Chief Financial Officer	Nicholas JT Gray	+44 (0)20 7886 3900	nick.gray@mrunderwriting.com
Claims Director	Alison C Cook	+44 (0)20 7886 3900	alison.cook@mrunderwriting.com
Compliance Director	Timur (Tim) Coskun	+44 (0)20 7886 3900	tim.coskun@mrunderwriting.com
Other Executive Director(s)	Oliver J Crabtree	+44 (0)20 7886 3900	oliver.crabtree@mrunderwriting.com
	Dominick JR Hoare	+44 (0)20 7886 3900	dominick.hoare@mrunderwriting.com
	Mark C Watkins	+44 (0)20 7886 3900	mark.watkins@mrunderwriting.com
Non-Executive Director(s)	Thomas E Artmann	+44 (0)20 7886 3900	central@mrunderwriting.com
	John A Cooper	+44 (0)20 7886 3900	central@mrunderwriting.com
	Edward N Noble	+44 (0)20 7886 3900	central@mrunderwriting.com
Company Secretary	Timur (Tim) Coskun	+44 (0)20 7886 3900	tim.coskun@mrunderwriting.com

SYNDICATES MANAGED IN 2009

SYNDICATE NUMBER	457 Watkins Syndicate		
Active Underwriter (Joint)	Dominick JR Hoare	+44 (0)20 7886 3900	dominick.hoare@mrunderwriting.com
Appointed	2001		
Active Underwriter (Joint)	Oliver J Crabtree	+44 (0)20 7886 3900	oliver.crabtree@mrunderwriting.com
Appointed	2001		
Main Areas of Underwriting	Space; Marine Liability; Energy; Cargo; Accident & Health; Yachts; Specie; War		
YEAR	CAPACITY £m		
2009	260		
2008	260		
2007	260		

BACKGROUND INFORMATION

Ownership	Munich Re Underwriting Ltd is controlled by the Munich Re Group of Bavaria, Germany
Date of Incorporation	1977
Former Names	MFK Underwriting Agencies Limited to 1996
	Apollo Underwriting Limited to 1997
Syndicates merged into 457	None

Navigators Underwriting Agency Ltd

Address	7th Floor
	2 Minster Court
	Mincing Lane
	London EC3R 7BB
Telephone	+44 (0)20 7220 6900
Fax	+44 (0)20 7220 6901
Contact Email	communications@navg.com
Website	www.navg.com

SENIOR MANAGEMENT

Title	Name	Telephone	Email
Chairman (Non-Executive)	Henry JM Blakeney	+44 (0)20 7220 6900	hblakeney@navg.com
Chief Executive Officer	Paul V Hennessy	+44 (0)20 7220 6900	phennessy@navg.com
Chief Financial Officer	Tracey O Lillington	+44 (0)20 7220 6900	tlillington@navg.com
Chief Operating Officer	Stephen R Coward	+44 (0)20 7220 6900	scoward@navg.com
Underwriting Director	Richard P Bardwell	+44 (0)20 7220 6900	rbardwell@navg.com
Claims Director	David Paveling	+44 (0)20 7220 6900	dpaveling@navg.com
Compliance Officer	Kate Hillery	+44 (0)20 7220 6900	khillery@navg.com
Non-Executive Director(s)	H Clay Bassett JR	+44 (0)20 7220 6900	cbassett@navg.com
	Christopher Duca	+44 (0)20 7220 6900	cduca@navg.com
	Stanley A Galanski	+44 (0)20 7220 6900	sgalanski@navg.com
	Dr Paul Kelly	+44 (0)20 7220 6900	pkelly@navg.com
Company Secretary	Steven Luck	+44 (0)20 7220 6900	sluck@navg.com

SYNDICATES MANAGED IN 2009

SYNDICATE NUMBER	**Syndicate 1221**
Active Underwriter	Richard P Bardwell +44 (0)20 7220 6900 rbardwell@navg.com
Appointed	2005
Main Areas of Underwriting	Marine Liability; Offshore Energy; Cargo & Specie; Non-Marine Property Liability; Onshore Energy; Excess Energy Liabilities; Excess Energy Liabilities; Lawyers Professional Liability; Engineering & Construction; Blue Water Hull; Marine Excess of Loss Reinsurance; Directors & Officers Liability

YEAR	CAPACITY £m
2009	122
2008	123
2007	140

BACKGROUND INFORMATION

Ownership	Navigators Underwriting Agency Ltd is controlled by Navigators Group of New York, USA, listed on the New York Stock Exchange
Date of Incorporation	1978
Former Names	Mander Thomas & Cooper (Underwriting Agencies) Limited to 2001
Syndicates merged into 1221	552, 1023

Newline Underwriting Management Limited

Address	Suite 5/4
	London Underwriting Centre
	3 Minster Court
	Mincing Lane
	London EC3R 7DD
Telephone	+44 (0)20 7090 1700
Fax	+44 (0)20 7090 1701
Contact Email	enquiries@newlineuml.com
Website	www.newlineuml.com

SENIOR MANAGEMENT

Title	Name	Telephone	Email
Chairman (Non-Executive)	Andrew A Barnard	+44 (0)20 7090 1700	abarnard@odysseyre.com
Chief Executive Officer	Carl A Overy	+44 (0)20 7090 1700	covery@newlineuml.com
Chief Financial Officer	Paul Clayden	+44 (0)20 7090 1700	pclayden@newlineuml.com
Chief Operating Officer	James (Dick) RF Micklem	+44 (0)20 7090 1700	dickmicklem@newlineuml.com
Chief Information Officer	James (Dick) RF Micklem	+44 (0)20 7090 1700	dickmicklem@newlineuml.com
Chief Underwriting Officer	Philip T Foley	+44 (0)20 7090 1700	pfoley@newlineuml.com
Chief Actuary	Neil Duncan	+44 (0)20 7090 1700	nduncan@newlineuml.com
Claims Director	Robert B Kastner	+44 (0)20 7090 1700	rkastner@newlineuml.com
Independent Review Director	Simon T Fradd	+44 (0)20 7090 1700	sfradd@newlineuml.com
Compliance Officer	James (Dick) RF Micklem	+44 (0)20 7090 1700	dickmicklem@newlineuml.com
Other Executive Director(s)	James (Dick) RF Micklem	+44 (0)20 7090 1700	dickmicklem@newlineuml.com
	Brian D Young	+44 (0)20 7090 1700	byoung@newlineuml.com
Non-Executive Director(s)	Richard S Donovan	+44 (0)20 7090 1700	rdonovan@odysseyre.com
Company Secretary	James (Dick) RF Micklem	+44 (0)20 7090 1700	dickmicklem@newlineuml.com

SYNDICATES MANAGED IN 2009

SYNDICATE NUMBER	**1218 Newline**		
Active Underwriter	Philip T Foley	+44 (0)20 7090 1700	pfoley@newlineuml.com
Appointed	2002		
Main Areas of Underwriting	UK & International Liability Insurance		
YEAR	CAPACITY £m		
2009	80		
2008	85		
2007	85		

BACKGROUND INFORMATION

Ownership	Newline Underwriting Management Ltd is controlled by Odyssey Re Holdings Corp, listed on the New York Stock Exchange
Date of Incorporation	1996
Former Names	Slipframe Design Limited to 1996
	TIG Syndicate Management Limited to 1999
Syndicates merged into 1218	None

Novae Syndicates Limited

Address	71 Fenchurch Street
	London EC3M 4HH
Telephone	+44 (0)20 7903 7300
Fax	+44 (0)20 7903 7333
Contact Email	novae@mconsulting.co.uk
Website	www.novae.com

SENIOR MANAGEMENT

Title	Name	Telephone	Email
Chairman (Executive)	Allan M Nichols	+44 (0)20 7903 7300	anichols@novae.com
Chief Executive Officer	Jeremy R Adams	+44 (0)20 7903 7300	jadams@novae.com
Finance Director	Mark A Hudson	+44 (0)20 7903 7300	mhudson@novae.com
Chief Information Officer	Clive L Murray	+44 (0)20 7903 7300	cmurray@novae.com
Group Chief Underwriting Officer	Peter C Matson	+44 (0)20 7903 7300	pmatson@novae.com
Group Claims Director	Jonathan A Boyns	+44 (0)20 7903 7300	jboyns@novae.com
Compliance Director	Stephen J Heming	+44 (0)20 7903 7300	sheming@novae.com
Other Executive Director(s)	Jonathan LJ Butcher	+44 (0)20 7903 7300	jbutcher@novae.com
Non-Executive Director(s)	Oliver RP Corbett	+44 (0)20 7903 7300	ocorbett@novae.com
	William (Bill) J Davis	+44 (0)20 7903 7300	bdavis@novae.com
	Matthew K Fosh	+44 (0)20 7903 7300	mfosh@novae.com
	John M Massey	+44 (0)20 7903 7300	jmassey@novae.com
	John RW Thirlwell	+44 (0)20 7903 7300	jthirlwell@novae.com
Company Secretary	Mark J Turvey	+44 (0)20 7903 7300	mturvey@novae.com

SYNDICATES MANAGED IN 2009

SYNDICATE NUMBER	Novae Syndicate 2007		
Active Underwriter	Jonathan LJ Butcher	+44 (0)20 7903 7300	jbutcher@novae.com
Appointed	2007		
Main Areas of Underwriting	Aviation Reinsurance; Bloodstock; Cargo; Energy; Financial Institutions; Fine Art & Specie; General Liability; Management Liability; Medical Malpractice; International Casualty; Marine; Political Risk; Professional Indemnity; Property; Terrorism		

YEAR	CAPACITY £m
2009	360
2008	360
2007	360

Novae Syndicate 1007, 1010, 1115, 1203 in Run-off (open year: 2002)

Run-Off Manager	Information not available

Novae Syndicate 1241 in Run-off (open year: 2002)

Run-Off Manager	Jeremy Richard Adams

BACKGROUND INFORMATION

Ownership	Novae Syndicates Ltd is controlled by Novae Group plc of London, listed on the London Stock Exchange
Date of Incorporation	1986

Former Names	Spreckley Villers Hunt & Co Limited to 1993
	Spreckley Villers Burnhope & Co Limited to 1997
	SVB Syndicates Limited to 2006
Syndicates merged into 2007	575, 1007 (see above), 1234 (see above), 1415, 2147

Omega Underwriting Agents Limited

Address	4th Floor
	New London House
	6 London Street
	London EC3R 7LP
Telephone	+44 (0)20 7767 3000
Fax	+44 (0)20 7488 9639
Contact Email	info@omegauw.com
Website	www.omegauw.com

SENIOR MANAGEMENT

Title	Name	Telephone	Email
Chairman (Non-Executive)	Roger B Morgan	+44 (0)20 7767 3000	info@omegauw.com
Managing Director	Andrew J Adie	+44 (0)20 7767 3000	andrew.adie@omegauw.com
Financial Director	Jeremy B Raishbrook	+44 (0)20 7767 3000	jeremy.raishbrook@omegauw.com
Chief Operating Officer	Mark I Daly	+44 (0)20 7767 3000	mark.daly@omegauw.com
Underwriting Director	John D Robinson	+44 (0)20 7767 3000	john.robinson@omegauw.com
Compliance Officer	Andrew D Smith	+44 (0)20 7767 3000	andrew.smith@omegauw.com
Non-Executive Director(s)	Walter M Fiederowicz	+44 (0)20 7767 3000	info@omegauw.com
	Ian W Mercer	+44 (0)20 7767 3000	info@omegauw.com
	John F Powell	+44 (0)20 7767 3000	info@omegauw.com
Company Secretary	Andrew D Smith	+44 (0)20 7767 3000	andrew.smith@omegauw.com

SYNDICATES MANAGED IN 2009

SYNDICATE NUMBER	GS Christensen & Others Non-Marine Syndicate 958		
Active Underwriter	John D Robinson	+44 (0)20 7767 3000	john.robinson@omegauw.com
Appointed	1995		
Main Areas of Underwriting	Non-Marine; Property		
YEAR	CAPACITY £m		
2009	249		
2008	249		
2007	249		

BACKGROUND INFORMATION

Ownership	Omega Underwriting Agents Ltd is controlled by Omega Insurance Holdings Ltd of Hamilton, Bermuda, listed on London Stock Exchange
Date of Incorporation	1997
Former Names	Fossildrift Limited to 1998
Syndicates merged into 958	None

Pembroke Managing Agency Limited

Address	2nd Floor
	3 Minster Court
	Mincing Lane
	London EC3R 7DD
Telephone	+44 (0)20 7337 4400
Fax	+44 (0)20 7337 4401
Contact Email	hq@pembrokeunderwriting.com
Website	www.pembrokeunderwriting.com

SENIOR MANAGEMENT

Title	Name	Telephone	Email
Chairman (Non-Executive)	Robert (Bob) J Wallace	+44 (0)20 7337 4400	hq@pembrokeunderwriting.com
Managing Director	Mark C Butterworth	+44 (0)20 7337 4400	mark.butterworth@ pembrokeunderwriting.com
Finance Director	Justin AS Wash	+44 (0)20 7337 4400	justin.wash@pembrokeunderwriting.com
Underwriting Director	Mark H Wheeler	+44 (0)20 7337 4400	mark.wheeler@pembrokeunderwriting.com
Head of Risk Assurance	Philip Hicks	+44 (0)20 7337 4400	philip.hicks@pembrokeunderwriting.com
Claims Director	Gillian E Barnes	+44 (0)20 7337 4400	gillian.barnes@pembrokeunderwriting.com
Compliance Officer (Services provided by Chaucer)			
	Lorraine Webb	+44 (0)20 7337 4400	lorraine.webb@chaucerplc.com
Other Executive Director(s)	Christopher D Brown	+44 (0)20 7337 4400	christopher.brown@ pembrokeunderwriting.com
	Timothy ABH Glover	+44 (0)20 7337 4400	tim.glover@pembrokeunderwriting.com
Non-Executive Director(s)	Allan Kaufman	+44 (0)20 7337 4400	hq@pembrokeunderwriting.com
Company Secretary	Philip Hicks	+44 (0)20 7337 4400	philip.hicks@pembrokeunderwriting.com

SYNDICATES MANAGED IN 2009

SYNDICATE NUMBER	4000 Pembroke (PMA)		
Active Underwriter	Mark H Wheeler	+44 (0)20 7337 4400	mark.wheeler@ pembrokeunderwriting.com
Appointed	2004		
Main Areas of Underwriting	Financial Institutions; Professional Liability ; Specie & Fine Art; Kidnap & Ransom		
YEAR	CAPACITY £m		
2009	95		
2008	73		
2007	73		

BACKGROUND INFORMATION

Ownership	Pembroke Managing Agency Ltd is controlled by Ironshore Inc of The Cayman Islands
Date of Incorporation	2006
Former Names	None in last 20 years
Syndicates merged into 4000	None

QBE Underwriting Limited

Address	Plantation Place
	30 Fenchurch Street
	London EC3M 3BD
Telephone	+44 (0)20 7105 4000
Fax	+44 (0)20 7105 4019
Contact Email	enquiries@uk.qbe.com
Website	www.qbeeurope.com

SENIOR MANAGEMENT

Title	Name	Telephone	Email
Chairman (Non-Executive)	Frank O'Halloran	+44 (0)20 7105 4000	enquiries@uk.qbe.com
Deputy Chairman (Executive)	Vincent McLenaghan	+44 (0)20 7105 4000	enquiries@uk.qbe.com
Chief Executive Officer	Steven P Burns	+44 (0)20 7105 4000	enquiries@uk.qbe.com
Chief Financial Officer	David J Winkett	+44 (0)20 7105 4000	enquiries@uk.qbe.com
Chief Operating Officer	John D Neal	+44 (0)20 7105 4000	enquiries@uk.qbe.com
Chief Underwriting Officer	Peter E Grove	+44 (0)20 7105 4000	enquiries@uk.qbe.com
Underwriting Director(s)	Ashis M Bathia	+44 (0)20 7105 4000	enquiries@uk.qbe.com
	David A Constable	+44 (0)20 7105 4000	enquiries@uk.qbe.com
	Matthew F Crane	+44 (0)20 7105 4000	enquiries@uk.qbe.com
	Emilio A Di Silvio	+44 (0)20 7105 4000	enquiries@uk.qbe.com
	Doron Grossman	+44 (0)20 7105 4000	enquiries@uk.qbe.com
	Robert BM Johnston	+44 (0)20 7105 4000	enquiries@uk.qbe.com
	Bernard Mageean	+44 (0)20 7105 4000	enquiries@uk.qbe.com
	Colin R O'Farrell	+44 (0)20 7105 4000	enquiries@uk.qbe.com
	Jonathan W Parry	+44 (0)20 7105 4000	enquiries@uk.qbe.com
	Graham S Rayner	+44 (0)20 7105 4000	enquiries@uk.qbe.com
	Terence J Whittaker	+44 (0)20 7105 4000	enquiries@uk.qbe.com
Chief Actuarial Officer	Philip A Dodridge	+44 (0)20 7105 4000	enquiries@uk.qbe.com
Risk Management Director	Ian D Beckerson	+44 (0)20 7105 4000	enquiries@uk.qbe.com
Compliance Director	Ian D Beckerson	+44 (0)20 7105 4000	enquiries@uk.qbe.com
Non-Executive Director(s)			
(Independent)	Philip V Olsen	+44 (0)20 7105 4000	enquiries@uk.qbe.com
(Independent)	Brian W Pomeroy, CBE	+44 (0)20 7105 4000	enquiries@uk.qbe.com
(Independent)	Howard M Posner	+44 (0)20 7105 4000	enquiries@uk.qbe.com
Company Secretary	Sharon M Boland	+44 (0)20 7105 4000	enquiries@uk.qbe.com

SYNDICATES MANAGED IN 2009

SYNDICATE NUMBER	**QBE Casualty Syndicate 386**		
Active Underwriter	David A Constable	+44 (0)20 7105 4000	enquiries@uk.qbe.com
Appointed	2003		
Main Areas of Underwriting	Non-Marine Liability		
YEAR	CAPACITY £m		
2009	340		
2008	340		
2007	339		

SYNDICATE NUMBER	**QBE Syndicate 2999**		
Active Underwriter	John Neal	+44 (0)20 7105 4000	enquiries@uk.qbe.com
Appointed	2009		
Main Areas of Underwriting	Reinsurance; Marine & Energy; Non-Marine Liability; Property; Aviation		
YEAR	CAPACITY £m		
2009	720		
2008	780		
2007	780		

SUB-SYNDICATES OF 2999			
Syndicate Number	**QBE Reinsurance Syndicate 566**		
Underwriter (Managing Director)	Jonathan W Parry	+44 (0)20 7105 4000	enquiries@uk.qbe.com
2009 Capacity £m	245		
2008	290		
2007	245		

Syndicate Number	**QBE Marine & Energy Syndicate 1036**		
Underwriter (Managing Director)	Colin R O'Farrell	+44 (0)20 7105 4000	enquiries@uk.qbe.com
2009 Capacity £m	215		
2008	210		
2007	220		

Syndicate Number	**QBE Syndicate 1886**		
Underwriter (Managing Director)	John D Neal	+44 (0)20 7105 4000	enquiries@uk.qbe.com
YEAR	CAPACITY £m		
2009	95		
2008	100		
2007	35		

Syndicate Number	**QBE Property Syndicate 2000**		
Underwriter (Managing Director)	Bernard Mageean	+44 (0)20 7105 4000	enquiries@uk.qbe.com
YEAR	CAPACITY £m		
2009	75		
2008	85		
2007	195		

Syndicate Number	**QBE Aviation Syndicate 5555**		
Underwriter (Managing Director)	Emilio A Di Silvio	+44 (0)20 7105 4000	enquiries@uk.qbe.com
YEAR	CAPACITY £m		
2009	90		
2008	95		
2007	85		

BACKGROUND INFORMATION

Ownership	QBE Underwriting Ltd is controlled by QBE Insurance Group Ltd of Sydney, Australia
Date of Incorporation	1971
Former Names	Michael Payne & Company to 1986
	Janson Green Limited to 1999
	Limit Underwriting Limited to 2007
Syndicates merged into 386	1156
Syndicates merged into 2999	45, 79, 566, 724, 1036, 1215, 1223, 1234, 2724

R J Kiln & Co Limited

Address	106 Fenchurch Street
	London EC3M 5NR
Telephone	+44 (0)20 7886 9000
Fax	+44 (0)20 7488 1848
Contact Email	*See below*
Website	www.kilngroup.com

SENIOR MANAGEMENT

Title	Name	Telephone	Email
Chairman (Executive)	Edward G Creasy	+44 (0)20 7886 9000	*For Senior Management email addresses*
Chief Executive Officer	Charles AS Franks	+44 (0)20 7886 9000	*R J Kiln & Co Limited wishes us to guide*
Finance Director	James W Dover	+44 (0)20 7886 9000	*you to its website*
Chief Operating Officer	Elizabeth M Walsh	+44 (0)20 7886 9000	
Director of Underwriting	Richard CW Lewis	+44 (0)20 7886 9000	
Group Director of Underwriting	Robert D Chase	+44 (0)20 7886 9000	
Compliance Officer	Keith N Grant	+44 (0)20 7886 9000	
Other Executive Director(s)	Shingo Batori	+44 (0)20 7886 9000	
	Roger A Bickmore	+44 (0)20 7886 9000	
	Paul M Culham	+44 (0)20 7886 9000	
	Robin G Hargreaves	+44 (0)20 7886 9000	
	Andrew N Hitchcox	+44 (0)20 7886 9000	
	David J Huckstepp	+44 (0)20 7886 9000	
	Paul M Letherbarrow	+44 (0)20 7886 9000	
	Stephen D Mathers	+44 (0)20 7886 9000	
	Timothy P Prifti	+44 (0)20 7886 9000	
	Bruce D Shepherd	+44 (0)20 7886 9000	
Non-Executive Director(s)	Ian Brimecome	+44 (0)20 7886 9000	
(Independent)	Paul W Hewitt	+44 (0)20 7886 9000	
(Independent)	Paul Wilson	+44 (0)20 7886 9000	
Company Secretary	Keith N Grant	+44 (0)20 7886 9000	

SYNDICATES MANAGED IN 2009

SYNDICATE NUMBER	**Kiln Life 308**		
Active Underwriter	Catharine J Toomey	+44 (0)20 7886 9000	cathy.toomey@kilngroup.com
Appointed	2003		
Main Areas of Underwriting	Life Insurance		
YEAR	CAPACITY £m		
2009	15		
2008	15		
2007	15		

SYNDICATE NUMBER	**Kiln Combined Syndicate 510**		
Joint Underwriters			
Accident & Health	Tim Prifti	+44 (0)20 7886 9000	tim.prifti@kilngroup.com
Aviation	Paul Letherbarrow	+44 (0)20 7886 9000	paul.letherbarrow@kilngroup.com
Marine & Special Risks	Paul Culham	+44 (0)20 7886 9000	paul.culham@kilngroup.com
Property & Special Lines	Robin Hargreaves	+44 (0)20 7886 9000	robin.hargreaves@kilngroup.com

Reinsurance	David Huckstepp	+44 (0)20 7886 9000	david.huckstepp@kilngroup.com
Risk Solutions	Dan Trueman	+44 (0)20 7886 9000	dan.trueman@kilngroup.com
Main Areas of Underwriting	Accident & Health; Aviation; Marine & Special Risks; Property & Special Lines; Reinsurance; Risk Solutions		

YEAR	CAPACITY £m
2009	630
2008	588
2007	735

SYNDICATE NUMBER	**Kiln Catastrophe Syndicate 557**		
Active Underwriter	David J Huckstepp	+44 (0)20 7886 9000	david.huckstepp@kilngroup.com
Appointed	2007		
Main Areas of Underwriting	Catastrophe		

YEAR	CAPACITY £m
2009	120
2008	120
2007	120

SYNDICATE NUMBER	**Kiln Mathers 807**		
Active Underwriter	Lloyd Tunnicliffe	+44 (0)20 7886 9000	lloyd.tunnicliffe@kilngroup.com
Appointed	2008		
Main Areas of Underwriting	Property; Personal Accident; Medical Classes		

YEAR	CAPACITY £m
2009	120
2008	120
2007	120

SYNDICATE NUMBER	**Tokio Marine Kiln Syndicate (TMKS) 1880**		
Active Underwriter	Stephen D Mathers	+44 (0)20 7886 9000	stephen.mathers@kilngroup.com
Appointed	2008		
Main Areas of Underwriting	Part of the reinsurances of Tokio Marine Group businesses including Kiln		

YEAR	CAPACITY £m
2009	325
2008	–
2007	–

BACKGROUND INFORMATION

Ownership	R J Kiln & Co Limited is a wholly owned subsidiary of Tokio Marine & Nichido Fire Insurance Co., Ltd
Date of Incorporation	1962
Former Names	R J Kiln & Co (No.1) Limited to 2003
	R.J. Kiln & Co Limited to 2003
Syndicates merged into 308	None
Syndicates merged into 510	123, 603, 955
Syndicates merged into 557	None
Syndicates merged into 807	None
Syndicates merged into 1880	None

SA Meacock & Company Limited

Address	4th Floor
	15 St Helen's Place
	London EC3A 6DE
Telephone	+44 (0)20 7374 6727
Fax	+44 (0)20 7374 4727
Contact Email	linda.mailoudi@sameacock.com
Website	None at present

SENIOR MANAGEMENT

Title	Name	Telephone	Email
Chairman (Non-Executive)	Sir FD David Thomson Bt	+44 (0)20 7374 6727	linda.mailoudi@sameacock.com
Chief Executive Officer	David A Thorp	+44 (0)20 7374 6727	david.thorp@sameacock.com
Chief Financial Officer	Nicholas NS Ford	+44 (0)20 7374 6727	nicholas.ford@sameacock.com
Chief Operating Officer	Karl W Jarvis	+44 (0)20 7374 6727	karl.jarvis@sameacock.com
Underwriting Director	Michael J Meacock	+44 (0)20 7374 6727	michael.meacock@sameacock.com
Claims Manager	Sean Farrelly	+44 (0)20 7374 6727	sean.farrelly@sameacock.com
Independent Review Director	David KL White	+44 (0)20 7374 6727	linda.mailoudi@sameacock.com
Compliance Officer	Karl W Jarvis	+44 (0)20 7374 6727	karl.jarvis@sameacock.com
Other Executive Director(s)	Alec Taylor	+44 (0)20 7374 6727	alec.taylor@sameacock.com
Non-Executive Director(s)	James M Meacock	+44 (0)20 7374 6727	linda.mailoudi@sameacock.com
Company Secretary	Karl W Jarvis	+44 (0)20 7374 6727	karl.jarvis@sameacock.com

SYNDICATES MANAGED IN 2009

SYNDICATE NUMBER	727 SA Meacock & Others		
Active Underwriter	Michael J Meacock	+44 (0)20 7374 6727	michael.meacock@sameacock.com
Appointed	1967		
Main Areas of Underwriting	US Property; Casualty		
YEAR	CAPACITY £m		
2009	74		
2008	74		
2007	74		

BACKGROUND INFORMATION

Ownership	SA Meacock & Company Ltd is owned by the Executive Directors
Date of Incorporation	1996
Former Names	SA Meacock, previously operated as a partnership with origins dating from 1910
Syndicates merged into 727	None

Sagicor at Lloyd's Limited

Address	1 Great Tower Street
	London EC3R 5AA
Telephone	+44 (0)20 3003 6800
Fax	+44 (0)20 3003 6999
Contact Email	info@sagicor.eu
Website	www.sagicor.com

SENIOR MANAGEMENT

Title	Name	Telephone	Email
Chairman (Non-Executive)	Dodridge D Miller	+44 (0)20 3003 6800	duncan.reed@sagicor.eu
Chief Executive Officer	Geoffrey M Halpin	+44 (0)20 3003 6800	geoffrey.halpin@sagicor.eu
Chief Financial Officer	Histasp A Contractor	+44 (0)20 3003 6800	histasp.contractor@sagicor.eu
Chief Operating Officer	Gary L Ross	+44 (0)20 3003 6800	gary.ross@sagicor.eu
Underwriting Director	Geoffrey M Halpin	+44 (0)20 3003 6800	geoffrey.halpin@sagicor.eu
Claims Director	Gary L Ross	+44 (0)20 3003 6800	gary.ross@sagicor.eu
Compliance Officer	Duncan J Reed	+44 (0)20 3003 6800	duncan.reed@sagicor.eu
Other Executive Director(s)	George Sweatman	+44 (0)20 3003 6800	george.sweatman@sagicor.eu
	Elisabetta Tenenti	+44 (0)20 3003 6800	elisabetta.tenenti@sagicor.eu
Non-Executive Director(s)	Bjorn Jansli	+44 (0)20 3003 6800	duncan.reed@sagicor.eu
	John M Mantz	+44 (0)20 3003 6800	duncan.reed@sagicor.eu
	Jerome B Nice	+44 (0)20 3003 6800	duncan.reed@sagicor.eu
	Philip NW Osborne	+44 (0)20 3003 6800	duncan.reed@sagicor.eu
	Ravi C Rambarran	+44 (0)20 3003 6800	duncan.reed@sagicor.eu
Company Secretary	Duncan J Reed	+44 (0)20 3003 6800	duncan.reed@sagicor.eu

SYNDICATES MANAGED IN 2009

SYNDICATE NUMBER	Syndicate 44		
Active Underwriter	Christopher J Ray	+44 (0)20 3003 6800	duncan.reed@sagicor.eu
Appointed	2003		
Main Areas of Underwriting	Life		
YEAR	CAPACITY £m		
2009	5.5		
2008	2		
2007	2		

SYNDICATE NUMBER	Syndicate 1206		
Active Underwriter	Geoffrey M Halpin	+44 (0)20 3003 6800	geoffrey.halpin@sagicor.eu
Appointed	2005		
Main Areas of Underwriting	Personal Accident; Property; D&O; Sabotage; Terrorism; Treaty & Liability		
YEAR	CAPACITY £m		
2009	Information not disclosed		
2008	101		
2007	60		

BACKGROUND INFORMATION

Ownership	Sagicor at Lloyd's Ltd is controlled by Sagicor Financial Corporation of Barbados, listed on the London and Trinidad & Tobago Stock Exchanges
Date of Incorporation	1995
Former Names	Flighthare Limited to 1995
	Owen & Wilby Underwriting Agency Limited to 1999
	Gerling at Lloyd's to 2007
Syndicates merged into 44	None
Syndicates merged into 1206	None

Spectrum Syndicate Management Ltd

Address	2nd Floor
	6 Bevis Marks
	London EC3A 7HL
Telephone	+44 (0)20 7283 2646
Fax	+44 (0)20 7621 0975
Contact Email	newbusiness@spectrumins.com
Website	www.spectrumins.com

SENIOR MANAGEMENT

Title	Name	Telephone	Email
Chairman (Non-Executive)	John R Hustler	+44 (0)20 7283 2646	john.hustler@btconnect.com
Deputy Chairman (Executive)	Michael J Wells	+44 (0)20 7283 2646	mike.wells@spectrumins.com
Chief Executive Officer	Richard J Murphy	+44 (0)20 7283 2646	richard.murphy@spectrumins.com
Finance Director	David B Yandell	+44 (0)20 7283 2646	david.yandell@spectrumins.com
Chief Operating Officer	Kim T Fox	+44 (0)20 7283 2646	kim.fox@spectrumins.com
Director of Underwriting	James W Mann	+44 (0)20 7283 2646	jim.mann@spectrumins.com
Chief Actuary	Stavros Martis	+44 (0)20 7283 2646	stavros.martis@spectrumins.com
Non-Executive Director(s)	Jerome Breslin	+44 (0)20 7283 2646	newbusiness@spectrumins.com
Chief Legal Counsel	C Mark Everest	+44 (0)20 7283 2646	mark.everest@spectrumins.com
Company Secretary	Julie J Marshall	+44 (0)20 7283 2646	julie.marshall@spectrumins.com

SYNDICATES MANAGED IN 2009

SYNDICATE NUMBER	**RenaissanceRe Syndicate 1458**		
Active Underwriter	James (Jamie) R Lewis +44 (0)20 7283 2646		newbusiness@spectrumins.com
Appointed	2009		
Main Areas of Underwriting	Commercial Property; Specialty Lines		
YEAR	CAPACITY £m		
2009	70		

SYNDICATE NUMBER	**Pembrace Syndicate 2112**		
Active Underwriter	Randolph Roppelt	+44 (0)20 7283 2646	newbusiness@spectrumins.com
Appointed	2007		
Main Areas of Underwriting	Contractors' Commercial General Liability ('CGL'); Creditor Insurance		
YEAR	CAPACITY £m		
2009	70		
2008	70		
2007	34		

Syndicate 53 P L D Denis & Ors in Run-Off (open years: 1998, 1999, 2000)

Run-Off Manager	Richard John Murphy

BACKGROUND INFORMATION

Ownership	Spectrum Syndicate Management Ltd is controlled by the management
Date of Incorporation	1973
Former Names	AR Mountain & Son Limited to 2002
Syndicates merged into 2112	None

Sportscover Underwriting Ltd

Address	3 Minster Court
	Mincing Lane
	London EC3R 7DD
Telephone	+44 (0)20 7398 4080
Fax	+44 (0)20 7398 4090
Contact Email	info@sportscover.com
Website	www.sportscoverunderwriting.com

SENIOR MANAGEMENT

Title	Name	Telephone	Email
Chairman (Non-Executive)	Robert (Bob) J Wallace	+44 (0)20 7398 4080	dominic.ford@sportscover.com
Chief Executive Officer	Matthew S Riley	+44 (0)20 7398 4080	matthew.riley@sportscover.com
Finance Director	Belinda J Taylor	+44 (0)20 7398 4080	belinda.taylor@sportscover.com
Director of Underwriting	Peter JR Nash	+44 (0)20 7398 4080	peter.nash@sportscover.com
Director of Claims	Peter JR Nash	+44 (0)20 7398 4080	peter.nash@sportscover.com
Compliance Director	Dominic VT Ford	+44 (0)20 7398 4080	dominic.ford@sportscover.com
Other Executive Director(s)	Christopher P Nash	+44 (0)20 7398 4080	chris.nash@sportscover.com
Non-Executive Director(s)	Andrew G Ripley	+44 (0)20 7398 4080	dominic.ford@sportscover.com
Company Secretary	Dominic VT Ford	+44 (0)20 7398 4080	dominic.ford@sportscover.com

SYNDICATES MANAGED IN 2009

SYNDICATE NUMBER	**3334 Sportscover Syndicate**		
Active Underwriter	Christopher P Nash	+44 (0)20 7398 4080	chris.nash@sportscover.com
Appointed	2009		
Main Areas of Underwriting	Amateur Sports; Professional & Semi-Professional Sports; Leisure Business		
YEAR	CAPACITY £m		
2009	20		
2008	15		
2007	15		

Sportscover Underwriting Ltd (continued)

BACKGROUND INFORMATION

Ownership	Sportscover Underwriting Ltd is controlled by Wild Goose Holdings Group
Date of Incorporation	2008
Former Names	None
Syndicates merged into 3334	None

Starr Managing Agents Limited

Address	3rd Floor
	140 Leadenhall Street
	London EC3V 4QT
Telephone	+44 (0)20 7337 3550
Fax	+44 (0)20 7337 3551
Contact Email	None
Website	www.cvstarrco.com

SENIOR MANAGEMENT

Title	Name	Telephone	Email
Chairman (Non-Executive)	Nicholas CT Pawson	+44 (0)20 7337 3550	nicholas.pawson@cvstarrco.com
Chief Executive Officer	Steven G Blakey	+44 (0)20 7337 3550	steven.blakey@cvstarrco.com
Chief Financial Officer	Michael Toran	+44 (0)20 7337 3550	michael.toran@cvstarrco.com
Chief Operating Officer	Ralph Bull	+44 (0)20 7337 3550	ralph.bull@cvstarrco.com
Chief Underwriting Officer	Mark Patterson	+44 (0)20 7337 3550	mark.patterson@cvstarrco.com
Compliance Officer	John S Moffat	+44 (0)20 7337 3550	john.moffatt@cvstarrco.com
Other Executive Director(s)	Christopher E Hancock	+44 (0)20 7337 3550	christopher.hancock@cvstarrco.com
	David Stewart	+44 (0)20 7337 3550	david.stewart@cvstarrco.com
Non-Executive Director(s)	Paul A Chubb	+44 (0)20 7337 3550	paul.chubb@cvstarrco.com
	David S French	+44 (0)20 7337 3550	david.french@cvstarrco.com
	Richard N Shaak	+44 (0)20 7337 3550	richard.shaak@cvstarrco.com
Company Secretary	John S Moffat	+44 (0)20 7337 3550	john.moffatt@cvstarrco.com

SYNDICATES MANAGED IN 2009

SYNDICATE NUMBER	1919 CV Starr		
Active Underwriter	Christopher E Hancock	+44 (0)20 7337 3550	christopher.hancock@cvstarrco.com
Appointed	2006		
Main Areas of Underwriting	Aviation; Marine; Technical Risks		
YEAR	CAPACITY £m		
2009	225		
2008	180		
2007	97		

SYNDICATE NUMBER	**2243 FRC**		
Active Underwriter	David Stewart	+44 (0)20 7337 3550	david.stewart@cvstarrco.com
Appointed	2007		
Main Areas of Underwriting	Energy & Technical Risks		
YEAR	CAPACITY £m		
2009	35		
2008	30		
2007	10		

BACKGROUND INFORMATION

Ownership	Starr Managing Agents Ltd is controlled by CV Starr & Co Inc of New York, USA
Date of Incorporation	2007
Former Names	None in last 20 years
Syndicates merged into 1919	None
Syndicates merged into 2243	None

Talbot Underwriting Ltd

Address	Gracechurch House
	55 Gracechurch Street
	London EC3V 0JP
Telephone	+44 (0)20 7550 3500
Fax	+44 (0)20 7550 3555
Contact Email	central@talbotuw.com
Website	www.talbotuw.com

SENIOR MANAGEMENT

Title	Name	Telephone	Email
Chairman (Non-Executive)	Michael EA Carpenter	+44 (0)20 7550 3500	michael.carpenter@talbotuw.com
Chief Executive Officer	CN Rupert Atkin	+44 (0)20 7550 3500	rupert.atkin@talbotuw.com
Chief Financial Officer	Nigel D Wachman	+44 (0)20 7550 3500	nigel.wachman@talbotuw.com
Claims Director	Gillian S Langford	+44 (0)20 7550 3500	gill.langford@talbotuw.com
Independent Review Director	Anthony J Keys	+44 (0)20 7550 3500	central@talbotuw.com
Compliance Director	Jane S Clouting	+44 (0)20 7550 3500	jane.clouting@talbotuw.com
Other Executive Director(s)	Mark S Johnson	+44 (0)20 7550 3500	mark.johnsonr@talbotuw.com
	Julian G Ross	+44 (0)20 7550 3500	julian.ross@talbotuw.com
Non-Executive Director(s)	Joseph E Consolino	+44 (0)20 7550 3500	central@talbotuw.com
	Edward J Noonan	+44 (0)20 7550 3500	central@talbotuw.com
	George P Reeth	+44 (0)20 7550 3500	central@talbotuw.com
	Verner G Southey	+44 (0)20 7550 3500	central@talbotuw.com
Company Secretary	Jane S Clouting	+44 (0)20 7550 3500	jane.clouting@talbotuw.com

Talbot Underwriting Ltd (continued)

SYNDICATES MANAGED IN 2009

SYNDICATE NUMBER	TAL Syndicate 1183		
Active Underwriter	James E Skinner	+44 (0)20 7550 3500	central@talbotuw.com
Appointed	2008		
Main Areas of Underwriting	Marine: Cargo, Energy, Marine Hull, Marine Trades, Marine & Energy Liability, Political Risk, Terrorism, War and Yachts		
	Non Marine: Contingency, Bloodstock/livestock, Accident/health, Financial Institutions, Property Direct and Facultative, Property facilities		
	Treaty: General Aviation, Aviation War, Space, Non Marine Risk and Catastrophe, Marine		

YEAR	CAPACITY £m
2009	400
2008	325
2007	325

BACKGROUND INFORMATION

Ownership	Talbot Underwriting Ltd is controlled by Validus Holdings Ltd of Hamilton, Bermuda
Date of Incorporation	1987
Former Names	Minimar (34) Limited to 1988
	Venton Underwriting Agencies Limited to 1999
	Underwriters Re Agencies Ltd to 2000
	Alleghany Underwriting Ltd to 2001
Syndicates merged into 1183	None

Travelers Syndicate Management Ltd

Address	Exchequer Court
	33 St Mary Axe
	London EC3A 8AG
Telephone	+44 (0)20 3207 6000
Fax	+44 (0)20 3116 2180
Contact Email	trv5000@travelers.com
Website	www.travelers.co.uk/lloyds

SENIOR MANAGEMENT

Title	Name	Telephone	Email
Chairman (Non-Executive)	Barnabas J Hurst-Bannister	+44 (0)20 3207 6000	bhurstba@travelers.com
Chief Executive Officer	Martin P Hudson	+44 (0)20 3207 6000	mphudson@travelers.com
Chief Financial Officer	Michael J Gent	+44 (0)20 3207 6330	mgent@travelers.com
Finance Director	Sonny Kapur	+44 (0)20 3207 6101	skapur@travelers.com
Chief Operating Officer	Anthony (Tony) J Dilley	+44 (0)20 3207 6851	tdilley@travelers.com
Underwriting Director	Steve G Eccles	+44 (0)20 3207 6246	seccles@travelers.com
Claims Director	Simon N Catt	+44 (0)20 3207 6217	scatt@travelers.com
Ceded Reinsurance & Review Director	Paul M Cusition	+44 (0)20 3207 6870	pcusition@travelers.com
Compliance Officer	Anthony (Tony) J Dilley	+44 (0)20 3207 6851	tdilley@travelers.com
Non-Executive Director(s)	Graham J McKean	+44 (0)20 3207 6000	trv5000@travelers.com
	M Fraser Newton	+44 (0)20 3207 6000	trv5000@travelers.com

| Company Secretaries | Graham K Jones | +44 (0)20 3207 6263 | gjones2@travelers.com |
| | Michael DL Vernon | +44 (0)20 3207 6231 | mvernon@travelers.com |

SYNDICATES MANAGED IN 2009

SYNDICATE NUMBER	**5000 Travelers at Lloyd's**		
Active Underwriter	Stephen Eccles	+44 (0)20 3207 6246	seccles@travelers.com
Appointed	2006		
Main Areas of Underwriting	Accident & Special Risks; Aviation; Global Property; Marine; Power & Utilities		
YEAR	CAPACITY £m		
2009	Information not disclosed		
2008	230		
2007	260		

Syndicate 340 J P Tilling & Ors in Run-Off (open years: 2000, 2001)

Run-Off Manager	Stephen Gordon Eccles

BACKGROUND INFORMATION

Ownership	Travelers Syndicate Management Ltd is controlled by The Travelers Companies Inc. of Minnesota, USA
Date of Incorporation	1996
Former Names	Minimar (336) Limited to 1996
	Gravett & Tilling Syndicate Management Limited to 1998
	St Paul Syndicate Management Limited to 2000
	St. Paul Syndicate Management Limited to 2004
	St. Paul Travelers Syndicate Management Limited to 2008
Syndicates merged into 5000	183, 227, 314, 340, 582, 1191, 1211, 2227, 2341

Whittington Capital Management Ltd

Address	33 Creechurch Lane
	London EC3A 5EB
Telephone	+44 (0)20 7743 0900
Fax	+44 (0)20 7743 0901
Contact Email	jon.francis@whittingtoninsurance.com
Website	www.whittingtoninsurance.com

SENIOR MANAGEMENT

Title	Name	Telephone	Email
Chairman (Non-Executive)	Thomas A Riddell	+44 (0)20 7743 0900	jon.francis@whittingtoninsurance.com
Chief Executive Officer	Stephen P Cane	+44 (0)20 7743 0900	stephen.cane@whittingtoninsurance.com
Chief Financial Officer	Anthony JR Gordon	+44 (0)20 7743 0900	anthony.gordon@ whittingtoninsurance.com
Chief Operating Officer	Luke N Barnett	+44 (0)20 7743 0900	luke.barnett@whittingtoninsurance.com
Underwriting Director	Stewart K Laderman	+44 (0)20 7743 0900	stewart.laderman@ whittingtoninsurance.com
Claims Director	Gary L Griffiths	+44 (0)20 7743 0900	gary.griffiths@whittingtoninsurance.com
Compliance Officer	Luke N Barnett	+44 (0)20 7743 0900	luke.barnett@whittingtoninsurance.com
Other Executive Director(s)	Helen M Westcott	+44 (0)20 7743 0900	helen.westcott@whittingtoninsurance.com

Whittington Capital Management Ltd (continued)

Non-Executive Director(s)	Digby FC Murphy	+44 (0)20 7743 0900	jon.francis@whittingtoninsurance.com
	David KL White	+44 (0)20 7743 0900	jon.francis@whittingtoninsurance.com
Company Secretary	Julie M Wilson	+44 (0)20 7743 0900	julie.wilson@whittingtoninsurance.com

SYNDICATES MANAGED IN 2009

SYNDICATE NUMBER	**1910 Arrow**		
Active Underwriter	Tom Milligan	+44 (0)20 7743 0900	tom.milligan@gs.com
Appointed	2008		
Main Areas of Underwriting	Property Catastrophe		
YEAR	CAPACITY £m		
2009	125		
2008	65		
2007	–		

SYNDICATE NUMBER	**1955 Barbican**		
Active Underwriter	Mark J Harrington	+44 (0)20 7743 0900	mark.harrington@whittingtoninsurance.com
Appointed	2008		
Main Areas of Underwriting	Property Casualty		
YEAR	CAPACITY £m		
2009	120		
2008	75		
2007	–		

SYNDICATE NUMBER	**WR Berkley Syndicate 1967**		
Active Underwriter	Michael (Mike) A Sibthorpe +44 (0)20 7743 0900 msibthorpe@wrbsyndicate.com		
Appointed	2009		
Main Areas of Underwriting	Property; Accident. The Syndicate also provides an international underwriting platform for clients of other WR Berkley member companies.		
YEAR	CAPACITY £m		
2009	55		
2008	-		
2007	-		

Syndicate 376 Alleghany in Run-Off (open year: 2001)

Run-Off Manager	Gary Leonard Griffiths

BACKGROUND INFORMATION

Ownership	Whittington Capital Management Ltd is controlled by Whittington Group of Singapore
Date of Incorporation	1985
Former Names	Shangford Limited to 1985
	BPC Participation Limited to 1986
	BPC (Partners) Limited to 1990
	BPC Underwriting Agencies Limited to 1993
	Whittington MLP Limited to 1994
	Whittington Syndicate Management Limited to 1996
	Murray Lawrence Corporate Limited to 1998
	Amlin Capital Management Ltd to 1999
	Whittington Capital Management Limited to 2000
	Omni Whittington Captial Management Ltd to 2006

Syndicates merged into 1910	None
Syndicates merged into 1955	None

XL London Market Ltd

Address	XL House
	70 Gracechurch Street
	London EC3V 0XL
Telephone	+44 (0)20 7933 7000
Fax	+44 (0)20 7469 1071
Contact Email	info@xlgroup.com
Website	www.xlinsurance.co.uk

SENIOR MANAGEMENT

Title	Name	Telephone	Email
Chairman (Non-Executive)	Philip O Sheridan	+44 (0)20 7933 7000	info@xlgroup.com
Chief Executive Officer	tba		
Chief Financial Officer	Simon C Barrett	+44 (0)20 7933 7000	simon.barrett@xlgroup.com
Claims Director	Martin D Turner	+44 (0)20 7933 7000	martin.turner@xlgroup.com
Other Executive Director(s)	Jonathan F Ibbott	+44 (0)20 7933 7000	jonathan.ibbott@xlgroup.com
	Eileen E McCusker	+44 (0)20 7933 7000	eileen.mccusker@xlgroup.com
	Arabella Ramage	+44 (0)20 7933 7000	arabella.ramage@xlgroup.com
	Neil D Robertson	+44 (0)20 7933 7000	neil.robertson@xlgroup.com
Non-Executive Director	Richard JW Titley	+44 (0)20 7933 7000	info@xlgroup.com
Company Secretary & Compliance Officer	Graham L Brady	+44 (0)20 7933 7306	graham.brady@xlgroup.com

SYNDICATES MANAGED IN 2009

SYNDICATE NUMBER	**1209 XL London Market**		
Active Underwriter	Neil D Robertson	+44 (0)20 7933 7000	neil.robertson@xlgroup.com
Appointed	2009		
Main Areas of Underwriting	Hull; Liabilities; Offshore Energy; Cargo; Fine Art & Specie; Bloodstock; International Aviation		
YEAR	CAPACITY £m		
2009	230		
2008	230		
2007	230		

BACKGROUND INFORMATION

Ownership	XL London Market Ltd is a wholly-owned subsidiary of XL Capital Ltd of Hamilton, Bermuda, listed on the New York Stock Exchange
Date of Incorporation	1980
Former Names	Towergate Underwriting Agencies Limited to 1985
	Alston Brockbank Agencies Limited to 1993
	Brockbank Syndicate Management Limited to 2000
	XL Brockbank Ltd to 2002
Syndicates merged into 1209	588, 861, 990

Companies – Run-Off Agents

Capita Managing Agency Limited

Address	40 Dukes Place
	London EC3A 7NH
Telephone	+44 (0)870 523 4567
Fax	+44 (0)870 162 4566
Contact Email	insurance@capita.co.uk
Website	www.capitainsuranceservices.co.uk

SENIOR MANAGEMENT

Title	Name	Telephone	Email
Chairman (Non-Executive)	Eric SC Stobart	+44 (0)870 523 4568	insurance@capita.co.uk
Managing Director	John B King	+44 (0)870 402 7614	john.king@capita.co.uk
Chief Financial Officer	William Scott	+44 (0)870 402 7575	william.scott@capita.co.uk
Compliance Officer	John S Hale	+44 (0)870 402 7591	john.hale@capita.co.uk
Other Executive Director(s)	Philip Dietz	+44 (0)870 402 7658	philip.dietz@capita.co.uk
	John S Hale	+44 (0)870 402 7591	john.hale@capita.co.uk
	Richard TA Morgan	+44 (0)870 402 7278	rick.morgan@capita.co.uk
	Timothy Shenton	+44 (0)870 402 7900	tim.shenton@capita.co.uk
Non-Executive Director(s)	Sarah M Wilton	+44 (0)870 523 4568	insurance@capita.co.uk
Company Secretary	Capita Company Secretarial Services Limited		

SYNDICATES MANAGED 2009

Syndicate Number	**991**		
Run-Off Manager	Harvey Simons	+44 (0)870 523 4567	harvey.simons@capita.co.uk
Appointed	2003		
Open Year(s)	1998, 1999, 2000		
Syndicate Number	**1688**		
Run-Off Manager	Philip Dietz	+44 (0)870 402 7658	philip.dietz@capita.co.uk
Appointed	2006		
Open Year(s)	1999, 2000, 2001		
Syndicate Number	**1900**		
Run-Off Manager	Philip Dietz	+44 (0)870 402 7658	philip.dietz@capita.co.uk
Appointed	2003		
Open Year(s)	2001		
Syndicate Number	**5500**		
Run-Off Manager	Philip Dietz	+44 (0)870 402 7658	philip.dietz@capita.co.uk
Appointed	2008		
Open Year(s)	2007, 2008		

Capita Managing Agency Limited (continued)

BACKGROUND INFORMATION

Ownership	Capita Managing Agency Ltd recently merged with Capita Syndicate Management Ltd.
	It is controlled by Capita Group Plc, quoted on the London Stock Exchange.
Date of Incorporation	2000
Former Names for both entities	BPD Kellet & Co Ltd to 1993
	Turret Run-Off Services Limited to 2001
	CMGL to 2008
Syndicates 'Reinsured to Close' into 991	None
Syndicates 'Reinsured to Close' into 1688	None
Syndicates 'Reinsured to Close' into 1900	None
Syndicates 'Reinsured to Close' into 5500	None

Cavell Managing Agency Ltd

Address	9-13 Fenchurch Buildings
	London EC3M 5HR
Telephone	+44 (0)20 7780 5850
Fax	+44 (0)20 7780 5851
Contact Email	compliance@cavell.co.uk
Website	www.rqih.co.uk

SENIOR MANAGEMENT

Title	Name	Telephone	Email
Chairman (Non-Executive)	John P Tilling	+44 (0)20 7780 5850	compliance@cavell.co.uk
Chief Executive Officer	Robin E McCoy	+44 (0)20 7780 5850	compliance@cavell.co.uk
Chief Financial Officer	Appointment not made		
Chief Operating Officer	John GF O'Neill	+44 (0)20 7780 5850	compliance@cavell.co.uk
Director of Claims and Reinsurance	Stephen T Clarke	+44 (0)20 7780 5850	compliance@cavell.co.uk
Compliance Officer	James A Willsher	+44 (0)20 7780 5850	compliance@cavell.co.uk
Other Executive Director(s)	Simon P Amies	+44 (0)20 7780 5850	compliance@cavell.co.uk
	Michael Bell	+44 (0)20 7780 5850	compliance@cavell.co.uk
	Peter AG Green	+44 (0)20 7780 5850	compliance@cavell.co.uk
	Ken E Randall	+44 (0)20 7780 5850	compliance@cavell.co.uk
	James A Willsher	+44 (0)20 7780 5850	compliance@cavell.co.uk
Non-Executive Director(s)	Alan C Pollard, MBE	+44 (0)20 7780 5850	compliance@cavell.co.uk
	Michael G Smith	+44 (0)20 7780 5850	compliance@cavell.co.uk
Company Secretary	James A Willsher	+44 (0)20 7780 5850	compliance@cavell.co.uk

SYNDICATES MANAGED 2009

Syndicate Number	**102 Goshawk Syndicate**		
Run-Off Manager	Robin E McCoy	+44 (0)20 7780 5850	compliance@cavell.co.uk
Appointed	2003		
Open Year(s)	2001, 2002, 2003		

(continued)

Cavell Managing Agency Ltd (continued)

Syndicate Number	**3330 Advent s.2 RITC**
Syndicate Contact	John GF O'Neill +44 (0)20 7780 5850 compliance@cavell.co.uk
Appointed	2009
Open Year(s)	2001, 2002

BACKGROUND INFORMATION

Ownership	Cavell Managing Agency Ltd is controlled by Randall & Quilter Investment Holdings plc, listed on the London Stock Exchange
Date of Incorporation	2003
Former Names	None in last 20 years
Syndicates 'Reinsured to Close' into 102	56, 203, 212, 236, 256, 310, 342, 380, 500, 501, 577, 584, 662, 667, 697, 765, 797, 872, 873, 950, 1048, 1114, 1142, 1143, 1178, 1179, 2021
Syndicates 'Reinsured to Close' into 3330	2

Duncanson & Holt Syndicate Management Limited

Address	40 Dukes Place
	London EC3A 7NH
Telephone	+44 (0)870 402 7278
Fax	+44 (0)870 162 4541
Contact Email	rick.morgan@capita.co.uk
Website	None at present

SENIOR MANAGEMENT

Title	Name	Telephone	Email
Chairman & Chief Executive Officer	Joseph R Foley	+44 (0)870 402 7278	-
Chief Financial Officer	Andrew (Andy) G Ripley	+44 (0)870 402 7278	-
Compliance Officer	Richard (Rick) TA Morgan	+44 (0)870 402 7278	rick.morgan@capita.co.uk
Other Executive Director(s)	Angus M Sladen	+44 (0)870 402 7278	-
Non-Executive Director(s)	Peter L Doyle	+44 (0)870 402 7278	-
	George E Lloyd-Roberts	+44 (0)870 402 7278	-
Company Secretary	Richard (Rick) TA Morgan	+44 (0)870 402 7278	rick.morgan@capita.co.uk

SYNDICATES MANAGED 2009

Syndicate Number	**957 G Absalom & Ors**
Run-Off Manager	David F McElhiney +44 (0)870 402 7278 -
Appointed	2008
Open Year(s)	1997, 1998, 1999

Syndicate Number	**1101 B P Theakston & Ors.**
Run-Off Manager	David F McElhiney +44 (0)870 402 7278
Appointed	2008
Open Year(s)	1997, 1998, 1999

Duncanson & Holt Syndicate Management Limited (continued)

BACKGROUND INFORMATION

Ownership	Duncanson & Holt Syndicate Management Limited is controlled by the Unum Provident Corporation
Date of Incorporation	1995
Former Names	None in last 20 years
Syndicates 'Reinsured to Close' into 957	None
Syndicates 'Reinsured to Close' into 1101	None

Ridge Underwriting Agencies Limited

Address	100 Leadenhall Street
	London EC3A 3BP
Telephone	+44 (0)20 7173 7000
Fax	+44 (0)20 7173 7800
Contact Email	info.uk@ace-ina.com
Website	www.acelimited.com

SENIOR MANAGEMENT

Title	Name	Telephone	Email
Chief Financial Officer	Philippa M Curtis	+44 (0)20 7173 7711	philippa.curtis@ace-ina.com
Claims Director	R Peter Murray	+44 (0)20 7173 7709	peter.murray@ace-ina.com
Other Executive Director(s)	Richard V Pryce	+44 (0)20 7173 7396	richard.pryce@ace-ina.com
Compliance Officer	Adrian W Missen	+44 (0)20 7173 7000	adrian.missen@ace-ina.com
Company Secretary	Adrian W Missen	+44 (0)20 7173 7000	adrian.missen@ace-ina.com

SYNDICATES MANAGED 2009

Syndicate Number	**1171 RGB Life**		
Run-Off Manager	Russell Burgess	+44 (0)20 7173 7000	info.uk@ace-ina.com
Appointed	2000		
Open Year(s)	1998, 1999, 2000		

BACKGROUND INFORMATION

Ownership	Ridge Underwriting Agencies Limited is controlled by ACE Ltd, part of the ACE Group of Companies of Zurich, Switzerland
Date of Incorporation	1958
Former Names	Golding, Drury & Co Ltd to 1990
	RGB Underwriting Agencies Ltd to 2000
	Ace (RGB) Agencies Ltd to 2000
Syndicates 'Reinsured to Close' into 1171	None

RITC Syndicate Management Limited

Address	3rd Floor
	117 Fenchurch Street
	London EC3M 5DY
Telephone	+44 (0)20 7220 8899
Fax	+44 (0)20 7220 8898
Contact Email	ritcwebenquiry@ritcsm.com
Website	www.ritcsm.com

SENIOR MANAGEMENT

Title	Name	Telephone	Email
Chairman	Anthony G Hines	+44 (0)20 7220 8899	ritcwebenquiry@ritcsm.com
Chief Executive Officer	Nigel HJ Rogers	+44 (0)20 7220 8899	ritcwebenquiry@ritcsm.com
Chief Financial Officer	Roy Katzenberg	+44 (0)20 7220 8899	ritcwebenquiry@ritcsm.com
Chief Operating Officer	Appointment not made		
Underwriting Director	J Nicholas C Wooldridge	+44 (0)20 7220 8899	ritcwebenquiry@ritcsm.com
Claims Director	Dinah J Gately	+44 (0)20 7220 8899	ritcwebenquiry@ritcsm.com
Independent Review Director	Appointment not made		
Business Development	Christopher P Hare	+44 (0)20 7220 8878	ritcwebenquiry@ritcsm.com
Compliance Officer	Roy Katzenberg	+44 (0)20 7220 8899	ritcwebenquiry@ritcsm.com
Non-Executive Director(s)			
(Independent)	Steven Fass	+44 (0)20 7220 8899	ritcwebenquiry@ritcsm.com
(Independent)	Donald C McCrickard	+44 (0)20 7220 8899	ritcwebenquiry@ritcsm.com
	William L Spiegel	+44 (0)20 7220 8899	ritcwebenquiry@ritcsm.com
	Ravi P Yadav	+44 (0)20 7220 8899	ritcwebenquiry@ritcsm.com
Company Secretary	Shirley L Blakelock	+44 (0)20 7220 8899	ritcwebenquiry@ritcsm.com

SYNDICATES MANAGED 2009

Syndicate Number	**5678**
Run-Off Manager	J Nicholas C Wooldridge +44 (0)20 7220 8899 ritcwebenquiry@ritcsm.com
Appointed	2007
Open Year(s)	Information not available

BACKGROUND INFORMATION

Ownership	RITC is controlled by Syndicate Re, A.I.
Date of Incorporation	2006
Former Names	None in last 20 years
Syndicates 'Reinsured to Close' into 5678	None

RiverStone Managing Agency Limited

Address	2nd Floor
	Mint House
	77 Mansell Street
	London E1 8AF
Telephone	+44 (0)20 7977 1600
Fax	+44 (0)20 7977 1687
Contact Email	None
Website	www.rsml.co.uk
Registered Office	Park Gate
	161-163 Preston Road
	Brighton BN1 6AU

SENIOR MANAGEMENT

Title	Name	Telephone	Email
Chairman	Appointment not made		
Chief Executive Officer	Nicholas C Bentley	+44 (0)20 7977 1600	nick.bentley@rsml.co.uk
Chief Financial Officer	Lorna A Hemsley	+44 (0)20 7977 1600	lorna.hemsley@rsml.co.uk
Operations Director	Luke R Tanzer	+44 (0)20 7977 1600	luke.tanzer@rsml.co.uk
Claims Director	Appointment not made		
Independent Review Director	Appointment not made		
Head of Assurance	Stephen Osborne	+44 (0)20 7977 1600	-
Non-Executive Director(s)	Dennis C Gibbs	+44 (0)20 7977 1600	-
	William F Goodier	+44 (0)20 7977 1600	-
	Anthony J Keys	+44 (0)20 7977 1600	stephen.osborne@rsml.co.uk
Company Secretary	Fraser Henry	+44 (0)1273 792 104	fraser.henry@rsml.co.uk

SYNDICATES MANAGED 2009

Syndicate Number	Syndicate 3500
Run-Off Manager	N/A
Appointed	2005
Open Year(s)	2005

BACKGROUND INFORMATION

Ownership	Riverstone Managing Agency Limited is a wholly-owned subsidiary of RiverStone Holdings Limited
Date of Incorporation	1996
Former Names	Cornbay Limited to 1996
	Kingsmead Underwriting Agency to 2003
Syndicates 'Reinsured to Close' into 3500	271, 506

Shelbourne Syndicate Services Limited

Address	5th Floor
	9-13 Fenchurch Buildings
	Fenchurch Street
	London EC3M 5HR
Telephone	+44 (0)20 7481 4681
Fax	+44 (0)20 7481 4832
Contact Email	roger.durowse@shelbournegroup.com
Website	None at present

SENIOR MANAGEMENT

Title	Name	Telephone	Email
Chairman (Non-Executive)	George N Cochran	+44 (0)20 7961 0810	
Chief Executive Officer	Sean J Dalton	+44 (0)20 7961 0810	
Chief Financial Officer	Clifford E Murphy	+44 (0)20 7961 0810	
Chief Operating Officer	Appointment not made		
Underwriting Director	Appointment not made		
Claims Director	Appointment not made		
Compliance Officer	Roger H Durowse	+44 (0)20 7961 0810	roger.durowse@shelbournegroup.com
Other Executive Director(s)	Andrew D Elliott	+44 (0)20 7961 0810	-
Non-Executive Director(s)	Timothy J Hanford	+44 (0)20 7961 0810	-
	Richard J Harris	+44 (0)20 7961 0810	-
	Phillip C Martin	+44 (0)20 7961 0810	-
Company Secretary	Roger H Durowse	+44 (0)20 7961 0810	roger.durowse@shelbournegroup.com

SYNDICATES MANAGED 2009

Syndicate Number	**529**
Run-Off Manager	Andrew D Elliott +44 (0)20 7961 0810 andrew.elliott@shelbournegroup.com
Appointed	2008
Open Year(s)	1998, 1999, 2000

Syndicate Number	**2008**
Run-Off Manager	Andrew D Elliott +44 (0)20 7961 0810 andrew.elliott@shelbournegroup.com
Appointed	2008
Open Year(s)	Started in 2008

BACKGROUND INFORMATION

Ownership	Shelbourne Syndicate Services Limited is controlled by Shelbourne Group Limited
Date of Incorporation	1994
Former Names	Rowan (47) Limited to 1994
	Pro Management Limited to 2001
	Pro Syndicate Management to 2008
Syndicates 'Reinsured to Close' into 529	None
Syndicates 'Reinsured to Close' into 2008	205, 588, 862, 1121, 1236

Companies – Members' Agents

Alpha Insurance Analysts Limited

Address	150 Minories
	London EC3N 1LS
Telephone	+44 (0)20 7264 2133
Fax	+44 (0)20 7264 2134
Contact Email	info@aianalysts.com
Website	www.aianalysts.com

	2009	2008
Capacity managed (£m)	293	248
Members (Number)	152	118

SENIOR MANAGEMENT

Title	Name	Telephone	Email
Chairman (Non-Executive)	WS Clive Richards, OBE	+44 (0)20 7264 2133	info@aianalysts.com
Managing Director	A James Sparrow	+44 (0)20 7264 2148	james@aianalysts.com
Finance Director	*Appointment not made – outsourced*		
Executive Director & Analyst	Emily L Apple	+44 (0)20 7264 2146	emily@aianalysts.com
Other Executive Director(s)	Emma Royds	+44 (0)20 7264 2132	emma@aianalysts.com
Non-Executive Director(s)	Alan C Lovell	+44 (0)20 7264 2133	info@aianalysts.com
	Michael J Meacock	+44 (0)20 7264 2133	info@aianalysts.com
Analyst	Chandon Bleackley	+44 (0)20 7264 2147	chandon@aianalysts.com
Compliance Officer	Jennifer (Jenny) SC Doyle	+44 (0)20 7264 2151	jenny@aianalysts.com
Company Secretary	Andrew S Fox	+44 (0)20 7264 2133	info@aianalysts.com

BACKGROUND INFORMATION

Ownership	Alpha Insurance Analysts Limited is owned by management and private individuals
Date of Incorporation	1994
Present Management in Operation since	2007
Former Names	Minmar (253) Limited to 1994
	CBS Analysts Limited to 2007

Argenta Private Capital Limited

Address	Fountain House
	130 Fenchurch Street
	London EC3M 5DJ
Telephone	+44 (0)20 7825 7200
Fax	+44 (0)20 7825 7212
Contact Email	privatecapital@argentaplc.com
Website	www.argentaplc.com

	2009	2008
Capacity managed (£m)	896	969
Members (Number)	661	699

SENIOR MANAGEMENT

Title	Name	Telephone	Email
Chairman (Non-Executive)	Lord Brabourne	+44 (0)20 7825 7200	privatecapital@argentaplc.com
Managing Director	Graham J White	+44 (0)20 7825 7182	graham.white@argentaplc.com
Finance Director	Marcus G Warner	+44 (0)20 7825 7262	marcus.warner@argentaplc.com
Head of Client Management	David Monksfield	+44 (0)20 7825 7139	david.monksfield@argentaplc.com
Client Services Director(s)	Trevor R Bird	+44 (0)20 7825 7131	trevor.bird@argentaplc.com
	Guy B Hudson	+44 (0)20 7825 7241	guy.hudson@argentaplc.com
	W David Robson	+44 (0)20 7825 7200	privatecapital@argentaplc.com
	Alan W Tucker	+44 (0)20 7825 7135	alan.tucker@argentaplc.com
Head of Research	Jeremy M Bray	+44 (0)20 7825 7174	jeremy.bray@argentaplc.com
Technical Director	Robert P Flach	+44 (0)20 7825 7179	robert.flach@argentaplc.com
New Business Director	James A Mackay	+44 (0)20 7825 7288	james.mackay@argentaplc.com
Non-Executive Director(s)	Andrew J Annandale	+44 (0)20 7825 7239	andrew.annandale@argentaplc.com
	David BK Harrison	+44 (0)20 7825 7200	privatecapital@argentaplc.com
	Paul F Sandilands	+44 (0)20 7825 7200	paul.sandilands@argentaplc.com
Compliance Director	Christopher JR Fairs	+44 (0)20 7825 7100	chris.fairs@argentaplc.com
Client Director(s) & Consultant(s)	Fiona A Blood	+44 (0)20 7825 7178	fiona.blood@argentaplc.com
	Michael RP Doughty	+44 (0)20 7825 7237	michael.doughty@argentaplc.com
	Peter T Fletcher	+44 (0)20 7825 7232	peter.fletcher@argentaplc.com
	Neil L Geisa	+44 (0)20 7825 7200	neil.geisa@argentaplc.com
	Milka Jacoby	+44 (0)20 7825 7180	milka.jacoby@argentaplc.com
	Jacquie A Phillips	+44 (0)20 7825 7230	jacquie.phillips@argentaplc.com
	John R Robson	+44 (0)20 7825 7177	john.robson@argentaplc.com
	Robin CG Taylor	+44 (0)20 7825 7291	robin.taylor@argentaplc.com
Research	Andrew Brooks	+44 (0)20 7825 7132	andrew.brooks@argentaplc.com
	Andrew M Colcomb	+44 (0)20 7825 7176	andrew.colcomb@argentaplc.com
Agency Manager	Kevin Jackson	+44 (0)20 7825 7258	kevin.jackson@argentaplc.com
Company Secretary	Christopher JR Fairs	+44 (0)20 7825 7100	chris.fairs@argentaplc.com

BACKGROUND INFORMATION

Ownership	Argenta Private Capital Limited is a subsidiary of Argenta Holdings plc, an unquoted holding company
Date of Incorporation	1962
Former Names	Sedgwick Forbes (Lloyd's Underwriting Agents) Limited to 1986
	Sedgwick Lloyd's Underwriting Agents Limited to 1996
	Sedgwick Oakwood Lloyd's Underwriting Agents Limited to 2000
	SOC Private Capital Limited to 2004

Hampden Agencies Ltd

Address	85 Gracechurch Street
	London EC3V 0AA
Telephone	+44 (0)20 7863 6500
Fax	+44 (0)20 7863 6555
Contact Email	hal@hampden.co.uk
Website	www.hampden.co.uk

	2009	2008
Capacity managed (£m)	1,473	1,529
Members (Number)	1,145	1,173

SENIOR MANAGEMENT

Title	Name	Telephone	Email
Chairman (Executive)	Nigel J Hanbury	+44 (0)20 7863 6502	nigel.hanbury@hampden.co.uk
Chief Executive Officer	Neil LC Smith	+44 (0)20 7863 6562	neil.smith@hampden.co.uk
Chief Financial Officer	Nicholas D Lewis	+44 (0)20 7863 6507	nicholas.lewis@hampden.co.uk
Chief Operating Officer	Mark J Tottman	+44 (0)20 7863 6504	mark.tottman@hampden.co.uk
Executive Director & Head of Research	Alistair T Wood	+44 (0)20 7863 6570	alistair.wood@hampden.co.uk
Executive Director & Compliance Officer	David A Cant	+44 (0)20 7863 6573	david.cant@hampden.co.uk
Other Executive Director(s)	Nicholas HD Carrick	+44 (0)20 7863 6526	nick.carrick@hampden.co.uk
	Charles GC Oliver	+44 (0)20 7863 6621	charles.oliver@hampden.co.uk
	Stephen M Wilcox	+44 (0)20 7863 6530	stephen.wilcox@hampden.co.uk
Non-Executive Director(s)	Sir Adam N Ridley	+44 (0)20 7863 6500	adam.ridley@hampden.co.uk
	Lord Strathclyde	+44 (0)20 7863 6500	hal@hampden.co.uk
	Sarah M Wilton	+44 (0)20 7863 6500	sarah.wilton@hampden.co.uk
Names Executive(s) & Consultant(s)	Timothy CJ Andrews	+44 (0)20 7863 6586	tim.andrews@hampden.co.uk
	Andrew NC Bengough	+44 (0)20 7863 6500	andrew.bengough@hampden.co.uk
	Giles R Berkeley	+44 (0)20 7863 6524	giles.berkeley@hampden.co.uk
	Timothy C Bruce	+44 (0)20 7863 6566	tim.bruce@hampden.co.uk
	Stuart H Buchanan-Smith	+44 (0)20 7863 6535	stuart.buchanan-smith@ hampden.co.uk
	David J de M Coulthard	+44 (0)20 7938 4321	david.coulthard@hampden.co.uk
	Nicholas J D'Ambrumenil	+44 (0)20 7863 6546	nicholas.dambrumenil@hampden.co.uk
	Stuart M Elswood	+44 (0)20 7863 6595	stuart.elswood@hampden.co.uk
	Jonathan N Green	+44 (0)20 7863 6577	jonathan.green@hampden.co.uk
	John W Hayter	+44 (0)20 7863 6500	john.hayter@hampden.co.uk
	Charles GL Hulbert-Powell	+44 (0)20 7863 6537	charles.hulbert-powell@hampden.co.uk
	Christopher AG Keeling	+44 (0)20 7863 6542	christopher.keeling@hampden.co.uk
	Stephen Lumley	+44 (0)20 7863 6551	stephen.lumley@hampden.co.uk
	John SM Mocatta	+44 (0)20 7863 6534	john.mocatta@hampden.co.uk
	Richard A Page	+44 (0)20 7863 6515	richard.page@hampden.co.uk
	Alexander CM Raven	+44 (0)20 7863 6559	alexander.raven@hampden.co.uk
	W Roger P Sedgwick Rough	+44 (0)20 7863 6547	roger.sr@hampden.co.uk
	Richard MA Watson	+44 (0)1332 873 332	richard.watson@hampden.co.uk
	Gregory C White	+44 (0)20 7863 6553	gregory.white@hampden.co.uk
	Nigel ER Wood	+44 (0)20 7863 6571	nigel.wood@hampden.co.uk

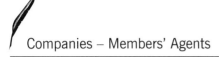

UNDERWRITING RESEARCH TEAM

Chairman	Nicholas HD Carrick	+44 (0)20 7863 6526	nick.carrick@hampden.co.uk
Research Team	John EH Francis	+44 (0)20 7863 6548	john.francis@hampden.co.uk
	Mark Isaacs	+44 (0)20 7863 6500	mark.isaacs@hampden.co.uk
	William W Lewis	+44 (0)20 7863 6572	william.lewis@hampden.co.uk
	Nicholas WL Nops	+44 (0)20 7863 6543	nicholas.nops@hampden.co.uk
	Michael J Wake-Walker	+44 (0)20 7863 6564	michael.walker@hampden.co.uk
Company Secretary	Hampden Legal plc	–	–

BACKGROUND INFORMATION

Ownership	Hampden Agencies Ltd is owned by Hampden Capital plc, the holding company for the Hampden Group
Date of Incorporation	1994
Former Names	Dealimport Limited to 1994
	Falcon Agencies Limited to 1998

ICP General Partner Limited

Address	Unit C25
	Jack's Place
	6 Corbet Place
	London E1 6NN
Telephone	+44 (0)20 7392 8480
Fax	+44 (0)20 7392 8481
Contact Email	info@inscap.co.uk
Website	www.inscap.co.uk

	2009	2008
Capacity managed (£m)	72	77
Members (Number)	1	1

SENIOR MANAGEMENT

Title	Name	Telephone	Email
Chairman (Non-Executive)	tba		
Chief Executive Officer	The Hon Charles AA Harbord-Hamond	+44 (0)20 7392 8480	charles.hh@inscap.co.uk
Finance Director	James RV Brandon	+44 (0)20 7392 8480	james.brandon@inscap.co.uk
Compliance Officer	Andrew S Fox	+44 (0)20 7392 8480	andrew.fox@inscap.co.uk
Non-Executive Director(s)	Robert FM Adair	+44 (0)20 7392 8480	info@inscap.co.uk
	Lord JP Marland of Odstock	+44 (0)20 7392 8480	info@inscap.co.uk
Company Secretary	Andrew S Fox	+44 (0)20 7392 8480	andrew.fox@inscap.co.uk

ICP General Partner Limited (continued)

BACKGROUND INFORMATION

Ownership	ICP General Partner Limited is owned by ICP Holdings Limited, which in turn is owned by management and other private shareholders
Date of Incorporation	1994
Present Management in Operation since	2006
Former Names	Globewalk Limited to 1994
	Murray Lawrence (Underwriting Agents) Limited to 2000
	CBS Services No 2 Limited to 2005
	CBS General Partner Limited to 2007

Lloyd's Members Agency Services Ltd (LMAS)

Address	Fidentia House
	Walter Burke Way
	Chatham
	Kent ME4 4RN
Telephone	+44 (0)1634 392 090
Fax	+44 (0)1634 392 081
Contact Email	lloyds-lmas@lloyds.com
Website	www.lmas.co.uk

SENIOR MANAGEMENT

Title	Name	Telephone	Email
Chairman (Non-Executive)	Jock Worsley, OBE	+44 (0)1634 392 090	lloyds-lmas@lloyds.com
Managing Director	Paul Box	+44 (0)1634 392 082	paul.box@lloyds.com
Chief Financial Officer	*Handled by the Corporation of Lloyd's*		
Names Director	Angela Kerr	+44 (0)1634 392 083	angela.kerr@lloyds.com
Compliance Officer	Angela Kerr	+44 (0)1634 392 083	angela.kerr@lloyds.com
Non-Executive Director(s)	Christopher Hare	+44 (0)1634 392 090	lloyds-lmas@lloyds.com
	Luke Savage	+44 (0)1634 392 090	lloyds-lmas@lloyds.com
	Graham White	+44 (0)1634 392 090	lloyds-lmas@lloyds.com
Names Executive(s)	Chomps Kaeowsri	+44 (0)1634 392 087	chomps.kaeowsri@lloyds.com
	Jenny Inkpen	+44 (0)1634 392 084	jennifer.inkpen@lloyds.com
	Tony Skelt	+44 (0)1634 392 088	anthony.skelt@lloyds.com
	Cliff Talbot	+44 (0)1634 392 085	clifford.talbot@lloyds.com
Company Secretary	Angela Kerr	+44 (0)1634 392 083	angela.kerr@lloyds.com

BACKGROUND INFORMATION

Ownership	LMAS is a wholly owned subsidiary of the Corporation of Lloyd's, with an independent Board of Directors. It acts as a Members' Agent to manage the run-off affairs of approximately 4400 former active Lloyd's members.
Date of Incorporation	1990
Former Names	Corenotion Limited to 1990
	Additional Underwriting Agencies (No.8) Limited to 1994

Active Syndicates –
Ownership, Capacity, Gross Written Premium

Syndicates – Ownership, Capacity and Gross Written Premium

Syndicate No	Managing Agency	Capacity £m 1 Jan[1] 2009	Capacity £m 1 Jan 2008	Capacity £m 1 Jan 2007	GWP £m 31 Dec 2008	GWP £m 31 Dec 2007	3rd Party Capital, % 31 Dec 2008
33	Hiscox Syndicates Ltd	750	700	875	885	996	27
44	Sagicor at Lloyd's Ltd	5.5	2	2	1	2	-
218	Equity Syndicate Management Ltd	452	420	420	555	569	36
260	KGM Underwriting Agencies Ltd	73	54	50	63	49	40
308	R J Kiln & Co Limited	15	15	15	15	14	50
318	Beaufort Underwriting Agency Ltd	201	201	201	159	130	53
382[2]	Hardy (Underwriting Agencies) Ltd	250	110	110	116	108	-
386	QBE Underwriting Ltd	340	340	340	412	436	30
435	Faraday Underwriting Ltd	250	250	325	258	258	-
457	Munich Re Underwriting Ltd	260	260	260	333	309	-
510	R J Kiln & Co Limited	630	588	735	757	678	47
557	R J Kiln & Co Limited	120	120	120	38	35	100
566[3]	QBE Underwriting Ltd	245	290	245	(see Syndicate 2999)[3]		-
570	Atrium Underwriters Ltd	125	125	125	133	117	75
609	Atrium Underwriters Ltd	200	215	215	194	173	75
623	Beazley Furlonge Ltd	146	158	164	197	179	94
727	SA Meacock & Company Ltd	74	74	74	68	63	91
779	Jubilee Managing Agency Ltd	30	30	38	34	29	86
780	Advent Underwriting Ltd	135	135	151	163	137	-
807	R J Kiln & Co Limited	120	120	120	126	145	49
958	Omega Underwriting Agents Ltd	249	249	249	329	282	84
1036[3]	QBE Underwriting Ltd	215	210	220	(see Syndicate 2999)[3]		-
1084	Chaucer Syndicates Ltd	545	445	485	642	526	-
1176	Chaucer Syndicates Ltd	32	28	28	26	22	44
1183	Talbot Underwriting Ltd	400	325	325	383	344	-
1200	Argo Managing Agency Ltd	326	326	314	409	325	22
1206	Sagicor at Lloyd's Ltd	N/A	101	60	127	56	-
1209	XL London Market Ltd	230	230	230	265	210	-
1218	Newline Underwriting Management Ltd	80	85	85	104	90	-
1221	Navigators Underwriting Agency Ltd	125	123	140	174	149	-
1225	AEGIS Managing Agency Ltd	200	183	221	246	240	-
1231	Jubilee Managing Agency Ltd	45	54	46	47	51	-
1274	Chaucer Syndicates Ltd	135	135	-	150	-	100
1301	Chaucer Syndicates Ltd	75	75	72	78	69	100
1318	Beaufort Underwriting Agency Ltd	35	-	-	-	-	-
1400	Max at Lloyd's Ltd	125	125	125	48	64	-
1414	Ascot Underwriting Ltd	470	450	625	506	538	-
1458	Spectrum Syndicate Management Ltd	70	-	-	-	-	100
1861	Marlborough Underwriting Agency Ltd	100	82	120	80	97	-
1880	R J Kiln & Co Limited	325	-	-	-	-	-
1886	QBE Underwriting Ltd	95	100	35	(see Syndicate 2999)[3]		-
1910	Whittington Capital Management Ltd	125	65	-	90	-	100
1919	Starr Managing Agents Ltd	225	180	97	233	91	-

1– in accordance with Lloyd's rules syndicates can also commence at quarter days, capacity figure will then be as per the date of the syndicate's commencement. 2 – 3820 merged into 382. 3 – GWP of Syndicates 566, 1036, 1886, 2000 and 5555 is included in umbrella syndicate 2999

Syndicates – Ownership, Capacity and Gross Written Premium

Syndicate No	Managing Agency	Capacity £m 1 Jan[1] 2009	Capacity £m 1 Jan 2008	Capacity £m 1 Jan 2007	GWP £m 31 Dec 2008	GWP £m 31 Dec 2007	3rd Party Capital, % 31 Dec 2008
1955	Whittington Capital Management Ltd	120	75	-	66	-	100
1965	Argenta Syndicate Management Ltd	30	30	15	12	8	-
1967	Whittington Capital Management Ltd	55	-	-	-	-	100
2000[3]	QBE Underwriting Ltd	75	85	195	(see Syndicate 2999)[3]		-
2001	Amlin Underwriting Ltd	825	825	1000	842	901	-
2003	Catlin Underwriting Agencies Ltd	1094	1094	1094	1318	1215	-
2007	Novae Syndicates Ltd	360	360	360	315	274	6
2010	Cathedral Underwriting Ltd	300	300	300	229	212	42
2012	Arch Underwriting at Lloyd's Ltd	100	-	-	-	-	-
2112	Spectrum Syndicate Management Ltd	70	70	34	14	12	100
2121	Argenta Syndicate Management Ltd	130	113	89	132	95	60
2243	Starr Managing Agents Ltd	35	30	10	32	2	100
2468	Marketform Managing Agency Ltd	120	100	100	122	110	71
2488	Ace Underwriting Agencies Ltd	285	330	400	437	393	-
2525	Max at Lloyd's Ltd	42	42	42	43	42	98
2526	Max at Lloyd's Ltd	32	32	32	30	30	64
2623	Beazley Furlonge Ltd	624	656	697	837	753	-
2791	Managing Agency Partners Ltd	401	401	459	282	342	57
2987	Brit Syndicates Ltd	525	600	525	714	647	-
2999[3]	QBE Underwriting Ltd	720	780	660	852	978	-
3000	Markel Syndicate Management Ltd	170	170	175	238	197	-
3010	Cathedral Underwriting Ltd	30	30	20	16	4	-
3210	Mitsui Sumitomo Insurance Underwriting at Lloyd's Ltd	340	340	340	353	360	-
3334	Sportscover Underwriting Ltd	20	15	15	15	13	100
3622	Beazley Furlonge Ltd	7	-	-	-	-	-
3623	Beazley Furlonge Ltd	33	1	-	0	-	-
3624	Hiscox Syndicates Ltd	80	-	-	-	-	-
3820[2]	Hardy (Underwriting Agencies) Ltd	-	75	65	56	41	-
4000	Pembroke Managing Agency Ltd	95	73	73	66	59	-
4020	Ark Syndicate Management Ltd	222	170	114	226	89	-
4040	HCC Underwriting Agency Ltd	54	54	54	47	51	13
4141	HCC Underwriting Agency Ltd	16	12	-	19	-	-
4242	Chaucer Syndicates Ltd	84	84	84	64	38	86
4444	Canopius Managing Agents Ltd	450	410	450	484	469	7
4472	Liberty Syndicate Management Ltd	715	830	917	951	1045	-
4711	Aspen Managing Agency Ltd	160	88	-	78	-	-
5000	Travelers Syndicate Management Ltd	N/A	230	260	320	295	-
5151	Montpelier Underwriting Agencies Ltd	143	143	47	62	8	-
5555[3]	QBE Underwriting Ltd	90	95	85	(see Syndicate 2999)[3]		-
5820	Jubilee Managing Agency Ltd	63	42	44	56	64	86
6103	Managing Agency Partners Ltd	40	43	43	16	18	100
6104	Hiscox Syndicates Ltd	52	34	-	23	-	100
6105	Ark Syndicate Management Ltd	28	20	-	23	-	100
6106	Amlin Underwriting Ltd	50	-	-	-	-	100

Capital Providers &
Classes of Business

Sources of Capital 2002 - 2008

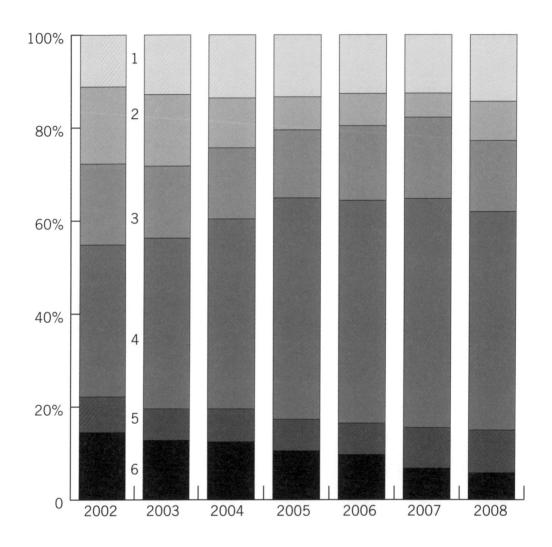

1 ▨ Worldwide Insurance Industry
2 ▨ Bermudian Insurance Industry
3 ▨ US Insurance Industry
4 ▨ UK Listed and other corporate
5 ▨ Individual members - Limited
6 ▨ Individual members - Unlimited

Source: Lloyd's

Leading Capital Providers 2007 & 2008

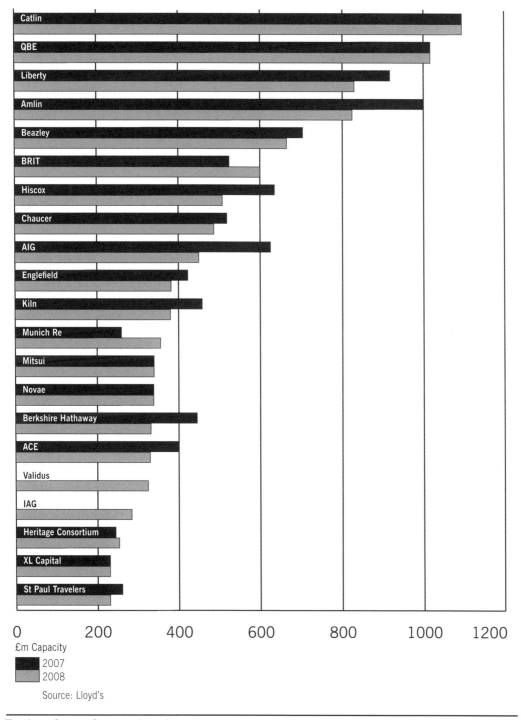

£m Capacity
- ■ 2007
- ▨ 2008

Source: Lloyd's

Business Profile 2008

Class of Business Split

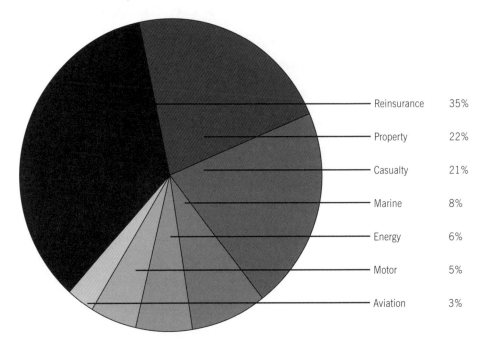

Reinsurance	35%
Property	22%
Casualty	21%
Marine	8%
Energy	6%
Motor	5%
Aviation	3%

Geographical Split

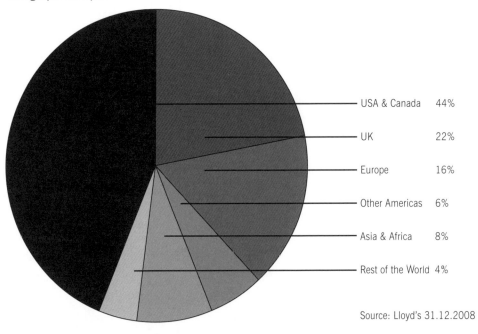

USA & Canada	44%
UK	22%
Europe	16%
Other Americas	6%
Asia & Africa	8%
Rest of the World	4%

Source: Lloyd's 31.12.2008

Agencies

Agencies

The Lloyd's Agency Network consists of almost 330 Lloyd's Agents and a further 330 Sub-Agents. The first Lloyd's Agency appointments were made in 1811, primarily for the provision of shipping movements and casualty information. Although most Agents still carry out this function, their main role today is one of conducting or arranging surveys on ships and cargoes for insurers and commercial interests throughout the world. Almost 200 Agents have also been granted authority to adjust and settle claims arising under Lloyd's certificates of insurance.

GENERAL CONTACT DETAILS

Address	Lloyd's Ground Floor
	One Lime Street
	London EC3M 7HA
Tel	+44 (0)20 7327 6677
Fax	+44 (0)20 7327 5255
Email	lita@lloyds.com
Website	www.lloyds.com/worldwide
Controller of Agencies	Karen Bizon

Albania
Durres

Algeria
Algiers

American Samoa
Pago Pago

Angola
Luanda

Antigua and Barbuda
Antigua

Argentina
Buenos Aires

Australia
Adelaide
Brisbane
Fremantle
Sydney

Austria
Vienna

Azerbaijan
Baku

Bahamas
Freeport
Nassau

Bahrain
Bahrain

Bangladesh
Chittagong

Barbados
Holetown

Belarus
Minsk

Belgium
Antwerp

Belize
Belize City

Benin
Cotonou

Bermuda
Bermuda

Bolivia
La Paz

Botswana
Gaborone

Brazil
Manaus
Recife
Rio de Janeiro
Santos
Sao Luiz

Brunei Darussalam
Bandar Seri Begawan

Bulgaria
Varna

Burundi
Bujumbura

Cambodia
Phnom Penh

Cameroon
Douala

Canada
Edmonton
Halifax
Montreal
Toronto
Vancouver

Canary Islands
Las Palmas de Gran Canaria
Santa Cruz de Tenerife

Cape Verde
St. Vincent

Cayman Islands
Grand Cayman

Chile
Santiago

China
Beijing
Dalian

Agencies

Guangzhou
Hong Kong
Qingdao
Shanghai
Tianjin

Christmas Island
Christmas Island

Colombia
Bogota

Congo
Matad
Pointe Noire

Cook Islands
Rarotonga

Costa Rica
San Jose

Cote D'ivoire
Abidjan

Croatia
Rijeka

Cuba
Havana

Curacao
Curacao

Cyprus
Limassol

Czech Republic
Prague

Denmark
Aalborg
Aarhus
Copenhagen
Esbjerg

Djibouti
Djibouti

Dominica
Dominica

Dominican Republic
Santo Domingo

Egypt
Alexandria
Cairo
Port Said

El Salvador
San Salvador

Eritrea
Asmara

Estonia
Tallinn

Ethiopia
Addis Ababa

Falkland Islands
Stanley

Faroe Islands
Torshavn

Fiji
Suva

Finland
Helsinki
Turku

France
Bordeaux
Brest
Cherbourg
Le Havre
Lorient
Marseille
Nantes
Paris
St. Malo

French Polynesia
Tahiti

Gabon
Libreville

Gambia
Banjul

Georgia
Batumi

Germany
Berlin
Bremen
Duisburg
Hamburg
Mannheim
Munich

Ghana
Accra

Gibraltar
Gibraltar

Greece
Piraeus

Greenland
Nuuk

Grenada
St George's

Guatemala
Guatemala City

Guinea
Conakry

Guinea-Bissau
Bissau

Guyana
Georgetown

Haiti
Port au Prince

Honduras
Puerto Cortes

Hungary
Budapest

Iceland
Reykjavik

India
Chennai
Kandla
Kochi
Calcutta
Mumbai
New Delhi
Visakhapatnam

Indonesia
Jakarta

Iran
Bandar Abbas
Teheran
Baghdad
Umm Qasr

Ireland
Dublin
Limerick

Israel
Ashdod

Italy
Bari
Genoa
Livorno (Leghorn)
Naples
Palermo
Rome

Trieste
Venice

Jamaica
Kingston

Japan
Kobe
Yokohama

Jordan
Amman

Kazakstan
Almaty

Kenya
Mombasa
Nairobi

Korea, Republic of
Seoul

Kuwait
Kuwait

Latvia
Riga

Lebanon
Beirut

Liberia
Monrovia

Libyan Arab Jamahiriya
Benghazi

Lithuania
Klaipeda

Madagascar
Antananarivo

Malawi
Blantyre

Malaysia
Kota Kinabalu
Kuala Lumpur
Penang

Malta
Malta

Martinique
Martinique

Mauritania
Nouadhibou
Nouakchott

Mauritius
Mauritius

Mexico
Coatzacoalcos
Guadalajara
Mexico City
Veracruz

Mongolia
Ulaanbaatar

Montenegro
Bar

Morocco
Agadir
Casablanca

Mozambique
Beira
Maputo

Nepal
Kathmandu

Netherlands
Amsterdam
Rotterdam

New Caledonia
Noumea

New Zealand
Auckland
Wellington

Nicaragua
Managua

Nigeria
Lagos
Port Harcourt

Norfolk Island
Norfolk Island

Norway
Kristiansand
Narvik
Oslo
Trondheim

Oman
Muscat
Salalah

Pakistan
Karachi

Panama
Balboa
Cristobal
Panama City

Papua New Guinea
Lae
Port Moresby
Rabaul

Paraguay
Asuncion

Peru
Lima

Philippines
Manila

Poland
Poznan

Portugal
Azores
Lisbon
Madeira
Oporto

Puerto Rico
San Juan

Qatar
Doha

Reunion
Reunion

Romania
Bucharest

Russia
Moscow
Novorossisk
St. Petersburg
Vladivostok

Rwanda
Kigali

Samoa
Apia

Sao Tome and Principe
Sao Tome

Saudi Arabia
Dammam
Jeddah

Senegal
Dakar

Serbia
Belgrade

Seychelles
Victoria

Sierra Leone
Freetown

Singapore
Singapore

Slovenia
Koper

Somalia
Berbera
Mogadishu

South Africa
Cape Town
Durban
Johannesburg

Spain
Barcelona
Bilbao
Cadiz
Ceuta
Corunna
Ferrol
Gijon
Madrid
Malaga
Palma
Valencia
Vigo

Sri Lanka
Colombo

St. Helena
St. Helena

St. Kitts and Nevis
St. Kitts and Nevis

St. Lucia
St. Lucia

St. Vincent and the Grenadines
St. Vincent (WI)

Sudan
Khartoum
Port Sudan

Sweden
Gothenburg
Helsingborg
Malmo
Stockholm
Visby

Switzerland
Basel
Neuchatel

Syrian Arab Republic
Aleppo

Taiwan
Taipei

Tanzania, United Republic Of
Dar-es-Salaam

Thailand
Bangkok

Togo
Lome

Tonga
Tonga

Trinidad and Tobago
Trinidad

Tunisia
Tunis

Turkey
Iskenderun
Istanbul
Izmir
Mersin

Uganda
Kampala

Ukraine
Odessa
Mariupol

United Arab Emirates
Abu Dhabi
Dubai

United Kingdom
Bristol
Grangemouth
Hull
Liverpool
London

United States
Anchorage
Baltimore
Boston (MA)
Charleston
Chicago
Honolulu
Houston
Los Angeles
Miami
Mobile
New Orleans

New York
Norfolk
Portland (ME)
Portland (OR)
San Francisco
Savannah
Seattle
Tampa
Wilmington

Uruguay
Montevideo

Uzbekistan
Almaty (Kazakstan)

Vanuatu
Port Vila

Venezuela
Caracas

Vietnam
Hanoi

Virgin Islands (British)
Tortola
St. Croix
St. Thomas

Yemen
Aden
Hodeidah

Zambia
Lusaka

Zimbabwe
Harare

International Offices

Introduction

Lloyd's international offices are a valuable resource for the Lloyd's market and a key part of Lloyd's commitment to its customers worldwide.

Each office provides a range of services to support the Lloyd's market in conducting business in a country.

Principally they offer the following:

- Maintaining strong and close relationships with leading brokers, insurers, local regulatory authorities and insurance industry associations

- Providing Lloyd's businesses with extensive local commercial knowledge and market information, both in person and through the Lloyd's Worldwide section of the Lloyd's website

- Enhancing Lloyd's reputation through strong customer support

- Working to raise Lloyd's profile and assisting with Lloyd's promotional activity

- Acting as underwriters' legal representatives in respect of service of suits

- Assisting in public authorities tender processes in certain EU countries.

GENERAL CONTACT DETAILS

Contact	Kevin Reeves
Position	Head of Operations International Markets
Address	One Lime Street
	London EC3M 7HA
Tel	+44 (0)20 7327 6264
Email	kevin.reeves@lloyds.com
Website	www.lloyds.com

Australia

Name	Keith Stern
Position	Lloyd's General Representative Australia
Address	Lloyd's Australia Limited
	Level 21
	123 Pitt Street
	Sydney NSW 2000
	Australia
Tel	+61 (0)2 9223 1433
Fax	+61 (0)2 9223 1466
Email	keith.stern@lloyds.com

Austria

Name	Dr Harald Svoboda
Position	Lloyd's General Representative Austria
Address	Kubac, Svoboda & Kirchweger
	Rechtsanwälte
	Kantgasse 3
	A-1010 Wien
	Austria
Tel	+43 (1) 7130713
Fax	+43 (1) 7132421
Email	harald.svoboda@ksk-lawyers.com

Belgium

Name	Alexis Fontein
Position	Lloyd's General Representative Belgium
Address	Lloyd's
	c/o D'Hoine & Mackay
	Schaliënstraat 30
	2000 Antwerp
	Belgium
Tel	+ 32 (3) 470 2309
	+ 31 (10) 50 66600
Fax	+ 32 (3) 470 2317
	+ 31 (10) 50 19593
Email	a.fontein@hvd.nl
	alexis.fontein@lloyds.com

Brazil

Name	Marco Antonio de Simas Castro
Position	Lloyd's General Representative Brazil
Address	Avenida Rio Branco nº 85 16º andar (parte)
	CEP 20040-004 Rio de Janeiro
	Brazil
Tel	Tel: 55 (21) 3849-4425
Email	marco.castro@lloyds.com

Canada

Name	Deborah Moor
Position	President
Name	Sean Murphy
Position	Attorney in Fact in Canada for
	Lloyd's underwriters
Address	1155, rue Metcalfe
	Suite 2220
	Montréal H3B 2V6
	Québec
Tel	+1 (514) 861 8361
	+1 (514) 864 5444
Fax	+1 (514) 861 0470
Email	info@lloyds.ca
	lineage@lloyds.ca

China

Name	Eric Gao
Position	Lloyd's General Representative for Lloyd's
	Reinsurance Company Limited
Address	Lloyd's Reinsurance Company (China) Ltd.
	33rd Floor, Azia Centre
	1233 Lujiazui Ring Road
	Pudong
	Shanghai 200120
Tel	+86 (21) 6162 8200
Fax	+86 (21) 6162 8250
Email	info@lloyds.com.cn

Cyprus

Name	Marianna Papadakis
Position	Lloyd's General Representative Cyprus
Address	Lloyd's Cyprus Limited
	199 Arch Makarios III Avenue
	Limassol 3608
	Cyprus
Tel	+44 (0)20 7327 6802
Fax	+44 (0)20 7327 5255
Email	marianna.papadakis@lloyds.com

Denmark

Name	Jes Anker Mikkelsen
Position	Lloyd's General Representative in Denmark
Address	Langelinie Allé 35
	DK-2100
	Copenhagen
	Denmark
Tel	+ (45) 7227 0000
Direct	+ (45) 7227 3586
Fax	+ (45) 7227 0000
Email	jam@bechbruun.com

France

Name	Anne-Gaëlle Leillard
Position	Lloyd's General Representative France
Address	4 rue des Petits Pères
	75002 Paris
	France
Tel	+ 33 (0) 1 42 60 43 43
Fax	+ 33 (0) 1 42 60 14 41
Email	lloydsparis@lloyds.com

Germany

Name	Burkard von Siegfried
Position	Lloyd's General Representative Germany
Address	Niederlassung für Deutschland
	Gärtnerweg 3
	60322 Frankfurt
	Deutschland
Tel	+ 49 (0)69 5970253
Fax	+ 49 (0)69 550926
Email	burkard.vonsiegfried@lloyds.com

Greece

Name	Marianna Papadakis
Position	Lloyd's General Representative Greece
Address	Lloyd's Greece SA
	25A Boukourestiou Street
	106 71 Athens
	Greece
Tel	+30 (210) 363 9156
Fax	+30 (?10) 363 9362
Email	marianna.papadakis@lloyds.com
London Tel	+44 (0)20 7327 6802
London Fax	+44 (0)20 7327 5255

Hong Kong

Name	Alex Faris
Position	Lloyd's General Representative Hong Kong
Address	Lloyd's
	Suite 1220
	Two Pacific Place
	88 Queensway
	Hong Kong
Tel	+ 852 2918 9911
Fax	+ 852 2918 9918
Email	afaris@lloydshk.com.hk

Ireland

Name	Eamonn Egan
Position	Lloyd's Country Manager for Ireland
Address	70 Sir John Rogerson's Quay
	Dublin 2
	Eire
Tel	+353 (1) 6 313 600
Email	eamonn.egan@lloyds.com

Israel

Name	Jonathan Gross
Position	Lloyd's General Representative in Israel
Address	Gibor Sport Building
	7 Menachem Begin Road
	Ramat Gan 52521
	Israel
Tel	+972 (3) 612 2233
Fax	+972 (3) 612 3322
Email	jgross@lloyds.co.il

Italy

Name	Enrico Bertagna
Position	Lloyd's General Representative Italy
Address	Lloyd's
	Corso Garibaldi, 86
	20121 Milan
	Italy
Tel	+39 (0) 2 637 888 1
Fax	+39 (0) 2 637 888 50
Email	reception@lloyds.it

International Offices

Japan

Name	Iain Ferguson
Position	Lloyd's General Representative Japan
Address	Lloyd's Japan Inc
	Otemachi Financial Center 17F
	1-5-4 Otemachi
	Chiyoda-ku
	Tokyo 100-0004
	Japan
Tel	+0081 (3) 3215 5297
Fax	+0081 (3) 3215 5295
Email	i.ferguson@lloyds-japan.co.jp

Malta

Name	Mark Gollcher
Position	Local Director of Lloyd's Malta Ltd
Address	Lloyd´s Malta Ltd.
	19 Zachary Street
	PO Box 268
	Valletta VLT 1133
	Malta
Tel	+356 25691500
Fax	+356 21234195
Email	contact@gollcher.com

Namibia

Name	Peter Grüttemeyer
Position	Lloyd's General Representative in Namibia
Address	c/o Ohlthaver & List Trust Company (Pty) Ltd
	Carl List Haus
	No. 27 Fidel Castro Street
	PO Box 16
	Windhoek
	Namibia
Tel	+264 (61) 207 5236
	+264 (61) 207 5111 Switchboard
Fax	+264 (61) 234 021
Email	peter.gruttemeyer@olfitra.com.na

Netherlands

Name	Alexis Fontein
Position	Lloyd's General Representative
	for the Netherlands
Address	Hudig Veder & Co
	Debussystraat 2
	3161 WD RHOON
	The Netherlands
Tel	+31 (10) 506 6600
Fax	+31 (10) 501 9593
Email	a.fontein@hvd.nl
	alexis.fontein@lloyds.com

New Zealand

Name	Mr Scott Galloway
Position	Lloyd's General Representative
	in New Zealand
Address	c/o Hazelton Law
	Level 3
	101 Molesworth Street
	PO Box 5639
	Wellington
	New Zealand
Tel	+64 (4) 472 7582
Fax	+64 (4) 472 7571
Email	scott.galloway@hazelton.co.nz

Norway

Name	Espen Komnaes
Position	Lloyd's General Representative for Norway
Address	Komnaes Braaten Skard DA
	Ruseløkkveien 6 Pb. 1661 Vika,
	N - 0120 Oslo
	Norway
Tel	+47 (23) 11 45 60
Fax	+47 (23) 11 45 70
Email	komnas@kbco.no

Poland

Name	Witold Janusz
Position	Lloyd's General Representative Poland
Address	Lloyd's Polska Sp. z o.o.
	Warsaw Financial Center
	13th Floor
	ul. Emilii Plater 53
	00-113 Warszawa
Tel	+48 (602) 247 478
Email	witold.janusz@lloyds.com

Singapore

Name	Simon Wilson
Position	Lloyd's General Manager for Singapore
Address	Lloyd's of London (Asia) Pte Ltd
	One George Street
	#15-01/06
	Singapore 049145
Tel	+65 6538 7088
Fax	+65 6538 7768
Email	simon.wilson@lloyds.com.sg

South Africa

Name	Amit Khilosia
Position	Lloyd's General Representative for South Africa
Address	Lloyd's South Africa
	7th Floor
	The Forum
	2 Maude Street
	Sandton
	2146
Tel	+27 (11) 884 0486
Fax	+27 (11) 884 0384
Email	amit.khilosia@lloyds.com

Spain

Name	Sr. D. Juan Arsuaga
Position	Lloyd's General Representative Spain
Address	Calle José Ortega y Gasset 7, 1ª Planta
	Edificio Serrano 49
	28006 Madrid
	Spain
Tel	+44 (0)20 7327 7900
	+34 (91) 426 2312
Fax	+34 (91) 426 2394
Email	juan.arsuaga@lloyds.com

Sweden

Name	Eva Lindberg
Position	Lloyd's General Representative for Sweden
Address	Stureplan 4c
	4th Floor
	Stockholm 114 35
	Sweden
Tel	+46 (0)8 463 1111
Fax	+46 (0)8 463 1010
Email	eva.lindberg@lloyds.com

Switzerland

Name	Graham West,
Position	Lloyd's General Manager for Switzerland
Address	Lloyd's Versicherer
	Zweigniederlassung Zürich
	Seefeldstrasse 7
	8008 Zürich
	Switzerland
Tel	+ 41 (44) 266 6070
Fax	+ 41 (44) 266 6079
Email	graham.west@lloyds.com
	silvia.soltermann@lloyds.com

USA

ILLINOIS

Name	Maryanne Swaim
Position	President
Address	Lloyd's Illinois Inc
	181 West Madison Street
	Suite 3870
	Chicago
	Illinois 60602-4541
	USA
Tel	+1 (312) 407 6200
Fax	+1 (312) 407 6229
Email	maryanne.swaim@lloydsillinois.com
	info@lloydsillinois.com

KENTUCKY

Name	Patrick Talley
Position	President
Address	Lloyd's Kentucky Inc.
	314 West Main Street
	Frankfort
	Kentucky 40601-1808
	US
Tel	+1 (502) 875 5940
Fax	+1 (502) 223 5531
Email	pat.talley@lloydskentucky.com

NEW YORK

Name	tba
Position	President and Director
Address	Lloyd's America Inc
	The Museum Office Building
	25 West 53rd Street
	14th Flo
	New York
	NY 10019
	USA
Tel	+1 (212) 382 4060
	+1 (212) 382 4090
Fax	+1 (212) 382 4070
Email	c/o sue.langley@lloyds.com

US Virgin Islands

Name	Hank Feuerzeig
Position	Lloyd's General Representative for the USVI
Address	Lloyd's Attorney in Fact
	Dudley Topper and Feuerzeig
	Law House
	1A Frederiksberg Gade
	Charlotte Amalie
	St Thomas
	US Virgin Islands 00802
Tel	+1 (340) 715 4443
Fax	+1 (340) 715 4400
Email	hfeuerzeig@DTFLaw.com

Zimbabwe

Name	Mrs Emilia Chisango
Position	Lloyd's Principal Officer in Zimbabwe
Address	c/o KPMG
	Mutual Gardens
	100 The Chase (West)
	Emerald Hill
	Harare
	Zimbabwe

Mailing address

	PO Box 6
	Harare
	Zimbabwe
Tel	+ 263 (4) 302600/303700
Fax	+ 263 (4) 303699
Email	emiliachisango@kpmg.co.zw

International Licences

International Licences

Lloyd's is licensed to underwrite business in certain territories subject to the laws and regulations of those territories. Lloyd's may be able to accept risks proposed from countries that are not on the list below in certain circumstances and in accordance with the laws and regulations of those countries.

GENERAL CONTACT DETAILS

Contact	Rosemary Beaver
Address	Lloyd's Ground Floor
	One Lime Street
	London EC3M 7HA
Tel	+44 (0)20 7327 6677
Fax	+44 (0)20 7327 5255
Email	lita@lloyds.com
Website	www.lloyds.com/worldwide

Insurance business

Listed below are the territories in which Lloyd's is licensed or eligible to undertake insurance business. The licences and eligibility relate to direct insurance. Reinsurance business can also be undertaken in these and many other territories.

Anguilla	Grenada	Norway
Antigua	Guernsey	Papua New Guinea
Australia	Hong Kong SAR	Poland
Austria	Hungary	Portugal
Bahamas	Iceland	Romania
Barbados	Ireland	Singapore
Belgium	Isle of Man	Slovakia
Belize	Israel	Slovenia
Bermuda	Italy	South Africa
British Virgin Islands	Jamaica	Spain
Bulgaria	Japan (ii)	St Kitts & Nevis
Canada	Jersey	St Lucia
Cayman Islands	Latvia	St Vincent
Cyprus	Liechtenstein	Sweden
Czech Republic	Lithuania	Switzerland
Denmark	Luxembourg	Trinidad & Tobago
Dominica	Malawi	United Kingdom
Estonia	Malta	US (iii)
Finland	Mauritius	US – Illinois (iv)
France (i)	Monaco	US – Kentucky (v)
Germany	Namibia	US – Virgin Islands (vi)
Gibraltar	Netherlands	Vanuatu
Greece	New Zealand	Zimbabwe

i)   France and its overseas departments, territories and territorial collectives.

ii) Through Lloyd's Japan Inc. only.

iii) Lloyd's is an eligible surplus lines insurer in all US jurisdictions except for Kentucky and the USVI. Lloyd's is licensed in Illinois, Kentucky and the USVI. Lloyd's is an accredited reinsurer in all US states.

iv) Lloyd's is authorised to write both licensed and surplus lines business in Illinois.

v) Lloyd's cannot do business on a surplus lines basis from Kentucky.

vi) Lloyd's cannot do business on a surplus lines basis from USVI.

Reinsurance business

Lloyd's is specifically registered or licensed to write reinsurance business in the following territories:

Argentina	Colombia	Labuan
Brazil	Ecuador	Mexico
Chile	Guatemala	Venezuela
China	Honduras	

Life business

Lloyd's is licensed or eligible to write life insurance in the following territories listed below:

Antigua	Grenada	Netherlands
Austria	Guadeloupe	New Caledonia
Bahamas	Hong Kong SAR	Norway
Belgium	Hungary	Poland
British Virgin Islands	Iceland	Portugal
Bulgaria	Ireland	Reunion
Cayman Islands	Isle of Man	Romania
Cyprus	Israel	Saint Barthelemey
Czech Republic	Italy	Saint Martin
Denmark	Jamaica	Slovakia
Estonia	Jersey	Slovenia
Falkland Islands	Latvia	South Africa
Finland	Liechtenstein	Spain
France	Lithuania	Saint Vincent
French Guiana	Luxembourg	Sweden
French Polynesia	Malawi	United Kingdom
Germany	Martinique	Zimbabwe
Gibraltar	Mauritius	
Greece	Monaco	

Brokers

A

AAA Insurance & Reinsurance Brokers Ltd

Address 6 Gracechurch Street
London EC3V 0AT
Tel +44 (0)20 7220 8000
Fax +44 (0)20 7220 8001
Web www.aaairb.co.uk

AFL Insurance Brokers Ltd

Address Suite 2/5
3 Minster Court
Mincing Lane
London EC3R 7DD
Tel +44 (0)20 7220 7712
Fax +44 (0)20 7929 3327
Web www.aflib.com

Afro-Asian Insurance Services Limited

Address First Floor
11/12 London Fruit & Wool Exchange
56 Brushfield Street
London E1 6HB
Tel +44 (0)20 7375 7420
Fax +44 (0)20 7375 0972
Web www.afroasian-insurance.com

Alsford Page & Gems Ltd

Address Minories House
2-5 Minories
London EC3N 1BJ
Tel +44 (0)20 7456 0500
Fax +44 (0)20 7456 0600
Web www.apg.net

Alston Gayler & Co Ltd

Address 100 Leadenhall Street
London EC3A 3BP
Tel +44 (0)20 7626 5252
Fax +44 (0)20 7626 5030

Alwen Hough Johnson Ltd

Address 2 Minster Court
Mincing Lane
London EC3R 7BB
Tel +44 (0)20 7398 2600
Fax +44 (0)20 7623 8940
Web www.ahjltd.co.uk

Anglo French UK Limited

Address Holland House
4 Bury Street
London EC3A 5AW
Tel +44 (0)20 7220 4433
Web www.afunet.co.uk

Anglo Pacific Consultants (London) Ltd

Offices 4-7 Granary Court
9-19 High Road
Chadwell Heath
Romford
Essex RM6 6PY

Tel +44 (0)20 8597 5656
Fax +44 (0)20 8597 5678

Aon Benfiled Italia S.p.A

Address Via Andrea Ponti 10
20143 Milano
Italy
Tel +39 02 818 02 237
Fax +39 02 818 02 803
Web www.aon.com

Aon Ltd

Address 8 Devonshire Square
London EC2M 4PL
Tel +44 (0)20 7623 5500
Fax +44 (0)20 7621 1511
Web www.aon.com

Apex International Reinsurance Brokers Limited

Address St Clare House
          30 - 33 Minories
          London EC3N 1PE
Tel   +44 (0)20 7977 5290
Fax   +44 (0)20 7977 5299

ARB International Ltd

Address The Matrix
          9 Aldgate High Street
          London EC3N 1AH
Tel   +44 (0)20 7377 0123
Fax   +44 (0)20 7377 2738
Web   www.arbint.co.uk

Arthur J Gallagher (UK) Ltd

Address 9 Alie Street
          London E1 8DE
Tel   +44 (0)20 7204 6000
Fax   +44 (0)20 7204 6001
Web   www.ajginternational.com

B

Bannerman Rendell Limited

Address Peek House
          20 Eastcheap
          London EC3M 1EB
Tel   +44 (0)20 7929 3400
Fax   +44 (0)20 7929 3600
Web   www.bannermanrendell.com

Bar Professions Limited

Address 4th Floor
          6 Minories
          London EC3N 1BJ
Tel   +44 (0)20 3150 0100
Fax   +44 (0)20 3150 0101
Web   www.barprofessions.com

Baronsmead Partners LLP

Address 5th Floor
          21 Bruton Street
          London W1J 6QD
Tel   +44 (0)20 7529 2300
Fax   +44 (0)20 7529 2301
Web   www.baronsmead.com

BDB Ltd

Address 40 Lime Street
          London EC3M 7AW
Tel   +44 (0)20 3102 8000
Fax   +44 (0)20 3102 8009
Web   www.bdbltd.co.uk

Beach & Associates Ltd

Address 6th Floor
          2 Seething Lane
          London EC3N 4AX
Tel   +44 (0)20 7680 8390
Fax   +44 (0)20 7680 8388
Web   www.beachandassociates.com

Bell & Clements Ltd

Address 55 King William Street
          London EC4R 9AD
Tel   +44 (0)20 7283 6222
Fax   +44 (0)20 7283 8222
Web   www.bellandclements.com

Benfield Asia Pte Ltd

Address 80 Raffles Place #42-01
          UOB Plaza 1
          048624
          Singapore
Tel   +65 6532 7797
Fax   +65 6532 0081/82
Web   www.benfieldgroup.com

Benfield Ltd

Address 55 Bishopsgate
          London EC2N 3BD
Tel   +44 (0)20 7578 7000
Fax   +44 (0)20 7578 7001
Web   www.benfieldgroup.com

Benfield Paris

Address 11 rue Scribe
Paris 75009
France
Tel +33 1 44 63 13 00
Fax +33 1 42 81 45 26
Web www.benfieldgroup.com

Bennett Gould & Partners Ltd

Address 15 St Helen's Place
London EC3A 6DE
Tel +44 (0)20 7588 8052
Fax +44 (0)20 7588 5507
Web www.bgpltd.com

Berry Palmer & Lyle Ltd

Address 150 Leadenhall Street
London EC3V 4TE
Tel +44 (0)20 7375 9600
Fax +44 (0)20 7929 4499
Web www.bpl-global.com

Besso Ltd

Address 8-11 Crescent
London EC3N 2LY
Tel +44 (0)20 7480 1000
Fax +44 (0)20 7480 1280
Web www.besso.co.uk

BISYS Hanleigh

Address Suite 153 1 Paragon Drive
Montvale
New Jersey
USA
07645
Tel +1 201 505 1050
Fax +1 201 505 1051
Web www.bisysinsurance.com

Blackmore Borley Limited

Address 52 Lime Street
London EC3M 7NP
Tel +44 (0)20 7929 4616
Fax +44 (0)20 7929 4626
Web www.blackmoreborley.com

Bloemers & Partners Ltd

Address Room 783
1 Lime Street
London EC3M 7HA
Tel +44 (0)20 7256 3460
Fax +44 (0)20 7626 6678
Web www.bloemers.com

Bluefin Insurance Services Ltd

Address Fountain House
130 Fenchurch Street
London EC3M 5DJ
Tel +44 (0)20 7338 0111
Fax +44 (0)20 7294 0115
Web www.bluefingroup.co.uk

BMS Group Ltd

Address One America Square
London EC3N 2LS
Tel +44 (0)20 7480 7288
Fax +44 (0)20 7488 9837
Web www.bmsgroup.com

BMS Intermediaries Inc

Address 5005 LBJ Freeway
Suite 700
Dallas
Texas
USA
75244
Tel +44 (0)20 7480 7288
Fax +44 (0)20 7488 9837

Bowood Partners Ltd

Address 1st Floor
33 Lombard Street
London EC3V 9BQ
Tel +44 (0)20 7397 4400
Fax +44 (0)20 7397 4444
Web www.bowood.co.uk

Broker Network London Markets

Address	3rd Floor
	107 Fenchurch Street
	London EC3M 5JF
Tel	+44 (0)1423 554106
Fax	+44 (0)20 7816 7201
Web	www.brokernetwork.co.uk

Butcher Robinson & Staples International Ltd

Address	Collegiate House
	9 St Thomas Street
	London SE1 9RY
Tel	+44 (0)20 7397 5000
Fax	+44 (0)20 7407 1076
Web	www.brasil.co.uk

Butcher Robinson & Staples Ltd

Address	Collegiate House
	9 St Thomas Street
	London SE1 9RY
Tel	+44 (0)20 7397 5000
Fax	+44 (0)20 7407 1076
Web	www.brasil.co.uk

Butcher Robinson & Staples Marine Ltd

Address	Collegiate House
	9 St Thomas Street
	London SE1 9RY
Tel	+44 (0)20 7397 5000
Fax	+44 (0)20 7407 1076
Web	www.brasil.co.uk

C

Camberford Law Plc

Address	2 Royal Exchange
	London EC3V 3DG
Tel	+44 (0)20 7623 9111
Fax	+44 (0)20 7623 9444
Web	www.camberford-law.com

Carroll & Partners Ltd

Address	63 St Mary Axe
	London EC3A 8LE
Tel	+44 (0)20 7645 4600
Fax	+44 (0)20 7623 6922
Web	www.carroll-londonmarkets.co.uk

Carroll Insurance Group Ltd

Address	2 White Lion Court
	Cornhill
	London EC3V 3NP
Tel	+44 (0)20 7623 2228
Fax	+44 (0)20 7283 7181
Web	www.carrollinsurance.co.uk

CBC UK Ltd

Address	Mansell Court
	69 Mansell Street
	London E1 8AN
Tel	+44 (0)20 7265 5600
Fax	+44 (0)20 7702 4784
Web	www.cbcuk.co.uk

Channing Lucas & Partners

Address	St Clare House
	30-33 Minories
	London EC3N 1PE
Tel	020 7977 5700
Fax	020 7702 9276
Web	www.clpinsurance.co.uk

Chesterfield Insurance Brokers Ltd

Address	St Clare House
	30-33 Minories
	London EC3N 1DD
Tel	+44 (0)20 7481 1683
Fax	+44 (0)20 7488 1919
Web	www.chesterfieldgroup.co.uk

CityNet Insurance Brokers Limited

Address 1st Floor
108 Fenchurch Street
London EC3M 5JR
Tel +44 (0)20 7488 7950
Fax +44 (0)20 7488 7951
Web www.citynet.eu.com

CJ Coleman & Co Ltd

Address Portsoken House
155 Minories
London EC3N 1BT
Tel +44 (0)20 7488 2211
Fax +44 (0)20 7488 4436
Web www.cjcoleman.co.uk

CKRe Ltd

Address 1st Floor Valiant House
4-10 Heneage Lane
London EC3A 5DQ
Tel +44 (0)20 7929 7017
Fax +44 (0)20 7626 1891
Web www.ckre.co.uk

Clegg Gifford & Company Ltd

Address 7 Eastern Road
Romford
Essex RM1 3NH
Tel +44 (0)1708 729500
Fax +44 (0)1708 729501
Web www.cglloyds.co.uk

COBRA London Markets Limited

Address 110 Fenchurch Street
London EC3M 5JT
Tel +44 (0)20 7204 0014
Fax +44 (0)20 7204 0019/20
Web www.cobralm.com

Cogent Resources Ltd

Address 50 Fenchurch Street
London EC3M 3JY
Tel +44 (0)20 7469 6300
Fax +44 (0)20 7469 6399
Web www.cogent-resources.com

Colemont Insurance Brokers Ltd

Address 4th Floor
Centurion House
24 Monument Street
London EC3R 8AJ
Tel +44 (0)20 7621 8560
Fax +44 (0)20 7621 8561
Web www.colemont.com

Commercial Risks (UK) Limited

Address New Loom House
101 Back Church Lane
London E1 1LU
Tel +44 (0)20 7702 2103
Fax +44 (0)20 7488 9792
Web ww.commercialrisks.co.uk

Contractsure Ltd

Address 9-13 Fenchurch Buildings
Fenchurch Street
London EC3M 5HR
Tel +44 (0)20 7709 1366
Fax +44 (0)20 7709 1367
Web www.contractsure.co.uk

Cooper Gay & Co Ltd

Address 52 Leadenhall Street
London EC3A 2EB
Tel +44 (0)20 7480 7322
Fax +44 (0)20 7481 4695
Web www.coopergay.com

Corrie Bauckham Batts Ltd

Address Suite 405
New Loom House
101 Backchurch Lane
London E1 1LU
Tel +44 (0)20 7895 6500
Fax +44 (0)20 7488 4159
Web www.cbbltd.co.uk

COSCO (Hong Kong) Insurance Brokers Ltd

Address Room 4701
COSCO Tower
183 Queen's Road
Hong Kong

Tel   +852 2809 6711
Fax   +852 2547 2180
Web   www.coscoins.com.hk

Cosmos Services Company Ltd

Address   3rd Floor
          Minories House
          2-5 Minories
          London EC3N 1BJ
Tel   +44 (0)20 7335 1001
Fax   +44 (0)20 7335 1002
Web   www.cosmos-rs.co.uk

Crescent Global UK Limited

Address   148 Leadenhall Street
          London EC3V 4QT
Tel   +44 (0)20 3178 7631
Fax   +44 (0)20 3178 7630
Web   www.crescentglobal.com

Crest Underwriting Ltd

Address   No 10 The Courtyard
          Kilcarbery Park
          Nangor Road
          Dublin 22
          Republic of Ireland
Tel   +353 1 461 1550
Fax   +353 1 461 1570
Web   www.crestunderwriting.ie

Crispin Speers & Partners Ltd

Address   St Clare House
          30-33 The Minories
          London EC3N 1PE
Tel   +44 (0)20 7977 5700
Fax   +44 (0)20 7702 9276
Web   www.cspinsurance.com

Croton Stokes Wilson Limited

Address   Suite 505
          New Loom House
          101 Backchurch Lane
          London E1 1LU
Tel   +44 (0)20 7867 5888
Fax   +44 (0)20 7867 5900

Culver London Limited

Address   Suite 53
          The London Fruit and Wool Exchange
          Brushfield Street
          London E1 6EX
Tel   +44 (0)20 7456 1300
Fax   +44 (0)20 7456 1312
Web   www.culverinsurance.com

D

Dashwood Brewer & Phipps Ltd

Address   Independent House
          7 Cutler Street
          London E1 7DJ
Tel   +44 (0)20 7626 3711
Fax   +44 (0)20 7283 4175
Web   www.dashwood.co.uk

Decus Insurance Brokers Limited

Address   117 Fenchurch Street
          London EC3M 5DY
Tel   +44 (0)20 3178 6515
Web   www.decusbrokers.co.uk

Denis M Clayton & Co Ltd

Address   Landmark House
          69 Leadenhall Street
          London EC3A 2DB
Tel   +44 (0)20 7480 6410
Fax   +44 (0)20 7488 9022
Web   www.towersperrin.com

Dublon Insurance Brokers Limited

Address   Holland House
          4 Bury Street
          London EC3A 5AW
Tel   +44 (0)20 7220 4448/9

E

Elliott Special Risks LP

Address   Suite 810
        130 Adelaide Street West
        Toronto
        Ontario
        Canada
        M5H 3P5
Tel   +1 416 601 1133
Fax   +1 416 601 1150
Web   www.elliottsr.com

Endeavour Insurance Services Limited

Address   Suite 503
        New Loom House
        101 Backchurch Lane
        London E1 1LU
Tel   +44 (0)20 7895 6550
Fax   +44 (0)20 7895 6555
Web   www.endeavouris.co.uk

EPG Insurance Services Ltd

Address   Gallery 4
        Lloyd's Building
        12 Leadenhall Street
        London EC3V 1LP
Tel   +44 (0)20 7816 7145
Fax   +44 (0)20 7816 7146
Web   www.epginsurance.co.uk

European Brokers Alliance Limited

Address   5-10 Bury Street
        London EC3A 5AT
Tel   +44 (0)20 7929 7711
Fax   +44 (0)20 7929 7733
Web   www.eba-london.co.uk

European Insurance and Reinsurance Brokers Ltd

Address   8-11 Crescent
        London EC3N 2LY
Tel   +44 (0)20 7480 1117
Fax   +44 (0)20 7480 1287

Execution Ltd

Address   The Old Truman Brewery
        91 Brick Lane
        London E1 6QL
Tel   +44 (0)20 7456 9191
Fax   +44 (0)20 7375 2007
Web   www.executionlimited.com

F

FirstCity Partnership Ltd

Address   13-15 Folgate Street
        London E1 6BX
Tel   +44 (0)20 7247 6595
Fax   +44 (0)20 7410 4818
Web   www.firstcity.com

FP Marine Risks Ltd

Address   4th Floor
        5 Royal Exchange Buildings
        London EC3V 3NL
Tel   +44 (0)20 7397 4920
Fax   +44 (0)20 7397 4921
Web   www.fp-marine.com

G

Genavco Insurance Ltd

Address   Third Floor
        Michael's House
        10-12 Alie Street
        London E1 8DE
Tel   +44 (0)20 7702 4300
Fax   +44 (0)20 7702 4585
Web   www.genavco.co.uk

Genesis Insurance Brokers Limited

Address   148 Leadenhall Street
        London EC3V 4QT
Tel   +44 (0)207 743 8810
Fax   +44 (0)207 743 8811

Giles Insurance Brokers Limited

Address Suite 110
1 Royal Exchange Avenue
London EC3V 3LT
Tel +44 (0)207 464 4230
Fax +44 (0)870 400 9411
Web www.thebroker.co.uk

Gina Fitzgerald Ltd

Address 150 Leadenhall Street
London
EC3M 5AD
Tel +44 (0)20 7702 0855
Fax +44 (0)20 7702 0854

Glencairn Ltd

Address 71 Fenchurch Avenue
London EC3M 5AD
Tel +44 (0)20 7558 9200
Fax +44 (0)20 7548 9701
Web www.glencairngroup.com

Gresham Insurance Brokers Ltd

Address First Floor
28 Great Tower Street
London EC3R 5AT
Tel +44 (0)20 7280 8600
Fax +44 (0)20 7280 8680
Web www.greshamlondon.com

Griffiths & Armour Global Risks Ltd

Address 145 Leadenhall Street
London EC3V 4QT
Tel +44 (0)20 7090 1106
Fax +44 (0)20 7090 1101
Web www.griffithsandarmour.com

Grimme Butcher Jones Ltd

Address Suite 2.07
New Loom House
101 Backchurch Lane
London E1 1LU
Tel +44 (0)20 7264 0420
Fax +44 (0)20 7481 2156
Web www.gbj-ltd.co.uk

Grosvenor Brokers (America) LLC

Address 20 St Dunstan's Hill
London EC3R 8HL
Tel +44 (0)20 7337 6800
Fax +44 (0)20 7337 6828
Web www.grosvenorbrokers.com

Groupe Eyssautier

Address 37-39 rue de la Bienfaisance
Paris 75008
France
Tel +33 1 44 82 10 60
Fax +33 1 42 33 85 31
Web www.groupe-eyssautier.com

Guest Krieger Ltd

Address 68 Cornhill
London EC3V 3QX
Tel +44 (0)20 7283 6644
Fax +44 (0)20 7623 7548
Web www.guestkrieger.com

H

H W Wood Ltd

Address The Baltic Exchange
38 St Mary Axe
London EC3A 8BH
Tel +44 (0)20 7398 9000
Fax +44 (0)20 7398 9001
Web www.hwint.com

Harel (UK) Ltd

St Clare House
30-33 Minories
London EC3N 1PE
Tel +44 20 7977 5293
Fax +44 20 7702 9276

Harman Kemp North America Ltd

Address	Roman Wall House
	1-2 Crutched Friars
	London EC3N 2HT
Tel	+44 (0)20 7782 0537
Fax	+44 (0)20 7782 0538
Web	www.hknal.com

Hayward Aviation Ltd

Address	Harling House
	47-51 Great Suffolk Street
	London SE1 0BS
Tel	+44 (0)20 7902 7800
Fax	+44 (0)20 7928 8040
Web	www.haywards.net

HBA Ltd

Address	14 Fenchurch Avenue
	London EC3M 5AT
Tel	+44 (0)845 618 0120
Fax	+44 (0)20 7481 0484
Web	www.hba.eu.com

Heath Lambert Ltd

Address	133 Houndsditch
	London EC3A 7AH
Tel	+44 (0)20 7560 3000
Fax	+44 (0)20 7560 3231
Web	www.heathlambert.com

Hispania Risk Broker Correduria de Seguros y Reaseguros S.A.

Address	Paseo de la Habana 50 Bajo Dcha
	28036 Madrid
	Spain
Tel	+34 91 359 50 80

Houlder Insurance Services Ltd

Address	Michael's House
	10-12 Alie Street
	London E1 8DE
Tel	+44 (0)20 7980 3800
Fax	+44 (0)20 7980 3814
Web	www.houlder.co.uk

Howard Global Insurance Services Ltd

Address	Third Floor
	19-21 Great Tower Street
	London EC3R 5AR
Tel	+44 (0)20 7626 2185
Fax	+44 (0)20 7626 2191

Howden Insurance Brokers Ltd

Address	Bevis Marks House
	Bevis Marks
	London EC3A 7JB
Tel	+44 (0)20 7623 3806
Fax	+44 (0)20 7623 3807
Web	www.howdengroup.com

HRH Reinsurance Brokers Ltd

Address	3rd Floor
	71 Fenchurch Street
	London EC3M 4BR
Tel	+44 (0)20 7481 6111
Fax	+44 (0)20 7481 6112
Web	www.hrh.com

HSBC Insurance Brokers Ltd

Address	Bishops Court
	27-33 Artillery Lane
	London E1 7LP
Tel	+44 (0)20 7247 5433
Fax	+44 (0)20 7377 2139
Web	www.insurancebrokers.hsbc.co.uk

I

Insurance Marketing Ltd

Address	26 Alie Street
	London E1 8DE
Tel	+44 (0)20 7977 5406
Fax	+44 (0)20 7977 5409

Integro Insurance Brokers Ltd

Address 2nd Floor
100 Leadenhall Street
London EC3A 3BP
Tel +44 (0)20 7444 6000
Fax +44 (0)20 7444 6001
Web www.integrogroup.com

International Professional Risks Limited

Address Boundary House
7-17 Jewry Street
London EC3N 2HP
Tel +44 (0)20 7488 4144
Fax +44 (0)20 7488 3373
Web www.iprins.com

International Risk Solutions Ltd

Address 12 Camomile Street
London EC3A 7AS
Tel +44 (0)20 7621 2934
Fax +44 (0)20 7929 2387
Web www.int-rs.com

Iris Insurance Brokers Ltd

Address 7th Floor Maitland House
Warrior Square
Southend-on-Sea
Essex
SS1 2JN
Tel +44 (0)1702 456341
Fax +44 (0)1702 618901
Web www.irisib.com

J

James Hampden Insurance Brokers Ltd

Address Bury House
31 Bury Street
London EC3R 5AR
Tel +44 (0)20 7398 8080

Fax +44 (0)20 7398 8081
Web www.jameshampden.com

Jardine Lloyd Thompson Ltd

Address 6 Crutched Friars
London EC3N 2PH
Tel +44 (0)20 7528 4000
Fax +44 (0)20 7528 4500
Web www.jltgroup.com

Jardine Lloyd Thompson UK Ltd

Address 6 Crutched Friars
London EC3N 2PH
Tel +44 (0)20 7528 4444
Fax +44 (0)20 7528 4500
Web www.jltgroup.com

JB Boda & Co (UK) Ltd

Address New London House
6 London Street
London EC3R 7LQ
Tel +44 (0)20 7488 1236
Fax +44 (0)20 7488 4942
Web www.jbboda.net/london.html

JIS (Chile) Limited

Address Luis Thayer Ojeda 0180 Oficina 311
Providencia
Santiago
Chile
Tel +56 2 334 4865
Fax +56 2 334 4861
Web www.jischile.cl

JLT Reinsurance Brokers Limited

Address One America Square
London EC3N 2JL
Tel +44 (0)20 7466 1300
Fax +44 (0)20 7528 4500
Web www.jltgroup.com

John B Collins Associates (UK) Limited

Address   11th Floor
           1 Minster Court
           Mincing Lane
           London EC3R 7AA
Tel   +44 (0)20 7220 8900
Fax   +44 (0)20 7220 8901
Web   www.jbcollins.com

John Holman & Sons Ltd

Address   22 Billiter Street
           London EC3M 2RY
Tel   +44 (0)20 7977 8200
Fax   +44 (0)20 7977 8201
Web   www.holmans.co.uk

K

K M Dastur & Company Limited

Address   10 Fenchurch Avenue
           London EC3M 5BN
Tel   +44 (0)20 3008 6066
Fax   +44 (0)20 7663 5948

Kinetic Insurance Brokers Limited

Address   7th Floor
           50 Fenchurch Street
           London EC3M 7HS
Tel   +44 (0)20 7283 9142
Fax   +44 (0)20 7283 8964
Web   www.kineticbrokers.com

Kite Warren & Wilson Ltd

Address   1st Floor
           19-21 Great Tower Street
           London EC3R 5AR
Tel   +44 (0)20 7929 5555
Fax   +44 (0)20 7929 6666
Web   www.kwwltd.com

L

LIBG Ltd

Address   Wigham House
           Wakering Road
           Barking
           Essex IG11 8PJ
Tel   +44 (0)20 8557 2300
Fax   +44 (0)20 8557 2430
Web   www.larkinsurance.co.uk

Lloyd & Partners Ltd

Address   One America Square
           London EC3N 2JL
Tel   +44 (0)20 7466 6500
Fax   +44 (0)20 7466 6565
Web   www.lloydandpartners.com

Lockton Companies International Ltd

Address   6 Bevis Marks
           London EC3A 7AF
Tel   +44 (0)20 7933 0000
Fax   +44 (0)20 7933 0915
Web   www.uk.lockton.com

London Market Insurance Brokers Ltd

Address   London Underwriting Centre
           3 Minster Court
           Mincing Lane
           London EC3R 7DD
Tel   +44 (0)20 7617 4740
Fax   +44 (0)20 7617 4754
Web   www.lmib.co.uk

London Special Risks Ltd

Address   Minster House
           42 Mincing Lane
           London EC3R 7AE
Tel   +44 (0)20 7459 9200
Fax   +44 (0)20 7488 9300
Web   www.londonspecialrisks.com

Longreach International Ltd

Address 4th floor
20-21 Tooks Court
London EC4A 1LB

Tel +44 (0)20 7421 7555
Fax +44 (0)20 7421 7550
Web www.longreachint.com

Lonsdale Insurance Brokers Ltd

Address 24 Creechurch Lane
London EC3A 5JX
Tel +44 (0)20 7816 0028
Fax +44 (0)20 7816 0029
Web www.lonsdaleib.com

Lothbury UK Limited

Address Fleur De Lys Court
112 Houndsditch
London EC3A 7BD
Tel +44 (0)20 7929 2105
Fax +44 (0)20 7816 7235
Web www.lothburyuk.com

Lucas Fettes & Partners Ltd

Address 22 Rathbone Street
London W1T 1LA
Tel +44 (0)20 7413 0999
Fax +44 (0)20 7631 0058
Web www.lucasfettes.co.uk

M

Mar Risk Services Limited

Address 150 Minories
London EC3N 1LS
Tel +44 (0)20 7264 2029
Fax +44 (0)20 7264 2040

Marine Aviation & General (London) Ltd

Address 10 Eastcheap
London EC3M 1AJ

Tel +44 (0)20 7398 4010
Fax +44 (0)20 7398 4011
Web www.maglondon.com

Market Insurance Brokers Ltd

Address 107 Fenchurch Street
London EC3M 5JF
Tel +44 (0)20 7264 1100
Fax +44 (0)20 7264 1111
Web www.mib.co.uk

Marnix Europe Limited

Address River Plate House
7-11 Finsbury Circus
London EC2M 7AF
Tel +44 (0)20 7826 8693
Fax +44 (0)20 7826 8695

Marsh Ltd

Address Tower Place
London EC3R 5BU
Tel +44 (0)20 7357 1000
Fax +44 (0)20 7929 2705
Web www.marsh.co.uk

Meridian Risk Solutions Ltd

Address Valiant House
4-10 Heneage Lane
London EC3A 5DQ
Tel +44 (0)20 7648 5177
Fax +44 (0)20 7623 6868
Web www.meridianrsl.com

Miles Smith Broking Ltd

Address Birchin Court
20 Birchin Lane
London EC3V 9DU
Tel +44 (0)20 7283 0040
Fax +44 (0)20 7220 0860
Web www.milessmith.co.uk

Miller Insurance Services Ltd

Address Dawson House
5 Jewry Street
London EC3N 2PJ

Tel   +44 (0)20 7488 2345
Fax   +44 (0)20 7410 2321
Web www.miller-insurance.com

N

N.I.B. (UK) Ltd

Address 3rd Floor
        71 Fenchurch Street
        London EC3M 4BR
Tel   +44 (0)20 7488 4696
Fax   +44 (0)20 7480 5895

Nausch Hogan & Murray Inc

Address 11-13 Crosswall
        London EC3N 2JY
Tel   +44 (0)20 7481 4161
Fax   +44 (0)20 7702 1719
Web www.nhmurray.com

NCG Professional Risks Ltd

32 Lombard Street
London EC3V 9BQ
Tel   +44 (0)20 7283 2393
Fax   +44 (0)20 7220 4199
Web www.ncgpi.co.uk

Newman Martin and Buchan Ltd

Address NMB House
        17 Bevis Marks
        London EC3A 7LN
Tel   +44 (0)20 7648 8800
Fax   +44 (0)20 7648 8890
Web www.nmbinsurance.com

Norman Butcher and Jones Ltd

Address NBJ House
        2 Southlands Road
        Bromley
        Kent BR2 9QP
Tel   +44 (0)20 7337 4060
Fax   +44 (0)20 7337 4061
Web www.nbj.co.uk

O

OAMPS Insurance Brokers Ltd

Address 40 Lime Street
        London EC3M 7AW
Tel   +44 (0)20 7929 6880
Fax   +44 (0)20 7929 6889
Web www.fairmontinsure.com

Oval International Limited

Address Osborn House
        74-80 Middlesex Street
        London E1 7EZ
Tel   +44 (0)20 7398 1000
Fax   +44 (0)20 7398 1400
Web www.theovalgroup.com

Oxygen Insurance Brokers Ltd

Address 117 Fenchurch Street
        London EC3M 5DY
Tel   +44 (0)870 114 2643
Fax   +44 (0)870 114 2644
Web www.oxygeninsurance.com

P

Pana Harrison (Asia) Pte Ltd

Address 371 Beach Road
        #03-01/02
        Keypoint
        Singapore
        199597
Tel   +65 62948966
Fax   +65 62981500
Web www.panaharrison.com

Paragon International Insurance Brokers Ltd

Address 140 Leadenhall Street
        London EC3V 4QT
Tel   +44 (0)20 7280 8200
Fax   +44 (0)20 7280 8270
Web www.paragonbrokers.com

Parker Norfolk & Partners Ltd

Address Norway Chambers
         Weavers Lane
         Sudbury
         Suffolk CO10 2EZ
Tel   +44 (0)1787 379937
Fax   +44 (0)1787 375528

Paul Napier Limited

Address 4th Floor
         120 Fenchurch Street
         London EC3M 5BA
Tel   +44 (0)20 7648 7400
Fax   +44 (0)20 7648 7401
Web   www.paulnapierlimited.co.uk

Platus

Address 13-15, rue Taitbout
         75009 Paris
         France
Tel   +33 (0)17 27 12 57
Fax   +33 (0)17 27 12 57
Web   www.platus.eu

Price Forbes & Partners Ltd

Address 6th Floor
         2 Minster Court
         Mincing Lane
         London EC3R 7PD
Tel   +44 (0)20 7204 8400
Fax   +44 (0)20 7204 8404
Web   www.priceforbes.com

Priest & Co Ltd

Address 13 Woodbrook Crescent
         Billericay
         Essex CM12 0EQ
Tel   +44 (0)1277 633166
Fax   +44 (0)1277 632314
Web   www.priestco.com

Primary Group Intermediary Services Ltd

Address 4th Floor
         47 Mark Lane
         London EC3R 7QQ
Tel   +44 (0)844 209 0103
Fax   +44 (0)844 209 0104
Web   www.pg-is.co.uk

PYV Ltd

Address 10 St Mary at Hill
         London EC3R 8EE
Tel   +44 (0)20 7626 6789
Fax   +44 (0)20 7626 6567
Web   www.pyv.co.uk

R

Ramon International Insurance Brokers Ltd

Address 3rd Floor
         24 Creechurch Lane
         London EC3A 5EH
Tel   +44 (0)20 7369 0250
Fax   +44 (0)20 7369 2050
Web   www.ramon.co.uk

Rasini Vigano Ltd

Address Pinnacle House
         23-26 St Dunstan's Hill
         London EC3R 8HN
Tel   +44 (0)20 7626 4448
Fax   +44 (0)20 7626 4420
Web   www.rva.it

Rattner Mackenzie Ltd

Address Walsingham House
         35 Seething Lane
         London EC3N 4AH
Tel   +44 (0)20 7480 5511
Fax   +44 (0)20 7481 3616
Web   www.rattnermackenzie.com

RFIB Group Limited

Address   Staple Hall Stone House Court
          87-90 Houndsditch
          London EC3A 7NP
Tel   +44 (0)20 7621 1263
Fax   +44 (0)20 7623 6175
Web   www.rfib.co.uk

RIB Reinsurance International Brokers Spa

Address   Corso di Porta Romana 122
          20122 Milan
          Italy
Tel   +39 02 584711
Fax   +39 02 5847 1247
Web   www.ribgroup.com

RK Carvill & Co Ltd

Address   St Helen's
          1 Undershaft
          London EC3A 8JT
Tel   +44 (0)20 7929 2800
Fax   +44 (0)20 7929 1604
Web   www.carvill.com

RK Harrison Insurance Brokers Ltd

Address   52 Leadenhall Street
          London EC3A 2BJ
Tel   +44 (0)20 7456 9300
Fax   +44 (0)20 7456 9399
Web   www.rkharrison.com

RL Davison & Co Ltd

Address   Bury House
          31 Bury Street
          London EC3A 5AH
Tel   +44 (0)20 7816 9876
Fax   +44 (0)20 7816 9876
Web   www.rldavison.co.uk

Robertson Taylor Insurance Brokers Ltd

Address   33 Harbour Exchange Square
          London E14 9GG

Tel   +44 (0)20 7510 1260
Fax   +44 (0)870 114 2644
Web   www.robertson-taylor.co.uk

Ropner Insurance Services Ltd

Address   Boundary House
          7-17 Jewry Street
          London EC3N 2HP
Tel   +44 (0)20 7488 4533
Fax   +44 (0)20 7481 0830
Web   www.ropnerins.co.uk

S

Safeonline LLP

Address   St. Clare House
          30/33 Minories
          London EC3N 1DD
Tel   +44 (0)20 7977 0333
Fax   +44 (0)20 7977 4969
Web   www.safeonline.com

SBJ Global Risks Limited

One Hundred Whitechapel
London E1 1JG
Tel   +44 (0)20 7816 2000
Fax   +44 (0)20 7816 2429
Web   www.sbjgroup.co.uk

Seascope Insurance Services Ltd

Address   57 Mansell Street
          London E1 8AN
Tel   +44 (0)20 7488 3288
Fax   +44 (0)20 7481 4499
Web   www.seains.com

Senior Wright Ltd

Address   Boundary House
          7-17 Jewry Street
          London EC3N 2FX
Tel   +44 (0)20 7680 5750
Fax   +44 (0)20 7680 5777
Web   www.seniorwright.co.uk

Brokers

Smith Bilbrough & Co Ltd

Address 77 Gracechurch Street
         London EC3V 0AG
Tel   +44 (0)20 7816 4500
Fax   +44 (0)20 7816 4540

Somerville Market Solutions Ltd

Address 145 Leadenhall Street
         London EC3V 4QT
Tel   +44 (0)20 7648 1370
Fax   +44 (0)20 7648 1371
Web   www.somerville.co.uk

Special Contingency Risks Ltd

Address 30 Fenchurch Street
         London EC3M 5AD
Tel   +44 (0)20 7088 910
Fax   +44 (0)20 7088 910
Web   www.scr-ltd.co.uk

Special Risks Insurance Brokers Ltd

Address 5-7 St Helens Place
         London EC3A 6AU
Tel   +44 (0)20 7638 0778
Fax   +44 (0)20 7628 0772

SSL Insurance Brokers Ltd

Address 6th Floor
         140 Leadenhall Street
         London EC3V 4QT
Tel   +44 (0)20 7220 1110
Fax   +44 (0)20 7220 1120
Web   www.sslins.com

Strategic Insurance Services Ltd

Address 46-48 East Smithfield
         London E1W 1AW
Tel   +44 (0)845 345 6611
Fax   +44 (0)845 458 9633
Web   www.sis-l.com

Swinglehurst Ltd

Address 11th Floor St Clare House
         30-33 Minories
         London EC3N 1DD
Tel   +44 (0)20 7977 6700
Fax   +44 (0)20 7480 6996
Web   www.swinglehurst.co.uk

T

Tasker & Partners Limited

Address 70 St Mary Axe
         London EC3A 8BE
Tel   +44 (0)20 7623 4133
Fax   +44 (0)20 7621 9811
Web   www.taskerpartners.com

Texel Finance Ltd

Address 17-19 Alie Street
         London E1 8DE
Tel   +44 (0)20 7481 3030
Fax   +44 (0)20 7481 6600
Web   www.texelfinance.com

The Underwriting Exchange Limited

Address 52/54 Gracechurch Street
         London EC3V 0EH
Tel   +44 (0)20 7398 8100
Fax   +44 (0)20 7398 8100

Thompson Heath & Bond Ltd

Address 107 Leadenhall Street
         London EC3A 4AF
Tel   +44 (0)870 751 5077
Fax   +44 (0)870 756 9340
Web   www.thbgroup.com

Towergate London Market Limited

Address 77 Leadenhall Street
         London EC3A 3DE
Tel   +44 (0)20 7712 6000
Fax   +44 (0)20 7712 6001
Web   www.towergate.co.uk

Brokers

Tyser & Co Ltd

Address	12 Camomile Street
	London EC3A 7PJ
Tel	+44 (0)20 3037 8000
Fax	+44 (0)20 3037 8010
Web	www.tysers.com

U

United Insurance Brokers Ltd

Address	69 Mansell Street
	London E1 8AN
Tel	+44 (0)20 7488 0551
Fax	+44 (0)20 7480 5182
Web	www.uib.co.uk

W

W Denis Insurance Brokers Plc

Address	Brigade House
	86 Kirkstall Road
	Leeds LS3 1LQ
Tel	+44 (0)113 243 9812
Fax	+44 (0)870 705 2085
Web	www.wdenis.co.uk

Walsham Brothers & Co Ltd

Address	4 Fenchurch Avenue
	London EC3M 5BS
Tel	+44 (0)20 7623 2711
Fax	+44 (0)20 7623 7987
Web	www.walshams.co.uk

WBA Srl

Address	U-329 Business Centre
	52 Upper Street
	London N1 0QH
Tel	+44 (0)20 7288 6018
Fax	+44 (0)20 7288 6017
Web	www.wbasrl.com

Willis Limited

Address	The Willis Building
	51 Lime Street
	London EC3M 7DQ
Tel	+44 (0)20 3124 6000
Fax	+44 (0)20 3124 8223
Web	www.willis.com

Windsor Partners Ltd

Address	2 America Square
	London EC3N 2LU
Tel	+44 (0)20 7133 1200
Fax	+44 (0)20 7133 1500
Web	www.windsor.co.uk

WT Butler & Co Ltd

Address	8 Queen's Gate Place Mews
	London SW7 5BQ
Tel	+44 (0)20 7589 1532
Fax	+44 (0)20 7584 2252

Associations

Association of Lloyd's Members (ALM)

Contact	Linda Evans/Pat Saunders
Address	6th Floor
	100 Fenchurch Street
	London EC3M 5LG
Telephone	+44 (0)20 7488 0033
Fax	+44 (0)20 7488 7555
Contact Email	mail@alm.ltd.uk
Website	www.alm.ltd.uk

ALM BOARD

Title/Name	Company/ Position	Telephone No	Email
Chairman			
Michael Deeny		+44 (0)20 7488 0033	mail@alm.ltd.uk
Deputy Chairman			
Sir Adam Ridley	Hampden Agencies Ltd		
	Non-Executive Director	+44 (0)20 7488 0033	mail@alm.ltd.uk
Chief Executive			
Anthony Young		+44 (0)20 7488 0033	mail@alm.ltd.uk
Other Board Members			
Dr Paul Kelly (Honorary Treasurer)	Navigators Underwriting Agency Ltd		
	Non-Executive Director	+44 (0)20 7488 0033	mail@alm.ltd.uk
Professor Tim Congdon, CBE		+44 (0)20 7488 0033	mail@alm.ltd.uk
Nigel Hanbury	Hampden Agencies Ltd		
	Chairman	+44 (0)20 7488 0033	mail@alm.ltd.uk
Paul Hipps		+44 (0)20 7488 0033	mail@alm.ltd.uk
Marcus Johnson	N W Brown & Co Ltd		
	Chief Executive	+44 (0)20 7488 0033	mail@alm.ltd.uk
Alan Lovell (co-opted June 2006)	Alpha Insurance Analysts Ltd		
	Non-Executive Director	+44 (0)20 7488 0033	mail@alm.ltd.uk
Peter Morgan, MBE		+44 (0)20 7488 0033	mail@alm.ltd.uk
Consultant			
Edward Vale		+44 (0)20 7488 0033	edward.vale@alm.ltd.uk
Senior Administrator			
Linda Evans		+44 (0)20 7488 0033	linda.evans@alm.ltd.uk
Company Secretary			
Anthony Young		+44 (0)20 7488 0033	mail@alm.ltd.uk

BACKGROUND INFORMATION

About the ALM	The ALM is one of two representative voices of Names at Lloyd's. The ALM's mission is to represent and advance the interests of Names whether they participate on an unlimited or a limited liability basis. Names provide £2.4 billion of capacity to underwrite in the Lloyd's Market, and the majority of Names are members of the ALM. The ALM organises conferences for Names and the Market and also provides publications which give financial analysis of Lloyd's syndicates, MAPA's, corporate vehicles, Managing Agencies and Members' Agencies.
ALM Membership	ALM membership or associate membership is open to all past or present underwriting or prospective members of Lloyd's, participating investors or partners in Lloyd's limited liability vehicles, and those individuals and companies having professional relationships with such members.

Lloyd's Market Association (LMA)

Contact	Louise Maisey
Address	Suite 358
	One Lime Street
	London EC3M 7DQ
Telephone	+44 (0)20 7327 3333
Fax	+44 (0)20 7327 4443
Contact Email	lma@lmalloyds.com
Website	www.lmalloyds.com

LMA BOARD

Title/Name	Company/ Position	Telephone No	Email
Chairman			
Paul A Jardine	Catlin Group Ltd		
	Chief Operating Officer		
		+44 (0)20 7327 3333	lma@lmalloyds.com
Deputy Chairman			
Barnabas J Hurst-Bannister	Travelers Syndicate Management Ltd		
	Chairman	+44 (0)20 7327 3333	lma@lmalloyds.com
Chief Executive			
David H Gittings	Lloyd's Market Association		
	Chief Executive	+44 (0)20 7327 4151	david.gittings@lmalloyds.com
Other Board Members			
David A Constable	QBE Underwriting Ltd		
	Active Underwriter Casualty Syndicate 386		
		+44 (0)20 7327 3333	lma@lmalloyds.com
Tom RC Corfield	Liberty Syndicate Management Ltd		
	Active Underwriter Syndicate 4472		
		+44 (0)20 7327 3333	lma@lmalloyds.com
Charles Franks	Kiln Group R J Kiln & Co Ltd		
	Group Chief Executive	+44 (0)20 7327 3333	lma@lmalloyds.com
Nick H Furlonge	Beazley Furlonge Ltd		
	Director of Risk Management		
		+44 (0)20 7327 3333	lma@lmalloyds.com
Richard A Hextall	Amlin Underwriting Ltd		
	Group Finance Director		
		+44 (0)20 7327 3333	lma@lmalloyds.com
Lawrence A Holder	Cathedral Underwriting Ltd		
	Managing Director	+44 (0)20 7327 3333	lma@lmalloyds.com
Andrew J Kendrick	ACE European Group		
	Chairman and CEO	+44 (0)20 7327 3333	lma@lmalloyds.com
Nick Marsh	Atrium Underwriters Ltd; Atrium Underwriting plc		
	Executive Chairman; Director of Corporate Underwriting		
		+44 (0)20 7327 3333	lma@lmalloyds.com
Jeremy Pinchin	Hiscox		
	Group Claims Director	+44 (0)20 7327 3333	lma@lmalloyds.com
Bob A Stuchbery	Chaucer Syndicates Ltd		
	Underwriting Director	+44 (0)20 7327 3333	lma@lmalloyds.com

Associations

Lloyd's Market Association (LMA) (continued)

Company Secretary
Patricia Hakong
Lloyd's Market Association
Head of Financial and Regulatory Policy
+44 (0)20 7327 4872   patricia.hakong@lmalloyds.com

MANAGEMENT TEAM

Title	Names	Telephone No	Email
Chief Executive Officer	David Gittings	+44 (0)20 7327 4151	david.gittings@lmalloyds.com
Market Liaison Director	Mel Goddard	+44 (0)20 7327 8334	mel.goddard@lmalloyds.com
Head of Claims	Tim Willcock	+44 (0)20 7327 8373	tim.willcock@lmalloyds.com
Head of Underwriting	Neil Smith	+44 (0)20 7327 8333	neil.smith@lmalloyds.com
Head of Professional Standards	Terence (Terry) Hayday	+44 (0)20 7327 8384	terry.hayday@lmalloyds.com
Head of Financial and Regulatory Policy	Patricia Hakong	+44 (0)20 7327 4872	patricia.hakong@lmalloyds.com
Head of Market Processes	Robert (Rob) Gillies	+44 (0)20 7327 8377	robert.gillies@lmalloyds.com
Operations Manager	Charlotte Myers	+44 (0)20 7327 8371	charlotte.myers@lmalloyds.com
Head of IT	Peter Griggs	+44 (0)20 7327 8380	peter.griggs@lmalloyds.com

BACKGROUND INFORMATION

About the LMA	The LMA is the representative voice of the Lloyd's underwriting community. All Managing Agents at Lloyd's are members, together managing an underwriting capacity of around £16 billion. Through the LMA the interests of Lloyd's Underwriters, Managing Agents and Members' Agents are represented wherever decisions need to be made that affect the market. The purpose of the LMA is to identify and resolve issues of particular interest to the underwriting community and, working in partnership with the Corporation of Lloyd's and other partner associations, to influence the course of future market initiatives. The LMA holds an annual Black Tie dinner for members and market colleagues.
LMA Structure	The LMA is governed by a Board made up of senior market practitioners who are elected by the membership, appointed by market sectors or co-opted for their expertise. The Board sets the Association's priorities and is supported by the three major policy committees – Finance, Underwriting and Claims. Specific market sector committees support the Underwriting Committee and a structure of specialist business panels and advisory groups provides the market input and expert knowledge necessary for the LMA's day-to-day work, ranging from production of standard wordings and clauses to consultation on capital issues. An additional four policy committees underpin the structure and address issues faced by the whole market.
LMA Membership	The LMA's constitution provides for two categories of membership. Full Membership is open to Managing Agents and Members' Agents operating at Lloyd's. Currently, all eligible businesses are members. Associate Membership is open to individuals, companies or organisations which are trading partners of a Lloyd's Managing or Members' Agent.

High Premium Group (HPG)

Contact	Howard Evans
Address - Administration	Forge House
	Lower Road
	Forest Row
	East Grinstead RH18 5HE
Telephone	+44 (0)1342 824 811
Fax	+44 (0)1342 825 767
Contact Email	highpremiumgroup@hotmail.com
London Office	+44 (0)20 7823 6980

MANAGEMENT STRUCTURE

Title/Name	Company/ Position	Telephone No	Email
Chairman			
Lady Rona Delves Broughton		+44 (0)20 7823 6980	highpremiumgroup@hotmail.com
HPG Committee			
HJ Mervyn Blakeney	Navigators Underwriting Agency Ltd		
	Chairman (Non-Executive)		
		+44 (0)20 7823 6980	highpremiumgroup@hotmail.com
Chantal Davies		+44 (0)20 7823 6980	highpremiumgroup@hotmail.com
Diarmid Glencairn Campbell		+44 (0)20 7823 6980	highpremiumgroup@hotmail.com
Nigel J Hanbury	Hampden Agencies Ltd		
	Chairman	+44 (0)20 7823 6980	highpremiumgroup@hotmail.com
The Hon Charles AA Harbord-Hamond			
	ICP General Partner Ltd		
	Chief Executive Officer	+44 (0)20 7823 6980	highpremiumgroup@hotmail.com
Tom Hindmarch		+44 (0)20 7823 6980	highpremiumgroup@hotmail.com
David Monksfield	Argenta Private Capital Ltd		
	Head of Client Management		
		+44 (0)20 7823 6980	highpremiumgroup@hotmail.com
Patrick Moore		+44 (0)20 7823 6980	highpremiumgroup@hotmail.com
Dr Bruce Nicholson		+44 (0)20 7823 6980	highpremiumgroup@hotmail.com
A James Sparrow	Alpha Insurance Analysts Ltd		
	Managing Director		highpremiumgroup@hotmail.com
Charles (Charlie) Sturge			highpremiumgroup@hotmail.com
William (Billy) Whitbread		+44 (0)20 7823 6980	highpremiumgroup@hotmail.com
Vivian Wineman		+44 (0)20 7823 6980	highpremiumgroup@hotmail.com
Founder Member & Honorary Member			
Oliver Carruthers		+44 (0)20 7503 2104	ocarruthers@blueyonder.co.uk
Executive Secretary			
Howard Evans		+44 (0)1342 824 811	highpremiumgroup@hotmail.com

(continued)

Associations

High Premium Group (HPG) (continued)

BACKGROUND INFORMATION

About the HPG

The High Premium Group is the other representative voice of Names at Lloyd's. It was set up in 1994 to represent the interests of Lloyd's members who underwrite large amounts. It currently has about 300 members and includes Limited Liability Partnerships (LLPs) and NameCos as well as unlimited liability members. The HPG committee has also co-opted senior management of Members' Agents. The HPG has no official status within Lloyd's but is regularly consulted about any proposed changes in the Lloyd's market that are likely to affect members; together with the ALM it automatically receives relevant consultation documents.

For example they:
- talk to syndicates about issues which affect their Members and try to find satisfactory solutions;
- find new opportunites for private capital participation in the market;
- watch market developments and alert members to potential problems.

HPG Membership

The criterion for membership is underwriting of at least £1 million.

HPG Events

The HPG Chairman and committee of private capital providers meet each month to review market developments. The HPG with its Lutine Luncheon Club is holding monthly luncheons in various London Clubs which feature a market speaker and serve as a forum for the exchange of ideas and dissemination of analysis and information vital to continuing underwriting. The lunches also offer a convivial meeting place for old friends and other Names.

Clubs and Societies

Brokers' and Motor Underwriters' Cricket Club (BROMUCC)

Main Contact	Stewart Hayden
Address	HSBC Insurance
	Academy Place
	Brook Street
	Brentwood
	Essex CM14 5NQ
Telephone	+44 (0)8456 052 052
Contact Email	stewart.hayden@hsbc-insurance.co.uk
Website	None at present

Chairman	Stewart Hayden	+44 (0)8456 052 052	stewart.hayden@ hsbc-insurance.co.uk
Honorary Secretary	Colin Jones	+44 (0)20 7469 0159	–
Honorary Treasurer	Kevin Walsh	+44 (0)8456 052 052	–

Membership The Brokers' and Motor Underwriters' Cricket Club has no membership as such. Once a year a fundraising race night is held and is open to all those involved in motor underwriting. Anyone interested to join should contact Stewart Hayden for further details.

Background It has been over thirty years since an informal match between Lloyd's Motor Brokers and Lloyd's Motor Insurers led to a permanent fixture. Since then the club has organised itself into a philanthropic force, as surplus cash was donated to numerous charities. Since its formation BROMUCC has raised thousands of pounds for many worthy causes.

Founded The Brokers' and Motor Underwriters' Cricket Club was established in 1978.

Lloyd's Art Group

Main Contact	Susannah Hubert
Address	223 Highbury Quadrant
	London N5 2TE
Telephone	+44 (0)7789 071 887
Contact Email	info@lloydsartgroup.co.uk
Website	www.lloydsartgroup.co.uk

Chairman (Joint)	Martin Hitt	+44 (0)7771 882 549	martin.hitt@aon.co.uk
Chairman (Joint)	Susannah Hubert	+44 (0)7789 071 887	susannah@lloydsartgroup.co.uk
Honorary Secretary	Susannah Hubert	+44 (0)7789 071 887	susannah@lloydsartgroup.co.uk
Honorary Treasurer	Martin Hitt	+44 (0)7771 882 549	martin.hitt@aon.co.uk

Membership There is a £20 joining fee. Members are invited to exhibit up to 3 pieces of work In the Lloyd's Art Group annual exhibition. The Lloyd's Art Group is open to members of the Lloyd's Market community including employees of Lloyd's Brokers and the Company Market whether working or retired, and to their immediate families.

Background	The Lloyd's Art Group comprises some 30 artists – painters, printmakers, sculptors, photographers – who have a connection with Lloyd's and the London insurance market. There is an annual exhibition every November in the Old Library at Lloyd's. The event showcases the work of its members and 15% of the profits are donated to the Coombe Trust Fund. This Trust mainly provides holidays and respite to disadvantaged families, the elderly and disabled children. The Lloyd's Art Group has also an ongoing exhibition at the Brokers Wine Bar in Leadenhall Market.
Founded	The Lloyd's Art Group held its first exhibition in 1963, organised by the founders David Dubery (Hartley Cooper), Peter Lovick (Benfield, Lovick and Rees) and Reg Lymon, all Lloyd's Brokers.

Lloyd's Choir

Main Contact	Brian Bendle
Address	c/o Lloyd's
	One Lime Street
	London EC3M 7HA
Telephone	+44 (0)20 7648 4120
Contact Email	bbendle@priestco.com
Website	www.lloydschoir.plus.com

Chairman	Brian Bendle	+44 (0)20 7648 4120	bbendle@priestco.com
Honorary Secretary	Michael James	+44 (0)7951 921 028	james@mandk.fsbusiness.co.uk
Honorary Treasurer	Andrew Crozier	+44 (0)7710 259 204	a.j.crozier@qmul.ac.uk

Membership	Annual membership consists of three terms and is £100pa or £40 per term. Concessionary rates are available. This fee covers all music and the professional fees of the music director and accompanist. The Lloyd's Choir has some 75 members of which about 50 are regular active members. Members are drawn largely, though not exclusively from the insurance, financial, and banking communities within the City.
Background	In addition to its annual orchestral concert, the Lloyd's Choir gives three concerts a year, usually at St Katharine Cree Church. The Choir also sings masses and evensongs at St Katherine's, as well as at weddings and memorial services throughout the year, including the Lloyd's Branch of the Royal British Legion Remembrance Service each November. In 1999 the Choir released a CD of 'a cappella' folksong arrangements under the title 'City Folk' followed by a second CD in 2006.
Founded	The Lloyd's Choir was formed in 1922 by Geoffrey Toye, a Member of Lloyd's and professional conductor in London theatres. The Lloyd's Choir first performed in the Underwriting Room at the Royal Exchange, a former home of Lloyd's.

Lloyd's Cricket Club

Main Contact	Mark Bromage
Address	c/o Lloyd's
	One Lime Street
	London EC3M 7HA
Telephone	+44 (0)7771 633 683
Contact Email	mbromage@nhmurray.co.uk
Website	None at present

Chairman	David Sibree	+44 (0)20 7522 8103	david.sibree@aonbenfield.com
Honorary Secretary	Mark Bromage	+44 (0)7771 633 683	mbromage@nhmurray.co.uk
Honorary Treasurer	John Parry	+44 (0)20 7327 1000	john.parry@lloyds.com

Membership

£10 pa. Those interested should contact Mark Bromage or another Committee Member for an application form. The application form is also available from the match managers at each game.

Background

The Lloyd's Cricket Club usually plays six or seven regular fixtures annually and sometimes additional matches against sides touring in the UK. The flagship game is against the Stock Exchange CC (a fixture now in its 58th year) and 2008 also saw Lloyd's CC win the inaugural City Twenty20 Competition, beating the Stock Exchange and Baltic Exchange XIs on the way! In 1978 the Lloyd's Cricket Club undertook its first overseas tour to Hong Kong from which the team returned undefeated and since then it has toured on several more occasions with varying degrees of success, as well as playing touring sides and taking part in charity matches. In 2004, the Club toured Bermuda and in 2009 is embarking on a trip to Singapore and Malaysia, playing the national teams of both. The Club holds a biennial black tie dinner.

Founded

The Lloyd's Cricket Club was formally established in 1974. However, matches have been played by Lloyd's representative elevens since at least 1922. The Club was founded by Bertie Brasier, a well-known Lloyd's Underwriter and great character.

Lloyd's Croquet Society

Main Contact	David Viner
Address	c/o Lloyd's
	One Lime Street
	London EC3M 7HA
Telephone	+44 (0)20 7623 1819
Contact Email	david.viner@charlestayloradj.com
Website	None at present

President	Bronek Masojada	+44 (0)20 7448 6012	bronek.masojada@hiscox.com
Chairman	Andrew Deans	+44 (0)1628 783 891	andrew.deans@clifton-owen.co.uk
Honorary Secretary	David Viner	+44 (0)20 7623 1819	david.viner@charlestayloradj.com

Clubs and Societies

Honorary Treasurer	Nigel Wachman	+44 (0)20 7550 3500	nigel.wachman@talbotuw.com
Other Committee Member(s)	Malcolm Beacham	+44 (0)1444 482 841	malcolm@beacham.co.uk
	Edward Brookfield	+44 (0)20 7902 7800	ebrookfield@haywards.net

Membership

£25 pa. Application forms can be obtained from the Honorary Secretary. The Lloyd's Croquet Society is open to members of the Lloyd's and London Market community such as Underwriters, Brokers, Service Providers, etc. There are currently some 100 members of the Society.

Background

The Lloyd's Croquet Society is the only outside organisation able to rent lawns at the Hurlingham Club on a regular basis and has been lucky enough to have had two superb lawns for use every Monday evening. The Lloyd's Croquet Society has many non-playing members who enjoy the annual black tie dinner and a core of keen croquet players willing to take on any new opposition. The current President, Bronek Masojada, follows past Presidents Colin Murray and John Stace in generously supporting the Society.

The Society plays at Hurlingham on Monday evenings between April and September, usually a total of 16 evenings, from 6pm until dusk. A midsummer evening on the lawns is an enjoyable experience. The playing skills of the members vary from handicaps of 24 (maximum) to 4, membership is thus not restricted to the experts. Handicaps even out playing abilities in the internal knockout tournaments. During the season the Society plays an evening against Lloyd's Yacht Club, and occasionally against Lloyd's Golf Club and the Council of Lloyd's. The annual dinner is in May at the Carlton Club.

Founded

The Lloyd's Croquet Society was started in 1985 by Thomas Coles and Paul Torrington, who promptly and very shrewdly attracted many members by holding a summer ball at the Hurlingham Club.

Lloyd's Croquet Society Honours Board
As displayed in Lloyd's

Presidents		Chairmen	
1985 - 1995	CK Murray	1985 - 1986	WT Coles
1996 - 2003	JL Stace	1987 - 1988	APT Harker
2004 -	BE Masojada	1989 - 1991	WT Coles
		1992 - 1994	PG Torrington
		1995	MJ Beacham
		1996 - 2000	G Everington
		2001 - 2005	EDH Brookfield
		2006 - 2007	MJ Beacham
		2008 -	ARW Deans

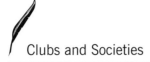
Lloyd's Fly Fishing Society

Main Contact	Brian Fitzsimmons
Address	Windmolen
	White Horse Road
	East Bergholt
	Suffolk CO7 6TU
Telephone	+44 (0)1206 299 400
Contact Email	brianfitzs@aol.com
Website	www.lloydsflyfishers.co.uk

President	Antony Pinsent	–	apinsent@btinternet.com
Chairman	James Kalbassi	+44 (0)20 7382 2400	jkalbassi@paragonbrokers.com
Honorary Secretary	Brian Fitzsimmons	+44 (0)1206 299 400	brianfitzs@aol.com
Honorary Treasurer	Richard Hughes	+44 (0)1730 893 146	richardh@potwell.me.uk
Other Committee Member(s)	Andrew Bathurst	+44 (0)20 7220 1110	bathurst@sslins.com
	Ken Carter	+44 (0)1672 514 050	carter@mantongrange.com
	Edmund Eastwood	+44 (0)20 7480 6320	edmund.eastwood@bmsgroup.com
	Simon Edwards	+44 (0)20 7626 4404	simon.edwards@leviathanfacility.com
	Adam Fox	–	adamngfox@aol.com
	James Leeper	+44 (0)1982 836 969	jleeper609@aol.com
	Charles Lindley	+44 (0)20 7357 3525	charles.a.lindley@marshmc.com
	Steve Willis	+44 (0)1844 278 606	fivepenny@btinternet.com

Membership	There is a fee of £35 for the first year and £15 pa thereafter. Application forms are available on the Lloyd's Fly Fishing website or via the Honorary Secretary. There are currently some 260 members, many of whom take an active interest in the fishing and social calendar.
Background	The Society has fishing available on a mile of the Itchen, about 3 miles of bank on a River Kennet fishery near Hungerford and a lovely 3 mile stretch of the River Avon in the Woodford Valley. All these are available by prior arrangement with the Secretary and are listed online on the main booking schedule. The website is regularly updated with fishing events.
Founded	The Lloyd's Fly Fishing Society was founded in 1987 by Alan Parry as the 'leading light' along with Andrew Bathurst, Roger Bradley and Brian Fitzsimmons who all share the common interest.

Lloyd's Fly Fishing Society Honours Board
As displayed in Lloyd's

Presidents			Chairmen	
1987 - 1992	A Parry		1987 - 1992	A Bathurst
1993 - 1999	MD Martin		1993 - 1995	JY Bogue
2000 -	AAM Pinsent		1995 - 1996	JC Davies
			1997 - 2001	EC Russell
			2002 -	JR Kalbassi

Clubs and Societies

Lloyd's Football Club

Main Contact	David Flint
Address	KPM Search
	13 Austin Friars
	London EC2N 2JX
Telephone	+44 (0)20 7680 1986
Contact Email	d.flint@kpmsearch.co.uk
Website	None at present

President	Brian Caudle	+44 (0)20 7743 8202	brian.caudle@adventgroup.co.uk
Chairman	Graham Bell	+44 (0)20 7456 0514	graham.bell@apg.net
Honorary Secretary	Gary Bass	+44 (0)7766 056 889	gary.bass@mobileemail.vodafone.net
Honorary Treasurer	Chet Ahmet	+44 (0)20 7782 0060	chet.ahmet@jltre.com
First Team Manager	David Flint	+44 (0)20 7670 1986	d.flint@kpmsearch.co.uk
Club Captain	Bradley Maltese	+44 (0)20 7782 0060	bradley.maltese@jltre.com

Membership There is no joining or annual membership fee. New members are usually recommended to the Club, whereby they are subsequently invited to play at a match in order to qualify for a squad position. Those interested should contact David Flint.

Background The Lloyd's Football Club is a friendly-based Club preferring to promote and enhance the dual interests of the Lloyd's Market and the Corinthian principles of fair play and the 'beautiful game' rather than competitive competition. The team has always been a representative side made up of employees of both underwriting organisations and broking houses. The Club has a long-standing and historical playing relationship with the London Stock Exchange, Sandhurst Military Academy and the Universities of Oxford, Cambridge, London and Cardiff. The team now plays up to ten fixtures in each season along with up to five veteran fixtures, the primary aim of which is to promote the interests of the Lloyd's Market. The Lloyd's Football Club organises many international tours including Amsterdam to New York. Socially, the Club organises a charity dinner which is a five-a-side competition in memory of former Chairman, Matthew Harding.

Founded The Lloyd's Football Club was founded in 1952 by Perry Cranmer, who remained President of the Club until his death.

Lloyd's Golf Club

Main Contact	Simon Clapham
Address	c/o Lloyd's
	One Lime Street
	London EC3M 7HA
Telephone	+44 (0)7774 995 710
Contact Email	sclapham@hotmail.co.uk
Website	www.lloydsgolfclub.com

President	Charlie Davies	+44 (0)20 7623 5500	–
Honorary Secretary	Simon Clapham	+44 (0)7774 995 710	sclapham@hotmail.co.uk
Honorary Treasurer	Jonathan Turnbull	+44 (0)7747 038 736	jonathan.turnbull@rfib.co.uk
Captain	Charles Cantlay	+44 (0)20 7623 5500	–

Membership

Prospective members need a Proposer supported by an Officer and six Members of the Club. The Club is open to those who have been working within the Lloyd's Market for a minimum of 2 years and are also a member of a recognised golf club with a handicap of 18 or less. There are currently some 500 members who have either worked for a Lloyd's Underwriting Agent or a Lloyd's Broker.

Background

The Club has played an influential role in the Society of Lloyd's over the last 115 years and some say it ran Lloyd's for many years! The Lloyd's Golf Club's Committee consists of four officers and eight members. There are approximately 27 matches a year which are played on various courses including Walton Heath, Royal St George's, the Berkshire and Rye Golf Clubs. There are also 3 meetings a year where members are invited to join. In addition, there is an annual dinner which in recent years has been held at the Merchant Taylors' Hall.

Founded

The Lloyd's Golf Club was formed by six members of the Lloyd's Market in 1894.

Lloyd's Golf Club Honours Board

As displayed in Lloyd's

Presidents

1895	A Borwick	1939	SW Bullock
1896	DA Howden	1940 - 1945	World War II
1897	DA Howden	1946	FMM Carlisle, MC
1898	GD Hardy	1947	TA Miall
1899	John H Luscombe	1948	MW Drysdale
1900	John H Luscombe	1949	I Ayscough
1901	WHP Leslie	1950	WS Gray
1902	SA Boulton	1951	LH Savill
1903	CC Blogg	1952	GE Thomson
1904	R Graham Murray	1953	M Illingworth
1905	Raymond Beck	1954	GW Harper
1906	Sir John H Luscombe	1955	Walter Barrie
1907	Edward Beauchamp	1956	KG McNeil
1908	Col DA Kinloch	1957	G MacG Harper
1909	EE Cooper	1958	PW Milligan
1910	RB Lemon	1959	DG Kennedy
1911	CE Heath	1960	WN Dru Drury
1912	CI de Rougemont	1961	AC Grover
1913	HG Poland	1962	John Lewis
1914	Percy Janson	1963	RT Hawes
1915 - 1919	World War I	1964	EB Pope
1920	SA Boulton	1965	PR MacKinnon, DSC
1921	Sir Fred Hall, MP	1966	AC Showden, MBE
1922	AL Sturge	1967	Henry Dumas, MC
1923	Ernest E Adams	1968	RW Sturge
1924	AC Turner	1969	CT Letts
1925	AH Hobdell	1970	AC Sturge, MC
1926	WHP Leslie	1971	JP Hine
1927	ER Pulbrook	1972	IHF Findlay
1928	CEW Austin	1973	Francis Perkins, DSC
1929	Sir Percy Mackinnon	1974	MP Henderson, TD
1930	EL Jacobs	1975	NR Frizzell
1931	AR Mountain	1976	CDD Gilmour
1932	HC Malyon	1977	PW Kininmoth
1933	Percy Hargreaves	1978	KB Ohlson, MC, TD
1934	GC Rogers	1979	HK Padfield
1935	FG Hall	1980	JG Hogg
1936	Harvey Bowring	1981	ERH Bowring, MC
1937	P D'Ambrumenil	1982	HR Rokeby-Johnson
1938	Neville Dixey	1983	J Groom

Lloyd's Golf Club Honours Board (continued)

Presidents (continued)

1984	JNE Butcher	1997	AF Jackson
1985	JJP Hine	1998	Sir David Rowland
1986	DJ Barham	1999	WD Robson
1987	WJ Uzielli	2000	PA Truett
1988	IR Binney	2001	PM Franklin-Adams
1989	BL Evens	2002	RC Cunis
1990	CJB Needham	2003	IC Agnew
1991	FE Hughes-Onslow	2004	BM Roddick
1992	PW Bedford	2005	PJR Webb
1993	MV Williams	2006	GD Gilchrist
1994	WNM Lawrence	2007	T Kemp
1995	CF Frizzell	2008	WRP Sedgwick Rough
1996	Sir Alexander Graham, GBE	2009	CM Davies

Captains

1895	AL Tweedie	1932	JA Roddick
1896	C Wintle	1933	WH Maslen
1897	SA Boulton	1934	AW Street
1898	WHP Leslie	1935	AB Dick-Cleland
1899	CC Blogg	1936	HWE Leslie
1900	HBL Sedgwick	1937	SW Bullock
1901	JH Morrison	1938	Leslie Wimble
1902	R Graham Murray	1939	VAB Dunkerly
1903	R Graham Murray	1940 - 1945	World War II
1904	Raymond Beck	1946	I Ayscough
1905	HL Boyd	1947	WS Gray
1906	PR Selby	1948	LH Savill
1907	Col D A Kinloch	1949	GE Thomson
1908	W Sydney Smith	1950	M Illingworth
1909	EC Bambridge	1951	WG Henderson
1910	CE W Austin	1952	AC Grover
1911	AD Hanbury	1953	PW Milligan
1912	Col Sidney Wishart	1954	WN Dru Drury
1913	Fred Hall, MP	1955	TGL Ashwell
1914	Fisher Dilke	1956	CB Gilroy
1915 - 1919	World War I	1957	AEM Gale
1920	Geoffrey Head	1958	GT Todd
1921	Ernest E Adams	1959	E Squire
1922	AC Turner	1960	John Lewis
1923	AH Hobdell	1961	EB Pope
1924	Percy Janson	1962	BH Gilbert
1925	Harvey Bowring	1963	AC Snowden, MBE
1926	Guy BC Howard	1964	Henry Dumas, MC
1927	BI Franklin-Adams	1965	MW Nesbitt, DFC
1928	E Geoffrey Toye	1966	AC Sturge, MC
1929	MW Drysdale	1967	Mark Palmer
1930	FW Clark	1968	CT Letts
1931	GC Rogers	1969	DA Colls, MBE
		1970	ERN Clifford-Smith

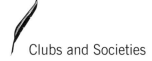
Lloyd's Golf Club Honours Board (continued)

Captains (continued)

1971	WD McClure, MC	1990	MV Williams
1972	NR Frizzell	1991	CF Frizzell
1973	CDD Gilmour	1992	WNM Lawrence
1974	PW Kininmonth	1993	Sir Alexander Graham, GBE
1975	KB Ohlson, MC , TD	1994	WD Robson
1976	HK Padfield	1995	AF Jackson
1977	JG Hogg	1996	PA Truett
1978	JNeE Butcher	1997	RC Cunis
1979	HR Rokeby-Johnson	1998	PM Franklin-Adams
1980	J Groom	1999	IC Agnew
1981	WJ Uzielli	2000	BM Rodick
1982	KF Rust	2001	GD Gilchrist
1983	JJP Hine	2002	T Kemp
1984	TJ Stubbs	2003	PJR Webb
1985	DJ Marchant	2004	WRP Sedwick Rough
1986	WA Lake	2005	CM Davies
	JC Woods	2006	SM Wilcox
1987	CJB Needham	2007	WJ Bushell
1988	FE Hughes-Onslow	2008	RHA Clark
1989	PW Bedford	2009	CPT Cantlay

Lloyd's Lawn Tennis Club

Main Contact	Howard Pountney		
Address	c/o Lloyd's		
	One Lime Street		
	London EC3M 7HA		
Telephone	+44 (0)1494 763 547		
Contact Email	None at present		
Website	None at present		
Life President	Howard Pountney	+44 (0)1494 763 547	–
Chairman	Matthew Simson	+44 (0)20 7984 8788	matt.simson@britinsurance.com
Honorary Secretary	Carl Moore	+44 (0)20 7280 8200	cmoore@paragonbrokers.com
Honorary Treasurer	Alistair Yardley	+44 (0)20 7357 2402	alistair.yardley@guycarp.com

Membership   Interested parties should contact the President or Honorary Secretary.

Background   The main purpose of the Lloyd's Lawn Tennis Club is to meet informally in the field of sport and thus to promote and harmonise relationships. In line with other Lloyd's clubs, Lloyd's Lawn Tennis Club has ventured abroad to meet and play tennis with players involved with the business of insurance. Countries visited include on several occasions the United States and also Australia, Bermuda, Finland, France, Hong Kong, India, Netherlands, New Zealand, Thailand, Sweden and Switzerland. The Club has always been well received and many mementos have been exchanged. Each trip has been recorded photographically. At home, the matches played are against teams representing the banks, barristers, the House of Commons, the Law

Society and the other professional bodies and businesses. Members have cultivated many new friends and engendered much goodwill for Lloyd's by their efforts.

Founded	The Lloyd's Lawn Tennis Club was founded in the 1960's by Howard Pountney.

Lloyd's Market Association Events Group

Main Contact	Louise Maisey
Address	c/o Lloyd's Market Association
	Suite 358
	One Lime Street
	London EC3M 7DQ
Telephone	+44 (0)20 7327 4938
Contact Email	louise.maisey@lmalloyds.com
Website	www.lmalloyds.com

Chairman	Robert Smith	+44 (0)20 3102 3241	robert.smith@maxatlloyds.com
Honorary Secretary	Louise Maisey	+44 (0)20 7327 4938	louise.maisey@lmalloyds.com
Honorary Treasurer	Steven Luck	+44 (0)20 7220 6926	sluck@navg.com
Other Committee Member(s)	Paul Element	–	–
	Liz Hargreaves	–	–
	Tamara Haylock	–	–
Other Committee Member(s)	Anthony Hipperson	–	–
	Shelley Young	–	–

Membership	There is no joining fee. Those interested in attending events organised by the Group should contact the Honorary Secretary Louise Maisey. Members of the Lloyd's Market Association Events Group represent themselves and not the businesses they work for. It is open to any employee, partner or director of any underwriting agency at Lloyd's, any firm acting as a licensed Lloyd's adviser or any other organisation deemed appropriate by the Committee.
Background	This Group, formerly known as the Under 35s Underwriting Agents Group, organises events for the younger people in the insurance market to network with each other. Events organised by the Group include quiz nights, wine tasting, a black tie dinner, and Christmas drinks. All members can attend functions and events, and are eligible to vote or stand for election to the Committee. The Committee comprises eight members drawn from across the Group's constituencies.
Founded	The Lloyd's Market Association Events Group was established in 1999 by the Lloyd's Underwriting Agents' Association.

Lloyd's Motor Club

Main Contact	Brian Hunt
Address	c/o Lloyd's
	One Lime Street
	London EC3M 7HA
Telephone	+44 (0)20 7898 6212
Contact Email	secretary@lloydsmotorclub.com
Website	www.lloydsmotorclub.com

Chairman	Roger Earl	+44 (0)20 8948 1714	chairman@lloydsmotorclub.com
Honorary Secretary	Brian Hunt	+44 (0)20 7898 6212	secretary@lloydsmotorclub.com
Honorary Treasurer	Derrick Rowe	+44 (0)20 7173 7597	treasurer@lloydsmotorclub.com
Membership	Bob Bradbury	+44 (0)20 7696 8516	membership@lloydsmotorclub.com
Magazine Editor	Jonathan Suckling	+44 (0)20 7264 2228	magazine@lloydsmotorclub.com

Membership

£20 pa or £100 for life. Membership is open to Members of Lloyd's and those involved in the Lloyd's and London Insurance Company Market.

Background

There are currently some 750 members of the Lloyd's Motor Club. The Lloyd's Motor Club initially ran its own sprint meetings at Brands Hatch and Lydden Hill in the 1950s until the Club expanded its sporting activities when it was invited to the Eight Clubs in 1968 and participated in its annual event at Silverstone. It is a club that believes in the future of motorsport and has many members active in areas ranging from Le Mans and international rallies through to karting and Club level racing. For members wishing to take the plunge into motorsport there is a wealth of friendly experience to be called upon for information, support and advice. For those who have no wish to join the fray, but still want to 'feel' the experience of motorsport, LMC organise a number of 'track days' each year, when it is possible to try your own car on some of the UK's most famous circuits. This includes the long-standing track days at Goodwood and an annual kart racing meeting at Buckmore Park. The Club also organises manufacturer forums, factory and museum visits. The bi-annual Club dinner is traditionally held at the Royal Automobile Club in Pall Mall.

Founded

The Lloyd's Motor Club was founded in 1951 by several motor enthusiasts in the London Insurance Market, following an upsurge of interest in motoring and motor sport after the Second World War.

Lloyd's Rugby Club

Main Contact	Richard Nemeth
Address	BRS International Ltd
	Collegiate House
	London SE1 9RY
Telephone	+44 (0)20 7397 5075
Contact Email	nemeth@brsint.com
Website	None at present

Chairman	Ralph Sharp	+44 (0)20 7247 6595	ralph.sharp@firstcity.com
Honorary Secretary	Richard Nemeth	+44 (0)20 7397 5075	nemeth@brsint.com
Honorary Treasurer	John Cutts	+44 (0)20 7550 3500	john.cutts@talbotuw.com
Membership	Lucian Roberts	+44 (0)20 7626 0486	lucian.roberts@catlin.com
Captain	Matthew Fitzegerald	+44 (0)20 7456 1134	matt.fitzgerald@executionlimited.com
Vice-Captain	James Templeman	+44 (0)20 7648 7118	jtempleman@thbroup.com

Membership	Those interested should contact the Honorary Secretary Richard Nemeth or Lucian Roberts. The Lloyd's Rugby Club is open to all who work in or are connected with the Lloyd's and London Insurance Market.
Background	The Club currently plays around ten games each season mainly on Wednesday evenings. The annual sevens tournament is held in May at Richmond Athletic Ground and some 30 teams compete in what has become the largest event of its kind in the South East of England. Many firms entertain their clients in the marquees at what has become a major sporting and social occasion for the London Insurance Market. In May 2008 the Club won the inaugural City League knock-out competition, beating BNP Paribas in a well-contested final at Charlton Park. Touring is also an important part of the Club's activities. Over the past 30 years matches have been played in Argentina, Australia, Canada, Chile, Malaysia, Singapore, South Africa and the United States as well as closer to home. The Club also plays in sevens and tens tournaments around the UK and in Europe. The Club played the opening match in the Bermuda Classic rugby tournament in November 2008 and will be playing China, Hong Kong and Singapore in 2009. A formal dinner is held every year at the end of November and many guests from all sectors of the market join current and former players.
Founded	The Lloyd's Rugby Club was founded in 1920 to play against the London Stock Exchange.

Lloyd's Saddle Club

Main Contact	John Manning Mocatta
Address	Hampden Agencies Ltd
	85 Gracechurch Street
	London EC3V 0AA
Telephone	+44 (0)1277 210 495
Contact Email	junesykes@btinternet.com
Website	www.ridinglondon.com

Chairman (Joint)	John Manning Mocatta
	+44 (0)20 7863 6534 john.mocatta@hampden.co.uk
Chairman (Joint)	Richard Heathcote – –
Honorary Secretary	June Sykes +44 (0)1277 210 495 junesykes@btinternet.com
Honorary Treasurer	No appointment at present
Membership	£10 pa. The Saddle Club is open to all those with a connection to the Lloyd's Market. Application forms can be obtained from any of the Committee members.
Background	The Lloyd's Saddle Club ran very prestigious events in the 1970s and 1980s when it sponsored a variety of equestrian events including a polo match in which Prince Charles participated. It also organises annual stable visits for its members. The Club is now strongly affiliated with the London Riding Club which organises various riding events, drinks parties and lectures. The London Riding Club also has access to riding facilities across the country.
Founded	The Lloyd's Saddle Club was founded in 1976.

Lloyd's Shotgun Club

Main Contact	Andrew Briant
Address	c/o Lloyd's
	One Lime Street
	London EC3M 7HA
Telephone	+44 (0)20 7398 0102
Contact Email	lloydsgunclub@btinternet.com
Website	www.lloydsclayclub.com
President	Ray Watson +44 (0)20 3150 0103 raywatson@barprofessions.com
Chairman	Andrew Briant +44 (0)20 7398 0102 andrew.briant@compassuw.co.uk
Honorary Secretary	Charlotte Warr +44 (0)20 7780 5341 lloydsgunclub@btinternet.com
Honorary Treasurer	Lt Colonel Michael White TD
	+44 (0)20 7481 2695 hwhite@beachandassociates.com
Club Auditor	Jim Evans +44 (0)1483 474 134 jim.evans@ukgateway.net
Legal Officer	Stephen Jarvis +44 (0)20 7623 2011 stephen.jarvis@incelaw.com
Stats Officer	Ray Watson +44 (0)20 3150 0103 raywatson@barprofessions.com
Safety Officer	Charlotte Warr +44 (0)7976 533 313 lloydsgunclub@btinternet.com
Game Secretary	Andrew Briant +44 (0)20 7398 0102 andrew.briant@compassuw.co.uk
Membership	There is a £25 joining fee and £25pa thereafter. Application forms can be downloaded from the Club website. The Lloyd's Shotgun Club has over 100 members made up of underwriters, brokers, lawyers, and many others involved in the insurance industry.

Clubs and Societies

Background	In 2007, the Club ran over 12 shoots from Holland and Holland to the Bisley Shooting Ground, including both clay pigeon and game shooting. There are six or seven clay events, a few simulated pheasant days, and four to five game days. Annuals dinners and annual general meetings are held in Lloyd's.
Founded	The Lloyd's Shotgun Club was founded in April 1995 by Andrew Briant and Lt Colonel Michael White TD.

Lloyd's Shotgun Club Honours Board
As displayed in Lloyd's

Club Presidents		Club Championship	
1995 - 1998	Sir David Rowland	1995	Ray Barry
1998 - 2001	Ray Busbridge	1996	Ray Barry
2002 - 2005	Ray Barry	1997	Ray Watson
2006 -	Ray Watson	1998	Ray Watson
		1999	Michael White
		2000	Michael White
		2001	Michael White
		2002	Andrew Briant
		2003	Michael Headland
		2004	Brian Chick
		2005	Brian Chick

Lloyd's Ski Club

Main Contact	Magnus Eriksson		
Address	Willis Ltd		
	51 Lime Street		
	London EC3M 7DQ		
Telephone	+44 (0)20 3124 8546		
Contact Email	erikssonm@willis.com		
Website	www.lloydsskiclub.com		
Patron	John Boyagis	–	–
President	Antony Barrow	+44 (0)20 7469 6300	antony.barrow@cogent-resources.com
Honorary Secretary	Magnus Eriksson	+44 (0)20 7448 8546	erikssonm@willis.com
Honorary Treasurer	Scott Lawrence	–	slawrence@tokiomarineglobal.com
Captain	Filippo Guerrini Maraldi	+44 (0)20 7456 9394	filippo.guerrini-mar@rkharrison.com
Race Organiser	Amin Momen	+44 (0)20 7371 9111	amin@momentum.uk.com

Membership	£15 pa. Membership is open to all those in the Insurance/Reinsurance fraternity. For membership enquiries please contact the Honorary Secretary, Magnus Eriksson.
Background	From the 1980s the Lloyd's Ski Club organised various skiing competitions which were sponsored by international broking houses. The Ski Club now sends 3 teams to participate in the City of London Ski races which take place in Courmayeur. Among recent successes, Lloyd's 1 team, consisting of Filippo Guerrini Maraldi, Antony Barrow, Alessandro Guerrini Maraldi and Chris Oliveira, won both the Super G and Parallel Slalom events in Courmayeur at the City Ski Championships in March 2007.

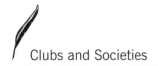

Past Presidents of the Club have been Kenneth McNeil (1957-1968), Colwyn Sturge (1969-1977), and John Boyagis (1978-1992).

Founded　　The Lloyd's Ski Club was founded in 1957 by John Boyagis as a social Club for those who enjoyed going to the Alps.

Lloyd's Under 30's Non-Marine Group

Main Contact	David Morris
Address	c/o Lloyd's
	One Lime Street
	London EC3M 7HA
Telephone	+44 (0)20 7550 3500
Contact Email	david.morris@talbotuw.com
Website	www.lloydsu30s.co.uk

Chairman	David Rothstein	+44 (0)20 7357 2425	david.rothstein@guycarp.com
Honorary Secretary	David Morris	+44 (0)20 7550 3500	david.morris@talbotuw.com
Honorary Treasurer	Imogene Ahmad	+44 (0)20 7170 9073	imogene.ahmad@cathedralcapital.com
Other Committee Member(s)	James Chicken	–	–
	Andy Cochrane	–	–
	Katie Cupman	–	–
	Gemma Higgins	–	–
	Mark Hiles	–	–
	Steve Hoes	–	–
	Richard Shreeve	–	–
	Nick West	–	–

Membership　　There is no fee to join this Group. Those interested in attending the social events organised by the Group should register online. Membership is open to all those under the age of 30 years who are engaged in the Lloyd's Non-Marine market.

Background　　The Lloyd's Under 30's Non-Marine Group aims to provide a forum for topical comment and to encourage members to be aware of the many rapidly changing facets of the Insurance industry as a whole and in particular those that affect the Lloyd's Non-Marine community. The Group has always believed that one of the most effective ways of enhancing this awareness amongst its membership is to hold trips every second year to the United States to visit markets, new and old that are important to the Lloyd's Non-Marine community. The tour parties have traditionally been made up of circa 30 people from a wide section of the market, being Underwriters and Brokers of varying classes of Non-Marine insurance and reinsurance business. The Committee also runs a number of social events throughout each year such as seasonal parties and golf days to allow younger members to network and strengthen their contacts within the Lloyd's community in a less formal environment. The Group is committed to making charitable donations with the profits from such events to causes deemed worthy and with an association to Lloyd's and the people who work within.

Founded　　The Lloyd's Under 30's Non-Marine Group was established over thirty years ago.

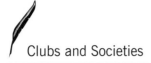

Lloyd's Yacht Club

Main Contact	Clodagh Mitchell		
Address	Allied World		
	22 Billiter Street		
	London		
	EL3M 2RY		
Telephone	+44 (0)20 7480 4436		
Contact Email	secretary@lloydsyachtclub.com		
Website	www.lloydsyachtclub.com		

President	Brian Stewart	–	info@lloydsyachtclub.com
Honorary Secretary	Clodagh Mitchell	+44 (0)20 7480 4436	secretary@lloydsyachtclub.com
Honorary Treasurer	Luke Savage	–	treasurer@lloydsyachtclub.com
Commodore	Darren Powell	+44 (0)7769 741 975	commodore@lloydsyachtclub.com
Vice-Commodore	Liz Lotz	+44 (0)7798 744 012	vc@lloydsyachtclub.com
Rear-Commodore (Sailing)	Lawrence Nicholls	–	sailing@lloydsyachtclub.com
Rear-Commodore (Club)	Liz Lotz	–	club@lloydsyachtclub.com
Admiral	Paul May	–	info@lloydsyachtclub.com
Vice-Admiral	Peter Young	–	info@lloydsyachtclub.com
Solicitor	Tony Allen	–	info@lloydsyachtclub.com
Other Committee Member(s)	Tom Bailey	–	info@lloydsyachtclub.com
	Spencer Clark	+44 (0)7513 044 514	info@lloydsyachtclub.com
	Clive Hassett	–	info@lloydsyachtclub.com
	Ed Hilier	+44 (0)7841 562 978	info@lloydsyachtclub.com
	Michael Hook	+44 (0)7825 427 154	info@lloydsyachtclub.com
	Kevin Miligan	+44 (0)7921 239 570	info@lloydsyachtclub.com
	Philip Oxford	+44 (0)7711 070 132	info@lloydsyachtclub.com
	John Pawley	–	info@lloydsyachtclub.com
	Gavin Stanley	–	info@lloydsyachtclub.com

Membership
£60 pa plus £30 joining fee. Concessionary rates are available. Membership to Lloyd's Yacht Club is open to anyone who has a connection to the insurance market and who is interested in sailing. Application forms are available online.

Background
The Lloyd's Yacht Club runs several sailing and social events during the year in addition to regular Club sailing weekends. There is racing and cruising aboard the Lutine and several racing opportunities on board the Lutine Belle. Highlights include the Illingworth Trophy – a new JOG race to La Trinite, home of French sailing, Cork Week and Cowes Week on board Lutine Belle, South Coast Rally, and the Lutine Lineslip Regatta. The first running of the Club's South Coast Rally for some years took place in June 2008. It also offers Lutine, a Swan 53, for charter activity, with day charter rate, including the skipper, varying from £500 to £1,500 according to the season. The Lloyd's Yacht Club supports various charities, including Solent Protection, Aqualung Trust, Ahoy and Jubilee Sailing Trust. The annual dinner at the end of the season provides a chance to get the crews back together.

Founded
In 1936, five individual members of Lloyd's set out from Gosport in an informal race to Cherbourg. The yachts were disparate in design and size, the only rules were

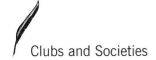

the rules of Sea and there was no handicapping. The start was by the wave of a handkerchief and the finish self-timed at the entrance to Cherbourg harbour.

The owners and crews met up at a café that evening to find the winners and losers and it was during that meal that the format of a yacht club was first mooted.

The following year, 1937, a similiar informal race took place and that evening the basis of membership and the rules of Lloyd's Yacht Club were hammered out. It was agreed that membership should be limited to Members of Lloyd's by right, and to those who had a ticket to work in The Room at Lloyd's, provided they had a proposer and seconder. However, the gestation period was elephantinely long, twenty two months.

Only in 1938 was the Club officially formed.

Lloyd's Yacht Club Honours Board

As displayed in Lloyd's

Admirals		Commodores	
1958 - 1973	AJ Whittal	1938 - 1958	AJ Whittal
1973 - 1989	FA Howarth	1958 - 1963	KG Poland
1989 - 2003	BA Stewart	1963 - 1974	FA Howarth
2003 - 2006	J Newton	1974 - 1989	BA Stewart
2006 - 2008	DH Moreton	1989 - 1994	JAN Hoare
2008 -	PAJ May	1994 - 1997	JAW Read
		1997 - 2000	J Newton
		2000 - 2003	DH Moreton
		2003 - 2006	PAJ May
		2006 - 2008	P Young
		2008 -	D Powell

The Story of Lutine

In 1949 the Lloyd's Yacht Club was presented with a Swordfish dinghy. She was the first Club boat and was named Lutine. It was a not an unreasonable name for a dinghy, as the English translation is a sprite or mischievous fairy. However, there were weightier historical reasons behind the name.

La Lutine in the storm that was to prove fatal

It all goes back to 1793 when a French flotilla, lying in Toulon, was surrendered to the British by French Royalists, anxious that the ships should not fall into revolutionary hands. Amongst them was a 36 gun frigate called La Lutine.

Admiral Lord Hood placed this prize under Admiral Nelson. After two years service, she was sent to Gibraltar for a temporary refit and thence to England. Entered in the navy lists as HMS Lutine at the end of 1795 she was dispatched to Woolwich as a tender. As the war dragged on, Lutine, after a complete refit, was pressed back into active service on convoy duties, and in 1799 was stationed at Great Yarmouth.

Now, the turmoil of war had had its effects on British mercantile trade and in the early autumn of 1799 the Hamburg-based agents of London merchants faced the distinct possibility of having to default on bills of merchandise. To prevent this, it was arranged that sufficient money be sent to Hamburg, via Cuxhaven, to meet the bills as they fell due. The total amount involved was £1.4 million, the equivalent spending power today would be £55 million.

As the sum involved was so high, the merchants applied to the Admiralty for a Navy ship to act as transport, as the seas at that time were swarming with privateers and enemy ships, a lone merchantman was easy prey. The Admiralty consented and HMS Lutine was selected for the task.

The treasure, in gold and silver coins and bars, went by wagon with an escort from the London banks to Great Yarmouth, where it was stowed aboard Lutine in Yarmouth Roads, awaiting her orders to sail. As well as her officers and men, HMS Lutine carried representatives of the London banks travelling as passengers.

On the morning of October the 9th in a fair wind the frigate set sail. The wind rapidly gained force, becoming a severe gale from the north-northwest. At around midnight the same day, 130 miles from Great Yarmouth, HMS Lutine foundered on a sandbank off the Dutch islands of Vlieland and Terschelling and sank instantly. Her precious cargo went down with her, as did her complement of officers, men and passengers.

That cargo was insured in full at Lloyd's. How many members Lloyd's had in 1799 is unknown – many of the Society's records perished in a subsequent fire. Estimates put the figure at 200, meaning each of them today would have to pay £275,000 to meet the loss – as all those members did in 1799 and promptly.

Despite numerous salvage attempts, only a small number of gold and silver bars were ever recovered until in 1858 the wreck yielded £100,000 in bullion and its most symbolic treasure – the ship's bell, weighing 80 pounds.

At some time in the 1890s, the bell was hung in the Lloyd's underwriting Room in the Royal Exchange and rung when news of overdue ships was received. Since then it has been hung in the Room in all subsequent Lloyd's buildings; currently the Lutine Bell hangs in the Caller's Rostrum in the centre of the Room, a piece of history. On rare occasions nowadays it is struck once for bad news and twice for good as, for example, when Reconstruction & Renewal was concluded.

Each successive yacht of the Lloyd's Yacht Club has carried the name Lutine on her transom. Subsequent owners of those vessels have not been allowed to retain that name.

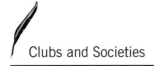

Lutine Golf Society

Main Contact	Stephen Cappell
Address	47 Lambardes
	Longfield
	Kent DA3 8HX
Telephone	+44 (0)1474 872 629
Contact Email	stevechappell@yahoo.com
Website	None at present
Honorary Secretary	Stephen Chappell +44 (0)1474 872 629 stevechappell@yahoo.com

Membership   The Lutine Golf Society is open to External Members of Lloyd's ie Names who do not work in the market. Those interested in becoming a member should contact Stephen Chappell. The Society currently has some 50 members.

Background   The Lutine Golf Society plays some nine fixtures per year including some against WIGS. Members play 'lovely courses and have a wonderful time'.

Founded   The Lutine Golf Society was founded 20 years ago by Christopher Cox.

Marine Under 35's Insurance Group

Main Contact	Laura Bloomfield
Address	Hill Dickinson
	Irongate House
	22-30 Duke's Place
	London EC3A 7HX
Telephone	+44 (0)20 7280 9109
Contact Email	laura.bloomfield@hilldickinson.com
Website	www.marineu35.com

Chairman	Isabella Virvilis	–	isabella.virvilis@amlin.co.uk
Honorary Secretary	Laura Bloomfield	+44 (0)20 7280 9109	laura.bloomfield@hilldickinson.com
Honorary Treasurer	Laura Bloomfield	+44 (0)20 7280 9109	laura.bloomfield@hilldickinson.com
Other Committee Member(s)	Clare Aylwin	–	caylwin@navg.com
	Vicky Hayward	–	vicky.hayward@aspeninsurance.co.uk
	Tom Houston	–	tom.houston@hiscox.com
	Duncan Hayward	–	duncan_hayward@ jltagnewhiggins.com
	Ross Taylor	–	ross.taylor@libertygroup.co.uk
	Tom Hillary	–	thomas.hilary@marsh.com
	Louise Jones	–	joneslm@willis.com
	Samantha Dunning	–	samantha.dunning@catlin.com
	Marcus Tobin	–	marcus.tobin@britinsurance.com
	Christopher Touhey	–	christopher.touhey@markelintl.com

Membership   There is no joining fee for this Group. Please contact Laura Bloomfield to be added

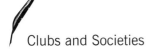

to the mailing list which informs members of upcoming events. The Marine Under 35's Insurance Group is open to anyone under the age of 35 who is working in or associated with marine insurance business. The group currently has around 300 members.

Background The Marine Under 35's Insurance Group is a large and diverse group that is involved with a range of educational and social events for young professionals working in the London marine insurance market. The group is a non-profit making organisation, which relies on the efforts of a 12-person committee. The aim of the Group is to promote education and interest in all aspects of marine insurance, to educate members of the marine insurance market and to facilitate socialising, interaction and debate between members of the market.

Each year an educational tour abroad is held and this is usually rotated among the marine hull, cargo, and liability markets and the marine energy markets. These tours usually have 10–20 participants, sponsored by their companies but travelling under the name of the Marine Under 35s Insurance Group. The current chairman of the group committee leads the trip. The purpose of the educational tour is to provide the group with the ability to visit relevant clients, insurance counterparts, shipyards, ships and other related marine visits. The trip is designed to promote knowledge and interaction between people who work in the London market.

Founded 1990s.

Royal British Legion, Lloyd's Branch

Main Contact	Regina Bond
Address	c/o Lloyd's
	Room 805
	One Lime Street
	London EC3M 7HA
Telephone	+44 (0)20 7327 4672
Contact Email	british.legion@lloyds.com
Website	None at present

Chairman	Mark Drummond Brady		
		+44 (0)20 7327 4672	british.legion@lloyds.com
Honorary Secretary	Bill Seakens	+44 (0)20 7327 4672	british.legion@lloyds.com
Honorary Treasurer	Hannah Poulton	+44 (0)20 7327 4672	british.legion@lloyds.com
Administrator	Regina Bond	+44 (0)20 7327 4672	british.legion@lloyds.com

Membership £11 pa plus £4 for branch fee. The Royal British Legion, Lloyd's Branch is open to all those connected to the Lloyd's Market. The Lloyd's Branch has approximately 200 members, many of which are ex-servicemen themselves.

Background The aim of the Lloyd's Branch of the Royal British Legion is to raise money from Lloyd's and the London insurance market for ex-servicemen in need. It supports existing RBL homes in providing facilities for residents, for example Lloyd's Library in Galanos House, Birmingham, and the provision of specialist care beds and mattresses for various homes. The Lloyd's Branch holds an annual dinner at Lloyd's to entertain residents of RBL homes, ex-servicemen's associations and

military hospital patients. A remembrance ceremony and service is also organised at Lloyd's. The City Poppy Appeal originated with the Lloyd's Branch and raises many thousands of pounds for the Royal British Legion. Members of the Lloyd's Branch are also encouraged to partake in their own fund raising activities. Mark Drummond Brady recently rowed down the Thames raising money for the charity.

Founded	The Royal British Legion, Lloyd's Branch was founded in 1947.

The Room Rifle Club

Main Contact	Kim Gibbs
Address	Argenta Holdings plc
	Fountain House
	130 Fenchurch Street
	London EC3M 5DJ
Telephone	+44 (0)20 7825 7175
Contact Email	kim.gibbs@argentaplc.com
Website	None at present

Chairman	Andrew Briant	+44 (0)20 7398 0102	andrew.briant@compassuw.co.uk
Honorary Secretary	Kim Gibbs	+44 (0)20 7825 7175	kim.gibbs@argentaplc.com
Honorary Treasurer	Julian Bayne	+44 (0)20 7548 1888	jbayne@glencairngroup.com

Membership	£25 pa plus £25 joining fee. The Room Rifle Club is open to all those connected to the Lloyd's market. Those interested in joining the Club should contact Kim Gibbs. Prospective members are invited to attend a guest open day and are granted a 3 month probation period before becoming a full member.
Background	The Room Rifle Club meets five or six times a year and specialises in 7.62mm target rifle shooting at Bisley at 300 to 1,000 yards. Club members have travelled overseas to take part in events in Germany, Guernsey and Switzerland. A family day is also organised in July for novices. Team events are organised for the internationally recognised Bisley Imperial Meeting. Team events are organised for the annual IRC competition which takes place in two parts, one in May and the other in September. Events are also sometimes linked with the Shotgun Club.
Founded	The Room Rifle Club was founded in 1955.

The Three Rooms Club

Main Contact	Vernon Ashford
Address	Lloyd's
	One Lime Street
	London EC3M 7HA
Telephone	+44 (0)20 7623 9916
Contact Email	threerooms@tiscali.co.uk
Website	None at present

Chairman	Don Coombe	+44 (0)20 7623 9916	info@coombetrust.co.uk
Deputy Chairman	Brian Wilkin	+44 (0)20 7623 9916	threerooms@tiscali.co.uk
Honorary Secretary	Vernon Ashford	+44 (0)20 7623 9916	threerooms@tiscali.co.uk
Honorary Treasurer	Anthony Barrable	+44 (0)20 7623 9916	threerooms@tiscali.co.uk
Assistant Treasurer	Terry Pitron	+44 (0)20 7623 9916	threerooms@tiscali.co.uk
Honorary Secretary of			
The Three Rooms Charitable Trust	Brian Wilkin	+44 (0)20 7623 9916	threerooms@tiscali.co.uk
Membership Secretary	John McKeigue	+44 (0)20 7623 9916	john.mckeigue@besso.co.uk
Assistant Membership Secretary	John Bristow	+44 (0)20 7623 9916	threerooms@tiscali.co.uk
Editor of the Quill Newsletter	Peter Westoby	+44 (0)20 7623 9916	threerooms@tiscali.co.uk
Other Committee Member(s)	Peter Fisher	+44 (0)20 7623 9916	threerooms@tiscali.co.uk
	Dudley Staines	+44 (0)20 7623 9916	threerooms@tiscali.co.uk
	John Tuff	+44 (0)20 7623 9916	threerooms@tiscali.co.uk
	David Weekes	+44 (0)20 7623 9916	threerooms@tiscali.co.uk
	Peter Wright	+44 (0)20 7623 9916	threerooms@tiscali.co.uk

Membership

£15 pa, life membership is £150 or £75 for those over 70. To qualify for membership, an applicant has to demonstrate a minimum period of 30 years working at Lloyd's, for a Lloyd's broker, at an underwriting box, with an Underwriting Agent, or with the Corporation of Lloyd's. There are currently approximately 950 members.

Background

The Three Rooms Club (formerly the 'New Three Rooms Club') was initially founded for those who worked in the 'three rooms' of the Royal Exchange, the Lloyd's 1928 building (the site where Lloyd's stands today) and the Lloyd's 1958 building opposite. The Three Rooms Club has now evolved into an 'old boys Club' which allows current and former Lloyd's people to keep up-to-date with other members. The Club meets twice a year, including for the AGM.

The Three Rooms Club also presents Long Service awards for 45 years of service in Lloyd's. This year, Long Service awards were made to Paul Barnes, Charles Skey, Robert Jensen, John McKeigue, David Tyler and Martin Glassborrow.

The Club also runs the Three Rooms Charitable Trust set up in 1988 by Terence Higgins, Ronald A (Dusty) Miller, James W Bragg and C Roy Hill. To date nearly £80,000 have been donated to over 190 UK based charitable organisations which have been proposed by members.

Founded

The Three Rooms Club was founded in 1961

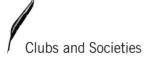

Under 35's Reinsurance Group

Main Contact	Emma Karhan		
Address	Guy Carpenter & Company Ltd		
	1 Tower Place		
	London EC3R 5BU		
Telephone	+44 (0)20 7357 2131		
Contact Email	emma.karhan@guycarp.com		
Website	www.under35s.com		

Chairman	Emma Karhan	+44 (0)20 7357 2131	emma.karhan@guycarp.com
Honorary Secretary	Tom Graham	+44 (0)20 7397 9700	tom.graham@chaucerplc.co.uk
Honorary Treasurer	Johanna Ewen	+44 (0)20 7481 0010	johanna.ewen@incelaw.com
Media and Debate	Joanne Jolly	+44 (0)20 7643 7502	jjolly@blg.co.uk
Sports and Social	Tom Horrell	+44 (0)20 7680 8383	thorrell@beachandassociates.com
Other Committee Member(s)	Manuel Almenara	+44 (0)20 3124 8704	almenaram@willis.com
	Vicky Baxter	+44 (0)20 7903 7661	vbaxter@novae.com
	Robert Burnside	+44 (0)20 7505 7223	robert.burnside@aon.co.uk
	Sophie Chapman	+44 (0)20 7480 0276	sophie.chapman@bmsgroup.com
	Tom Chivers	+44 (0)20 7105 4048	tom.chivers@uk.qbe.com
	Stuart Dale	+44 (0)20 3003 6873	stuart.dale@sagicor.eu
	Katy Gunyon	+44 (0)20 7398 2627	k.gunyon@ahj-ltd.co.uk
	George Harris-Hughes	+44 (0)20 7782 0060	ghhughes@hwsltd.com
	Rhett Hewitt	+44 (0)20 7933 7717	rhett.hewitt@xlgroup.com
	Jaimie Hunter	+44 (0)20 7357 2333	jaimie.l.hunter@guycarp.com
Administration	Jenny Wilson	+44 (0)20 7551 8366	jenny.wilson@incelaw.com

Membership	The Under 35s charges no entrance or subscription fee and those interested should enroll on the Group's website. The Group is open to anyone under the age of 35 years who is engaged in or associated with the reinsurance business.
Background	The Under 35s Reinsurance Group has developed over the years to become a large and diverse group engaged in a variety of educational and social activities in the reinsurance market. Throughout the year, the group arranges several educational events including underwriting and business planning seminars, geo-hazard and weather workshops, risk visits and many other topical seminars to help members keep abreast of the changing market place. Since 1975 the Under 35's have also organised various educational visits abroad to places such as the USA, Australia and New Zealand, Indonesia, Taiwan, Singapore and Canada and several in the UK. Each trip provides invaluable overseas experience and contacts for the participating individuals and their sponsoring firms.
Founded	The Under 35's Reinsurance Group was established In 1972 to give younger reinsurance practitioners a voice in the market.

Charities

Charities

Lloyd's Benevolent Fund

Contact	Raymond G Blaber (Secretary)
Address	Lloyd's Benevolent Fund
	One Lime Street
	London EC3M 7HA
Telephone	+44 (0)20 7327 6453
Email	raymond.blaber@lloyds.com
Website	www.lloyds.com

TRUSTEES

Chairman	Richard C Cunis	Information not available
Deputy Chairman	Timothy Kemp	Formerly HSBC Insurance Brokers Ltd, Executive Director
Trustees	Brian Wilkin	The Three Rooms Charitable Trust, Trustee
	David W Higgins	Formerly Novae Syndicates Ltd, Executive Director
	Nicholas (Nick) C Marsh	Atrium Underwriters Limited, Director of Corporate Underwriting
	Gordon David Gilchrist	Formerly RJ Kiln & Co Ltd
	Stephen M Wilcox	Hampden Agencies Ltd, Executive Director

Background and Objectives	The Lloyd's Benevolent Fund is a registered charity which aims to assist all those in need who work or have worked within the Lloyd's community. Dependants are also eligible for assistance at the discretion of the Trustees. Financial assistance is provided in the form of grants and practical help is also given for those unable to cope with everyday problems.
Founded	1829
Registered Charity Number	207231

Lloyd's Charities Trust

Contact	Victoria Mirfin (Secretary)
Address	Community Affairs
	Lloyd's
	One Lime Street
	London EC3M 7HA
Telephone	+44 (0)20 7327 6144
Contact Email	communityaffairs@lloyds.com
Website	www.lloyds.com

TRUSTEES

Chairman	Graham White	Argenta Private Capital, Managing Director
Trustees	Holly Bellingham	Marketform Managing Agency Limited, Chairman
	Grahame Chilton	Aon Group, Vice Chairman
	David Gittings	Lloyd's Market Association (LMA), Chief Executive
	Lawrence Holder	Cathedral Underwriting Limited, Managing Director
	Sue Langley	Lloyd's, Director Market Operations & North America

Charities

Brian Pomeroy	QBE Underwriting Limited, Non-Executive Director
John Spencer	Heritage Managing Agency Limited, Non-Executive Director
Anthony Townsend	Brit Syndicates Limited, Non-Executive Chairman
Iain Webb Wilson	Hiscox Syndicates Limited, Non-Executive Director

Background and Objectives

The Lloyd's Charities Trust is the grant making charity for the Lloyd's market. The Trust is managed by the Trustees and is supported by a Secretariat based in the Community Affairs team at Lloyd's. The costs of its administration are currently borne by the Corporation of Lloyd's, which has a long tradition of providing charitable support to a wide range of national and international charities. Donations are made by the Trust to a number of charities focusing on children and young people; social welfare development and medical health projects.

The Lloyd's Special Award has been running since 2007 and is an annual award of £50,000 to a charity making a positive contribution to an issue or subject of interest to the Lloyd's market. The Trust works with and supports three partner charities over a three year period. The theme for 2007-2010 is 'At Risk' and the partner charities have been selected on the basis of providing innovative projects to support some of those most at risk at home and abroad. The current partner charities for 2007-2010 are Coram, England's oldest children's charity, which aims to develop and promote best practice in the care of vulnerable and at risk children, FARM-Africa, which works with poor African farmers, helping them to produce more food for their families, and the Samaritans, who are available 24 hours a day to provide confidential emotional support for people.

Lloyd's Charity Challenge

The Lloyd's Charity Challenge kicked off on 3 June 2008 with the goal of raising as much money as possible for the three Lloyd's Charities Trust's partner charities: Coram, FARM-Africa and the Samaritans. The 2008 Challenge Champions were Marketform and Beazley. Marketform were crowned the 'Challenge Champions' for their achievement in raising over £70,000 over one month, the largest amount raised by any of the teams. Runners-up prizes were also awarded to Argenta and Hiscox who, along with Marketform, were the top three fundraising teams with all three teams being awarded a day out in private boxes at the Glorious Goodwood races. The accolade of 'Challenge Creatives' was awarded to Beazley who, in the view of the judges, had approached the Charity Challenge in the most creative way and had 'thrown their heart and soul' into it with a non-stop schedule of fundraising activities. The Beazley team has been able to celebrate their success in a box at the first ever rugby match held at the new Wembley Stadium - Barbarians vs Australia.

Lloyd's Market Charity Awards

Launched in 2007 by Lloyd's Charities Trust, the Awards recognise and support charities of importance to people working in the market. Market employees applied for £1,000 donations for UK registered charities supported by them through either voluntary or fundraising commitment. The 70 applications received demonstrated a high level of charitable and community involvement from individuals working within the market.

Founded

1953

Registered Charity Number

207232

Lloyd's of London Tercentenary Foundation

Contact	The Secretary, Lloyd's of London Tercentenary Foundation
Address	One Lime Street
	London EC3M 7HA
Telephone	+44 (0)20 7327 5921
Email	communityaffairs@lloyds.com
Website	www.lloyds.com

TRUSTEES   The Lloyd's of London Tercentenary Foundation has been given a dispensation by the Charity Commission from publishing the names of its Trustees.

Background and Objectives   Lloyd's Tercentenary Foundation was established to commemorate Lloyd's 300th anniversary. Its principal objective is funding research in the fields of medicine, science, safety, the environment, engineering and business. Over the years a number of research Fellowships were awarded to post-doctoral candidates of outstanding merit who are designated Lloyd's Fellows.
Two Lloyd's Fellowships were awarded for research into the Earth's core where the magnetic field is generated and for the study of Antarctic fossils to determine the effects of climate change.

Following a four-year partnership with the Royal Commission for the Exhibition of 1851, Lloyd's Tercentenary Foundation is moving in a new direction in 2009 to support research teams working on specified projects. New individual fellowships are not therefore currently being offered.

Founded	1988
Registered Charity Number	298482

Lloyd's Patriotic Fund

Contact	Victoria Mirfin (Secretary)
Address	Lloyd's Patriotic Fund
	One Lime Street
	London EC3M 7HA
Telephone	+44 (0)20 7327 5921
Fax	+44 (0)20 7327 6368
Email	communityaffairs@lloyds.com
Website	www.lloyds.com

TRUSTEES

Chairman	Clive I de Rougemont	Formerly C I de Rougemont & Co, Members Agent
Trustees	Anthony M F	
	Asquith LVO	Information not available
	Graham Findlay	Price Forbes & Partners Ltd, Executive Director
	Michael Hardingham	Formerly CRS Group (London) Limited, Executive Director
	Patrick Holcroft OBE	RFIB Group Limited, Chief Executive Officer

Christopher Klein   Information not available

Matthew F Newton   Travelers Syndicate Management Limited,
Non Executive Director

Charles H A Skey TD (past immediate Chairman)
Edwards & Payne (Underwriting Agencies) Ltd,
Chairman & Underwriter Syndicate 219

Maxwell (Max) Taylor Mitsui Sumitomo Insurance Underwriting at Lloyds Ltd,
Non-Executive Chairman

Lord Levene of Portsoken KBE (ex officio)
Chairman of Lloyd's

Background and Objectives

The Lloyd's Patriotic Fund is the oldest naval and military charity of its kind, established in 1803 to raise funds for victims of the Napoleonic War. With increased global conflict and UK military personnel serving overseas, the Fund's support is as vital now as ever, and financial assistance is available for ex-servicemen and women, their widows and dependants. The fund pays particular attention to cases of real need, especially those with chronic ailments or those who live in poverty. Through its working relationship with SSAFA Forces Help, grants are made for exceptional expenses, essential domestic items, utility bills and home adaptations for those who are disabled. Assistance is also given to Gurkha pensioners and children of service personnel at nominated schools.

The Fund is divided into a number of individual funds. The General Fund provides assistance to men and women of the Royal Navy, Army, Royal Marines and Royal Air Force, (including widows, orphans and dependent relatives, who at the Trustees discretion are fitting recipients). The Hugh Steward McCorquodale Memorial Fund was set up with the same Beneficiaries as the General Fund. The Edwin Hampson Mackintosh Fund was set up for the benefit of the Royal Navy and their dependants. The Janson Fund assists officers of the Royal Navy, Army and the Royal Marines and their dependents, mainly in the form of grants towards the education and maintenance of their children.

Founded

The General Fund was set up in 1803, the Hugh Steward McCorquodale Memorial Fund in 1901, the Edwin Hampson Mackintosh Fund in 1916 and the Janson Fund originates from 1918.

Registered Charity Number

210173

Lloyd's Patriotic Fund

Past Chairman and Secretaries

CHAIRMEN – 1803 TO DATE	
1803	Sir Brook Watson
1803 - 1810	Sir Francis Baring
1810 - 1823	John Julius Angerstein
1823 - 1827	Robert Shedden
1827 - 1855	George Shedden
1855 - 1872	William Shedden
1872 - 1873	William Saunders
1873 - 1901	Sir Charles Wigram
1901 - 1915	Herbert de Rougemont
1915 - 1927	Percy Janson
1927 - 1939	Charles de Rougemont
1939 - 1955	Sir Percy MacKinnon
1955 - 1977	Ernest de Rougemont, CBE
1977 - 1995	David Beck, MC
1995 - 2005	Charles Skey, TD
2005 - Present	Clive de Rougemont

SECRETARIES – 1803 TO DATE	
1803 - 1828	J P Welsford
1828 - 1864	J P Lines
1864 - 1897	J Millington
1898 - 1902	J Cadwallader
1903 - 1914	Major TD Inglis
1915 - 1927	Lt Col AN St Quintin, OBE
1927 - 1940	Brig Gen WH Usher Smith, CB CBE DSO
1941 - 1946	SW Burghes
1946 - 1947	GC Newby
1947 - 1963	Mrs LR Spicer
1963 - 1968	Capt GN Rawlings, DSO DSC RN
1968 - 1980	AJ Carter
1980 - 1985	J Gawler
1989 - 1992	Mrs JH Bright
1993 - 1994	Miss BA Lowden
1994 - 2005	Mrs L Harper
2005 - Present	Ms Vicky Mirfin

Community Programme

Mentoring in the Community

As I am a war baby, I am fortunately too young to remember much at all about the war itself. However, I can remember the consequences such as rationing (especially sweet rationing) and the poverty pervading London at the time. My family lived in a council flat in the London Borough of Hackney and we were surrounded by bomb sites. My friends and I used the bomb sites to the full, they were a massive playground. From Old Street Station we could see St Paul's Cathedral, which was one of the few buildings left standing. It was an adventurous time to grow up.

My parents worked hard to feed and clothe my two sisters and me. They were very strict but set high standards and we knew how to behave. All three children were encouraged to study hard at school and to get the best education possible. I was a slow learner but they never gave up on me and I finally left school at the age of 17 with 5 GCE 'O' levels.

I spent my whole career in the City, where I started in 1959, as an insurance clerk. My parents' work ethic stood me in good stead and I gained professional qualifications and taught myself something about the law. I held many posts in the insurance industry including becoming the millennium President of our professional body, the Chartered Insurance Institute.

Driven by a desire to put something back into the community, which had given me so much, I started mentoring in 2004. I currently have four mentees – three 16 year old students from Bishop Challoner Catholic Collegiate School and one 18 year old from Tower Hamlets College. I hope I can inspire them to fulfil their own aspirations and to be ready to help as much as I can. They have all become friends and I get enormous pleasure and satisfaction from the work we do together.

Reg Brown

Former Active Underwriter Syndicate 702 (retired)
Octavian Syndicate Management Ltd
For Full Profile please see People at Lloyd's Section

Community Programme

Main Contact	Victoria Mirfin
Address	Community Affairs
	Lloyd's
	One Lime Street
	London EC3M 7HA
Telephone	+44 (0)20 7327 6144
Contact Email	communityaffairs@lloyds.com
Website	www.lloyds.com/community

Management Board

Nick Furlonge	Chairman, Lloyd's Community Programme Director, Beazley
Nick Adams	former Executive Director, Chaucer Syndicates Ltd
Paul Buchanan	London Director, Business in the Community
Julian James	Executive Chairman International Operations, Lockton International
Jane Owen	Director of Sustainability, Aon Ltd
John Spencer	Non Executive Director, Heritage

Background and Objectives

Lloyd's Community Programme celebrates its 20th anniversary this year thus making it one of the longest-running community involvement schemes in the City of London. The programme provides volunteering opportunities for individuals and companies at Lloyd's to give their time and share skills in an effort to improve the opportunities of people living in the local community.

Over 50 underwriting agencies, insurance brokers and other associated companies who form part of Lloyd's insurance market, pay an annual membership donation which is used to fund the Lloyd's Community Programme's projects. The unique collaborative nature of the programme has encouraged a sense of community – both within the market itself as well as with neighbouring boroughs.

Lloyd's Community Programme has worked to address some of the main socio-economic challenges of Hackney and Tower Hamlets in East London, an area that has some of the highest social deprivation statistics in Britain.

Lloyd's Community Programme has gone from strength to strength. In 2008 more than 900 volunteers from more than 60 companies in the Lloyd's market took part in a range of volunteer opportunities in East London. This year it aims to reach a target of 1,000 volunteers.

There is a wide range of volunteering opportunities for Lloyd's people to get involved with. This includes helping children with literacy and numeracy skills, sports coaching, developing skills to help young people get a job, sharing skills with community leaders or even lending a hand on a local city farm.

Current Projects

Student mentoring at Tower Hamlets College
Coaching for the Lloyd's Cricket Cup at the Oval
Reading and Number Partners at Harry Gosling Primary School
Mucking in at Spitalfields City Farm
Mentoring at Shoreditch Police Station
Word Alive! at The National Theatre

Application for funding

Lloyd's Community Programme funding is available to projects in Hackney
and Tower Hamlets that fall within one of the 6 key themes. Priority is given to
projects that provide opportunities for people from the market to get involved as
volunteers. All funds are currently committed to ongoing partnerships.

Founded

Launched in 1989 by HRH the Prince of Wales.

COMMUNITY PROGRAMME MEMBERS

Ace European Group Ltd
Advent Underwriting Ltd
Amlin Plc
Aon Ltd
Ascot Underwriting Ltd
Atrium Underwriting Plc
BMS Group Ltd
Barlow Lyde & Gilbert LLP
Beazley Group Plc
Benfield Group Ltd
Bowood Partners Ltd
Brit Insurance Holdings Ltd
Canopius Managing Agents Ltd
Capita Group Plc
Catlin Underwriting Agencies Ltd
Chaucer Syndicates Ltd
Clyde & Co LLP
Cooper Gay & Co. Ltd
Denis M Clayton & Co Ltd
Dewey & LeBoeuf LLP
Edwards Angell Palmer & Dodge UK LLP
Ernst & Young LLP
Faraday Underwriting Ltd
Glencairn Ltd
Hardy Underwriting Group Plc
Heath Lambert Group Ltd

Hiscox Plc
John Holman & Sons Ltd
HSBC Insurance Brokers Ltd
Ince & Co LLP
Jardine Lloyd Thompson Group Plc
Kiln Plc
Liberty Syndicate Management Ltd
Lloyd's
Lockton Companies International Ltd
Markel International Ltd
Marketform Group Ltd
Mazars LLP
Miller Insurance Services Ltd
Munich Re Underwriting Ltd
Navigators Underwriting Agency Ltd
Newline Underwriting Agents Ltd
Novae Group Plc
Omega Underwriting Agency Ltd
PricewaterhouseCoopers LLP
QBE Insurance Group Ltd
Reynolds Porter Chamberlain LLP
Talbot Underwriting Ltd
Travelers Syndicate Management Ltd
Xchanging Claims Services Ltd
XL London Markets Ltd

Lime Street Ward

Lime Street Ward and The City of London

Lime Street Ward is one of the 25 Wards of the City of London. Each Ward, or electoral division, elects one Alderman and a number of Councilmen, based on the size of the electorate, to the City of London Corporation. Also known as the Court of Common Council, this Council is the main decision-making body through which the City operates and is headed by the Lord Mayor.

Lime Street itself is named after the medieval lime producers and sellers of the area; lime being an ingredient in the mortar used in the construction of buildings of the time and made by burning limestone in kilns. The area is unique in one respect as it was the only ward with one church, St Helen's Bishopsgate, within its boundaries, which is quite remarkable given the number of churches in the Square Mile.

Today Lime Street is home to the largest insurance market in the world. At the centre is Lloyd's at Number One Lime Street, surrounded by many insurance companies in the buildings that hug the narrow streets of the area. Close by is the Baltic Exchange, the world centre of shipping information, which moved along from its location on St Mary Axe, where the 'The Gherkin' now stands, following extensive bomb damage to the previous building in 1992. The Baltic Exchange started in similar circumstances to Lloyd's in the 'Virginia and Baltick Coffee House' on Threadneedle Street in 1744 and has moved several times during its lifetime.

Another large centre of trade was to be found in Leadenhall Market, where in the mid-fourteenth century poultry was permitted to be sold by 'foreigners', which was to say anybody who came from outside London. In about 1377, these same 'foreigners' were permitted to sell cheese and butter, with leather and wool being added later.

The present boundary of Lime Street Ward

The name Leadenhall comes from a large mansion with a leaden roof, behind which the market was established. The leasehold was sold by the Neville family along with its estate to the City Corporation in 1408. Purchased by Sir Richard (Dick) Whittington, Lord Mayor of London, he presented it to the Corporation in 1411. The mansion, market and surrounds were destroyed in the Great Fire of 1666, but reconstructed soon after. The current building was constructed in 1881 as a market for a wider range of goods including meat, poultry, plants and fish.

During the 18th century a gander called 'Old Tom' managed to escape execution and became a great favourite in the market and was fed at the local inns. Following his death at the age of 38 in 1835, he lay in state in the market and was buried there.

Under Leadenhall Market are the remains of a large Roman Basilica and Forum, as this part of the City was the Roman administrative centre. No longer a market as such, the area is now home to many retail businesses.

The City of London

The City combines its ancient traditions and ceremonial functions with the role of a modern and efficient local authority. It looks after the needs of its residents, businesses and of the over 320,000 people who come to work in the 'Square Mile' every day. Amongst local authorities, the City of London is unique; not only is it the oldest in the country, but it also operates on a non-party political basis through its Lord Mayor, Aldermen and members of the Court of Common Council.

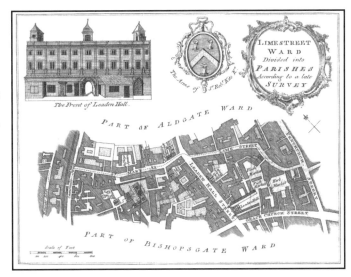

A map of Lime Street Ward sometime after the Great Fire of London

The Office of Lord Mayor dates back to around 1189, the first year of the reign of King Richard I, the Lionheart. In 1215 his successor, King John, sealed the Magna Carta at Runnymede and in the same year sealed another charter giving the Barons of the City of London (today's 25 elected Aldermen of the 25 Wards in the Square Mile) the right to choose their own Mayor.

The Court of Common Council sits every four weeks in Guildhall and works through issues arising from the City's various committees. Its main business focuses on the reports of the committees as well as Members' questions and motions. It also includes approving certain applications from individuals for the Freedom of the City, through to approving the formation of new livery companies. The Court also has responsibilities for overseeing the management of Mansion House – through the Private Secretary to the Lord Mayor – and can also make nominations to the Court of Common Council for the appointment of Aldermen on Corporation committees. The Court meetings are open to members of the public.

As well as sitting on the Court of Common Council, the 25 Aldermen also sit on the Court of Aldermen. This court was originally responsible for the entire administration of the City, but its authority was reduced with the development of the Court of Common Council in the fourteenth

century. Meeting nine times a year in the Aldermen's Court Room at Guildhall, the Court of Aldermen is also summoned and presided over by the Lord Mayor.

The current Lime Street Ward representatives are Alderman Sir John Stuttard, Christine Cohen OBE, Dennis Cotgrove BA and Elizabeth Rogula.

Leadenhall Market with the Lloyd's Building in the background

Representing the Ward

Elizabeth Rogula pictured on the day she was elected to the Court of Common Council at The Guildhall

Elizabeth Rogula has worked in the Lloyd's market for more than 25 years and is a Common Councillor for Lime Street Ward. Elizabeth first took up this role having won a by-election on 17 July 2008, and was recently re-elected for a four year term in March 2009. The City is a huge part of her life, both professionally and personally.

Says Elizabeth, "Being elected to represent the voters of Lime Street Ward is a huge honour and privilege and I have enjoyed the last year immensely. I sit on the Markets Committee (which represents Billingsgate, Spitalfields and Smithfield markets) and also the Community and Children's Services Committee. Each month, the Court of Common Council sits at Guildhall, which is the historic centre of City government and is presided over by the Lord Mayor.

"I am very lucky to have attended some magnificent functions at Guildhall and Mansion House over the last year, and my only concern has been the occasions when the gentlemen wearing their ceremonial dress, particularly the Lord Mayor, have looked *more glamorous than the ladies!*" she added.

Lime Street & Cornhill Ward Club

Main Contact	Ann Benson
Address	Hilbre Farmhouse
	Douglas Road
	Rotherfield
	East Sussex TN6 3QT
Telephone	+44 (0)1892 852682
Contact Email	annbenson179@yahoo.co.uk
Website	www.limestreetward.co.uk

Officers

President	Sir John B Stuttard MA –	+44 (0)20 7213 4590
	Alderman of Lime Street Ward	col-eb-tc@cityoflondon.gov.uk
Vice President	Sir David HS Howard Bt –	
	Alderman of Cornhill Ward	col-eb-tc@cityoflondon.gov.uk
Master	Alistair RS Bassett Cross	
Upper Warden	Stanley ST Liu	
Lower Warden	Stephen J Hatton BA MBA FCA FCMA	
Honorary Secretary	Ann B Benson	+44 (0)1892 852682
		annbenson179@yahoo.co.uk
Honorary Treasurer	Christopher J Otter FCA	
Assistant Honorary Secretary	Daphne E Cave	
Other Committee Members	C Vernon Ashford	
	Roseanne Bowman	
	Peter C Cave	
	James TL Cross	
Ex Officio Member	Elizabeth Rogula CC	+44 (0)7827 449336
		elizabeth.rogula@cityoflondon.gov.uk
	Gregg R Spence	
	Simon C Tuff I Eng	
	Tina Wishart	
	Jonathan AG Woodrow FCII MRAeS	
Ward Beadle	Stephen Kipping	

COMMON COUNCILLORS (EX OFFICIO MEMBERS OF THE COMMITTEE)

LIME STREET WARD

Deputy	Mrs Christine Cohen OBE CC	+44 (0)20 7359 9796
		mail@christinecohen.co.uk
	Dennis Cotgrove CC	+44 (0)20 7482 3345
		dennis.cotgrove@cityoflondon.gov.uk
	Elizabeth Rogula CC	+44 (0)7827 449336
		elizabeth.rogula@cityoflondon.gov.uk

Cornhill Ward

Deputy	Rev'd Stephen Haines CC
	Peter Dunphy CC

Lime Street Ward

Membership	£20 pa. Application forms can be obtained from the Honorary Secretary. The Club is open to all members working or being associated with the Wards of Lime Street and Cornhill.
Background	Members of the Ward Clubs, which were originally formed as ratepayers associations, include Liverymen, Freemen, Common Councilmen, City professionals and residents who look to promote and encourage interest in the City's affairs and to help maintain the high traditions and prestige of the City. They also offer support to the Alderman of the Ward, the Deputy and Common Councilmen in carrying out their duties on behalf of the City of London and, in particular, the Ward itself. The Club holds an annual Civic Luncheon at Guildhall, an AGM dinner and a variety of social events for members. It is also involved in a number of charitable activities.
	Each year the Ward Club holds a Carol Service in the church of St Peter-upon-Cornhill. There is also a Service there prior to the Ward Club's annual Civic Luncheon, which is held in the presence of The Rt Hon The Lord Mayor.
Founded	1946

INDEX – People Profiles